BLOOD AND N

RONALD HUTTON is professor of history, U
many books including, most recently, *The Druids: A History, Debates in Stuart History,*
and *Witches, Druids, and King Arthur: Studies in Paganism, Myth, and Magic.*

BLOOD AND MISTLETOE

THE HISTORY OF THE DRUIDS IN BRITAIN

RONALD HUTTON

YALE UNIVERSITY PRESS
NEW HAVEN & LONDON

For information about this and other Yale University Press publications, please contact:
U.S. Office: sales.press@yale.edu www.yalebooks.com
Europe Office: sales@yaleup.co.uk www.yalebooks.co.uk

Set in Adobe Caslon by IDSUK (DataConnection) Ltd.
Printed in Great Britain by Hobbs the Printer, Totton, Hampshire

Library of Congress Cataloging-in-Publication Data

Hutton, Ronald.
  Blood and mistletoe : the history of the Druids in Britain / Ronald Hutton.
    p. cm.
  Includes bibliographical references and index.
  ISBN 978-0-300-14485-7 (ci : alk. paper)
  1.   Druids and druidism—History. 2.   Great Britain—Religion.   I. Title.
  BL910.H88 2009
  299'.160941—dc22

                                                                         2008044642
A catalogue record for this book is available from the British Library.

ISBN 978–0–300–17085–6 (pbk)

The paper used for the text pages of this book is FSC®certified. FSC (The Forest Stewardship Council®) is an international network to promote responsible management of the world's forests.

10 9 8 7 6 5 4 3

CONTENTS

ILLUSTRATIONS

14. S. F. Ravenet, *The Druids; or the Conversion of the Britons to Christianity*, engraving, 1752, after F. Hayman. Wellcome Library, London.
15. *Noah's Ark During the Flood*, fresco, *c.* 1100. Abbey Church, Saint-Savin-sur-Gartempe, France. Lauros/Giraudon/Bridgeman Art Library.
16. 'The Wicker Image of the Druid' from Aylett Sammes, *Britannia Antiqua Illustrata*, 1676. The Art Archive.
17. 'R. Mills, The Treasurer of the Grand Lodge of Druids', engraving, 1832, frontispiece from the *Druids' Magazine*. Wellcome Library, London.
18. *A Sketch of the Grand Lodge as it Appeared on 1 March 1832*, engraving, 1832. Wellcome Library, London.
19. Procession of Salisbury Lodge of Druids, 27 June 1832. © Salisbury & South Wiltshire Museum.
20. Robert Cruickshank, *Iolo Morganwg*, *c.* 1875. © The National Library, Wales.
21. John Martin, *The Bard*, oil on canvas, *c.* 1817. Yale Center for British Art, Paul Mellon Collection, New Haven.
22. William Blake, 'The Voice of the Ancient Bard', plate 31 from *Songs of Innocence*, 1789, relief etching with watercolour. Yale Center for British Art, Paul Mellon Collection, New Haven.
23. W. O. Gellers, *The Druids' Sacrifice*, engraving, 1832. © Salisbury & South Wiltshire Museum.
24. Benjamin Robert Haydon, *William Wordsworth*, oil on canvas, 1842. National Portrait Gallery, London. Giraudon/Bridgeman Art Library.
25. Frontispiece of William Kingston's *Eldol the Druid*, 1874. Fortean Picture Library.
26. Gaetano Zancon, *An Indian Widow Burns to Death with her Husband's Body*, coloured engraving, nineteenth century. Private collection. Stapleton Collection/Bridgeman Art Library.
27. *Hindu Goddess Kali Dancing on Siva*, colour lithograph. Private collection. Archives Charmet/Bridgeman Art Library.
28. The Rocking Stone on Pontypridd Common. Author's photograph.
29. *Dr William Price in Ceremonial Costume*, lithograph, nineteenth century. National Museum Wales.
30. The Ancient Order of the Druids ceremony at Stonehenge. © Salisbury & South Wiltshire Museum.
31. Head of the stone serpent avenue on Pontypridd Common. Author's photograph.
32. Title page of the official magazine of the Ancient Order of Druids, 1909.
33. Robert MacGregor-Reid, Chosen Chief of the Druid Order, during the ceremony to mark the Autumnal Equinox of the Sun on Primrose Hill, London, 23 September 1957. Keystone/Getty Images.
34. Stonehenge, the Dawn Ceremony on the summer solstice, 21 June 1956. Photo by Harry Kerr/BIPs/Getty Images.

ACKNOWLEDGEMENTS

A s the work on which this book is based was the same as that carried out for its predecessor, *The Druids*, my debts of gratitude are the same; but they are so great that they need to be repeated. Many specific kindnesses are recorded in the notes to the book; so only the overarching group is acknowledged here. The Arts and Humanities Research Council provided most of the funding for my research, and with it an assistant, Dr Joanne Parker, who was a wonderful partner and has launched her own very promising career, presently at Exeter University, on the strength of it. My department at Bristol welcomed Joanne and gave me a year of reduced teaching in which to complete the project. The Order of Bards, Ovates and Druids functioned as a research council in its own right, both collectively and in the person of its present Chosen Chief, Philip Carr-Gomm. He bestowed a grant for the preliminary research, and lent me books and sent me photocopied documents from his order's own archive and library, built up by him patiently over many years of collecting.

I am also grateful to the staff of the many public libraries and archives that I have visited in the course of the project; they were almost invariably kind and helpful. Once more I single out for special mention those of the Wiltshire Archaeological and Natural History Society Library; the Salisbury and South Wiltshire Museum; Cardiff University Library's Salisbury Collection (especially Peter Keelan); and Hywel Matthews at Pontypridd Public Library. To this list of heroes and heroines I would here add another: John Goodchild, owner and custodian of the remarkable collection of materials relating to friendly societies that is housed underneath Wakefield Public Library. He welcomed me and supplied documents for me with marvellous care and interest. When I offered to buy him lunch as a return for his efforts, he refused it simply to disprove the saying that nobody ever gets anything for nothing. As a result, I can bear witness that at Wakefield an archival monument to English philanthropy and fraternity is tended by a living one.

The final tribute is to Ana Adnan, for her constant companionship and support throughout this project, as many others.

INTRODUCTION

W hat's in a name? Where Druids are concerned, it seems, almost everything. It is very doubtful that anything like as much excitement would subsequently have been attached to these characters of ancient north-western Europe if the Greeks and Romans who wrote about them had simply called them by their own common words for priests or seers. It was the use of a unique native term, translating to modern English as 'Druid', which made them seem special and noteworthy: an order set apart from the rest of their own society and from other religious functionaries of their own time and of others. This put the seal on the indication, in those same ancient texts, that these particular priests and seers had indeed been unusual and distinctive in some way; elevated above their own peoples and unlike the priests of other societies. The world has been trying to make sense of them ever since.

Among the modern peoples who have made the ancient Druids into important figures in their imagination are the Irish, Germans, French, Scots, English, Welsh, Americans, Canadians and Australians (more or less in that order). The relationship between each of these and the figure of the Druid would make a full study in itself: the present one confines itself to the three major historic peoples of the island of Britain. It may well be that, collectively, these have thought about Druids, or acted out being Druids, more intensely and for a more sustained period than any of the others. That, at any rate, seems to be what the face of the existing evidence shows; but further research may serve to disprove it. At any rate, it can be confidently asserted that the British relationship with Druids has been a long and complex one, and that a study of it can tell us some interesting things about the changes in British culture during the past half millennium. To focus on this relationship, rather than on the ancient figures themselves as most books concerned with Druids have been wont to do, is not to deny the potential worth of a quest for the Druidry of prehistory. It is certainly not to suggest that archaeology does not have very important things to tell us about the European Iron Age, as about every other period. It may well be, in addition, that at any point excavation could turn up evidence of decisive value for our knowledge of the 'original' Druids. This book does suggest, however, that so far such evidence has not – at least by any general agreement – been forthcoming, and that it is likely that any relevant artefacts uncovered by future archaeology will be the subject of considerable controversy before commanding any better acceptance. Why this should be so, and why the textual sources for the ancient Druids are likewise very difficult to evaluate, is the subject of the first chapter of the work that follows. By contrast, it can be argued with some confidence that an analysis of the way in which Druids have been regarded in later ages rests on solid data and can be used to draw some sustainable conclusions; at least after a process of discussion and debate.

This book is the second major outcome of a research project that I carried on between 2000 and 2007. The first was a book published by Hambledon Continuum in 2007, entitled *The Druids*. That earlier book, as was made clear in it, represented both a trailer for the present one and a work in its own right. It was more explicitly written for a popular market and was divided into thematic chapters, each examining an aspect of the way in which Druids had been regarded in Britain since 1500. Most of the material in it is reworked in the present book, but there are points at which the first book deals with different matters, and the present one occasionally refers to the first rather than repeats it. Nor shall I repeat explanations for stylistic touches, such as my use of the term 'Druidry' rather than 'Druidism', which I provided in detail in the former work. None the less, in virtually every respect, the present book is the heavyweight of the two, and the main published outcome of the research project. For one thing, it is three and a half times as large, enabling it to cover all issues tackled in the first book in much greater depth, and to discuss many more. Its format is chronological, proceeding period by period and allowing a full integration and comparison of the material from each.

It also provides a full scholarly apparatus, meaning that it discusses in detail its use of sources and their nature, and explains and defends its approach to each aspect of its huge subject. However, the fact that I have just defined, in lay terms, what a 'scholarly apparatus' means indicates that it is also deliberately written in a style that should make it accessible to anybody interested in the subject. Full source references are provided to every part of the text, and where the work cited is scarce there is also a guide to where a copy can be located. Normally, when undertaking a research topic and budgeting for the time and effort likely to be needed, I read everything that I can locate which has been written on the topic already, and note down the original sources employed in it. Then I estimate that there are probably about as many sources again that nobody has yet used. This is a rule of thumb that works for the kinds of subject on which I have generally written, though it would clearly not suit many others. In the case of attitudes to Druids, it broke down completely, because the unused sources outnumbered those already employed by about six to one. I had at first intended to compile a full bibliography of references, but realized that this would be pointless: in the years between 1700 and 1730, when the British interest in Druids was just picking up, there were already hundreds of points at which they were mentioned in published works, and the volume just kept on swelling after that. I therefore confined myself to discussions of them in which any significant opinions were aired; and that proved a big enough task in itself. I am well aware that each of the chapters of this book could have been made the basis of a volume in itself, and hope that it will encourage others to do so, contextualizing and interrelating writings on or illustrations of Druids in a particular period with other themes within it.

In the preface to a book published in 1965, the great archaeologist Stuart Piggott praised a famous cartoonist, Osbert Lancaster, for prefacing a book of his own by stating his class, religion, race, tastes and district of residence. Piggott commented that 'similar acts of self-revelation' would contribute greatly to an understanding of scholarship. Having said that, he proceeded to offer no such list of his own attributes, although he did present his own (pessimistic) view of humanity instead. From the vantage point of the next century, there seem to have been two reasons why Piggott might have avoided taking his own advice. One was that, at the time at which he wrote, professional historians and prehistorians were expected to transcend personal tastes and prejudices when presenting their material, adhering to a rigorous code by which evidence might be uncovered and interpreted. This was, after all, a large part of the reason why they were respected as professionals; and such a view lingers with some force until the present.

The force is due to the fact that to some extent it is correct, but it conceals a deeper truth. Professional scholars are trained in techniques that enable them to detect and present material, and conventions that permit it to be properly investigated. Both (usually) prevent taste and prejudice from seriously distorting the transmission of evidence and discussion of it. None the less, the perceptions that individual investigators form of their subject matter, and the messages that they receive from it, are conditioned to a very important extent by their genetic and social programming. That is one reason why the study of the past always remains so vibrant and exciting, and why different scholars, even at the same time and from similar backgrounds, gain differing lessons from it. The realization of this fundamental truth, in recent decades, has inspired the new academic fashion for 'reflexivity', the willingness to consider why it is that we see our subjects of study in the way in which we do. I am personally very keen on this, and a few years ago devoted a book to the issue of how it has operated among historians specializing in the Stuart period of British history. The other problem with following Lancaster's prescription, however, is that it isn't really an answer to the challenge of achieving reflexivity. A mere list of attributes, though revealing in some respects, is simply not adequate to the task of explaining why scholars approach material as they do. The identities of most, as of most human beings, are more fluid, complex and subject to cross-currents and qualifications than a series of labels would suggest.

With this is mind, I am not going to follow the Lancaster model myself, but, to enable readers to understand better why I wrote this book, and what I wanted it to do myself, I am going to say a few things about my relations with two groups who are discussed in it: professional archaeologists and modern Druids. By profession and vocation, I am a historian. Indeed, to some extent history occupies the space in my life filled in that of others by religion or spirituality. It defines much of the way in which I come to terms with the cosmos, and with past, present and future. In my adolescence, however, I gave as much time and enthusiasm to archaeology. I served on the committee of the local archaeological society and took part in its excavations, and also engaged in or visited some of the most important 'digs' of the period between 1965 and 1976, including Pilsdon Pen hill fort, Ascott-under-Wychwood long barrow, Hen Domen castle, and a temple site and catacomb in Malta. Between 1966 and 1969 I visited every prehistoric chambered tomb surviving in England and Wales, and wrote a guide to them, for myself and friends. Had I chosen to carry on down that path, and been lucky enough, I probably would have turned into Tim Darvill. On choosing a university subject, however, I settled for history, for which I had an equal taste and probably more aptitude, and which had more jobs in it. In addition, archaeology at that period was heading into a close alliance with the social sciences, which took it in a direction in which I did not myself want to go. None the less, while an undergraduate I took a course under the leading archaeologist of my university, Glyn Daniel. He was already becoming unfashionable at that time (1975), but we had a common interest in megalithic tombs, and I also thought that I would learn more from an old lion, contemplating changing times, than from the local eager beavers of the 'New Archaeology'. I think I was correct: Daniel and I were very different people, but, despite his cantankerous public persona, he proved more engaging, and more interested in a diversity of opinion, than many of the young radicals whom I also met at that time.

After that I settled down to become a historian, but retained an interest, and kept up with developments, in the study of British prehistory. In 1989 the pull became too much, and I began to write a book on what was currently known of the religions of the ancient British Isles. It was published in 1991, and I have been in and out of topics related to archaeology ever since. I also multiplied my friendships and acquaintances with British archaeologists in general, of whom one in particular has significance for the present book: Stuart Piggott. I got to know him towards the very end of his life, and was as impressed by his continuing force of personality, liveliness and erudition of mind, and breadth of interests, as I was shaken by his moments of savagery.

History is one of the most porous of disciplines, so that most of its practitioners have an alternative one, in which they could readily have made a career instead. These other fields include anthropology, sociology, art and literary criticism, criminology, religious studies, classics and modern languages: mine just happens to be archaeology. Having said that, I am not simply a passive consumer of what its practitioners provide: at moments, when it enters areas of what I take to be my own expertise, I pass comment on it, and I also have a general stance with regard to how its data may be interpreted. This is at one with my attitude to historical interpretation, but usually even stronger because of the particular limitations of material evidence. I am one of those scholars who emphasize the range of conclusions that different experts may, with the same validity, draw from the same sources, and the need for the greatest possible plurality of perceptions and voices to be applied to the process. I would still claim a leading role for professional experts in retrieving and presenting evidence, but would seek to provide as much as possible for the general public to draw its own (varied) conclusions from that evidence. In this, I position myself within a spectrum of opinion that runs through both disciplines, and sometimes starkly divides practitioners of each.

My relationship with modern Druidry began much more recently than that with archaeology, for the simple reason that the kind of Druid with whom I am acquainted has not been in existence for long. This acquaintance has something of a prehistory of its own, in that I knew some of the people who were to become leading Druids, at first or second hand, in previous decades. I did not, however, become aware of them as Druids until 1989. Thereafter, some of them took a keen interest in me because of the book on ancient paganism that I published in 1991. The one who initially had the greatest impact on my life was Tim Sebastion, chief of the Secular Order of Druids. It was difficult to come within range of Tim and avoid such an impact: he had more energy and vision than almost anybody else I have met, directed both to improving the world radically and to mobilizing everybody else around him into work for his latest – enormous, thrilling, exhausting and over-ambitious – project to do so. In my case he swept me up by inviting me to be a speaker at a large conference he was organizing at Avebury. It is typical of his breadth of interest and dynamism that he should have heard of my work and decided to recruit me. It is equally typical that he had not actually read the book, and so signed me up for an event intended to advocate a position (the continuous survival of pagan traditions in Britain to the present) which I could not adopt. The clincher of our friendship was that, having made that discovery, he did not mind a bit. It was at Tim's conference that I properly got to know Philip Carr-Gomm, Emma Restall Orr, John Michell, Rollo Maughfling, Philip Shallcrass and other people who feature prominently in the history (to date) of modern Druidry. Fate decreed that, during Tim's final illness, he was placed in a hospital a few miles from my home, so that I became one of his most regular visitors. I was among those present on his last day of life, and this book is dedicated to his memory.

Druids of Tim's sort, however, do not actually feature in it. Only three chapters, indeed, are concerned with the twentieth century; the bulk of them deal with the earlier period in which Druidry was most important in national culture as a whole. It would have been wonderful to deal with the most recent manifestations of Druidry, as with representations of Druids in fictional works published or filmed since 1950. To have done so, however, would have produced a book too long to be publishable. None the less, contemporary Druids have greatly contributed to parts of it. The largest of their organizations, the Order of Bards, Ovates and Druids, has been of immense assistance to me, as my endnotes regularly chronicle, and indeed renders the same service to any serious scholar. As I am painfully and embarrassedly aware, this is also the order which has a published history, at least as represented by its previous chief, which has been most comprehensively undermined by my own work. The fact that it does not seem to mind reinforces my debt of gratitude to it, and is of a piece with Tim Sebastion's cheerful dismissal of the importance of our differences over historical interpretation.

Contemporary Druidry is not the central spiritual tradition of my own life; it is not even my favourite one among those which make up the current range of Britain's 'alternative' spiritualities. Still, I find its tenets attractive and exciting, because they are deeply concerned with two phenomena, the natural history and prehistory of Britain, which are old and enduring loves of my own. Few things can divide people more effectively, of course, than common enthusiasms; but the Druids with whom I have dealt have been so remarkably lacking in dogmatism, let alone fundamentalism, that a serious clash has never developed. Inevitably this has been a self-selected sample – the less amenable and tolerant Druids will not have come into contact with me – but those in it are still remarkable. They have a capacity for generosity and a gift for friendship, of which I have just provided two examples among many, which at least matches that of any other group of people whom I have encountered in a fairly long and adventurous life.

In the last analysis, however, this book is about neither archaeology nor Druidry, but about the British, and the way in which they have seen themselves, their island, their species and their world.

1

THE RAW MATERIAL

The Druids may well have been the most prominent magico-religious specialists of some of the peoples of north-western Europe just over a couple of thousand years ago; and that is all we can say of them with reasonable certainty. They left no accounts of their beliefs and practices, and so our impressions of them depend ultimately on images produced in other cultures or at later periods. These images are the foundation of all that follows in this book; the basic material from which later concepts of Druidry were constructed. They are vivid and compelling, which is why their effect has been so enduring. They are also, without exception, problematic, controversial and possibly fallacious, and there is no sure way out of the problems that they present to a historian.

By far the most influential of these images were produced by ancient Greek and Roman authors. This is partly because the writers concerned lived during or soon after the time at which Druids were active, and so were arguably closer to their subject than any other authority. It is also, however, because of the tremendous enduring impact of classical literature on later European culture; these representations of Druids featured in familiar and beloved texts. This being so, it is worth noting how few these representations actually are: the total number of them can be encompassed within a dozen pages of relatively large print.[1] Their very scarcity has lent them an additional importance and prominence. As they are to feature repeatedly throughout the rest of this book, it is necessary to summarize them in chronological order and to point out the problems of each as evidence. Such an enterprise may seem an obvious one, yet it has rarely been undertaken. The passages concerned are, to scholars of Iron Age and Roman Britain, among the most familiar and frequently quoted in ancient literature. For the most part, however, they have been lifted from their original texts and then submitted to analysis by comparison with each other and with relevant data provided by archaeology and medieval Irish sources. There has been little attempt, especially in recent years, to look at each in the context of the work that contained it, and in the light of what experts in Greek and Roman culture currently think of the authors concerned. Without such an attempt, however, no real appraisal of their value can be made.

It is reasonably certain that people who were called (something like) Druids were in existence by 200 BCE, because they were apparently mentioned in two Greek books of about that date: a history of philosophy by Sotion of Alexandria and a treatise on magic, commonly but wrongly attributed to Aristotle. Both are lost, but they were quoted over four centuries later by Diogenes Laertius, whose work does survive.[2] *If* he cited them accurately, one or both of them said that among a list of wise or holy men of foreign peoples were the *Druidas* of the *Keltois* and *Galatais*. The former term, the origin of the modern word 'Celts', was used vaguely for the tribes north and west of the Alps. The latter name may indicate the Galatians, a people who had cut their way through the Balkans to settle in Asia Minor, or the Gauls, the inhabitants of what are now France, Belgium and Germany west of the Rhine. So, we can be fairly (though not absolutely) sure that there were Druids around by 200 BCE, but not of where they were or what they were doing.

For a view of that we have to wait another one and a half centuries, for the arrival of the earliest original text to describe them. This is also the fullest, and the only one left by an author who might have had first-hand experience of the subject: Julius Caesar. As such he is our star witness, and the one from whose testimony many later accounts or impressions were to be wholly derived. It appeared in his history of his conquest of Gaul for the Roman Empire, in the 50s BCE. This was probably compiled, in the main, from the dispatches that he had written from the battlefronts, but at one point he enriched his narrative by inserting a description of Gallic society in the manner of a learned geographer of his time. The account of Druids appears in this.[3] Caesar was one of the most remarkable and influential individuals that the world has known, equally talented as a soldier, politician and writer. He was extraordinarily clever, ruthless and unscrupulous – a master tactician both as a general and as an author – and this needs to be remembered when reading him.[4] Until recently it has generally been forgotten, because his combination of tremendous achievements, expert self-representation and a tragic and premature death has made him one of the most admired figures in Western history and lent apparent credibility to all his writings.

He stated that in Gaul there existed only two classes of respected person: *druides* and *equites* (literally 'horsemen', probably meaning warriors). The former were concerned with 'divine worship, the due performance of sacrifices, public and private, and the interpretation of ritual questions'. They taught many young men as pupils, and acted as arbitrators and judges in almost all disputes, private or public, including those relating to crimes and arguments over inheritances and territorial boundaries. If anybody refused to accept the decision that they imposed, they had the power to decree the complete social ostracism of that person. They all recognized the authority of a single leader, who held the post for life. At the death of each of these chiefs a new one was chosen, either because of his obvious pre-eminence, or by vote, or by armed conflict. At a certain time each year they all met at a holy place in the territory of the Carnutes, at the geographical centre of Gaul, to decide legal cases from all parts. Caesar recorded that Gauls believed that the 'rule of life' of the Druids had first been developed in Britain, and he added that those who wanted to learn most diligently how to perform it still went there to study. This could be taken to suggest that Britain was a place of unusual learning, but in a different part of his book Caesar gave the opposite impression. He himself twice launched invasions of the island as a subsidiary operation of his conquest of Gaul, and wrote in his account of these that the native British population, dwelling in the interior, dressed in skins, lived on milk and meat because they did not till the soil, and held their wives in common.[5] All this was based on hearsay, as Caesar never penetrated the interior but stayed in the south-eastern corner which he claimed had been settled by culturally superior agricultural tribes from Gaul. The point of the passage was to convey to Roman readers a sense of profound barbarism, and thereby, implicitly, provide an excuse for Caesar's not proceeding with the conquest of an island which was inhabited by such primitive, despicable and unprofitable people.

Caesar went on to say that Druids usually held aloof from war, and so were excused military service and the taxes raised to pay for it. The vocation of *druides* was prestigious, many young men volunteering for it and many more being pushed into it by their families. He had heard that in Druidic schools pupils learned many verses by heart, and that some took twenty years to complete their training. Druids did not think it proper to set their teachings down in writing, although they used Greek script for other transactions. Caesar believed that this restriction was intended both to keep their doctrines secret and to cultivate their powers of memory. He was, however, sure of their greatest teaching: 'that souls do not perish, but after death pass from one to another'. This doctrine was considered to have the practical benefit of inducing Gallic warriors to fight with reckless courage, because they believed that death was only the entry to a new life. *Druides* also had 'many discussions concerning the stars and their movement, the size of the cosmos and the earth, the world of nature, the powers of deities', and taught their conclusions to their pupils.

In a third section Caesar concentrated on their role in human sacrifice, for which he explicitly stated that they were employed as 'administrators'. Such sacrifices were made, or vowed to be made, by people in mortal danger from either disease or violence, who believed that by offering deities the life of another they would be spared themselves. At times mass sacrifices were made: colossal figures of woven twigs were built, filled with living human beings and set on fire. The individuals selected to suffer were preferably those convicted of serious crimes; but if none were available then innocent victims were killed instead. To this information Caesar added two snippets at slightly later points: that Druidic teaching reputedly held that all the Gauls were descended from a common ancestor, Dis, and that the German tribes, to the east of the Rhine, had no *druides* 'to regulate divine worship'.

Other parts of his survey of Gallic customs provide more context for his statements about Druids. He recorded that the deities worshipped were very similar in form to those venerated by the Romans: a god of arts, travel and commerce, a god of healing, a goddess of arts and crafts, a god who 'rules over the sky', and a war god. Of these, the god of arts, travel and commerce was the most popular and frequently honoured. After victory in battle, all the captives and booty were dedicated to the god of war, the living things being sacrificed to him and the inanimate objects piled up in heaps which were henceforth believed to belong to the deity alone. Caesar also recorded that the Gauls held magnificent funerals, in which they burned with the corpse all possessions, including living creatures, which had been precious to the dead person during life. He added that until 'a generation ago' slaves had been included among the possessions that had been destroyed in this manner.

All this is presented with clarity and confidence, as if from personal observation; the few occasions when Caesar admits to relying on hearsay are explicitly distinguished. It is true that when he discussed regions in which he never himself set foot, he could include misinformation: among his description of the beasts of the German forest is one of a unicorn.[6] Gaul, however, he came to know extremely well, and, if Druids were indeed major figures in its society, he should have had ample opportunity to meet and observe them. This being the case, it is the more remarkable to confront a problem that has beset scholars ever since it was first noticed in 1891.[7] Given the importance that Caesar attributed to the Druids, and their apparent centrality in Gallic society, one would expect them to feature prominently in his long and detailed description of his conquest of the region; but they are completely invisible in it. Nor do they appear at all in his account of his two expeditions to Britain. They are only mentioned, in fact, in that self-contained survey section on native customs, which does not seem to have any relevance to his practical experiences in Gaul. That this is not simply an authorial policy on Caesar's own part is strongly suggested by the fact that his history of the Gallic war was continued after his death by another Roman politician, Aulus Hirtius, who also made no mention of Druids in his depiction of the action.

Three different strategies have been developed to cope with this paradox. One is to suggest that Caesar's (and Hirtius's) narrative of operations did not call for comment on the normal religious and judicial activities of local society, as by definition those operations created an abnormal situation.[8] The problem with this is that, according to Caesar's own record, the spiritual functions of the Druids were enhanced in emergencies. The second solution is to suggest that in his account of native culture Caesar was actually lifting passages from the work of an earlier writer, and so describing a system that had ceased to exist by his time.[9] This is also credible, but Caesar nowhere admitted to such quotation, even though to do so would protect him against being held responsible for possible errors in his account, and spoke as if what he was describing was in the present and (mostly) at first hand.

The third solution to the puzzle is that he misrepresented the Druids to suit his own purposes. Nobody who deals with the information conveyed by Caesar's writings should forget the assertion made by a Roman historian, Gaius Asinius Pollio, that Caesar 'was too quick to believe others' accounts of their actions and give a false account of his own actions, either on purpose or through forgetfulness'.[10] There is no doubt that from Caesar's own point of view, the system that he portrayed was a dream package. His Druids were educated and wise enough to represent a society worth including in the Roman Empire, organized enough to pose a serious potential political threat, and barbaric enough to make their conquest a mission of civilization. Their practice of human sacrifice was one that had become by his time viewed with special repugnance by Greeks and Romans and one of the litmus tests of savagery. The reference to Britain as the heartland of their tradition made Caesar's own incursions into that land seem more significant and glorious. The challenge for any historian, therefore, is to decide how many of the details of this portrait were created or reworked by him to fit such a convenient end product. Stuart Piggott felt that he might have invented the annual meeting and the office of presiding chief. Daphne Nash thought it 'not unlikely' that he 'greatly exaggerates' both the centralization of the Druidic system and its connection with Britain. Other historians and archaeologists have similarly thought his account of their power and degree of organization to be embellished.[11] Sean Dunham and Bernhard Maier have both been more specific, suggesting that his portrait consisted of a straightforward projection of the Roman system of priesthood on to an alien people. Most of the characteristics that Caesar ascribes to the Druids are, in fact, the religious functions of Roman senators, and his projection of them on to Gallic society would give a much stronger impression that the Gauls were worthy of incorporation into the Roman state and were sufficiently similar to be incorporated fairly easily. Likewise, his portrayal of the German tribes as a completely different, and much less sophisticated, sort of people justified his decision to halt his conquests at the Rhine.[12]

Suspicion that all this is the case is strengthened, though not wholly confirmed, by the only independent witness that we possess from the period: Caesar's colleague among the Roman political elite, Marcus Tullius Cicero. In a note on divination, the latter commented that he had met a Gallic Druid, Divitiacus of the Aedui tribe. This man had claimed to Cicero to be learned in the ways of the natural world, and he made predictions, sometimes from observing the flight of birds and sometimes spontaneously.[13] The Gaul concerned was also a friend of Caesar, who called him by what seems to have been the more authentic version of his name, Diviciacus. Caesar wrote quite a lot about him, because he was the most steadfast native ally of Rome. He never, however, called him a Druid; Diviciacus is represented, rather, as a leading Gallic politician and spokesman for his tribe in an assembly of chiefs. Far from holding aloof from war, he guided the Roman army on campaign and led a war band of his own tribe in support of it. Sean Dunham has made this one prop of his argument that Caesar's account of Druids as a special caste is misleading, and that *druides* was in fact simply a Latinization of the native term for the religious function of chiefs and leading aristocrats of Gaul. Roman senators, after all, doubled as priests just as Diviciacus seems to have done.[14]

It may be observed in passing that Cicero duplicated Caesar's ambivalent attitude towards the Gauls, as people with a culture worthy of both respect and condemnation. As noted, he portrayed Diviciacus as a person of at least apparent wisdom based on Druidic tradition. When Cicero defended his friend Fonteius against charges of misgoverning a Gallic tribe, however, he did so with the argument that as the Gauls engaged in human sacrifice they were barbarians, and so their testimony could not be trusted in a court of law.[15] Like Caesar, he may simply have been reflecting the truth in both cases; but he may equally have been distorting it, consciously or not, to suit his purpose.

After the time of Caesar and Cicero, another hundred years may have elapsed before any more contemporary testimony about Druids was provided. This gap is partly filled, however, by probable retrospective evidence, referring to an earlier period than that of Caesar. In the late first century BCE, Greeks and Romans began to take a more systematic interest than before in the peoples and cultures that inhabited their world and its fringes, stoked by the dramatic expansion of Roman rule into these borderlands. The result was a flowering of works of historical geography, and three of these mentioned Druids. All were the work of authors who had no personal experience of them and relied on the writings or testimony of others. The first to publish, in 36 BCE, was Diodorus of Sicily, Diodorus Siculus, who produced a survey of the Roman world and lands on its borders as a preface to a history of the Greeks and Romans. It may be noted that the contemporary figure whom he most admired was Julius Caesar, and some scholars have thought that Caesar inspired him to write his book.[16] Diodorus had both much less interest in, and less information concerning, north-western Europe than the Mediterranean and Near Eastern lands: he himself seems only to have set foot in Italy, Sicily and Egypt. None the less, he included sections on both Britain and Gaul. The former section placed even greater emphasis on the primitive nature of the British than Caesar had done, calling them a simple and poverty-stricken folk who lived in homes made of reeds or logs. The latter contained some information on religious customs and traditions. It began by saying that the Gauls believed 'the Pythagorean doctrine', that human souls 'are immortal and after a prescribed number of years they commence a new life in another body'. This gave their warriors a complete lack of fear of death. Diodorus added that he had heard that this belief in the survival of the soul was so strong that some Gauls cast on to funeral pyres letters written to the dead person, in the belief that he or she would be able to read them.

He continued by telling of the existence among the Gauls of poets and singers called *bardous*, who composed praises and satires. In the same society were deeply respected philosophers and theologians called *drouidas*, and renowned soothsayers who foretold the future by watching the flight of birds and examining the entrails of victims. The most important divinations, reserved for emergencies, were made by stabbing a man fatally in the chest and observing his death throes to see the pattern of his limbs and blood flows. Diodorus stressed that no sacrifice was performed without the assistance of a 'philosopher', because these men were especially practised in dealing with deities and seeking their blessings. They were held in such respect that armies about to join battle would halt obediently if they came between the opposed ranks to stop the conflict. This proved that 'even among the most savage barbarians anger yields to wisdom'. Diodorus added that the Gauls were accustomed to execute criminals by impaling them in groups, and prisoners of war by burning them to death as offerings to their deities at the beginning of harvest. He commented that these customs were examples of their 'savage ways' and 'outlandish impiety'.[17]

The next author was Strabo, who finished writing in the 20s CE. For most of his life he seems to have lived in Asia Minor, though he visited most eastern parts of the Roman Empire, and came as far west as Italy. He declared that among all the Gallic peoples three kinds of men were held in exceptional honour: the *bardoi* who were singers and poets, the *o'vateis*, who were diviners and experts in the natural world, and the *druidai*, who studied 'moral philosophy' as well as the workings of nature. Of these, the *bardoi* were clearly the *bardous* of Diodorus, the exact equivalent of the medieval bards of Celtic-speaking peoples. His unique word *o'vateis* is just a rendering into Greek of the Latin word *vates*, signifying prophets or soothsayers; the parallel term in Gallic would have been *vatis*.[18] The implication of his description of them is that their knowledge of the natural world was related to their speciality of predicting events. Strabo recorded that the Gauls in general believed that 'men's souls, and also the universe, are indestructible, although both fire and water will at some time or another prevail over them'. His *druidai* were particularly respected for their sense of justice, and so entrusted with deciding cases of murder and arbitrating in tribal wars, even (as Diodorus had said) halting the combatants when they were lined up for battle. The individuals whom they judged to be guilty of crimes were turned into human sacrifices, and the *druidai* thought that the larger the quantity of people offered in this manner, the better the harvest would be. No sacrifices could take place without *druidai* being present, and the forms that these rites took included stabbing a man in the back and divining the future from the manner in which he writhed, shooting victims with arrows, impaling them in shrines, or burning them to death in a colossal figure of straw and wood, together with cattle and wild animals. Strabo went on to say that the Romans had abolished these cruel practices.[19] In another section of his work of geography he gave a generally poor impression of the (still independent) British, asserting that they were in some respects simpler and more barbarous than the Gauls: some of them were ignorant of agriculture and could not even make cheese from milk. Their land was largely covered in forest, and they had no permanent habitations, constructing and then abandoning a succession of temporary settlements.[20]

Other sections of his account of Britain and Gaul added further details which were to be used by modern historians of Druidry. One stated, with a sneer at the 'simplicity', 'folly' and 'arrogance' of the Gauls, that they wore golden collars round their necks and golden bracelets on their arms, and that those of any importance had garments dyed and worked with gold. In another place he added that there was reputed to be a small island somewhere off the mouth of the River Loire, which was inhabited only by a colony of Samnite women (a tribe known historically only in southern Italy) who dedicated their lives to the worship of the god Bacchus, or Dionysos. No man was allowed to land there, and when the women wished to mate, they crossed to the mainland to do so. Once a year, they ritually removed the roof of the temple, and rebuilt it before sunset on the same day. If one of them dropped the load of material that she was carrying for the purpose, the others tore her to pieces and carried the mangled parts of her body around the temple with wild shouts. It was said that, every time, one of them was designated in advance to suffer this dreadful fate. This sensational passage was often to be quoted in later accounts of Druidic custom, and sometimes still is. It may be noted that, whatever the literal truth of what is described, no god equivalent to Bacchus or Dionysos is attested by the material remains of native Gaul and Britain, or in medieval Irish literature; the account, as said, seemingly calls the women a foreign colony.[21]

Strabo was quite a thorough and scrupulous scholar, but in regions of which he had no personal experience, which included Gaul and Britain, he was naturally totally reliant on his sources. These were, overwhelmingly, Greek, and the Roman authors he knew were both few and – at times – in bad copies. His account of Gaul contains serious mistakes of geography – for example, he places the Aquitani people in the centre of the region, whereas they lived in the south-west – apparently because the version of Caesar's book on the Gallic war that he used was itself imperfect.[22] His description of native customs is associated with the tribes that had lived in the northern part of Gaul, beyond the Rhône and Garonne valleys. Strabo stated explicitly that he was not speaking of the way that the peoples concerned lived in his own time, when they had long been under Roman rule, but 'as we understand that they existed in former times'.[23] He was fond of naming the sources which he used, but it is notable that he never did this for his passages concerning Druids, or the women on the island. They appear to be gossip, perhaps picked up on his visit to Italy.

When speaking of the modes by which the Gauls had carried out human sacrifices, he quietly distanced himself from the information by using the construction 'it is said'. For his account of the women, he took another step back in distance. He commenced and ended it with the expression 'they say', as though the information was not associated with any of the reputable scholars whom he quotes liberally elsewhere. He then hinted strongly that he did not believe it himself, by going on immediately to tell another story of native divination techniques, commenting that this was 'even more obviously fictitious' than the one about the island. Occasionally archaeology can test one of Strabo's assertions. It is certainly true that the Gauls delighted in golden collars – the famous 'torques' of twisted metal – and bracelets, because these have been found by excavation. On the other hand, Gallic costume was still worn in his own time, and might even have been seen at Rome, while the native religious customs had (as stated) been altered, and leave no such clear presence in the material record. Moreover, at times archaeology invalidates his information: for example, the assertion that the British of his time had no permanent settlements. Strabo had, like Caesar, a patent motive for exaggerating the poverty of British culture, for he followed his account of it with an argument that it vindicated the Roman failure to conquer the island up till his time; the place was not worth the cost of occupation.

The third and last of these authors was Pomponius Mela, a Spaniard by origin who seems to have been based in Rome. He is known for a short summary of the geography of his world. In this he commented that by his time (in or around 40 CE), Roman law had reduced human sacrifice to a furtive practice among the Gauls. He added that the *druidas* could still be respected as teachers of wisdom, claiming to know 'the size and shape of the world, the movements of the heavens and the will of the deities'. They met in secret either in caves or in remote valleys, and educated young Gallic nobles in courses lasting up to twenty years. Only one of their teachings was widely known – 'that souls are eternal and that there is another life in the world below' – and this was put about widely because it made the Gauls in general braver in battle. Because of this belief, also, they burned or buried with the dead objects that they had needed in life, and had formerly even deferred the completion of business and the payment of debts until they arrived in the next world. Some had willingly flung themselves on to funeral pyres in order to accompany the dead person to a new life immediately.[24] Pomponius added a story about an island of priestesses, differing from that quoted by Strabo. His island lay between Britain and Gaul, and had nine women vowed to perpetual virginity and serving an oracle. The Gauls called them Senae and believed that they could raise storms with their songs, change themselves into animals, cure any diseases and predict the future.[25]

Modern scholars have devoted much time to discussing the sources used by all three writers. It was once suggested that Strabo was adding a little extra information to a medley of Caesar and Diodorus, and that Pomponius was just a rehash of Caesar with a few imaginative flourishes.[26] The last of those arguments may still stand, although it is also possible that Pomponius was quoting another authority or authorities, now completely lost. In the case of Diodorus and Strabo, the situation has been made to seem simpler. Since the 1950s there has been a widespread consensus that behind the description of Gaul given in both lies a single lost source: the work of a Greek philosopher from Syria, Posidonius, who visited south-eastern Gaul in the early first century BCE. It has also been proposed that Posidonius represents the earlier authority whom Caesar might have been quoting for his set portrait of Gallic society.[27] If this is the case, then pretty well all that is recorded of Druids before Roman conquest disrupted their society and authority rests on the indirect testimony of one traveller.

Specialists in the period have therefore come to speak of a 'Posidonian tradition' of Greek and Roman writing about the ancient Druids which is characterized by the two apparently contrasting aspects of all the accounts given above: that Druids were at once quite sophisticated thinkers and scientists, with a firm belief in the immortality of the soul, and practitioners of large-scale human sacrifice by a variety of cruel means. They could therefore be both respected and abhorred. Both parts of this picture have been undermined by different modern scholars. Stuart Piggott, Daphne Nash and David Rankin suggested that Posidonius exaggerated the sophistication of Druidic teaching by imposing Greek concepts of philosophy upon it, and that he romanticized tribal peoples as representatives of primitive innocence and natural wisdom.[28] If these writers think that he might have rose-tinted the Druids, others suggest that he blackened them. Jane Webster and Peter Berresford Ellis have drawn attention to his admiration for Rome, and accused him of acting as a propagandist for it by tainting the Gallic tribes with barbarism.[29] Piggott noticed that the description of human sacrifice by shooting to death with arrows is odd, because archery is not mentioned in any accounts of the warfare of the Gauls or related peoples.[30] Webster has added the caution that as Posidonius only visited one corner of Gaul, everything he reported may have been true only of that one region.[31] All aspects of the Posidonian tradition, apparently our most reliable for the recovery of the ancient Druids, have therefore been called into question.

The problem is, however, worse than that: there may, in fact, have been no Posidonian tradition. Posidonius's lost text was certainly very influential, and was quoted specifically by a number of subsequent Graeco-Roman authors, but there are no references to Druids in these clearly attributed extracts. Instead the accounts of Druidry appear only in passages that may (or may not) have come from him.[32] When those in Caesar, Diodorus and Strabo are compared, they show some overlap but also significant differences. Caesar's description of the inter-tribal Druidic organization is unique to him, and his account reads so differently from those of the other two authors that there has been a recent tendency to conclude that his account was not derived from Posidonius at all, or was at best slightly influenced by him.[33] That leaves Diodorus and Strabo, who are much more similar but also have several discrepancies of detail. It was suggested above that Strabo may be read as saying that some (at least) of his information on Gallic society was picked up by word of mouth. He and Diodorus may both have been repeating stories that were circulating in Rome during the period a generation or two after the conquest of Gaul. All that can be concluded is that we have absolutely no secure knowledge of the sources used by any of these authors for their comments on Druids, and therefore of their date, their geographical framework or their accuracy. We can only discern that, wherever it came from and however true it was, the dualistic image of the Druid, as at once wise and learned and a specialist in horrific acts of sacrifice, was standard among Greek and Roman writers by the first century CE.

Thereafter it split into its two component parts. Roman authors retained the image of barbarism, which features prominently in their memories of the destruction of the Druidic system after its incorporation into their empire. Writing in the early second century CE, Suetonius recorded that, after the completion of the conquest of Gaul, the emperor Augustus had ruled that nobody could be both a Druid and a Roman citizen. This would automatically discourage the more ambitious members of the native ruling elite from becoming Druids. Claudius, reigning in the 40s CE, took the final step of banning 'the barbarous and inhuman religion of the *druidae* in Gaul' and 'very thoroughly suppressed it'.[34] Suetonius did not say whether this was done because it had become weakened to the point at which suppression was easy, or because it had survived so well as to prove that it would not disappear naturally. Moreover his source may have been at fault, because Gaius Plinius Secundus (commonly called Pliny the Elder), writing in the 70s CE, said that the ban occurred under Claudius's predecessor, the emperor Tiberius. Then, he said, a decree was issued against the *druidae* of Gaul and the 'whole tribe' of native soothsayers (*vates*) and healers (*medices*) there. He added soon after that the world owed a huge debt to Rome for ending 'the monstrous cult, whereby to slaughter a man was an act of great piety, and to eat his flesh most beneficial'.[35] It is not absolutely certain that this refers to the Druids, but some later writers have assumed that it did, and that cannibalism may accordingly be added to the list of atrocities with which they may be charged. If Pliny had aimed this comment at the Druids, however, he already undermined it himself. He had reported rumours of cannibal tribes in parts of Asia far beyond those of which the Romans had any certain knowledge. While admitting that these might seem incredible, he urged his readers to give them credit, because Greek mythology included traditions of cannibals in the remote European past and because 'quite recently' the 'peoples beyond the Alps' had practised human sacrifice, 'which is not far removed from eating human flesh'.[36]

There is, in fact, rather an obvious distinction between the two practices; they may be associated, but one does not necessarily equate to the other.

Shortly before Pliny exulted over the suppression of Druidry, the Roman poet Marcus Annaeus Lucanus (commonly known as Lucan) was recalling its past in tones of equal horror. He portrayed *druidae* in Caesar's time as leaders of a tradition of 'barbarous rites' and 'sinister customs'. He mocked them for claiming exclusive knowledge of the divine world and teaching 'that the same spirit has a body again elsewhere' and 'that death is but one point in a continuous life'. Their rites were declared to have been carried on in the depths of forests. At another point Lucan provided a description of a sacred grove that had allegedly existed directly outside Marseilles at the time, a hundred years before Lucan's own, when Julius Caesar was besieging the city. Marseilles was, however, actually a Greek colony, in a part of Gaul that had long been under Roman rule, and was under siege as part of a Roman civil war. Logically, therefore, this ought to have been a Greek, and not a Gallic, sacred place. It got in the way of Caesar's intended siege works, and also offered much-needed wood for the building of them, and so he ordered the grove to be felled. His men hesitated to touch the sacred trees, so he struck the first axe-blow himself and, as he sustained no harm, the soldiers then followed his command. Lucan could not resist embellishing it with a lurid description of the grove itself: 'interlacing boughs enclosed a space of darkness and cold shadows, and banished the sunlight far above ... gods were worshipped there with savage rites, the altars were heaped with hideous offerings, and every tree was sprinkled with human blood'. No birds or beasts dared enter it, and not even the wind, but the branches moved of their own accord and water fell from 'dark springs'. 'The images of the gods, grim and rude' were uncouth blocks formed of felled tree trunks. 'Legend also tells', added Lucan, that 'yew trees fell and rose again, phantom flames appeared among the trunks, and serpents glided between them'. No humans ever entered the grove except its priest.

Lucan had three apparent purposes in this passage. The first was to illustrate Caesar's capacity for ruthless leadership. The second, as James Masters has emphasized, was to send up one of the traditional themes of Greek and Roman literature: the horror of destroying a sacred grove, as a place that combined beauty and sanctity. By making the grove itself a place of horrors, Lucan reversed the theme and strengthened his credentials as a daring and innovative author, something he clearly aspired to be.[37] The third was to spice up his account of the siege. He had an imagination that later generations would term Gothic; later in the poem, for example, his readers encounter a witch who is capable of raising the dead, rendering cornfields infertile and pulling down the moon from the sky. It is not known whether his contemporaries would have taken such passages seriously, or whether he intended them to do so. As another specialist in Lucan's work, Frederick Ahl, has said of it, 'history is the raw material ... not its purpose'.[38] Furthermore, Lucan never mentioned the Druids themselves in connection with the grove at Marseilles, and it was in a part of Gaul not associated with them, at least by Caesar's time. None the less, the description of it was to be quoted repeatedly in later centuries, out of context, as if it were an objective piece of ethnography providing an insight into Druidic religion. At another point, when listing Gallic tribes of Caesar's time, he added a reference to a nameless people 'who propitiate with horrid victims ruthless Teutates, and Esus whose savage altars make people shudder, and Taranis, whose altar is no more benign'. All three of these gods are attested from inscriptions as actual Gallic deities, later honoured under Roman rule; again, Lucan gives the impression of a barbarous religion. As well as slighting Druids, he poked fun at the Gallic *vates* and *bardi* for their verses sung in praise of dead heroes.[39]

Modern historians have debated the reasons for, and context of, this campaign of repression and vilification. Some have argued that the testimony of the classical writers should be taken at face value, and that the Greeks and Romans were genuinely horrified by the Gallic addiction to human sacrifice. Their hostility to the Druids was therefore cultural and not political, and part of what these Mediterranean peoples saw – with some justice – as their mission to civilize the known world.[40] Others have reasoned that the Druids being a focus of Gallic regional identity and tradition meant that they had to be degraded or destroyed as an essential step in the consolidation of Roman rule.[41] The debate has never reached a resolution, and it is hard to see how, given the state of evidence, it could. Those who have seen the Gallic Druids as actual leaders of resistance to Rome – at least after Roman enmity to them became clear – have drawn attention to a statement by the Roman historian, Cornelius Tacitus, that they used their reputation for prophecy to encourage a revolt against Roman rule in CE 69. Against this view it has been argued that Tacitus could merely have been reporting a rumour that had reached Rome, and that was itself inspired by prejudice against Druids.[42]

Tacitus bequeathed another account of alleged Druidic resistance to Rome, and one that has had a particular impact on British writers. It described how the Roman governor of Britain, Suetonius Paulinus, led an army to the far end of what is now north Wales at the opening of the 60s CE. Caesar had, as said, recorded the belief (for the truth of which he himself did not vouch) that Britain was the birthplace of the whole Druid system. Pliny, having mentioned the suppression of that system in Gaul, went on in the same passage to state that the arts and rites that he associated with Druids were still celebrated fervently among the British (in the 70s). This being the case, it is again worthy of comment that only one paragraph in the accounts of the Roman conquest of two-thirds of Britain mentions their presence. Admittedly, those accounts are much more episodic and less detailed than the histories of the occupation of Gaul (above all, Caesar's own) but, again, it seems odd that there should be such silence with respect to Druids had they been as essential to the workings of society and politics as Caesar had suggested.

That exceptional paragraph in Tacitus is, however, one of the most dramatic pieces of writing to be left by a Roman historian. It portrayed what happened when Paulinus's force faced the island of Mona (later Anglesey) across a narrow strait:

On the (opposing) shore stood the enemy host, with its dense array of armed men, among whom dashed women in black attire like Furies, with hair dishevelled, waving flaming torches. All around were *druidae*, raising their hands to the sky and shouting dreadful curses, which terrified our soldiers who had never seen such a thing before; so that, as if paralysed, they stood still and exposed their bodies to wounds. Then, swayed by their general's appeal and their own mutual incitements not to be scared by a bunch of frenzied women, they carried the standards forward, hacked down all resistance and burned their enemies with their own torches. An occupying force was imposed on the conquered, and their groves, dedicated to inhuman superstitions, were destroyed. They had believed it, indeed, a duty to drench their altars in the blood of prisoners and to consult their deities through human entrails.[43]

The degree of terror initially experienced by the Roman soldiers seems to confirm what the passage itself also apparently states, and the rest of the recorded history of the conquest of Britain suggests: that it was extremely rare for Druids to engage in active resistance to the invaders. On the other hand, it is also possible to read the text as stating that it was the black-clad women, and not the Druids, whom the invaders found novel and frightening. No indication is provided of who these women actually were and what they represented, if the victors ever bothered to find out: whether female Druids (the first ever mentioned in an ancient text), priestesses of some parallel religious system, human representations of native war goddesses, or just the military equivalent of cheerleaders. It was also very unusual for Romans to destroy the sacred places of the peoples whom they conquered, and this suggests either that those of Anglesey were especially associated with hostility to Rome or with human sacrifice, or that the destruction was part of a package of retribution for unusually determined resistance (like the razing of the Jewish temple of Jerusalem a decade later). It should be noted that Tacitus never stated explicitly that Anglesey was an especially important place to Druids, although it is possible to draw that inference from his text. He explained instead that Suetonius chose it as a target because it was densely populated – which meant that it would make an important conquest and yield good booty – and that it had given refuge to people who had resisted Roman rule in other parts of Britain and therefore posed a potential threat. Indeed, there is some evidence that there was no special association between Anglesey and Druidry. Suetonius had to abandon it soon after his conquest, and it was retaken all over again by a subsequent governor of Britain, Gnaeus Julius Agricola, eighteen years later. Once again it was a major stronghold of native resistance, and Tacitus himself reported its second, and final, capture by the Romans, without ever mentioning Druids (or women).[44]

It has to be admitted, however, that the dramatic scene on the shores of the Menai Strait may have no basis in reality at all. One of the most recent scholars of Tacitus, E. W. Black, has stated flatly that Tacitus cannot be trusted as an authority on first-century Britain.[45] This is because, writing about fifty years later, he relied on earlier written material, of variable quality, and – possibly but not certainly – the memories of participants in some of the events concerned. This material he then reshaped to suit his own rhetorical purpose. David Braund has reinforced this last point: 'it would be facile in the extreme to treat artful Tacitus as no more than a reporter of events'.[46] It is impossible to tell whether the Tacitean description of the Roman attack on Anglesey rested ultimately on an account written soon after the action or on a recollection made long after the event, or was a pure fiction invented to liven up a narrative and to pander to Roman prejudices against barbarians. Those who wish to take it literally can point to an excellent candidate for an eyewitness of the scene concerned: the future governor Agricola, who served on Suetonius's staff, might have been present as Anglesey was attacked, and was Tacitus's own father-in-law.[47] Those who prefer to emphasize the unreliable nature of the story can highlight the purpose it serves in the narrative. To the Roman mind, savages were influenced by women, prone to superstition, given to noisy, dramatic and overblown displays of valour, and indulged in horrible religious rites. Tacitus's cameo of the fall of Anglesey incorporated all of these very economically, with the inevitable polemical addition that Roman courage, steadiness and common sense proved more than equal to them and freed another part of the world from another ghastly cult.

Pliny, however, remains the writer who claims to say most about the Druids of the first century, largely because he was a natural historian and so incorporated examples of their beliefs and usages with regard to plants. In his most famous passage he declared that in Gaul their most sacred tree was the oak, and their most sacred plant or shrub the mistletoe found growing on an oak tree. He added that they worshipped in groves of oak and required leaves of it to be present for any of their rites. From this he proposed the possibility that the very word 'druid' derived from the Greek name for that tree. He added that mistletoe actually grew on it very rarely, and that when it was found there, the Gallic *druidae* gathered it according to a particular rite. If possible this was held on the sixth day after a new moon, because (Pliny added) they reckoned their months and years, and their larger, thirty-year, cycles, according to the progression of moons. They called the mistletoe by a term signifying 'the all-healing'. Having made preparations for a sacrifice and banquet beneath the tree, they led thither two white bulls and prayed to the moon as the healer of all things. Clad in a white robe, the officiating priest (*sacerdos*) climbed the oak and cut the mistletoe with a golden sickle, so that it fell into a white cloak held ready for it. The 'victims' (presumably but not necessarily the bulls) were then killed, with a prayer to the relevant god that the plant would be as effective as possible. They believed that, administered in a drink, it made barren animals fertile and was proof against all poisons. Pliny ended this account with a sneer: 'such are the religious feelings held by many peoples towards trivial things'.[48]

At another point he said that Druids believed that the *selago* plant warded off all kinds of evil and its smoke cured diseases of the eyes; he described a rite needed to cut it, by a man clad in white, with bare feet and divested of iron, but did not specifically state that this was Druidic. He was more exact about a water plant that he said Druids called *samulos*, and which they thought to be effective in preventing disease in cattle. This, he added, they gathered with the left hand, when fasting, and avoiding looking behind them, and laid in the drinking troughs of the beasts.[49] He added (with another swipe at their credulity or capacity for deceit) that they treasured objects that looked like small, hard-shelled, pocked apples. These they believed to be a form of egg, secreted by groups of snakes and having the power to win the favour of rulers and ensure success in lawsuits. They taught that it had to be snatched from the serpents in a 'soldier's cloak' on a certain day of the moon.[50] Pliny had seen one of these things; from his description, Stuart Piggott has plausibly suggested that it consisted of the fused egg-cases of a species of whelk found in Atlantic waters;[51] we shall, however, never know the truth. Nor can it ever be certain what sorts of plant *selago* and *samulos* were; the former has variously been identified as a kind of moss, or savin plant, and the latter as a type of water pimpernel, anemone or brook-lime.[52]

Pliny also provided a spicy anecdote about native British religious customs, which was to have a great impact on the imagination of modern writers: that 'at certain sacred rites' the wives and daughters-in-law of the Britons 'march along naked', having stained the whole of their bodies almost black with the dye of the woad plant.[53] This was provided as another example of the folly of 'remote tribes', and is part of his general disdain for the customs of barbarians.

In general, the value of Pliny's information as a scholar spans a spectrum between two extremes. When discussing the Mediterranean world, which he knew himself, in which he was primarily interested and on which he had the best information from others, he was sometimes an accurate writer. At the other extreme are the fables that he reports concerning peoples in lands with which the Romans had no direct contact. He populated the middle of the Sahara desert with the Atlantes, who did not have personal names and never dreamed when asleep, the Trogodytae, who ate only snakes and lacked the power of speech, the Blemmyis, who had no heads and whose eyes and mouths were in the centre of their chests, and the Satyris, who were half-goat. Along the upper Nile he reported the Nigroi, whose king was said to have a single eye in the centre of his forehead, and the Cynamolgi, who had dogs' heads. In the Himalayas was the region of Abarimon, whose people had feet turned backwards on their legs, and somewhere in the north of Russia were the Arimapsi, who also had one eye in the centre of their foreheads and fought griffins to steal their gold. Indian tribes included the Monocoli, who had only one leg, with a huge foot that they could use as a sunshade when lying on their backs, and the Astomi, who lived only on perfume, inhaling nourishment through their nasal membranes. And so on, and so on.[54]

The problem for our present concerns is that Britain and Gaul lie in the hazy area between these two extremes. Britain was half conquered and half known. Gaul was now becoming more Romanized and familiar, but Pliny was dealing with aspects of its native society that had mostly been removed by Romanization and so now existed in an imperfectly recorded past. Moreover, as can be seen from his extension of the definition of cannibalism, he was quite capable of manipulating information to the discredit of peoples whom he regarded as barbarians. He also recorded completely inaccurate data from his own society: among many examples, that the smell of lamps being put out usually induced miscarriage, and that menstrual blood made crops barren and fruit fall off trees, blunted the edges of knives, and killed men who had intercourse with a woman producing it at the dark of the moon.[55] One of the recent authors on Pliny, Mary Beagon, has stated bluntly that he has become regarded 'as a mine of misinformation, if not actual fantasy', and that his main value is as an exemplar of the beliefs of his own place, class and time.[56]

Pliny was unusually scrupulous in citing the existing books from which he had taken his information; indeed, he may have done this more often than any other ancient author. It is therefore significant that none of his references to Druids have any such attribution. This suggests – though it does not prove – that they came to him by word of mouth. He had visited the extreme south of Gaul – under Roman rule since long before Caesar's time – and also served in the army in Germany.[57] He had ample opportunity to pick up gossip about what Gallic Druids had been supposed to have done, or were supposed to be doing, and more concerning British customs; but we have absolutely no means of judging its worth. What may be much more confidently ascertained is the use to which Pliny put the data that he gathered. His basic cultural attitude was summed up in the line: 'The one race of outstanding eminence in virtue among all the races in the whole world is undoubtedly the Roman'.[58] He was prepared to accord the Greeks credit for notable contributions to civilization, but the peoples outside the Greek and Roman world had, by definition, to be inferior on every count. This has an obvious bearing on his treatment of Druids, but they fared still worse in his text because of his assimilation of them to another target of his polemic: magicians. He was determined to denounce human attempts to manipulate apparent supernatural power as a degeneration of both religion and science. Furthermore, he portrayed them as un-Roman, a compound of superstition and fraud foisted on his own society by less virtuous peoples.[59] He turned the Druids into exemplars of both qualities, referring to them interchangeably as *druidae* and as *magi* (his general term for magicians).

It has often been noted that Pliny's Druids have none of the judicial and philosophical functions mentioned by writers in the previous century, and seem to have become folk magicians and folk healers, akin to the later European cunning men, rather than philosopher-priests. This has been ascribed to the dramatic decline in their status that would have resulted from the Romanization of Gallic society and the prohibition of the sacrifices at which they had officiated.[60] It is a reasonable supposition, but not quite secure enough to write straight into history because, after all, Pliny was mainly interested in their medical teaching and, conversely, it is possible that earlier writers had exaggerated their learning and social authority. Another striking development is that Roman authors of the first century CE – Pomponius, Lucan and Pliny – associate Druids with secluded natural places, whereas the earlier commentators put them at the centre of aristocratic society. This change has likewise been ascribed to the results of Roman conquest and persecution, forcing them into hiding.[61] Again, the explanation is sensible, but it is also possible that the Druidic schools were always isolated from mainstream society. Tacitus, after all, had written of sacred groves on Anglesey when the Romans arrived there; however, they were also planted around many Greek and Roman shrines and need not imply a particularly close relationship between Druidry and the natural world even if the passage itself is not a fiction. Pliny was more specific that they had a special relationship with oak trees, though it is curious, if that was the case, that no other author mentions it. His guess that the very word 'Druid' might be related to the Greek one for 'oak' was still widely accepted by scholars in the mid-twentieth century.[62] It has now been largely abandoned. Behind all the Graeco-Roman names for these figures lies an original Gallic term, reconstructed by modern scholars as *druis*. That seems in turn to be related to Indo-European terms signifying powerful or extensive knowledge, so could just mean 'wise one' or 'one who knows much'.[63]

Pliny and Tacitus conclude between them the list of ancient writers who accused the Druids, either specifically or as part of native Gallic or British society, of committing human sacrifice. The moment seems opportune, therefore, to sum up what can be said about the subject, as it is represented in those texts. In a different work, I have provided a 'narrow' definition of it, which seemed most defensible and sustainable when discussing views of the ancient Druids.[64] This treated human sacrifice as a religious system that demanded the killing of people as part of the worship of its deities. On further reflection, it seems fairer here to broaden it to include any taking of human life as an intrinsic component of a spiritual belief system, whether it be done to honour divine beings, to predict the future, to provide a dead leader with companions in the next world, or to provide the foundations of buildings with greater strength. There are many societies in the historical record who certainly engaged in such practices, in many parts of the world, including both North and South America, Polynesia, Africa, India and China. On the other hand, many – apparently the majority – have not, and the question here is into which category those that had Druids should fall. In my previous remarks on the subject, I pointed out that other customs, much more widespread in humanity, could resemble human sacrifice in externals and so be confused with it, but were essentially distinct from it, such as the ritualized execution of criminals and murder of prisoners of war. They could, of course, overlap, in that cultures that sacrificed humans would often prefer criminals and prisoners as their victims, to inflict the minimum damage on their own population; but they are not at basis the same. I concluded in that earlier work that the Greek and Roman sources for Druidry are not, as we have received them, of sufficiently good quality to make a clear and final decision on whether the sacrifice of people was indeed a part of their belief system, and I stand by that opinion here.

What is beyond doubt is the cultural role that human sacrifice occupied in the minds of the people who wrote the ancient texts on which most subsequent authors have depended for their information on Druids. In the words of one recent commentator, J. Rives, it was 'part of a complex and wide-ranging Graeco-Roman discourse about civilisation and religion'. In his words, by alleging it against other cultures, 'Greeks and Romans were able to confirm their opinion of their own cultural superiority by attributing to a foreign people a practice that they considered cruel and perverse'. Whereas Greeks deployed the charge against barbarians, Romans increasingly used it also against suspected groups within their own society, such as Jews, Christians, political conspirators and magicians. Human sacrifice became for them a general marker of bad religion. Rives accepts that in some cases it may well have been practised by the foreign peoples concerned, although, in the case of the Druids, he regards the evidence as 'ambiguous'.[65] Another recent author, Lautaro Roig Lanzillotta, has agreed that human sacrifice 'served not only as a way of opposing the civilisation of the Graeco-Roman world to the barbarism outside it, but also as a means to draw a line between culture and humanity and barbarity and inhumanity within the same cultural world'.[66]

His particular interest was in the charge levied by pagan inhabitants of the Roman Empire against early Christians among them, of committing child murder or sacrifice, together with cannibalism, sexual orgies and incest. He pointed out, as Rives had done, that the same charges were made in turn by Christians, both then and later, against adherents of heretical forms of or counterparts to their own religion, while that of ritual child murder was also alleged by them against Jews. It interested Lanzillotta that historians have tended to reject such accusations when made against Christians and Jews, who have left writings of their own and remain culturally significant in modern society, while believing them of heretics, who have lacked both advantages. It may be commented, fairly obviously, that Druids have suffered from the same handicaps as the heretics. The unanswered, and probably unanswerable, question is whether pagan Romans were any more just to Druids than they were to Christians, or than Christians were to Jews.

These, then, were the Roman sources of the first and second centuries, which together with the writers of the last century BCE were to provide posterity with most of its concepts of what a Druid should have been. The other aspect of the earlier tradition, of the wise native philosophers and holy men, also continued, but it did so mainly at the far end of the Roman Empire and in Greek sources. It was associated in particular with the great metropolis of the Hellenistic world, Alexandria. The earliest in sequence of the authors who wrote in this tradition is Dion Chrysostom, who flourished at the opening of the second century CE, and who listed the holy or wise men of various foreign peoples. At the end of this list, he commented that 'the *Keltoi* have men called *druidas*, who concern themselves with divination and all branches of wisdom.' He added that kings depended so heavily on their advice that they were the true rulers of their societies.[67] A hundred years later the Christian saint Clement of Alexandria argued that the Greeks had originally learned much of their wisdom from cultures which they had latterly regarded as those of barbarians. He asserted that Pythagoras had been taught by Assyrians, *Galatoi* and the Indian Brahmins. Again, it is hard to tell whether Galatians or Gauls were meant by the second term. In addition he made an inventory of six foreign peoples who had schooled the Greeks in science and philosophy: among them (apparently with the belief that they were distinct) were the *druidai* of the *Galatoi* and the 'philosophers' of the *Keltoi*.[68]

Shortly after Clement, Hippolytus wrote that the *druidai* of the *Keltois* 'applied themselves thoroughly to the Pythagorean philosophy', having been taught it by a former slave of Pythagoras himself, a Thracian called Zamolxis, who came to them as a missionary after his master's death. They were regarded as prophets by their own people 'because they can foretell certain events by the Pythagorean reckoning and calculations', and also practised sorcery. Hippolytus added that this description was intended as a riposte to those who asserted that the knowledge of different peoples was not interconnected.[69] At around the same time in the third century, Diogenes Laertius drew up another list of foreign cultures that had allegedly produced philosophers before the Greeks. He, however, distanced himself from this hypothesis, attributing it to others; and it was at this point that he provided the reference to

Sotion and the pseudo-Aristotle, four hundred years before, that was cited above. He went on to say that those who held this idea also said that the *gymnosophistas* (literally 'naked wise men') of India and the *druidas* 'make their pronouncements by means of riddles and dark sayings, teaching that the gods must be worshipped, and no evil done, and manly behaviour maintained'.[70] That last saying has the ring of a triad, a classic literary form used by peoples speaking Celtic languages in the Middle Ages, and so could be an actual translation of a Druidic teaching in Gallic. On the other hand, it could, in context, equally have come from India or have been coined by Diogenes or one of his sources to sum up a foreign opinion; the Greeks were also capable of thinking in units of three, hence the three Fates and the three Graces.

There remain two sources in Latin, though the first one was produced by a Greek. He was Ammianus Marcellinus, the great fourth-century historian. For his few comments on the Druids, however, he quoted an earlier writer called Timagenes, who is generally (but not securely) identified with a Greek who had worked in Rome in the later first century BCE. His first extract from this lost book stated that the *drasidae* taught that some of the population of Gaul was aboriginal, but that the rest had immigrated from beyond the Rhine and from the isles to the west (presumably Britain and Ireland). In a longer section, he reproduced the information that the Gauls had been taught the arts of civilization by the *bardos*, *euhagis* (apparently a corruption of *o'vateis*) and *drasidas*. The *bardos* celebrated the deeds of famous men in epic verse, accompanied by the lyre. The *euhagis* 'strove to understand the sublime truths of nature'. The *dryaridae* (clearly to Ammianus or Timagenes an alternative term for *drasidas*) were 'men of a higher genius, members of the secret fellowship of the Pythagorean teaching; they were uplifted by investigations into secret and profound things; and with contempt for mortal lot they pronounced the immortality of the soul'.[71] The distortion of the Gallic words is so bad here (extending to inconsistency) that either Timagenes was quoting somebody else with imperfect understanding or Ammianus was using a garbled copy of Timagenes.

To this clutch of Greek authors can be added a Roman one: a geographer called Valerius Maximus who wrote in the first half of the first century CE. He included an account of one custom of the natives of Gaul: 'it is said that they lend each other money that is repayable in the next world, so firmly have they been persuaded that human souls are immortal. They ought to be called fools, were it not for the fact that what these trouser-wearers maintain was believed by the civilized Greek Pythagoras.'[72] Trousers, to a Greek or Roman of the period, were the costume of barbarians; the words translated as 'civilized Greek' in this passage were summed up curtly in the original by the single term *palliatus*, 'wearing a proper Greek cloak'. Ancient society – like most others – functioned largely on prejudices activated by a person's appearance.

Put together, this group of sources is vulnerable to disputation in both general and particular respects. The general problem with them is that they seem to be written mostly by people who were even more removed in geography and time from the societies that had produced the Druids than the other authors who dealt with them, and even more dependent on second- and third-hand testimony. They are certainly briefer and less detailed than the descriptions given in the more hostile accounts, and can be dismissed as the work of intellectuals constructing a myth of noble savages with which to criticize their own civilization. Their respectful accounts of Druidic philosophy could be countered, like those in the 'ambivalent' tradition of Diodorus, Strabo and Pomponius, as a projection of Greek concepts on to badly understood native traditions. Against all this may be lodged the suggestion that these authors were not contaminated by the prejudices and vested interests of the other writers, and felt none of the same need to promote Roman imperialism. Some indeed, as Greeks, could consider themselves to have been victims of it just as the Gauls and British were. The admiring tradition of classical writing on the Druids was actually older than the hostile one, providing that we accept the validity of the references to Sotion and the pseudo-Aristotle. With that provision, it was also more sustained, spanning six hundred years, while the denunciations were concentrated into the two centuries of the Roman conquest and its immediate aftermath. The more admiring set of texts cannot, therefore, be either confidently accepted or rejected as valid testimony.

The particular problem concerns the link with Pythagoras. Virtually nothing is known about him but his name, as he is represented neither by a body of teachings nor by a set of historical facts. In this he and his immediate followers have much in common with the Druids themselves, except that Greek and Roman writers were more interested in them than in the Druids and so wrote more about them. All the most informed of those writings, however, have been lost. What is clear is that upon his reputed life-story and teachings was based a tradition of belief that developed and altered over the following millennium, and that images of Pythagoras and his school changed with the tradition. Most experts agree that he must have taught that the soul was a senior partner of the body, and somehow survived death, and most of those favour the idea that this survival took the form of the rebirth of individual souls on this earth in new mortal bodies, human or animal. This tradition became one of the most common tenets of later forms of 'Pythagoreanism', together with a belief in the divine power of numbers. This latter doctrine eventually gave Pythagoras a reputation as a scientist which is entirely missing from the earlier writings on him.[73]

Since classical authors were comparing the Druids with a Greek thinker and his disciples who were effectively legendary themselves, any attempt to discuss historical relationships between Druidry and the 'original' Pythagoreans must be futile. What can be analysed are the relationships that Greeks and Romans perceived between Druidical teachings and Pythagorean philosophy as they were thought to have been by, and after, the last century BCE. Here there is an obvious linkage: that Caesar and Diodorus stated as the best-known philosophical doctrine of the Druids the belief in the transmigration of souls to new bodies after death that was also associated with Pythagoreanism. This striking comparison would in itself have caused ancient authors to associate the two, and the new reputation of Pythagoras as a scientist would eventually have been joined to the reputation of the Druids as experts on the natural world to suggest (as Hippolytus did) that Druidical science was based on Pythagorean principles. There is, however, a problem even with this neat conclusion. Some of the authors quoted above credited the Gauls with beliefs concerning an afterlife that were sharply at variance with those associated with Pythagoreanism.

These appear in Pomponius, Lucan and Valerius Maximus – all sources of the early to mid-first century CE – and consisted of the assertion that the Gallic tribes firmly believed in the reincarnation of human beings after death in their familiar bodies and their familiar society in a parallel world. Valerius attributed this doctrine to Pythagoras, but was badly wrong to do so, as it represents a completely different concept from the Pythagorean one of rebirth of the soul in a different body in the same world. All that they had in common is that the soul survives in a new frame, and the moral and social implications of the two are utterly different. It might be argued that the later accounts represented hostile distortions of the earlier, purer, representations of Druidic doctrine made by Diodorus and Caesar. Archaeology, however, suggests otherwise, producing consistent evidence of the burying of goods in Gallic and British graves that strongly suggests an assurance that their owner would need them in a different world. It is possible, therefore, that the earlier reports crediting the Druids with the actual Pythagorean doctrine of transmigration of souls were based on a misunderstanding of Gallic culture by somebody steeped in Greek philosophy.[74] With that, any certainty as to the relationship between Druids and Pythagoreans dissolves completely. The lost reality may have lain anywhere on a spectrum between an actual mission by a disciple called Zamolxis to Gaul and Britain to a complete misidentification of native belief made by a Greek visitor and then propagated in Graeco-Roman literature.

The question of what happened to the Druids is left unanswered in the classical literature. Suetonius and Pliny both stated that the Druids had been suppressed by imperial decree, but Pliny then proceeded to write as if they still existed, raising the possibility that only their political power and religious role had been destroyed. If that was the case, it would explain the remaining references to them in ancient texts, three of which appear in the series of potted biographies of Roman emperors written in the fourth century CE and known collectively as the *Augustan History*. In each of these a Gallic *dryas* or *drydis*, or a group of *druidae*, makes a prophecy to an emperor or future emperor that turns out to be perfectly accurate.[75] All these alleged incidents took place in the third century, and in all of them, although the term for the person or people making the predictions is related to Druid, the prophets concerned are clearly female. In one case she is the landlady from whom the emperor-to-be is renting a billet during his service in Gaul. These are the first and only appearances of female Druids, by name, in the whole of ancient literature. It is possible that they had always been present in Gallic society. It is possible that, with the annihilation of their religious and political role, the Druids as a whole were reduced to local healers, soothsayers and folk magicians, and came to include women as part of this loosening of their social identity. It is also possible that terms related to Druid were being applied, by Roman authors who knew little of Gaul and the Gallic language, to kinds of magical practitioner very different from the original Druids.

It is noteworthy that the classical writers treated these late Gallo-Roman 'Druids' as a socially unimportant group of people who had occasional real gifts of prediction and so possessed value at moments. They were certainly not regarded as threatening, and the writing of hostile accounts of Druidry died out during the early second century, after the Romanization of Gaul and Britain was completed. In their place remained the casual references to female soothsayers, and the memories of Druids as wise men of the past that continued in Greek tradition. By the fourth century, Gallo-Roman aristocrats and scholars had come to refer proudly to Druid ancestors: the poet Ausonius hailed two of his learned friends as descendants of the *druides* and *druidae* of north-western Gaul. In each case he stated that the descent was only reputed, suggesting that it derived from a now remote and semi-legendary period.[76] It seems that Druids had achieved the transformation that Scottish Highlanders and Native Americans were to undergo many centuries later: from being regarded as savages and menaces to being viewed as romantic and admirable, once the civilization that was doing the viewing had destroyed or absorbed them.

Readers unfamiliar with the ancient sources for Druids, and who were following the present discussion comfortably until about the point at which it passed Strabo, may now be completely bewildered by the number of writers represented, and the problems with each. What needs to be clear is that all of them may be correct or all may be wrong. We may be in possession of a relatively large quantity of valuable data or we may have none at all. Although the information is collectively internally compatible, some of it may be wildly inaccurate and some accurate in the last detail. We have no objective means whatsoever of consigning any of it to one category or the other. In default of such a means, historians and prehistorians have in practice tended to privilege or blend particular items of information according to a number of instinctual predispositions. These include whether they identify more with an imperial power or with the traditional peoples being colonized by it; what their relationship is with modern Celtic nationalisms or Druid movements; whether they are specialists more in Greek or in Latin texts; whether they respond to authority with automatic reverence or automatic resentment; whether they take an optimistic or a pessimistic view of human nature; and whether their literary purpose is to absorb an accepted view into a wider work or to challenge an accepted view in order to make a mark on a subject.

The contrasting results of these predispositions are very plain. To Stuart Piggott it seemed obvious that the hostile view of Druids taken by ancient authors was more realistic, and the admiring one just intellectual reverie. He decided that they were essentially a barbarian priesthood, learned by the standards of their own peoples but deeply implicated in sacrificial rites.[77] To Peter Berresford Ellis it was equally self-evident that all Roman sources could be largely discounted as imperial propaganda; that their more detailed descriptions all rested on Posidonius, who fervently admired Rome; and that the more respectful Greek texts were the only group that could be taken as objective. His Druids were not priests, but a learned class equivalent to Hindu Brahmins, and one against whom the charge of human sacrifice remained entirely unproven.[78] Nora Chadwick went further, calling them true philosophers, whom no ancient author had directly associated with the killing of humans.[79] Anne Ross has had no problem with accepting that the ritual slaughter of human beings was central to Druidic practice and has concluded that they were pre-eminently tribal priests and diviners, to be equated more with the shamans of other traditional peoples than with classical philosophers.[80] This is also broadly the view of Barry Cunliffe and Miranda Aldhouse-Green.[81] Jean-Louis Brunaux visualized them as an order of holy men who lived in pagan monasteries devoted to worship, wisdom and (advanced) science, and were brought out to give sanctity to public occasions. As such, their presence was needed to dignify sacrifice but they would never have performed an act of bloodshed.[82] Hilda Ellis Davidson conceived of them as priests, teachers and judges, and warned against an 'exaggeration' of their role in ritual killing.[83] Jane Webster has taken the classical sources to show that there was no fixed role for them, and that their nature and duties evolved constantly through recorded ancient history.[84]

This is a restricted sample of recent expert opinions, published or republished during the past two decades. There is a tendency in it for archaeologists to be harsher on Druids than specialists in literary sources, but attitudes clearly differ markedly within those disciplines as well as between them. What must be obvious is that the classical sources have represented for them the equivalent of colours on an artist's palette, to be selected and combined more or less at will to construct strikingly different portraits. Where these very recent, professional scholars have behaved in this manner, even when exposed to all the modern academic apparatus of forensic training and peer-group review, it is hardly surprising that earlier writers and artists did so to the same, or a much greater, degree.

* * *

For over three hundred years, the images of Druids produced in Britain have not depended entirely on the ancient texts, although these have been by far the most important source for the subject. They have been combined with two other sorts of evidence, both of which have increased in prominence over time. The first of these consists of material remains, which were first studied through the fieldwork of early antiquarians and now depend mainly on the survey and excavation techniques of modern archaeology. Most of the scholarly writings on Druids published during the past half century have been the work of experts in the Iron Age and Roman periods; and in this as in many other respects, it was long expected that they would unearth significant new evidence to complement and correct that provided by a fixed and unreliable group of classical texts. The problem here is that to date not one single artefact or image has been unearthed that can undoubtedly be connected with the ancient Druids.

In lieu of such discoveries, archaeologists have adopted one of two strategies. One is to assume that since Druids were apparently so central to ancient Gallic and British society, virtually any remains of that society, and especially those associated with ritual, can be connected to them.[85] The problem with this, of course, is that since the literary sources have left such unreliable accounts of their position and activities, it is not clear to what the remains concerned are being connected. The other approach is to identify specific finds with Druids; and this bears more extended consideration. The common difficulty here is that none of these identifications has been without some potential for alternative interpretation, and a quick look at some case studies should serve to illustrate it. In 1991 the burial of a man was found at the Kentish coastal town of Deal and dated to somewhere in the last two centuries BCE. He had been buried with a sword, shield and bronze crown or head-dress. Because of the last of these, the excavator suggested he might have been a Druid, but that he also might have been a king; and indeed he could have been either, both or neither.[86] Four other metallic head-dresses are known from Iron Age sites in England and Wales. Andrew Fitzpatrick has pointed out that they are unlike helmets of the period and most similar to artefacts found on Romano-British temple sites, which have been plausibly interpreted as ritual garb for priests. He has also suggested, however, that before the Romans arrived, they might have been worn by tribal chiefs who combined the roles of rulers and functionaries of religion, rather than by religious specialists such as Druids.[87]

In 1996 a cremation burial was excavated at Stanway, near Colchester, which was part of a high-status cemetery used by the native aristocracy during the years 40 to 60 CE. As the Romans took Colchester in the year 43, this would suggest that most of it dated from the period immediately after their conquest, and that the noble families represented there were some who had adapted to Roman rule. This particular grave attracted great interest because it contained a set of surgical instruments, making it the earliest unequivocal evidence of a medical practitioner in Britain, and the instruments some of the oldest in the world. With them were a set of rods, which may have been used for divination, as part of the work of diagnosis. The instruments combined Greek and Roman features with some from British and Gallic culture, and the grave also contained British brooches and both native pottery and some imported from Roman Gaul and Spain. The obvious conclusion to draw was that the grave's occupant had been part of a local noble household, in the manner of the private physicians retained by wealthy Romans. The excavators, however, chose to highlight the possibility that he might have been a Druid who had continued to operate after the Romans arrived. In the published excavation report, Ralph Jackson claimed that it was 'hard to avoid' this conclusion, while Nina Crummy, more temperately, thought it 'too specific' while adding that it was 'not inconsistent' with the evidence.[88] In the publicity put out for the report in the magazine *British Archaeology*, written by the principal members of the authorial team, it was the Druidical interpretation that was given full emphasis: the cover headline was 'The Druid Who Saw The Romans Invade UK'.[89] It is indeed a possibility; but somehow others that are also compatible with the data, such as that the dead man was a Gallo-Roman doctor hired by the local nobility as part of their adaptation to Roman ways, who was given some native brooches and pottery, were not discussed.

Between the 1970s and the 1990s, large Iron Age ritual sites were excavated at Gournay-sur-Aronde and Ribemont-sur-Ancre in northern France. From their dating they would have been the work of the powerful Gallic people known as the Belgae, who were subsequently to be conquered by Caesar. The sites were large rectangular enclosures of timber and mud-brick. At Ribemont the bones of hundreds of young men had been broken, crushed and then burned in crematoria that had themselves been made of human skeletal remains. Around the outer wall, eighty headless male bodies had been displayed along with weapons of war. At Gournay about two thousand weapons and pieces of armour had been hung around the inner precinct or set up on the gateway, in individual suits. In both places, also, there were abundant deposits of animal bones, from feasting, sacrifice or both. The two sites represent the largest collections of weaponry yet found from the Northern European Iron Age. The excavator, Jean-Louis Brunaux, declared that they confirmed the reports of human sacrifice among the Gauls given by Caesar and Diodorus; the remains were those of enemies who had been killed in battle or taken prisoner and then ritually slaughtered, and their bodies burned or displayed as offerings to deities.[90] A British archaeologist, Martin Brown, subsequently suggested instead that they might have been war memorials to dead warriors of the tribe who were given the honour of being cremated or set up on display after death at these holy places, in reward for their courage. The missing heads of the bodies around the wall of Ribemont would, according to this explanation, have been ritually committed to another venerated spot, such as a river.[91]

New investigations have left both explanations seeming possible, but also admitted a third. In the 2000s fresh excavations were undertaken at Ribemont, which confirmed the huge quantity of remains present at the site – thousands of human bones and thousands of weapons – and the fact that all seemed to date from the same period, near the beginning of the third century BCE. They also revealed a grave in which the bodies of about twenty individuals had been interred with weapons, and a second enclosure in which several dozen more had been laid. Both sets of people were treated with more apparent honour than those hung on the wall or turned into building material for crematoria. The interpretation now being made of the site is that it was a memorial and shrine erected after a single enormous battle, in which the bodies of slain enemies were displayed as trophies and those of warriors of the winning side were given dignified burial. Centuries later, after the Roman conquest, a Gallo-Roman temple complex was built over it.[92] Gournay now looks both more and less similar to Ribemont. It is more so, in that it likewise contained human bones as well as weaponry, and in particular skulls, which were hung or fixed up with the metal objects. As at Ribemont, the remains were overwhelmingly those of young men. It is less similar, in that it does not appear to commemorate a single event. Its construction certainly seems to be more or less contemporary with Ribemont, but deposits of material there continued for about one and a half centuries. It was abandoned at the end of the second century BCE, and the site later occupied by another, small, Gallo-Roman temple. Jean-Louis Brunaux, the excavator, now interprets it even more firmly as the sanctuary of a war god, to whom the heads and equipment of defeated enemies were dedicated as trophies and offerings.[93] It may be seen that there are now three explanations of the sites: as scenes of human sacrifice, commemoration of the beloved dead, and war temples at which the bodies and trappings of dead enemies were displayed. All are in fact entirely compatible with each other, but the actual evidence supports the last two more directly than the first. What is very clear, as Professor Brunaux points out, is that the discovery of these complexes completely refutes the conclusion that has often been drawn from Pliny, that the Gallic tribes worshipped in groves and other natural places, and did not construct impressive sanctuaries.[94] It is a further reminder of the pitfalls of relying on classical texts.

Similar problems have attended the question of the survival or disappearance of the Druids. To John Drinkwater, the material evidence testified overwhelmingly to the rapid Romanization of the Gallic aristocracy in the hundred years after conquest. This would, to him, in itself have soon sounded the death knell for the Druidic system that depended on those aristocrats. He has suggested that the decrees of Tiberius and Claudius were aimed at a vanishing tradition, already confined to the (literal) backwoods after one generation.[95] Anthony King drew attention to the same process of Romanization, with an exactly opposite conclusion. He pointed out that the great majority of native shrines continued in use, being rebuilt as stone temples, with cult images and inscriptions after the Roman pattern. This continuity of religion suggested to him a continuity of personnel, so that either the Druids were not involved in mainstream religion or (and, as he thought, more likely) they remained in charge of it: 'anti-druid decrees were probably unenforceable'.[96]

At times particular classes of artefacts have been used as evidence for the subject. John Creighton has studied the coins minted in south-eastern Britain during the last three centuries before the Roman occupation. He has suggested that the designs on them are often similar to images perceived by humans in states of altered consciousness, and may be associated with Druids in their capacity as seers. Since these designs waned in use as the names of kings appeared on coins, he thought this indicated a growth of royal at the expense of Druidic power. He related this to the fact that Iron Age shrines seemed to cluster along tribal boundaries until the last century before the Roman conquest, as if the Druids who staffed them acted as arbitrators between chiefs. In his reading, by that final century shrines were found near centres of political power, suggesting again a waning of Druidic influence.[97] All this may be true, providing that the coin designs are indeed trance-related images and not local stylizations of Greek coinage patterns, and that we have a large enough sample of known Iron Age shrines on which to base such conclusions. Both provisos, however, are in doubt.

Andrew Fitzpatrick has drawn attention to a small but distinctive group of swords, with short blades and handles in the form of human bodies, made across a large tract of Western and Central Europe in the later Iron Age. Nine bear distinctive stamps on the blades, usually a circle on one side and a crescent on the other. He suggested that these could be solar and lunar symbols, associated with the calendar and therefore with the Druids who were experts in the heavens, and thus in the reckoning of time, according to some Greek and Roman writers. It followed that these rare swords might have been carried by them as part of their insignia.[98] So they might indeed, if we discount the problems – acknowledged by Fitzpatrick – that nine is a small sample from which to generalize; that similar designs are sometimes found on other kinds of Iron Age sword; that they may not represent heavenly bodies at all; and that the short swords with the special handles are also found in parts of Europe not associated with Druids in the ancient literature. Fitzpatrick has gone on, however, to challenge the whole view of a distinctive caste of Druids spread uniformly across north-western Europe. What archaeology has found instead, he suggests, are certain objects, like the swords and like pairs of enigmatic spoons uncovered in a few British graves, which may have ritual connotations. As the graves concerned are both rare and in all other respects normal, he concludes that there was probably a great range of local special-ists who carried out between them the functions that Roman writers attributed to Druids, rather than one unified Druidical order or society responsible for the lot.[99] It is an interpretation which does rather call into question the utility of the very term 'Druid' for the archaeology of the Iron Age.

Two particular finds have been used above all to support different views of the Iron Age Druids, and between them neatly characterize the two aspects of the classical representation of them: the barbaric and the learned. The first is Lindow Man, the partial remains of a human body found in Lindow Moss, Cheshire, in August 1984. They consisted of the head, upper torso, arms and part of the right leg of a high-status male who had died in his twenties, all preserved by the peat bog to a degree which made forensic analysis possible. Three years later more of the legs and parts of the lower abdomen were recovered, but added little to the conclusions already drawn from the existing evidence by a large team of experts brought together by the British Museum to examine it. The report of that team, published in 1986, concluded that the man had been a victim of ritual killing. His skull had been fractured, his neck broken with a garrotte and his jugular vein severed, to produce a 'triple death' of such careful elaboration that it was hard to resist the conclusion that a major element of ritual had been involved.[100] At first tentatively dated between the fifth and third centuries BCE, and then more firmly to the period shortly before or during the Roman conquest of the region, he fitted into a society long associated (because of the Graeco-Roman writers) with human sacrifice. The same writers had identified the Druids with this, and there was a further piece of evidence to link them to Lindow Man: his stomach contained traces of mistletoe pollen, and Pliny had spoken of this plant as especially treasured by them. Furthermore, this particular body fits into a much broader context of human remains found in bogs across Northern Europe from Ireland to Germany and Denmark, which had often suffered severe acts of violence before and at death and can be dated to the Iron Age. These have commonly been interpreted as good evidence for human sacrifice.[101] As a result of all these factors, the body has regularly featured in works on Iron Age ritual and religion ever since as the best proof that the ancient British ritually killed and deposited human beings, as some classical authors had asserted.[102] It was arguably the most sensational find made by British archaeology during the 1980s and is perhaps the most carefully investigated human body on record. It has become one of the prize exhibits of the British Museum.

The interpretative status of the find is, however, thoroughly insecure, for two reasons. The lesser is its dating. The standard method used for determining the time at which artefacts went into the soil is by analysing radiocarbon in them, and human remains usually respond well to this. The first tests on the Lindow corpse suggested that it belonged to the Roman or post-Roman period, and subsequent refinement of these put it near the beginning of the Roman occupation. The problem with such an attribution is that ritual killing of humans was both legally and socially unacceptable to Roman and Romanized society, and Druids had apparently ceased to operate in it, or at least to have any connection with sacrifice. The location of the man's death in the pre-Roman period was achieved at first by ignoring the radiocarbon dates as unsound and then by taking advantage of the fact that the possible range of these dates extended back to a point before the Romans arrived. Since the discovery of more remains at Lindow Moss in 1987 it has become accepted that one or two other human bodies had been deposited in the bog, and these other remains date more firmly to the Romano-British period. Advocates of the theory of ritual killing have therefore had to put up the suggestion that the practice was carried on in secret in this thinly inhabited area of the Roman province, by natives habituated to the old ways. The problem with this, of course, is that there is no unequivocal evidence that there was a native tradition of ritual slaughter of humans to continue: Lindow Man had achieved his importance because he had been supposed to represent that evidence.[103]

The bigger problem is that, whatever his date, the pathology underlying the diagnosis of a 'triple death' by violence is itself unsafe. The diagnosis was made by a pathologist from a major London hospital, Iain West. The body was also examined soon after discovery, however, by a different expert, Robert Connolly of Liverpool University, who reached different conclusions. He considered that the man's neck had been broken by another of the blows, administered by a blunt instrument, which had fractured his skull in two places. To him, the supposed garrotte was simply a necklace, to hold a pendant or pendants which had been removed before he was put into the bog or which had corroded away there. He thought the gash over the jugular had been caused by damage to the body after it had been laid in the peat, perhaps associated with those peat-cutting operations that had divided the corpse itself into pieces.[104] If he is correct – and the matter can no longer be resolved after this lapse of time and the application of conservation treatment – then the ritual elements of the man's death disappear and he was the victim of robbery and murder or else of execution. The other body or bodies found in the Moss is or are represented by too many fragments to make a comparable attempt at diagnosis possible. The mistletoe pollen in the stomach amounted to just four grains, and though it could have arrived there by the eating of the plant's berries, it could just have blown on to the man's last meal or been breathed in.[105] There is no intention here of suggesting that Connolly's interpretation was the correct one, and West's was wrong. What is being proposed is that there was a difference of expert opinion, and that this, and the dating question, make the evidence in this case particularly difficult to evaluate. Nor does the wider context remove any of the difficulties. None of the other bodies retrieved from the bogs across Northern Europe have been conclusively shown to be victims of human sacrifice. Many or all may in fact be, but for each some alternative explanation is possible: notably that they had been criminals executed for heinous offences. These considerations mean that if Lindow Man appears at all in present discussions of the ancient Druids, he should not do so as a central piece of evidence.[106]

The archaeological artefact used most often to highlight the ancient image of Druids as scholars and scientists is the Coligny calendar. This was found in the Bresse district of south-eastern France in 1897, in the ruins of what had been a Gallo-Roman temple, and was written in Roman characters. From this context it has been dated to the later second century CE, and so is a part of the history and culture of the Roman

Empire. It also, however, represents a system of marking time not found elsewhere in that empire and was kept in the native, Gallic, language; it is indeed the most extensive surviving text in that language, and indeed in any early Celtic one, that has been discovered so far. It can be considered at least reasonably possible that the calendar embodies pre-Roman native ideas, and as such it has taken its place ever since its discovery in discussions of native Gallic customs and of Druidic belief. An entirely typical recent set of references to it in that context can be found in a book by Miranda Aldhouse-Green. At one point she calls it 'perhaps the most important archaeological document which can be quite firmly linked with the Druids'. At another she suggests that 'the Druids were almost certainly involved in the drawing up of the Coligny calendar', and that it was 'probably used' by them. At a third, she adds that 'it is probable that the Coligny calendar was a Druidical device'.[107] The qualifications applied in these phrases may be vestigial, but their presence is highly significant; it is a fair presumption that the Romanized Gauls who made the calendar were using a system developed before they lost their independence over two centuries before, but it cannot be proven by any means apparent thus far.

Having established that fundamental fact, it may next be asked what the calendar actually tells us; and here its condition at the time of discovery is crucially important. It was found in 153 bronze fragments, representing between them less than half of the original document. The beginning and end are lost, and only two months are wholly represented out of a probable original total of more than sixty. The text is full of notations, using a system of abbreviation that needs interpretation in itself. This means that any conclusions to be drawn from it must be based on a conjectural reconstruction; and here the fun begins. Stuart Piggott found a nineteen-year cycle in it (of the sort advocated by the Greek Meton), while the French scholars P.-M. Duval and G. Pinault have discerned a thirty-year one (influenced in part by what Pliny said about Druidical time-keeping).[108] Garrett Olmsted announced three different cycles in the same system: a twenty-five-year one, a thirty-year one and a longer one.[109] Part of this confusion results from the fact that there is no firm agreement on the place in the fragments at which the solar year is supposed to begin, or where in that year the individual months can be located.

During the 1990s two different American academics published judgements on the calendar. One was Olmsted, who employed a computer to simulate the paths of sun and moon through the surviving portions. He revealed a scheme of 'pure mathematical beauty and precision', which ensured that 'Gaulish druids could predict, hundreds of years into the future, lunar and solar positions to within one day in 455 years!' It proved that they were genuine philosophers and scientists, producing 'the most accurate solstice predictor in the ancient world'.[110] The second scholar was Stephen McCluskey. He found an attempt to reconcile solar and lunar calendars that had created a year on average almost two days out. The result was 'clearly too approximate to be continued indefinitely without further adjustment', and so he decided that one very good reason why the Druids were recorded as studying the movements of heavenly bodies was that they were too scientifically weak to operate a calendar which did not need constant empirical correction.[111] Olmsted's scientific marvels therefore transform into backwoodsmen struggling to run a system of time-keeping that needed annual adjustment. When experts equipped with the latest technology can reach such different conclusions, the rest of us can only look on in wonder. Before leaving the subject, it may be worth recording Jean-Louis Brunaux's comment that in its names for months, its intercalary system, and its dual division of the year, the Coligny calendar is similar to some used by the ancient Greeks, and may represent only a local version of the latter.[112] Certainly the Greek colony of Marseilles would have been one obvious route for such influence.

What should be obvious from this quick survey is that archaeology has so far failed to settle the question of which of the classical images of the Druids were true or false. This is because the evidence that it has turned up is itself in need of interpretation, and the interpretations made have tended to rely on the privileging of certain ancient texts over others. Scholars have remained trapped in a circle from which the work of spade, trowel and sieve might have been expected to rescue them. It may do so yet. There is a real possibility that a thorough study of the material evidence for ritual in the Iron Age will produce conclusions regarding the nature of the Druids – or whether the whole category of 'Druids' should be discarded by specialists in the period – that can be sustained and generally accepted. Furthermore, it is true that only an archaeologist – or a team of archaeologists – can undertake this task. To date, however, it has not been achieved.[113]

*   *   *

The other category of source that has been used to supplement or complement the classical accounts of the Druids consists of actual or possible references to them in medieval Irish and Welsh literature. Such references have been employed for this purpose since scholarly analysis of the subject began in Britain at the start of the eighteenth century, while in Ireland the production of literary images of Druids and attempts to write objective histories of them blend into one another almost seamlessly. None the less, this Celtic vernacular literature has made less of an impact on the British than the Graeco-Roman authors, for two reasons. One is that British education has always focused much more closely on ancient Greek and Roman than Celtic works (which is why, of course, ancient Greek and Latin texts *are* 'Classics'). The other is that the Irish and Welsh texts have often been considered less trustworthy, as the surviving versions were all produced centuries after the conversion of the peoples concerned to Christianity, a process usually presumed to involve the abandonment of Druidry. As such they represent retrospective accounts of a long-vanished culture, whereas the Greek and Roman authors were either contemporary to what they were describing, or drawing on written sources or memories that were still relatively recent. To this argument, the partisans of the Celtic literature have always responded that it was created by societies in which Druids had actually flourished, and so is free from the taint of prejudice, hostility and misunderstanding that can so easily be discerned or presumed in the classical authors.

Until recently the latter position was greatly strengthened by a presumption that dominated the study of medieval Irish literature from the mid-nineteenth to the late twentieth century. This was that the epic tales in that literature were based on stories that had originated in pre-Christian times and been preserved in a flourishing oral tradition of recitation and repetition until they were written down at various times in the early and high medieval periods. They were the cultural property of an elite of bards whose social position and training, like the tales they told, had survived the coming of Christianity almost unchanged. This supposition was based on two very plausible pieces of evidence. One was that Greek and Roman writers, as shown, had commented on the role played by bards in Gallic society, which was precisely equivalent to that which they fulfilled among those later speakers of Celtic languages, the medieval Irish and Welsh. The other was that the Irish epics were set in what was explicitly a pre-Christian native culture, represented with apparent sympathy and admiration, and so seemed very unlikely to be compositions of the medieval Christians who had compiled the manuscripts in which they came to survive. Furthermore, as Ireland had never been conquered by the Romans, Druids would presumably have flourished there until the start of the Middle Ages and the coming of literacy to their own people. This seemed to increase the probability of the transmission of authentic memories of them to the written records.

During the 1980s these attitudes began to wane among specialists, under the impact of both of the two main scholarly tools that could elucidate the matter: textual analysis and archaeology.[114] The former drew attention to the fact that the medieval Irish epics showed none of the familiar features of orally transmitted stories, so apparent in other works from early literatures such as the poems of Homer. The Irish works are mostly in prose, not verse, and lack a formulaic structure, or the repetition of key phrases, or alliteration, rhyme, rhythm, metre, assonance and other devices used to commit works to memory. They bear, in fact, every sign of works that had been composed as literature from the beginning. Archaeologists discovered that the royal centres that featured in the stories had indeed existed in pagan times, but not as the residential halls confidently portrayed by the medieval writers. They had instead been complex ceremonial centres, often open to the sky. The later authors either knew of their former importance because of a lingering tradition that had not preserved an accurate record of their form or purpose, or else were simply making guesses based on the sight of ruins in the landscape. The buildings, dress and war gear of the people in the epics were those of the Middle Ages, not of the Iron Age. The animals described in them include some species never found in Ireland and others that were introduced after the coming of Christianity. It might be riposted that genuinely old stories were just being retold in contemporary trappings, much as Shakespeare staged the undoubtedly historical events of the death of Julius Caesar in Elizabethan costume. Shakespeare, however, was working with texts that had descended from Caesar's own time, and the medieval Irish authors had no such sources on which to draw for their pre-Christian past. In 1992 J. P. Mallory summed up an emerging consensus when he declared that 'in general, no matter what games one attempts to play with the data, it is impossible to make a convincing case for an Iron Age date' for the earliest recorded Irish epics.[115]

This begs the question of why medieval Christian Irish writers would have tried to recreate the glories of a pagan and prehistoric world; but it is one which has now been effectively solved. It is clear that by the seventh century Irish monasteries had already become some of the powerhouses of Western civilization, outdoing the inhabitants of Britain in their knowledge of Greek and Latin texts and production of manuscripts. They were familiar not only with the Bible and other important early Christian writings but with some of the most celebrated works of pagan Greece and Rome. During the succeeding half millennium they worked hard both to produce a great literature of their own and to locate themselves within the broad framework of European history as established by classical writers. In this wholly successful venture, they drew on ideas and images from the Bible and other Christian texts and from classical Greek and Latin works, mixing them up with a great deal of native tradition. We have no real idea, however, of how much of this tradition was genuine and how much was invented for lack of anything better. Certainly the authors were attempting to convince readers and listeners that it was authentic, setting tales at sites by then long abandoned, referring to political systems that no longer existed and including styles of verse that were old-fashioned by the time the rest of the stories were composed. What can never be known is whether any of their material was based on genuine oral traditions deriving from pre-medieval times and, if so, which of it.[116]

The passages referring to Druids – which are more numerous than those in the classical texts – all fall into this category of data that may be either authentically remembered or the product of medieval fantasy. Scholarly treatment of them has accordingly depended on the same range of personal predispositions and contexts that produced the widely divergent evaluations of the images of Druids found in Graeco-Roman authors. We can be sure that the pagan Irish had Druids, because neither the prominence of the latter in classical texts nor the medieval Irish knowledge of the texts concerned was great enough in itself to bring about their introduction into so many native tales. The native terminology for them is also persuasive: close enough to the Gallic to seem like a genuine equivalent in a related Celtic language. This suggests that, from Ireland to Gaul, the pre-Roman native peoples possessed either similar functionaries or a similar function that could be matched to certain people and associated with the term rendered in modern English as 'Druid'. The most common Irish words for such a person were *drui*, *draoi*, *drua* and *drai*, pronounced (certainly) 'dree', and possibly 'dry' as well. The Druids of the Irish texts are not carbon copies of those found in the classical accounts: they have no general chief or assembly, no distinctive doctrines, no association with sacrifice, no special reverence for the oak and no consistent priestly functions. On the other hand they have enough in common to suggest a similar role in Iron Age Gallic, British and Irish society: they are the wisest and most learned people of their time, with multiple roles and overall a broad responsibility for understanding and interpreting the cosmos, and act as advisers to local political leaders. None of this, however, is sufficient to answer the problem of whether their specific appearances in the stories represent what they actually did, as opposed to what medieval writers wanted them to have done. It is time to examine these appearances in more detail.

The Druids of the Irish epics are, pre-eminently, magicians. The words *druidecht* or *draideacht* (or variants of them), literally meaning 'druidry' or 'druidcraft', feature as a general term for magic, both in the medieval literature and in Irish folklore recorded up to the nineteenth century. In the literature, Druids operate like wizards in stories all over the world: they perform feats physically impossible to humans in the apparent world, by uncanny means. They curse and blight humans and districts, raise storms and fogs, cause glamour and delusion, confer invisibility, inflict thirst and confusion on enemy warriors, transform people into animal shape or into stone, subdue and bind them with incantations, and raise magical barriers to halt attackers.[117] Occasionally details are provided of the rites involved in the casting of such spells. One tale mentions a famous blind Druid of the Ossory district, who decided to rout a band of invaders by 'burning a wisp and sending a hornless red cow' towards them.[118]

A number of reflections can be made on this pattern. One is that it makes the category of Druid very porous. In some tales Druids are evidently a distinct category of specialist. In others, the act of working magic makes anybody a Druid while it is being worked, irrespective of what she or he is for all the rest of the time. Thus, in the Fenian Cycle of stories, dating in various reworkings from the twelfth to the nineteenth centuries, giants and warriors are called by the terms approximating to Druid if they have acquired the ability to cast a few spells, even though that ability is a sideline to their main identity and activities. The terms are usually applied to them only with respect to their magical activities.[119] Other (apparently) specific types of person are also commonly credited in the medieval literature with a propensity to wield arcane powers, above all the highest class of poet, the *fili* or *ollamh*, and the blacksmith. Some of these are clearly the equal of Druids in such skills, while in certain texts the identity of magicians slides back and forth between labels. For example, in *Baile in Sca'il* ('The Phantom's Frenzy'), the High King Conn goes on to the ramparts of his fortress of Tara with three *druid* and three *filid*. On perceiving an unusual phenomenon, he asks one of the poets, not one of the Druids, to interpret it. The *fili* then goes off to work the necessary rites in a thoroughly 'Druidic' way, and indeed is called a Druid later in the story.[120] The tale of the adventures of the sons of the High King Eochaid Mugmedon features 'Sithchenn the Druid', who is called in to judge which of those sons should become heir to Eochaid's throne. Sithchenn is described in the next sentence as 'the blacksmith who was in Tara', and it is added that his reputation as a Druid derived from his gift of prophecy.[121] In a number of narratives, Druids are presented as one component of a set of specialists in esoteric arts who serve royal courts: thus we read of 'Druids and seers', 'sages and Druids' or 'Druids and poets' being collectively given, or achieving, tasks that require spell-casting: where the 'sages' are itemized, they turn out to consist of poets and legal experts. The terms *dichetal filedh*, 'poet's incantation', and *dichetal druadh*, 'Druid's incantation', are employed as if they were in practice identical.[122]

Some authors have used this blurring of categories to suggest that on the coming of Christianity, the Druids simply metamorphosed into poets, relinquishing their religious functions to the clergy of the new faith but keeping all the others. This is a long-established interpretation, and has been restated recently by Peter Berresford Ellis, Dáithí Ó hÓgáin, Christian-J. Guyonvarc'h and John Minahane.[123] The benefit of this tactic is that it permits the teachings of the medieval Irish bardic schools to be represented, to a greater or lesser degree, as those of the Druids themselves. If this belief is adopted, then the apparently lost wisdom of pagan Druidry can in theory be disinterred from much later records, by a process of selection based on the criteria, and instincts, of individual scholars.[124] It may well be perfectly correct, but for lack of any Irish literature from the pagan period we have no means of testing it. In this situation, the identification of particular texts and passages of texts as echoes of ancient Druidry is more or less arbitrary, and none of these exercises can be proven.[125] A countervailing possibility remains that the overlap or blending of the roles of Druid and poet (etc.) represented a genuine medieval confusion about what had actually gone on in ancient Ireland.

A second reflection that can be made on the Irish identification of Druidry with magic is that it almost certainly does reflect an ancient reality. One of the functions of magico-religious specialists in traditional societies is generally to attempt to ensure military success for their own people and to blight or repel enemies. The Druids on Anglesey who called down imprecations upon the legions of Suetonius Paulinus were – whether they themselves actually existed or not – fulfilling a stereotypical role. The story of the second battle of Maigh Tuired provides a good example both of how important this role was in medieval Irish perceptions of the former Druids and (again) of how complex a set of specialists could be associated with it. It portrays an army about to engage in the battle being supported by spells put on its opponents by its *druide*, but also its *deoguhairi* ('cupbearers'), *corrgunechai* (specialists in a type of curse involving standing on one leg with one arm outstretched and one eye closed), *filid* (poets, of course) and *ban-tua* (sorceresses).[126] This account, however, also provides a fine case study of how difficult it is to evaluate this sort of description as an echo of historical practice. The battle concerned was not part of Ireland's 'human' history, or pseudo-history, but fought between two mythical or legendary races of superhuman being. Moreover the text itself seems to be a late medieval reworking of an eleventh- or twelfth-century reworking of a probable eighth-century original, and it is impossible to attribute the passage cited above to any particular layer in this sequence of authorship. We can suppose that the ancient Druids were indeed wielders of arcane weaponry against the foes of their communities, but cannot tell whether any of the specific examples of this function provided in the medieval sources represent a memory of past reality.

A third reflection that can be made on the image of Druids as sorcerers is that Irish literature commonly presents them not merely as magicians, but as the wrong sort of magician, using devilish powers and ending up defeated by Christian missionaries who have the power of a true god behind them and so can accomplish greater wonders. This is part of a broader pattern in which Druids function as the foremost literary representatives of the evils of ancient paganism. In the words of the editor of the lives of Irish saints, Charles Plummer, they 'meet us at every turn as the chief, if not the only, opponents of the new faith'.[127] The saints who feature as victors over Druids include Berach, Ruadan, Colum Cille (known to the British as Columba), Mochuda, Fintan of Dun Blesci, Molaise and (pre-eminent in this as in all other respects) Patrick himself.[128] The tradition of the Druid as the main foe and victim of the saint began when Irish literature itself first appeared, and persisted till the seventeenth century.[129] It may well reflect a reality, of Druids as the leaders of pagan resistance to conversion, but there are severe problems in accepting the portrait of them given in the stories of the Christian holy men, even leaving aside the supernatural elements.

This is well illustrated by what are probably the earliest known tales of this kind, in one of the oldest surviving pieces of Irish literature: the life of Patrick written by Muirchú in the seventh century.[130] Composed in Latin, it described how the saint confronted the High King Loegaire at his court at Tara, and how the king was surrounded by *scives*, magi, *aurispices*, *incantatores* and 'all other practitioners of the dark arts'. Out of this string of Roman terms for magicians and soothsayers, scholars usually pick the most elevated, the magi, as signifying Druids. It is certainly they who take the lead in identifying Patrick to their ruler as a dangerous enemy, and opposing him with their arcane skills. He defeats them all with miracles, in the course of which their two leaders are killed. Muirchú, however, makes it plain that he is not just repeating a native tradition, whether related to actual events or not, but producing an Irish equivalent of scriptural episodes. By doing so, he sought to establish Ireland firmly as a Christian country as blessed as Israel had been. He expressly compares Loegaire and his magicians to Nebuchadnezzar and his magi, and Tara to Babylon, and Patrick's destruction of the magus Lochru to the duel of the apostle Peter with Simon Magus. Another parallel is equally clear but implicit: the competition of the saint and his followers with the other leading magus echoes details of that of the prophet Elijah with the priests of Baal.[131] A further Bible story probably lies behind this and many of the other legendary confrontations of Irish saints with Druids: that of the contest between Moses and Aaron and the magicians of Pharaoh. Under normal circumstances, it would be wise to conclude that there may well originally have been a major confrontation between Patrick and the royal Druids at Tara, but that the hagiographer, writing a couple of hundred years later, might have dressed it up in biblical terms in order to promote the Christian credentials of his people. The circumstances are, however, not normal: for once, we have a means of checking a later medieval account, in the form of documents from the time that it describes.

These consist of two letters written by Patrick himself, one representing an auto-biography and both dealing with the difficulties of his work as a missionary in an Ireland that was still then largely pagan.[132] They are probably, if we exclude memorial stones from the category of literature, the only literary works to survive from the British Isles in the whole of the fifth century. They are also the only authentic texts for the career of the historical saint, and they never mention Druids; the people cited as giving him trouble are either local kings or hostile Christians. There is also no reference at all to the dramatic confrontations at Tara. This does not mean that Druids did not play any part in the opposition that Patrick encountered, nor does it prove that the whole narrative of his encounter with Loegaire is a fiction invented after his time. The lack of detail he provides for most of his activities may well conceal evidence in support of both points. His letters do, however, strongly suggest that the importance of Druids in countering his missionary work was inflated in later centuries under the influence of biblical parallels, and that Patrick's visit to Tara was

given a pivotal importance that it never possessed – if it ever occurred at all – to suit
later political preoccupations. If this is true of the relatively early lives written of
Patrick, it is likely to be even more so of the bulk of accounts of Irish saints, which
are much later in date and separated in some cases by several centuries from the times
of the individuals whom they celebrate.

The only appearances of Druids in documents attributed to Patrick himself occur in
some that are generally thought to have been composed after his death. One of these
consists of a set of canons allegedly issued by him and his companions, and probably
dating in reality from the sixth century. One ordains that to swear an oath before a
'haruspex' (diviner) 'as pagans do' is an offence as serious as murder or adultery, and
carries an equivalent penance.[133] The term used is a version of a standard Latin one for
a soothsayer and is generally, though not certainly, translated as 'Druid'; and the direction seems to reflect a genuine pagan legal custom. The other of these documents is the
so-called *Lorica*, or 'breastplate' of Patrick, a prayer for divine protection that may just
possibly be the work of the saint himself but is not recorded before the ninth century.
The dangers listed in the prayer include 'spells of women, smiths and *druad*'.[134]

The impression given by these two sources – that Druids did not represent the
bulwark of paganism in the face of the Christian challenge, but were just one element
of the society that Christianity was trying to reform – is reinforced by the Irish law
codes. These are also relatively early texts, composed between the sixth and ninth
centuries, and their practical and functional nature suggests that they do provide
insights into a genuine set of relationships. Their hostility to Druids is sometimes
obvious, but the latter are regarded as a nuisance, and as one item among several in
need of reform, rather than as arch-enemies. Most famous in this respect is *Bretha
Crólige*, which declared against three figures traditionally respected in Irish society, as
fit only for repudiation: the Druid, the satirist and the raider. This repudiation,
however, only consisted of reducing the level of care that a householder was expected
to give them if they fell sick to that granted to a prosperous farmer, no matter how
much more noble their actual social rank happened to be.[135] Another legal manual,
Uraicecht Brecc, blandly includes Druids among the lesser varieties of people with
crafts or skills to offer, such as physicians, smiths, harpists and artisans. This may be
an insult, degrading them from a former equivalent status with poets, but it also
implies a measure of acceptance for their role, whatever that was.[136] Ecclesiastical
sanctions, such as those recommended in penitentials (the books of penances
recommended for specific sins), are – as one might expect – harsher. One such code
of penances classes magi with heretics, adulterers and 'a cruel man vowed to evil' as
those persons who get seven years on bread and water. Another denies remission from
penance to those guilty of *druithdechta*. The tract *Altram Tige dá Medar* classes
together *draídecht* and *díabaltacht*, 'druidry' and 'devilry'.[137]

These references could quite plausibly be read as proof of an embittered hostility
between Druids and early Irish Christians; but a linguistic problem hangs over the
terms used. If *druidecht* and its variants had become used as a blanket expression for
all forms of magic, what may be reflected in these condemnations is the animosity
of medieval Christianity towards magic in general (i.e. human manipulations of any

supernatural power outside the formal framework of the Church's procedures) rather than towards a particular group of people called Druids. A parallel difficulty attends the relationship between Druid and saint. It has long and frequently been noted that the figure of the classic medieval Irish saint – a mighty and combative figure with power over the forces of nature and an effective propensity for cursing – may well have taken on the characteristics of the pagan Druid. Certainly saints, as represented in their (much) later hagiographies, were stereotypes; the transformation of the historical Patrick, as represented in his writings, into the hero of the lives written of him later represents a classic, and unusually well-documented, example of this. It may be proposed here, however, that the traditional suggestion that a stereotype of a Druid is turned into one of a saint assumes that the medieval Irish knew more about the ancient Druids than they may have done. If they actually had no better idea of how Druids behaved than of the true nature of pagan ceremonial centres or of Iron Age costumes and technology (matters which have been determined by archaeology), then the process might even have worked in reverse. First the Christian scholars of the seventh to ninth centuries constructed a stock image of how a saint should be, based mainly on Old Testament models but also on existing, continental, lives of saints (just as Patrick's autobiography seems to have been based on his reading of the much more famous one by Augustine). This process is clear enough. It may be argued that then they could have constructed a stock image of a Druid to put up against the saint in the place of the evil magicians of existing Hebrew and Christian legend, and invested him with qualities that were a mirror-image of those of the saint.

A fourth major reflection on the medieval Irish identification of Druidry with magic is that by far the most important single function of Druids as represented in the stories is as diviners. This is a complex role that covers five different categories of operation. The first of these is straightforward prophecy: the (apparently) spontaneous prediction of major events.[138] The second is a more deliberate form of divination by which measures are taken to produce a foresight of what is to befall a particular kingdom or its ruler.[139] The third is the ability to interpret or explain an unusual occurrence: an apparently meaningful dream experienced by a king, a peculiar natural phenomenon, and so on.[140] The fourth is a knowledge of the luck or potential that attends specific days or numbers.[141] The fifth is the use of methods to reveal the whereabouts of missing people or objects.[142] There can be little doubt that divination must have been one of the duties of the ancient Druids, in Ireland and elsewhere, if only for the reason that most traditional societies have had specialists in this skill. It was associated with the Gallic Druids by Graeco-Roman writers, and one of the few interpretations of the Coligny calendar on which there seems to be general scholarly agreement is that it marks specific days as lucky or unlucky.

The problem is whether any of the methods of divination employed by Druids in the Irish epics can be treated as historical, or whether all should be classed as possible or probable inventions of medieval authors trying to imagine how ancient pagans would have behaved. We hear of events being predicted from the movement of clouds and of water, by use of a gaming board (similar to that of chess), from the sound of the wind and from the casting of rods marked with special characters.[143] The glossary *Cóir*

Anmann interprets the name of the famous legendary Druid Mogh Ruith as meaning 'Magus rotarum, the devotee of the wheels, for it is by wheels that he used to make his *taiscéladh druidhechta* or magical observation'.[144] This looks like a classic piece of guesswork by an Irish author familiar with Latin, based on the similarity of the respective Irish and Latin words. One of the most famous rites of divination to emerge from the literature is the *tairb-feis*, or 'bull-dream', by which the identity of a successor to a kingdom would be revealed in a dream to a man who had gorged himself on the meat and broth of a white bull. An incantation was sung over him before he went to sleep. Two references to this custom survive.[145] In one, it is not specified that Druids sing the charm, but in the other it is. Both treat the ritual as one belonging to a dead past, and there is no sure way of knowing whether they represent a genuine memory of a pagan custom or a literary tradition concocted after such memories had passed away.

The same is true of the method prescribed for gaining one of the great arcane skills commonly attributed to Irish Druids, poets and sages: the *imbas forosnaí* or 'knowledge of enlightening', which seems to denote a general ability to make predictions or interpret signs. The recipe appears in *Sanas Chormaic*, 'Cormac's Glossary', a work probably compiled in stages between the years 900 and 1100. It describes how *filid* or poets would gain the power by chewing a piece of red pig, dog or cat and putting it on a flagstone behind a door. The practitioner would then sing an incantation over it, offer it to deities and then call the latter to enlighten him. If that did not do the trick, he would sing incantations over the palms of his hands on the following day, call the divinities to him again, lay his palms on his cheeks and fall asleep. If he was not disturbed (and it was customary to post a friend to ensure that this did not occur), he would awake with the power. The entry in the glossary added that the ritual had been abolished on the arrival of Christianity, as it represented an offering to demons.[146] The problem, of course, is to reckon the likelihood either that it had been remembered across the centuries since it had disappeared, or that the entry was taken from an earlier, and reliable, literary source. Both eventualities are possible, and it could well be argued that, as the symbolic use of the human hand features in medieval charms, this strengthens the credentials of this story as a relic of actual pagan custom.[147] However, it is still possible that it was an invention. The glossary is not a reliable authority in some other respects – its explanations of the meanings of the names of the festivals of Beltane and Imbolc, and of the word 'Druid' itself, have been rejected by modern linguists as misplaced guesses.[148]

The practice of divination presupposes a greater knowledge of the natural and divine world than is common to humans, and so in itself it would fit Irish Druids for the roles of sages and scientists that were attributed to their Gallic counterparts. These roles are not, however, very prominent in the medieval literature; to be a magician is not really the same as being a scholar or philosopher, and the Irish texts, as said, emphasize the magician. When references to their knowledge of the cosmos do occur, the Druids tend to be represented as quacks. One law tract, for example, celebrates a legendary Christian lawyer called Connla Cainbhreathach, 'who used to contend with the Druids, who said it was they that made heaven and earth, and the sea etc., and the sun and moon, etc.' He challenged them to make the sun and moon shine from the north, and when they failed he bid them believe in his (true) faith instead.[149] It is a matter for personal instinct whether anything more lies behind this account than evangelical invention. One of the biographers of Patrick, Tírechán, who wrote in the late seventh or early eighth century, asserted that Irish magi believed in 'the day of the Lord's judgement', which they called 'the day of erdathe'.[150] What this meant, and whether it was anything more than a projection of Christian belief, is unknown. It is also unclear whether the various supernaturally skilled physicians who appear in the Irish literature should be regarded as memories of a healing aspect to the work of the ancient Druids. It may or may not be significant that when Druids themselves feature as curing people in the stories, the malady is one of rage or madness, rather than a physical ill.[151]

There are, however, grander glimpses of them in the medieval sources, which seem to reflect more closely the role attributed to their Gallic counterparts by Caesar and a few other ancient writers: that of judge and arbitrator. There is the reference to swearing oaths before a haruspex mentioned above, though if this does mean a Druid it may merely indicate that the latter could invite deities to witness the act rather than function as some kind of authority himself. The legal tract Bretha Nemed toísech contains the line 'a defeat against odds [and] setting territories at war confer status on a Druid'.[152] This could mean that Druids had the power to determine whether kingdoms were at war or peace, and directed military efforts. It could, however, also have other meanings; for example, a reference to the Druidic role as prophet or soothsayer, which could be enhanced by pronouncements in time of war. In general the earlier, seventh- and eighth-century, sources clearly distinguish the role of brithemain (judge or lawgiver) from that of Druid.[153]

The epics also contain one super-Druid, Cathbad or Cathub, who features in the Ulster cycle of stories that was put together between the seventh and twelfth centuries. In Mesca Ulad, 'The Drunkenness of the Men of Ulster', he is described as somebody who 'arbitrated between the rulers' of that province. The story asserts that it was forbidden for even the greatest king in it to speak before his Druids did, and it was Cathbad who spoke first of those.[154] In the Ulster epic par excellence, Táin Bó Cuailnge, 'The Cattle-Raid of Cooley', he is shown as himself the father of the paramount king, and always having a hundred pupils learning 'Druid lore' from him.[155] He is, then, a Druid who matches those of Gaul, as described by the authors of the first century BCE: a mighty judge, teacher and arbitrator exerting authority over tribal leaders. This is precisely how he, or his kind, might have been in ancient Ireland, and from the nineteenth century to the present the portraits of him have been treated as good evidence for historical reality.[156] Kim McCone, however, has suggested that they were composed by medieval clerical authors anxious to exalt the political power of churchmen as the implied successors of such great spiritual leaders.[157] It is as impossible to argue away this point as it is to prove it. Cathbad's social and political status is certainly unusual in respects other than those that relate to his Druidry. In Compert Conchobuir, 'The Conception of King Conchobur', he is depicted as the leader of a freelance band of warriors, who wins battles by combining physical strength and dexterity with magic. Bloodthirsty and ruthless, he gains land for himself (and so establishes himself as a legitimate and independent power in Ulster) by kidnapping an heiress and giving her the choice of marrying him or being killed.[158] As in the case of other characters in the literature, therefore, his Druidry consists of the addition of a knowledge of non-physical powers to more routine talents and a 'secular' role.

At regular intervals other morsels have been picked from the medieval Irish texts to provide apparent evidence for the nature of the ancient Druids. Some have drawn attention to a passage in Tírechán's life of Patrick, stating that a Druid and eight companions who attempted to murder the saint were dressed in white tunics. Combined with Pliny's description of a white-robed 'priest' cutting the mistletoe from the oak, this has been used to prove that Druids wore white robes, from Ireland to Gaul.[159] Writers who have wished instead to assimilate them to tribal shamans prefer a single section of *The Siege of Drom Damghaire*, in which the Druid Mogh Ruith is portrayed at one point as donning a 'dark grey hornless bull's hide' and a 'white speckled bird headpiece', before flying up into the air.[160] The costume is supposed to equate to the caftans and head-dresses worn by some Siberian shamans, and the literal flight of the tale is held to represent instead the spirit of the shaman going forth into an otherworld. Those who have desired them to be parallels to Christian clergy have extracted references from three texts to the use by Druids of a pagan equivalent to baptism, and a couple of others to their wearing of tonsured hair like Christian clerics.[161] Such exercises do not consider the odds for or against the likelihood that all these images result from the capacity of medieval writers for creation or projection. Conversely, Kim McCone has pointed out that the three potent orders of humanity who feature in the tales – kings, poets and Druids – match the triad of *reges*, *prophetae* and *sacerdotes* (kings, prophets and priests) found in the Latin version of the Old Testament used by the scribes who wrote the tales. He has drawn attention to a specific judicial ordeal cited in the literature, the *airisem oc altóir*, whereby an accused person would walk nine times around an altar and then drink water over which a Druid had pronounced an incantation: the guilty would choke. It sounds authentically Irish, but actually echoes a process found in the biblical Book of Numbers.[162] The obvious counter-argument is that these parallels are coincidental and that the Irish texts represent native Iron Age customs. We can never know the truth.

For later authors inclined to take a negative view of Druidry, a favourite pair of passages occurs in the *Dindshenchas*, or collections of lore associated with places, compiled in the eleventh or twelfth century. One such place was Maigh Slecht, a plain now in County Cavan, and a prose text describes how the greatest idol in Ireland once stood there, a figure of gold called Crom Cróich. Around it were twelve lesser idols, of stone. This passage adds that 'the firstlings of every issue and the chief scions of every clan' were killed as offerings to it, and at each feast of Samhain, 1 November, the High King of Ireland led all the people to prostrate themselves before it. They flung themselves to the ground so hard that three-quarters of them perished each time. Hence the name Maigh Slecht, 'Plain of Prostrations'.[163] More information appears in a verse version of the *Dindshenchas*. There the idol is called Crom Crúaich, and it is declared that 'the firstborn of every offspring and the firstborn of every family' was sacrificed to it. This consumed a third of the children of Ireland; their blood was poured around the idol, and the people doing so asked for good yields of milk and corn in return. These atrocities continued until St Patrick took a sledgehammer to the idols and brought them down.[164] This story appears in turn to have been based on one in the *Tripartite Life of Patrick*, written at some point between the eighth and eleventh centuries and regarded by scholars as the latest and most fantastic of the early medieval biographies of the saint. This describes how Patrick found on Maigh Slecht the chief idol of Ireland, an image of gold and silver called Cend Crúiach, 'Bloody Head', accompanied by twelve other idols of brass. He expelled the demons that inhabited them and drove the idols themselves into the ground. There is no mention of sacrifices. The Maigh Slecht story sounds, therefore, like a medieval Christian fantasy, developing over time and growing more lurid with each retelling. The one note of realism in it is the description of the remains of the sanctuary that accompanies the story in the *Tripartite Life*, which was said to be still in existence at the time when the text was composed, with the idols buried up to their heads in earth and a mark left by St Patrick's staff visible on top of the biggest. It seems likely that a genuine pagan sanctuary had existed on the spot – perhaps of standing stones – which was linked to the lurid fable concocted about Patrick.[165]

Jacqueline Borsje has recently revisited these texts, and all those which make apparent reference to human sacrifice in pre-Christian Ireland. She has suggested, plausibly, that the Maigh Slecht tradition was assembled out of a number of ideas and themes in earlier works. These include Old Testament references to idols of brass or gold, to child sacrifice, and to idols in Patrick's own, genuine writings, and to the saint smashing the head of a dragon, meaning paganism in general, in Muirchú's earlier life of him. She has linked the full development of the story to a new interest in human sacrifice as a pagan custom, shown by Irish writers around the year 1100. This included a translation of Lucan's *Pharsalia*, reminding us that the authors concerned could imbibe such ideas from Greek and Roman texts as well as the Bible. Dr Borsje concludes that the stories about Maigh Slecht seem 'to be more a key towards understanding in what way the pre-Christian past was viewed in the Middle Irish period than a key to disclose knowledge about the historical veneration of Cenn Cruiach'.[166] It seems hard to disagree with that interpretation.

The issue of whether the ancient Irish practised human sacrifice (with the implication that Druids would, in that case, have led it) was a subject for vigorous debate in the late Victorian and Edwardian periods. The controversy was kindled by two Catholic Irish academics in 1873, as part of a literary movement intended to give the British a better consciousness of the high cultural achievements of ancient and medieval Ireland. In doing so, of course, they were seeking to counter the frequent assertions or implications made by British writers of the time, joined by some members of Ireland's own Protestant Ascendancy, that the native Irish were an inferior race, unfit for self-government and unworthy of respect. Inevitably, they picked on the deficiencies of the medieval sources to argue that there was no good evidence for such sacrifices among the ancient Irish.[167] At the end of the century, the Irish nationalist leader Douglas Hyde cast further doubt on the tale of Maigh Slecht, suggesting that the references to the offering of children were insertions made by a medieval monk imitating the references in the Old Testament.[168] This case was reinforced in 1903 by Patrick Weston Joyce, who called the story of the killings on Maigh Slecht 'an invention pure and simple', adding his opinion that 'no human beings were ever sacrificed in Ireland . . . to any other idol'. Joyce then proceeded, however, to undermine his own argument, in two ways. First, he accepted the existence of the idols to which the sacrifices were allegedly made, though not the sacrifices themselves; even though the evidence for the former was hardly better than that for the latter. Second, he declared that there was reason to believe that human sacrifices had been made; not to idols, but to consecrate the foundation of a building, and to avert natural disasters.

To justify this view, he cited two other medieval texts. One was a version of the famous *Life* of Columba, the saint who carried Christianity from Ireland to the native peoples of Scotland in the sixth century. It told of a follower of the saint called Odrán or Oran, who volunteered to die so that his body, interred in the Scottish isle of Iona, would act as a protective force for the island and scare away the demons that had inhabited it hitherto. This occurred, and Iona subsequently became the base for Columba's missionary work. The other story came in the tale of *The Courtship of Becuma*, and was set at the time of a dreadful famine, brought upon Ireland as divine punishment for a great crime committed by a woman. It was decided to kill a boy and sprinkle his blood on the doorposts of Tara, to avert the curse. Instead, a wonderfully formed cow appeared to those about to make the offering, and took his place, achieving the same beneficial effect.[169]

These qualifications afforded a prime opportunity for authors on the other side of the Irish Sea, who challenged the whole case. One was a great scholar of Irish medieval literature, Kuno Meyer, who called the tale of Maigh Slecht entirely believable, because it fitted the classic model of a primitive fertility cult, as imagined by authors of his time. This was an era in which many folklorists and historians of religion believed that all ancient paganism had essentially consisted of cults to promote the fertility of the land and its inhabitants; a theory which is now almost completely abandoned. As further proof of his argument, Meyer cited another version of the story of the famine already quoted by Joyce, in the text *Echtra Airt mic Cuinn ocus Tochmarc Delbcháime*. In this, Druids had advised that a dearth caused by the king marrying the wrong woman would be averted if the son of a sinless married couple was killed and his blood mixed with the earth. Instead a cow was offered in the lad's place, brought by his mother.[170] Meyer was seconded by another notable authority on Celtic literatures, this time a Scot: John Arnott MacCulloch. His key argument was that there was clear proof that other ancient races at the same level of development as the ancient Irish had practised human sacrifice, so there was no reason to grant the Irish any special benefit of the doubt. As his clear proof, he cited the ancient Greek and Roman claims of the practice in Gaul. He also called the rites on Maigh Slecht a classic example of a primitive fertility cult, and added another medieval text as support for this view, taken from the twelfth-century *Leabhar Gabhála Éireann*, the Book of Invasions. This was a mythical history of Ireland, and the passage concerned related how one of the legendary races said to have populated the island in prehistoric times, the Nemedians, paid two-thirds of their children in tribute to a race of monsters called the Fomorians, every year. This is not an obvious reference to religious rites, and the context is clearly a fantastic one, but MacCulloch interpreted it as another example of an early agricultural cult requiring the blood of humans. He repeated as further evidence the stories of the famine and of Columba's monk, used before, and accused the critics of the idea that the Irish had sacrificed human beings of having been blinded by nationalist prejudice; he, of course, regarded his own opinions as entirely scientific and objective.[171] The debate now ended, as the granting of independence to the majority of Ireland removed the context that had inspired it.

Jacqueline Borsje has recently revisited the most frequently cited of the stories that were used to underpin that of Maigh Slecht by the participants who argued that the ancient Irish had committed human sacrifice. She suggests that the story of the projected sacrifice of the son of a sinless couple is not, in its origins, Irish at all, but based on a Welsh legend that will be considered below. Mixed in with it were the biblical traditions of the intended sacrifice of Isaac by Abraham and the sprinkling of sacrificial blood on doorposts to protect the Israelites in Egypt. As for the tale of the self-sacrifice of the follower of Columba (whether or not this constitutes human sacrifice as generally understood), it does not appear in the early life of Columba, but in one dated to 1169. It then became very popular, being repeated in different versions over the succeeding centuries. Once again, it appears to be a twelfth-century addition to earlier tradition, product of a time when, inspired by biblical and Graeco-Roman references, Irish writers were taking an interest in the topic of human sacrifice.[172]

Another example of the problems arising from selective quotation and credibility concerns the issue of female Druids. In general, medieval Irish literature represented women as having their own, formidable, tradition of magic, which was distinguished from that of Druids, who are almost always male: examples have been given above from the *Lorica* of Patrick and the tale of the Second Battle of Magh Tuired. There are also a few references to women Druids, as such. In *Acallam na Senorach*, 'The Colloquy of the Old Men', there briefly appears a *bandrúi* (literally 'woman-Druid'). One recension of *Táin Bó Cuailnge* features six *druid*, half of whom turn out to be female. Most famous is the account of the boyhood of the hero Fionn mac Cumhail, who was fostered with 'Fiacail son of Cochenn and Bodbmall the druidess and the Gray One of Luachair'.[173] All through the twentieth century these texts have featured as evidence that ancient Irish Druids admitted women.[174] This is natural enough, and may be the truth, but there are two different sorts of problem with it. One is the wearyingly familiar one: that any references to Druids in this literature may be the product of medieval fantasy, governed by very loose conventions of what could or could not be portrayed. The second has also featured before: that the term 'Druidry' was commonly used as a blanket term for magic. This is its sense, for example, in *Torchmarc Étaíne*, 'The Wooing of Etain', where a wicked woman learns spells from a Druid foster-father and thus gains the power of 'Druidry'. That being the case, the meaning of the three references to female Druids may not signify that 'women and men could both be Druids' so much as simply that 'women and men could both work magic'. Most medieval writers chose to put such women in a separate category from male magicians, but a few did not, just as some preferred clear categories of male magic-workers (Druids, poets, smiths, etc.) and some did not.

A final issue to be considered when evaluating the Irish evidence for ancient Druidry is the early medieval script known as *ogam* or ogham. In its heyday this was employed for inscriptions on stone monuments in Ireland and western Britain, though it occasionally reappeared in manuscripts after its use on monuments died out during the seventh century. It was well designed for putting messages on upright stones, consisting of a series of straight lines arranged in different patterns that could be placed with particular ease along the sharper edges of a monolith. The proclamations that it made were purely functional, apparently consisting of memorials to dead dignitaries, although it is possible that some of these stones were placed as territorial markers. It is therefore the script itself that is of interest in the context of Druidry. For most of the twentieth century it was placed firmly in that context, by the work of two experts, Eoin MacNeill and R. A. S. Macalister. Since the Middle Ages there had been an assumption that ogham was ancient, and predated Christianity, and these authors now appeared to place that belief on a scholarly footing. To MacNeill 'the Ogham tradition . . . was pagan to the last' and associated with the Druids. Macalister agreed, believing it to have been created as a sign language used for secret communication by the Druids of the Gallic tribes that had settled northern Italy, around 500 BCE. In his interpretation, it then spread through a supra-tribal Druidic organization (which formed an ancient equivalent to Freemasonry) all over north-western Europe until it was finally turned into a script in Ireland with the coming of Christianity.[175] Alongside this interpretative tradition was another, also medieval in origin: that each or virtually every letter in the ogham alphabet was named from a tree or plant having it as an initial. This made it, in a sense, an expression of the nature of trees. The references in classical authors of the first century CE to the setting of Druidical rites and teachings in woods or groves formed a natural harmony with this scholarly doctrine to reinforce a sense of the script as having a fundamental association with the Druids and their concept of the cosmos.[176]

In recent years every aspect of this picture has been abandoned by the most prominent specialists in the subject. First to go was the association with trees, disposed of in an article by Howard Meroney back in 1949.[177] His attack on the idea was not the first; it had been presaged by Charles Graves in the 1840s and indeed seems to be obvious to anybody who studies the relevant sources. The link with trees and plants had been made in a trio of later medieval Irish texts, produced at a time when the meaning of the script had ceased to be understood and speculations concerning it were growing. All these texts now exist only in chaotic fourteenth-century versions. They proposed between them and within themselves a range of possible interpretations of the ogham alphabet: one, for example, suggested that its signs were equivalent to the names of heroes. The connection with the plant kingdom was, however, the most popular, and it does not stand up to linguistic analysis. Only five of the twenty-five ogham characters have definite equivalents with tree names. The medieval authors involved, in Meroney's words, 'violently construed' a dozen more to try to make them seem to have them. In many cases the correspondences given were tentative and multiple: for example, the sign *ceirt* was aligned in one text to 'apple tree or holly in the forest or rowan or aspen'. The actual phonetic equivalents of the alphabet are far more diverse. Five, as said, are associated with trees, but the others with words for 'fear', 'ingot', 'rag', 'fork', 'trick', etc. If there is any meaningful system implied in these, it is not readily apparent.[178]

This is probably the best place for a brief digression concerning the place of trees in medieval Irish texts, with special relevance to Druids. Pliny, of course, had stated unequivocally that the sacred tree of the Gallic Druids was the oak. There is no sign of any such association in Ireland. If there is a tree that seems to have been especially linked with Irish Druidry, it is the rowan, alias the mountain ash or quickbeam. This appears in rites of divination worked by Druids in two medieval stories: in *The Life of Berach* they sit on hurdles of rowan wood, and in *The Siege of Drom Damghaire* they make a fire of it.[179] In later Irish folklore it has a tremendous reputation as *fid na ndruad*, 'the Druid's tree' or just 'the magical tree', employed in a range of spells. A. T. Lucas, however, has launched an attack on the whole concept of the rowan as a sacred or numinous tree to the ancient Irish, pointing out that it has no such status in the earliest texts. Instead, he suggests, veneration of it was introduced by the large-scale Viking settlement of Ireland in the ninth and tenth centuries, bringing a Scandinavian tradition in which it features prominently. Instead, the trees that represented local landmarks and meeting places in the earliest texts are the ash, oak, yew, walnut and hawthorn, and especially the first three. What these all have in common is simply size and availability; they were the most imposing species growing widely in Ireland in the early Middle Ages.[180] This would make a fit with the classes of tree given in the eighth-century legal tract *Bretha Comaithchesa*, which groups together as the 'noble' species the oak, hazel, holly, yew and ash, and possibly the pine and apple; the determinant here is utility. The rowan features as a 'commoner'.[181] If its prominence in later folk tradition really is due to Viking influence, it shows again through what a thick filter anything resembling pre-Christian tradition had to pass before it reached the twelfth-century and later versions in which most of the texts mentioning Irish Druids now exist.

The disappearance of trees from consideration of the meaning of ogham still left the theories of MacNeill and Macalister intact, but these have now been comprehensively rejected by the experts in the field who have published since the mid-1980s: Anthony Harvey, Damian McManus and Catherine Swift.[182] They have agreed that the specific evidence offered in support of those theories dissolves on inspection. Harvey could not find anything pagan in the script itself, as it had forms for 'abbot', 'bishop' and other Christian terms. He suggested that Latin and ogham had been adopted together as the earliest forms of Irish literacy, and that the practice of writing had been taken over from the Romano-British world. He allowed, however, that there was a possibility that this had occurred before the coming of Christianity. McManus concurred with all those points, but emphasized more strongly that it was also possible that the script was itself a Christian invention. It had apparently appeared at around the time the new faith reached Ireland and was associated with inscribed stones that were themselves copied from models found in already Christianized parts of Europe. There is no sign in the medieval epics that it was regarded as a secret means of communication, and although it was sometimes shown as used in works of magic, it was not treated in the stories as magical in itself. The most recent of the three writers, Swift, has also been the least compromising in this regard, suggesting that the appearance of ogham stones in Ireland is a map of early Christian communities, and that the script was inherently associated with the new religion. There is not much room left in all this for the Druids.

Despite this, it is possible that some could still be made for them. Putting together the work of these three scholars with others who have published on early Irish literacy in recent decades, it is clear that we actually know very little about the origins of ogham.[183] The majority of the inscribed stones date from the fifth and early sixth centuries, putting them within the Christian period, but there is a chance that some are fourth-century, and pre-Christian. The script itself may be older, and could have developed at any point between the first and fifth centuries because it is based on a type of Latin that flourished during that period. It is true that its most obvious purpose is to inscribe stones, and that current thought favours a date of invention towards the end of the span of time suggested above. None the less, it was almost certainly used on wood as well as stones, and its employment in that context may significantly predate the appearance of it on monoliths. There is no agreement whatsoever concerning where it first appeared, whether in Ireland, Britain or on the Continent. All this uncertainty leaves a real chance that it had some connection with paganism and Druids before being adopted by the Christian Irish. On the other hand, it must also be admitted that there seems now to be not one single piece of solid evidence for such a connection.

It remains briefly to consider the evidence of medieval Welsh literature. The brevity is the result of two factors. One is that the Welsh texts are both smaller in number and more limited in nature than those from Ireland. The second is that, as potential sources for pre-Christian tradition, they suffer from all the problems of the Irish material, but with an enormous additional complication: the intrusion of Rome. Ireland presents the spectacle of a native prehistoric society making a transition to a medieval one in its own fashion. Wales became part of the Roman province of Britain, before reverting to the rule of independent princes who remained in many respects Romanized – indeed the impact of Roman culture is actually more apparent there after the withdrawal of imperial rule than before. Furthermore, those post-Roman rulers were either already Christian or in the process of becoming rapidly Christianized. Traditions of the Druids had therefore a much larger filter to traverse in order to reach the mental world of medieval scribes.

This probably in itself explains the fact that, while Irish literature abounds in Druids, medieval Welsh texts may not mention them at all. They make occasional references to an individual being called a *dryw* and to characters called *derwydon*. These are usually, and quite credibly, regarded as medieval Welsh versions of 'Druid' and 'Druids', though this is not absolutely certain, and *dryw* in particular could mean 'wren', a bird commonly associated with magic. Assuming that the *derwydon*, at least, are supposed to be Druids, it is notable that they feature in a much more restricted context than in Irish literature, functioning entirely as prophets. Thus, the poem *Armes Prydein*, which is usually dated to the tenth century, includes the line 'dysgogan derwydon meint a dervyd', often translated as 'Druids foretell all that will happen', although the current standard edition of the text hedges its bets by rendering *derwydon* as 'wise men'.[184] One of the poems in the Book of Taliesin, *Kat Goddau*, which could have been composed at any time between the eleventh and fourteenth centuries, speaks of *Derwydon* who prophesy to (King) Arthur, apparently predicting Noah's Flood, the Crucifixion and Doomsday.[185]

If the term was intended to signify Druids, two interpretations of its status can be made. One is that the medieval Welsh authors had preserved a memory of ancient Druidry which had somehow persisted through all the centuries and cultural changes since the Roman conquest. The other is that the word was coined under the influence of contemporary Irish literature, which (as shown) prominently featured Druids, especially in the role of diviners. The first would allow for the persistence of some kind of native tradition, while the second would turn the references into a slight borrowing from a foreign literature which may itself have been based largely or wholly on invention. Certainly Welsh texts show a much greater sense of the importance of Ireland and the Irish than the latter do of the Welsh, and there is an occurrence of prominent Irish literary characters such as the gods Lugh and Manannan as occasional and quasi-human figures in the Welsh canon. The possibility of borrowing may be strengthened by the late Anglo-Saxon words *dry* and *drycraeft*, meaning 'magician' and 'magic' respectively.[186] As nobody has ever suggested that the early English had Druids of their own, this looks like a straightforward translation into their language of the Irish *drai* and *draidecht*. The trading, scholarly and religious contacts between England and Ireland in the early Middle Ages, starting with the resort of English scholars to Irish schools and the conversion of Northumbria by Irish clerics in the seventh century, and accentuated by the Viking merchant network, were quite ample enough to account for such a transfer.

For the sake of completeness, one more reference needs to be considered. It occurs in the *Historia Brittonum*, a Latin work composed in the 820s but claiming to draw upon earlier traditions and records. One passage deals with the ambition of the legendary or semi-legendary post-Roman chieftain Guorthïgïrn, later known as Vortigern, to build himself a fortress. To decide how best to do so, he summons magi, who refer back for information in turn to a 'council of the magi throughout Britain'. When the place is determined and problems are experienced in building the stronghold, they advise on the sacrifice of a special child to overcome them; and a story of marvel and prophecy ensues. This story is sometimes anthologized with accounts of the ancient Druids,[187] and it may indeed preserve a memory of a general meeting of them in Britain to match that portrayed by Caesar in Gaul. On the other hand, it may simply reproduce or refer to Old Testament images of a tyrant with his attendant evil magicians, as Muirchú had done in Ireland almost two centuries before.

This means that to use medieval Welsh literature as a source of information for ancient Druidry, as many people have done for over two centuries, it is necessary to practise on a grand scale what has also been attempted in the case of the Irish sources. That is, to treat the medieval Welsh poets collectively as the heirs to the Druids and the preservers of their traditions, and to illustrate this by selecting particular texts that conform to what the person making the selection thinks that ancient Druid teaching should have been. It is always possible that this process actually is picking up remnants of pre-Christian belief and custom, but demonstration of the fact is bedevilled by all the problems already noted in the case of the Irish material. The case would be much better made had any of its proponents, to date, had the necessary linguistic expertise to point to archaic elements in the texts concerned. So far, the works especially favoured by authors searching for traces of Druidry (which will be considered later in this book) have not attracted much attention from specialists in Welsh philology, for the simple reason that they have not been regarded as particularly early, but as classic products of the central or later Middle Ages.[188]

* * *

So this is how an Iron Age Druid is fashioned: from selected parts of Greek, Roman, Irish or Welsh texts usually mixed with archaeological data.[189] The process of selection made to compose the result is more or less an arbitrary one, determined by the instincts, attitudes, context and loyalties of the person engaged in it. Virtually none of the ingredients employed have the status of solid material, judged by any objective standards of textual or material evidence, and the little that has that status is not sufficient to produce a detailed or finished result. This is the case today, as has been suggested by the survey made above of recent publications, but it has been equally true ever since the inhabitants of Britain began wanting to have Druids in their thought-world again about half a millennium ago. The manner in which these ancient and medieval images of them have been put to use is therefore a perfect case study of the way in which the modern British have liked to think and feel: about humanity, nationhood, religion, morality and the cosmos. The raw materials for the construction of ancient Druids, so frustrating for a prehistorian or ancient historian, have resulted in a wonderful subject for a student of modernity.

2

$$\approx\!\!\ll$$

THE DRUIDS TAKE SHAPE

W ith the possible exception of a few Welsh poets, nobody in medieval Britain was interested in Druids; and in this respect the situation reflected that which obtained all over continental Europe. They simply had no obvious part to play in the medieval European imagination: they did not promote the glory of Christendom, or the claims of any royal or noble families, or the collective pride of towns or monasteries, nor did they inspire people to achievements of military prowess and chivalry. They did not even function well as hate-figures, having nothing especially demonic or exotic about them. They are not wholly missing from the record, being mentioned in passing by historians such as Adam of Bremen, but no attempt was made to discuss them or to relate them to contemporary concerns.

This situation ended abruptly in the last decade of the fifteenth century, as part of the transition between what have conventionally been defined as the medieval and the early modern periods. One of the main cultural forces associated with that transition was the humanist movement in scholarship, which embodied, among other aims, the project of recovering and building upon the knowledge of the classical ancient world. A vital aspect of this work consisted of the recovery, collation, edition and publication of ancient Greek and Roman texts, including most of those that made reference to Druids. These were rapidly pressed into the service of one of the other features of the period, a major development in the long process by which the European 'peoples' of the early Middle Ages were converted into the nation states of the nineteenth and twentieth centuries. It took the form of a celebration of the historic identities and achievements of people who shared a common language, culture and past, as 'nations'; and in this process Druids could at last play a significant part, as the nearest thing that ancient northern Europe had produced to scientists and philosophers. The sudden appearance of them for this purpose is, indeed, an argument in itself for the retention of the conventional break between the medieval and early modern periods at the end of the fifteenth century.

First off the mark were the Germans, against all the apparent logic of the classical sources: nobody had hitherto located the Druids in Germany and Caesar had explicitly stated that they were not to be found there. These apparently simple facts counted as nothing against two powerful historical forces. The first was the reaction of German writers and artists, proud of the cultural achievements of their homeland during the Middle Ages, against the reputation which the ancient Mediterranean writers had given it as a region of barbarism and ignorance. Contemporary Italians, as the most obvious heirs of the Romans, were inclined to harp on these old stereotypes in order to score political points. The other force was provided by the fact that one of the most wealthy, sophisticated and dynamic parts of early modern Germany was the Rhineland, much of which had been part of the Roman province of Gaul. Its authors could quite legitimately claim ancient Gallic culture, which included the Druids, as their inheritance, and apply it to a new German identity. The work was started with remarkable speed and confidence by two friends belonging to a network of Rhenish patriots. One was Johannes Trithemius, Abbot of Sponheim, who completed a history of the Carmelite order of friars in 1492. In this, he hailed the Druids as spiritual ancestors of the Carmelites, being a respected order of pagan clergy who dwelt in cities, forests and villages alike. Trithemius was interested in them not only as a monk but as an occultist; he was also deeply concerned with the use of ritual magic to make direct contact with divine beings, and so the reputation of the ancient Druids as sorcerers and as keepers of the secrets of the natural world was an attraction rather than a deterrent to him. He called his own abbey 'home of the Druids', and was hailed as a Druid by members of his literary circle.[1]

The most influential of the latter was Conrad Celtis, often regarded as the most fervent of German humanist scholars. He disposed of the problem of what Druids were doing in ancient Germany by declaring as known fact that they had fled across the Rhine from the persecution of the Romans, and been given sanctuary by the free tribes in the German forests. There was, of course, no evidence to back up this story; but also none positively to refute it. Having got the Druids to Germany, Celtis had to establish that they were worth having, and did so without qualification. In his vision, they were the most admirable figures of the ancient northern world, being priests devoted to the pristine worship of a single god who did not demand material sacrifice and was venerated in simple groves of trees. Furthermore, they were great scholars, expert not only in their own traditions of wisdom but in the whole of Greek learning. In Celtis's reimagination of history, they eventually became Christians, to which their own faith naturally tended, and converted Germany to this new and better religion.

Celtis realized instinctively that to seize the imagination of readers, his Druids had both to possess visual form and to be linked to antiquities in the German landscape, and he achieved both targets in one story. This described how he had stayed with a friend at a monastery near Regensburg in Bavaria, and seen six stone images built into the cloister wall. Each was seven feet high, and wore a hooded mantle. Their beards hung to the top of their legs, their feet were bare, and their faces were inclined downwards and severe in expression. Each held a book and a staff, of the design associated particularly with the Cynic school of Greek philosophy. To Celtis there was no doubt that these were not representations of Greek sages but of the Druid refugees to Germany and, as the statues vanished long ago, it is impossible to assess the worth of his judgement. What it achieved was to give the world in general a striking impression of what the Druids had actually looked like, to fill the gap left by the absence of literary or artistic evidence in the ancient sources.[2] His work had a rapid and understandable impact, and by the time of his death in 1508 he had established the Druids as major figures in the German historical imagination, where they were to remain for the rest of the early modern period. A long succession of writers accepted and augmented the view of them that he and Trithemius had developed. The most prominent in the next generation was Johannes Aventinus, who depicted them as the scholar-monks of a wholesome religion based on the veneration of heroic ancestors and service of a single deity.[3]

By then the French had appropriated them as well, and with more obvious reason as the boundaries of France, even by that period, incorporated most of ancient Gaul. The Gallic Druids could therefore be made much more directly ancestral to French culture, and in the form into which the Germans had transmuted them they represented particularly attractive forebears. The process was given further assistance from an Italian – one of a nation which, ironically, usually exemplified the Mediterranean contempt for northern peoples. He was a Dominican friar, Giovanni Nanni, whose work appeared in 1498. Like the Germans, Nanni Latinized his pen-name to take his place in the international commerce of scholarship, and was generally known as Annius Viterbensis; in English, Annius of Viterbo. The greatest problem for northerners attempting to write the early history of their own lands was a total absence of reliable information of the sort that the ancient Greek and Roman authors, and the Bible, appeared to provide for the Mediterranean world. Annius offered it, by publishing what he represented as fragments of hitherto unknown works by genuine classical authors. Between them they provided an outline history of north-western Europe that neatly spanned the gap between Noah's Flood and the beginning of the historical sources identified up to that time. It was framed around the reigns of successive kings, of whom the first was Samothes, grandson of Noah and ancestor of the peoples whom classical writers called Celts. He was said to have taught the art of writing and left descendants who became pre-eminent in learning among Europeans. His immediate successors founded many schools and towns. The third king to reign after him, Druiyus, established the order of Druids, and the fourth one, King Bardus, that of Bards, to foster and propagate the sophisticated culture developed by their forebears. Collectively, they and their subjects taught literacy, poetry and science to the Greeks.[4]

The only question still in doubt is whether Annius made all this up himself, or whether he acted as the mouthpiece for somebody else: the existing evidence points strongly to the former. The polemical point of his work was to undermine humanist scholarship in general and its admiration for ancient Greece in particular. It immediately provoked critics, who wondered why his quotations were not in the usual literary style of the authors to whom he credited them, and why he never produced the manuscripts that he claimed to have discovered. The names of his kings sounded suspiciously as if they had been invented out of the groups and institutions that they were supposed to have founded. By the seventeenth century, international scholarship was coming to reject his history, although it was not completely consigned to the realms of myth and forgery until the nineteenth. In the sixteenth, however, it was just too convenient to be disregarded by many German and French authors, providing them as it did not merely with a complete account of the development of their nations but with a claim to cultural pre-eminence in the earliest times; and the Druids were now lodged clearly within that claim. Annius's work was slow to make an impact – it was not taken up with any great enthusiasm in discussions of Druidry for over fifty years – but its impact was all the greater, when it came, for the long maturation of its acceptance by the international scholarly world. That impact was compounded, in turn, by the fact that the same intervening period had seen the Druids firmly established as heroic forebears in various different nations.

It seems to have been Symphorien Champier, in a series of publications between 1508 and 1517, who first presented them to the French as noble ancestors, functioning as the leading philosophers and scientists of a sophisticated civilization and preaching doctrines such as the immortality of the soul that paved the way for Christianity. This view of them was developed for the remainder of the century by writers such as Jean Picard, Pierre de la Ramée, Charles de Bouelles, Guy Lefèvre de la Boderie and Noel Taillepied. It was Picard, publishing in 1556, who made the earliest extended discussion of them in French, and he brought in Annius to bolster and extend the portrait sketched out by Champier.[5] Taillepied was the first author, in any language, to devote an entire book to them; it appeared in 1585.[6] Most of these were aware that the ancient representations were not entirely flattering, and reacted by trying to talk such blemishes away: thus, they argued that human sacrifice was an unimportant fringe activity of Druids; or was a universal practice among early pagans, than whom they were no better in this single respect; or was believed to be an act of redemption that led to eternal life for the victim.[7] Such apologetics became less restrained as the seventeenth century opened, and reached their apogee in the work of a historian of Chartres, Sébastian Rouillard, who published in 1609. As interest in Druids began to revive near the end of the Middle Ages, Chartres had become identified with the place 'in the territory of the Carnutes' where those of Gaul had met each year according to Caesar.[8] It was not the only claimant for this honour, another being the town of Dreux to the west, but its partisans made the identification with the most consistent determination. They did so largely because it had acquired a well-justified reputation as a centre of sanctity and learning during the Middle Ages, because of its magnificent twelfth-century cathedral which was the site both of a major school and of a cult of the Virgin Mary. By the early sixteenth century the Druids and the Christian cult had been united, in a story that the cathedral itself had been founded by them in recognition of a prediction that they had made there of the birth of a saviour to a virgin.

Rouillard picked up these existing beliefs, and the previous French eulogies to Gallic Druidry, and ran with them. He got rid of any unpleasant assertions that Greek or Roman authors had made about the Druids by declaring all such statements to have been lies or misunderstandings. In his reading the Romans became the villains of the story, being idolaters, polytheists, makers of blood sacrifices and persecutors of Christianity, while the Druids were simply the finest people in the ancient world.

They were the discoverers of literacy, science and philosophy, which they had taught to the Greeks in general and Pythagoras in particular, and their religion had been designed to prepare the world for Christianity. Their gods had all represented different aspects of Christ himself, the oak tree had been their symbol of his Cross, with the mistletoe hanging on it standing for the Crucifixion, and all the details of the cutting of it, as recounted by Pliny, had looked forward to aspects of the life of Jesus or of Roman Catholic ritual. Rouillard repeated the tale that Druids had predicted the virgin birth, and stated that the accusations made against them of sacrificing humans had been misunderstandings of their preoccupation with the coming self-sacrifice of the Christian saviour.[9]

This celebration of Druidry by the early modern French was truly 'national', in three key respects. First, its authors came from various parts of France. Second, many of them wrote in the French language itself, rather than the international scholarly one of Latin. Third, it penetrated beyond intellectual circles to become part of the mental equipment of cultured people in general. When the physician François Rabelais published his comic tales in 1552, he could already refer to 'our ancient Druids' as familiar and beloved figures.[10] In making them into admired ancestors, however, the French had to reckon with a more serious problem than the less appealing characteristics with which ancient writers had invested Druidry: Caesar had stated categorically that it had been taught to the Gauls by the British.[11] The Italian tendency to regard France as backward and unsophisticated was reproduced by the French with regard to the inhabitants of Britain; and above all the English, as the Hundred Years War had bequeathed a powerful mutual animosity. The higher patriotic Frenchmen drove the reputation of the Gallic Druids, the greater the opportunity they presented to the peoples of Britain to identify their island as the place that had, through Druidry, given the arts of civilization to all Europe. All the components were in place for a mighty turning of nationalist tables.

Initially, it seemed as if this might be starting to occur, as the Druids were swiftly taken up, as heroic ancestors, by the British nation most intimately connected with France: its frequent diplomatic and military ally, the kingdom of Scotland. It can be no accident that, having been absent from the medieval histories of the Scots, they suddenly appeared in a book about Scotland published in Paris in 1526, and written by a Scotsman who had studied in that city when the first French works extolling the Druids as national heroes were appearing. He was Hector Boece, and he fitted Druidry into a process of historical invention in which late medieval Scots had already begun luxuriantly to indulge. Anxious to prove the superior antiquity of their kingdom to that of their traditional rivals, the English, they were populating Iron Age Scotland with scores of kings who belonged entirely to the realm of legend. Boece continued this process of elaborating a mythical history. At one point he related a story of how the thirteenth king of Scots, Iosyne, entertained two shipwrecked priests from Spain who persuaded him and his subjects to forsake idolatry and follow the true faith of one god. The next king, Finnanus, opened the way for the return of paganism by tolerating it alongside monotheism, but he also instituted clergy to administer the purer faith. Here Boece mixed together themes from Caesar and Tacitus. Like the Gallic Druids of the former writer, these Scottish priests had a Grand Master and regular assemblies, and controlled judicial decisions as well as religious affairs. Tacitus had portrayed the British Druids as present on the island of 'Mona', which could be taken from this to have been especially associated with them. From his description there is no doubt that he was referring to Môn, or Anglesey, off the coast of Wales. Boece, however, claimed Mona for Scotland by identifying it as the Isle of Man, which had been part of the kingdom of Scotland in the early Middle Ages.[12]

He also sensed, as Celtis had done and as the French were doing at Chartres, the need to locate his nation's ancient religion in particular places and surviving physical relics. He added that a later (though equally imaginary) king of Scots, Manyus, had ordered temples to be built to the national religion, consisting of rings of stones with the greatest towards the south, to be used as the altar. Here he was clearly referring to the so-called 'recumbent-stone circles' found in the neighbourhood of Aberdeen and representing one of the most striking categories of late Neolithic ritual monument. It can hardly be a coincidence that Boece was a regent of the university at Aberdeen. He did not mention the Druids specifically in connection with them, but his text made such an association natural to infer, and when a translation of his history was made into Scots verse by William Stewart in 1535, Druids were stated specifically as having charge of these temples.[13]

For a time it looked as if the co-option of the Druids as spiritual ancestors of Catholic clergy might damn them in the eyes of Protestant Scots. One of the landmark works of Reformation historiography was the history of Scotland published by George Buchanan in 1582. It dismissed Druids in a jeering sentence which spoke of their 'superstition', which 'so addled the minds' of Britons and Gauls.[14] What rescued them was a further swing of religious policy, which reintroduced aspects of the old Church, such as bishops and seasonal ceremonies, into the new one. As part of this, it became possible once more to admire Druids as forebears. In 1639 the religious primate of the kingdom, John Spottiswoode, Archbishop of St Andrews, completed a history of the Church of Scotland that had been commissioned from him by royal command. He was learned enough in the classical texts to acknowledge that all that they said of Druids was not good, and he thought it impious to suggest, as some of the French had done, that they had been allowed foresight of the coming of Christ to an extent denied to the biblical prophets. On the other hand, he could still assert that they had been the best of all heathen priests, living with dignity and wisdom, contributing well to the public affairs of their people, having considerable learning, and teaching 'that there was one only God, and that it was not lawful to present him in an image: that the souls of men did not perish with the bodies, and that after death men were rewarded according to the life they lived on earth'. Like the Catholic Boece, the Protestant Archbishop was anxious to present them as fitting predecessors of the Scottish prelates. Spottiswoode followed Boece's nationalist lead in setting the centre of their organization and the meeting-place for their assembly in the Isle of Man. Indeed, he went further, in making this island the seat of their primate, who presided over them as he did over the Scottish Church of his own time.[15]

With the Scots thus taking advantage of the example provided by the Germans and French, the other peoples of the British Isles had even more apparent incentive to do so. The Irish, after all, had Druids built into their national literature, which was to receive a new stimulus in the early modern period in the face of British and Protestant aggression. The Welsh could claim to be the direct descendants of the ancient Britons, and their own literature already incorporated possible references to Druidry. The English had the greatest reason to annex it to their history, possessing a traditional claim to political leadership of the whole archipelago and a rivalry with the French in which the new continental admiration for Druidic wisdom could be turned to powerful polemical effect. Both they and the Welsh were also engaged, by the mid-sixteenth century, in a fresh burst of nationalist history-writing, propelled by their breach with the medieval Church which created a new interest in the distinctive religious traditions of their island. All this should have produced a celebration of the Druids in Tudor England, Wales and Ireland that was even more passionate, euphoric and unrestrained than that already undertaken by continental authors. The truly significant fact is that it did not.

* * *

The reasons for the relative neglect of Druids in Ireland and southern Britain during the sixteenth and seventeenth centuries are complex, and differ between the peoples concerned. The Irish writers who wrote to answer English Protestant propaganda were by definition Roman Catholics, and here the native tradition that had represented Druids as the main opponents of Christian saints weighed in heavily. It can be seen in action very effectively in the archetypal nationalist work produced in this period, Geoffrey Keating's account of Ireland from the earliest times until the high Middle Ages, completed in the mid-1630s. Druids featured in it wherever they had already been included in the medieval sources on which most of the first part of the book was based. The existing hostility to them was, however, sharpened at points and made still more meaningful to readers of the Bible: in one place, for example, they were portrayed as adoring a golden calf in the manner of the Israelites punished by Moses. Keating, like Boece, embedded his Druids in the landscape and the physical remains of the past by associating them with prehistoric monuments: in his case the megalithic chambered tombs of the Neolithic and Bronze Ages. The contrast between the two authors is, however, most revealing, for Keating represented the tomb-chambers as having been altars for sacrifice, beneath which the Druids bathed themselves in the blood of victims.[16]

The Welsh were also engaged in the production of nationalist histories by the mid-sixteenth century, to justify and contextualize the Reformation that authors like Keating were doing their utmost to resist. One of their greatest Tudor scholars, Humphrey Llwyd, was anxious to grab back Tacitus's Druid island of Mona from the Scots, and restore its true identification with Môn, alias Anglesey. Having achieved this, however, he was too faithful to Tacitus's account of the island to find its ancient inhabitants attractive, commenting on their 'idolatry and absurd religion'.[17] His friend Sir John Price made an attempt to relate the Druids to the later Welsh bards who were the main repositories of patriotic tradition. He did so, however, only in passing and by using an apparent linguistic similarity that was probably mistaken: the existence of the word *prydydd* (which Price wrote as *prydruid*) as one term for a poet.[18] Erroneous or not, his attempt was still highly significant in explaining the neglect of Druids by most early modern Welsh writers: the patriotism of the latter was constructed around the medieval princes who had resisted English and Norman aggression, and the bards who had given that struggle literary expression. Compared with these figures, the ancient history of Britain was at once too badly recorded and too generalized to be of much service.[19] The pattern persisted for a long time. At the end of the sixteenth century another Welsh scholar, Maurice Kiffin, declared flatly that he did not believe that any Druidic doctrine had come down to the historic bards.[20] One hundred years later a famed poet, Henry Vaughan, replied from his home in Breconshire to an English scholar anxious for information on Druids. He explained that as neither the latter nor the ancient bards had left literature, little of value could be known about them. He could find no evidence that they had anything in common with the medieval bards, a highly literate and sophisticated society of authors who were the direct ancestors of people like himself.[21]

The failure of the English to take up Druids with enthusiasm was seemingly the most fortuitous. It is possible that the Druids' identification with French and Scottish nationalism may have been a deterrent in itself. The neglect of them, however, may just come down to the fact that, of the first three authors to refer to them in England, one made a misreading, one was an Italian, and one went mad. The misreading was the work of a poet, Alexander Barclay, who published a stanza in 1509 which mocked 'Druydans' for running 'in vain about /In their mad feasts upon the hill of yde / Making their sacrifice with furor noise and shout/ When their madness setteth their wit aside'.[22] The 'hill of yde' is Mount Ida, either the peak of that name near Troy or (more probably) the one in Crete, and Druids were never associated with those regions; Barclay had probably got them mixed up with the frenzied priests of the Asiatic goddess Cybele.[23] The Italian was the famed humanist scholar known in English as Polydore Vergil, hired by Henry VII to write the first properly researched history of England. The result was published at Basle in 1534, and was at once too scrupulous and too insensitive to English prejudices to make much of the Druids. It quoted Caesar and Tacitus on them and, while admitting their learning, dismissed them as 'priests of heathen religion, saying their accursed prayers'. To compound their marginalization, Vergil accepted Boece's award of Mona to the Scots, as the Isle of Man.[24] His disregard for beloved English legends (such as those of King Arthur) and the changed political circumstances produced by England's breach with the Roman Church made a replacement for his work immediately desirable. Henry VIII gave the job to John Leland, an enthusiastic supporter of religious reform who had studied at Paris in the 1520s and should thus have been well aware of the patriotic potential of Druids. By 1545 Leland had written a book that placed them at the head of the tradition of British learning, although he added that their religion was still inferior to the true one, of Christ.[25] At that point, tragically, he went permanently insane, and his work remained unpublished for almost two centuries.

The manuscript was read by his friend, John Bale, who succeeded him as England's foremost antiquarian. As an ardent Protestant propagandist, however, Bale initially had other uses for Druids, whom he chose to turn into exemplars of all that was wrong with pagan and Roman Catholic priests alike. Mixing the pseudo-histories of Annius of Viterbo and various earlier medieval authors with the diatribes of Hebrew prophets against the heathen, he constructed a new condemnation of them that was published in 1546. In this, they had arrived in Britain from Athens, and set themselves up to live like chaste hermits in the forest. Having won the respect of the populace and been put in charge of sacrifices, they proceeded to feast on the latter while keeping whores whom they decked with jewels. He cited Boece's view that they had worshipped one god and rejected the grosser aspects of ancient paganism, but immediately countered this by quoting Pliny against them, as evil sorcerers. In this lurid guise, they made their first 'genuine' appearance in English.[26] Later, in exile on the Continent, Bale absorbed enough of the favourable Franco-German representations to come round to Leland's view and publish a recognition of their precocious contribution to British learning, based on the fantasies propagated by Annius.[27] But he never provided an extended eulogy of them to compensate for the attack that he had made previously.

This token recognition of their honourable place in British scholarship appeared in works by Englishmen produced in the next generation. When John Caius published a history of Cambridge University in 1568, he hailed them as its original founders.[28] In his Protestant account of the development of English Christianity, the first Elizabethan Archbishop of Canterbury, Matthew Parker, quoted Caesar on the knowledge of the Druids, and the respect in which they were held, while still adding that they had to give way to the true faith.[29] These references, with Bale's retraction of his former condemnation, appeared to establish for them a favourable place in the works of English intellectuals. All three passages, however, were brief, limited in their approval, marginal to the main purpose of the works in which they appeared, and composed in Latin for the consumption of an international scholarly elite. What were still missing were major publications in the vernacular language of the sort now so familiar in France, which offered the Druids as home-grown heroes to a patriotic domestic audience: and two of those were now to appear in England, representing very different, though equally effective, approaches to the writing of national history.

One was published in 1577, in the form of the first edition of the bumper history of Britain and Ireland produced by a team of writers co-ordinated by Raphael Holinshed. Their aim was certainly nationalist in the sense that it was intended to foster a sense of communal pride and historic depth among subjects of the Elizabethan English state. It was not, however, sponsored by the government or linked to any one faction within the regime or any one strain of religious loyalty, and it represented a number of different approaches to the national past.[30] The two sections that dealt with Druids reflected all these characteristics. Both were the work of William Harrison, a strenuous evangelical Protestant, but were composed in different national contexts and reflected different foundation myths. The first took a 'British' perspective and was based on the fictions of Annius of Viterbo, enriched with medieval legends and glosses put upon them by more recent writers such as Bale and Caius. In this reworking, Annius's King Druiyus was fleshed out as a great scholar and theologian who taught belief in a single omnipotent deity: a god who was merciful to the godly and punished the wicked, had created the world and would end it, and had given humans immortal souls. Druiyus instituted the Druid order to propagate this true and good faith, but it eventually became decadent. It first developed the false theory of transmigration of souls between bodies, and then fell into polytheism and the veneration of the oak tree, and wore distinctive clothing, like Catholic clergy, so that its members would immediately be revered wherever they went. Likewise the bardic order founded by Druiyus's son Bardus commenced as scholar-priests little different from Druids save in their use of poetry and song, and degenerated into minstrels praising mortal deeds instead of divinity.

Despite this, Harrison's Druids long remained great champions of learning and civilization, teaching the Gallic peoples religion and philosophy. Their main college was on the British mainland, but they had smaller schools in the isles of Wight, Anglesey and Orkney which sent representatives to general synods held in Britain. Things only really began to go badly wrong with them after the arrival of a new royal family led by Albion, a descendant of Egyptian kings who had taught sorcery and 'unnatural lust'. He introduced idolatry, and thereafter the deities venerated by the British multiplied considerably in number and the practice of human sacrifice was imported. The Druids also acquired a more elaborate hierarchy, with three archpriests ruling from London, York and Caerleon over twenty-five local 'idol-churches'. None the less, British religion still remained less contaminated by polytheism and superstition than that of the Romans. In the second century of the Christian era, the emperor Antoninus abolished Druidry throughout his domains and, rather than adopt vile Roman paganism, the sub-king of Britain, Lucius, sent to the Pope for Christian missionaries. They duly arrived and converted Lucius, his court and many of the former Druids, turning Britain into the first nation generally to adopt Christianity. Thus ended the first of the pseudo-histories in which the Holinshed compilation made a place for Druids. The second pseudo-history came in its section dealing with Scotland, where Harrison copied Boece's assertions about the institution of them as pagan equivalents to bishops, by King Finnanus. He stressed their initial virtue and later corruption by power, and paid respect to Welsh feeling by noting that the Druid base of Mona might have been either the Isle of Man or Anglesey.[31]

What was thus provided was a pair of mythologies based upon traditions that had been evolving ever since the eighth century, but given a distinctively Protestant slant. A notion of the tendency of true religion, provided by divine revelation, to undergo corruption and distortion over time is of course built into Christianity, through the Old Testament. With it is the associated concept of the periodic restoration of the true faith, by processes of divinely inspired reformation and purification. Protestantism, however, had a natural tendency to emphasize those processes very strongly, and Harrison's Druids represented a dress rehearsal for the clergy of the medieval Western Church: godly and devout products of a genuine religious revelation who had gradually turned to error and ungodliness over many generations, until their replacement by a restored version of the true faith became imperative. To Harrison, of course, the latest restoration of true religion had been the Protestant Reformation. In his history, just as many clerics of the medieval Church had converted to the reformed faith in the sixteenth century (among them Leland and Bale), so many Druids had turned Christian under Lucius; and that earlier conversion pointed to Britain's destiny as a land of unusually pure and zealous Christianity. It was a composite story that well fulfilled the basic aim of the Holinshed project: to provide the Elizabethan English with a heroic and edifying sense of the British past and of their own relationship with it.

The other major publication of the period to mention Druids was conceived in the year in which the first edition of the Holinshed history was published; and represented another example of the influence of continental scholarship on British attitudes. In this case the scholarship concerned was embodied in the great Flemish geographer Abraham Ortelius, who visited England in 1577. He stayed with a young Westminster schoolmaster, William Camden, who was acquiring a reputation for his study of the physical remains of the British past. Ortelius was already interested in Druids, having corresponded with the Welsh historian Humphrey Llwyd over the correct identification of the island of Mona.[32] He persuaded Camden to write a book on British antiquities which would give European scholars an enhanced sense of his nation's importance within the ancient and early medieval worlds.[33] The result was published, in Latin, in 1586, under the title of *Britannia*. As a work produced as a contribution to international scholarship, according to the highest standards of research, it did not make any grand claims for the Druids, or associate them with rulers such as Druiyus, Bardus and Albion. Instead it alluded briefly to them as practitioners of a heathen religion, relying firmly on ancient Roman sources.[34]

As the years passed, and the book went through successive, and ever enlarged, editions, Camden's attitude to them changed. He still confined his authorities to the classical sources that represented 'genuine' history, but quoted these at greater length and more favourably to the Druids. The process culminated in 1610, when the final and biggest version of the book was translated into English. It had turned, after all, into a patriotic work intended primarily for a domestic market. The ancient sources on which he relied for information on Druids, especially Caesar, were quoted at length and lightly trimmed to highlight the passages that dealt with the Druids' learning and social importance. Most impressive, he quoted two early Christian writers, Tertullian and Origen, as saying that they had predisposed the British to receive the Christian faith, by acknowledging only one god.[35] Here was the claim that German and French writers had been making for them over the past hundred years, apparently anchored in real ancient texts and contextualized specifically in the Druidic homeland of Britain.

Actually, Camden only had one witness, because Tertullian merely boasted that by his time, under the later Roman Empire, even some of the (remote) British had adopted Christianity. It was Origen who apparently provided the testimony, and he did not mention Druids as such; rather, as Camden read him, he stated that the British had believed in a single god before the coming of Christ, and it could be reasonably inferred from this that the Druids had been responsible for that belief. Camden had, however, made a classic mistranslation. He had not realized that Origen had been posing a rhetorical question: that of whether, before the coming of Christ, peoples as marginal as the British and the Berbers had believed in one deity. The implied answer was clearly negative, allowing Origen to proceed to his point, which was that, by his time in the third century, Christianity had carried that message even to these far-flung regions.[36] Camden's knowledge of Greek, or that of his informant, had not been up to the understanding of the passage. Later in the seventeenth century other scholars spotted the mistake,[37] but it was embedded in a work of huge popularity and influence, justly respected for the generally high quality of its erudition and research.

Between them, and in their very different ways, Holinshed and Camden had provided the English with a vision of ancient Druidry that, while not as adulatory as that developed by continental neighbours, turned the Druids into spiritual and ethnic ancestors worthy of admiration and celebration, firmly positioned in the nation's story. It could be expected that henceforth they would become major characters in the English imagination, familiar heroes of poetry and prose and of works of historical fact and fiction alike: 'our' Druids, as they had long been for the French. Once again, what should have been anticipated failed to happen.

* * *

There are no Druids in Shakespeare. This simple fact deserves closer inspection than it has received hitherto, because he had both the opportunity and the means to deal with them. He wrote a play, *Cymbeline*, which is set in ancient Britain, and (famously) he relied heavily on Holinshed's volumes for much of his impression of national history. Apparently he felt that Druids lacked dramatic potential, and would have no automatic resonance with his audiences. That they also lacked it with playwrights is strongly suggested by their first actual appearance on the English stage, in John Fletcher's melodrama *Bonduca*, which was written shortly after *Cymbeline*, in the period 1611–14.[38] Its subject was Boudica's rebellion against the Romans; Druids were mentioned twice in it and entered the stage once. In each case, their role was made clear: all they did was sing, of the deeds of the glorious dead. In other words, Fletcher had got them hopelessly mixed up with bards.[39] Nor did the more sophisticated world of the royal court cope better with them, two decades later. On the night of Shrove Tuesday 1633, Thomas Carew presented a masque in which ancient Britain briefly paid its homage to the reigning sovereign, Charles I. It did so, colourfully but vaguely, in a 'Chorus of Druids and Rivers'.[40] Things were slightly more precise at a court entertainment three years later, when a Druid popped up to urge the king to direct his clergy to suppress Puritan preachers. This at least showed that the author had registered that Druids had been some kind of priesthood, and is another interesting indication that they were more favoured by people who liked hierarchy and ceremony in a church. None the less, it was no more than a cameo appearance.[41]

In popular literature, Druids fared rather worse. A playwright and hack writer contemporary to Shakespeare, Thomas Nashe, published a prose satire in 1594 which showed how bad an image Druids could acquire in populist works. To Nashe, they had simply been evil foreign sorcerers, who made ripe figures for fun. They 'dwelt in the Isle of Man' and were 'lousy' with attendant demons: 'had they but put their finger and thumb into their neck, they would have plucked out a whole nest of them'.[42] Almost twenty years later, a pamphlet describing the trial of some people accused of witchcraft in Northamptonshire built on Nashe's image. It was aimed against the many people in England who, even at that date, doubted the reality of witchcraft, and as one proof of its reality, cited the 'ancient records of the witches called Druides, in old time confined into the Isle of Man'.[43] These writings afford the best proof that, at a popular level, the adoption of the Druids by the Scots as respected ancestors counted against them in England; Druidry was not just bad, it was foreign.

In attempting to offset such impressions, the accounts found in Holinshed and Camden had to vie with sophisticated objections as well as ignorance and confusion. Between 1590 and 1605 the main hostile Roman accounts of Druids were all translated into English, so that they could be read by those who could not manage the good Latin editions already available in print.[44] As a result of this, and the commentaries of the different scholars, the Druids had arrived in the historical consciousness of most educated English people by the early seventeenth century; but there was no general agreement as to what they were doing there, and whether they should be welcome. The ancient messages were just too mixed, and so were the modern. Who, for example, were the 'definitive' Druids in Holinshed: the wise and pious priests of good king Druiyus, or their degenerate and bloodthirsty descendants whom the Greeks and Romans encountered? Faced with such data, writers had no escape from tumbling into selectivity, inconsistency or uncomfortable acts of balancing and qualification.

In the year 1606 somebody using the initials 'W. B.' brought out an English edition of Ortelius's book of maps of the world. He was clearly a person of considerable erudition, who cited all the main classical sources and had read German writers such as Celtis; he knew enough philology to reject Pliny's suggestion that the word 'Druid' derived from 'oak', relating it instead to 'wisdom'. His Druids were, however, not gentle philosophers but the priests of tribal peoples who killed their old folk and late-comers to feasts, and converted the skulls of their enemies to drinking vessels.[45] A dozen years later it was the turn of the English cartographer, John Speed, to try his hand at a historical survey to accompany his book of maps of Britain. He began uncompromisingly by declaring that the religion of the ancient British had been one of 'diabolical superstition', involving idol worship and human sacrifice. When he came to discuss the Druids, however, fifty pages later, he represented them as somehow detached from the beliefs and practices of their own people. He respectfully summarized Camden's view that they had facilitated the conversion of their people to the way of Christ, and mentioned the French writers who had credited them with predicting the virgin birth. He then added a fragment of his own to this evolving mythology by suggesting that the Roman emperors had banned Druidry because it 'savoured too much of Christianity'.[46]

Poets were able to produce no more consistent an impression than geographers. In 1621 William Slatyer published a history of Britain in verse, with a portrait of Druids that celebrated their virtuous early years as represented in Holinshed, and referred only briefly and obliquely to their fall from grace.[47] The writer to treat of them most often in stanzas was, however, Michael Drayton, whose willingness to return repeatedly to the subject merely increased the potential for confusion. In general, he spoke of them as malevolent and powerful magicians, inhabiting gloomy groves, riding chariots drawn by dragons, killing plough horses, and feeding demon-familiars on human gore;

in his eyes they were as much a menace to their own people as witches were supposed to be. He managed to invest even Pliny with a new level of hostility towards them, retelling the famous episode of the mistletoe-gathering with talk of their 'strong fury' and 'bloodied hands', and of how 'the murmuring woods even shuddered as with fear'. Yet at another point he could speak of 'the fearless Druids, that ministered the laws, and were so truly wise'.[48] When publishing his most famous work, in 1612, Drayton supplemented his own views with those of a historical commentator, his friend John Selden who was one of the most learned Englishmen of his generation. Selden had read the classical sources and an extensive range of the continental literature on Druids. He contemptuously rejected the historical romances of Annius and Boece, corrected Camden's misreading of Origen, and recognized that the derivation of the word 'Druid' was obscure (though he admitted a preference for the 'oak' option).

In view of this, it is remarkable that he produced one of the most blatant apologies for the ancient Druids ever published in early modern Britain, and one that acted as an implicit reproof to much of what Drayton had written about them in the same book. He himself misread Pliny's passage that credited them with believing that the mistletoe healed all ills, to turn it into evidence that they venerated an all-healing deity. Having thus substituted one textual error for another, he went on to retain for the Druids the title of the most Christian pagans in ancient Europe, and to declare their superiority to the Greeks and Romans, in particular. He applauded their morality in stopping wars (as Diodorus and Strabo had said), and confirmed for them another accolade, of having acquired learning before the Romans, by suggesting that their doctrines resembled not only those of Pythagoras but those of the Hebrew Cabbala. Both of these were believed to predate the rise of Rome from obscurity. The result of all this was to present them as fit heroes for the Protestant English; like many people of his time and faith, Selden regarded blows struck against the prestige of the ancient Romans as landing automatically upon Roman Catholics. At one point he admitted that his paragons had been charged with human sacrifice, and simply declared that he proposed to ignore this.[49]

Selden had already developed this attitude to Druids, for he had summarized it in a Latin history of English law that he had published two years before.[50] He held to it for the rest of his long life; in notes left unpublished at his death in 1654, he honoured their 'natural wisdom' and the exceptional respect in which their people held them, and added that, having heard the Christian message, they became 'the leaders of the blind people in a better way, and unto a better hope; and held forth that light'.[51] Selden's affection for them seems to have derived from his political programme, which was to argue, with the full apparatus of his tremendous learning, that the laws of England were derived ultimately from free assemblies of its people and were thus outside the power of monarchs operating by themselves.[52] This was, of course, a contribution to the debate that commenced under James I, and continued until late in the Stuart period, over the ultimate origins of authority in the state. In Selden's work, Druids featured as guardians of customary law, meeting in regular conventions to discuss and interpret it. As such, they functioned as the ancient British ancestors of the later English parliaments and the founders of a tradition of common law, the two institutions that represented in his view the true fount of legitimacy and the bulwark of liberty in his nation. In part, at least, he may have been led into these ideas by another great champion of the antiquity and authority of Parliament under the early Stuarts, Sir Edward Coke, who had declared that the common law of England had been established, or at least nurtured, by Druids.[53]

If writers such as Drayton and Selden could differ sharply even when friends, and when contributing to the same work, so too could individual authors have dramatic changes of mind. An exemplar of this process is one of the most enduringly famous of all to write on Druids in the period: John Milton. In his first references to them, in poems from the 1630s, he made Fletcher's error of confusing them with bards.[54] His treatment of them was warm; he had, after all, mistaken them for fellow poets. By 1644, in his pamphlets calling for legal reforms, he had absorbed the admiring view of them as sages, almost certainly from Selden's notes to Drayton's poem, and was augmenting it by declaring that the Druids (conceived of essentially as British) had taught wisdom not merely to the French and Pythagoras but to the ancient Persian magi.[55] It seems that he then read some of the classical texts concerning them for himself, and had a terrible shock; for by the time he completed his history of Britain, in 1647, he had swung to the opposite stance. He referred to Druids huffily as 'a sort of priests or magicians', whom he could not call philosophers even if they might have studied Pythagoras's teachings. They were 'men reported facetious and ambitious', 'part of a barbarous and lunatic rout' on Anglesey, and presided over a people who (according to Caesar) had savage and immoral customs. Caesar had also said that the Druids had possessed a single leader, like a Christian archbishop, and so Milton's hatred of prelates was aroused as well as his contempt for savages. He declared that the arrival of the Romans was essential to civilize the ancient British, and never thereafter wrote about Druids.[56]

Nor was there any greater consistency in how they should be regarded among those engaged in the partisan religious controversy that was one of the features of the period. It has already been demonstrated how French and German Catholics and a Scottish Catholic and Protestant could enlist Druids as forerunners of their own forms of religion; English authors were more at odds with each other over the propriety of this tactic. Both Harrison and Camden had, after all, employed it in the English Protestant cause with significantly different sources and arguments. In 1615 the Anglican Bishop of Llandaff, Francis Godwin, wrote a history of episcopacy in Britain which treated Druids simply as opponents. In his reading, the true agents of divine providence had not been them but the Romans, who had prepared the way for Christianity by 'pulling up the weeds of that so long continued superstition' of Druidry.[57] His attitude may have helped to provoke a Catholic apologist, Richard Broughton, to restate the case for them as prophets of Christianity who were easily converted to it and thereafter became enthusiastic missionaries. He cleverly drew both on the French writers and on Protestants such as Caius and Speed, whose work he subverted for his own ends.[58]

Sometimes members of the same Church could clash directly over the issue. In the 1650s, the Anglican minister Thomas Fuller published a history of British religion, in which he lambasted the ancient inhabitants of the island as idol- and devil-worshippers and condemned the notion that they had been monotheists or paved the way for Christianity. He drew a reply from another Anglican cleric, Peter Heylyn, to the effect that he had misunderstood the true doctrine of the Druids, who had preached the existence of a single supreme god served by lesser divinities who functioned much as saints did in Roman Catholicism. In return, Fuller grumbled that nobody had mistaken the ancient Greeks as anything but pagans who had venerated false deities, even though they had believed in a king of the gods. With that, the argument petered out. It may have been sharpened by the fact that, although both Fuller and Heylyn were royalists during the Civil War, the former had opposed the royal religious policies of the 1630s, with their emphasis on ceremony and hierarchy, and the latter strongly supported them. Likewise, the former had conformed to the Church of the republican regimes of the 1650s while the latter held firmly aloof from it. In that sense they were different kinds of Anglican churchman. None the less, the gap between them was neither wide nor fixed, and they subsequently became friends, and were both appointed as royal chaplains when the monarchy was restored.[59]

The British Druids therefore entered the second half of the seventeenth century much as they had been at the opening of the first: mostly ignored by the Welsh, treated by the Scots as hazy if respectable ancestors, and employed by the English as literary figures whose role and identity mutated constantly according to the author. Whereas the Scots had linked them to tangible ancient remains, in the English and Welsh imagination they were consigned to long-vanished woodland groves; their invisibility in the landscape was proportionate to the lack of agreement over their historical meaning. Their one big chance to break out of this pattern seemed to be thwarted in 1655. It was in that year that John Webb, a pupil of the celebrated architect Inigo Jones, edited and published a report on the likely origins of Stonehenge, which had been commissioned from Jones, as surveyor of the royal works, some thirty-five years before by King James I. Jones commenced his study by considering and dismissing various possible identities for the builders of the monument, including the Druids. His arguments against associating them with it were entirely reasonable: that no classical author had claimed that they were great architects or located them within stone temples; that the design of Stonehenge was unique among the ancient monuments of Britain; and that, in particular, nothing like it had ever been recorded on Anglesey, the stronghold of British Druidry.[60] Jones and Webb then went on, notoriously, to misrepresent the structure and dimensions of the site to support an argument that it had been built by the Romans. This, in itself, was to start a debate, but not one in which anybody immediately pleaded the cause of the Druids (the other contenders put forward were the Danes): for the time being it seemed that they had been wiped off the physical landscape even more effectively than before.

In 1652 Elias Ashmole, soon to be famed as a scholar of the natural sciences and the founder of Oxford University's museum of antiquities, edited an anthology of English poetry on scientific and quasi-scientific subjects. He felt that he needed to give the Druids a place in the early story of English learning, but had no real idea of what that should be. As a result, he honoured and dismissed them in a single phrase, as 'the famous and mysterious Druydae'.[61] The words perfectly sum up the position which they had acquired in British history by that decade.

* * *

This situation was to change slowly during the following half century, because of a number of different developments. A vital part in them was to be played by Oxford University: Cambridge might have been claimed to have begun as a Druidic foundation, but its great rival was to contribute considerably more to the cultural history of Druidry. In 1655 a fellow of Merton College, Edmund Dickinson, used the university press to put out a Latin treatise on different aspects of antiquity. It had an appendix which attempted to reconcile biblical with classical mythology, mainly by using the evidence of language; for example, it was suggested that Hercules and Joshua had been the same person. The technique was applied to Druids, and the way in provided by Pliny's derivation of their name from the word for 'oak'. As Abraham had taught the true and divinely revealed religion of the Old Testament beneath the 'oak trees' of Mamre in Palestine, this apparent connection was made the basis for an argument that the Druids had learned their theology from the patriarch himself, and that their teachings had therefore (initially, at least) represented the pure faith of the Hebrew patriarchs.[62] Gossip around Oxford asserted, confidently and enduringly, that the treatise published by Dickinson as his appendix had actually been written by a former colleague of his at Merton. This was Henry Jacob, a brilliant young philologist who had gone completely mad and been deprived of his fellowship in 1648, dying in 1652.[63]

Whatever the truth of the matter, the argument took hold at Oxford and was repeated with much enlargement and massive learning within ten years by a fellow of Magdalen College, Thomas Smith. The latter used his remarkable linguistic expertise to argue that Abraham had imparted the true religion not merely to the Druids but to the Brahmins of India. Smith worked, moreover, according to exemplary standards of scholarship, proceeding slowly and thoroughly from point to point and buttressing his deductions with quotations printed in the original script of his Greek, Syriac, Hebrew and Arabic sources, so that fellow experts could check his translations. His book provides a classic illustration of how a completely erroneous theory, based ultimately on mere wish-fulfilment, can be argued with admirable learning and logic.[64] By the mid-1660s, therefore, this small group of Oxford philologists had pioneered a new route by which the Druids could be connected to the Hebrew patriarchs and the revealed religion of the true god, guided by first-class research and genuine texts and bypassing the increasingly implausible claims of Annius of Viterbo. Their work was to be cited, frequently and continually, for the next hundred years.

A second development by which Druidry was to be made more familiar and more meaningful to the British began with a gathering of Wiltshire landowners at Marlborough Castle, seat of the Seymour family, at Christmas 1648. It can hardly be coincidental that it was held as the national political crisis centred on London, that was to culminate in the execution of King Charles I and the abolition of the monarchy and House of Lords, was rapidly intensifying. The Seymours were ardent royalists, and seem to have wanted to discuss these developments with friends, even if in the event they proved to be as impotent a set of onlookers as all the rest of the king's adherents. On 7 January they and their guests rode out to hunt hares on the Marlborough Downs, and the chase led them down to the village of Avebury. Among them was a young man called John Aubrey, from a junior branch of a family of Welsh squires, who had grown up in Wiltshire and had developed from childhood a love of ancient and medieval remains. What ensued has become part of the foundation epic of British archaeology. Aubrey noticed that part of the village was enclosed in a huge earthwork, the interior of which was set with stones that appeared to form circles. He left the hunting party to explore it, and realized that he was looking at an impressive ancient monument that nobody seemed to have noticed before. The appearance of the book on Stonehenge by Jones and Webb six years later stimulated his interest in such sites, and further opportunities for him to examine the remains at Avebury were provided in the later 1650s by his friend James Long, a former royalist colonel excluded from public life by the republican governments. Long had taken to using the village as a base for autumn hawking holidays, and regularly invited Aubrey to join him.[65]

The next great transformation of national politics produced a further twist in the story, as the restoration of the monarchy in 1660 was followed by the foundation of the Royal Society in London to promote British science. Aubrey and Long were both made early members, and in July 1663 the society discussed the megalithic complex at Avebury and directed the two men to consider a project for excavations there. In August two other leading members presented Aubrey to the newly restored king, Charles II, who was excited enough by his description of the site to visit it himself when on progress in the following month. Charles and his brother and heir, James, were both impressed, and commanded Aubrey to produce a written account of it and of other ancient monuments in its vicinity. He began at once, and the eventual result was the manuscript of a book that Aubrey provisionally entitled *Templa Druidum*, the main argument of which was that Avebury and the other prehistoric stone circles of Britain and Ireland, including Stonehenge, had been religious structures erected by the prehistoric British, and probably associated with the rites of the Druids.[66]

This much is beyond dispute. What nobody has considered systematically is how and when Aubrey came by this idea. He himself never explained this, in contrast with the vivid pen-portrait that he provided of his discovery of Avebury. Clearly the very title of his projected book embodies the argument, but the manuscript of it that survives is embedded in a revised and extended work dating from the period 1694–5.[67] The title was certainly already in place by March 1673, when a friend of Aubrey's referred to it in a letter.[68] This is the earliest secure dating for it, but it was probably adopted as soon as he began to carry out the fieldwork for the book ten years before. The surviving version of *Templa Druidum* is mostly concerned with Avebury itself, where Aubrey began surveying almost as soon as the king instructed him to do so.[69] The conclusion to it is dated 1665, which could be taken as a solid terminal point for the development of his basic ideas were it not for the fact that Aubrey was clearly stating it from memory, and his remembrance of events was insecure. Initially, he wrote beside the date the name of the home in Wiltshire at which he believed he was living at the time, only to cross it out later on further reflection and put the name of a different residence.[70] On balance, however, it seems most likely that he had developed his characteristic ideas concerning stone circles by the mid-1660s.

The question of how he developed them is likewise ultimately indeterminate, although some suggestions can be made. One is that his attention was drawn to Druids during a visit that he made to Ireland in July 1660, when he saw a version of the New Testament in which the Three Wise Men were described as Druids.[71] Another is that this interest was reinforced, or engendered from the start, by his visits to Oxford in the 1660s, when members of the university were drawing attention to the subject. He certainly made these visits, at times specifically to buy books: it was in a bookshop there in 1667 that one of his most important friendships began.[72] He also owned both of the works that had advanced the case that the Druids were pupils of Abraham.[73] Unfortunately, there is no evidence that he had read either before 1673: he certainly had not heard of the one by Dickinson before it was recommended to him in 1694.[74] The third explanation is the most likely and secure: that his attention was drawn to the Druids by the argument against their association with Stonehenge, made by Jones and Webb in 1655. As said, he himself recorded that their book was important to his developing thought, and its contention that nothing like Stonehenge existed elsewhere may have grated against his own discovery of the Avebury circles and his belief that they and Stonehenge represented monuments of the same ancient culture. It seems, however, to have been the Scots who provided the vital impetus to his decision to identify this culture firmly with the native British and provisionally with their Druids. He himself, in his draft conclusion dated 1665, credited Sir Robert Moray and Lord Yester with the information that similar stone circles were found in parts of Scotland that the Romans had never reached.[75] Moray was a fellow member of the Royal Society, and had been present during the royal visit to Avebury and taken his own notes on the site; so he would almost certainly have imparted this information to Aubrey as early as 1663.[76] It was reinforced when, as a result, Aubrey read Boece and Spottiswoode, the great Scottish histories that mentioned and extolled Druids and, in the case of Boece, linked them to prehistoric circles.[77] In this manner, the early and sustained warmth shown towards Druids by the Scots finally came south to bear rich fruit.

It was, however, slow to ripen. By 1665, if his date can be trusted, Aubrey had a book prepared that boldly and clearly advanced his argument for the origins of the stone rings. Its great case study consisted of Avebury, but it added data from other sites and its argument was based on the existence of stone circles across much of Britain and Ireland. It made the simple and powerful point that because the distribution of these monuments was so wide, it could only be accounted for by crediting them to the pre-Roman inhabitants of these islands. As their structure had no obvious practical function, they were fairly clearly ceremonial structures ('temples'), and as the religious experts of the ancient British and Irish were the Druids, the latter could be logically associated with them. So the work concluded. Aubrey decided to add an appendix to it devoted to Stonehenge, so bringing this most famous and enigmatic of Britain's ancient remains into the picture, giving his book added polemical power and fulfilling the royal command to survey that site as well. The work was done, and the whole volume duly dedicated to Charles II.[78] Aubrey was now ready to lob a bomb-shell into the international scholarly community; but he shrank from the act.

The basic reason for this was that John Aubrey simply couldn't write a book; he was, rather, a natural jotter-down of notes. Almost by accident, in *Templa Druidum*, he had created something very like a compact, punchy, publishable text, and now his natural inclination to tinker kicked in. His decision to tack on a large appendix was the first symptom of this ailment, and it was reinforced by a natural timidity, probably enhanced by the financial and emotional disasters that rocked his personal life in the late 1660s.[79] Having got his manuscript ready for the press, he decided to shelve it until he had gathered more data from Wales and Scotland that might make his argu-ment unassailable.[80] Then he resolved to broaden the whole work to a general survey of ancient monuments and customs in Britain, of which *Templa Druidum* would be only the first section. In May 1680 he told a friend that he had decided to name this enlarged book *Monumenta Britannica*, to imitate the famous work that the Danish scholar Olaus Worm had published on the antiquities of his own land.[81] In a private note he admitted to himself that he could be more certain of ascribing most of the monuments to the (ancient) British than to the Druids.[82] In that letter of May 1680 he had announced that the enlarged manuscript was now ready to be made into a fair copy and sent to press; but another decade passed without this happening.

None the less, Aubrey's ideas were not wholly without effect, although not in print. He was a very gregarious man, and the letters quoted above show how he discussed his project with friends, who were themselves notable scholars. News of his views must have spread through some at least of the nation's networks of intellectuals, together with the favourable account of the origins of Druidic thought propagated by the Oxford fellows cited above. It may also be, in addition, that the political climate of the restored monarchy was kinder to Druids than that which had prevailed earlier. Although there had been nothing like a clear correspondence between confessional loyalties and attitudes to the subject, Catholics, and Anglicans like Heylyn who were enthusiastic proponents of ceremony and hierarchy, tended to regard Druids with more sympathy, and evangelical Protestants to treat them with less. It is possible that the dominance of English public life by churchmen of Heylyn's hue, ushered in by the Restoration, softened accounts of the ancient British priesthood.

Whatever the reason, those accounts did tend to grow more appreciative. When Aubrey's friend Anthony Wood published his history of Oxford University in 1674, he prefaced it by quoting Caesar and Strabo to restate the idea, mooted since the Tudor period, that the Druids were the founders of British scholarship.[83] In 1678 a royal chaplain, Thomas Jones, wrote to prove that the Church in Britain was older than that of Rome, and had never been subject to it. Behind that early native Church he positioned the Druids, as teachers of 'sublime and unparalleled metaphysics', espe-cially 'touching God and soul and holy discipline' which had made them responsive to Christianity. He repeated the tradition that they had instructed the Greeks, and added the thought that the medieval wizard Merlin might have been a scientist preserving 'a relic of the Druidean philosophy'.[84] At some point in the period between 1681 and 1699 the courtier and diplomat Sir William Temple drafted a history of

England, in which he hailed the Druids as teachers of 'justice and fortitude', living simply in the woods: 'their food of acorns, berries or other mast; their drink water: which made them respected and admired, not only for knowing more than other men, but for despising what all others valued and pursued, and by their great virtue and temperance, they were suffered patiently to reprove and correct the vices and crimes, from which themselves were free'.[85] It is interesting to observe that the same warming of attitude took place among authors associated with the more radical wing of English Protestantism, but with more qualification. In 1671 occurred the death of Thomas, Lord Fairfax, the general who had commanded the New Model Army that had won the Civil War for Parliament in 1645–6. After his demise the oak woods at his seat of Nun Appleton in the soft countryside of central Yorkshire were felled for profit, and his cousin Brian Fairfax composed a poem to complain of this action. He asserted that, in contrast with this modern greed, when the 'learned Druids taught, / Then it was sacrilege to cut a tree; / To wound an oak – to offend a deity'. He was careful, however, to add that Lord Fairfax himself had surpassed the Druids in virtue, because what he had studied in the shade of the trees had been the Bible.[86]

It also helped the growing reputation of the Druids that for the first time readers of English were provided with a means to visualize them. The classical and Irish accounts had not carried pictorial illustrations of them, nor had the works of earlier British writers. In 1676, however, a lawyer called Aylett Sammes brought out a history of ancient Britain which combined novel theories with visual aids. The former were based on a suggestion made by a French philologist, Samuel Bochart, who had concluded that there were marked similarities between Hebrew and Welsh, which could be explained by the influence of ancient Phoenician traders operating between Palestine and Britain. The Phoenicians had certainly been the first great mariners and colonists of the ancient Mediterranean, getting from their homeland on the Lebanese coast as far as Spain, and it required only a little imagination to push their voyages further out into the Atlantic. Sammes approved Bochart's work, and extended it to suggest that the Phoenicians had also intoduced bards to Britain, as religious teachers who explained the doctrine of the immortality of the soul; thereby providing a plausible historical mechanism whereby the ideas of Abraham could have been transported to the far end of Europe. Subsequently, in Sammes's reimagining, the Druids arrived on the same Phoenician vessels, probably from Greece and bringing with them Pythagoras's concept of the transmigration of souls, with which they replaced the purer and better bardic teaching. They also degraded the bards into poets and singers, replacing them as priests and setting up primates to oversee the north and south of the island, with one probable supreme chief over all. Tactfully splitting the difference between Scots and Welsh, Sammes seated one primate in Man and the other in Anglesey. Although he regarded the Druids as inferior to the earlier bards, he still thought highly of them, praising them for their virtuous lives and their preparation of the British for the reception of Christianity. He accepted that they had sacrificed humans, but suggested that their victims were enemies or evildoers, turning the rites into no more than public executions.[87]

There is, in fact, no evidence that the Phoenicians ever reached British shores, or even got anywhere near them; but their utility as a means of getting Old Testament religion to Britain meant that they were to sail through the imagination of writers on the ancient British past for the next two hundred years or more. It was, however, Sammes's illustrations, and not his text, which were to have the enduring impact. He accorded this section of his book just two. One was of an actual Druid, and was taken ultimately from the only ancient image that anybody had claimed to represent one: that portrayed in the statues that Conrad Celtis had seen in the cloister wall in Bavaria, almost two centuries before. Sammes had read of these in a book by John Selden, and his picture copied the account there exactly, showing a wise-looking old man with a long beard, a hooded cloak and robe, and a staff. It was to establish the dominant portrait of a Druid for the modern British. Four pages later, however, Sammes balanced this benevolent and sympathetic icon with another, by printing an imagined representation of the burning alive of a crowd of human victims in one of the giant wicker figures described by Caesar. Given the fact that Sammes was an apologist for Druids, he may not have intended the negative impact that his representation of this huge wicker male figure, filled with writhing bodies, was to have on perceptions of ancient British paganism, right down to, and including, the world of late twentieth-century cinema.[88]

Meanwhile, the University of Oxford was engaged in further work that would promote public consciousness of ancient Druidry. It commenced with an initiative taken in 1692 by a young Fellow of Queen's College, Edmund Gibson, who decided to edit a new and extensively revised edition of Camden's *Britannia* which would display to the public the advances in knowledge of the British past made in the course of the century.[89] He assembled a team of about thirty contributors, of whom four are of special importance for the present subject. Two were young Oxford scholars like Gibson himself. The more remarkable was Edward Lhuyd, who had just been appointed to manage the university museum. Although he is remembered primarily as a linguist, his talents extended to making major contributions to the developing fields of botany, geology and prehistory.[90] In connection with the last, he has been called the first Welsh archaeologist,[91] and indeed he was a self-conscious Cambrian patriot, working hard to advance knowledge of the land and heritage of Wales. He was entrusted with the additional material for all the Welsh chapters of the projected volume. Following a pattern which will recur in this book,[92] Lhuyd was himself marginal to the nation that he was to honour with such passion, being born and brought up over the English border in Shropshire, the illegitimate son of a minor Welsh gentleman. He never lived in Wales itself, making his whole adult career in Oxford. The other young member of the initial editorial team who has relevance to the present subject was Thomas Tanner, then still an undergraduate at Gibson's college. He was given the chapter in the *Britannia* on his native Wiltshire, and took the crucial step of bringing John Aubrey into the project by persuading him to lend his unpublished manuscript on ancient monuments and to discuss the ideas embodied in it.[93]

Tanner's interest apparently gave Aubrey the push which he had needed to resume his work and to deal with the doubts concerning it that had accumulated in his mind. Once again, Scotland played a crucial role in guiding his thoughts, this time in the shape of James Garden, Professor of Theology at the university of Aberdeen, the city set just to the east of that striking group of monuments, the 'recumbent-stone circles', that had moved Boece's imagination almost two hundred years before. At this critical moment Aubrey established a correspondence with Garden, which lasted from mid-1692 to mid-1693 and confirmed all his earlier suppositions.[94] The Scot began by answering his enquiries with the discouraging news that there seemed nothing in either place-names or folklore to connect the Aberdeenshire circles to Druids. None the less, he did agree that such a connection might 'rationally' be made, and went on subsequently to defend this view. He pointed out that the classical authors had regularly associated Druids with bards, who had remained a feature of Gaelic Scottish society; which suggested that Druids had also formerly been present. He added that in Ross-shire the local people associated megalithic monuments with *Druineach*, meaning 'the clever ones', which might signify Druids (though Garden admitted that the locals themselves used it as meaning Picts).

Aubrey had developed three conceptual problems in particular when dealing with his theory, and the good professor dealt with all of them. One was that ancient authors themselves did not represent Druids as worshipping in stone monuments. The reply was that most of those authors had not dealt with the setting for ritual at all, but they broadly agreed that Druids had been priests, and throughout the ancient world priests had been represented as using stone altars. The second problem was that more recent authorities had considered megalithic structures to have been tombs for heroes or dignitaries, and not temples. Garden answered that it was inherently unlikely that the distinguished dead would have been carried to such remote places as those in which the monuments were found, and that such human remains as had been found at them had probably the same relationship to them as graves had to a Christian church. Aubrey's final worry was that the classical texts had commonly portrayed Druids as worshipping in groves, not stone circles; and to this came the simple answer that the trees could well have disappeared, or been removed, during the many centuries since.

These letters had such a powerful effect on the old English antiquary that he had them incorporated into his manuscript of *Monumenta Britannica*, which he now set to work finally to complete and publish. The book that he had written almost three decades before was now only the first part of a two-volume work on monuments and customs, and was itself padded out with further data. Its argument remained the same: that stone circles had been the temples of the ancient British and could therefore be plausibly suggested to have been the setting for Druid rites. This second proposal remained more tentative than the first, and although Aubrey had now added a section on the probable beliefs of the Druids, it was almost devoid of personal speculation or excitement. It consisted, instead, of quotations from the main classical texts that dealt with the subject, and citations of modern works such as those by Edmund Dickinson and Thomas Smith. The only touches characteristic of Aubrey were the mention of German and Welsh folk beliefs concerning birds, which he believed could derive remotely from Druidical traditions.[95] It is possible that his enthusiasm for Druids was more evident in conversation than on paper. Many years later a Kentish antiquary, John Batteley, recalled showing him a strigil found in a Roman fort – a bronze instrument used for scraping skin clean as one of the usual processes of Roman bathing – upon which Aubrey exclaimed, 'Behold the golden sickle with which the Druids used to cut mistletoe.' Batteley continued that the old man 'was apt superstitiously and idly to wrest almost everything to the religion and worship of the Druids'.[96] This may be good evidence that Aubrey's emotional involvement with the subject was indeed more passionate than his writings suggest. On the other hand, Batteley may have built on this single remark about the strigil, and Aubrey's general association with the interpretation of prehistoric rings as Druid temples, to credit him with an obsession that he did not actually have.

What is very clear is that, during the period between 1692 and 1695, he was unusually preoccupied with Druids as he struggled to get his book into print, and keen to discuss them with anybody available. One of those willing to abet him was the fourth of the individuals roped into Gibson's network of collaborators who have significance for the present book: a tall, lean, dark-haired young Ulsterman called John Toland who turned up in Oxford in 1693.[97] Toland's background made him a most unusual figure in that setting, for he was of native Irish stock, from the peninsula of Inishowen, and had been brought up a Roman Catholic. It was his conversion to Protestantism during his adolescence which had won him ecclesiastical patronage powerful enough to launch him into an education that had already taken him through the universities of Glasgow, Edinburgh, Leiden and Utrecht.[98] His learning was impressive, and his command of the Irish language made him a scholar of considerable potential; Gibson rapidly engaged him as a consultant for the improvement of the section of the *Britannia* on Ireland. The collaboration was, however, brief, for Gibson almost immediately found Toland's 'insolent conceited way of talking' insufferable.[99] Lhuyd agreed, commenting that he had 'as little a share as may be of modesty or conscience; and [was] one of the best scolds that I ever met with'.[100] It was, however, the radicalism of the religious and political opinions which he had acquired, and the brashness with which he expressed them, that turned Oxford against him more than his personality in itself. One furious don described Toland to the Archbishop of Canterbury as 'trampling on ye Common Prayer Book, talking against the scriptures, commending commonwealths, justifying the murder of K[ing]. C[harles]. 1st, railing against priests in general'.[101] By the second half of 1694 the Vice-Chancellor had ordered him out, and he was off to London and a still more controversial career.

His conversations with Aubrey in Oxford had, however, left a lasting impression on him. The sweet-natured English antiquary got on well with the fiery Irish youth, and they continued to meet after the latter's forced removal to the capital.[102] Many years later Toland paid tribute to the old man's influence, admitting that Aubrey was the first person whom he had encountered to have the idea that prehistoric stone circles were Druidic temples, and recalling how he had shown Toland the letters from Garden as the necessary confirmation of this theory. Toland also added, however, that '[neither] the facts he knew, nor the reflections he made, were what I wanted'.[103] This last statement, while it may have reflected Toland's appetite for self-glorification, was probably true enough; his newly acquired hatred of clergy was not easily reconciled with an interest in ancient priests. He would make this reconciliation, to great effect, but that was yet far in the future.

By July 1693 Aubrey was actively seeking a publisher for *Monumenta Britannica*, even while he was still adding material to it.[104] In 1695 he at last delivered it to one Awnsham Churchill, who hung on to it while he negotiated with the author over the financial terms on which it was to be put out. The argument was still in progress when Aubrey died, at Oxford in 1697.[105] Churchill's problems with the projected book were well justified, and were shared by that born editor, Edmund Gibson, when he saw the manuscript. Gibson was aghast, and embarrassed, to find that 'the accounts of things are so broken and short, the parts so much disordered and the whole such a rhapsody, that I cannot but wonder how that poor man could entertain any thoughts of a present impression'.[106] Thirty years of trying had not rendered Aubrey any more capable of producing a finished work of literature: thinking that he had erected a palace of learning, he had given the world a builder's yard of piled materials instead. None the less, the materials had undoubted value, and Churchill retained the manuscript which had by chance ended up in his hands, for the use of future scholars.

The likelihood that such scholars would wish to consult it was greatly increased by the appearance of Gibson's edition of the *Britannia* in 1695. It was a high-profile, much-admired publication that did a great deal to define the view that educated British people took of their past; and Gibson felt able to edit a still further enlarged version in 1722. It established as credible, or even orthodox, the interpretation of the megalithic monuments of Britain as holy places of its prehistoric inhabitants. In addition, Tanner and Lhuyd introduced readers to John Aubrey's theory that they had been built under the direction of the Druids, for use in their ceremonies. Both were careful not to give this theory direct endorsement, but they supported it in more subtle ways. Tanner presented it as only one of a number of explanations that had been offered for the construction of Stonehenge, but he explicitly rejected its main competitors, to state his belief that the monument was the work of the native British in pre-Christian times. Lhuyd repeatedly cited additional pieces of Welsh evidence that fitted Aubrey's conjecture. This was all the braver in that he had come under direct pressure to avoid doing this: in the course of his work for the volume, a leading antiquarian, John Woodward, had written to him repeatedly to convince him that megalithic monuments were post-Roman. Those who suggested otherwise, especially Aubrey, in his opinion allowed 'too much to fancy'.[107] By putting things as they did in the new *Britannia*, Tanner and Lhuyd managed at the same moment to avoid accepting personal responsibility for the hypothesis if it proved controversial, to offer it in an attractive manner, and to give its aged exponent full credit for it.[108] Thus, at the end of the seventeenth century, the ancient Druids were suddenly turned into a vivid part of the cultural heritage of the English and Welsh as well as of the Scots, by becoming associated – at least potentially – with a very large number of the physical remains of the British past.

* * *

The story of the first three decades of the eighteenth century is one of how this concept began to settle into the British consciousness and to engender new works in turn. The revised *Britannia* had appeared, quite self-consciously, in the period at which a revised Britain was being created, by the union of the states of England and Scotland in 1707 and the final collapse of the Welsh bardic tradition during the second half of the seventeenth century. Traditional national identities were being renegotiated, and the figure of the Druid was emerging as one of the symbols around which a genuinely common, British, past could be constructed for all the different historical peoples and cultures of the island. It was probably the influence of Gibson's volume that caused this figure to be familiar enough by 1710 for the polished London essayist Joseph Addison to use the word 'Druid' as humorous slang for a clergyman when writing in the *Tatler*.[109] In 1706 Henry Purcell contributed music to a revived version of Fletcher's play *Bonduca*, and gave its Druids lyrics for their songs, calling on divine powers to defend Britain against its enemies.[110] The revised *Britannia* probably also served finally to convince the average British reader that the Druid island of Mona had been Anglesey and not Man, as Lhuyd threw his patriotic weight behind this argument.[111] Lest any remain doubtful, in 1702 a Londoner, Thomas Brown, wrote a tract which restated that argument in patient and thorough detail; to drive the point home, Brown's work was published as an appendix to a semi-official account of the Isle of Man itself, produced by a former governor. His essay also did something to increase a sense of the Druids as mystics with very wide horizons, by suggesting that their alleged doctrines sounded more similar to those of the Hebrews, Egyptians and Indian Brahmins than those of the Greeks.[112]

The publication of descriptive accounts of Britain's neighbouring small islands was itself a feature of the period, for two apparent reasons. The more important was to give the British, in an age of union, a better overview of their archipelago and a better sense of the resources that might be exploited in its outlying portions. The lesser, but still significant, was the threat of invasion and rebellion presented by the existence of an exiled royal family, that of the main House of Stuart which had been driven to the Continent in 1688. The Scottish Highlands and Islands soon emerged as the main focus of support for it and as the natural bridgehead for French or Spanish forces invading to restore it; and, this being the case, the government needed precise information on the seaways along which such attempts would be made. The study of Man was preceded in 1693 by one of the northern isles of Orkney and Shetland, and succeeded in 1703 by one of the Hebrides. Both of these went swiftly into subsequent editions. For the purposes of the present book, they make a significant contrast. The former mentioned the huge prehistoric circles of Orkney mainland, and added that the local people thought they had been pagan temples – a comment that gave further comfort to Aubrey in his own views – but did not mention Druids.[113] The study of the Hebrides, however, put the Druids in the foreground of its discussion of the islands' past.

It may be suggested, once again, that the influence of the new *Britannia* might have been behind so dramatic an alteration. Ironically, the Scottish sections of Gibson's volume did not pay attention to Druidry, despite the now long tradition of its association with the Scots. This was because they had been entrusted to Sir Robert Sibbald, an Edinburgh physician who had little interest in ancient history and had taken up the idea (floated in England during the mid-seventeenth century but excitingly avant-garde for the Scots) that megalithic monuments were the work of the Danes; his views had intimidated Aubrey until Garden came to the latter's rescue.[114] The efforts of Tanner and Lhuyd had, however, more than compensated for Sibbald's neglect, and the book on the Western Isles effectively carried on where they had left off. It was, ironically, inspired by Sibbald himself, who had proposed the project and entrusted it to a native of the Isle of Skye, a fellow doctor called Martin Martin, who explored the region systematically at the end of the seventeenth century.[115]

Martin's technique for putting a spotlight on the Druids was simple. The Gaelic society of his time, in the Scottish Highlands and Islands, still gave high status to bards as poets, historians, propagandists and leaders of secular ritual. Martin declared, as if it were a fact needing no argument, that they had taken all these functions from the ancient Druids. In large part, therefore, the role of the latter could be reconstructed from that of the medieval and early modern bards: reciting the pedigree of a new chief at his inauguration, haranguing an army before battle to arouse its courage, and so on.[116] In this respect Martin was the ancestor of all those modern scholars who have assumed that medieval bards inherited and propagated Druidic teachings. Martin, however, went further. When introducing readers to the spectacular megalithic circle and avenues at Callanish, on Lewis, he stated not only that the local people believed them to have been a heathen temple, but that they had told him that a 'Chief Druid or Priest' had stood at the centre of the circle to address the worshippers. When speaking of the traditional festival of Beltane, which opened in May, he declared with equal confidence that the Druids had had all fires in each community extinguished and would not allow any to be relit until the householders had paid their tithes to them in full. They had also, he continued, marked the festival by burning criminals between two fires: as a Presbyterian Scot, Martin was more suspicious of priests in general than the Catholic Boece or the Episcopalian Spottiswoode had been.[117]

Martin therefore not merely reinforced the association between Druids and mega-liths, and asserted that they had made a permanent impact on Gaelic society, but actu-ally suggested that memories of them remained strong in the oral tradition of the Hebrideans. If true, this is a point of major importance in any reconstruction of the history of Druidry and of its legacy, but doubt has been cast on it, for good reason. The author of the best extant book on literary images of Druids, A. L. Owen, discov-ered an undated letter from Martin to Lhuyd, following the former's visit to Callanish, in which he described the monuments and what the locals said of them but omitted references to Druidry. Instead he reported that some of the islanders called them 'false men', apparently meaning petrified human beings. The implication is that Martin later added the reference to the 'chief Druid' himself, to suit his own purposes. Owen also found a wide-ranging account of Highland beliefs and customs by an unknown author which had been sent to Sibbald, who had copied it in turn to Lhuyd. It went to some effort to collate the explanations that the natives provided for stone circles, finding that these attributed them to giants or early Christian monks, or called them the burial places of heroes or the temples of pagans; but none apparently mentioned Druids.[118] The suspicion that Martin was imposing his Druids on actual local beliefs and customs is further strengthened by his reference to Beltane. Other accounts of early modern Gaelic societies mention the customs of extinguishing and rekindling household fires at that festival, and of passing between two bonfires in order to gain ritual protection against danger in the coming summer.[119] Martin remains, however, the only one to associate them with local traditions of the payment of Druidic tithes or the sacrifice of malefactors.

The suspicion must stand, therefore, that he was using Druidry to spice up his account; but, whether it is just or not, there is no doubt about the impact of his book. His own patron Sibbald subsequently published as proven fact the statement that 'many vestiges' of Druidry still survived in northern Scotland and its islands.[120] By the 1720s Scottish scholars were starting routinely to describe the prehistoric monuments of their nation as Druidic temples even when, as in the case of the Iron Age towers known as 'brochs', it was much more apparent that their function was defensive rather than religious.[121] Meanwhile, the same process was at work in Wales, under the influence of Edward Lhuyd. He may have been cautious when bringing Druids into his discussion of Welsh antiquities in the new *Britannia*, but his contribution had a decisive effect in encouraging the British to regard their own prehistory as something exciting and admirable in itself, rather than as an appendage to the study of the Greek and Roman worlds and always to be viewed through the eyes of the latter.[122] He promoted this shift not merely in his publications but in his research methods, by building up a network of correspondents across Wales, hundreds strong, who supplied him with data. Most were parish clergy, whom he contacted with a set questionnaire seeking information about their localities; some, inevitably, were inspired by this to become antiquaries in their own right. Lhuyd was aiming to produce a multi-volume work on the natural and human heritage of Wales, which would almost certainly have been one of the greatest products of British scholarship. Its first volume, in 1707, dealt with philology and made the decisive recognition that Gaelic, Welsh, Manx, Cornish and Breton belonged to a distinctive group of languages, to which he gave the name 'Celtic'. Lhuyd's health had, however, never matched the strength of his intellectual abilities and ambitions, which may indeed have undermined it further. He died suddenly in 1709, leaving his notes in no fit state for further publication.[123]

His enquiries provoked the greatest interest in Druids, logically enough, in the island which he had helped to reclaim for them: Anglesey, or Môn. In particular, they aroused the enthusiasm of two clergymen serving parishes on the shore of the Menai Strait, occupying pretty well exactly the ground on which the Druids would have stood to curse the Roman soldiers in the account provided by Tacitus. Moreover, the same terrain was thickly studded with megalithic monuments, which could now readily be linked to that event. Lhuyd actually published in the *Britannia* information provided by one of those clerics, the rector of Newburgh, which related two local place-names to Druidry and identified a particular site as a likely focus for sacrificial rites.[124] It was his neighbour to the east, however, the vicar of Llanidan, who not only became one of Lhuyd's correspondents but set up as an author in his own right. This was Henry Rowlands, who finally published his famous book on the history and monuments of Anglesey in 1723.[125] It was designed to be a local case study of the most important kind, using a close reading of the textual and physical evidence for a particular county to make propositions that had relevance for the history of a whole continent. To achieve this, Rowlands accumulated and employed the familiar data from the Bible and the Greek and Roman classics, alongside brand new material provided by philology and archaeology, including his own fieldwork in Anglesey. His book included a number of plans and illustrations, produced with the same scrupulous care: the drawing of a Druid was taken directly from that in Aylett Sammes's book, which had seemed in turn to be based on the best scholarly authority. Rowlands was patient and meticulous, again, in circulating copies of earlier drafts of his work in manuscript, for criticism by experts in the relevant fields; the second half of the book which resulted was taken up with systematic answers to objections that had been raised to the manuscript of the first half.[126] He was careful to insist that his suggestions were no more than conjectures. As in the case of Thomas Smith and the oaks of Mamre, his conclusions may have been wrong, but his methodology was impeccable. His problem was the same as Smith's: that two of the vital building-blocks of his argument – contemporary approaches to the Bible and to philology – happened to be flawed.

The infant discipline of philology had embraced the idea that frequent apparent similarities between the form of words indicated a family relationship between languages. This was, long afterwards, disproved by a much greater body of research and data: it is the structure of languages that puts them into groups and not similar word-forms, which are often coincidental. It has already been noted that the French scholar Bochart had discovered seemingly close phonetic comparisons between Hebrew and Welsh, and this idea was soon taken up by the Welsh themselves.[127] Much more was riding on it than an exercise in linguistics: with the collapse of the bardic tradition and the increasing integration of Wales into the developing British state, the Welsh language was starting to give ground seriously before English. A claim for it as an ancient one akin to that of the Scriptures, which had survived with unusual purity, might go far to rescue it and the distinctive cultural identity that largely depended on it.[128] Rowlands took up that claim in a big way and applied it systematically to the Welsh names for natural features and prehistoric monuments. From this he concluded that Britain had first been settled by people speaking Hebrew; and the Bible strongly suggested that this would have been during the repeopling of the earth following Noah's Flood.

If this were the case, then these first settlers would also have brought with them the faith revealed directly by the true God to the Hebrew patriarchs: 'some of the rites and usages of that true religion, pure and untainted in their first propagating of them'.[129] Rowlands accordingly used the Book of Genesis to interpret local prehistoric remains: to him the chambers of megalithic tombs, denuded of their covering mounds by erosion, had been altars for first-fruit sacrifices according to the divine injunction to Noah, and cairns were imitations of those raised by Jacob. His Druids were, initially, the priests of this religion, and their entirely justified reputation as scholars and scientists had been due to their closeness to the Hebrew patriarchs who had received the divine truth, and to whom had also been imparted the laws of nature.

He followed Selden in believing that their mystical teachings had a strong resemblance to those of the Hebrew Cabbala, explicable by their common ancestry. He adapted Strabo's threefold division of their order, into true Druids who acted as theologians, Ovates (in his Welsh rendering, 'ofyddion') who carried out the priestly duties, and Bards who sang. He interpreted Tacitus as indicating that Anglesey had been a particular stronghold of theirs, and argued from this that it had functioned as a kind of 'mother church' for ancient Wales. His Druids suffered a classic biblical fall from grace, becoming 'abominably corrupted, and perverted into the grossest heathenish fictions and barbarities', including human sacrifice. As a result, they ended up both militarily and morally inferior to the Romans, who performed a service for the British by destroying them and so preparing the ground for the coming of the restored true faith, of Christ.[130] Rowlands thus repeated what was essentially the story in Holinshed, but removing the bogus history of Annius to leave what virtually all people of his time regarded as the impeccable authority of the Old Testament, and linking it to physical remains in the fashion of the new antiquarian studies. He also gave his own people, the Welsh, a particular claim to regard themselves as having a special relationship with ancient Druidry; not just because of the importance of Anglesey to that tradition, and the significance of its megalithic remains, but through its literature. He became the first scholar to argue directly that Druidic teaching had been preserved in medieval Welsh poetry; and particularly in the collections of bardic lore known as triads.[131]

Three years after the appearance of Rowlands's book, the public could read another ambitious attempt to put Druids firmly into the landscape and history of the British Isles, this time from John Toland, and representing the ultimate product of that interest that had been fostered in him by John Aubrey during his youth. In the intervening years Toland had won some fame and much notoriety as the author of works which preached the same extreme radicalism that had got him run out of Oxford. His writings on Druids were composed in a period of tremendous optimism and creativity for him, the late 1710s, when a government of which he approved had taken charge of Britain and he was apparently at the height of his literary powers. Those writings represent a curious phenomenon. On the one hand, Toland described them as the result of researches extending back many years, which had turned him into the world expert on the subject, whose work, when complete, would remove the necessity for any further publication on it.[132] While this claim provided proof (if any were needed) that he had not grown any more modest in the long years since he had annoyed Gibson and Lhuyd, he also furnished evidence that it was not wholly unfounded. He had indeed read, or appeared to have read, all the literature on the antiquities of northern Europe, by English, Irish, French and Danish authors,[133] as well as all the relevant classical Greek and Latin texts and (as the decisive factor in his claim of mastery) a range of medieval Irish sources. He may have cut some corners in this research – it has been suggested that many of the Irish texts he cited were quoted not from the originals but from their appearance in the books of other scholars[134] – but it was still an impressive achievement. Its intention was to establish him, once and for all, as a major intellectual figure rather than as merely a political pamphleteer.

What he produced, however, was only an interim report, neatly summed up by the modern writer Leslie Ellen Jones as 'somewhere between a dissertation prospectus and a grant proposal'.[135] In Toland's own word, it was just a 'specimen' of forthcoming work.

It took the form of three letters written to his most consistent patron, the Whig politician Viscount Molesworth, between June 1718 and April 1719. They were designed to be circulated among wealthy and influential people, in order to solicit funding for a six-month expedition which Toland proposed to undertake in order to complete his researches. Specifically, he needed to visit Scotland and Ireland, to view prehistoric monuments and to read manuscripts. His letters were therefore contrived to whet the appetite of prospective sponsors while not giving too much of even his existing discoveries away. He explicitly excluded from discussion, for example, the ideas of the Druids concerning divinity, the soul, the natural world and the heavens, with all of which he promised to deal extensively as part of a projected four-volume book.[136] That book, however, was never written, because his advertising gambit failed; he did not attract the necessary funding, and never carried out the research. Instead his political allies lost power, his finances collapsed, and then his health gave way, so that he died in 1722. His three letters on Druids were published in a posthumous collection of his writings put out four years after that.

They thus represent a firework display of ideas, rather than a sustained and finished treatise, and are different in kind from each other. The first was designed to press the Druids into the abiding preoccupation of his adult life, his campaign against established churches, by vilifying them as the direct ancestors of all that he opposed in the religions of his own day. Thus, 'no heathen priesthood ever came up to the perfection of the Druidical', meaning that it was the most cunning in the entire ancient world in ensuring that priests retained political and social power and the ordinary people remained ignorant and subservient to them. To Toland, 'the *history of the Druids*, in short, is *the complete history of priestcraft*' (his emphases), and functioned as a warning against the impostures and deceits of clergy in his own time. By understanding the way in which these ancient priests had starved their flocks of knowledge, terrorized them with the threat of excommunication, and appropriated their wealth, he believed, people would be able to reject clerical power and pretension in the present.[137] Toland also supplied his own description of the appearance of Druids, blending Celtis's philosophers with other hints in classical and medieval texts to produce figures in long robes and beards, short-haired, carrying staves and wearing Pliny's Druidic 'eggs' encased in gold about their necks. He also adapted the three-rank system for their order, with Bards and Ovates as the lesser ranks, from whom Druids proper were distinguished by white surplices. In Ireland, he declared, the three levels were marked by different colours of tartan, and everywhere women could be found in all the ranks.[138]

He did acknowledge some virtue in their beliefs, conceding that they professed 'the two grand doctrines of the eternity and incorruptibility of the universe and the incessant revolution of all beings and forms'.[139] This has caused some commentators on Toland's treatment of Druids in the letter to suggest that it was ambivalent and inconsistent,[140] but it is hard to sustain this in view of the savage condemnation of them with which it opens. What he seems to have been saying is that even priests who had some inkling of the great truths of the cosmos would pervert them for their own ends, and so priesthood was evil in itself. Certainly this is how this letter was read at the time, and such a reading played a significant part in ensuring that Toland did not receive the patronage for which he was angling. He sent a slightly earlier draft of it to the Whig Lord Chancellor, Thomas Parker, of whose powerful favour he had hopes, only to have it rejected by Parker as an argument which 'he did not understand but which he suspected to be levelled against Christian priests'.[141] This suspicion was, of course, entirely justified.

The rebuff may explain why he called off the anticlerical bombardment in his succeeding two letters, which had different objectives. The second, started ten days after he got the bad news from the Chancellor, was concerned with drawing attention to a visible legacy of Druidry, in the megalithic monuments and folk customs of the British Isles, and especially of their Gaelic regions. Here Toland was exploiting his Irish roots, but his ability to do so directly was limited by the fact that he had left Ulster as an adolescent and that his studies in Scotland had been undertaken before Aubrey had given him an interest in Druids and prehistoric temples. As a result, he was totally dependent on the writings of others, a fact that jarred with his determination to present himself as the pre-eminent expert and lent urgency to his doomed project of a research expedition. His tactic was therefore to take ideas and descriptions from existing books or manuscripts and to improve on them with his own intellectual and imaginative powers, giving minimal or no credit to the authors on whom he relied for his data. He bought a copy of the second edition of Martin's survey of the Western Isles, and covered it with scribbled comments, ridiculing the author for his limitations and the islanders for their backwardness and superstition;[142] before stealing large amounts of material from it. He was particularly interested in the description of Callanish, which, relying wholly on Martin's information, he proceeded to interpret as a temple laid out by the Druids to represent a circle with wings, in honour of the sun, the seasons, the winds, the signs of the zodiac, and the moon, using the nineteen-year cycle called 'metonic' by the ancient Greeks. Having learned about the two large megalithic circles in the centre of Orkney, from the book on the Northern Isles, he declared that these had been dedicated respectively to the sun and the moon. Apparently he had heard of Rowlands's theory that what we now know as megalithic tombs were Druidic altars, because he stated it, with special reference to Wales (which suggests his source). From all these second-hand data he concluded that Druids always performed their rites in a stone circle with an altar at the centre. There is actually a Neolithic tomb in the middle of the main circle at Callanish, which Toland made his type specimen for all Druidic temples. In fact it is very unusual to find the two types of monument combined, but Toland got round this problem – which was obvious even from his limited information – by asserting that in most cases either the circle or the altar had been removed by later human depredations. He followed Irish texts in claiming (with more reason) that the bonfires still ritually lit in many regions of Britain and Ireland, at the festivals of Beltane, Midsummer and Hallowe'en, were remnants of Druidic religion.[143]

Although his arguments in this second letter were less overtly hostile to churchmen, they still contained swipes at the character of the Druids. One in particular was to become very influential. It concerned a natural phenomenon, found sparsely in the granite and sandstone areas of Britain: boulders that the process of weathering or action of glaciers has left balanced on top of others, so they can be rocked from side to side. Geologists are now certain that they are wholly the work of natural forces, but eighteenth-century scholars were inclined to credit them to human hands. Toland included them with megalithic monuments as the work of the Druids, and saddled them with a vivid fantasy. He asserted that they had been erected to manipulate the system of justice, so that an accused person would be invited to rock the stone, only to find it immobilized by a lever secretly activated by one of the Druids presiding. As soon as the wretched person withdrew, the lever was released and the stone again rocked easily, making the guilt of the accused apparently attested by divine authority. Alternatively, Druids could use the same method to acquit a guilty person of whom they approved. In Toland's words, 'by this pretended miracle, they condemned of perjury or acquitted, as their interest and affection led them'.[144] As rocking stones were never constructed by humans, and there is no evidence whatever that Druids were associated with them, Toland was almost certainly wrong. None the less, his image of the stones as instruments of Druidical injustice and tyranny was to reappear in publications, both of fiction and of non-fiction, for the following three hundred years.

The snub from Parker and the completion of the first two letters all occurred within two weeks in the summer of 1718. More than nine months passed before Toland completed the third letter, and its form suggests that, as his prospective sponsors were insufficiently attracted by either of its predecessors, he was making one last try, with a new angle. This was to catch the attention of the many people who knew and admired ancient Greek and Roman literature, by integrating Druids into the world that had produced it and suggesting how great a debt that world owed to them. Once again, he was drawing on existing ideas, and elaborating them. From Aylett Sammes he took the idea that the Gallic god Ogmius could be associated with the classical hero Hercules, who could thus be regarded as having a 'Celtic' origin. He went further, to link Ogmius to the Irish ogham script, copying from the medieval manuscripts that he had read (or heard of) the error that it was based on a tree-alphabet. He also picked up and turned to his purpose one of the most attractive of Greek legends: that of the land of Hyperborea. This appears in some of the earliest Greek writings as an idyllic region lying so far north that it was actually beyond the Arctic zone ('behind the north wind') and so enjoyed a fertile and mild climate. Its inhabitants were supernaturally blessed, suffering no disease, old age or strife, and giving themselves up wholly to music, dance and religion; which is why their god was Apollo, divine patron of the arts. No Greeks ever got there, but there was a tradition that the Hyperboreans had once visited Greek lands. Most of the texts that mentioned Hyperborea put it beyond Scythia, a region roughly covering the modern Ukraine; which would make it lie in theory somewhere at the back of Arctic Russia or Siberia. Diodorus Siculus, however, quoted the lost work of a Greek geographer called Hecataeus, who identified it as an island at least as big as Sicily, lying north of 'the Celtic territory'. This latter phrase could put it anywhere beyond what is now France and Germany. He added (from Hecataeus or some other source) that it had a capital city and a 'spherical' temple to Apollo, and that the god himself visited it every nineteen years, after each metonic cycle of the rising and setting of the moon was completed.[145]

The information provided by Diodorus, of course, made Britain one of the possible candidates for the identity of Hyperborea. Toland was by no means the first author to point this out, but he gave his own twist to the suggestion by asserting that it had actually represented the Hebrides, as he had read of them in Martin, with its great temple being the megalithic complex at Callanish; this was helped by mistranslating 'spherical' as 'circular'. The Hyperborean best known to the Greeks had been a man called Abaris, who had reputedly visited Pythagoras and whose historical existence remains as hazy as most of the details of that philosopher's life. The idea that Abaris had been a British Druid was already in the air – Rowlands argued that, as the Druids spoke a form of Welsh, his actual name had been ap Rees[146] – and Toland took it up in a big way. He made Abaris a Hebridean cultural ambassador (in full Gaelic dress), and promised prospective supporters that his forthcoming book would reveal everything that this Druid had taught the Greeks, including the metonic cycle, and solve for good the old problem of whether Pythagoras had learned from the Druids, or vice versa.[147] It was all in vain; and having shot this final bolt he gave up the whole project.

He did, however, give a passing mention to Druids in the work to which he now turned instead, and which proved to be the last major project that he would live to complete: his book *Pantheisticon*, published in 1720.[148] It was a blueprint for a society that would operate on the model of Plato's *Symposium*, as a dining club dedicated to the discussion of philosophical subjects. The intended membership was characterized as being 'pantheists', a term which Toland thus gave to the world. He defined them as believing that the world was created and is directed by a great maker, whose intentions could be discerned by studying the laws and operations of nature; in this sense his pantheists were nature's priests. As models and ancestors for them, he praised a list of Greek and Roman philosophers and moralists, plus the Chinese sage Confucius, and also the Druids. He now praised the latter as 'men of an elevated genius' who 'kept up to the strictness of their brotherly union (as the authority of Pythagoras has decreed)' and 'were versed in the knowledge of the most abstruse things and . . . lifted up by the contemplation of the sublimest mysteries'.[149]

Unlike most of Toland's work, *Pantheisticon* was published in Latin, which suggests that he intended it for a more select, scholarly and genteel readership than his norm. What has never been satisfactorily established is how seriously he meant some or all of it to be taken, and what its significance actually was.[150] Certainly his praise of Druids makes a remarkable contrast with the abuse that he had heaped on them only two years before. In the absence of any sure sense of the purpose and tone of the book, there are three possible explanations for the change. One is that Toland had in fact altered his opinion. Another is that, having discovered that his vilification of them had provoked hostile reactions on the part of the sort of patron he wanted, he was developing the more positive treatment that he had displayed in 1719. If that was the case then the contrast was tactical. The third possibility is that in these final, laudatory, remarks he was actually joking; though in that case it is also unclear whether his intended readership was expected to take him seriously. When circulating the manuscript of the work among his friends, he referred to it as a 'foolery'.[151]

In many respects the writing of history, even in the late twentieth century, has been an act of ancestor-worship, and in this context it matters that most of the works about early authors on Druids have been produced by archaeologists and experts in Celtic Studies. These modern scholars have, naturally enough, tended to value those authors according to the extent to which they managed to promote their own disciplines by discovering or anticipating ideas which were later to be important to them, thereby contributing to the advancement of human knowledge. This being the case, Henry Rowlands, for all his patient, honest, logical, intelligent and innovative work, has been labelled as naïve, misguided and a bad influence on scholarship, while the more mercurial, unscrupulous and opportunist Toland has been praised for his modernity and contributions to learning.[152] It is notable in this context that modern Druids have recognized Toland as an ancestor and ignored Rowlands.[153] Both men, in fact, were enterprising scholars intent on turning a cultural disadvantage – of deriving from the Celtic-speaking fringe of the new British superstate – into an asset. Rowlands noted ruefully that medieval Irish literature was much more helpful to a historian of Druidry than that of his own land;[154] but he tried to get round that, as said, by suggesting that the Welsh triads preserved Druidic teaching, and by exploiting the rich potential for fieldwork among the monuments of his island. Toland employed his knowledge of Irish to use the very texts that Rowlands had envied. Neither was immediately successful in persuading the English to take an interest: Toland's whole venture failed, while, although Rowlands did attract a long enough list of subscribers to launch his book, he still felt it necessary or desirable to publish in Ireland instead of England.

The two were also similar in one fundamental respect, which made them absolutely typical of their age: the core or wellspring of the attitudes of each man lay in his strong religious beliefs. Rowlands's, however, were absolutely orthodox as befitted a minister of the established Church, and Toland's were extremely heterodox. In essence Toland's principles represented a lifelong furious rejection of his Roman Catholic upbringing, which he had rapidly extended to all established Churches, including those Protestant denominations that had rescued him from rural obscurity and paid for his excellent education. As such he had become part of that important if marginal strand of the European Reformation that rejected the mediation of professional clergy in favour of a direct relationship between human beings and their deity; a strand that had been well established in England and Wales since the 1640s. This conversion experience made him, inevitably, adopt a politics that supported governments prepared to tolerate Protestants who worshipped outside their national Churches; initially, this made him favour republics, as represented by the Dutch state and the Cromwellian Protectorate in Britain, but he became a firm supporter of the claims of the House of Hanover to the succession to the British crown, as he believed (rightly) that it would provide what he wished. Toland was also very much part of his time in that he belonged to a tendency within radical Protestantism that gave increasing importance to reason, rather than divine possession or revelation, in the understanding of the deity's plan for humanity.[155] In 1694 he had made a profession of faith that identified him firmly as a Christian, and there is no reason to believe that he ever abandoned this position.[156] He also, however, held with equal consistency to belief in a 'natural religion' that could only be achieved if clerical doctrine and self-interest were brushed out of the way.[157] He was very much a man of his time, in addition, in believing that true religious toleration and the expression of popular will were not desirable ends, as the real need was to tolerate or give power only to people with the right ideas: he was a firm supporter of the continued oppression of his own people, the Roman Catholic Irish, by a Protestant ruling class, on the grounds that their opinions were the most dangerous of all.[158]

All this has important implications for Toland's attitude to ancient history in general, and that of the Druids in particular. He was exactly in period, also, in that he assumed that his view of religion had to be the correct one for all ages and places and therefore that which had been revealed by his one god to all humanity in early times. Accordingly, he sought traces of it in old religious systems, by 'restoring' the teachings of ancient sages to show how they conformed to what he preached himself. His favourite sources were ancient Greek (Pythagorean and Platonist) and Indian, but he also respected the Persians and Egyptians – at least as they were represented by early modern scholarship – and some of the ancient Hebrews, attempting to turn Moses into an exemplar of civic leadership. He coined the term 'pantheism' for the primordial and true religious faith to which he was trying to return humans.[159] This all makes sense of his treatment of Druids, in whose teachings he had to claim to find traces of that original faith, even while he excoriated them for corrupting it by representing the most acute ancient form of that 'priestcraft' that was to manifest later in Christianity. His view was, of course, a deliberate, and highly ironic, mirror-image of that now well-established early modern tradition that had treated them as preparing the way for the true faith of the Gospels. Because of his dislike of scriptural authority, which was one aspect of his dislike of any authority other than his own ideas, Toland escaped the trap that had claimed Rowlands and many others: of trying to assimilate the Druids, and all the ancient British, to a version of history set forth in the Old Testament. His lack of interest in philology rescued him from the errors attendant on those who ventured too rashly into that new science. For these reasons his view of the British past was indeed to appear more attractive to later generations than those of most of his contemporaries. To congratulate him on this, as a pioneer or a discoverer, is natural but perhaps to miss the point. He was like a person who blundered on to the right path out of a maze, while others, like Rowlands, chose the wrong one on equally rational grounds.

In the first three decades of the eighteenth century, there were still signs that the Druids could be ignored or marginalized by those writing national history. Thomas Hearne, one of the great historical scholars of his generation, commented in 1715 that their famed learning could not have amounted to much, as the ancient authors had agreed that the British were savages; in his view it was the Romans who had brought real civilization to his island.[160] In 1723 a Wiltshire vicar, Thomas Twining, published a book to prove that the Romans had built the Avebury circles and their related monuments.[161] There was certainly both a growing role for Druids in the British imagination and a growing awareness of them as the main figures of the earliest known period of national history. The Northamptonshire squire Edward Dryden, who died in 1717, changed his family motto to 'Ancient as the Druids'.[162] More generally, the number of publications that mentioned them, whether works of history, poetry or drama, increased markedly after 1700. Almost all did so briefly, however, and with no consensus on how they should be regarded, or whether they should be regarded at all. The three positions that could be adopted towards them – that they should be admired, deplored or dismissed – were all articulated as passing comments in works published between 1700 and 1730.[163] The confusion between Druids and bards remained a feature of poetry.[164] None the less, the work of Oxford University, in propagating the Renaissance Scottish notions that the Druids were both worthy of serious attention and associated with the land's most impressive prehistoric monuments, was starting to have an impact on the English and Welsh.[165] That this was not more pronounced had been largely a matter of circumstance: Aubrey's shortcomings as an author; the association of the new ideas with individuals from the less influential peoples of the archipelago (Scots, Welsh and an Irishman); and – perhaps above all – the caprices of mortality. Lhuyd had died before most of his promised work had been produced, Rowlands before his book appeared, and Toland with his relevant writings unpublished. To bring the Druids home properly to the British, somebody was needed to champion their cause who was part of the English intellectual establishment and blessed with sufficient time to mature, publish, develop and defend arguments at length. The stage was set; but the main character had yet to appear on it.

➤❦

3

THE DRUIDS TAKE OVER

The question of how far individuals shape history is one of the great traditional debating points among historians; and tends to revolve around two different propositions, which might be termed the 'hard' and 'soft' forms of the issue. The former asserts that there are individuals great enough to wrest the course of events from what might be considered their natural outcome; effectively to change the processes of history. The latter merely proposes that economic, social, cultural and political forces can all lead towards a certain result, but that this result will be delayed until the right person comes along to precipitate it. The contention of this chapter is that the second, 'soft', formulation is relevant to the history of modern British attitudes to Druids: that by the early eighteenth century all the circumstances existed to turn them into major figures in the national imagination, but that the appearance of an effective advocate was needed to make this happen. That person was William Stukeley.[1] He is a person for whom abundant evidence survives, in the form of dozens of published and unpublished works by his own hand, diaries and notebooks, correspondence, drawings and sketches, and comments made on him and his ideas by many contemporaries. He was also much painted, drawn and engraved, by himself and others, his strong yet fleshy face, with its large straight nose, challenging eyes and stubborn mouth facing us out of one frame after another. Because of all this information, rather than despite it, his career and beliefs have been a matter for contention between modern scholars.

For almost half a century, the standard view of him was that established in the famous biography by Stuart Piggott, which appeared in 1950 and went into a second edition in 1985.[2] This book reinforced a prevailing view that Stukeley had probably been the most important of the early forerunners of the discipline of archaeology, and was therefore one of the major figures in the history of British scholarship. It also, however, emphasized that he deserved this credit only for the early period of his activity, in the 1710s and 1720s, when according to Piggott he surveyed and interpreted ancient monuments with an admirable objectivity and rationality. This ended in the late 1720s when he was ordained into the Church of England and henceforth devoted his life to defending its doctrines with reference to the evidence of ancient remains. The result, in Piggott's view, was a tragedy, in which he distorted and misrepresented his former research to conform to a fantastic set of religious ideas. These credited Britain's megalithic monuments to the ancient Druids, whom he regarded as the ancestors of later Anglican Christianity. His new obsession with them turned him into something of a laughing-stock in his old age, and not merely caused posterity to undervalue his fieldwork but abetted a general decline in British studies of antiquities, which lasted until the nineteenth century.

This was an interpretation which seemed to be supported by the known evidence, and fitted well the mood of British intellectual culture in the mid-twentieth century. That mood extolled rationalism and regarded progress in knowledge and technological prowess as the greatest achievement of humanity. It led scholars to praise or blame their predecessors according to the contribution which the latter seemed to have made to the development of academic disciplines into their modern form; and this is what Stuart Piggott did with Stukeley. Piggott himself was among the founders of the professional practice of archaeology, and it was one aspect of his greatness that he fostered the study of early modern antiquaries as an integral part of the self-awareness of that profession. His view of Stukeley immediately secured wide acceptance and long maintained it: in the single year 1979 it could be reproduced both in Aubrey Burl's famous scholarly study of the Avebury monuments, and in a novel by Penelope Lively.[3]

It was a different study of the Avebury complex, in 1991, which provided the first major challenge to the Piggott portrait. Produced by Peter Ucko, Michael Hunter, Alan Clark and Andrew David, this included an account of Stukeley's career which stressed the essential continuity of his ideas. It argued that, at the time of his much-admired early fieldwork, he had already developed an all-embracing interpretation of prehistoric monuments as expressions of the rites and symbols of the ancient Druids, which he merely elaborated in later years.[4] This view was strongly reinforced by the first comprehensive study of Stukeley's thought in its contemporary context, published in 2002 by a former pupil of Michael Hunter, David Haycock. This was especially valuable in its analysis of its subject's hitherto neglected scientific writings, which identified him securely as an admirer of Sir Isaac Newton. It showed how Stukeley had followed up two of Newton's greatest projects – to understand the natural world and (thereby) to understand the divine plan that underpinned it – while attempting to do so in more orthodox Anglican religious terms than Newton himself. To Haycock, the only real change which occurred around the time of his subject's ordination was that henceforth Stukeley continued this work from inside the ranks of the clergy.[5]

These publications have not caused a controversy, being generally accepted to date as a genuine progression of knowledge; and with good reason. Stuart Piggott himself generously put on record his acceptance of the criticism of his ideas by Peter Ucko and his fellows.[6] In large part this has simply been due to the fact that the successive interpretations of William Stukeley's work have been based on an expanding body of source material. Piggott's pioneering research had been heroic, but he had missed a large quantity of manuscripts containing writings by Stukeley which were now housed in several different archives.[7] This new evidence leaves no doubt that Stukeley always had a strong streak of mysticism and interpreted ancient remains in accordance with set notions concerning the nature of primitive religion.

All this said, there is still a difficulty with the interpretation of his thought in terms of continuity and consistency: that it does not itself exactly fit the evidence. In a letter to an unknown friend, announcing his decision to enter the ministry in 1729, Stukeley acknowledged that it would surprise the recipient and many others. He portrayed his change of mind as a genuine conversion, a mighty act of divine grace 'in throwing rubbish out of my thoughts'.[8] His fellow antiquary Thomas Hearne recorded that his friends thought him 'mad', and one of them, Roger Gale, indeed commented that his reinvention as a churchman had 'surprised all the world with the utmost astonishment'.[9] It is true that in later life Stukeley did try to play down the extent of his conversion experience and to insist on essential continuity in his attitudes. In a pair of memoirs written after 1747 he declared that he had always been 'of a religious turn', and had a 'religious turn of mind'.[10] He wrote the same thing to the Archbishop of Canterbury at the start of 1747, though with a hint that his piety might have been less obvious during his earlier life.[11] The contrast between these retrospective comments and those he made at the time of his ordination raises two different, though compatible, suspicions. One is that he was rewriting his personal history to give a better impression of consistent Anglican piety, both to his own Archbishop and to posterity. The other is that he was telling the truth about his essentially religious nature, but that the content of his beliefs altered at the end of the 1720s. It will be argued here that both these possibilities are in fact correct.

One of the aspects of his life on which Stuart Piggott and David Haycock agreed was that he only became deeply interested in ancient monuments after the age of thirty. Born in 1687, the son of a Lincolnshire lawyer, he chose to follow a medical career because of his youthful enthusiasm for the natural sciences. This derived in turn from a deeper love: for structure, form and design. In the course of his life he enjoyed equally the dissection of dead bodies, the excavation and surveying of ancient remains, the sketching of architecture and the contemplation of the stars, as part of a personal quest for an underlying message and purpose in their composition. This was blended with a powerful aesthetic sense, for Stukeley was a compulsive artist who was forever drawing people, landscapes and monuments. This fascination with composition and creation was the root of his sense of religion, and it is wholly in character that his first major philosophical and religious treatise, drafted in 1717, was devoted to the making of the cosmos. It was a sustained attempt, using an elaborate mixture of his own observations, ancient science and philosophy, and the writings of recent scholars such as Newton himself and the Jesuit Athanasius Kircher, to defend a literal belief in the creation story contained in the Book of Genesis. This may sound like an expression of fundamentalist Christian faith, but it reads more as an emotional reaction against contemporaries who believed that the universe was both timeless and randomly put together. For Stukeley it was vitally important that the natural world was united by and fitted for a purpose that humanity might discover, or rediscover: in his words, 'a curious and voluminous book, and we to be the readers of it'.

Furthermore, he had a strong personal sense of immanent divinity within it, so that the cosmos itself might be considered a deity: 'eternal, immense, without beginning or end, sacred, all in all'. His yearning for immanence and interconnectedness was not well served by the Christian Scriptures, but it found rich nourishment in the ancient traditions of Platonism and Pythagoreanism, which spoke of a united cosmos streaming out from an original great divine being.[12]

This major early work displays another abiding characteristic of Stukeley's thought, which he summed up in a later essay as an urge 'to go up to the fountain head'.[13] By looking for the origin of both physical phenomena and human ideas, he believed that he had the best chance of understanding their true nature. It was this impulse that led eventually to his interest in the form and purpose of prehistoric monuments, which seemed to him to promise an understanding of the earliest, and therefore purest, forms of human religion. This alteration can be seen dramatically in one of his notebooks, which was commenced in 1717 as a collection of data on medicine, but turned at the end of 1718 into one of information on megalithic monuments.[14] Stuart Piggott spotted the development behind this change of focus: Stukeley's friendship with the Gale family, a father and two sons with a dedicated interest in the British past. The father had made or acquired a transcript of John Aubrey's unpublished *Monumenta Britannica* – or at least of some of it – and this was lent to Stukeley by one of the sons. It came as a revelation to him, and he copied out whole sections of it into the notebook, following them with further information on prehistoric remains apparently taken from manuscripts compiled by Edward Lhuyd, and now lost.

He had known of megaliths before, but did not identify in the least with the builders, whom he called 'unpolished people',[15] and it was the discovery of Aubrey's work that revealed to him the extent and importance of Britain's prehistoric remains. He immediately acquired an obsession with them, and in that sense may fairly be termed the last and greatest of Aubrey's converts to an interest in British prehistory and an association of it with the Druids. At the opening of the very next summer he began to build on Aubrey's own fieldwork by starting a programme of drawing and surveying at Avebury and Stonehenge which was to last on and off for six years and be extended to several other prehistoric sites.[16] Into those initial transcriptions from Aubrey's manuscript, he interpolated the line 'the Druids are said to have conversed with eagles as Pythagoras' (did).[17] Having had his attention drawn to the ancient British sages, he immediately linked them to the Greek philosophical traditions that had already inspired him.

A number of clues exist as to his religious attitudes during this celebrated period of fieldwork. One lies in an event which occurred in London during July 1722: the foundation of a Society of Roman Knights to foster interest in the ancient history of Britain.[18] The whole membership took nicknames drawn from native British and Gallic personalities recorded in the history of the Roman period, and all but one chose the name of a tribal chief. The exception was Stukeley, who assumed that of a Druid, or rather of a presumed one. The name was Chyndonax, and was taken from an inscription on a cremation burial from the Roman period which had been dug up in Burgundy in 1598. Although undoubtedly a native Gallic one, there was nothing whatsoever to associate it with the Druids. It had in fact been found with an inscription to the late Roman god Mithras, and the person named seems to have been identified as a priest of this mystery religion, of Mithraism; indeed, it is possible that the name itself was misread. Such, however, was the enthusiasm for Druidry among French antiquarians at the time that the discoverer published a little book celebrating his find as a Druidic burial.[19] One of the reasons why the ancient Druids had long seemed so inaccessible and intangible was that they were almost wholly anonymous: the names of none were known from Britain, and of all those of Gaul only Divitiacus or Diviciacus was identified in the sources. There were plenty named in Irish literature, but neither the French nor the British of the early modern period wished to identify with the native Irish, who were regarded by both as a barbarous people whose fate in this period was to be subjugated and civilized by the English. The Burgundian find, therefore, apparently doubled the number of names available for the original Druids of Britain and Gaul, and Stukeley duly became Chyndonax in the Society of Roman Knights. He came to like the name so much that he retained it for the rest of his life, among his friends and in his writings. The fact that he chose it at all indicates that he was singled out among the Knights by his mystical interests and inclination to identify personally with the ancient priesthood. This indication is strongly reinforced by the tendency of his fellow members to refer to him affectionately thereafter as 'the Druid' in conversation and correspondence.[20]

The greatest source of evidence for his views during these years consists of the surviving manuscripts of a multi-volume work that he planned to publish on the basis of his field observations, and which he seems to have begun in the course of 1723. Two of these are now kept at Cardiff, and one at Oxford.[21] They were intended to represent Stukeley's revelation to the world of his discoveries about ancient Britain, and were never published. Instead, he incorporated material from them into books that he brought out almost twenty years later; and here lies a major textual problem which has not been adequately recognized. Many of the pages of the earlier manuscripts were scored through by Stukeley, though still more or less readable, and some were cut out and are missing altogether. He presumably carried out this work at the time when he was writing up his later books. We can never know what was on the missing pages, and this predicament leaves us with two opposed possibilities. One is that Stukeley simply incorporated the vanished material wholesale into his subsequent volumes; in which case his ideas in the early 1720s would have borne a closer resemblance to his later, published, views than is now apparent. Alternatively, he may have destroyed evidence of opinions which were completely irrelevant, or even embarrassing, to his position in the later period; and certainly such opinions do survive at points in the manuscripts, even in the mutilated or defaced condition in which they now exist.

This being so, it is impossible to be absolutely certain of Stukeley's thought in the period of his famous fieldwork, and there is a second major problem with the manuscripts that he intended to reflect it. In their present condition they are not finished texts but notebooks, in which polished sections of prose intended apparently for publication later became interleaved and decorated with further, more careless, jottings. They therefore consist of layers of material entered at different times over three or four decades, and mostly undated. It is easy to distinguish between the hand-writing used by Stukeley in the 1710s and early 1720s and the heavier and larger hand that he employed from the 1730s. There is, however, a transitional period between them – crucial for the development of his thought – in which different entries may be virtually contemporary or else separated by years, and there is no obvious way of telling which is the case.

The way to reconstruct his ideas in the form which they took at the time when he began to write his intended books in 1723 is to strip the text in the manuscripts down to its basic form – the polished and continuous passages – by ignoring all the addi-tional jottings. When this is done, a consistent and dramatic argument does appear: Stukeley's belief in a primeval religion which had been shared by all the peoples of the remote past, simply because it was the natural one for primitive humanity to embrace. As such, it was not spread by missionaries but arose spontaneously from 'the same common reason in mankind'.[22] It was focused on the veneration of a single all-powerful and indivisible god, in whom Stukeley himself believed, stating that 'the first ages held an unity of the Divine Being' and 'it is no less an argument of imperfection to make Him more than one than to make Him parts and members or less than infi-nite, eternal'.[23] In support of the existence of this mighty being, and of the belief of the entire ancient world in that existence, he cited a series of pagan Greek philosopers and the Graeco-Egyptian Hermetic texts. He furthermore asserted that the stone circles of the British Isles represented the same concept in physical form, and that circular monuments representing the one deity were universally the earliest temples of the human race. The unbroken and repetitive figure of a circle was 'the most expressive of the nature of the deity without beginning or end'.[24]

Stukeley also, however, believed that the ancients had venerated the main compo-nent parts of the divine creation – the heavenly bodies, the earth and the four elements – and recognized the numbers and musical harmonies on which the universe had been constructed. To him this understanding and architectural embodiment of cosmological principles was a further expression of the fundamental goodness and truth of their religion.[25] Peter Ucko and his colleagues have shown how he built it into his interpretation of the Avebury monuments, believing that while the great stone circle represented the one god, the two smaller circles inside honoured the sun and moon, and two more, which he thought had existed at the ends of stone avenues running out of the big circle, were dedicated respectively to the earth and to the god Mercury, as spirit of air and guide of souls to the underworld after death.[26] In the summer weeks that he spent making drawings and plans of the huge grey sandstone megaliths under the chalk downs, Stukeley was partly enjoying a holiday, partly trans-ported by the thrill of scientific discovery, and partly a man whose ears were full of the music of the spheres.

He brought the same complex of attitudes to another ancient ritual landscape, in an account which he wrote in March 1724 as an intended appendix to one of these volumes. The complex concerned consisted of the three stone circles and some outlying settings of megaliths situated in and around the Somerset village of Stanton Drew. Weathered beautifully into patterns of green, red and pink, their stones drowse above the meanders of the little River Chew, flanked by limestone hills. Characteristically, it had been Aubrey who had first drawn the attention of scholars to their significance, in his unpublished manuscript; equally in character, he had been too diffident to make a proper inspection and plan of the stones because most were in a field under crops. Now Stukeley, more ambitious, more thorough and more forceful, became the first person to map the site out in its entirety, and to interpret it. He argued that it represented a celebration of the sacred truths embodied in astronomy, chemistry, mathematics and music, and associated in ancient literature especially with Pythagoras, 'the Archdruid as I venture to call him'. The main circle was dedicated to the planets, and the lesser to the sun and moon, while the other stone settings were shrines to earth and water.[27] Not surprisingly, he found similar cosmological principles in the design of Stonehenge itself, its successive circles and horseshoes of stones representing the Neoplatonic model of the universe as a series of spheres from which 'the divine influences of the archetypal mind descend thro' the sidereal world to the elementary'.[28] To Stukeley this model was objectively real.

His taste for Greek philosophy, and his belief in the essential unity and ubiquity of primeval religion, did not prevent him from extolling the British Druids as the finest representatives of that true old faith. He declared them (without producing evidence) to have been superior even to Pythagoras in their doctrine of the fate of the soul, in that they taught that humans could only reincarnate in bodies of their own kind, while the Greek believed that they could be reborn as animals as well: Stukeley clearly found this latter idea repugnant.[29] He acknowledged that continental European pagans had degenerated into idolatry, which he defined (following the ideas of several previous writers, including Newton) as the worship of ancestral humans as though they were deities.[30] None the less, he insisted that the Druids had not shared in this, continuing instead to venerate 'the types and symbols of the supreme mind'.[31] Even their alleged practice of human sacrifice was explained and extenuated in his work as the ritualized execution of criminals.[32]

In contrast with this passion for Druidry, the same writings show an indifference to Christianity. There is a striking absence of quotation from Scripture, his unitary concept of deity seems explicitly to deny the doctrine of the Trinity, and there is even a swipe at Christ's followers: he recorded his belief that the largest trio of stones at Stonehenge, which has lain broken during recorded history, might have been toppled 'in a blind act of Christian zeal'.[33] The one book of the Bible for which he showed respect in these writings was Genesis, to which he had devoted such attention in 1717; and this seems to be because it offered the clearest account of that creation of the cosmos in which he was so interested. To accept Genesis is not in itself to be a Christian, and while citing it he reminded readers that the myths of many nations contained complementary stories of the same great event. He went on immediately to imply denial of the exclusive truth of Christian revelation, by adding that many peoples also had the idea of 'a God immediately derived from parent to son . . . but as to its particular modes and forms there may not perhaps be so much in reality as furious zealots and narrow-minded enthusiasts are willing to inculcate'.[34]

It seems hard to avoid the conclusion that, during the early to mid-1720s, Stukeley was what his contemporaries called a 'deist', an umbrella term for somebody who believed in a single omnipotent deity whose works were manifested in the natural world and regarding whom Christianity did not necessarily offer the whole truth.[35] As Frank Manuel showed, almost half a century ago, the deist school of thought developed in England during the seventeenth century, flourished there in the early eighteenth, and was exported from there to parts of the Continent.[36] It was itself a product of the recognition, by many European scholars, that there were certain basic similarities between religions practised by peoples in many different parts of the world; a perception that was made possible, in turn, by the tremendous increase in contact between Europeans and other continents since 1500. In the course of the Stuart period, orthodox members of the Church of England had begun to argue that ancient Greek, Roman and Egyptian religion contained echoes of genuine divine revelation. Deists took this suggestion further, by removing claims for a uniquely exalted character for the Christian revelation, although they commonly still credited that revelation with virtue and importance, and some accepted the divinity of Christ himself. Toland himself was one of the most controversial authors in this tradition, and his place in it, and in the wider pattern of belief at this period, should be clear from the discussion of him in the previous chapter.[37] Anglican polemicists responded to the challenge of deism by representing ancient paganism as a preparation of European humanity for the Christian message, imperfect in comparison, but perfectly compatible, with it. Both sides of the debate tended to agree that humans had a natural goodness and religiosity, and that paganism had tended to become corrupted in the course of time, so that its original virtues had largely degenerated into superstition and idolatry by Roman times, especially among common people. This fitted the view of history and of human nature built into the Bible, and – as said before – especially favoured by Protestants. Both parties in the debate were also frequently preoccupied with that attempt to reconstruct the origins of religious practice and belief which featured so strongly in Stukeley's work. The twin focuses of these discussions – the nature of primeval religion, and its relationship with Christianity – were incorporated into the mythology and symbolism of Freemasonry, which was spreading rapidly through English society in the 1710s and 1720s.

Stukeley was thus, in many respects, an intellectual of his place and time; but in others he was a truly remarkable one during the 1720s. His lack of interest in Christianity, and his passionate personal engagement with Platonist and Pythagorean ideas, represented a very unusual combination indeed. It may be relevant that his interest in Freemasonry was initially intense enough for him to found his own lodge soon after his initiation in 1721, but that it waned so rapidly that he seems to have abandoned participation a short time after that.[38] He clearly did not find in it an answer to his intellectual and spiritual needs. This set of characteristics makes him very difficult to categorize during this period. To term him a deist would be both defensible and misleading, given how much he differed in some qualities from most who have been given that label. The same problem attends a description of him as a 'freethinker', another contemporary term and one which is certainly accurate but too vague, and begging too many questions, for comfort. He could quite justifiably be called a pagan Neoplatonist, and that is the most precise definition of his beliefs as revealed in his writings at this time. He himself, however, chose to be known as a 'Druid', and the fact that he was so solitary in that self-ascription is itself a powerful testimony to the markedly individual nature of his ideas.

Those ideas, moreover, continued to develop rapidly, in response to new data. Peter Ucko and his partners have suggested that in the course of 1724 he came to modify his interpretation of the Avebury monuments because of his failure to find objective evidence of a stone circle at the end of one of the stone avenues leading from the main ring. This transformed his image of the whole complex from a neatly balanced set of circles and avenues to the design of a gigantic snake crossing a circle.[39] Such a reading of his work seems to be correct, but the process is difficult to date precisely. No such problem exists with another key discovery that he made at this time, of a set of earthworks on the edge of the Humber marshes near Barrow, which he visited on 25 July 1724. It seems in fact to be the remains of a motte and bailey castle from the Norman period.[40] Stukeley, however, dug into tumuli situated nearby and found prehistoric cremation burials similar to those which he had uncovered in the round barrows near Stonehenge. He therefore identified the monument as a prehistoric temple of a form not recognized before, of a circle with curved patterns around it.[41] In the following year he came across a second set of earthworks (from his drawings, also probably medieval) on Navestock Common, Essex, which he interpreted as another of the same kind.[42] He was later to develop the notion that they belonged to a distinctive class of Druidic 'alate' or 'winged' temples.[43]

At the same time he was acquiring a greater respect for the ancient Egyptians, whom he had relegated earlier to being just one of many peoples who had shared the original and true religion.[44] He had been encouraged in his researches at Stonehenge by the Earl of Pembroke, whose seat lay only a short distance away at Wilton. Between surveying the prehistoric remains, Stukeley had studied the famous collection of ancient sculpture displayed at the mansion, including what seems to have been a statue of an official from the Late Dynastic period of Egyptian history. It had been mistaken instead for one of the goddess Isis, and in November 1724 he wrote a treatise on its hieroglyphs, which he deciphered using the system and the framework of cosmological interpretation provided for the ancient Egyptian script during the previous century by Athanasius Kircher. This was also wrong, but Stukeley had complete faith in it, and employment of it led him to a conclusion comfortingly and excitingly in harmony with his developing beliefs: that the Egyptians 'had obtained an excellent notion of the Supreme Being and of the order of the world, of the admirable connexion and relationship between superior and inferior things'. This order, of course, turned out to be that of the Neoplatonists whom he so much admired, and above all that of Proclus, a fifth-century pagan Athenian in whose cosmology solar and lunar intelligences conducted the emanations of the Supreme Mind through the stars to the mundane world. The latter was filled with spirits, who connected creation with creator in an admirable and harmonious manner, and with hidden cosmic sympathies and antipathies that wise humans needed to understand. Stukeley, finding all this apparently represented on the Egyptian statue at Wilton, declared that the Egyptian priests had therefore been outstandingly wise, and had imparted some of their occult knowledge to the Hebrew prophet Moses.[45] As a result of all these apparent discoveries, Stukeley seems to have set about a new process of research, raking through records of ancient iconography for images of winged circles and of circles with serpents passing through them, which he rationalized to his concept of an emanating supreme deity. He filled pages in the backs of his existing manuscripts, and blank spaces in the earlier sections, with notes on them and on esoteric traditions concerning snakes. The Avebury complex was now transformed in his notes into a gigantic expression of this latest scheme of universal ancient symbolism.[46]

It was still not a Christian scheme, but an elaboration of his existing system of belief. He now saw the Egyptians and Druids as the supreme masters of the skill of designing temples that represented the true nature of the 'World Soul' of ancient Platonic thought, so that rites enacted in them would ensure that the influence of the great deity 'must needs be drawn down and his presence more constant and conversant'.[47] They were, in brief, engines for the practice of theurgy, an ancient term designating ceremonies intended to bring human practitioners into spiritual union with the divine that had been advocated by the Neoplatonic philosophers. This reading of them perfectly suited the tone of his life after he withdrew suddenly from London to his native Lincolnshire in June 1726, settling as a country doctor at Grantham. For ten years he had been an active part of the intellectual life of the capital, prominent in its learned societies and with powerful friends and allies, of whom the Earls of Pembroke and Winchelsea were the most socially impressive. It was part of his pattern of dramatic conversion experiences that he rejected this existence with a speed and lack of warning that surprised his social world and for which, many years later, he felt obliged to account in a memoir.[48] He supplied a number of lesser reasons for the change, such as the healthier nature of rural living, but his main one was that, having spent seven years waiting for his 'great friends, who had encouraged me in the pursuit of antiquarian studies' to 'make some provision for me', he had lost faith in them. This sense of betrayal was bitter enough to make him forsake their company and the whole metropolitan orbit in which they operated. It was an explanation that he provided to other scholars who visited him at Grantham, in the more general terms that he had not received the 'encouragement' that he had expected from 'the public'.[49] If true, it seems that Stukeley's work on Druids, like Toland's research project, had foundered for lack of the aristocratic patronage that was needed by an author without substantial private means and without the public respectability or appeal that would win subscriptions. It is possible that the nature of his religious ideas itself contributed to this failure.

The drawing of such conclusions is made the more difficult by the fact that Stukeley's own best friends did not entirely understand him. They were all aware that he had flounced out of London with extreme ill humour: in what one of them, Alexander Gordon, termed a 'pett'.[50] In case they had not realized this for themselves, one of his first actions on quitting the capital had been to send a standard letter to most of them, informing them that he intended never to communicate with them again.[51] Joan Evans suggested many years ago that the cause of his anger was a falling out with the Society of Antiquaries, which included many of these friends, because of his failure to make available the minute books that he kept as the main part of his office as the society's first secretary.[52] This may be the whole truth of the matter, but it is not what he said himself about it, as quoted above, and so the suspicion at least must remain that he felt his work to be insufficiently appreciated and supported. His companions sustained his rebuff to them – while remaining unsure of its cause – with the greater ease because of their expectation that he would relent; which is exactly what occurred. It was part of his general volatility: in the words of another of them, Roger Gale, his 'whimsical, unsettled sort of temper'.[53] His rebellious and noncon-formist streak of character, which was one of his great strengths as a scholar, could shade into straightforward eccentricity. In 1725 he had taken against the fashionable wearing of wigs, and begun to wear his own hair in public, cut short, as a visible badge of difference, loudly preaching its superiority. Gestures like this inspired his compan-ions with a mixture of admiration and ridicule.[54] Certainly, to judge from their surviving correspondence, none of them seem to have been deeply interested in his idiosyncratic religious ideas.

What is also certain is that he maintained those ideas after his withdrawal into rural seclusion. In his memoir he commented that he 'went down in the country intending to pass my days in finishing my studies upon the Druids',[55] and he designed his new home as a fit setting for the work. In a letter to his friend Samuel Gale, in October 1727, he described his study as adorned with Roman antiquities, 'as my bedchamber adjoining with Egyptian, which become prophylactic, and drive off all evil'. Within these sanctuaries, he portrayed himself as conversing with 'the immortal ghosts of Virgil, etc, with the old sages and prophets of Egypt, that first disseminated wisdom through the world'.[56] His gardens were likewise laid out as a sacred land-scape, including 'a temple of the Druids, as I call it', consisting of concentric circles of hazels and evergreens modelled on the design of Stonehenge, with an apple tree grown with mistletoe at the centre. He also constructed a 'tumulus' beside the temple and (first of all) a 'chapel', which contained a Roman altar and other ancient artefacts.[57]

These places were intended as settings for actual rites. The altar had a camomile bed sown in front of it to give sensual pleasure to the experience of kneeling before it. One of Stukeley's major changes of lifestyle on moving to the provinces had been to marry, and he and his wife endured the tragedy of two successive miscarriages. After the first, in July 1728, Samuel Gale wrote to Stukeley urging him to 'assemble the sacred college of the Druids' and devise rituals to 'avert the anger of the Gods and draw down blessings' on his lady.[58] It is not apparent what, if anything, Stukeley did in response, but when the same misfortune was repeated in October, he buried the foetus in the camomile bed, 'with ceremonies proper to the occasion'.[59] There is no evidence whatever in his many surviving letters and papers that he actually had a 'college of Druids' or any other group with which to practise regular pagan cere-monies. Gale's letter may, accordingly, just have reflected the banter that their circle had often applied to him in his perceived role as its 'Druid'; though the subject was an odd one for light treatment and Stukeley's own rites at his child's interment seem to have been sincere. As so often in the case of classically educated Europeans who imitated pagan monuments and ceremonies between the fifteenth and early twentieth centuries, it is very hard to tell where play-acting ended and genuine religious behaviour began. Given Stukeley's tendency to passionate enthusiasm, and his strong streak of mysticism, however, it is difficult to believe that all this was less than half serious.

It does make the more intelligible the amazement of his friends when he suddenly reinvented himself as an Anglican clergyman in the summer of 1729, and the more credible his portrayal of the experience as one of genuine and dramatic conversion. The reasons for it can probably never be known. Stuart Piggott suggested that material considerations may have been most important, as Stukeley grew weary of the hard and inadequately paid career of a country doctor and decided that a Church living would better allow him the lifestyle that he wanted. There is certainly evidence in his letters and memoirs to support this argument.[60] While recognizing it, David Haycock emphasized that ordination was 'a natural progression from the religious faith he had exhibited in all his work'.[61] It must be obvious from what has been suggested above that this statement is in one sense absolutely right and in another absolutely wrong. If the reconstruction of Stukeley's attitudes in the 1720s made here has been correct, then towards the end of the decade he became frustrated by the private, idiosyncratic and lonely spiritual system that he had developed for himself. However well supported this system was by ancient texts, there was only one form of religion on offer in early Georgian England which could be practised in public and with the full support of a national and local community, and in which he could effectively operate as a priest: and that was Christianity.

He presented his conversion to two different audiences, in slightly differing form. To the Archbishop of Canterbury, whom he approached directly for ordination and for support in obtaining a good benefice, he characterized himself as an antiquarian eager to use his knowledge to defend the doctrines of the Church of England against contemporary criticism.[62] In particular, he promised to substantiate that of the Trinity, which had come under increasing attack during the previous thirty years.[63] This was certainly a sincere ambition, because he announced it privately to his friends, but he seems at first to have presented it to the latter as part of a broader project of 'reconciling Plato and Moses, and the Druid and Christian religion';[64] in other words, of showing how the private beliefs that he had embraced earlier were compatible with Christianity and could contribute to an understanding of it. An expression of the confusion of his thought at this period may be found in a letter he wrote to one friend, the medical doctor Robert Thomlinson, which its Victorian editor dated to the pivotal year 1729. He began by saying that Christian institutions represented 'the highest pitch of morality that ever was presented to the world'. Having extolled the social virtues of Christianity, he then proceeded to deny one of its key beliefs, by expressing a personal belief in reincarnation, buttressed by apparent personal memories of past lives. One at least of these had been illustrious: 'I could tell you who I was once several ages ago, and whose name you have very often read, but that would seem a little too much to praise myself'. He ascribed his instinctual interest in the remains of the past to 'a desire of being acquainted with those times wherein I had formerly made some sort of figure ... only to be lamented because I was obliged to return under the cover of another body whence I may in some measure account for that strange affection I always had for that notion of Pythagoras's transformation'. Having thus reaffirmed his identity as some sort of Pythagorean, he checked himself and asserted that only Christ, as the second person of the one true deity, had allowed humanity the opportunity to see the deity himself in his glory.[65]

Certainly he never reneged on his conversion, and it served him well. Almost immediately the Archbishop helped him into a lucrative parish living in an elegant Lincolnshire town, Stamford. A decade later he moved back to the capital, and another benefice in one of its most fashionable districts, while he acquired new noble patrons in the form of the Dukes of Ancaster and Montagu. Through all this successful career development he continued to pour out his ideas about the history of religion: in the published works on which his reputation came to rest, in letters, sermons, hymns, poems and autobiographical notes; and in dozens of surviving manuscript treatises, many of which were privately circulated or read to societies. He also embodied them in yet further jottings in his unpublished works from the 1720s. These ideas now took new and distinctive forms, even while reusing much of his existing material. One was, as he had promised, to defend Christianity in general and the doctrine of the Trinity in particular, by showing that both had been built into the primeval religion shared by all humanity in the first period after the creation of the world. Famously, he reinterpreted the pattern of the winged circle and serpent on which he had decided that Avebury was built, to act as a representation of the three persons of the deity.[66] More generally he argued that the original religion had conceived of the supreme being in triple form.[67] He represented the Druids as having foreknowledge of Christ's mission, including his birth from a virgin and his cruci-fixion: a belief summed up in the famous declaration at the opening of his book on Stonehenge, that Druidic religion was 'so extremely like Christianity, that in effect, it differed from it only in this; they believed in a Messiah who was to come into the world, as we believe in him that is come.'[68]

As part of this change of tack, he could no longer speak of a primeval faith that had occurred naturally and spontaneously to all humanity. Instead, the true religion had to have been revealed by the deity to chosen evangelists in a particular holy land and diffused outwards by them from that point, as the Bible had specified. It had, in fact, to be embodied in the teachings given to Abraham, who thus became the first Druid.[69] As Stuart Piggott noticed, his need to bring in Abraham drove him back on the published theories of earlier English authors, and most of all Aylett Sammes, to find a mechanism that would get those teachings to Britain: it was provided by them in the shape of Phoenician colonists led by the 'Tyrian Hercules'.[70] This new scheme of things made the ancient Egyptians redundant, and his love affair with them at an end. In 1742 he informed a society founded specifically to study their remains that they were not greatly to be admired, as they had gained all their learning from

Abraham and subsequently perverted his true religion into the worship of animals and human heroes.[71] Whereas he had largely ignored the Scriptures in his former search for ancient wisdom, he now studied the Old Testament closely as the primary text for it. During the 1730s and 1740s he devoted as much care to drawing conjectural restorations of Solomon's temple, the tabernacle of Moses and the breastplates of Hebrew priests, as he had in the previous two decades to drawing ancient and medieval monuments.[72] His interest in antiquities was not itself diminished, and indeed remained a lifelong passion, but it was now accompanied by, and often placed in the context of, his biblical studies.

He persisted in his argument that ancient pagan philosophy and mythology contained authentic traces of divine revelation, but with a very significant twist: the only authentic revelation was now that recorded in the Bible, and so the traces of it were deformed and misunderstood remnants. Indeed, Stukeley now argued that the whole of ancient paganism had consisted of such misunderstandings.[73] Stukeley had always viewed the idolatry of the historic ancient religions as a degeneration, but had deemed it the result of understandable error. Now he recognized the existence of a force of supernatural evil in his hitherto beautiful and unified cosmos. By 1735 the paganism of the Egyptians, Greeks, Romans and their neighbours had become to him 'the most turbid mixture of corruption', produced by both 'the malice of the devil' and 'the wickedness of humanity'.[74] In a later note added to the study of Stonehenge that he had written in the mid-1720s, he declared that the ancient Thracians had been corrupted by 'the devil and the contagion of their neighbours'.[75] His belief in reincarnation had now evaporated: in 1757 he wrote a treatise attempting to locate, in outer space, the regions of heaven and hell to which spirits were consigned after judgment.[76] To his congregations he preached sermons, based on scriptural texts, which threatened damnation to sinners and held out the hope of salvation to the truly repentant.[77]

In many ways these alterations transformed him into a much more orthodox and familiar sort of thinker for his place and time. They situated him far more easily in the established debates over the nature and significance of primitive religion, described above, as a continuator of the orthodox Anglican tradition. He remained very unusual, however, in two respects: his knowledge of prehistoric monuments and his passionate affection for the British Druids. Just as before, he exempted the latter from the strictures that he had applied to most ancient pagans, but he now turned them into the vital link between the pure religion of Abraham and that of Anglicanism. In these later years, indeed, his preoccupation with them became obsessive in a way that it had not been before, so that he was constantly finding them hidden behind English place-names and monuments from later periods, and identifying his favourite friends and potential patrons with them.[78] He also engaged in flights of apparent pure fancy in the detailed reconstruction of their rites, very different from the careful reasoning from evidence (whether or not the evidence itself was faulty) which had marked his earlier work. Thus, by the 1750s he had decided that they wore long dark habits over long-sleeved white linen surplices, and fastened purple mantles over these with golden brooches. At the autumn equinox they adorned their temples and selves with oak leaves and sprigs of heather, sacrificed oxen, and erected a T-shaped cross inscribed with sacred names. At the spring equinox they sacrificed rams and wore anemones; at the summer solstice they offered pigeons and donned sprigs of vervain and foxglove flowers; at midwinter they killed goats and cut mistletoe for decoration; and so on and on.[79] His new tendency to shed caution in his speculations was noted by at least one of his most loyal friends, Roger Gale, who warned him in 1737 that a treatise he had just written, arguing that the icons of pagan deities were accurate portraits of the main characters of the Book of Genesis, outran the limits of credibility.[80] Reading through the manuscript works composed during the last two decades of his life, it is easy to see why an observer could note that they regularly moved meetings of the Society of Antiquaries to hilarity.[81] Even in the context, and by the standards, of their own time, they have ridiculous aspects. One of the franker and more perceptive retrospective verdicts on him was provided by Bishop Warburton, who commented that 'there was in him such a mixture of simplicity, drollery, absurdity, ingenuity, superstition, and antiquarianism . . . a compound of things never meant to meet together'.[82]

In view of all this, it is important to note how much was achieved by Stukeley's two great books, that on Stonehenge, which appeared in 1740, and that on Avebury, which followed three years later. Had he died in the late 1720s or the 1730s, he would have represented another case such as those of Aubrey, Lhuyd and Toland: of a marvellously fertile mind which had a limited impact on the public at large because some of its most significant work was either never completed or left unpublished in the author's lifetime. Stukeley survived, however, and accumulated the personal wealth needed to get his books through the press without the need of patrons or subscriptions; his second marriage, which brought him a handsome dowry, probably provided the crucial addition of funds. The result was a pair of large and very readable volumes, lavishly illustrated with his own beautiful plans and drawings: and their impact on all levels of literate society was tremendous and enduring.

They established, firmly and for ever, that the megalithic monuments of England, as of all other parts of Britain, were built by its prehistoric inhabitants, and not by the Romans, the Danes or the post-Roman British. They alerted readers to the richness, profusion and importance of these monuments, and especially to the complex at Avebury. They mapped out the ritual landscape there, and around Stonehenge, for the first time, and produced the technical terms by which certain aspects and categories of monument are known. If archaeologists still speak of the 'Sanctuary' at Avebury or the 'Avenue' and 'trilithons' at Stonehenge, or of megalithic 'coves', or of 'cursus' monuments or 'long barrows', this is because of William Stukeley's books. The latter were intended explicitly to stop the demolition of such ancient structures, which had greatly accelerated in some districts during Stukeley's lifetime, by giving people an enhanced sense of their value. In this ambition they may have succeeded, as the destruction of the Avebury stones, which he had observed with such bitterness during his fieldwork there, slowed considerably after the appearance of his book on them. He promoted the study of local antiquities, especially by members of the professional classes to which he himself belonged. His linkage of prehistoric monuments to the patriarchal religion of the Old Testament was in an existing scholarly tradition, and may well have served to enhance their value still further in the eyes of many readers, and render the study of them still more respectable to country clergymen. As part of this achievement, he associated the ceremonial monuments of prehistoric Britain firmly with the Druids, not as an interesting possibility (which is what Aubrey had achieved) but as a dominant and orthodox belief.

David Haycock has demonstrated the influence of Stukeley by proving the impact of his ideas on a selection of learned authors working in the late eighteenth and early nineteenth centuries.[83] His findings can be complemented at a more populist level by the major example of attitudes to Stonehenge. Before Stukeley's book on it appeared, the dispute over the monument's age was still very much alive, and an omnibus edition of the main competing ideas regarding this, published in the previous century, was brought out in 1725. The balance of scholarly opinion seems to have continued at that time to favour a date that was Roman or later.[84] This situation makes a complete contrast with that expressed in the guidebooks to provincial Britain that began to appear in the late eighteenth century, to service the domestic tourist industry that was a product of the greater ease and safety of travel in that period.[85] Five of them published between 1785 and 1798 dealt with Stonehenge, and all of them credited the Druids as its designers: four specifically cited Stukeley as the person responsible for this opinion.[86] Two of them referred to megalithic monuments in other parts of England as likewise Druidical, and an early guide to the Lake District put the stone circles of that region into the same context.[87] As for the national network of antiquarians, the simplest possible insight into the shift in its opinion is provided by the first ten volumes of *Archaeologia*, the journal in which the Society of Antiquaries began to publish selected papers from its proceedings in the 1770s. Right across the island of Britain, striking prehistoric remains of all kinds were automatically credited to Druids, without argument:[88] a complete contrast with the situation which had obtained before Stukeley published his two big volumes. To revisit the controversy to which the opening of this chapter referred, this is an excellent proof of the impact a single human being can have on national culture, given favourable circumstances.

It also, however, embodies an irony. Stukeley wanted to be honoured, primarily, not as somebody who had produced a better knowledge of British antiquities as such, but as one who had furthered human understanding of the nature of the cosmos, and through it of the nature of divinity. His religious ideas, though recognized in some of the references to his work cited above, made far less impact on his contemporaries, and on posterity, than his drawings and his dating of monuments. This was partly because people were less inclined to accept them, or less interested in them, and partly because of another accident of publishing. He had advertised his books on Stonehenge and Avebury as the first two of a series entitled 'Patriarchal Christianity, or A Chronological History of the Origin and Progress of True Religion and of Idolatry'.[89] The other five volumes of this were designed, according to their titles, to embody his wilder ideas regarding the relationship between the biblical and pagan religions, and they were never written. Always prone to violent fits of rapture and animosity, and changes of plan, he scrapped the rest of the project on discovering that his deal with the publishers of *Stonehenge* and *Abury* was yielding them too large a share of the profits, and he could not secure a better one for the remaining books.[90] As ever, he was a curious balance of the mystic and the mercenary, of audacity and caution, and the result in this case may have enhanced his later reputation, as most of his sillier notions remained out of print. He continued to expound them in lectures and circulated manuscripts, however, until his death in 1765. Here is, therefore, a further reflection upon the contribution made by his career to the debate over the role of the individual: for Stukeley, as for others, it proved much easier to make a major impact on the imagination of fellow humans than to determine the exact form which that impact would take.

It appears, moreover, as if both Stuart Piggott and his critics were right about Stukeley. They were unquestionably correct that his study of prehistoric monuments was inspired and informed by a profound religiosity which prescribed his interpretative framework for it. His intellectual life can no longer be divided into a reliable, rational and objective period before his ordination and a speculative and fantastic one after it. On the other hand, a major change of attitude did occur at the time of his ordination, and his scholarship did thereafter become more imaginative and less cautious. The story of the relationship between Christianity and Neoplatonism is a long and complex one, connecting figures as widely separated in time as Dionysius the Areopagite in the sixth century, Marsilio Ficino in the fifteenth, and C. S. Lewis in the twentieth. The career of William Stukeley seems to represent another episode in that relationship, illustrating something of what was, and was not, possible in the mental world of Georgian Britain.

*   *   *

Some further insight into the nature and limitations of Stukeley's influence can be gained by examining the work of two people who made particular use of his work and left great reputations, in very different fields, as a result. One is John Wood, a leading architect of eighteenth-century Britain and the person who, more than any other, turned Bath into one of the most celebrated and gorgeous of Georgian cities. The other is William Borlase, father of the study of Cornish prehistory and natural history.

Wood had in common with Stukeley a love of form and design combined with a strongly religious temperament, but expressed these traits with much more consistency. Eileen Harris has shown that he was a devout fundamentalist Christian who rejected the concept of the Trinity; which in contemporary Anglican terms made him a heretic. He was not alone in these beliefs, as a small but vocal number of authors were arguing against Trinitarianism in the early eighteenth century; Stukeley, as shown, switched from one side of the argument to the other. Somebody who fully shared the doubts regarding the division of the Christian god into Father, Son and Holy Ghost, but preferred to keep silent on the matter in public, was the dominant figure in contemporary science, Sir Isaac Newton. Stukeley himself was a devoted disciple of Newton, and Wood was another. In particular, Wood was influenced by Sir Isaac's *Chronology of Ancient Kingdoms Amended*, which appeared in 1728. As a fervent, if quietly unorthodox, Christian, Newton treated the Bible as the earliest reliable historical document, and identified the tabernacle of Moses as the first known piece of human architecture. He also argued against the contemporary admiration for the pagan Greek and Roman classics, deeming them unreliable in their assertions because they were the work of practitioners of false religion. His work was, further-more, imbued with an interest in the cosmological significance of numbers and measurements, and in the interpretations of ancient Hebrew buildings – above all, the temple of Solomon – as representations of the cosmos, and of history. In this respect, too, Stukeley and Wood were both his pupils.[91]

Newton's influence was greatly reinforced for Wood by a great upswelling of interest in Solomon's temple and Moses's tabernacle, which occurred in Western Europe at the same period and peaked in England in the 1720s. In the middle years of the decade a German architect exhibited wooden models of both buildings at London, which inspired Wood to make his own and to deliver lectures on them in 1726. The excite-ment over the mystic properties of architecture, and of ancient Hebrew structures in particular, was both a reason for and a consequence of the contemporary spread of Freemasonry, which claimed to represent a secret tradition of wisdom descended directly from Solomon's master builders. This all, naturally, added a thrilling dimen-sion to Wood's own craft, as an architect and builder, and – in contrast to Stukeley – he became profoundly influenced by Masonic symbolism. In his desire to claim a divine origin for his profession, he went further than any previous writers by asserting that all the classical orders of architecture employed by the Greeks and Romans had been stolen by them from the Hebrews. These orders were increasingly influential in English buildings, including those that he designed himself, and he seems to have had a powerful emotional need to uncouple them from the pagan civilizations of antiquity and link them to the Bible, and so to religious revelation. He asserted, indeed, that all the pagan peoples of the ancient world had engaged in a similar cultural larceny, and that the tabernacle of Moses, with dimensions dictated by the deity himself, was the origin of all human architecture. By the late 1730s he was working on a book to argue this case, even as he erected his first major buildings at Bath; and the successive versions of this work provide a remarkable insight into the way in which an author at this period could become emotionally involved with Druids.

The first draft of it was completed by 1737, when it failed to find an aristocratic patron and so got shelved.[92] This manuscript, now in Sir John Soane's Museum, London, asserted that the ancient Britons had no knowledge of architecture, art or science until the Romans arrived, bringing what they had learned from the Hebrews. Wood knew, however, of no surviving Roman buildings in Britain, and thought that the oldest edifice still in existence in the whole island was Llandaff Cathedral, centre of the diocese of south-east Wales, which he believed (quite wrongly) to be fifth-century. After his first attempt to obtain funding for the book failed, Wood changed his mind. He had now read Toland's posthumously published letters and had his eyes opened to the existence of prehistoric monuments and their presumed association with Druids. He was prompted by this to read other authors and got the idea that the Druids had received the religion of the ancient Hebrews; the chronology worked out by his hero Newton (following Aylett Sammes) suggested that they did so through Phoenician traders, soon after the building of Solomon's temple. He thus became interested in Stonehenge, and read the book on it by Jones and Webb, rejecting (in the light of his new reading) its conclusion that the monument was built by the Romans, but noting the number of stones recorded in it. From these he decided that it had been a Druidic temple based on the cycles of the moon. All this was added to his original manuscript in a series of revisions in a black ink which was also used for a building account and a draft letter to a friend inserted into the front and back of the book; the latter was becoming a collection of odds and ends. The insertions at front and back are dated March and May 1738, which reveals when the new turn in his thought occurred.[93]

The next stage in the development of his thought was precipitated by the appearance of Stukeley's book on Stonehenge, in 1740, which roused Wood to a fever of jealousy and ambition. Architecture in his period was a fiercely competitive profession, and he had just the temperament to match it. He was also both underemployed and humiliated, having just had his plans for a Grand Parade at Bath rejected. Furthermore, he seemed to secure just the patron whom he needed to support his plans to upstage Stukeley: the Earl of Oxford, a magnate keenly interested in history and prehistory, who turned up at Bath in early August.[94] With Oxford's encouragement, he immediately set to work on his own surveys of megalithic monuments, and commenced with the circles of Stanton Drew.[95] Wood was not just a passionate Christian and architect, but a fervent local patriot for his native Bath and nearby districts of Somerset. Stanton lay in one of these, and he duly incorporated his findings there into a second manuscript version of his book on architecture, which survives today in Bath Central Library.

In this, he proposed an interpretation of the circles as an exposition of Pythagorean cosmology, with the great circle representing the stars and the lesser two the sun and moon.[96] The similarity of this interpretation to Stukeley's is obvious, and may just be an illustration of the fact that thinkers living in the same society at the same time can reach parallel conclusions. After all, Pythagoras had featured prominently in the debates since the mid-seventeenth century on the nature of primitive religion, and his association with Druids had been highlighted by Toland. Toland had also credited Druids with building temples to the sun and moon. It must be noted, however, that Wood's biographers, Tim Mowl and Brian Earnshaw, have proposed a different line of descent for his new ideas: that they came directly from Stukeley. Wood had spent the formative years of his career in London, at the time when Stukeley was part of its intellectual life and gathering and discussing his data concerning megalithic monuments. Indeed, Wood's own friend and business partner, John Theobald, succeeded Stukeley as secretary of the newly formed Society of Antiquaries, to which Wood himself might have belonged. If so, he might have heard Stukeley expound his interpretation of Stanton Drew, and perhaps even read his manuscript treatise on its circles.[97] Such an argument is very convenient for the theme of this chapter, which is to cry up Stukeley's impact on perceptions of British prehistory. If it is accepted, however, it is hard to understand why Toland's work should have made such a dramatic impact on Wood over ten years later, and converted him from a belief that there were no prehistoric monuments in Britain.

Wood certainly made his own complete survey of the Stanton Drew circles, and his personal identification with Somerset drove his claims for them to greater heights. He declared that the Phoenicians had brought with them to Britain not merely the true religion of the Hebrew patriarchs but the design of Solomon's temple. The British Druids absorbed both and set about building monuments in imitation of the temple, of which those at Stanton became the chief. They were, in fact, the seat of the Druidic 'episcopacy', founded by a Phoenician leader, and the national headquarters of Druidry. As such, they were 'perhaps the finest example on earth of the Pythagorean system'. In case readers are wondering what Pythagoras had to do with Solomon, it needs to be understood that Wood believed that, just as all architecture derived ultimately from ancient Hebrew monuments, so Pythagoreanism, Zoroastrianism and the other great philosophical systems of early antiquity were all derivations of the revealed religion of Israel. In his scheme, the great circle at Stanton had been planned not merely as a temple of the stars but to embody symbols of the zodiac and of the earth, and as a residence and college for eighty Druids, led by their high priest, whose houses were built within the stones.[98]

Before the end of the year he had moved on to Stonehenge. His intention was to prove Stukeley wrong in his measurements and eclipse his conclusions, while giving credit for ideas to the ancient authors Caesar, Diodorus and Pliny, and to Toland, who were all safely dead and so could not be seen as rivals. He decided that Stonehenge had been built after Stanton Drew, and that the medieval legend that attributed its construction to the wizard Merlin had preserved the memory of a 'real' Merlin, an Archdruid. Its dimensions reflected the phases and movements of the moon, its trilithons were symbolic of the Roman moon goddess Diana, and the two kinds and colours of stone used in its construction represented the warring powers of good and evil, according to the religion of Zoroaster.[99]

Wood never got the hoped-for patronage, as Oxford suddenly died, but he decided to go it alone. Like Stukeley he had begun to identify personally with the Druids, for in 1741 he awarded himself a coat of arms, proclaiming that he was a gentleman of the 'ancient Britons' and displaying oak trees on a mound, quartered with crescent moons, symbols of Diana, who he had now decided was worshipped by the Druids under her Phoenician name of Onca.[100] He proceeded to issue his thoughts about the ancient world in a stream of books. First, in 1741, came his general theory of the origins of architecture in divine revelation, to the Hebrews.[101] Next was a history of Bath which he published in two parts in 1742 and 1743. In this, Stanton Drew was turned into the national university of Druidic Britain, while its capital became Bath itself, chief seat of the Druids and a city built of marble at a time when Rome was still made up of mud huts. In Wood's imagination, the steep limestone hills and valleys around his beloved home town became filled with ancient shrines to the heavenly bodies, above all to the sun god Apollo and the moon goddess Onca.[102] He followed Toland in claiming that Britain had been ancient Hyperborea, but whereas the Irishman had turned the most famous Hyperborean, Abaris, into a fellow Gael, Wood identified him with King

Bladud, the legendary founder of Bath itself. Wood's Abaris had gone on a fact-finding tour of the Middle East, meeting not only Pythagoras but Zoroaster and the builders of the second temple of Jerusalem, before bringing back his accumulated knowledge to the Druids of Britain. In this scheme of events the Romans had destroyed Druidic Bath and martyred its leading inhabitants, only to repent in the next generation. They had then rebuilt the city on its old model and invited back Druids to live and teach there; which enabled Wood to claim as Druidic the splendid ruins of the Roman city which were being revealed and admired in his lifetime. This was a parallel to the way in which his history of architecture enabled him to claim classical styles as Hebrew, likewise giving no credit to the pagan Greeks and Romans for them. It also allowed him to vent his hostility to Roman Catholics, by accusing their missionaries, sent by Gregory the Great, of finally suppressing the Druidic teachings.[103] In 1747 he rounded off his books with a short one on Stonehenge, presenting the conclusions that he had reached after his survey of it seven years before.[104]

In some respects Wood was even kinder to Druids than Stukeley; whereas the latter tried to explain away their ancient association with human sacrifice, the former simply ignored it. In others, he was more detached. He allowed that their veneration of the sun, moon and stars in their temples (as he and Stukeley read the evidence) represented a decline from the original and pure worship of the one true deity alone. In that sense they venerated idols, though their confinement of that tendency to the heavenly bodies, and their representation of these in abstract forms like circles, seemed to him a far lesser offence than the luxuriant polytheism of the classical ancient civilizations. He never doubted that Christianity was superior to Druidry, and found comfort in the sight of the medieval parish church at Stanton Drew, which dominated the village and its prehistoric remains; this he saw as a reminder of the triumph of true religion.[105] Wood and Stukeley were ironically similar in that the fieldwork in which they engaged, and which ultimately promoted the development of the discipline of archaeology, was accompanied in both by an attitude to history which was reactionary and outdated even for their own time. Both wanted to believe in the medieval history of Britain produced by Geoffrey of Monmouth, with its succession of legendary kings which had become discredited among leading scholars during the Tudor period. It was this work that had given Wood the characters of Merlin and Bladud.[106] Stukeley's enthusiasm for it, however, diminished with time, while Wood's remained one of the guiding themes of his thought. Furthermore, he united it with an equally literal acceptance of the forgeries of Annius of Viterbo.[107] In part this was due to the fact that he was a self-educated working man, who lacked both the temperament and the training for historical source criticism. His publications were certainly imaginative beyond a point that Stukeley reached even in his manuscript treatises, and his biographers have aptly suggested that he should be acknowledged 'not only as Bath's greatest architect, but as her first writer of historical fiction'.[108]

Stukeley and his friends naturally resented Wood's work, feeling with good reason that it abused Stukeley himself while preying on his ideas and inflating them with absurd elements. Stukeley thought it the 'most inveterate mixture of ignorance, malice and malevolence', Roger Gale called it 'a silly pack of stuff', while the Bishop of Gloucester dubbed Wood 'a great fool, and not less a knave'.[109] His ideas about the origin of architecture were indeed absurd even by the standards of his time, and his book on the subject failed to sell out in its first and only edition.[110] That on Stonehenge likewise seems to have been little noticed.[111] His work on Bath, however, sold well enough to justify the publication of both its second part and two further editions. In the West of England, indeed, it literally put the Stanton Drew monuments on the map. A chart of Bristol and its environs, made and sold by that city's Mathematical Academy in 1769, clearly marked them as 'Druidical stones'. Furthermore, it provided a detailed plan of them as a sub-set in the map; both megaliths and Druids had been turned into proud items of regional heritage.

Wood's main job, however, was not to write history or prehistory but to put up buildings, and in this respect as in all others they remain his true memorial. His masterpiece was the circular range of stately buildings at Bath, pierced by streets and enclosing an open space known as the Circus. After much discussion among architectural historians, there seems to be a general acceptance of the interpretation of this proposed by Timothy Mowl and Brian Earnshaw: that the design reflects Wood's esoteric interests.[112] It is based on the Masonic sign of a triangle within a circle, about which he had written, incorporates the mystical sequence of Druidic or Pythagorean numbers which he claimed to have found at Stanton Drew, and, as a sacred structure occupied by housing, reflected his concept of the great circle at Stanton as a Druidic college. As these were, in Wood's belief system, dimensions for building taught by the deity himself to Moses, the Circus became a permanent hymn of praise to the divine architect. Lest anybody miss, at a glance, its connection to Druids, he topped it with a row of giant stone acorns to represent a grove of sacred oaks. He also gave it superb acoustics, fitting the central space for ceremonies because words spoken aloud there are naturally amplified by the curve of the surrounding buildings. Functionally, the Circus is a series of residential blocks, and it was for these that Wood received his payment. Symbolically, it is the first Druidic temple to be erected in Britain since ancient times, created as the testimony of faith of a passionate, if highly unusual, Christian. It may, in fact, be the first stone temple ever built in the name of Druidry.

Wood died in 1754, the year in which William Borlase sprang to national attention. Borlase was rector of Ludgvan in the westernmost district of Cornwall, a granite upland studded with ancient monuments, including megaliths. In this respect his situation was similar to that of Henry Rowlands, and indeed the work of the latter was to feature prominently in the Cornishman's own. As his biographer, P. A. S. Pool, has shown, however, his interest in prehistory was slow to develop.[113] He was appointed to his living in 1722, by the influence of his father who was a leading local gentleman; a career in the Church was a suitable means of employment for younger sons of gentry at this time. It certainly suited his pious temperament, but (as he candidly admitted to Stukeley) he still became bored enough to need another outlet for his intellectual energies.[114] He gradually found it in antiquities, which in Cornwall had hardly been investigated before he undertook the work. His interest was first drawn to them by the discovery of a Bronze Age burial in a local barrow in 1728. He thought it to be Danish, together with the prehistoric monuments around it, in conformity with a major trend in scholarly thought during the previous century. His perceptions, together with his income, were broadened by his acquisition of a second living at St Just, at the very tip of the peninsula. In June 1738 he became excited by the discovery of basins apparently cut into the granite outcrops of that parish. They seemed to him to be older than the period of the Danes and designed to play a part in sacrificial rituals. At this point he made a deductive leap of the imagination, and hypothesized that they were 'therefore not improbably belonging to the secret rites of the Druids'.[115]

He was, in fact, completely wrong: geologists have since concluded that the basins concerned are the product of natural weathering. This mistake, none the less, fell into the category of what may be termed 'a fertile error'.[116] It inspired Borlase to write round seeking experts on Druids, a quest which was unsuccessful until the publication of Stukeley's book on *Stonehenge* provided what he was seeking.[117] The two men eventually had a brief but amiable correspondence,[118] and by 1750 Borlase had completed a book of his own. Four more years were required to advertise its existence and raise the subscriptions to pay for publication, but Borlase's network of clerical and gentry connections was very potent; among those who eventually put down money for the job were the Princess of Wales, the Archbishop of Canterbury, and the leading politician William Pitt.[119] The result was *Antiquities, Historical and Monumental, of the County of Cornwall*, the most accurate and comprehensive survey of a county's prehistoric remains produced up till that date. It made the author's reputation as a major scholar.

It also made the reputation of Cornwall as a great centre of prehistoric remains, especially that of Borlase's own home district, the westernmost hundred of Penwith, on which he had concentrated his main attention. His text was embellished with many beautiful illustrations of sites and artefacts, which gave expression and excitement to his long and careful discussions of different classes of monument. These were the rich fruits of his long years of effort expended on scrambling through bracken, gorse and heather to reach different sorts of weathered stones, cairns and ramparts. Most of the remains that he described – standing stones, dolmens and stone circles – he associated with the Druids. The first of these he represented as their idols, the second as their burial places, and the third as their settings for acts of worship and judgment. He sensibly concluded that Rowlands had been wrong in identifying megalithic chambers – the dolmens, cromlechs and quoits of popular terminology – as Druidic altars, because of the difficulty of climbing and balancing on top of them to perform sacrifices. Instead, he called them tombs, and modern scholarly opinion has endorsed his view. He went further, however, to bring in natural features – not merely the rock basins (which he now saw as holding water for ritual purifications) but also rocking stones and dramatically shaped granite formations – as sacred places of Druids. At moments he conceded that the latter had probably not erected these structures, but went on immediately to suggest that they had venerated them, enhanced them, and used them as platforms or ritual accessories. The result was, effectively, an enchantment of the Cornish landscape, filling its hills, heaths and moorlands with impressive vestiges of a vanished culture. In doing so Borlase spoke bluntly of the lack of fieldwork, and therefore of objective data, that had character-ized almost all previous writers on Druidry, especially Toland. He singled out Stukeley, alone, for praise of his 'learned and ingenious' character.[120]

Stukeley, however, was mightily offended by the book;[121] for he and the Cornishman differed fundamentally in their views of the nature of ancient Druidry. Borlase's reading of classical literature, and of the Old Testament, had left him with a loathing of ancient paganism, of which he regarded the Druids merely as having been one 'sect'. This sentiment seems to have been reinforced in him by a general pessimism about human nature and a hatred of Roman Catholicism, which he regarded as retaining – in its love of ceremonial, icons and mystification – many of the features of paganism. As a result, he rejected the idea that the pure religion revealed to the Hebrew patriarchs could have lasted long anywhere other than among the Jews: human depravity and Satan would have seen to that. He acknowledged that the Druids might have held some of 'the most elevate notions of the human soul, and the most certain persuasion of futurity', left over from the original divine revelations to Adam and Noah, but said that they mixed these with a 'total contempt of human life': 'the frequency of their human sacrifices shocks us, their magic exceeds belief, their oak worship looks singular and absurd'. They had induced, instead of the 'true fear of God, a gloomy kind of awe, and religious dread, consisting of the Grove, and Night-worship', and 'instead of the true purity of heart, a false superficial purity ... consisting of ablutions, white garments, outward sprinklings and lustrations'.[122] As part of this view of them, Borlase rejected the idea that they had arrived as part of a Phoenician colony, acting as a conduit for the teachings of Abraham. He bluntly (and rightly) called it the result of false philology, and declared that Britain had been peopled from across the Channel. If there were some striking similarities between forms of ancient paganism from the British Isles to the Near East, this was simply because Satan worked everywhere in similar ways. Borlase thought that the Romans had therefore been right to suppress Druidry as far as they were able, and that Christianity had done a splendid job in destroying it completely. In his imagination, moreover, the Druids had made many Christian martyrs before they succumbed.[123]

Borlase's biographer Pool has commented that 'by the standards of his own time his conclusions were sober and well argued, especially when compared with the wildly extravagant fantasies of Stukeley'.[124] This is certainly what Borlase himself wanted posterity to believe, but in his reconstructions of Druidic organization and practices he could be every bit as imaginative as the older scholar. To be sure, he based all of them on identified sources – classical texts, material remains, and the work of early modern authors – but the combination and interpretation he made was both arbitrary and personal. He informed readers that the Druidic hierarchy was divided into three main ranks, called (in ascending order) Vates, Bards and Druids proper, but that each of these had itself two divisions. Thus the whole system consisted of six grades, each with its own costume. There were also three different kinds of Druidess, ranging from those who lived like Catholic nuns, as virgins in their own communities, to those who saw men once a year, to those who lived with husbands.[125] Borlase's Druids worshipped in groves, which were designed to produce an atmosphere of gloomy mystery. They were usually on hills, bounded by a fence or bank and grown with trees consecrated with human blood. Each contained stone circles, images of deities, holy wells, caves for the instruction of the young, altars of different kinds for distinct varieties of sacrifice, law courts, cairns for holy fires, stone troughs or basins for holy water, and pens for sacred or sacrificial animals.

The rites were held at noon or midnight, with big assemblies at the new and full moons which were attended by the local nobility, common people being excluded. Ritual equipment included incense, tapers, candles and offerings of meat and fruit. The actions included the kindling of candles and torches from a sacred fire, sprinkling of celebrants with holy water, prayers, libations and blood sacrifices. Borlase's Druids were dressed in white, with diadems and crowns of oak leaves on their heads, five-sided shoes, a 'serpent's egg' pendant around the neck of each, and crescents embroidered on their robes. The younger were clean-shaven, the older bearded. Druidesses had white hair, white gowns, and linen cloaks fastened with clasps and brass belts, and went barefoot. Favourite sacrificial victims were bulls and human criminals or prisoners of war, but the need of the religion for human blood was such that a whole range of devices and excuses were employed to secure it. Borlase portrayed the Druids as out and out polytheists and idol-worshippers, with a pantheon of deities like any other ancient pagans, and poured scorn on the idea that they had any notion of the Trinity. He tried to save Stukeley's face by attributing the theory that they had to the Germans, but it must have been perfectly plain to informed readers who was in his sights. Borlase went on to make the Druids seem ridiculous as well as horrific, claiming that they had bickered constantly over whether to turn left or right during services, and regarded the earth as defiling, so that they would not inter their dead in it, or allow mistletoe and other greenery to touch it during rites.[126]

As Leslie Ellen Jones has recently pointed out, in the lushness of these descriptions there is more than a hint of prurient fascination.[127] Borlase took it for granted that 'after sacrifice, luxury and debauch ensued' among the celebrants, especially in the nocturnal ceremonies.[128] A telling – and to modern eyes, perhaps comical – example of the difference between him and Stukeley is provided by their differing treatment of that passage in Pliny describing how British women had paraded naked and dyed dark at religious assemblies. Stukeley (and Toland and Wood) had ignored it, while Borlase gave it a prominent position in his portrait of Druidical rites. He suggested that the nobility exposed their wives and daughters in this fashion to deaden the sensibilities of the young men to the scenes of horror attendant on the sacrifices.[129] There can be little doubt that his book owed its popularity not merely to its painstaking scholarship but to its lurid passages of historical fiction.

Whichever had more impact on individual readers, it transformed Cornwall's image among antiquarians from that of a virtually unknown corner of the nation to one possessed of some of the most important and celebrated concentrations of prehistoric remains. His own district of West Penwith was accorded particular celebrity, which it still retains in both the senses that he invited for it: as the setting of an unusually large, varied and spectacular group of monuments, and as a wild and romantic lansdscape covered with traces of a fascinating vanished culture. His representation of the district's Druidic past may actually have sunk into popular culture, because a century later folklorists were collecting traditions that the basins formed in the granite outcrops had been made by a race of vanished cannibal ogres, who had carried out sacrificial rites there on human victims.[130] In wider society, he must have reinforced the sense that Stukeley had provided of the importance and ubiquity of the Druids, and their association with megalithic monuments, which Borlase extended to striking natural features. At the same time he must have done much to destroy the good impression of them that Stukeley had striven so hard to foster. In the case of the latter's influence on Borlase, as in that which he had on Wood, it can be seen very clearly that a scholar can have a major, and permanent, impact on cultural perceptions, while remaining largely out of control of the form that impact takes.

* * *

Thus far it has been argued that William Stukeley was of pivotal importance in transforming the Druids into ubiquitous figures of the British historical imagination, and especially that of the English. It is necessary now to consider the possibility that they would have become much more prominent in British culture, at around the same time, even had Stukeley never been born. At first sight, it is possible to make a seemingly good argument that they would have done. This is because they were bound up in two of the most powerful forces in that culture during the eighteenth century. One has already been mentioned: the growth of a British identity, in the wake of the union of the kingdoms of Scotland and England, which could transcend traditional national rivalries within the island, and perhaps all over the British Isles. When that development was considered earlier, it was suggested that the Druid could make a potent contribution to it, as one of the very few figures whom the whole of the islands had in common during the past. That association was indeed made during the course of the century, as the subjects of the newly united kingdom came to have a sense of common purpose and nationhood. As British nationalism became more confident and aggressive, Druids could become embodiments of patriotism, especially in their role as co-ordinators or inflamers of resistance to the foreign menace represented by the Romans. Pliny's linkage of them to the oak proved exceptionally helpful here, as that tree became regarded as the vegetable symbol of Britain: the shelter of the British monarchy because the future King Charles II had hidden in one when in flight for his life, and the wood from which the royal navy, on which the security of the realm depended, was built.

Trees also came to the support of Druids in the case of the second great cultural movement that was to prove influential in altering public perceptions of them: Romanticism. One of their chief characteristics, as alleged by the first-century Roman authors, had been their propensity to teach and worship beyond the limits of civilization, in places such as woods and caves. Romanticism, as it took shape during the eighteenth century, depended partly on a belief that there was an inherent wisdom and virtue, as well as beauty, poetry and numinous divinity, in wild nature. It encouraged civilized people to seek out natural places that were apparently unaffected by human activity in order to renew their acquaintance with them as sources of cosmic knowledge and artistic and intellectual inspiration. The fact that Druids had habitually seemed to do exactly that made them easy objects for admiration on the part of those who were acquiring these new ideas. The patriotic and Romantic attitudes, although distinct in nature and origin, were very easily combined, so that woodlands, Druids and Britishness could all be blended into one powerful emotional brew.

There is, however, a problem in deciding how self-sufficient these developments were, and how detached from those represented by the antiquarians such as Stukeley. On the one hand the two groups of people concerned can easily be distinguished from each other: the view of Druids as priests and sages connected with megalithic monuments was propagated by scholars, and the association of them with patriotism and the natural world was mainly the work of poets. Furthermore, the images themselves hardly overlap: the Romantic concept of Druidry had little time for the prehistoric remains which were central to the antiquarian one. It can be shown that the former tradition was already developing in the 1730s, before Druidry had seized the imagination of the scholarly world. On the other hand, its early development was very muted indeed, whereas it flowered spectacularly after the appearance of Stukeley's books, following the same trajectory as the scholarly interest that those books inspired. It seems likely, therefore, that Stukeley may indeed be given much or most of the credit for the development of this other set of attitudes to Druidry, as well as for those which he embodied himself.

Some modern attempts had already been made to turn Druids into priests of nature. The association of them with rivers in a court masque of Charles I indicates how easily they could be assimilated into the national landscape, and in the same decade, the 1630s, a costume was designed for one in just such a royal entertainment, probably the same masque. It was by Inigo Jones, the great architect and impresario of the early Stuart kings, and showed a Druid as a figure with flowing hair, beard and robe, and bare feet, crowned with greenery; very much a woodland spirit.[131] In 1713 the poet William Diaper portrayed them as inhabitants of the greenwood and friends of its spirits:

> With sacred mistletoe the Druids crown'd
> Sung with the nymphs, and danc'd the pleasing round.

Diaper also credited them with both patriotism, in loving the unspoiled British landscape so well, and prophecy, taught to them by their friends the nymphs, which enabled them to foresee the evils of the Roman conquest.[132] None the less, such images were individual and widely separated in time and social space; they were not part of any continuous tradition.

It seems to be generally agreed that the first classic text of the Romantic Movement in England was James Thomson's huge poem *The Seasons*, published in sections between 1726 and 1730.[133] Thomson was a part of the literary world of London, dependent on aristocratic patronage and public acclaim for his living, and his poem represented a bold new initiative in both its form of verse and its subject matter. Although willing to praise the achievements of civilization, it was primarily a celebration of woodlands, and of rural life and traditional peoples. There were no Druids in it, but they featured in another of Thomson's most famous poems, 'Liberty' published between 1734 and 1736 and devoted to eulogizing British freedom. It did not have a lot of time for ancient Britain, dismissing it as 'Celtic night', but praised the Druids for inspiring its people (who were portrayed as forest-dwellers) to heroic patriotism, by promising them immortality after death.[134] Thomson was a Scot by birth and upbringing, and may have absorbed the respect for Druids that had been a theme of his national culture for over two hundred years. It may have counted for more, however, that he was also a great admirer of the poetry of Milton, who had been unfashionable for most of the previous eighty years because of his association with regicide and republicanism. He probably absorbed from it Milton's early affection for Druids, without noticing the dramatic change of opinion that occurred in the poet's later prose works.[135]

It may be observed, therefore, that the major themes of the Romantic celebration of Druidry – the association of Druids with British nationalism and a reverence for the natural world (and especially the woodland world) – were present in Thomson's pioneering work. They were, however, very loosely combined, and the Druids them-selves merited just one line in one very big poem. Only the seeds of the subsequent literary fashion were present before Stukeley published his books on Druids in 1740–43, and they sprouted in the wake of those works. In, or shortly before, 1744, one of the most famous English poets of the age, Thomson's friend Alexander Pope, made a plan for an epic on the theme of the settlement of Britain by Trojan refugees. This was the best known of the medieval legends that had by then long been discred-ited by serious scholars, and Pope's decision illustrates again how long an afterlife these legends had among writers of creative literature. He had long before, in 1713, associated oak trees with an essential Englishness, in his poem *Windsor Forest*. He had not, however, dealt with Druids, and now intended to make up for this by featuring them prominently, as the priests of the native population whom the Trojans encoun-tered. He conceived of them as gentle and harmless worshippers of sun and fire who offered fruits and flowers on their altars rather than blood sacrifices and were wise enough to realize that the strangers would be good for the land. Indeed they would be, because in Pope's vision the Trojans introduced a more rugged, heroic and patri-otic spirit into the Druidic flower-children who had led the Britons hitherto, and removed some of the 'superstition' in their beliefs and rites.[136] The result might have been one of the great works of English literature, but Pope died before he could write it. In 1747, one John Wheeler published a polemic entitled *The Modern Druid*,[137] which called on the British to preserve and extend their surviving oakwoods so that the navy should not lack for ships and (therefore) the nation for defenders. It held up the ancient British priesthood, with its reputed reverence for oaks, as an example to be followed.

Actual or intended works such as these were indications of the way in which such ideas were germinating, but they flowered most obviously among a network of poets based in and around Oxford and London. Thomson was one of these, and the others were Thomas Gray, William Mason, Joseph and Thomas Warton, and William Collins: names that between them largely embody the early Romantic Movement in

England. The mood that inspired much of their work is summed up in a list of possible subjects for poetry compiled by Joseph Warton when still a schoolboy at Winchester College in 1739:

> The solemn silence of the Pyramids. The dark gloomy scenes in mines. The fall of the Nile. Distant noises. Indian Brahmins wandering by their rivers. Medea's nightly spells. Meteors in the night. Gripping of a serpent or a crocodile. A lamp in a lone tower. Noises heard at Hell-Gates, that were shut. Extended prospects from Olympus. The flames of Etna seen in a dark night by strangers. Cassandra calling on Agamemnon, as he was dying. Pangs and struggles in drowning. Lapland witches, feasts and religion. Evening dances in Arcadia. Serpents fly from the rattlesnake. The effect of an eclipse on all the animal creation. Sudden thunder over a summer's day. Sailors' cries at sea in a stormy night. Traveller benighted. Two strong seas separated by an isthmus – or two angry lions by a wide river. The priest bleeding. Old men slaughtered . . .[138]

There were no Druids yet in this maelstrom of adolescent fantasy, but it is easy to see how they would have fitted in, and by 1746 they had arrived in Warton's verse: a hollow oak beside an English village is honoured as having possibly been the dwelling of a 'holy Druid old'.[139] In the previous year, Joseph's younger brother Thomas wrote an ode containing the belief that Druids had first discovered the benefits of contemplation while musing in 'oaken bowers'.[140]

The most significant poetic contributions to the subject in this period were made by Thomson, again, and William Collins who was one of the latter's greatest admirers. In 1748 Thomson completed his last major work, an allegorical poem called *The Castle of Indolence*. The hero was a knight, who was accompanied and counselled by a 'Bard, a little Druid-wight', 'sage and staid' called Philomelus. He was sweet-faced, wore russet brown, rode a 'milk-white palfrey' and played a 'British harp'.[141] This all sounds remarkably unlike a Druid, and makes one conclude that Thomson's love of Milton's poetry had caused him to perpetuate its error of confusing Druids and bards. What Philomelus sang about, however, is extremely significant. He preached a view of the cosmos as emanating from a supreme being, so humans had the opportunity of rising up, by efforts of will and learning, back along the chain of emanations through successive incarnations to reunite with the divinity. This is a clearly recognizable form of late antique Neoplatonism, and there is no doubt that for Thomson, as for Stukeley in the 1720s, it was a creed that the author treated as a personal belief as well as one identified with the Druids.[142] For both men, therefore, this attraction to ancient philosophy was associated with an attraction to heterodox religious ideas.[143]

The appearance of Thomson's poem was flanked by two by Collins which tackled the same subject. In 1747 he published his 'Ode to Liberty', inspired partly by Thomson's earlier poem and likewise designed to make the claim that Britain had become the true home and defender of human freedom in the modern world. It also perpetuated the old tendency to lump together Druids and bards, portraying the 'consorted Druids' of ancient Britain as singing of the patriotic achievements of its chiefs in a woodland shrine to the goddess Liberty.[144] Two years later he produced the second work, a tribute to Thomson himself, who had died suddenly of a chill caught while being rowed home along the Thames. He opened and closed the poem by hailing his hero as a Druid, a title probably the more effective in that he never explained it. Instead he justified it by association, portraying his dead friend and mentor as a poet who had loved and revered the countryside in general and woods in particular.[145] In works such as these, the Druids were being cut loose from their primary perceived ancient roles as priests and scientists, and turned into the spiritual ancestors of British nature poetry. There was, however, a deeper and more concealed relevance to Collins's comparison, for Thomson had, after all, held unorthodox religious views which he had credited to the Druids. Collins himself was also, at this period, alienated from Christianity, and its priesthood was said to be 'the thing he most derides'.[146] If his tribute to Thomson was intended to have this private resonance, then it was an ironic one, because the dead poet had been allegedly reconciled to the faith of Christ at the end of his life, and so was Collins to be.[147]

By the mid-1750s Joseph Warton (who loved Oxford University deeply all his adult life) was prepared to declare that poets would do better to celebrate wild and natural scenery, as stimulants to the creative imagination, than the universities. He made the Druids into key figures traditionally associated with such landscapes: 'The mention of places, incurably romantic, as the supposed habitation of Druids, bards, and wizards, is far more pleasing to the imagination, than the obvious introduction of Cam and Isis, as seats of the Muses.'[148] Three major works of literature were about to exemplify and reinforce those attitudes and to confirm the new enthusiasm for Druids as poetic heroes: *The Bard* by Thomas Gray, *Caractacus* by William Mason, and *Ossian* by James Macpherson. This was despite the fact that two of them, the first and last, never mentioned Druids at all.

Gray was another of the key figures in the development of Romanticism, and probably the best informed of all this group of writers on the subject of Druids. He had certainly read Stukeley, along with Caesar, Tacitus and Camden, and probably Rowlands, Toland and Borlase as well.[149] The result of all this work was to put him off the Druids as a subject, for he decided that none of the ancient sources for them were reliable, being 'fictions' or a 'half-dozen of old fancies' showing only 'how little we know of the characters and customs of the people'.[150] This was astute, as was his decision to write about the medieval bards instead, as more solid knowledge of them existed. In doing so, he also made a significant contribution to the creation of the new sense of British identity that was one of the achievements of his century. This creation consisted of three different, and interlocking, processes. The most important was the development of a shared sense of national character, based on the concept of the British as an island people with a glorious destiny, dedicated to freedom in political rights and (Protestant) religion and pitted against the powers of Popery and tyranny.[151] A corollary to this, however, was an enhanced sense on the part of the smaller traditional nations in the new consortium – the Scots and the Welsh – of their own history and cultural inheritance, employed to maintain their position as distinct units within a state clearly dominated by England. This has already played some part in the present story, and will become more prominent soon. The third process, which matched the second, was a new interest on the part of English intellectuals in Welsh and Scottish culture and a willingness to value it, as part of the consolidation of a partnership with these other British peoples. Apart from its political advantages, this willingness also promised to open up new cultural resources, in the form of native literatures, for authors and artists jaded with the overwhelming fashion for Greek and Roman models. Gray (himself a Londoner who had settled in Cambridge) was one of the most influential of these.[152]

In view of his rejection of the classical sources for Druids as fictions, it is heavily ironic that Gray proceeded to swallow whole a tremendous historical fantasy concerning Welsh bards: that the medieval English king Edward I had ordered their extermination. The genuine King Edward had certainly been the ruler who ended the independence of Wales and incorporated it into the English state, but he had made no move against the bards as a profession; indeed, the two centuries after the English conquest had seen some of their greatest achievements. The story that he had tried to destroy them was a myth that had appeared in north Wales during the early seventeenth century, partly to rally support for the vanishing bardic culture. It achieved belated widespread currency because it was repeated in Thomas Carte's influential history of England, published in 1747, and it was there that Gray came across it.[153] It gave him the subject for an epic poem, in which the last surviving bard, pursued by Edward's thugs through the wilderness of Snowdonia, is cornered on a crag above the River Conway and chooses to throw himself in it rather than yield to foreign tyranny. It expressed the new British patriotism in miniature, combined with a deep sympathy for the Welsh as a proud and distinctive people and the newly fashionable admiration for primitive cultures and wild scenery.

Accordingly, it made a huge impact when it was published in 1757, achieving a wide readership and subsequently inspiring no fewer than ten works of art.[154] As Gray knew well, Druids were not bards, but the distinction between the two was much hazier in the minds of others, as has been illustrated above. The visual interpretations of the poem, which all concentrated on the final dramatic confrontation above the Conway, portrayed the doomed hero as an ageing man with fiery eyes, streaming hair and beard, and robe; very similar to the now accepted image of the Druid. At the very least, Gray succeeded in instilling in his readers greater respect for that indigenous culture in which Celtic languages were spoken and Druids had existed, and from which bards emerged.

One of those whom he inspired was James Macpherson, who made a sustained attempt to induce the English and Lowland Scots literary worlds to admire the Highland Gaelic culture which represented Macpherson's own heritage. Between 1760 and 1763 he published three books of poetry, allegedly translated from the Gaelic and mostly representing epics he claimed were composed in Scotland in the third century. Collectively, they (and especially the last two) became known as 'Ossian' after the ancient author claimed for them.[155] Almost immediately doubts were raised as to how old Macpherson's sources actually were and how far he himself had improved on them and added to them in the process of translation. The resulting controversy lasted into the twentieth century, although there now seems to be agreement that he worked up folk stories into much more imposing pieces, and then claimed that these were ancient, rather than forged the poems wholesale. In his own lifetime, Macpherson won many admirers for them, and they became major influences on literary taste and perception in turn. There were no Druids celebrated in the 'Ossian' poetry; instead it conveyed a powerful sense of the majesty of Scottish scenery and the nobility of ancient British society, in an atmosphere of tragic gloom; perfectly (and deliberately) suited to the developing Romantic literary tastes. None the less, as Druids had been a part of the society and landscapes thus celebrated, they could only benefit from the interests and appetites that Macpherson's work aroused.

Between these two bodies of work, in 1759, came Mason's epic poem *Caractacus*, which focused directly upon Druids. Published in the great year of British victories over the French, from Canada to India, it played up to the swelling mood of patriotic fervour by letting readers have the best of both worlds in their attitudes to the Roman conquest of Britain. The native British were portrayed as heroic and noble barbarians, and their Druids as admirable, while the Romans were made into magnanimous conquerors who added to British culture the blessings of civilization and of reason, and so created a perfect blend that was eventually to produce an unbeatable nation. Mason himself was a friend and admirer of Gray, and a former Cambridge don who had won a patron in the Earl of Holderness and been made that magnate's chaplain with a parish living in Yorkshire. Gray wrote of his disciple, cruelly but accurately, that he 'reads little or nothing, writes abundance, and that with a design to make a fortune in it'.[156] *Caractacus* certainly displayed all these qualities. Mason had read Toland to improve his knowledge of Druids, and gained much other information on the historical context from Gray.[157] His poem was based on the Roman attack on Anglesey by Suetonius Paulinus. With an eye to its market, however, he mangled even the apparently known historical facts beyond recognition, transporting the genuine British hero Caractacus there from a different decade, and crediting the Romans with a gallantry completely at variance with everything in Tacitus's account of the attack.

His Druids, furthermore, were not Toland's, nor Stukeley's, but the romantic sages already established in the new movement in English poetry. The chief of them was a 'seer', dwelling in a 'shaggy cave', with his brotherhood occupying similar accommodation in the neighbouring cliffs, the 'Euvates' to his left and the Bards, who wore white robes and carried harps, to his right. They all meet at night in a sacred grove purified by sprigs of vervain dipped in dew, and sacrifice only white cattle; humans, Mason stated firmly, were offered up by the Gaulish (i.e. the French) Druids, but not by those of Britain. The latter's two great loves were represented as being peace and holiness, and their worship as directed towards the celestial spirits who preside over their majestic and wild land:

The airy tribe that on yon mountain dwell,
Even on majestic Snowdon: they, who never

Deign visit mortal men, save on some cause
Of highest import, but sublimely shrined,
On its hoar top in domes of crystalline ice
Hold converse with those spirits that possess
The sky's pure sapphire, nearest heaven itself.[158]

The result was a bestseller, which went through another edition before the end of the year and four more before 1777, when it was turned into a stage play as well.[159] Edward Snyder wrote a classic study of its influence on other British writers, and found that it was both profound and long-lived, lasting until the end of the century. So did Mason himself, and on his death in 1797 a fellow poet called for his burial beneath a 'central oak's mysterious shade', and dreamed of Druids, bards and 'dark-robed priestesses of the grove' attending the funeral rites.[160] In the previous year, the last of Mason's life, another author had coupled a tribute to him with praise of English woodlands, and fantasized that Druids still lived on in secret in their depths, having evaded the Romans and all subsequent conquerors.[161] Through the decades since the publication of *Caractacus* had stretched a succession of similar literary works, celebrating Druidry in verse as the religion which, more than any others, could be associated with the beauty, goodness and wisdom of the natural world, and of that of Britain in particular. Mason himself supplied some of them,[162] as did Thomas Warton.[163]

Of the other contributors, a few deserve special notice. William Waity and John Tait made a desperate effort to associate Druids with another of the century's most enduringly famous writers, Oliver Goldsmith, who had never himself shown any affection for them;[164] they suggested that the ancient Druids had retired into fairy-land, where they could 'hear the rules of love' in enchanted woods and spy on and admire modern poets like Goldsmith.[165] To the author of an anonymous poem of 1792, they had been the gentlest of all ancient priests, each one a 'foe to blood', and forbidding even animal sacrifice because of the possibility that a beast's body might contain a former human soul, reborn in it after death. He portrayed them processing to Stonehenge to make offerings of woodland fruits, ewe's milk, honey and wild grains, the female Druids wearing hoods bound with fillets and carrying oak branches. Inside the monument, the chief Druid made a speech extolling the virtues of peace.[166] To Thomas Maurice, it was impossible that a civilization as admirable as that of ancient Rome would have wiped out so sweet-natured and pious a people. In his reimagining, the Druids continued to practise all through the Roman period in Britain, assisting their conquerors in their opposition to barbarism, and only being exterminated by the savage Anglo-Saxons.[167] Another poet, William Mickle, felt obliged to admit that Druids were probably not as kindly in reality as he had portrayed them in his work, but insisted that he was showing them as they would have been in their earlier days, when the teaching of the Hebrew patriarchs was still strong in them.[168]

Others associated Druidry more with rugged scenery and stirring emotions than soft woods and gentle ways. The youngest to write in this fashion was a Cornish schoolboy called Richard Polwhele, who frequented the great bare ridge of Carn Brea overlooking the twin mining towns of Redruth and Camborne. There he found (as the visitor still does) the tumbled walls of an ancient fort among the rocks and under-growth, together with piled cairns and those granite basins that had excited Borlase. The work of Borlase coloured his perceptions, as he wrote of how the guardian spirit of the ridge remembered its ancient glories:

Still she sees the Druid train
(Reverend Chorus) sweep the lyre!
Still she hears the thrilling strain; –
Glows her heart with holy fire.
Richly robed the hoary sage
Still the mystic rites performs;
Silvered o'er his brow with age!
Still his frame devotion warms.

Young Polwhele hoped that his reveries on the hill would put him in contact with the same forces that had inspired the bards of the Druidic time, and advance his career as a poet.[169]

The first poem entirely devoted to Druids appeared in 1787, with a second part two years later. It was the work of John Ogilvie, the minster of Midmar in Aberdeenshire, who was in the unusual position of having a well-preserved stone circle standing right next to his parish church,[170] and, according to the general pattern in the wake of Stukeley's books, interpreted it as having been a Druidic temple. He commenced by declaring that he based his reconstruction of the rites that would have occurred within it entirely on classical texts; but he was clearly deeply influenced by the recent swelling of enthusiasm for Druids among his fellow poets. He portrayed Druids as dedicated to the arts of peace, the teaching of virtue to the young, and the worship of the one true god. Their chief was a silver-haired man robed in white, who dwelt in a dell of oaks and poplars and combined high-minded asceticism with a kindly understanding of human nature. His religion included priestesses, who were dedicated to divine service and virginity when young. The natives who revered him and his kind turned out to have thoroughly unlikely names such as Edgar and Florella; but then Ogilvie's ancient Britain was a never-never land, a primitive paradise of innocence, peace and joy equivalent to the Arcadia of classical literature. He concluded by declaring that such simple happiness now existed only in native societies far elsewhere in the world such as those of Tahiti and India.[171] Here he was plugging straight into one of the major literary themes of his generation: a new enthusiasm for the ancient concept of the noble savage, uncontaminated by the corruptions of civilized life and able still to enjoy the untroubled and natural existence of the first humans. This was itself an aspect of the new admiration and love for natural and rural settings which had appeared in the first half of the century. The discovery by Europeans of new tribal peoples in Asia, Africa and the Pacific, which was one of the most exciting features of the period, was immediately pressed into the service of this attitude. The islanders

of Polynesia in particular were made the exemplars of it; which is why Ogilvie highlighted Tahiti in his comparison. The predisposition of Europeans to admire the
primitive both produced a selective reading of the accounts of natives sent back by the
explorers and conditioned the manner in which the latter made their original reports.
In the words of the classic scholar of this subject, Hoxie Fairchild, 'by 1799 no traveller with an eye to publication would deal very harshly with savages'.[172] Pacific
islanders and Druids were equal beneficiaries of the fashion.

Given the new interest in Druids, and sympathy for them, it was inevitable that
somebody would turn them into a musical, and this was done in 1774 by John Fisher.
His *Masque of the Druids* set them in a woodland paradise so gorgeous that the
goddess Venus herself descended to bless their rites, and nature-spirits capered about
them. In this wonderland, both religion and daily life celebrated the natural bounty
and felicity of existence, and Druids pranced off to worship with the careless grace
normally associated with Arcadian nymphs and shepherds:

Holy Druids from your consecrated woods,
Rocky cliffs and silver floods,
From their margins fringed with flowers,
Hither move, forsake your bowers,
Strewed with hallowed oaken leaves,
Decked with flags and sedgy sheaves,
To yon bright dome straight repair,
But leave behind you all your care.

It was typical of the confusion with which all this goodwill towards them was
commonly mixed that Fisher thought the main deity of the Druids had been the
Anglo-Saxon god Woden.[173] The show was, at any rate, a success, having a series of
performances at Covent Garden in the winter of 1774–5.[174] The adaptation of
Mason's *Caractacus* was not the only appearance of Druids on the non-musical stage
during the period. As said, Shakespeare had ignored them in his *Cymbeline*. By
contrast they had a prominent place in a play with the same title written by Henry
Brooke in the mid-1770s; so much had taste changed.[175] Where professional drama
led, amateur dramatics cheerfully followed. In 1774 Lady Betty Hamilton became
engaged to marry Lord Stanley. Her family coat of arms displayed an oak tree, and
his country seat in Surrey was called the Oaks; the combination provided an irresistible theme for the party held at his home to celebrate the event. It included a
masque composed by Stanley's uncle, John Burgoyne, better known to history as
'Gentleman Johnny' and as the general who was to lead a British army to abject defeat
in the American War of Independence only a few years later. On that happy summer
night in 1774, however, he won a major social victory with a series of songs and
dances intended to compliment Lady Betty as 'The Maid of the Oaks'. They were
linked by speeches provided by a Captain Pigott, costumed as a Druid, who closed
the proceedings by pronouncing a solemn blessing on the engagement at an altar
erected beneath a large oak tree.[176]

For those who preferred a more martial spirit in their representations of the ancient British, Druids had their uses as well, and this was exemplified in 1780, when one of the finest poets of the age, William Cowper, wrote an ode on the rebellion of the British queen Boudica. He portrayed how, having been outrageously punished and humiliated by the conquering Romans, she sought counsel from a 'hoary chief' Druid, 'sage beneath a spreading oak'. Enraged and grieving, he prophesied the destruction of Rome itself and a glorious imperial future for Boudica's own British people, in its place. Once again Cowper was blending the figures of Druid and bard, calling his character both by turns and having him play a 'sweet and awful lyre'; and this was a confusion which generally worked to the advantage of Druids.[177] Certainly the poem helped further to establish them in the modern British mind as patriotic ancestors, and its popularity lasted into the twentieth century; indeed, until the end of the British Empire itself.[178]

Three works published in the year 1800 may serve to illustrate how deeply embedded an affection for Druids had become in British poets by the end of the century. To William Sotheby, they had not truly perished but were waiting in an enchanted cave, together with King Arthur and his knights, for the moment when Britain truly needed them again.[179] Richard Llwyd, while lauding the beauty and historic heritage of Anglesey, declared that they had taught all the most important and admirable tenets of the ancient Hebrew religion.[180] Most conventional for his time, and therefore most representative, was one Dr Darwin, who addressed his verses to an old oak tree and visualized how

Erst, when the Druid bards, with silver hair,
Poured round thy trunk the melody of prayer;
When chiefs and heroes joined the kneeling throng,
And choral virgins trilled the adoring song;
While harp's responsive rung amid the glade,
And holy echoes thrilled thy vaulted shade . . .[181]

With associations like these, stone circles had suddenly altered from disregarded collections of rock into numinous and highly desirable features of a landscape. A local author describing his favourite Cardiganshire view in 1796 commented on how 'the whole expanse around, of intermingled beauties, may continually feed the eye; where, if a Druid's temple never stood, a Druid's temple is unquestionably called for; and I cannot help experiencing a hope, that a rude imitation will one day there be placed.'[182] In other words, where megalithic monuments did not exist already they could be created, and they soon were. Before the end of the decade, the owner of an island in Derwentwater, one of the most popular parts of the newly fashionable Lake District, had 'improved' it with 'a chapel, a church, a fort with cannon and a Druid circle'.[183] This was what visitors now wanted to see.

It was also what aristocrats wanted to have in their gardens. After the publication of Stukeley's book on Stonehenge, his patron the Earl of Pembroke decided to build a small replica of the monument in the grounds of his mansion at Wilton. Pembroke was, however, a special case, being the local magnate in the Stonehenge district and himself keenly interested in antiquities; furthermore, it does not seem that the project was actually carried out. Stukeley's book on Avebury produced better results, for it inspired a young gentleman called Crow to lay out his estate in imitation of the prehistoric complex as the book had interpreted it. The great house itself was to represent the central temple, with newly planted avenues of elms imitating the stone rows that the book had declared to form the pattern of a huge serpent. The head of the snake was portrayed by a mound with a stone pillar on its summit. One of Stukeley's later patrons, the Duke of Montagu, reacted to his ideas by decorating the largest oaks in the park of his seat at Boughton with 'the names of Druids, stamped in lead and fastened to the trees'.[184] An admirer of his, the antiquary Francis Wise, landscaped the grounds of his home during the 1740s to include ponds, cascades, seats, a triumphal arch, the Tower of Babel, an Egyptian pyramid – and, of course, 'a Druid temple'.[185]

In the following three decades, this fashion spread beyond the circles immediately influenced by Stukeley's work. During 1785 a local militia on the Channel island of Jersey levelled the top of a hill to make a new parade ground. The work uncovered an elaborate Neolithic passage-grave, with a set of side-cells arranged around the main chamber. The islanders showed their affection for their governor at the time, General Henry Conway, by digging up the megaliths and shipping them to his Buckinghamshire mansion, Park Place, to be re-erected as a decoration for its grounds. A plaque inscribed in the local French was sent with them, proclaiming them to have been a shrine of the Druids; and the whole reassembled structure still stands, in the garden of a house at Henley, called Templecombe. Conway's cousin, Horace Walpole, hearing of the remarkable gift, spotted at once the dual influences that ultimately lay behind it: he observed in a letter to the general that 'Dr Stukeley will burst his cerements to offer mistletoe in your temple; and Mason, on the contrary, will die of vexation and spite that he cannot have "Caractacus" acted on the spot'.[186]

The Park Place tomb was not unique in being a genuine prehistoric structure pressed into service as a garden ornament; the Marquess of Anglesey was lucky enough to have another Neolithic chamber already standing on what became the lawn before his mansion. It was one of the series that line the Menai coast of the island, on which the Romans had landed and where Henry Rowlands had preached to his congregation and written his book. Both house and dolmen survive together today.[187] More often, of course, 'Druidical' structures had to be custom built, and took various forms. A 'Druid's throne and temple' constructed of 'pieces of . . . rock' were installed at another Welsh mansion, Piercefield Park, by 1759. An English gentleman, Sir Samuel Hellier, began to improve his seat of Wodehouse Wombourn by creating a mock-up of a medieval hermitage, complete with a mechanical hermit called Father Francis. By 1773 he had added a 'Druid temple'; apparently without a matching occupant. Likewise a Mr St John first ornamented his park at Dogmansfield, in the sandy heathlands of the Hampshire Barrens, with a 'Gothic arch'. By 1754 he had felt obliged to embellish that structure with 'an imitation of a British or Druid avenue . . . of large stones set up on end for half a mile'.[188] Before Stukeley brought out his books, nobody would have associated Druids with 'avenues'. In another part of the same county, at Fyfield, a clergyman called Henry White hired men to drag a four-ton boulder into a copse on his property in 1781, so that it could be set up there as a 'Druidical column'. In 1755 Thomas Wright published a *Book of Arbours*, to illustrate various different kinds of garden buildings and embellishments. One of the subscribers who paid for its publication was a Somerset gentleman, Sir Charles Tynte. He took a particular liking to the picture on the title-page, of a round thatched building supported on wooden pillars. A replica of this was subsequently erected in a wood in his park at Halswell, and named 'the Druid's temple'; as its form bore no resemblance to the megalithic monuments associated with Druids by Stukeley and his followers, the name was presumably inspired by the growing poetic tradition that located such temples in woods and other secluded places.[189] The wealthy aesthete William Beckford had a fake dolmen built in the grounds of his famous neo-Gothic mansion of Fonthill Abbey, as a matter of course. In Kent, the Earl of Darnley demolished a genuine megalithic monument and used the stones to build a 'Merlin's Grott' at his home of Cobham Park.[190] Some landowners built metaphysical arguments into their Druidical follies. In the park of his mansion at the southern end of Wiltshire, the eighth Lord Arundell of Wardour already had a ruined castle, his family's former residence which had been wrecked during the Civil War. During the 1790s, it was fashioned into one element in a landscape through which visitors could travel back through time. Starting with a mock-Gothic, recently built banqueting house, where they could be given food and drink, they moved on to the 'true' Middle Ages, in the form of the overgrown castle ruins. From there they progressed to the ancient world, in the form of a Druid circle, and so finally to a grotto decorated with falling water, ferns and fossils, to evoke the power of wild nature. The circle was a genuine prehistoric stone ring, from nearby Tisbury, which had been uprooted and transported to the site.[191]

The most elaborate Druidical monument of the age was erected at Swinton, in Yorkshire, on the orders of William Danby, after he had gone on holiday to the Lake District in 1795. He returned so full of enthusiasm for its scenery, including its Neolithic stone rings, that he redesigned the grounds of his mansion to echo it, putting in a lake with promontories and inlets, evergreen woods, huge boulders and (by 1803) a megalithic complex. This was, however, no straightforward stone circle of the Cumbrian sort, but a collection of trilithons, chambers, altars and monoliths intended to represent the elements and the signs of the zodiac; as if Stonehenge had mated with a Neolithic passage grave and produced offspring. It was a solid manifestation of the wildest theories of Stukeley and Wood concerning the Druidical attachment to Pythagorean mystical geometry. Less ambitious landowners were content to commission statues of Druids for their gardens, always represented in the fashion of Aylett Sammes's illustration as bearded and robed men, carrying staves and wearing a dignified expression. By 1780 these had appeared in the grounds of stately homes in Hampshire, Worcestershire, Wales and Staffordshire, while another decorated a conduit in the city of Chichester.[192] Only Sir Richard Hill, owner of Hawkstone Park, Shropshire, seems to have taken the additional step of installing a live one. By 1802 he had persuaded an anonymous retainer to take up residence in the grotto that was (and is) one of the spectacular follies constructed in his grounds. The job of this person was to dress up in Druidic robes every time he heard visitors approaching, and then to appear in the chapel of the grotto, bowing to its altar, in order to impress, delight or startle them.[193] In 1740 Druids had been marginal figures in the imagination of the English and Welsh; within fifty years they and their presumed monuments were virtually everywhere. They loomed out of books, strutted in plays, and peered through shrubbery.

4

THE DRUIDS TAKE FLESH

To his tribute to the Iron Age Druids in his poem in praise of Anglesey, cited earlier, Richard Llwyd appended a footnote which read: 'Such was the Druidism of the ancients: in that of the moderns, among other benevolent and patriotic tenets, there is one which it is impossible to contemplate without the highest gratification – the liberality with which it encourages and awards exertion, for saving the sufferers in cases of shipwreck.'[1] In other words, by the time he published this, Druids were no longer a thing of the past: they had reappeared in Britain and begun to deserve consideration as a contemporary phenomenon.

When exactly this happened may be a matter for dispute. One answer to the question was provided in 1990, by the posthumously published book on Druidry written by Ross Nichols, founder of the Order of Bards, Ovates and Druids.[2] This credited the origins of the modern Druid orders to John Aubrey, who decided in or around 1694 to revive a society of Druids called the Mount Haemus Grove, which he learned had been founded at Oxford in 1245, and disappeared at some point in the intervening years. He and his companions therefore 'began to wear the robes and carry out some of the ceremonies'. One of this Grove was John Toland, who brought a number of other Druid groups together in 1717 to found the order to which Nichols himself eventually belonged, and which had therefore survived continually from the early eighteenth century to his own time, and, indeed, to the present: the Universal Bond (commonly known simply as the Druid Order). This account of events is the most systematic and confident statement of the origins of the modern Druid orders that has yet appeared in print.

It is, moreover, certainly not Nichols's account alone, for it is also found in statements published earlier by the Circle of the Universal Bond itself. One of these, from the 1970s, provides further details for one portion of his story: that the Mother Grove or Grand Lodge of the order was proclaimed on Primrose Hill, London, at the autumn equinox of 1717, and given the Gaelic name of *Gairdeachas*. Its inaugural assembly was held at the Apple Tree Tavern, in the Covent Garden district of London, and was organized by Toland, who was acting on a suggestion made by Aubrey over twenty years before. Delegates from 'Druid centres' in London, York, Oxford, Man, Anglesey,

Cornwall, Scotland, Ireland, Wales and Brittany attended and elected Toland chief, aided by a Supreme Grand Council. The avowed purpose of the newly constituted order was to unite the activities of the disparate Druid groups 'to further the cultivation of the noblest and best in man and thus work for the restoration of the Golden Age'. The statement concluded by declaring that the Supreme Council and its chiefs had continued to honour these ideals ever since.[3] Its second chief was Stukeley.

Ross Nichols did not provide any evidence for his claims, describing them simply as derived from the tradition of his order, the existence of which was (he added) itself kept secret until the end of the nineteenth century. The parallel statement from the 1970s was equally barren of source references. As a symbolic representation of history they combine to work very well: the story told in the past two chapters of the present book has confirmed the central importance of Aubrey, Toland and Stukeley, successively and cumulatively, in creating the conditions in which Druids could reappear. It has also endorsed the role played by Oxford as a place in which much of this work of creation took place. If the version of developments presented by Nichols and the Universal Bond is treated as an esoteric teaching, by which major truths are offered in a concealed form, then it embodies much demonstrable history. Only if it is treated as a literal statement of fact are there problems with it; but if it is, then the problems are considerable. The context within which the Universal Bond's account of its own past was created, in the early and mid-twentieth century, will be reconstructed in detail in later chapters of the present work. For now, it is important to consider that account on its own merits.

The problems with it revolve around the central issue that Aubrey, Toland and Stukeley have all left considerable records of their private lives and thoughts, and in the case of none of them do these show any trace of membership of a Druid organization. This is linked to the fact that there is no reason why any of them would have needed to keep involvement in an organization of this kind such a close secret as to make necessary the destruction of every trace of it. Even in the twentieth century, the Druid order that claimed descent from them did not hold any beliefs, or engage in any rites, that would have been seriously dangerous to freethinkers in the years around 1700: Toland's professed doctrines were actually as outrageous as any later associated with the Druid order he was said to have founded.

Aubrey left many manuscript notes and jottings on his interests, some of which have been published in succeeding centuries, and large volumes of correspondence with friends and associates in Oxford; some of those people, such as Tanner, Lhuyd and Anthony Wood, left equally large quantities of private letters in turn. This material was used in discussions of his work during the previous chapter. None of it seems to contain any evidence that he either knew of a medieval Mount Haemus Grove or founded a group by that name himself. Neither of his biographers has come across any, and both portray him in the period around 1694 as old, ill, and distracted by his futile struggle to publish *Monumenta Britannica* and by a bad quarrel with his old friend Wood.[4] He did indeed belong to a group in Oxford at that time, which was to have vital significance for the history of Druidry, but this was not a grove but the circle of scholars working on the new edition of Camden. Edmund Gibson, and not Aubrey, was at its centre, and none of its members were very interested in Druids except Aubrey himself. His degree of personal identification with Druidry is doubtful.

The case of Toland is more complex. As discussed in the last chapter, his known pronouncements on Druids varied from the fiercely condemnatory to the warmly approving. Ross Nichols suggested that his hostile comments were intended to conceal his leadership of a Druid order, and would be taken as a joke by those who knew the truth.[5] If so, it does seem a rather curious joke to make, and begs the question of why his remarks on the subject were so inconsistent; a different explanation has been proposed. Toland was certainly intensely sociable, enjoying participation in various circles and salons both in Britain and on the Continent. His surviving manuscripts include the regulations for a dining club calling itself the Knights of Jubilation, founded by French Protestant refugees at the Hague in 1710 and dedicated to eating, drinking and merriment.[6] It is notable, however, that his own name is not on the list of members attached, and it is actually very hard to prove that he belonged to any formal society, lodge or order at any time or place. There were rumours at various times of his life, from his student days onward, that he was involved with secret clubs of radicals, but the truth of these is apparently impossible to establish.[7]

In this context, his last book, *Pantheisticon*, presents special problems. Nichols suggested that it could be 'a rather fantasticated description' of the Druid order that Toland had just founded.[8] Certainly it seemed to draw a direct parallel between Druids and the 'Socratic companions' whose views and society it was claiming to represent. It declared that the 'companions' 'strenuously ruminate upon the same studies, for which the Druids and Pythagoras made themselves so illustrious'. On the other hand, the book pays much more attention, and respect, to Greek and Roman sages than to Druids, and the declaration quoted above concludes by saying of the latter, 'yet the Pantheists allow not all their words and deeds; for where they depart from truth, there we also depart from them'.[9] This is a quite decided piece of distancing. Furthermore, it needs to be repeated that the work was presented as a project for a group that did not yet exist, rather than a portrait of one that did. He certainly never had the opportunity to put it into action, because his fatal illness began soon after.

What, then, of the very detailed account of the foundation of the Circle of the Universal Bond in 1717, in a private meeting at a tavern and a public proclamation at Primrose Hill? It seems to have been assembled by splicing together two real, and disconnected, historical events to create a mythical one. A Druid group certainly met on Primrose Hill at an autumn equinox in the eighteenth century, but it was the Gorsedd of the Bards of Britain (of which more later), and the year was 1792. Likewise a number of local groups of a common tradition met in London in 1717 to form a common organization with a chief and ruling council: but they were the Freemasons, who thereby founded their first Grand Lodge and launched Freemasonry on its modern career. The meeting took place on Midsummer Day, four lodges from different parts of London being present to make the union, and the moving spirit was not Toland, but a French Protestant refugee and close friend of Sir Isaac Newton, called John Theophilus Desaguliers. It does not seem to be recorded where the gathering occurred on

Midsummer Day, but the preliminary meeting of the four lodges, that decided on the union, was held at the Apple Tree Tavern.[10] As for the name *Gairdeachas*, it was that of the Mother Grove of the Universal Bond in the early twentieth century, to which this book will come.

Stukeley's case is different again. It was argued above that he very much wanted to be a Druid, and may possibly have been the first person in Britain since the end of the ancient world to have that desire. He was also not merely sociable but clubbable, and in the course of his life was a member of the Gentlemen's Society of Spalding, the Royal Society, the Society of Antiquaries, the Freemasons, the Society of Roman Knights, the Brazen Nose Society at Stamford, and the Egyptian Society.[11] He was just the sort of person who would have joined, and probably led, a modern order of Druids. However, it has also been argued that, although some of his friends encouraged him in his self-perceived role of Druid with banter and jollity, he could find nobody to share it with him; and this played some part in his decision to seek ordination into the national Church. None of his many surviving treatises, notes, poems, autobiographical jottings or bodies of correspondence suggest that he was part of an actual Druid society. The situation is complicated, however, by the fact that in middle and old age his increasing obsession with ancient Druidry, and his multiplying moments of fatuity, led him to hail his friends as fellow Druids. At times they played up to this fiction. In 1738 he obtained a home north of London, in a district that he and his chums the Gale brothers nicknamed 'Mount Haemus', after the peak in Greek mythology that is the home of the winds. Presumably it was in a breezy situation.[12] The correspondence between them, using this name, was published in the nineteenth century, and seems to have been the origin of the Universal Bond's story of a 'Mount Haemus Grove', though how that got transferred to Oxford is hard to say. At any rate, to the end of his life, Stukeley used the title of 'Druid of Mount Haemus'.[13]

In the 1750s, after his unhappy if lucrative second marriage, Stukeley turned for his emotional needs to successive women friends, to whom he gave nicknames like 'Hebe', 'Miriam' and 'Phoebe', and whom he hailed as Druidesses.[14] In this period, also, he gave the same title to a much grander lady, Augusta, the widowed Princess of Wales. When some Bronze Age axe-heads were discovered in the grounds of one of her residences, at Kew, Stukeley rode over to see them, and then sent a treatise to the princess providing his own explanation of their date and function. She invited him to wait upon her to speak further of the matter, and he was granted thirty minutes of audience on 5 October 1754, in which he expounded his theories regarding the Druids and thought her convinced by them. To his understandable delight, she proved to have read his book on Stonehenge.[15] That is where the direct relationship seems to have ended: the social gulf between them was too great for a friendship, and the princess was not really interested in ancient history. None the less, Stukeley continued to court her attention at intervals until the end of his life, giving her the title of 'Archdruidess of Kew'. He sent her another treatise on the ancient Druids,[16] and when he published a collection of sermons in 1763 he dedicated them to her under that title, and with the pseudonym of 'Veleda'.[17] This was in fact the name of a German prophetess who had featured prominently in the work of the Roman historian Tacitus, but, as that of no actual

Druidess was recorded in ancient sources, he was rather short of choice. He paid a similar honour to at least one other potential aristocratic patroness: another unpublished treatise was dedicated in 1761 to the Countess of Pomfret as 'Arethusa, Archdruidess of Rollright Temple'; this time he had to resort to classical mythology for a pseudonym.[18] What the ladies concerned thought of their designations goes unrecorded, and there is no evidence that they were ever part of any actual order. It is touchingly notable, too, that Stukeley was modest, and realistic, enough to reserve the title of Archdruidess for noblewomen, while he and his untitled lady friends remained mere Druid and Druidesses.

The simple truth seems to have been that there were not enough people around who were sufficiently impressed by the Druids or concerned with them to form the basis for any modern Druidic order before the late eighteenth century. It was the huge swelling of publications on them in the middle of that century, associating them with a British patriotic identity, which made possible the necessary willingness to identify with them. When groups of modern Druids appeared as a result, it was not among metropolitan intellectuals and aristocrats playing the semantic equivalent of party games, but among provincial gentry and among working-class people in the capital. To understand why this should have been, it is necessary to understand one of the main phenomena of Georgian Britain, its love affair with a particular kind of organization: the club.

* * *

The main historian of this phenomenon, Peter Clark, has calculated that, in the course of the eighteenth century, there may have been up to 25,000 voluntary societies meeting in the English-speaking world. He found over 130 different kinds of them in the British Isles during that period, including purely social clubs; associations for self-improvement or for philanthropy; groups for the promotion of pure science, art, commerce, music, medicine, gardening, agriculture, literature or industry, or of political, social and religious causes; groups set up for former members of educational institutions, or for present or past members of particular neighbourhoods, regions or nationalities; and organizations designed to enable the enjoyment of a wide range of specific games, hobbies and pastimes. Like most other forms of social life, such as assemblies, plays, balls, concerts and scientific lectures, they were mostly found in urban centres, although these could merely be small country towns. They were not purely a feature of Britain and its colonies, but continental equivalents were never as numerous, diverse, important and enthusiastically supported. This was partly because on mainland Europe older forms of organization, such as religious confraternities, trade guilds and bands of youths, had survived better, and partly because governments there tended to be more suspicious of people forming themselves into private societies, which might be tempted to discuss politics.

These clubs and associations were essentially a new kind of institution, which appeared in the course of the seventeenth century. Their earlier models were the medieval religious confraternities and trade guilds, but unlike the former they had no religious function, and unlike the latter they did not regulate the way in which people worked. They were also novel in the huge range of interests and purposes they embodied, and the amount of involvement in them by gentry, nobility and professional people. They were therefore essentially a product of British society in the period before industrialization, and first became important in London, from which they spread out to the English provinces and to Scotland and Ireland, and the colonies. Although nearly always restricted to men, the men concerned were drawn from a wide range of age groups and social backgrounds. Those who founded and led the societies were often food-sellers, innkeepers, printers and members of professions. In the seventeenth century, the groups they formed were preoccupied mainly with leisure activities. During the Georgian period, this was accompanied by an emphasis on personal and public improvement, which was joined in turn before 1800 by a growing stress on moral and social reform. By the middle of the eighteenth century, the image and concept of the voluntary society had penetrated every part of British social and cultural life. It was a feature of a nation which possessed, by general European standards, an extraordinarily large number of towns, remarkably high living standards, and unusually active social and physical mobility.[19]

Once the Druids became established as major figures in the British historical imagination, it became inevitable that some of these clubs and associations would take on their name. In the event, only three of them did so, but these were, in their different ways, more important than most. The first appeared on 15 October 1772, when eighteen of the most important inhabitants of the island of Anglesey founded an association to improve it, socially and economically. The one thing that most educated people knew about the island by that date was that it was supposed to have been a notable stronghold of the Druids. This fact, and the favourable impression that the British generally had of ancient Druidry during the period, ensured that the new body was called the Druidical Society. These were the modern Druids praised by Richard Llwyd. All that is known about them is summed up in two articles published in Wesh journals, but the authors of these had access to plenty of good material, consisting of the minute books and regalia of the society.[20]

What was agreed at the foundation of the group was that it would meet at the island's capital, Beaumaris, in the shadow of the great medieval castle built by Edward I. It would do so once a month, all who were present wearing a copy of a medal showing an oak tree on one side and a Druid's head between two oak boughs on the other. Everybody attending was to put some money into a box, and at the end some of this would be used to cover the cost of the ale consumed at the meeting – people who wanted wine or spirits would have to pay extra for them – and the rest added to a fund. Once a year, the group would decide, by majority vote, upon the causes on which the accumulated cash was to be spent. New members were to be proposed by any of the existing set, and accepted or rejected in a ballot. The business discussed at the gatherings was to be kept absolutely secret from outsiders. After seven years, as it grew impressively in numbers, the society acquired a hierarchy. At its head was an Archdruid, who presided over meetings and invested newcomers with their medals. He was supported by a Sub-Druid, who sat at the other end of a long table around which everybody gathered, and administered to new members the declaration required of all who joined: to attend the meetings, assist their business and obey the rules for them. There were also treasurers to look after the fund, a secretary to keep the minutes, and four regulators to show new members to their seats. As well as titles, the leading members were starting to acquire physical trappings: Archdruid and Sub-Druid wore ribbons round their necks, the Sub-Druid carried a wand, and the other officers had ribbons in their buttonholes.

In 1790 the entire membership was given a standard uniform of a dark blue coat, white waistcoat and breeches, and red stockings. The coat had a blue velvet collar bearing a button of yellow metal stamped with a Druid's head. Four silver cups were bought for the formal proposing of toasts. It was in the next decade that the society reached the peak of its success, with up to a hundred members. It had always been socially illustrious, two peers contributing the money for the striking of the original medal, and by 1800 it included more or less the whole social elite of the island, from the Marquess of Anglesey down to prosperous farmers and doctors. Its meetings were clearly very convivial, with payments for harpers to entertain them and waiters to serve drinks, but the serious business of the group lay in the application of its fund. This regularly supported the public hospitals at Chester and Liverpool, the nearest such institutions to Anglesey, as well as the Liverpool asylum for poor blind people. It also provided one-off payments to individuals on hard times, made grants to agricultural societies on the island, and offered rewards to farmers for the best planting of hedges, drainage of land, and crops of clover and potatoes. As Llwyd had noted, it also rewarded people who had saved lives at sea, around Anglesey's long and dangerous coastline. At its peak, between 1787 and 1800, the society was paying out an average 34 guineas per year.

During the early nineteenth century, enthusiasm for it began to wane, and by 1834 its minute book records anxiety over whether it could sustain the membership needed to continue. Ten years later, it formally concluded that this was impossible, and dissolved itself, dividing its remaining fund between the hospitals at Chester and Liverpool and a new one closer to hand, at Bangor, plus sums paid to ensure that a number of poor boys were apprenticed to trades, and to the Royal National Lifeboat Institution. It was wound up with the grace and generosity that it had displayed throughout its existence.

About seven years after the foundation of the Anglesey group, a Society of 'the Druids of Cardigan' was formed. It seems to have been designed chiefly to encourage the writing of poetry, and to have been the creation of an original genius, William Jones, who went on to earn a knighthood, a high judicial office in India, and the distinction of being the first truly great British scholar of Sanskrit literature, and the discoverer of the concept of the Indo-European family of languages. Jones was certainly its 'chief bard', and the group appears to have lasted for only a couple of years, dissolving as Jones himself moved on to other regions and ambitions.[21] None the less, it deserves a place in history as the second modern organization to bear the name of Druids. It may well have been inspired directly by the Druidical Society of Anglesey, as Jones stayed with one of the latter's leading members, Lord Bulkeley, while practising his profession as a barrister on the assize circuit in north Wales. The same work took him down to Cardigan, where he made the friends who formed the society with him.

The Druids of Cardigan existed chiefly, it seems, to enjoy literary picnics together during the season of the summer assizes, when Jones, who now himself lived in London, was in the area. Their favourite spot for these was underneath the ruined medieval castle of Cilgerran, which has a spectacular site on a wooded crag overlooking the River Teifi. There they would lunch on turkey pies, lobsters and crabs, cooling their wine in the river. Jones's verse, recited on these occasions, mostly celebrates the kinds of thing that would appeal to high-spirited young men: wine, the local scenery, and the local girls. It incorporated with this frivolity a sustained element of paganism, mostly taken from the Graeco-Roman classics so familiar to people of Jones's education: one of the drinking songs that he wrote for his Druids honours the nymph of a nearby spring, and all 'deities propitious'. At times, however, these religious trappings adorned more serious arguments. His poem 'On the Gods of Greece, Italy and India' proposed that the pantheon of Hindu deities should be given as much honour, by civilized modern people, as those of the Greeks and Romans. Most remarkable was his response to the Gordon Riots of 1780, in which Londoners had gone on a violent rampage in protest against proposed measures to improve the position of British Catholics. Jones was shocked into writing a poem which both made a passionate plea for religious tolerance and advanced the argument that behind all the main world religions lay the veneration of a single great ancient goddess, whose worship had united the human race. He seemed to suggest that a revival of her religion might be the cure for the evils of religious division and hostility:

> What means all this frenzy, what mad men are they,
> Who broil and are broil'd for a shade in religion?
> Since all sage inspirers one doctrine convey
> From Numa's wild nymph to sly Mohammed's pigeon.
> Then Druid arise,
> Teach the world to be wise,
> And the grape's rosy blood for your sacrifice pour,
> Th'immortals invoke,
> And under the oak
> Kneel, kneel, to the Goddess whom all men adore.

How seriously did he mean this? The evidence for any confident answer seems to be missing, and the Druids of Cardigan did not survive his disappearance from them, as the lure of India called him away eastward. There, like so many British, he found enduring renown, and an early grave.[22]

* * *

On 29 November 1781 there appeared the first modern society of Druids to be founded outside Wales. It took shape at the King's Arms tavern on the corner of Oxford Street and Poland Street in London's West End. Initially much less socially illustrious than the Welsh group, it was to become far larger, far more important and much longer-lasting; indeed, it flourishes to the present day. This was the Ancient Order of Druids. Little is known about its origins. Almost certainly, no records were kept of its proceedings during its earliest years. At the beginning of the 1830s, a sustained attempt was made to write the history of the order in successive issues of the journal that it published by that time, the *Druids' Magazine*. This would certainly have contained valuable information on its foundation and its development until the end of the eighteenth century. It is entirely possible that, by that date, members were still alive who had been present in 1781, and likely that people were active in the order who had spoken to others, now dead, who remembered its first years. Unfortunately, no copy seems now to survive of the first two issues of the journal concerned, which would have included this early material. All that a historian has to go on now are entries made in works published by the order in the first few decades of the twentieth century, by members who seem still to have had access to the missing issues, or to other sources that have also since disappeared.[23]

By the 1920s those sources had left the order with two different stories concerning its own origins.[24] One narrated that it had arisen from a group of minor merchants and artisans which had taken to meeting at the King's Arms simply to enjoy each other's company. In order to keep out intruders, its members decided to turn themselves into a formal society. After much discussion over the choice of a name, one of them, a Mr Hurle, proposed that which was adopted, with unanimous approval. He had a personal enthusiasm for the ancient Druids, as bringers of knowledge and the arts to the British, and improvers of the general condition of humanity. The aim of the new society was, above all, to serve and foster a love of music, together with virtuous living and good citizenship. Hurle became its first president, with the title of 'the most noble Archdruid', and two Bards to assist him. Rules were drawn up for membership and the conduct of meetings, and ceremonies adopted, with regalia to be worn by officers and an initiation rite for newcomers. The rules excluded all discussion of politics or religion, both to reduce any potential for division and to avoid arousing the suspicion of local or national authorities. Members were not asked to swear to keep the proceedings secret (as the Anglesey Druids had done, following the model of the Freemasons), but had to be of known good character, to be recommended by an existing member, and to follow the regulations established for the conduct of meetings.

The second story held that the group of friends meeting at the King's Arms had lost a member, who had died suddenly leaving his mother, who had depended on his support, destitute. The remainder, led by Hurle, decided to honour his memory by setting up a fund to provide for her, and this entailed the founding of a formal society. It was agreed that this would survive her death and provide a means by which the friends could help each other in time of need, following the (presumed) ancient Druidic ideal of brotherly love. The founders thus hoped to create, in miniature, an ideal human society. This account is, of course, perfectly compatible with the first, but there are two grounds on which to be more cautious of it. The first is that the former story was certainly taken from the lost first issue of the *Druids' Magazine*, and so is of proven early date, whereas no source is given for the latter. The second is that this second tale emphasized the essential nature of the order as a charitable body, which – as will be described fully below – it was certainly not, but which many members greatly wished that it could become. It therefore has the hallmarks of a nineteenth-century political myth; but there is no clear proof that it is one.

In 1932 the best historian that the Ancient Order of Druids itself has yet produced, Wilhelm North, commented that only three facts were known about its foundation: the date, the place, and the pivotal importance of Hurle. He added that it would be impossible ever to know for certain who Hurle himself was. He went on to suggest, however, that the contemporary records contained only one plausible candidate: a Henry Hurle who was a carpenter, surveyor and builder working at Garlick Hill, in the city of London, from 1769. This Hurle was obviously a man of some substance, spending thousands of pounds on building a row of houses at Pentonville. He belonged to the livery company of Carpenters, the trade body representing the most respectable members of this craft. He also represented his ward on the Common Council of the city from 1782 to his death in 1795, and held offices in his home parish of St James Garlick Hithe.[25]

With his usual exemplary honesty and austerity as a scholar, North added that 'absolutely nothing' was known of the order in its first twenty years of existence.[26] By that he seems only to have meant that no contemporary records survived from that period, because he proceeded himself to describe some developments in it, which are also found, with more detail, in publications by some of his colleagues in the order. Almost certainly, they are taken from the missing portions of the *Druids' Magazine*. The first notable event after the foundation of the original group was its development into an order, made up of separate bodies in different places which were united by a common allegiance. This must have been propelled by the success of the bunch of friends meeting at the King's Arms and the desire of people who knew them to imitate their example and be associated with them. The mechanism by which this could come about was copied, in both its structure and its terminology, from Freemasonry, the century's great template for a closed society that consisted of a network of local cells united within a national framework. Hurle's members seem to have decreed that the component bodies of their order would be termed 'lodges', after the Masonic name for local groups (taken in turn from the temporary dwellings put up by medieval masons). It named itself Lodge No. 1, and accepted a set of friends meeting at the Rose Tavern, in the Ratcliffe Highway, Wapping, as Lodge No. 2, on 21 August 1783.

The fact that Wapping was a raffish seaport district east of the city indicated how wide the appeal of the group that included Hurle had already spread, in both social and geographical terms. This impression is reinforced by the fact that the third lodge was established, soon after, in Westminster, the heart of the nation's political life and on the opposite side of the capital, in a physical and social sense, to Wapping. This sense of upward mobility combined with dynamism is confirmed by the later belief of the order that one of the most prominent of the age's politicians (though not the most respectable), Charles James Fox, was initiated into the Westminster lodge by Hurle himself. The fact that the lodge met at Fox's favourite inn was said to be one reason for his joining, though Wilhelm North suggested that his interest was reinforced by a desire to increase his popularity among the borough's voters. It is the easier to accept this tale as historical because a copy of the speech of welcome made by Hurle to Fox was still preserved in 1909. North added the belief, which was also preserved in the order, that Fox attempted to make a speech in the lodge to drum up support during the election of 1784, and was stopped because of the rule against the discussion of politics at meetings. To carpet a national leader in this way, so soon after foundation, seems a wonderful proof of the confidence and integrity of the fledgling order.[27]

A yet more effective, and definite, demonstration of its potency lay in its continued rapid expansion. By 1785 it had six lodges in London, and during that year it established its first in the provinces, at Ipswich. Ten years after Hurle and his chums had formalized their meetings at the King's Arms, their order had a chain of them, stretching across southern England from East Anglia and Kent to Bristol.[28] It is obviously worth asking what appeal it possessed, apart from its charismatic name, which could account for such immediate success. The answer seems to be that it filled a niche that no other society occupied: by providing a closed, safe, well-regulated space, spiced up by ritual and sweetened by conviviality, that was dedicated to music. Here the confusion between Druid and bard, common in England for almost two hundred years, achieved a particularly creative result. Members of the order were welcome to read poetry and discuss a range of scientific and artistic subjects, but their central activity was to play musical instruments and to sing. Their meetings provided a haven for prosperous working people who enjoyed chamber and choral concerts and wanted to perform as well as to listen.[29]

The mid-1790s brought in a period of crisis, produced by the outbreak of a major war with France, directed against the regime established by the French Revolution. This indirectly provoked the order's first schism, when some members who had enlisted in military units for the war brought their swords and pistols to a meeting at one lodge. The person presiding directed them to leave these in an anteroom, whereupon one of them took sufficient offence to resign and found his own Grand Select Order of Druids. In the event, it seems to have survived but a short time, and posed no serious threat to the parental body.[30] Much more damaging was the suspicion that the British government had begun to display towards closed societies of working men, for fear that they might prove to be breeding grounds of opinions sympathetic to those of the French revolutionaries. Here the Ancient Order of Druids was extremely vulnerable, despite its explicit prohibition of the discussion of political and religious matters. In 1793 legislation had been passed through Parliament to protect clubs and associations that had a charitable purpose, providing that they recorded their existence and nature in a central registry. The Ancient Order, despite the foundation story later told about it, was not explicitly or centrally a charitable organization, and so could not shelter under the new law. As a result, several of its lodges suspended meetings in 1794 and subsequent years, and some, including the prestigious one at Westminster, closed down altogether.[31]

It is a measure of the vitality of the order that it recovered rapidly as official disapproval slackened in the latter part of the decade, and reached the new century with twenty-two lodges intact. Among them was Lodge No. 1 that had been Hurle's own. The order had also slightly expanded its geographical range, the group furthest from London meeting at Dudley in the ironworking region of the West Midland Black Country. There followed a further, tremendous, burst of growth, as the organization was absolved from all doubt on the part of the authorities. By 1831 it had 193 lodges, with a total membership of over 200,000. They had reached America, Canada and India, but the main expansion had been into the industrial areas of the Midlands and North of England.[32] The order had also become much more visible, and accepted, in the lives of local communities. In 1807 three lodges in Birmingham organized a grand meeting for all those in the Midlands, including a parade by all participants through the city streets, wearing the regalia of their offices and decorations of their lodges. Seven thousand members took part, watched by huge crowds, and they further ingratiated themselves with the citizens by contributing £217, gathered in a collection among them, for the support of local hospitals.[33]

Some indication of what the lodge decorations paraded at Birmingham may have looked like is provided by a description of the annual festival that the local lodge was holding in the small Kentish market town of Dartford by the early 1830s. It decorated the town's Bull Hotel, where it usually met, with boughs of oak, numerous flags, and two silk banners with 'Druid devices'. In the centre of this display was a 'transparency' showing the ceremony of the gathering of mistletoe, as reported by Pliny. The room where the lodge gathered had its ceiling covered with another transparency, of an azure sky with the harp of Apollo in the centre. Around the walls were hung flowers, and twelve diplomas awarded to well-known members for unspecified achievements. The parish church rang its bells in honour of the event, and local brewers contributed bowls of punch. Proceedings consisted of speeches, songs and toasts. The Dartford lodge was an exceptionally dynamic and confident one at this time; it was the only one to open a 'Druid school' for children of members aged seven to thirteen, where they might be educated in the order's principles, as well as in general. This image of a harmonious and accepted relationship with the wider local community seems typical of that period.[34]

It was achieved at the price of some initial tension. The first foothold of the order in the West Midlands was established at Dudley in the ironworking region called the Black Country. In 1813 a Methodist living in the area published an attack on its local lodges as designed 'to promote alehouse conviviality, to revive ancient heathenism, and to plunge those who live in the nineteenth century into all the ignorance and barbarism of pagan Britain, when Druids were priests, and demons were objects of religious worship'. He cast scorn on the initiation ceremony, as – from what he had heard – degrading. The oath now demanded of new members was, in his opinion, 'illegal', 'irreligious' and 'absurd', though he did not specify what it was. Most significantly, he boasted of the fact that many ministers of dissenting chapels in the west Midlands had already excluded members of the order from their congregations, and Methodists were starting to do the same; his tract, which began as an article in the *Methodist Magazine*, was intended to encourage this process.[35] Eleven years later, a different sort of attack was made by a pair of anonymous hacks who purported to inform the public of a range of ceremonies used by the leading closed societies and orders of the time. The information provided bears no resemblance to anything known of the reality of these organizations. In the case of the Ancient Order (the importance of which, by this time, is indicated by its inclusion), readers were assured that the candidate for initiation was led in dressed in a black garment reaching to the middle of his thighs, with holes for arms. Druids concealed behind a curtain uttered yells and groans, and burned sulphur, to give an impression of hell. Then the Archdruid appeared with a battleaxe and threatened to kill the candidate unless he fled. If he stood fast, he was allowed to kneel before an altar and was given the secret password and sign of the order. He was told that Stonehenge was his national temple, and led round the company to be greeted by them.[36] That the order should be made the subject of such ridicule and exploitation by the 1820s, rather than direct denunciation, is itself a sign of growing acceptance, and indeed by the 1830s it seems to have been accepted, however grudgingly, even by the nonconformist Churches which had launched the earlier attacks.

At some point in the 1820s, it felt confident enough to issue a book of the rules and ceremonies to be used throughout its lodges by that date.[37] This began by declaring grandly that the purpose of the order was to increase the present and future welfare of mankind (the language of the order, like its membership, was wholly concerned with men). It added that part of this design was to keep alive the memory of the ancient community of Druids, as the chief source of power among the aboriginal British and their exclusive repository of knowledge. It proposed to unite all members in 'one fraternal bond of philanthropy', to collect information concerning the ancient Druids, and to inculcate, into the present, the social and moral teachings that had distinguished them. Unlike its ancient counterparts, it intended to make its knowledge available to all, preserving only enough secrecy in its proceedings to bond its membership together. Members had to be at least twenty-one years of age, and pay an entrance fee of 9s. 6d. (modest enough to allow in prosperous working men, but stiff enough to deter the poor). The initiation ceremony was compulsory, and anybody who divulged the signs and passwords used to recognize members would be expelled, as would anybody who voiced political opinions at a meeting.

The pamphlet provided the standard form of the initiation ceremony used by that date. As the blindfolded candidate entered the darkened meeting room he was greeted by a song of welcome, performed by all the others present. Candles were then lit and the blindfold removed. After he made his declaration to obey the order's rules, the candidate was given another chorus, extolling its ideals, and his head was bound with fronds of an evergreen plant or tree. He was then shown the mistletoe, as the sacred plant of Druids, and told of 'Togodubiline', the ancient founder of the order. This character is unknown to history, and was apparently invented by cobbling together two genuine names of ancient British chieftains, those of Togodumnus and his father Cunobelinus (this name, significantly, being used not in its classical form, but in that much better known from Shakespeare, as Cymbeline). The new-made Druid was now treated to a short lecture on the purposes of the order – of the sort used by Freemasons – and a third chorus, praising the bonds of friendship (to the tune of the National Anthem). With that the rite concluded. The booklet also contained the words for regular songs to be used at lodge meetings, culminating in the 'Finale Chorus' that closed each one, extolling drinking and music as the focal points of friendship. Sheets of the music to which each song was set were distributed to all lodges together with the pamphlet. Wilhelm North, in 1932, recorded details of the secret sign and password used in the early days of the Ancient Order, from a source now lost or not available to non-members. The sign was to seem to stroke a beard, twirl a hat around the head, and lay a finger against the lips; North recognized that these had been taken wholesale from another secret society, the Ancient and Honourable Society of Bucks, established in 1722. North did not provide the original password, but noted that it represented a uniting of names from two different ancient texts: which was, of course, how that of the mythical founder was formed, and, indeed, 'Togodubiline' probably was the word concerned.[38]

Visual evidence of the physical surroundings and trappings of the Ancient Order's meetings is provided by illustrations printed in its magazine in 1832.[39] One showed the Treasurer of Grand Lodge, enthroned with his insignia of office. The chair, which was presumably typical of those made for officers of the lodge by that time, is heavy, of carved wood, and has a wreath of oak leaves placed or incised on one side of its front. The confident-looking man upon it wears the brass-buttoned frock coat and linen stock of a prosperous member of the middle class of his time. Around his neck hangs a broad collar of satin or velvet, hung with three large brass ornaments, and a medal is suspended from a chain above it. The other picture is a sketch of a ceremony in the same lodge on 1 March of that year, set within a large hall decorated with hangings and greenery. Most of the members are grouped around tables on either side, with glasses in their hands, watching a procession of officers, clad in white robes, making its way towards the dais at the far end. A third picture of the order in action at this time is furnished by a coloured drawing of its Salisbury lodge, parading through that city to demonstrate in favour of reform of the system of parliamentary elections. The date is 27 June 1832, and they wear a variety of costumes and carry an assortment of objects. Some are in smart contemporary dress of frock coats and breeches, wearing collars and carrying staves with sickles on the end. Others are in full fancy dress as ancient Druids, with the same collars of the order but also wearing white robes and head-dresses and fake white beards; the standard image of the Druid ultimately derived from Conrad Celtis's statues. It is not clear whether these were made up for the occasion, or were actual ritual dress now used at the order's ceremonies. Nor is it certain what boys are doing in the procession, in modern dress with sashes tied about their torsos, carrying symbolic objects on cushions. One is an open book, another a human skull. The former is probably the Bible, and the latter a reminder of human mortality, but this is not made explicit.[40]

By the early 1830s, therefore, the Ancient Order of Druids had become one of the great voluntary organizations of the nation, characterized by remarkable vitality and self-confidence, and a clear potential for continued dramatic expansion. It contained within itself, however, a growing number of tensions and conflicts, which were to produce an intense crisis, and they revolved around two of the key components of its stated ideals: fraternity and philanthropy. The order might well be fraternal, with its emphasis on good-natured socializing and a common purpose and voice, summed up in the bonding of members in musical choruses. Brotherhood, however, did not imply equality. Within each individual lodge, the judgement of the presiding Archdruid was ultimately final. Above the level of the individual lodge came provincial Grand Lodges, which had the power to suppress any groups within their jurisdiction. Most important, the whole order was still, ultimately, ruled by Lodge No. 1 that had founded it, and to which Hurle had belonged. This had become known as the Grand Lodge of the whole order, imitating (again) the name of the body that ultimately governed English Freemasonry; and very grand it had become. The admission fee it charged was greater than that of any other lodge. In addition it levied regular financial dues on each lodge in the order, to be spent on its own needs, and had ultimate power to make policy and regulations for the order in general. Its endorsement was needed for the decisions of any provincial Grand Lodge to become effective. It had become steadily more opulent and imposing: a veteran member recalled in 1833 how, over the previous quarter of a century, he had seen it grow 'from the humblest meeting to the most splendid society in London'.[41] To complete these circles of hierarchy, in 1810 lodges had been given the power to create a formal inner ring within each, a Royal Arch Chapter, for wealthier and more genteel members who wished to widen the social distance between themselves and their social inferiors. Membership of this could only be conferred by those already in it. By the time the regulations were codified and published in the 1820s, only eight lodges had adopted this stratagem, but they were naturally among the richest and most important, and included the Grand Lodge itself.[42]

In adopting this mode of government, the order was entirely consistent with the spirit of Georgian England, which depended on the rule of elites, usually choosing and perpetuating their own membership, at all geographical, social and political levels. After all, the Freemasons, which had supplied the basic model for the Ancient Order, had achieved tremendous success by operating just such a system. The Georgian age was, however, coming to an end, and challenges were being mounted to the traditional oligarchies in one sphere of operation after another. The years 1829–34 saw the transformation of the British political system, with old restrictions on the membership of both Parliament and the town councils being removed and a standard set of qualifications for voters, and criteria for constituencies, imposed. It can be no coincidence that it was precisely in this period that the Ancient Order was torn apart by revolt. The issue that triggered the convulsion was embedded in the second of its professed aims: that of philanthropy.

As far as the more conservative members were concerned, it entirely fulfilled this aim, by fostering brotherly love – which is what the word means, in Greek – through sociability and conviviality. Even at this period, however, the term was acquiring an additional connotation, which has since become paramount: the giving of charity. This had hitherto, at no time, been the main purpose of the order; had it been so, then the mid-1790s would have been a far less traumatic period. Mutual charity was, however, the principal aim of a particularly successful and popular form of voluntary organization that had burgeoned during the eighteenth century: the friendly society, or benefit club.[43] This was established to pool and administer regular contributions from members, constructing a fund from which payments could be made to those unlucky enough to fall into poverty because of illness, unemployment or other accidents. It would also ensure them a proper burial when they died. In other words, such a society provided a consolidated insurance scheme for those within it. This essential function was combined with the socializing associated with most clubs, at regular meetings held at inns and taverns. Sometimes rituals, especially on initiation, and regalia, were added, and most had books of rules. Friendly societies became the only sort of voluntary association to achieve a major presence in rural as well as urban and industrial communities. By 1800 official figures, which must be underestimates as they depended on the willingness of such groups to report themselves for registration, suggest that about 40 per cent of the working population of London belonged to one, while in the Lancashire cotton-manufacturing town of Oldham, half of the adult male inhabitants did. Nottingham contained fifty-one such organizations, and it has been estimated that there were about 7,200 of them in England by 1801. They were mostly made up of artisans, but many included smallholders and labourers and some were middle class and run by gentry and members of professions. By the start of the nineteenth century, they had become the most important single means by which working people avoided becoming paupers. In the era of the Industrial Revolution, with its economically unstable and often physically dangerous new means of occupation, and its shattering of traditional supportive structures of kin and community, such a means had become particularly necessary.

Benefit clubs and friendly societies therefore had an obvious amount in common with the Ancient Order. Much of it was based on practical necessity. Inns and taverns were the obvious places to meet, because houses were generally too small, village halls did not exist, churches and chapels could not normally be used for profane purposes (and cut against the non-denominational nature of most voluntary organizations), and barns were generally uncomfortable, and dangerous to heat, and represented the exclusive property of one member. Publicans, by contrast, generally had accommodation of just the right kind, could provide refreshments, and generally welcomed the custom. Ritual, especially on initiation, communicated the meanings of membership, added colourful experiences to an often humdrum daily life, and created a collective identity in the group that was powerfully reinforced by their secretive and exclusive nature. It strengthened sentiments of sociability, and (frequently) of masculinity. A further similarity between friendly societies and the Ancient Order was added during the first three decades of the nineteenth century, with the appearance of national associations dedicated to mutual aid, divided into local lodges, on the model of the order (and, beyond it, of the Freemasons). The first and most famous were the Oddfellows, the Foresters and the Shepherds. All that distinguished the Druids from these, functionally, was that aid to distressed members was an optional and informal part of the Ancient Order's activities; but it was a significant distinction.

Although friendly societies were ubiquitous by 1800, their greatest strength was – for obvious reasons – in the expanding areas of new industry, in the Midlands and North of England. Lancashire, probably the most intensively industrialized of English counties at this time, had more members than any other, and it was the birthplace of the Oddfellows, the first of the nationwide, affiliated societies divided into lodges. It was in precisely these industrial areas that the Ancient Order of Druids underwent its main expansion in the 1820s, with accelerating success. Primarily – but by no means exclusively – from them now emanated growing demands that the order add the functions of a friendly society to those it already had. In theory, anybody could belong to such a society as well as the order. In practice, to do so would stretch both funds and time in a way uncomfortable for many workers, and so an increasing number of Ancient Order Druids thought that policy should change to meet their needs. In 1821 the Grand Lodge attempted to head off the problem by allowing individual lodges to use funds as they wished.[44] This, however, made more obvious the issue of the payments to the Grand Lodge itself, which were not generally applied to charity, and created a situation in which the poorer lodges, which were least able to meet the cost of providing insurance for their members, were precisely those in which the need for payments would be greatest.

The resulting crisis still took the order by surprise, and is chronicled, as it unfolded, in the pages of the order's magazine,[45] which commenced publication in 1831 and was itself a sign of the increasing confidence and sophistication of the whole society. In the first issue that survives, from 1832, the editor, Charles Letts (himself a Londoner, from the Aldersgate lodge) was still, for the most part, celebrating and honouring the order's achievements and praising the strength and opulence of the Grand Lodge as a symbol of the success of all. He did, however, comment that in an earlier issue he had taken up the cause of establishing a general 'fund for the relief of decayed Druids'. He added, bluntly, that the outside world viewed the order as 'a mere convivial body without any redeeming touches of utility'. He went on to note that the Grand Lodge had not supported the proposal for such a fund, but that junior lodges did, and invited the latter to petition the former for the institution of one. In the next surviving issue of the magazine, in 1833, Letts recorded that not only had such a request been made, but that over seventy of the lodges in Lancashire and Cheshire had added a demand that the Grand Lodge halve the fees that it required from the others, account for how it spent the money received, and call an assembly of delegates from the whole order to revise its laws. Control of the order was currently vested in a ruling body appointed by the Grand Lodge, termed a Council of Direction, and this now replied briskly to both proposals. It went some way to accommodating the first, by sanctioning the establishment of a general hardship fund; but it proposed to control this itself, even while the junior lodges supplied almost all the money. The demand from Lancashire and Cheshire was rejected completely. This answer precipitated a revolt. Some lodges combined to elect a United Provisional Committee to frame a new constitution for the order, by which its government would be vested in a national body consisting of every member who had served as Archdruid of a lodge. The response of the Council of Direction was to denounce the rebels and threaten their expulsion from the order, an action which provoked horror, and drew protests, from many other lodges.

On 30 July 1833 the Grand Lodge decided to appoint a sub-committee to find ways of allaying 'the excited feelings of the order', but this had still not reported by the end of the year: and before then, its task had become impossible. The Grand Lodge met repeatedly through the autumn to discuss short-term responses, and, although some within it called for conciliation and temperance, the reactionaries prevailed. On 7 October it voted to expel two of the rebel lodges, as an example to the others. In response, fifty lodges sent delegates to a meeting in London that opened on 16 December and was commissioned to revise the regulations by which the order was governed. Attempts were made there to reunite it, but all failed, and, at 2.30 on the morning of the 20th, the meeting resolved by sixty votes against seven to uphold the cause of the rebels, and secede from the order. In the words of Charles Letts, who was present and supported the resolution, 'it is scarcely possible to imagine the tumult created'. More than a hundred lodges – about half the total strength of the order – joined the secession, to form a United Ancient Order of Druids. Letts published his parting shot to his former comrades in the Ancient Order by declaring that those who left with him had 'passed from revelry to charity'.

The United Order was certainly a tremendous success. Thirteen years after its formation it had trebled its number of lodges, to 330 in England and Wales, with more overseas. Its main strength remained in the industrial North and Midlands, above all in Yorkshire, but its membership stretched from Cumberland to Kent, with three groups in south Wales. Its stated aims were 'social and intellectual intercourse' and 'general philanthropy and benevolence', and it was run by an elected Board of Directors.[46] Details of what life was like in its lodges are provided by the records created by the one that met at the Union Inn, in the market town and river port of Bewdley, lying on the banks of the Severn in Worcestershire.[47] They date from its foundation in 1843. The expressed aims of the order were now 'to promote friendship and Christian charity', and many of its rules were designed to protect its viability as a friendly society. Each prospective member had to be proposed by no fewer than two existing members, and had to be sound in mind and body; the lodge retained a surgeon to examine candidates if these conditions seemed to be in doubt. He had to be at least eighteen and at most forty years of age, and could not be in a physically dangerous occupation such as the armed forces or the police. The two people proposing him had to put up the sum of 2s. 6d. to do so, and he himself had to pay an initiation charge, according to his age, ranging from 15s. to £2 5s. The existing company was expected to vote to accept or reject him. Every person attending a lodge meeting had to pay 2s. each time, and to remain in the lodge a member had to attend at least five times per year, and to pay 2s. for each of the other meetings that he missed. Part of the fund thus accumulated was used for the lodge regalia, and for a fixed amount of beer at each gathering, but most went to provide sick pay and the expenses of funerals. Drunkards were expelled, both to keep the meetings decent and to remove another health risk from the membership.

The Union Lodge records give a good idea of what the meetings were like. They were held once a month, between seven and ten o'clock in the evening. The five that were compulsory were on four traditional quarter days that fell in the midst of each season and on which rents and wages were paid – Lady Day, Midsummer Day, Michaelmas Day and Christmas Day – and upon an annual feast day. The feast day would be marked by a formal procession if a majority of members wanted one. On the first lodge night after Lady Day each year (which would normally fall in April), members would elect or re-elect a board of officers. This was led by an Archdruid, who would preside over meetings and keep order. Forbidden behaviour included swearing, the singing of songs that were 'indecent', political or religious in nature, the interrupting of another member when he was addressing the company, and the leaving of the lodge room while a song or debate was in progress. The Archdruid was supported by a Vice-Arch, and accompanied by a Secretary to keep records, a Guardian to set up the room for meetings and keep an eye on the door to exclude strangers, two Bards (perhaps to lead the musical performances), and two 'Supporters' to aid the other officers. Everybody who entered the lodge room for a meeting had to give the secret sign of the order to the Archdruid before taking his seat. At the time when it was founded, the lodge had eleven members.

The creation of the United Ancient Order proved to be equally beneficial to the Ancient Order itself.[48] Purged of the tensions that had built up inside its original structure, it was able to embark immediately upon a fresh phase of expansion. Ten years after the traumatic events of 1833, it had already rebuilt its strength to a total of 381 lodges, almost double the number that it had achieved on the eve of the great secession. They occupied an even wider geographical area than those of the 1820s, and had once again achieved an especially dense concentration in the new industrial regions. Part of this success lay in the ability of the leadership to react swiftly and creatively to the order's massive losses. It did so by implementing many of the constitutional demands of the departing rebels, while rejecting their wish for a change in function. A grand committee of all past and present lodge chairmen met in 1834 to revise the regulations of the order, and its proposals were then approved by a majority of members. The Grand Lodge was left in charge of the order, recognizing all new lodges, composing its ceremonies, enforcing its laws and adding by-laws as it saw fit. It was itself now governed, however, by a committee made up of ten members from the Grand Lodge itself, balanced by ten former Archdruids of provincial lodges and led by three members elected from the ranks of both. Four of these were to retire each quarter and be replaced by freshly elected men. The Grand Lodge was still to receive annual payments from all the others, but had to send out accounts of how it spent the money. Any lodge could make subsidiary rules for itself, and turn itself into a miniature friendly society by establishing a charitable fund; though to do so involved a heavier annual tribute to the Grand Lodge. Furthermore, lodges in particular regions could form themselves into associations with a common store of money to bail out those that suffered a heavy run on their individual funds. The entrance fee was cut to 7s. The initiation ceremony was to remain uniform across the order, and taken from printed copies sent out by the Grand Lodge, but the passwords to lodges were to be changed every six months, to keep proceedings still more private. Every three years, lodges would send delegates to a national general meeting to discuss and review the order's affairs. It had achieved a balance of oligarchy and democracy typical of the Britain of the time.

Both halves of the former Ancient Order were therefore poised to make a significant contribution to Victorian culture; the more so in that by this time they were not alone among British voluntary societies in having adopted the identity of Druid. Since the 1820s a growing number of rivals and imitators had appeared; but this story, with that of the further enlargement of the family of groups descended from Hurle's people, must be held until the time comes to consider the relationships of the Victorians with Druids. For now, it is sufficient to attempt a final question: that of what these first British people to take the name of Druids perceived that name to represent. After all, by the late eighteenth century it had acquired not only high public visibility but a range of possible connotations. Was there a coherent vision in the Ancient Order, and later in the United Order as well, of what it meant to be a Druid; other, that is, than having a taste for music?

Four different sources go some way to providing an answer. One consists of the prefaces to the official handbooks published by the two orders and cited above. These conveyed a general belief that the ancient Druids had been possessed of certain admirable qualities, of which knowledge and impressive moral behaviour had been the most obvious. They were, however, extremely vague as to the nature of these virtues, and the earliest booklet issued by the Ancient Order, from the 1820s, also criticized the Druids for having failed to share their wisdom sufficiently with people at large. Furthermore, it admitted that there was a general lack of good information about them and declared the acquisition of more to be one of the purposes of the order, though it did not suggest how this might be achieved. The second source is also contained within those handbooks, and consists of the lists of lodges appended to them. It must be significant that the vast majority of these took their names simply from the pubs at which they met. Only a small minority – scattered across the nation – adopted some that had associations with the ancient world, and these covered the range that were familiar from the main literary works of the previous century: the oak tree, bards, sacred groves, altars, and the occasional patriotic hero such as Caractacus, who had been the most formidable opponent of the Roman invasion. This does not suggest that members in general thought very much, or hard, about their ancient role models.

The third source provides the views of those few in the order who did, and is made up of contributions to the magazine that was founded by Letts to serve the Ancient Order in 1831, and taken over by him to the United Ancient Order when it seceded.[49] Those on the 'original' Druids, by definition, represent the views of that relatively small number of members who were sufficiently interested in the subject to publish upon it. The most striking feature of these is their diversity. A few contributors clearly admired their ancient counterparts for their presumed learning, wisdom and charity, but more were equivocal, admitting at least the possibility that Druids had practised human sacrifice, and some were openly hostile and held that the modern order was much superior, like all Christian civilization, to pagan antiquity. The editor himself, at the moment of the great crisis of 1833, adopted the image of ancient Druidry presented since Holinshed: of just and wise leaders who became corrupted by bad religion and morality until they met a just end. He called on his fellows to 'copy their virtues and shun their vices'.[50]

The fourth source consists of a tract published by a member of the United Ancient Order who cared enough about the subject to deliver an address upon it to his local lodge and then to put it into print. He was a Yorkshire pub-owner, based in Bradford, and his publication appeared in 1835, when the breakaway order was still forming its own identity.[51] He had evidently read several of the scholarly books on Druids, and made reference through them to classical authors, whom he had not read himself and so sometimes misquoted. What emerged was an individual medley of the arguments of the books, taking a middle line. To him the Druids had practised a version of the true religion of the Old Testament patriarchs, which was corrupt, but not as severely so as most in the ancient world. They still believed in one supreme divinity, did not worship idols, and were great scientists and mechanics; these last qualities were given the prominence that one would expect from a working man living in one of the new industrial cities of the age.

Such a lack of any 'party line' regarding the ancient world, within the Ancient Order and United Ancient Order, testifies to the dynamism and freedom of opinion among their membership. It also, however, indicates a broader spectrum of opinion in British society. After all, these magazine entries, written by people who seem mostly to have been small merchants, tradesmen and artisans, provide a relatively rare glimpse into the opinions of people in the middle ranks of the early nineteenth-century British. They prove that, despite the huge elevation in the public profile of the Druids during the Georgian period, no greater consensus had been achieved on how they should be regarded, and imitated, since early Stuart times. This was, it seems, as true among the bulk of the population as it was among the intellectual elite.

5

IOLO MORGANWG

In 1772 the playwright Richard Cumberland produced a comedy of manners, *The Fashionable Lover*, which was acted at the Theatre Royal in Drury Lane and published as a text in the same year. It included a minor character called 'Dr Druid, the antiquarian'. There was nothing particularly Druidic about his interests, which covered the entire ancient world, and he was used to sending up the scholarly world of his time, as a pedantic buffoon. Nor was there anything remarkable about his name, given the fact that, by this date, Druids had come to stand, in the national imagination, for pretty well the whole of early Britain. What is noteworthy is just one feature of the character, obvious only when one reads his lines: Dr Druid is a Welshman.

Until now, as has been emphasized, there had been no special association between the Welsh in general and Druids. In their own cultural memory, and historiography, Welsh writers had found the Druids more or less superfluous, basing their own national identity on their medieval bards; and this had still been the situation at the end of the seventeenth century. Two major developments had occurred between then and the staging of Cumberland's play, which were to alter this situation permanently: Druids had suddenly become major figures to the British in general, and the Welsh bardic tradition had completely collapsed.[1] The Tudor Welsh scholars had still been proud of that tradition and eager to regard it as the vehicle for their nation's history and culture; and this was both understandable and apt, because it reached its pinnacle of achievement in the early sixteenth century. During the Elizabethan period, a decline set in, which led to an evaporation by the time of the later Stuarts. What had changed was the willingness of upper-class patrons to sponsor poetry of the accustomed sort. Around 1500 the typical poet composing in Welsh was a professional, serving a particular lord and belonging self-consciously to a body of high-ranking authors and performers who regarded themselves as the heirs of the celebrated bards of the early and high Middle Ages, such as Taliesin, Aneirin, Myrddin and Cynddelw. He would absorb his sense of this heroic past through oral teachings and the reading of manuscripts. He would meet with his fellows in assemblies known as *eisteddfodau*, at which they would compete for prizes in music and verse. By 1700 the typical Welsh poet was an amateur from humble stock, who composed in moments snatched from his regular work and had no connection with the gentry and aristocracy. The *eisteddfodau* were long gone, and the great medieval bards no more than names. Whether this development was a tragedy for Welsh culture is disputable: the new sort of poet had a wider audience and was much more free to choose between, and experiment with, forms of composition and sentiment. Furthermore, in the early eighteenth century, the *eisteddfod* was revived in a new and scaled-down form, as an informal gathering of local poets and grammarians to try out productions on each other in a tavern in a market town. The new poetic culture was, however, a far less effective and obvious vehicle for national history and collective tradition than the old.

The reasons for the change were complex. In large part they came down to the sheer success of the sixteenth-century Welsh in integrating themselves into a larger British superstate. They supplied that state with its royal family, the Tudors, some of its leading politicians, such as the Cecils (and, in the next century, the Cromwells), and its main political and religious myths, of King Arthur and the other early British kings, and of a native British Church, independent of the Roman one and more virtuous, which legitimized the Protestant one created at the Reformation. The problem with all this success was that it left the Welsh without much that was distinctively their own any longer. Between the mid-sixteenth and the mid-seventeenth centuries, the native upper classes began increasingly to take on the English language and the culture that went with it. This was not just to enable them to participate in, and profit from, the new superstate to best effect; it was also to enable them to conform to a more general new, Western European, norm of more sophisticated gentility. Court bards of the medieval kind had no place in that new world. As a result, by 1660 they had virtually disappeared, and their loss was as swift and complete in areas in which no English was spoken as in those in which it was making inroads.

Some limitation was imposed on the rupture in Welsh culture by the efforts of individual poets and scholars to record the surviving medieval material before it was forgotten. They wrote many manuscripts, but here another difficulty set in. The medieval and early Tudor poets had used a complex and abstruse system of imagery, symbolism and cross-reference, knowledge of which defined them as an elite and enabled them to keep outsiders at bay. That knowledge perished with the old bardic order, and by the late seventeenth century even people who keenly collected manuscripts of its work found that they could not understand them. They had lost the key to decipher many of the images and to identify many of the allusions in the poems and tales that had been preserved. In the early eighteenth century one scholar and translator of medieval Welsh, John Morgan of Matchin, wrote to a colleague that much of the traditional literature had become meaningless. By 1660, those who longed to preserve an older way of Welsh life still had a major remaining consolation. This was that an ancient and distinctive culture still existed at village level, among lesser landowners, smallholders, labourers and artisans. Over the following hundred years, however, this disappeared in turn, as the whole of Wales 'modernized'.

A reaction eventually set in against this process, designed to reconstruct a distinct Welsh nationalist culture, rooted in the past; and it began not in Wales itself but among Welsh people who had settled in London. There were three reasons for this. One was simply that the London Welsh commonly had more money than those who had remained at home, and so more resources to invest in cultural enterprises. The second was that they had more incentive to form themselves into clubs and societies to concert their efforts, as the metropolis was the original home of the new-style voluntary organizations, and brimming with them. The third, and perhaps the most important, was that exile in the British capital made Welsh people much more conscious of their identity as strangers and more inclined to be proud of it and seek respect from others. This is another manifestation of that phenomenon which was touched upon before when discussing Edward Lhuyd: the role of the outsider or borderer in fostering national identity. The first club that the London Welsh established was the Society of Ancient Britons, in 1715. This became in turn the inspiration for the Honourable Society of Cymmrodorion, founded in 1751. It was largely the creation of two brothers from Anglesey, Lewis and Richard Morris, and was designed to provide Welshmen in the city with a safe and friendly social space among their own kind, to aid those among them who had fallen on hard times, to promote the Welsh language, and – most important for our purposes – to study Welsh history and literature. It established a network of correspondence with scholars at home which aided the exchange of information and ideas, and encouraged the editing of old Welsh texts and publication of Welsh books. As such, it was attempting consciously to revive the system of cultural patronage that the native ruling class had long abandoned.

By 1770 many Welshmen in London thought that the Cymmrodorion were, in turn, becoming too hidebound and dominated by gentry. They founded a rival society, the Gwyneddigion, which was socially more humble, politically more radical, and even more directly concerned with the preservation and revival of traditional literature and music. It inspired still more societies with the same aims to appear in the capital over the next thirty years. It also sponsored the publication of a series of scholarly books, and a revival of the institution of the *eisteddfodau* on a larger scale and more traditional lines. In 1789 it provided prizes and publicity for competitions at Corwen and Bala, route centres in north Wales, which attracted poets and musicians from across the region. These were successful enough to turn the regional *eisteddfod* into a regular event in the northern half of the country. None of these efforts by London-based groups would have made much impact without the collaboration and encouragement of Welsh people who remained at home and shared the same enthusiasms. By 1790, the project of a national cultural revival, based partly on the retrieval and study of medieval texts, was well under way.

It was fairly clear that Druids could have a part to play in it. After all, the Welsh were the people in modern Britain who were descended most directly, in both blood and language, from the ancient inhabitants of the island who had included Druids. This not only meant that they could be most readily associated with them, but that there was a real possibility that their medieval literature, once properly collected, edited and analysed, might prove to contain traces of actual Druidical tradition. This was precisely what Henry Rowlands had suggested, back in 1723, and his book was put into a second, better and far more popular edition in 1766. In the course of the mid-eighteenth century Druidry and Welshness began, slowly and cautiously, to draw together. When, in 1751, Lewis Morris designed a coat of arms for the newly formed Honourable Society of Cymmrodorion, an 'ancient Druid' was one of the supporters. In case Morris needed any further encouragement in his interest in the subject, one of his personal friends was William Stukeley.[2] The most learned scholar in the network set up by the Morris brothers and the Cymmrodorion was Evan Evans. In 1764 he published the book which first began to reveal the treasures of medieval Welsh literary tradition to the British in general, *Some Specimens of the Poetry of the Antient Welsh Bards*. He reinforced the point made by Rowlands, that Druidic knowledge could be embodied in that tradition, but with particular respect to one body of verse: the mystical poems attributed to the very early Welsh bard Taliesin. Evans asserted that 'there is a great deal of the Druidical Cabbala intermixed in his works, especially about the transmigration of souls'.[3]

What he meant here was that in some of the Taliesin poems the author claimed to have passed through a series of previous shapes, animate and inanimate – such as a snake, a billhook, a spear, a stallion, a bull, a grain of wheat, a salmon, a dog, a stag, a spade, an axe, a pin and so forth – which could be read to represent previous lives, evidence of a doctrine of transmigration of the sort credited by Caesar to the Druids. His use of the word 'Caballa', however, deftly gave the problem with this interpretation away; for it already had its dual modern meanings of the great medieval system of arcane Hebrew cosmology, and of things that are hidden or difficult to understand. Evans was completely honest about this, calling the Taliesin poems 'very obscure', and earlier confessing that the best critics of medieval Welsh poetry hardly understood most of them.[4] The loss of the key to the bardic imagery, and of much of the oral tradition and associated bodies of literature on which it drew, meant that it was both very easy for a determined scholar to find apparent references to Druidic teaching in some of the surviving works, and virtually impossible to prove what they actually meant. This did nothing to stop Evans himself from appropriating Druids as ancestors of the Welsh in particular. In a long poem, *The Love of Our Country*, published in 1772, he hailed them as the first defenders of his nation (drawing of course on Tacitus's linkage of them with Anglesey) and the founders of Welsh poetry. He went on to assert that the medieval bards and early modern scholars of Wales had been their direct successors.[5] Three years later a guidebook to Anglesey was published, intended explicitly to build upon Rowlands's history. It stated as fact that medieval bardic verse contained Druid doctrines (of the immortality of the soul, and the existence of one god), and solved the problem of the identity of the black-clad women who had faced Suetonius's soldiers. To this author, they were simply the female natives of the island, who heroically preferred death to capture by the Roman enemy.[6] A powerful further sign of the increasing Welsh identification with Druids was the foundation of societies named after them, in Anglesey and Cardiganshire, as described earlier.

It counted for much that, not only were the Welsh becoming seriously interested in their ancestral relationship with Druids, but the English were themselves starting to set great store by the connection between Wales and Druidry. The significance of

Cumberland's play has already been noted. Thomas Carte's influential history of England, which appeared in 1747, drew attention to Henry Rowlands's suggestion that medieval Welsh poetry preserved Druidic teachings.[7] In 1783 an anonymous account of the great prehistoric monuments of Wiltshire was published at Salisbury. It relied heavily on Stukeley, as did most works on the subject by that time, but it also noted Rowlands's point, as of major potential importance.[8] In 1789 a novelist, Elizabeth Ryves, published a story about two English gentlemen, 'well known in the literary world', who earlier in that decade had taken a holiday in Wales 'to visit the villages in the neighbourhood of every place which is supposed to have been a seat of the Druids, and where they thought it probable the peasants might retain many traditions and customs which would throw light upon the imperfect account transmitted to us of their religious rites and ceremonies'.[9] This apparent fiction was clearly just an extension of what was already occurring in fact. In 1774 an English gentleman, Henry Penruddock Wyndham, made a tour of Wales. He returned with the comment that he had seen piles of stones in the countryside which he was certain had been made by shepherds clearing the fields for pastures, but which were now being identified to strangers as Druidic cairns. Two decades later, the great Wiltshire antiquarian Sir Richard Colt Hoare took a Welsh holiday and noted that any standing stones were by then being described, both by tourists and the locals who cannily pandered to their tastes, as monuments left by Druidic religion. This included some that had been set up only recently as posts against which cattle could scratch themselves.[10]

None the less, there was also some resistance to the idea that there was any special connection between Druids and Welsh, and anything praiseworthy in finding one. In 1786 William Warrington, chaplain to the Earl of Bessborough, wrote a patriotic history of Wales. He dismissed Druidry from it with the curt comment that it 'long established a boundless tyranny on the ruins of human reason'.[11] What was obviously needed, by this point, was an expert in medieval Welsh literature and bardic tradition capable either of supplying unequivocal evidence for a transmission of wisdom from Druids to bards, or else of showing firmly that there was no good evidence for such a transmission. The former result was, in the circumstances, clearly the more desirable one, and one person in particular now presented himself to deliver it. He is known to history by his bardic name of Iolo Morganwg.

* * *

There is still no full biography of Iolo in English, a fact which has limited both an appreciation of his own historical importance and an understanding of his impact on source material, amongst the British as a whole.[12] The research that made both of these things clear to readers of Welsh was published between the 1920s and 1950s by Griffith John Williams,[13] and there is a recent study of the man and his work in that language by Ceri Lewis.[14] For English-readers, until recently the best equivalent was a polished but short survey by Prys Morgan,[15] which could be supplemented by sections on Iolo in histories of eighteenth- and nineteenth-century Wales in general and of Glamorgan in particular. During the past few years, this situation has begun to be remedied by the team led by Geraint Jenkins at the Centre for Advanced Welsh and Celtic Studies of the University of Wales, which is producing both editions of

Iolo's own work and correspondence, and critical studies of his career, in English. A volume of essays that it published while this present book was being written represents the best overall consideration of the man and his relationships yet available.[16] One of the few areas that it did not cover, however, consisted of Iolo's attitudes to Druids and the system that he developed as a result of them.

Iolo was christened Edward Williams in 1747, having been born to a mother who loved literature and music and bewailed her status as the poor relation of local gentry, and who had been brought up by them and then turned loose to make her own way when she reached maturity. She married a stonemason, a literate and respectable man but one who represented a heavy fall from the social world that she had known as a girl. Young Edward was devoted to her, and she filled him with her enthusiasms, and her resentments. She also bequeathed to him her fragile health. He later described her as having been racked by asthma and consumption, as well as 'weak nerves'.[17] He certainly inherited the asthma, and by the early 1770s had taken to calming attacks with doses of laudanum, opium dissolved in alcohol. It was the period's standard painkiller and relaxant, and effective as such, but Williams rapidly became addicted to it for the rest of his life. It may, as Geraint Jenkins has argued, have affected his mind, making him prone to lose sight of the boundary between fact and fiction.[18]

Like so many patriots, he grew up in a borderland of the nation with which he was to identify passionately: Bro Morgannwg, the Vale of Glamorgan, a land of rolling little hills, set with woods, pastures and tilled fields, and villages gathered around medieval parish churches and manor houses on the English pattern. This was because it had been conquered by the Normans at the beginning of their thrust into Wales, and occupied by English and Flemish settlers. The latter had given their name to Williams's own village, Flemingston, which was one of the smallest in the district. Many of the native Welsh had survived the conquest, however, and more had come into the Vale later. Williams's first language was therefore English, and it remained so throughout his life, but he rapidly became a fluent speaker of Welsh too.[19] Owing to its marginal position, geographically and culturally, Glamorgan had never been prominent in Welsh culture. The princes who had led the resistance to Norman and English conquest had lived either further west or far to the north. There is no solid evidence to connect any of the great early bards with the region. By the end of the Middle Ages, the descendants of the conquering Norman lords had 'gone native' sufficiently to welcome and retain Welsh poets, but Glamorgan subsequently produced only one who could legitimately be regarded as a nationally famous figure: Lewis Morgannwg, who died in 1565.[20] By the time of his passing, the county had already been caught up in that general decline of the traditional bardic arts which was to affect the whole of Wales.

During the eighteenth century it also shared in the general revival of Welsh culture and its concurrent attempts to rediscover and preserve the national past. The local manifestation of this centred upon a group of poets and scholars living in the mountain country of Blaenau Morgannwg, those many valleys divided by hog-backed ridges that sweep down southward from the great peaks of the Brecon Beacons. It was then a poor country of rough grazing and woodland, making a contrast with the rich farmland of the Vale, but filled with mineral wealth that was just starting to be exploited by English ironmasters. Two of these upland literary men made a strong impression on the young Edward Williams: John Bradford, a weaver living in Betws Tir Iarll, and Edward Evan, a carpenter and glazier who preached in the noncon-formist chapel at Aberdare and held radical political as well as religious opinions. Closer to young Williams's home, at Coychurch, was Thomas Richards, a vicar who published a Welsh–English dictionary, and to the west at Neath lived Morgan Llewelyn, a schoolmaster and scholar of bardic literature. Both these men contributed further to his education, as did the brilliant local lexicographer John Walters, who taught him to read medieval Welsh.[21]

None, however, exceeded the influence of his mother, and her death in 1770 was the pivotal event of his youthful life.[22] It pushed him out into the world. In 1772 he published his first poems. The next year he left Wales, to spend four more years working at his trade in London and Kent. He himself was later to tell people that this was the direct result of a row with his father, over a job repairing the wall of a pasture. Edward had sat reading as usual while the other men went to the alehouse for lunch, and became so engrossed in his book that he failed to notice that pigs and poultry had got into the field from which the wall was designed to keep them out.[23] During this time in England, he met the leaders of the Welsh cultural revival who operated out of the capital, and whose strongholds were in the societies of the Cymmrodorion and Gwyneddigion. He was admitted to membership of the latter, a rare privilege for somebody from south Wales, as almost all the existing members (as the name of the club suggests) were from the north. His interest in his national past grew, and he copied manuscripts in the British Museum and the libraries of Oxford University. If he had not been aware of the burgeoning importance of Druids in the British consciousness, he was now, and he took care to visit Stonehenge and Avebury.[24] His reactions to the latter complex were an indication of things to come. He pronounced that they were certainly the remains of 'the grand seat of the Druids before the Roman invasion', so that Anglesey had simply been a refuge to which they had retired (thereby downgrading the claims for importance of north Wales, and of its people gathered in the Gwyneddigion). He confused many of the naturally occurring stones on the chalk hills above the Avebury temple with megaliths placed by humans, and so believed that he had discovered a great extension to the known monument. Finally, although he knew perfectly well that Stukeley had to be given the credit for bringing the whole set of structures to public attention and identifying them with the Druids, he tried to deny him as much as possible, rudely trying to score points off him for being wrong in details.[25]

When Edward made that visit, in 1777, he was already on his way home to Glamorgan, apparently with every intention of settling there. Four years later he got married, to a farmer's daughter called Margaret (Peggy) Roberts, who brought him a substantial dowry and lifelong love, aided by her lively, literate mind. She also even-tually gave him four children. What he could not provide in return was an income sufficient to support them all. By 1787 he had failed successively as a builder, a tradesman, a shopkeeper and a farmer, and spent time in a debtors' prison.[26] These misfortunes must have driven him to the opinion that a comfortable living could best be won by employing his three undoubted assets: his now considerable expertise in Welsh bardic literature; his own powerful literary ability; and his complete lack of scruple in deceiving and manipulating others. He had kept up a correspondence with leading members of the Gwyneddigion, and two of them became of crucial importance to his plan.

One was a man from the Myfyr valley of Denbighshire called Owen Jones, who took the nickname among his fellow Welshman (needed in a nation of relatively few personal and surnames) of Owain Myfyr. In the years in which Edward Williams had descended into penury, Myfyr's business in London, as a skinner and furrier, had thrived, and by the mid-1780s he had money to spare for his enthusiasms. The greatest of these was his native land itself – a compatriot described him as a 'red-hot Welshman' – and especially for its cultural heritage. His single portrait shows a bulky man, with a heavy, shrewd, resolute face and a determined mouth. He decided to revive, under the banner of the Gwyneddigion, a project of the London Welsh to edit and publish the masterpieces of medieval Welsh literature. The first in the intended succession of texts was the work of the fourteenth-century poet generally acknowledged as the finest in the whole of medieval Wales: Dafydd ap Gwilym.[27] As adviser for the task he chose another prominent member of the society who shared his passion for early Welsh poetry, a slim young man from Merionethshire with huge eyes and thin, petulant lips, who worked as a private tutor. He was called William Owen; because of his shyness, his nickname in London was William the Silent.[28] In 1788 Owen wrote to Edward Williams, asking for his help with the book.[29]

Both men were easy prey. Myfyr had already long thought Williams the best living scholar of the Welsh language and literature; Owen was by nature innocent, gullible and impressionable. When he received a sheaf of forged poems from Williams, represented as hitherto unknown works by Dafydd ap Gwilym, he incorporated them into the book as an appendix.[30] It was published in 1789 and made Williams's name among the metropolitan Welsh, whereupon he was ready for his next move. By this date the importance of the Welsh language and its literature, and its possible association with ancient Druidry, were becoming widely recognized by British people of letters as a whole. One of the settings in which it was discussed was the journal that provided the principal contemporary means for the exchange of scholarly information of all kinds, the *Gentleman's Magazine*. Its issues of June 1789 carried a long correspondence on the matter,[31] and Williams artfully built on this in a letter to the editor, written on 10 October.[32] It purported to be the work of a friend, sent on his behalf, which enabled him to praise himself with less restraint than a direct communication would have allowed. It portrayed him as 'a humble journeyman mason', sober, temperate, unworldly, reserved and bashful, with a vegetarian diet after the fashion of the ancient Pythagoreans. With this came the remarkable claim that only Glamorgan had retained the ancient customs of the bardic order which were once upheld all over Britain. These involved training by an existing bard, culminating in a series of examinations, followed by the initiation of a successful candidate into the mysteries of the order at a congress of bards assembled for the purpose. The letter asserted that only two men remained alive who had gone through that traditional process: Williams himself and Edward Evan of Aberdare, who could therefore reckon themselves the sole genuine descendants of the ancient bards. It was accompanied by some examples of his poetry, with an appeal to readers of the magazine to contribute money to publish an edition of it. Williams was attempting to accomplish two things in this manifesto. First, he was trying to present himself to the British as the Welsh equivalent of Scotland's Robert Burns: a simple poet of the people, living in an outlying region of the new British superstate and equipped with an innate talent strengthened by his closeness to nature and the simplicity of his life. Second, he was teasing the curiosity, and angling for the admiration, of his fellow Welsh, by declaring that the hitherto disregarded Glamorgan was actually the most important repository of traditional Welsh culture.

In 1791 he returned to London in a bid to follow up these aims in person, and remained there for four years, as one of the most active members of its Welsh literary colony. Hitherto, he had used the pen-name Iorwerth Gwilym (Edward Williams) in Glamorgan, and that of Iorwerth Morganwg (Glamorgan Edward) to the Gwyneddigion, which preferred territorial nicknames. Now he settled firmly upon a jollier, and less formal, abridgement of the second, to announce himself to the nation, and became 'Glamorgan Eddie': Iolo Morganwg.[33] His second period of residence in the capital coincided with one of excitement and dynamism among the Welsh there. Many of them had become committed, not merely to the promotion of their native culture, but to radical political reform in Britain as a whole, on the model just provided by the French Revolution. The Gwyneddigion, in particular, became committed to achieving that. In 1789, as the revolution in France began, Owain Myfyr wrote to a compatriot that 'freedom in land and Church is the aim of the Society, that is, that man shall be free in relation to his religion to follow his conscience . . . Freedom in the state means that man is subject to the laws of the kingdom but only those which are placed upon the best basis . . . that is his person and property are free . . . It is for these rights that the French are struggling at this moment, just as our ancestors have been doing for hundreds of years.'[34] These sentiments perfectly chimed with those of Iolo (as we may now call him), at least in many of his moods. As early as 1777, he had already written a poem which derided 'mad kings' and questioned the wisdom of fighting the French.[35]

As his political and religious views during these years have a direct bearing on his presentation of Druidry, it is necessary to take a closer look at them: and the material for this has been assembled and studied by Damian Walford Davies.[36] The letters that Iolo wrote from London between 1791 and 1795 frequently railed against the king and the established Church. In February 1795 he informed his wife that 'all systems of Church and Kingism [sic] are, as if with might and main, preaching Christianity out of this world'. At times he claimed to be descended from Oliver Cromwell, the principal leader of the only republic that Britain has known. His English friend Robert Southey later recalled that his favourite toast at this time had been to 'the three securities of liberty: All kings in hell; the door locked; the key lost'. He wrote a song to celebrate the acquittal of men charged with treason against the British monarchy in 1794, ridiculing 'spies and informers of state'. From the early part of that year onward, his papers were repeatedly being seized and examined by the authorities. His opposition to the war against France, which began in 1793, was based on two different and very powerful impulses: his sympathy, up to that point, for the revolutionary regime that was being attacked, and his loathing of war in general, which he regarded as a thing unnecessary in itself, and fostered by traditional monarchical regimes. At times, however, he emphasized that he was not hostile to forms of government as such. In June 1794 he wrote to a clergyman, 'I am no enemy to kings – and am a friend to every Church that retains some appearance of Christianity, and is not degenerated into the rank idolatry of Church-and-Kingism. I honour the minister (and not the less for his being termed priest) of every sect and party in religion who appears to have a true sense of piety . . . who never with parsonic shears fleeces the sheep of his fold . . . Let Churchism and Kingism be founded on their genuine and primeval principles of true religion, of piety towards God, benevolence and justice towards man, on the real rights of God and man, and I shall not much object to the models and externalities of either . . . I care not what title the Chief Magistrate may bear, whether it be King, Protector, President.' He added, however, that the present king and Church represented only 'tyranny and idolatry', and that he was willing to be martyred because of his opposition to them.

This reads like the reckless enthusiasm of a young man, drunk with the excitement of a cathartic moment of history; but Iolo was in his forties, and the beliefs he was expressing were in most respects embedded in him for life. The importance to them of his religious faith, in an essentialist form of Christianity which he believed to have been corrupted by the monarchies and established Churches of his day, must already be apparent. He was an admirer of the great revolutionary writer Tom Paine, but when Paine published an attack on Christianity itself, Iolo was appalled. Jesus mattered greatly to him, as his model of a social and religious reformer. In an undated note left among his manuscripts, he acclaimed Christ as the Prince of Peace, and lamented that the French – to whom he still wished success – had failed to follow Jesus's example and chosen instead the 'horribly sanguinary proceedings' of the reign of terror into which the revolution had degenerated by 1794. His understanding of Christian principles lay behind two other aspects of his ideology: his opposition to slavery and his vegetarianism, based on his tenderness towards animals.

This, then, was the physical and ideological context of Iolo Morganwg's revelation to the world of the ancient teachings of Druidry, which took place between 1792 and 1794. It took the form of two works of literature and an institution.

*   *   *

A historian interested primarily in Druids needs to ask three questions about Iolo's contribution to the subject: how his ideas developed, where they came from, and of what they consisted. The problem with the first is an almost complete lack of evidence. Iolo already claimed to be negotiating with a publisher for a book on the ancient history of Britain when he was working in Kent in the mid-1770s,[37] but nothing remains to indicate of what this work would have consisted. All that can be said with certainty is that his enduring system of ideas concerning ancient Druidry had been worked out, in all its essentials, by the time he returned to London. We know this, because he set about publishing a 'trailer' for it at once, and repeated his trick of using Owain Myfyr and William Owen as his dupes and stalking-horses.

Owen was working on the second volume in the series of publications of medieval Welsh poetry funded by Myfyr, consisting of the (alleged) work of the early medieval bard Llywarch Hen. This was the very body of poetry to which Rowlands had drawn attention, with the suggestion that Druidic ideas might be embedded in it. Iolo persuaded him, once more, to add a section of new material that he claimed to have discovered in Glamorgan. This time it was placed in the introduction, and appeared with the book in 1792.[38] It consisted of an account of the ancient bardic tradition of Britain of which Llywarch had once been a member. Iolo began by telling his readers that the foundation of that tradition had been a commitment to peace and goodwill, symbolized by the sky-blue robes, emblem of peace and truth, that bards wore as a sign of their rank (or, rather, Bards, for to Iolo these were not just any traditional poets and musicians but holders of a formal office in an institution). Their motto, which was also blazoned on the title-page of the book, was 'Y Gwir Yn Erbyn Y Byd', 'The Truth Against The World'. Iolo effectively took this as his own; as has often been noted, it was one of the many paradoxes of a man who built his own career on deceit. He went on to explain that a formal meeting of Bards was called a *gorsedd*, a Welsh term normally used to mean a mound or hillock. The early medieval laws of Hywel Dda, however, had extended it to signify a court or tribunal held in the open air, and this is the sense in which Iolo adopted it.[39] These meetings, he insisted, had always been held in the open air, in full view of the public, in a space defined by a circle of stones, with a larger one in the centre on which the presiding Bard would stand. Here he was crossing the authentic medieval Welsh tradition of bardic assemblies with the belief, made common by Stukeley, that Druids had met and worshipped in stone circles.

Iolo now expounded the doctrine of his medieval Bards, which he claimed to have been derived from that of the Druids, which in turn (as writers had now long argued) had been that of the patriarchs of the Old Testament. That derivation made it easy, he asserted, for Druids to accept Christianity when it arrived on their shores. It was based firmly on a belief in one god, the creator and ruler of the world. He had given living beings immortal souls, which migrated into new bodies when the existing bodies died. Human beings had been granted the free will to choose good or evil lives. If they preferred the latter, they were reborn as animals, and spent a while in that shape until given a chance to return to a human one in a subsequent life. Well-behaved humans would be reborn into the bodies of people who would grow into even better people, and the best would be removed from the mortal world altogether, into heaven. Well-educated people of Iolo's time would recognize the similarity between this theology and Hindu concepts of reincarnation, which were just starting to make an impact on British society.[40] He took care to camouflage the fact by declaring that, as the Hindus had also derived some of their ideas from the original religion of the patriarchs, the similarity was natural. What he had effectively done was to combine Christian and Hindu ideas to create a doctrine which made sense of Caesar's statement that Druids taught that souls were reborn in new bodies. He added that the human sacrifices carried out by the Druids had actually been executions of condemned criminals, and their religious aspect had been due to the need to appease a just god angered by the deeds of the people being put to death.

Iolo then went on to describe the divisions of the Bardic order, which consisted of the Bardd Braint (the true Bard), the Derwydd (Druid), the Ovydd (Ovate) and the Awenyddion. The last were disciples, being trained to take their place in one of the three other classes of Bard, and wore robes patched with blue, white and green. The Bardd Braint was dedicated to the performing arts and wore the blue robe described earlier. Druids were Bards who had become priests, or, after the coming of Christianity, ministers: here Iolo took care to emphasize again (following Stukeley) that 'the British patriarchal religion is no more than that of Noah, or Abraham, inimical to Christianity'.[41] According to Iolo, Druids were not superior to 'pure' Bards, but were Bards who had chosen to specialize in religion, and the instruction of youth; they wore white robes, as an emblem of sanctity, and tended to serve certain districts instead of roving as the Bardd Braint would do. The office of Ovydd was an honorary one, awarded to people who had distinguished themselves in science or literature, and a holder wore green, as a symbol of learning. This system was evidently Iolo's own, based on the famous description of the ranks of the ancient Gallic cultural elite by Strabo, filtered through the now well-known book by Henry Rowlands. Rowlands had noted that, of Strabo's three groups, bards were prominently found in medieval Welsh literature and Druids were occasionally mentioned in it (if *derwydd* actually meant Druid), but there seemed to be no equivalent to *vates*. Rowlands thought he had found one, in the term *Ovydd*. This was, in fact, the medieval Welsh version of the name of the Roman poet Ovid, and Iolo now copied Rowlands's mistake (of course, without any attribution to him) and incorporated it into the model of the bardic order that he was now designing.[42] The fact that Rowlands related the name *Ovydd* to *vates* was itself a misreading of Strabo's Greek, which put an 'o' to guide pronunciation in front of the word *vates*, as described in the first chapter of this book. So a spelling error joined with a textual misunderstanding gave Iolo the final division of his bardic system. The real significance, and value, of that system was that at last it fully integrated the ancient Druids with the medieval bards, and so linked Druidry firmly to the Welsh national tradition.

He now described the meetings of the ancient and medieval bards. The rules he revealed held that three Bards were needed to initiate a new one, except in an emergency, when a single one could create two others. This was clearly handy for Iolo, as he claimed to be the only genuine Bard still active. He explained that the great bardic assemblies had been held at the solstices and equinoxes, with lesser conventions, mostly for the instruction of disciples, possible at the new and full moons and the quarter days that commenced the seasons (the first day of November, February, May and August). At these meetings the Bards would stand bareheaded and barefoot, wearing their robes. Each meeting began with the unsheathing of a sword on the larger stone at the centre of the stone circle, which all Bards present then assisted to sheathe, as a sign of their commitment to peace. There had been provincial meetings for each of the great traditional kingdoms of Wales – Gwynedd, Powys, Dyfed and

Morganwg – in addition to the national assembly of the Bards of Britain. Bards guilty of criminal acts were removed or suspended from membership at these gatherings, the sword being raised against them as they were named three times.

The moral precepts of Iolo's bardic order declared that all men were inherently equal, though 'differently stationed in the state of humanity for the common good'. For any man to assume a natural superiority to another was to commit a great evil, 'and his soul will pass into the meanest worm'.[43] He went on to insist that in Britain Christianity had been led exclusively by the bardic order until the Catholic Church broke into it during the fifth century. Gradually, most of the bards of Wales accommodated themselves to the Catholic system, and in doing so forfeited their right to belong to the true order. Those who remained loyal to it were few, and were persecuted with especial venom by the English conqueror Edward I (here Iolo harnessed his claims to Gray's famous poem, *The Bard*). The last of them had remained in Glamorgan, and Iolo repeated his claim that he and his friend Edward Evan were the only two proper initiates left. He concluded this long introduction with examples of the teachings of the ancient and medieval bards, which summed up the attitudes that he had already explained and were embodied in triads. These were a medieval form of Welsh verse, used by the genuine bards, which gathered three things that had common characteristics. Lewis Morris had already drawn attention to their importance as a source for Welsh history. Rachel Bromwich, the main modern expert on them, estimated that two-thirds of those that Iolo published during his lifetime consisted of real medieval verses to which he had made significant additions. The remaining third were entirely composed by him.[44]

He was not so much describing a system that had existed in the past, as unveiling one that he intended to create in the present. It represented both his ideal for a bardic society (and indeed for society as a whole) and his ambition to set up institutions that would channel, preserve and reinforce the contemporary Welsh cultural revival. As soon as he arrived in London in 1791, he issued a proclamation in archaic Welsh, inviting all in the city who wished to become a Bard of the Isle of Britain to come to Primrose Hill, a few miles to the north, at nine o'clock on the longest day of the following year.[45] In his introduction to Owen's edition of the poems of Llywarch Hen, he informed readers that a 'revived' *gorsedd* of Bards had already taken place, in Wales at the vernal equinox of 1792. It had done so on Plynlimon, the highest mountain of central Wales, and consisted of Iolo himself and two others: thereby creating the three Bards who, according to his rules, could initiate more.[46] No account seems to survive of the gathering on Primrose Hill at the summer solstice of 1792.[47] By contrast, the meeting on the hill at the next cardinal point of the sun, the autumn equinox, was made the subject of a publicity campaign, with descriptions of it being sent to at least three different journals and newspapers.[48]

A stone circle was formed, exactly as described in Iolo's introduction to Owen's edition of Llywarch Hen, and a sword unsheathed and sheathed as was directed there. The Bards presiding were notable members of the London Welsh community: Iolo himself, Owen, Edward Jones, harper to the Prince of Wales, and David Samwell, a dark-haired, pockmarked, belligerent and lusty naval surgeon who had made his name by sailing the Pacific with Captain Cook. All the others held the rank of Ovate, only Iolo himself claiming that of Druid. The traditions of the Bards were recited (presumably by Iolo), and odes performed – in English – by Samwell on the rules of the bardic order and by Iolo on its 'ancient' mythology. Readers of the journals and newspapers concerned were informed that, if they were interested in Druidry, 'any regular Welsh Bard can in a few minutes give them a much better account of it than all the books in the world; and at the same time the most convincing proofs, that it is now exactly the same that it was two thousand years ago'. The emphasis on peace, made by the sheathing of the sword, carried an especially heavy political message at a time when Britain was drifting towards war with the revolutionary French republic. Lest anybody miss the radical credentials of the group, one published account ended with the announcement that at the next meeting, on the winter solstice, an ode would be read upon an ancient British chief called Rhitta Gawr. He, readers were informed, had been notable for making himself a robe out of the beards of tyrants. Iolo added an extract from a poem of his own, calling for the return of liberty to Britain. Later sources added the details – which cannot be verified – that the meeting had been watched by many curious spectators, and that among the initiations of Ovates made at it were two of women, Owen's wife Sarah Elizabeth and the writer Anna Seward. If this was true, Iolo's bardic society was not only radical in religion and politics, but had a feminist aspect as well.[49]

Iolo's Bards, Ovates and Druids met again on Primrose Hill at the winter solstice, now decked out in the colours of their different grades, with William Owen presiding. Iolo gave an address on the ancient bardic order, and poems were recited as before, but a new note was struck by Edward Jones, who led the company in a patriotic song, declaring loyalty to king and country, to the tune of the national anthem. It concluded:

Blessed is our happy land
Let us, a faithful band
Together cling;
Bold in the glorious cause,
George and Britannia's laws,
Shouting with loud applause,
God save the King.

This was clearly, and must have been deliberately, at variance with the tone of truculent radicalism expressed by Iolo. There were further signs of growing tension among the company, in that the business of that winter meeting concluded with the suspension of one Bard from the *gorsedd* and the degrading of another in rank, for unstated offences.[50] It is not certain how many more gatherings were convened by Iolo on Primrose Hill, or anywhere else around London.[51] The strains already apparent in the core group of the *gorsedd* split it open the following year, as both Edward Jones and David Samwell supported the government line, of war against the French revolutionaries, to which Iolo was opposed. By November 1792 relations had already deteriorated to the extent that Iolo and other Bards issued a challenge to Jones to meet them on the day of the next new moon, in the fields behind the British Museum. There he was to prove his continued fitness to be one of them.[52] No record survives of what, if anything, happened on this occasion. The clear achievement of Iolo during his remaining period in London consisted of the publication of his first book, *Poems, Lyric and Pastoral, in Two Volumes*, in 1794. He had been working towards it for almost thirty years, and it was the main objective, and labour, of his second stay in London. The process was, in the words of its historian, Mary-Ann Constantine, 'a nightmarish tangle of practical, financial and emotional difficulties'.[53] It also, however, rounded off the first, and crucial, stage in his reinvention of Druidry.

The book was really a composite of two very different works. One was what was promised in the title, a collection of poems that he claimed, correctly, to have written himself, and that was intended to stake his claim to be the Welsh equivalent of Burns. The other was a further account of the ancient bardic and Druidic tradition, as Iolo had now further developed it.[54] He now identified his source for the tradition as a manuscript written by Llywelyn Sion in about 1560. This was a characteristically shrewd trick, because Llywelyn Sion had been a genuine figure from that period, a landed gentleman seated in the Vale of Glamorgan who was a copyist of medieval texts and about whom little was known.[55] Like a good historian, Iolo next conceded that it might be objected that such a late document might not accurately preserve earlier tradition. To reassure readers, he referred them to the medieval poetry associated with Taliesin. Passages in this, he asserted, matched the beliefs that were set down in extended form in the sixteenth-century manuscript. What Iolo was in fact doing was placing a particular interpretation on some of the enigmatic allusions in the poems and then working it up in a new document to conform with the system of Druidry that he was concocting.

Once more he emphasized both his own attachment to Christianity and the natural harmony between the latter and ancient Druidry. He declared himself 'the friend of peace, benevolence, liberty, and the transcendently lovely Christian religion'.[56] This time he illustrated the way in which pagan Druidry had developed into a native British Christianity. In his model, the pagan Druids had believed that the souls of evil human beings passed on their deaths into the bodies of animals. His Christian Bards believed that souls passed through different levels, or circles, of existence, Christ having opened the way to the highest one for them. Iolo now named the lowest of these circles, as Annwn, well known in medieval bardic literature as an otherworld or (later) an underworld, peopled by non-human beings whom poets equated with fairies or demons. This he turned into a primeval level of creation, in which all animate beings originated. He then restated, and elaborated, his vision of a possible progress of souls from ferocious animals to gentler creatures, and so to better and better human beings.

All this he presented as the gift of the single all-powerful god. In humanity, he explained, good and evil were equally balanced, and people had the free will to choose between them. On the levels of existence above the human one, good predominated, increasingly, until eternal happiness was reached. On the first one above the human world, it became possible to remember past lives. Those people who deliberately sacrificed happiness in the mortal world for the good of others were promoted to the highest plane – Iolo's equivalent of heaven – as soon as they died. The souls of animals offered as sacrifices by the Druids were reborn more swiftly in human bodies, as a reward, or compensation. In this system, fortitude was the greatest virtue and pride the greatest vice. What Iolo had done, under the name of ancient Druidry, was to design a theology that rewarded virtue and punished vice in the Christian manner, and likewise depended on a single all-knowing and all-powerful creator god. At the same time it scrapped eternal damnation, getting round the problem of how a good deity could be other than benevolent to his creations. Iolo stressed again that this system had been combined with Christianity to produce the ancient British Church, led by converted Druids as its ministers. Even more than before, he turned Roman Catholicism into the villain of his story, accusing it of having introduced both a fiercer theology and a hierarchy of clergy: 'the old Welsh Bards kept up a perpetual war with the Church of Rome, and from it experienced much persecution'.[57] His implication was that all established Churches had absorbed the errors of Rome, and that true Christianity lay in a simpler and more egalitarian system, of the sort propounded by the more radical Protestant sects that had appeared in Britain since the seventeenth century. In his self-promoting letter to the *Gentleman's Magazine* in 1789, he had described himself as 'inclined to Quakerism'. In case readers missed the point, he declared in the preface to his collection of poems that 'there is too much priestcraft in every sect'.[58]

Iolo was clearly aware that his version of Druidry had to be corroborated by less equivocal sources than ambiguous passages in the Taliesin poems. He therefore appended a large new selection of triads embodying the teachings that he had just laid out. These he claimed to have found in a second manuscript from the collection of the useful Llywelyn Sion, and this time he specified where he had located it: in the possession of his friend Richard Bradford back in Glamorgan. Bradford was in no position to contradict this, having died almost ten years before,[59] and of course no such document was ever found; but the specific nature of the reference was impressive. The verses that he now published, and which he presented as a selection of those in the manuscript, confirmed his exposition of the Druidic teachings in every respect. They often had the glitter of epigrams. Thus, the three triumphs of the bardic order were learning, reason and peace. Its three duties were secrecy, invective against the unjust, and war against the lawless. The three unities of the cosmos were 'God, truth and liberty', and the three things that proceeded from them were 'life, goodness and power.' The three that caused humans to fall back to Annwn, and the need to be recreated from scratch, were pride, falsehood and cruelty. There was not much here that most Christians would find other than admirable, and nothing that would not be applauded by Christians of a radical hue. Having thus whetted the appetite of his readers, Iolo put out an advertising pitch: if enough people were prepared to fund the venture, he would rapidly publish all the triads he had discovered which embodied the ancient Druidic wisdom, both in the original early Welsh and in translation.[60]

It seems that this offer failed to attract sufficient response to launch such an enterprise. More important, though the collection of poems got generally favourable reviews,[61] it did not sell well enough to give Iolo a means of subsistence and did not attract further commissions. Reading the two volumes it is easy to suggest some reasons for this failure. Iolo had suffered bitter disappointments and delays in the course of getting the work published, and he could not resist venting his feelings in the preface. He took care to thank his friends who had saved the whole enterprise, including Owain Myfyr and William Owen, but unleashed his full fury on the 'indigence', 'envy' and 'betrayal by friends', and 'whispers by enemies' that he had suffered.[62] The result was to give a (wholly correct) impression of Iolo as a cantankerous and combative personality with whom it was difficult to do business. Furthermore, the publication of the work had put him in an ideological double-bind. Although radical friends and allies such as Tom Paine had subscribed money for it, the job could only be done with the support of the traditional aristocratic and ecclesiastical elite of the nation, who had, ever since ancient times, been the usual sponsors of scholarship and literature. Friends had duly managed to persuade a number of nobles, from the Prince of Wales downward, and bishops to subscribe funds to get the book out. Iolo, however, felt unable to compromise his revolutionary ideals to fit the reality of the help that he was getting. He therefore tried to have it both ways, by taking the money and yet still parading his hatred of what he termed 'priestcraft' and 'kingcraft', and 'scoundrelism, though captained by ever so *great a name*' (his emphasis).[63] He did so both in his preface and in several of the poems, and it is all too easy to imagine what most of the nobles and prelates who had provided their cash would have thought of such a response to their generosity. At any rate, Iolo had failed completely in his main objective in returning to London, which was to make a living from authorship. During his stay both his nerves and his body had suffered badly, and he had left his wife and children in desperate financial straits.[64] In 1795 he gave up and went back home to Wales, where he remained for the rest of his life, based in his childhood village of Flemingston.

* * *

Although he probably did not know it, Iolo had already done enough while in London to change the history of Britain, and of Wales in particular. His impact was greatly reinforced by the activities in which he immersed himself during the period of more than thirty years which remained to him after his return to Glamorgan. Money gradually became easier, as he resumed his original trade of stonemason, received further sums from friends in London, and could eventually draw upon first the labour, and then the earnings, of his devoted son, whom he had inevitably named Taliesin. Both pictures and descriptions of him are available for this period, to give him some physical as well as literary presence in the records. The set portrait of him, by a Colonel Taynton from the nearest town, Cowbridge, shows a man with a thatch of piebald hair, a thrusting nose, melancholy eyes and a wry mouth. Better known is the caricature of him by the contemporary cartoonist Robert Cruickshank, which exaggerates all these features, making the hair longer, greyer and more whip-like, the face more angular, the eyes more excitable, the nose and lips thinner, and the chin sharper. It also invests him with a nervous, pulsing energy that must be true to the life. A literary memoir of him in old age, which accompanied the caricature,[65] supplies many more vivid details. When travelling, he habitually dressed in a blue coat with brass buttons, with spectacles on nose and pencil in hand to enable him to read a book and take notes from it as he walked. He always had two canvas wallets with him, one slung before and one behind, to contain, respectively, a change of underwear, and books and papers. He probably could not have afforded to ride a horse had he wished to do so, but proclaimed that his legs were good enough to enable him to spare animals the burden of carrying him. Walking suited his restless temperament, and he often engaged in it, but he also spent much time at home in his cottage, and the same memoir provides some vivid images of him there. His asthma worsened until he could no longer breathe lying down, and so he slept sitting upright in a chair, with pens and paper set ready before him. He was a tireless talker, prone to irritable, angry and bitter outbursts but also greatly entertaining because of the sheer quantity of his knowledge on many subjects. His favourite refreshment consisted of vast quantities of tea, heavily mixed with milk and sugar; and, as before, he continued a prodigious consumption of laudanum.

This, then, was the man as he appeared to observers during his last three decades. His continued influence then, as before, took both literary and physical forms, and these may now be considered in turn. He contributed to one further publication concerned with Welsh history and literature, and this was, again, made possible by his old friend Owain Myfyr. The latter's business had prospered all through the 1790s, and in 1797 he sponsored a new literary project, a series of volumes that would contain all the leading medieval Welsh literature that had not already been edited and published. He wanted William Owen and Iolo to undertake the work between them, in London. Iolo refused to return to the capital, but was willing to discover material and send copies of it there if Owen would then prepare it for the press. This was agreed, and Iolo undertook a great deal of genuine research, including a tour of north and central Wales in 1799. His comments upon the manuscripts that he read there provide a key insight into part of his motivation for forging evidence. He was not interested in the Welsh past for its own sake, but as a way of improving the present and of increasing the reputation of the Welsh in it. The real medieval poetry and chronicles that he discovered simply did not contain the morality of pacifism, humanism and altruism that he wished people to adopt and with which he wanted his nation to be associated. Instead, he found (as all scholars do) mostly a celebration of – in his own words – 'infernally bloodthirsty princes'. He accordingly set to work, once again, to write the sort of thing he believed the genuine records should have produced, and pass it off as medieval.[66]

The trick worked on Myfyr and Owen, just as it had before. Both were impressed by the fake chronicles, triads and proverbs that Iolo sent them, the former declaring that they were proof that 'our ancestors were possessed of more extensive and correct knowledge of things than modern times have allowed them'.[67] As a result, Iolo made more and more extensive use of duplicity. The edition of texts appeared in three successive volumes, between 1801 and 1807, called collectively *The Myvyrian Archaiology* after its sponsor.[68] The first volume consisted of authentic bardic literature. Iolo introduced some of his forgeries into the second, though it was still mostly made up of genuine medieval works. The third volume, however, was filled with his fakes, in the form of triads;[69] it was, in one sense, the book that he had tried to get published in 1794, and its appearance in this form represented his revenge for the lack of support he had received then. Put together with those he had already got into print, in the edition of Llywarch Hen and with his own poems, they indeed represented a complete system of moral teachings of a kind that would impress any rational and generous-minded person, of his age and since. They show Iolo at his best, with a deep understanding of human nature and of the ways of the world, and a wry, realistic and perceptive sense of humour. Thus, in one triad the foundations of judgement are bold design, frequent practice and frequent mistakes; in another, the foundations of learning are seeing much, suffering much and studying much.

Iolo embodied in this material not merely morality but false history, filling in the many gaps in knowledge of the ancient Welsh past. Rachel Bromwich has teased out the way in which he developed the three dominant figures in his imagined version of events.[70] In the work of a genuine late medieval bard, Iolo Goch, he found a reference to a mythical emperor of Constantinople called Hu Gadarn, who had set a good example to his people by ploughing his own land. This character had been derived, in turn, from an earlier medieval romance about the historical emperor Charlemagne. Iolo now developed Hu into the hero responsible for the origins of Welsh culture. Another character, Prydain, featured in a real triad and some royal genealogies as a mythical conqueror of Britain, after whom the island was named. Nothing was known of him in these sources but his name, and so Iolo fleshed him out as the founder of the British state and of the bardic order. Dyfnwal Moelmut appeared in the genealogies, and the fantastic medieval history of Britain by Geoffrey of Monmouth had expanded his reputation by making him a codifier of laws. Iolo now invented triads that provided examples of the wise laws which Dyfnwal should have made.

The implications of his deceptions should not be underestimated. The *Myvyrian Archaiology* was designed specifically to introduce ordinary literate Welsh people to the glories of their heritage; and Iolo had sabotaged it. Deeming the actual literature of the bards to be inadequate, he had substituted an imagined early Wales of his own, and so cut off readers of the book – which indeed became a classic – from much of the real achievement of the medieval Welsh. In doing so, he had at once betrayed his friends and his country. After this he published nothing more on Welsh history and prehistory, and the possible reasons for this deserve some consideration. In part, his silence was a consequence of opportunity. All of his successes in getting his views into print hitherto had depended partly or wholly upon his two great friends and allies in London, and he now proceeded to quarrel with both. By 1807 Owain Myfyr had grown weary at last of Iolo's unreliability and ingratitude and the general burdens of supporting scholarship, and he abandoned both together. The rift put pressure in turn upon Iolo's friendship with William Owen, and it was widened by Owen's increasing personal affluence and success as a scholar, which provoked Iolo's jealousy. Iolo had long been inclined to mock and disparage Owen behind his back, and now this turned into open enmity.[71]

On the other hand, even when Myfyr was still willing to support Iolo, the latter had not taken full advantage of his opportunities. In 1802, Myfyr had offered him funding for the completion of his long-promised, full-scale history of the bardic tradition, and Iolo had first accepted the offer and then done nothing in response. In large part this was because of a second factor: Iolo's mercurial personality had led him into a new, and competing, enthusiasm. This was Unitarianism, an umbrella term for an attempt to put into action a simple and democratic version of Christianity that emphasized Christ's role as a reformer and teacher of liberty and pacifism rather than as a divinity. As such, it made a very good match with Iolo's own conception of what a religion should be, and, when a Unitarian Society of South Wales was founded in 1802, he was one of its leading members. He put his energy into this instead of completing the full account of British history that Myfyr was attempting to sponsor. One of his services to the new association was to draft its regulations, declaring that the aim of its members was to restore 'what appears to them to be the undebased religion of Jesus Christ'.[72] As a stonemason, he carved inscriptions for the first Unitarian chapels in Cardiganshire, and as a poet he composed thousands of hymns in Welsh to serve the new movement. His collection of them published in 1812 had the motto 'The Truth against the World' that he had claimed for the ancient bardic tradition.[73] In his representation, Unitarianism *was* the direct descendant, and modern form, of the ancient and pure religion of the Christianized British Druids.[74] His portrait of ancient Druidry had been intended to provide an example of the best possible civil and religious society, and Unitarianism now seemed to him to follow that example. It is small wonder that he gave it so much attention that might otherwise have been claimed by history.

All this said, it still does not seem likely that the element of distraction in Iolo's failure to publish a history book was more than a reinforcing factor, like his later lack of sponsorship. There is no evidence that he was ever capable of the self-discipline and the structural thinking needed to produce *any* sustained piece of writing. The best he could do was collect together essentially separate short pieces, as in his edition of poems or his hymnbook, or contribute essays or poems to works edited or composed by others. Geraint Jenkins has attributed this limitation directly to his addiction to opium, pointing out that it is a standard consequence of the drug,[75] and this may be the whole truth of the matter. The only hesitation involved in accepting it stems from the fact that John Aubrey did not need drug addiction to display precisely the same pattern; it may be that Iolo's problems were innate. As his consumption of opium began at around the same time as his literary career, there is no way of determining the issue. It is certain that he never completely gave up his ambition to give the world a full history of the bardic tradition he had invented. He continued to produce new materials for it, under the guise of copies of medieval or Tudor documents, and for the last ten years of his life urged his son Taliesin to undertake the work of editing and publishing them.[76] Taliesin was, however, at this stage too busy establishing his own career. The result was that Iolo filled his cottage at Flemingston with papers containing information on what he represented as medieval bardic and ancient Druidic teachings. These became, in themselves the main works on the subject that he bequeathed to posterity.

* * *

It is time now to examine these jottings, and see how his invented tradition developed, in his imagination, during his last three decades. Many of his later writings on it did not involve Druids, being concerned with the technical nature of bardic poetry and with the symbolic alphabet that his imagined Bards employed. Those that did took the form of short treatises that gave a general overview of ancient Druidry and its beliefs; a newly concocted Druidic creation myth; and a proliferation of precise terms for aspects of Druidic thought and practice that he had already devised. The most compact of his general overviews[77] began with the declaration that Druidic theology was essentially the same as that of the ancient Persian magi, Indian Brahmins, Phoenicians and Egyptians; in this, like many writers before him, he was following the biblical model of a single primeval religion. He added that bards were known to all early peoples, but that the system of Bards, Ovates and Druids had probably been developed in Britain. He then took a swing at the Romans, holding that they persecuted Druidry because it stood in the way of the priestcraft that they practised; to Iolo, ancient Romans were possessed of the same vices as the Roman Catholicism to which they later gave rise. By contrast, the Druids had eagerly embraced early Christianity, as yet uncorrupted by Rome. Roman Catholic missionaries, however, arrived in the fifth century and drove out true Christianity from most of Britain, leaving Wales as the principal refuge of the old, true faith.

Iolo next provided a picture of ancient British society, claiming that Druids were found everywhere, as the common teachers and priests of their time, whereas Bards, 'being of much superior character', only appeared in public at the great seasonal festivals. Here he was presenting a picture that suited better his new lifestyle, as a Bard who lived in comparative retirement and only sallied out for special occasions. He then berated modern Welsh writers for still commonly preferring Roman texts as sources of information for Druidry, when their own early writings and traditions (by which he meant his own versions of them) were much more accurate and informative. Finally, he returned to theology, repeating the central point that 'Bardism, or as commonly termed Druidism, is purely monotheistical and theosophical, it is as pure a specimen of the patriarchal, or primeval religion of the Word, as anywhere can be found . . . it is on that account valuable as it not only harmonizes with but confirms the truth of the ancient Jewish and regenerated Christian systems. It proves that God has in all ages and countries so ordered in His divine providence, that the evidence of His truths should never be lost.'

Despite all this, Iolo was very willing to create pieces of theology that were found in no other religious system, though they most resembled the Judaic and Christian.[78] One of these was his account of how the cosmos came into being. In this, the one deity first made light, which radiated from him as three rays. These represented the unity of creation, three in one (which has obvious echoes of the Christian Trinity), and were signified in Druidic and Bardic symbolism by three lines diverging from a single source. Iolo turned this symbol into the *nod cyfrin*, the mystical sign of Druidry and of the bardic order. Other pieces of fresh information concerned the circles of rebirth through which, in his theology of the 1790s, souls passed. He now gave all of them names. The lowest, where life was formed, was still Annwn. For the others, he coined new terms: the mortal world, and place of probation, was Abred. The sphere of heavenly bliss and immortality, where the best souls would end up, was Gwynvyd. Beyond that was the realm of Ceugant, which was reserved for the deity alone.

Iolo gave this theology a further optimism by declaring that, as one soul after another made the final ascent into Gwynvyd, Abred, the place of mortality and suffering, would eventually come to an end. This, of course, assimilated his 'Druidic' religious system further to a benevolent form of Christianity, and he extended this work. In another of his clusters of writing he declared that the medieval Bards had recognized Christ as God the Son, the younger form of God the Father, the 'Ancient and Unoriginated One'. He added the belief that anybody who performed seven works of mercy in the name of Jesus would win a passage to Gwynvyd. Once in Gwynvyd, all beings were equal in the love of the deity, no matter how many times they had fallen back before: Iolo had no time for the concept of saints, and made full use of the potential that the Christian Gospels contain for the belief that all souls are equal before their creator. He added a fall of angels on the Christian model, holding that the creator had originally made all living things to dwell in the bliss of Gwynvyd. They had, however, tried to invade his sphere of Ceugant, and become gods them-selves, whereupon he had flung them down into the cold, darkness and chaos of Annwn, to start the journey back to heaven through successive rebirths. One of the ways in which he continued to depart from Christianity was in his doctrine of rein-carnation, and what it implied for the unity of the natural world. He declared (through his fictitious Druids and Bards) that an evil man who had been reborn in the form of a worm had already recommenced the ascent towards heaven; and so nobody should tread on a worm without good cause.

Iolo also elaborated his own legendary history of the Welsh. He invented a myth that the three rays that issued from the creator were turned into letters by a hero called Einigan the Giant, as OIV or OIW, signifying the attributes of the deity as love, knowledge and truth, united in justice. Einigan then chose men, who were known by the collective name of Gwyddoniad, to commit them to memory and function as sages to his people, the ancestors of the Welsh. Hu Gadarn, 'the Mighty', led these people to Britain, and then they elected Prydain as their king, giving the island his name. He devised the system of Bards, Ovates and Druids, the privileges and customs of which were formulated by his successors, inspired directly by the deity. Iolo added that many people came to study in ancient Britain, but that the teachings given to them were always corrupted when they returned home. The true doctrine was therefore preserved only in Britain, and then in Wales. He also elaborated, repeatedly, the system that he had already devised by the 1790s. He declared that the Druidic names for the four cardinal points of the sun, and the great festivals that marked them, had been Alban Arthan (midwinter), Alban Eiler (spring equinox), Alban Hefin (midsummer) and Alban Elfed (autumn equinox). 'Alban' just means 'light' in Welsh, the substance from which Iolo believed all things had been created. He now stated that lesser meetings were held at any quarter day of the cycle of the moon, and were staffed by Druids, while Bards appeared mostly at the four great festivals. With some wishful thinking, he asserted that, although all ranks were equal in a *gorsedd*, Bards were given special honours outside it, in the form of lands and stipends to maintain them. He went into greater detail on such matters as how a stone circle was laid out for a *gorsedd* (with additional stones to form the pattern of the 'mystic sign').

A mechanism for the creation and multiplication of new local *gorseddau* was provided by his note that three properly initiated Bards could establish one between them. This system was given the potential to become a monopoly by his declaration that anybody who did not become a member of a *gorsedd*, through examination and initiation, was not regarded as a true Bard. Iolo devised an entire alphabet, which he claimed had been used by the ancient bards and Druids, and preserved by the bards in secret through the Middle Ages. He provided further information on the sources from which he purported to have taken this material. He still claimed to have found it in a manuscript made by Llywelyn Sion, but – lest readers think that Llywelyn might have made it up – added that this had been copied in turn, as notes in it showed, from an older manuscript by a medieval bard, Meyryg of Glamorgan. This, Iolo claimed, Llywelyn had read in the library at Raglan Castle; which had, notoriously, been destroyed in the Civil War, giving Iolo an obvious explanation for the fact that no other scholar had found or heard of the document concerned. Through all this myth-making he continued to produce moments of exquisite irony, whether or not it was ever conscious. He wrote a triad, for example, declaring that the three sorts of man who should never be made a Bard were 'a natural liar; an habitual wrangler; and one who is inevitably ignorant'.[79] Iolo himself was never the last of those, but he represented the first two more fully and consistently than most people have ever done.

All this information was jotted down higgledy-piggledy, on loose scraps of paper and the backs of old letters, bills and placards.[80] Often Iolo would compose several different versions of the same set of teachings, varying in details and sometimes contradicting each other. This pattern of working may have reflected the disorder of his mind and personality (with or without the aid of drug addiction), but it may also have been part of his skill as a forger. It reinforced the impression of a scholar copying information from many texts, all of them reflecting, in different ways, the same ancient teaching.

* * *

Iolo remained very much a man of action as well as words, and he continued to plant *gorseddau*. The Gwyneddigion Society kept bardic meetings going after his departure in London, advertising one on Primrose Hill, led by David Samwell, at midsummer 1798. After then, however, they seem to have vanished from the capital,[81] and the death of Samwell himself that year may have been the decisive blow. Instead Iolo developed them in Wales, and the historian of the institution of the bardic *gorsedd*, Dillwyn Miles, has retrieved most of what is known of the process.[82] It commenced as soon as Iolo got back, when he called one for the spring equinox of 1796, formed out of his old literary chums mixed with new friends with whom he was to be active in the Unitarian movement. It was to be held on one of the main hills of the Vale of Glamorgan, known to the Welsh as Bryn Owen, and to English-speakers as Stalling Down. Those attending were instructed to present work in the 'traditional' metres of the medieval Glamorgan bards, as specified by Iolo. Immediately he discovered that the political atmosphere in the provinces was less tolerant than that in the capital, and that his reputation as a revolutionary had made him a marked man among the local magistrates. As a hostile journalist put it, 'knowing the harlequin of the farce to be of democratic principles', the magistrates banned it. The next year Iolo tried again at midsummer, choosing Mynydd y Garth, one of the foothills of the mountains that cover northern Glamorgan and overlooking the point at which the River Taff gushes out from them. This was a safer distance from the gentry seats of the lowland, and the meeting duly took place, Iolo lecturing his fellows, in poetry and prose, on the religion and customs of the early Welsh.

Emboldened by this success, he proceeded both to convene a series of further *gorseddau* and to use them to air precisely the views of which the magistrates were most afraid. Three months after the Mynydd y Garth assembly, he held another closer to the Vale and his own home, on Forest Mountain north of Cowbridge. One of the activities there was to design a coat of arms for Napoleon, who was emerging as the leading soldier of the French republic which the British had by then been fighting for four years. The act was intended as a gesture of admiration for Napoleon, and the arms hailed him as a destroyer of tyrants. It did not escape the attention of the local justices; twelve of them watched the whole assembly, accompanied by a troop of mounted and armed vigilantes in case the proceedings stepped over the line between provocation and rebellion. In the following year, 1798, Iolo tried to repeat the pattern. He convened a *gorsedd* above the valley of the River Ogwr in the mountains above the north-west of the Vale, at the spring equinox. There he recited a poem on the rights of man. The magistrates were now determined to stop him. Iolo tried to throw them off his scent by advertising a midsummer assembly at Forest Mountain and then changing the location, by messages, to Mynydd y Garth. It was in vain; as he and his friends began their proceedings they were interrupted by a mounted troop of the local home guard, which forced them to disperse. Defiantly, Iolo sent out a summons to another meeting on Mynydd y Garth, at the autumn equinox, but there is no evidence that this was held.

Once again, the ageing radical tried to compensate for a failure in one region by starting afresh in another. During 1799 he travelled around north Wales, copying manuscripts for the *Myvyrian Archaiology*, and took the opportunity to hold a *gorsedd* there. It duly took place in October, on a hill overlooking the Menai Strait between the mainland and Anglesey, where once, according to Tacitus, the soldiers of Suetonius had massed to attack the island and its Druids. There he initiated three of Gwynedd's poets as Bards, including the currently most famous, Dafydd Ddu Eryri, and encouraged them to carry on the custom after his departure. Within four years, however, Iolo and Dafydd Ddu had fallen out over the former's insistence that his own poetic metres, those of Glamorgan, should be imposed on all Welsh Bards as the only authentic kind. Iolo now turned his attention to Unitarianism instead, and a decade seems to have passed before he revived the attempt to hold *gorseddau*. He did so, however, as soon as peace was at last firmly made between Britain and France and the French monarchy restored, in 1814. All suspicion of meetings as a focus for rebellion in league with a foreign enemy was now removed. Iolo called for a 'chair and eisteddfod' of bards to be held that year on 1 August, the date of the old Welsh festival that brought in autumn and also the time of a full moon.

He chose to locate it up in the mountain valleys of northern Glamorgan, Blaenau Morganwg, where he had always had friends interested in poetry and radicalism, and had recently made more. One of these was a poet and singer called Thomas Williams, with the bardic name of Gwilym Morganwg, who kept the New Inn at a place then called Newbridge, named after a miracle of eighteenth-century engineering, the longest single-span stone bridge in Europe, which arched gracefully across the River Taff. On the steep hillside to the east of the valley, opposite the end of the bridge, stood a natural wonder: one of those rocking stones which had been regarded as Druidic monuments because of the influence of Toland. It was a huge grey sandstone boulder weighing almost ten tons, poised on top of another so delicately that a child's hand could rock it.[83] In lieu of real megaliths, this was an excellent focus for ceremonies with a Druidic theme or tinge. Local people called it Yr Maen Chwŷf, the rocking stone. On the appointed day Iolo and his friends met at Gwilym's pub and then climbed up to the stone for the ceremony, led by Iolo and Gwilym and processing behind a banner. The theme of it was a celebration of the return of peace to the land, in keeping with Iolo's continuing association of the bardic order with pacifism. Gwilym himself contributed a notable poem to the day, and was duly initiated as a Bard. He convened another *gorsedd* at the rocking stone at midwinter, with an invitation to all Welsh poets to perform works on subjects which included brotherly love, peace, generosity, the excellence of the native language, and the history of the stone itself. Iolo was invited, and raised his own son Taliesin to the rank of Bard in the course of the proceedings. In subsequent years Gwilym continued to hold meetings at the stone or inside his inn, giving to the participants the collective name of 'Cymdeithas yr Maen Chwŷf', the Society of the Rocking Stone.[84]

For the first time, Iolo's *gorseddau* had taken root, and he was now on the verge of his greatest triumph in the field of bardic pageantry. It was given to him not by an advance in the cause of religious and political reform but by a precisely opposite development: defensive measures taken against religious nonconformity by the established Church that he continually denounced. The story of these events has now been pieced together by Geraint Jenkins, building on the work of Dillwyn Miles.[85] The source of them lay in the increasing numbers of Welsh people who were abandoning the official Church for dissenting Protestant denominations, mostly Congregationalist, Baptist and Methodist; Iolo's own Unitarians represented the extreme fringe of this movement. This was the more dramatic in that hitherto the people of Wales had been among the most religiously conservative in Britain. It was, however, of a piece with the transformation of its economic life, as a land of farmers, often on poor upland soils, was starting to turn into some of the major industrial regions of the world, based on the systematic exploitation of copper, coal and iron. By 1810 the ironworks of upland Glamorgan, where Iolo had found his steadiest friends and allies, were already the largest on the planet. The drift from the traditional parish churches to newly built chapels was also a reflection of that tremendous transformation of Welsh life which was a feature of the eighteenth century, consequent on the collapse of the traditional culture that had been passed on from the Middle Ages.

Faced with this challenge, by the first years of the nineteenth century some of the official clergy decided to link themselves to the revival of interest in traditional Welsh culture. In doing so, they hoped to secure a place for their Church in the new Wales, as an embodiment of a new Welsh nationalism. They earned the nickname of 'yr hen bersoniaid llengar', 'the old literary parsons'. Their chosen vehicles were local associations known as Cambrian Societies, founded in each of the traditional divisions of the country and centred on the institution of the *eisteddfod*, revived so recently by the London Welsh. It was at this point, indeed, that the Welsh who had remained at home began to take over leadership of the cultural revival from those who had moved to the metropolis. The leader of the movement was Thomas Burgess, Bishop of St Davids. He was himself a Hampshire-born Englishman, with ambitions to win promotion to an English see. This, however, only reinforced the fervour with which he championed the arts of his newly adopted nation, as part of his bid to prove himself worthy of greater honours. In 1818 one of his parish clergy at Carmarthen suggested that he found a Cambrian Society for Dyfed, the old Welsh province (once a kingdom) that roughly corresponded to his diocese. Burgess took up the idea with enthusiasm. Another aspect of his reforming zeal lay in his hostility to religious nonconformists, and especially Unitarians, whom he termed 'apostates' and 'blasphemers'. None the less, when the first meeting of the new society took place at Carmarthen in October, Iolo was invited to attend, because of his reputation as the leading expert in Welsh literature and tradition.

As Geraint Jenkins has demonstrated, although he was the only religious dissenter present and surrounded by orthodox clergy, Iolo took the meeting over by force of personality. All present agreed to hold an *eisteddfod* the following summer. When it opened, at the Ivy Bush Inn, Carmarthen, on 8 July 1819, Iolo repeated the trick of a takeover. Burgess, of course, presided over the opening session, which included more than two hundred guests, most drawn from the regional social elite. As soon as the Bishop had delivered a short speech of welcome, Iolo, whose formal status was only that of one of the judges, stood up and gave a fiery oration on the unique and glorious literary identity of the Welsh and the leading place of Carmarthen in it. He won thunderous applause. During the three days of competitions that followed, Burgess's parsons did very well, one of them, Walter Davies, winning three of the four major literary prizes. However, when the time came to enthrone Davies in the chair that had been the medieval symbol of a champion bard, Iolo again stole the scene. He pinned a blue ribbon on Davies's sleeve, as a sign of his reception as a Bard into what Iolo held to be the traditional bardic order. Audaciously, he proceeded to pin a white one on the sleeve of the Bishop himself, without any prior warning, and thus received him into that order with the rank of Druid.

Worse, from Burgess's point of view, was to come on the last day of the *eisteddfod*, as he watched helplessly while Iolo convened a *gorsedd* in the garden of the inn. The circle was marked out with pebbles, and Iolo's chum from Newbridge, Gwilym Morganwg, bore the ceremonial sword. Iolo's son Taliesin was also present, as was his old friend from London, Edward Jones, harper to the Prince of Wales, who was apparently reconciled to him now that the great divisive issues of war and revolution were gone. In the circle with them were three of the clergy of Burgess's official church, wearing their ribbons as Bards, and these joined in the ceremony of drawing and sheathing the sword and supported Iolo as he initiated a string of new Bards, Ovates and Druids. Among the new Ovates was a woman writer, Elizabeth Jones. At one point the outraged Bishop intervened and urged Iolo to conclude the proceedings swiftly, whereupon he was met with a flat refusal. Iolo went home satisfied, leaving a fuming Burgess, who vented his feelings in a letter to a fellow clergyman about the 'nonsense' and 'considerable improprieties' in the ceremony he had witnessed.[86] It was rumoured that he intervened personally to ensure that the *gorsedd* ceremony was not enacted when a Cambrian Society was formed for Powys and held its first *eisteddfod* at Wrexham in 1820.

The Bishop's group of nationalist clergy, who had originally produced the idea of hitching established religion to the nationalist revival, had other ideas. Some had, after all, taken part voluntarily in Iolo's rites at Carmarthen, and apparently liked them. One of them, David Richards, subsequently re-enacted the rites with three other clerics present in his churchyard at Llansilin, where the Berwyn mountains slope lush and green down to the English border. Two of the clerics had been initiated with him by Iolo at Carmarthen. Richards went on to hold an *eisteddfod* at the winter solstice of 1820, on one of the Kerry hills to the south of his parish, initiating more Bards and Ovates. Both events were attended by Walter Davies, who had been so prominent at Carmarthen, He then hosted one for a group of local clergy on the lawn of his own vicarage at Llangynyw, in the same county of Montgomeryshire, in November 1821. Among the guests was Iolo's old friend and collaborator, William Owen. Another was the heir of the English Earl of Shaftesbury, who had acquired an enthusiasm for Welsh culture and wanted to learn the language; to encourage him, Davies made him a Druid. Over the next twenty years, regional *eisteddfodau* in central and north Wales continued, occasionally, to include the *gorsedd* ceremony, and it persisted also as part of the gatherings held in upland Glamorgan, most notably by Gwilym Morganwg at Newbridge.[87]

* * *

It is a measure of Iolo's importance in the development of British views of Druids that, like Stukeley, he almost immediately provoked a rival and competitor, who took up his ideas and altered them into a new form. This was the role that John Wood and William Borlase had played with regard to Stukeley, and the part in Iolo's case was taken by a Welsh clergyman called Edward Davies, subsequently nicknamed 'Celtic' Davies. The relationship between the two men also has a parallel with that of John Toland and Henry Rowlands. Like Toland, Iolo was an adventurer and a political and religious firebrand, regarded with horror or disdain by many conventionally minded contemporaries. Like Rowlands, Davies was a minister in the established Church and a painstaking and scrupulous scholar, who attempted to fit what was apparently known of Druids by his time into a framework that supported orthodox religion. Both men were to have a considerable impact, but Iolo, simply by being so much less representative of mainstream opinion in his own age, was to enjoy a lesser success while yet living, and have a greater importance thereafter. In that, also, the parallel with Toland and Rowlands holds good.

Edward Davies was born on a hill farm in the Buellt district of mid-Wales, in 1756. As a boy he suffered two serious blows of fortune. First, some gunpowder exploded in his face, seriously damaging his eyes. Then he caught measles, which weakened his vision further, leaving him partly blind for the rest of his life and with the ever-present threat of a complete loss of sight. The local clergy inspired in him both a love of learning and a deep personal piety, so that before he reached the age of twenty he had already written fifty-six hymns. Like Iolo, he never got to university, but unlike him he did receive a grammar school education, and learned Greek, Latin and French, as well as having Welsh and English. He went on to combine his two enthusiasms by opening his own school in Herefordshire while taking on curacies in different parishes in that county. In his twenties he would perform divine service five times every Sunday and deliver three sermons, riding thirty miles in the process. In 1782 he moved to a richer and less exhausting position in Gloucestershire, as headmaster of Chipping Sodbury grammar school in the limestone hills above Bristol, and curate of a nearby parish. This, however, left him in the position of a Welshman exiled among parishioners and pupils who had a traditional contempt for his nation. As had happened among the Welsh in London, the experience only reinforced his admiration of, and interest in, the cultural heritage of his own people. He came upon the edition of the poems of Dafydd ap Gwilym, made by William Owen and contaminated by Iolo, and they fired an enthusiasm in him for medieval Welsh verse which was stoked by the correspondence on it in the *Gentleman's Magazine*. He wrote to both Owen and Iolo, who encouraged him in this enthusiasm, and during the 1790s he began to make and publish his own translations. The treble burden of teaching, ministering and research took a terrible toll on him, and from 1797 onward he was never entirely well. His greatest hope was to earn some position in the Church that would keep him even if he went completely blind.[88]

Poor Davies was therefore in a double-bind: the harder he worked on publications, the greater were his chances of earning such a sinecure, and yet the greater the strain on his eyes. His compromise was to give up teaching for a curacy in another south Gloucestershire parish, this time Olveston in the rich fields near the River Severn. An old school friend of his, Theophilus Jones, who had become a historian, set to work to help him. Jones contacted the chief justice who served the Brecon circuit of assize courts, George Hardinge, and Owen added his entreaties to this powerful man on Davies's behalf. The result was effective: Hardinge began talking to influential people about sending money to help Davies complete a book on the nature of the Celtic languages. In the end, he and other friends obtained 2,257 subscriptions, plus another 30 guineas in outright gifts, and the result was *Celtic Researches*, published in 1804.[89] This built on an idea, by now well established in eighteenth-century philology, that Welsh, Irish and Hebrew had developed from the same very ancient language. As part of this Davies said some nice things about Druids, whom he represented as high-minded philosophers deeply concerned with the nature of the deity, the soul, and life after death. He suggested that they had probably preserved more of the original religion revealed by the true god than any other heathens, so that 'notwithstanding their many and gross errors' they 'retained many of its vital and essential principles'.[90]

By now his relationship with Iolo had become complex.[91] As we know, Davies was originally inspired by Iolo and Owen to take an interest in medieval Welsh literature, and corresponded with both men.[92] Iolo sent him some of his own forged triads, and

Owen innocently fed him accounts of the ancient bardic order that had been passed to him, in turn, by Iolo.[93] In this manner, Iolo was ensuring that his false view of the Welsh past was embedded in the current research of others as well as being published directly to the world. Davies was not, however, entirely happy with this: not all of it accorded with what he was finding in the genuine medieval texts. His suspicions were strengthened when Iolo's portrait of the ancient bards and Druids first appeared in print, in the edition of Llywarch Hen. He complained to another Welshman who had knowledge both of the genuine medieval sources and of Iolo himself, John Walters, who lived near Iolo's home in the Vale of Glamorgan. Walters replied: 'I perfectly agree with you in your sentiments of Mr Owen's "Bardism": It is a *made dish*, cooked up from obscure scraps of the ancient bards and the Cabala (the pretended *arcana*) of the modern ones; a superficial acquaintance with the metempsychosis [the Pythagorean doctrine of rebirth]: and these ingredients spiced up with an immoderate quantity of wild invention. It is a species of Freemasonry.'[94]

This is a striking insight into how far informed readers could see into Iolo's deceptions from the very beginning. The trouble, however, lay in the 'obscure scraps of the ancient bards' that had gone into them. As everybody acknowledged that Iolo was genuinely learned in the old literature – perhaps uniquely so – it was a matter of guesswork to separate the real from the invented in his information. Davies therefore selected certain features of Iolo's portrait of Druidic doctrine and built them into his own sense of the past. Some he took directly from Iolo's published work: he was one of the subscribers to his edition of poems. Others were passed on to him by Owen, to whom Iolo confided features that he had added later to his vision of the past, as if they were new discoveries. In his one and only novel, published in 1795, Davies repeated the ideas that ancient bards wore sky blue, and preached harmony and peace.[95] *Celtic Researches* included in its portrait of Druidic belief and bardic custom the 'mystic sign' of the three diverging lines, the circles of rebirth, the secret alphabet, and the whole of Iolo's pseudo-history featuring Hu, Prydain and Dyfnwal. Iolo was one of the subscribers to this book, and on reading it he realized with horror the trap he had prepared for himself. His invention of so much false history was intended, in large part, to advance his own reputation and career. In some respects he had been too successful in the imposture, because his own creation was now taking on an independent life of its own, regarded as a body of data which any scholars could employ to their own benefit. Davies now seemed to be on the point of reaping the acclaim that Iolo had sought for himself, in part by using Iolo's own creations.

In a panic, Iolo wrote to his patron, Hardinge, protesting that only he had the true knowledge of the early literature required to produce a full history of the bardic tradition: 'not a man living has read the tenth part of the Welsh manuscripts I have read except my friend Mr William Owen'. By citing Owen, of course, he was reinforcing an impression that there were two independent authorities on his claimed tradition, while in reality he had given Owen all his information on it. He accorded Davies qualified praise, calling his book 'fuller of information from ancient writers respecting the Celtic than anything I have yet seen', while claiming that he had made serious mistakes. He then advertised to the judge his own prospective *History of the British Bards and Druids*, on which he had laboured for twenty years.[96] He had mistaken his man. As a senior judge, Hardinge already knew of Iolo's reputation as an agitator and heretic, and disliked him, while the criticism of Davies in the letter was not likely to endear him further. He forwarded it to Davies himself, curtly terming Iolo a 'knave'. The revelation that Iolo had attempted to deprive him of his most influential ally must have done much to turn Davies's suspicion into dislike, and this was strengthened by the advice of Davies's old friend and supporter Theophilus Jones. Jones wrote to him on the publication of *Celtic Researches*, warning him that the Druidic alphabet he had endorsed in it was the 'manufacture' of Iolo and Owen, and 'the behaviour of Mad Ned [Iolo] at last Cardiff Assizes, when he heard that you had inserted those letters in your book, convinces me that he feared detection. Owen is undoubtedly learned, and Williams has eccentric talents, but both are system mongers and I believe system makers.'[97]

Jones kept up the pressure for the following five years, as Davies worked on a second major book, devoted to the Druids. He expressed hope that Davies was 'exposing all the frauds and tricks' that Iolo had perpetrated, urged him to correct Iolo's 'insolence' and begged that 'he may be not spared'. With special reference to the *gorsedd* rites, he declared that 'all those monkey tricks exhibited at Primrose Hill by Owen and others have no more foundation and pretence for antiquity' than Iolo's claims to an unbroken descent of the true bardic tradition in Glamorgan.[98] Davies did not disappoint Jones. When the book that was to be his most famous work, *The Mythology and Rites of the British Druids*, appeared in 1809, it launched a savage attack on Iolo's version of Druidic and bardic history. It began by calling it 'in many respects, irreconcilable with the works of the ancient bards, or with the authority of the classical page'. It went on to assert that even a slight analysis of it would 'discover some marks of gross misrepresentation, if not of absolute forgery'. Some pages later it declared roundly that 'this is not the Druidism of history' and drew attention to Iolo's support for revolution and republicanism, suggesting that his system was invented to further these causes.[99] It could have given Iolo no satisfaction, on reading all this, to know that a large number of his inventions had gone undetected by Davies and provided some of the material on which the latter's own ideas, expressed in the new book, were based. Iolo drafted several replies to the charges against him, and managed to publish one of them in a journal nine years later, but none attempted systematically to refute what had been alleged. It was, after all, absolutely correct, and all Iolo could do in response was insult his critic, in general terms, as ignorant and foolish. The punch-line of his published response was that Davies's 'smattering knowledge of our language, our literary and bardic antiquities, etc has instigated him to publish what sooner or later will render him truly ridiculous'. Davies in turn felt that this completely removed any lingering restraint that he might have harboured in waging war directly on Iolo. When Bishop Burgess made his brief alliance with Iolo in 1818, Davies wrote him a near-hysterical letter warning him off it. It called the *gorsedd* ceremonies 'mummery', and termed Iolo and his friends 'infidels, freethinkers, fanatics, buffoons, republicans, anarchists'.[100]

Davies's *Mythology and Rites* became one of the most influential books on Druids to be published in the nineteenth century. It was based on works he had found in the libraries of various Gloucestershire gentry and Bristol antiquaries, and the public library at Bristol, in addition to the Welsh manuscript material of which he had obtained copies.[101] Like many historians since, and most social scientists, Davies believed that it was best to approach a mass of source material with a theoretical model in mind. The model could then be used to organize the material, and the material used to test the worth of the model. In his case, the one that he chose had been established thirty years before by a three-volume book called *A New System, or, An Analysis of Ancient Mythology*, written by Jacob Bryant. Bryant had been the pet scholar of the Dukes of Marlborough, provided by them with a comfortable income, lodgings at their gigantic country house, Blenheim Palace, and use of its famous library. He had enjoyed exactly the life of which Davies, and many another struggling writer of the age, dreamed. The book had made an analysis of what was known of the world's mythologies by that date, employing all the new information brought in by European journeys and conquests in other parts of the globe. Comparative religion and mythology had been a growth area for intellectuals in Western Europe ever since the seventeenth century, propelled by those same discoveries. Stukeley's speculations in the field have already been noted, and Bryant drew in turn on French scholarship of the 1760s for his own approach to it. This was based on the argument, in which Stukeley had dabbled, that figures in ancient European and extra-European myths had actually been characters in the Book of Genesis. That book represented their true reality, whereas their characters and activities in the myths were distorted memories, produced by the confusion of languages and decay of religion that had followed the dispersal of Noah's descendants. Bryant worked outward from the proposition that an event as cataclysmic as the biblical Flood, and the regrowth of all animal life from the survivors who had come out of Noah's Ark, should have left a huge impact on human memory. He and his French predecessor were certainly correct that myths of great floods have been recorded in different parts of the globe, and he built on this fact to relate one such story after another to the biblical experiences of Noah, his sons and their offspring.[102]

Bryant's book had enjoyed a huge success, and Davies kept himself up to date with work carried out by other writers as a result of it. One in particular caught his imagination: the work of a young Oxford don called George Faber, who had since gone on to become a country clergyman like himself. In 1803, at the end of his time at Oxford, Faber had published a book that added a further dimension to the Bryant thesis. It started from the standpoint that, if the biblical deluge had been the most dramatic single event in human history, the most dramatic and awe-inspiring phenomenon in the natural world was the sun, which brought light and heat each day. He therefore proposed that all ancient religion and myth had consisted of a mixture of sun-worship and memories of the Flood, with the veneration as deities of human beings who had featured in the earlier parts of the Book of Genesis.[103] In adopting the Bryant–Faber model as the theoretical basis of his analysis of the source for Druids, therefore, Davies was placing himself at the cutting edge of contemporary scholarship. He was using a system of explanation that was as powerful in its day as Marxism or structuralism was to be in ours. To Europeans at the opening of the nineteenth century, it had two tremendous attractions. First, it seemed to assimilate the new and disquieting information that had been arriving, regarding the very different religious beliefs and cultural traditions held by peoples in the rest of the world. Second, it made sense of these within a framework that seemed to prove that Christianity, and the Bible on which it was based, had taught the true history of humanity all along, and therefore was the true religion. The centrality of the biblical deluge to these analyses was also highly topical. Not only were flood traditions widespread, as said, but the first whispers were starting to pass through the European intellectual world that the new science of geology might pose some tough questions for Christians. It was starting to reveal that the earth might be considerably older than the Book of Genesis seemed to claim, and had contained many more ages, and species, than those represented there. Noah's Flood was destined, inevitably, to play a major part in the discussions of how, if at all, the lessons of the rocks might be assimilated to traditional biblical teachings. A model of comparative mythology that seemed to prove the literal truth of Genesis, and above all the story of Noah, was deeply reassuring to devout Christians.

The scholarly tradition of approaching evidence with a theoretical structure of explanation already in mind is one which is well suited to certain disciplines, and has achieved excellent results. It has, however, two inherent weaknesses. One is that explanatory models often have sell-by dates; they are formulated according to the cultural norms of particular places and times, and go out of fashion as times change. This was to be spectacularly true of that adopted by Davies. The other weakness is that practitioners of this method are not always able, or willing, to make the evidence a test of the model's worth. Very frequently, they select, organize and interpret the evidence itself in a fashion that seems to prove the model correct; and this was true of the one that Davies had chosen. Bryant's most recent biographer has described his book on mythology as 'a fantastic hodgepodge of spurious etymology . . . and riotous imagination'.[104] In applying these already flawed ideas to his own source material, Davies faced a situation which played up to the very worst weaknesses, and temptations, of the model-testing method: the now baffling nature of much Welsh medieval literature, which allowed huge latitude to both translation and interpretation. In other words, he could make of much of his evidence more or less what he wished.

Taliesin was remembered in Welsh medieval tradition as the greatest of the first generation of native poets known to history; the ninth-century *Historia Brittonum* located him in the late sixth century, and some of the poetry associated with him indeed connected him with kings who ruled at that time. It seems possible now that not a single one of the surviving poems credited to him is his own work. By the mid-twentieth century, half a dozen of them were regarded as still plausibly of sixth-century date. Recently, however, they have been claimed to contain a vowel form that did not develop until around 1050.[105] In any case, none of the half-dozen poems that have been deemed to be very early contain any of the arcane references which authors from Evan Evans's time thought might embody Druidic teaching. These are all in fifteen other poems in the collection, and all of these are ninth-century at the very earliest, and probably much later.

At the time of 'Celtic' Davies, however, all of the poems credited to, or associated with, Taliesin were believed to be his own work, and therefore to date from the sixth century. At such an early date, so soon after the conversion of the British to Christianity or even while that conversion was still in progress, they might very plausibly be thought to contain echoes of Druidic teaching. The same was true of other medieval poetry attributed to very early bards, such as a body of verse credited to Myrddyn, the wizard Merlin of later medieval romances, who was likewise supposed to have lived in the sixth century. From internal evidence – as will be shown – it was later recognized that it was written in the late twelfth or the thirteenth century, although it remains possible that it includes some older material. In the course of the eighteenth century it was added to the sources from which knowledge of ancient Druidry might possibly be gained. Thus equipped, with a misunderstanding of the nature and date of his main source material, an idiosyncratic translation of its contents, an additional body of evidence forged by Iolo, and a false model of historical explanation, Davies proceeded with his work. To many of his readers, of course, he appeared to have better material, a finer understanding of it, and a more sophisticated structure of analysis, than any author before him.

   He concluded that Druidic religion had centred upon the veneration of two great deities, representing the male and female forces of nature.[106] Its god was Hu, representing the sun, whose symbol was the bull, and who was in fact a distorted memory of Noah. His consort was the goddess of the earth, the Great Mother of all creation, who was actually a degenerate memory of Noah's Ark. He identified her with a character found in a genuine medieval tale (though one known now only in a seventeenth-century version)[107] as a sorceress who brewed a potion that conferred wisdom and poetic inspiration. Taliesin, according to this story, was the reborn form of a boy who drank the brew by mistake, and so gained its benefits. The bards of the high medieval period (from the eleventh century onward) treated her as their muse, the giver of the vital talent of composition. Her name in the medieval sources was most commonly given as Cyrridwen or Kerritwen. Davies now put it into its enduring modern form, as Ceridwen, and turned her into an ancient goddess, the presiding one of Britain. The shift in perception involved was signalled in his very choice of name. Sir Ifor Williams, the greatest twentieth-century expert in the Taliesin poetry, derived the original one from *cyrrid*, meaning 'crooked' and the positional mutation of *ben*, a woman.[108] The result, 'crooked woman', would suit her nature, in the legend, as a ruthless and selfish sorceress. In Davies's reworking it now translated as 'beloved and fair', a far better name for a mighty and deeply venerated divine being. By attempting to prove the truth of Genesis, he had created a modern goddess. He made other suggestions that were to remain influential long after their central and informing theology had been discarded. One was that the hero Arthur had once been a sun god, another of the names and forms of Hu, alias Noah. Another was that Neolithic chambered tombs had been designed as places for initiation into the Druidic mysteries, representing as they did the womb of Ceridwen. A third was that stone circles had represented Ceridwen's body (and so a dim memory of the Ark). As befitted a pagan religion that in his opinion had degenerated from the true one, and was (literally) based on mistakes, Davies's attitude to his imagined Druidry was condescending. He pronounced that it consisted of 'gloomy mazes of error', but that it had been only a little further removed from the pure religion of Noah than modern Roman Catholicism was from true Christianity.[109]

The book brought Davies the renown, and the comfortable life, that he had been seeking. Aided by the lobbying of his patron Hardinge, his fame won him a living as a full parish clergyman at last, back in his native Wales. He moved to the benefice of Bishopston, in the rich countryside of the southern Gower peninsula, next to the booming port and resort town of Swansea. In 1823 blindness at last closed in on him, whereupon his Bishop, who was none other than Burgess, got him a stipend for life from the Royal Society of Literature. Even in his enforced retirement he maintained a literary life, by publishing works on history, poetry and the Bible that he had written earlier, until his death in 1831.[110]

In an ironic, and slightly tragic, sense, Iolo Morganwg and Edward Davies had got the measure of each other. Davies had been absolutely correct in charging Iolo with inventing a British past in an effort to change his contemporary world into a form he thought better than any before. Iolo, in turn, was right that Davies's understanding of the medieval texts was superficial, and that subsequent generations of scholars would find him ridiculous. Both, however, were to make a great impression on the modern imagination.

* * *

It remains to be seen how much of an impact Iolo's view of Druids had upon his contemporaries, up to the time of his death. He had, after all, cunningly diffused it through various channels, planting it in what were supposed to be edited collections of source material, as well as expounding it in his own publications and through those of friends. The latter, in some cases, continued to propagate it in works undertaken on their own account and without Iolo's direct manipulation. His most loyal ally, William Owen, embodied it along with the legendary history that accompanied it, in a series of potted biographies of notable Welsh people that he published in 1803.[111] Edward Jones may have fallen out for a time with Iolo in the mid-1790s, but he consistently repeated what the latter had said of Druid organization and belief in his own books on Welsh literature and music.[112] The cumulative effect of all this dissemination on Welsh culture, at least, was summed up by one Welsh poet, William Williams, writing to another, the celebrated bard of Gwynedd, Dafydd Ddu Eryri, in 1806. He ranted that Iolo and William Owen between them had 'bewitched' the minds of ordinary people and 'cast down all accepted history'.[113]

A selection of surviving Welsh works from the period bears out some of this opinion. The author of a guide to south Wales relied on Iolo for some of his information on Glamorgan, and built him into the attractions of the county, extolling him as 'capable of doing the world more service, than the world seems willing either to receive or to return'. There is surely an echo of Iolo's grumbling in that passage, and he must have been delighted to read on and find himself characterized as a simple stonecutter who managed also to be a 'profound and sagacious' scholar, respected by gentry.[114] His representation of the past was built into works by others on Welsh history and law,[115] and was repeated wholesale in an account of the development of Wales as a nation written from the viewpoint of religious nonconformists, and especially Baptists.[116] This was a constituency to which Iolo's political and religious radicalism, a disadvantage when dealing with the leaders of British society, had a positive appeal; in many ways, it consisted of his own people. Another ally proved to be a John Hughes, who in 1816 published an early history of Britain which blended Iolo's work with Davies's, while still declaring Iolo to be the best man living to write a true history of the Druids.[117] More support was given to him, ironically, by that same Theophilus Jones who had been Edward Davies's friend ever since school and was to urge Davies to attack Iolo so bitterly in the later 1800s. In Jones's most famous work, his history of Breconshire, published in 1805, he gave a great deal of credit to Iolo's version of the past, for he included major features of it.[118] His subsequent fury was that of a conscientious man who felt deceived.

Jones's change of attitude and William Williams's tirade act as reminders that there was also a significant amount of resistance to Iolo's ideas amongst the Welsh. Whispers had been passing around them about the bogus nature of many of them, and the suspect quality of his material, since they were first published. In 1807, Iolo's own patron, Owain Myfyr, accused him directly of forging the poems that he had contributed to the edition of Dafydd ap Gwilym, as the last exchange in their foundering relationship.[119] Davies, as we know, published a full frontal attack, and another followed in 1824, from a Welsh barrister working in London, called John Jones. He produced a history of Wales which portrayed the ancient British as pagans who bowed to idols, worshipped many deities and practised cruel acts of human sacrifice. He called Iolo a good poet but a bad thinker, and claimed that Iolo had himself been taken in by the late medieval Glamorgan poets and scholars on whose work he had relied, and who had invented a false portrait of ancient bards and Druids.[120] In this manner, Iolo's careful covering of his tracks as a forger, by his citation of non-existent but plausible sources, could itself be turned against him. Jones was also a good enough philologist, and source analyst, to point out that the language, and many of the references, in poems credited to Taliesin and other early bards could only derive from a period after 1100.[121] This hit directly at Davies, as well as Iolo, and commenced the process of proper study and dating of medieval Welsh literature which continues to the present. It was possible, also, for scholars to incorporate aspects of Iolo's history into works on Wales while rejecting both his viewpoint and the possibility of ever knowing what was true. Such a one was David Williams, whose history of Monmouthshire appeared in 1796. He playfully and deftly revealed how the ancient evidence for Druidry could be legitimately used to draw a number of completely different conclusions, in a way of which any postmodernist critic of the present day might be proud. Thus he dismissed all ancient teachings as a 'tissue of illusion', and those of the Druids as 'cabbalistic revelries'.[122]

How much credit was given to any of these viewpoints by Welsh people in general, or even those particularly concerned with literature and scholarship, seems impossible to tell. It is tempting to take as the nearest thing to a normative reaction, if only because nobody challenged it, the judgement pronounced in a leading forum for Welsh letters, *The Cambrian Register*, in 1811. This anonymous contribution weighed up the charges made against Iolo by Davies, and Iolo's abusive reply (published in the same issue of the journal), and found both men wanting, and both praiseworthy. It thought Iolo too reliant on dubious sources, and too influenced by his love of liberty and human rights, and Davies too reliant on Bryant's theories, and too influenced by his own conservative instincts. It concluded that both had 'but a slender claim to the merit or praise of impartiality', but that both had 'greatly contributed to increase the knowledge of British antiquities'.[123] How far such a balanced, shrewd and generous verdict was typical, however, is an open question. It *is* rather curious that there was no immediate and major controversy over Iolo's assertions about the Welsh past, comparable with that which had raged over the authenticity of Macpherson's 'Ossian' poems, especially once Davies's book was at hand to stoke one. Perhaps nobody felt confident enough in their own scholarly powers, faced with such difficult source material, to start one.

All the work above was published in English, and could therefore be read freely throughout Britain, though only those who understood Welsh could, of course, participate in the arguments over sources. Iolo's own friendships, made in London, provided a direct channel by which his ideas could travel further into the English literary world. The main agent for this transmission was Robert Southey, who published an epic poem about a legendary Welsh hero, Madoc, regarded since the sixteenth century as a discoverer of America, and leader of a Welsh colony planted there, in the twelfth century. The American War of Independence had produced a new upsurge of interest in the story among the London Welsh, Iolo himself having forged some documents to support it.[124] Southey's poem, published in 1805, included not only a portrait of a medieval bardic *gorsedd*, taken directly from Iolo's representations, but an affectionate tribute to 'old Iolo' himself.[125] For English historians, to show awareness of the new information coming from Welsh sources was to display a scholarly sophistication, equivalent to their twentieth-century counterparts being able to quote ideas from French, German or Russian publications. Sir Richard Colt Hoare, who raised the study of prehistoric artefacts to a new level at this time, twice incorporated Iolo's material on bards and Druids into his books.[126] A gentleman signing himself 'S.R.M.' sent a letter to a Wiltshire newspaper in 1824 in which he artfully combined the opinions of Iolo and Davies, which he saw as shedding new light on his county's famous prehistoric monuments.[127] This may have been Samuel Rush Meyrick, who with Charles Hamilton Smith published a famous illustrated history of ancient Britain in 1815 which used Iolo's descriptions both for the text and for the gorgeous drawings that accompanied it. They also added selected information from Davies, as if the two writers complemented each other.[128] Less prominent publications by English historians also made use of Iolo's work,[129] and it was sometimes built into guidebooks. The team of writers who brought out a multi-volume one on the main sights of England and Wales, in 1814, showed how they had kept up with current scholarship by declaring that Stukeley's interpretation of Avebury was now out of date, and substituting one based on Iolo's pseudo-history. They matched this by reinterpreting Stonehenge in harmony with Davies's ideas, declaring that there, as well, Stukeley was now overtaken.[130]

Just as significant, in this context, was a pamphlet published by an English curate in 1824. He was based in Stoke-on-Trent, and, like Davies and many another clergyman before him, was trying to write his way to attention and preferment. He commenced his work with the declaration that the Welsh had now taken over the Druids for themselves, and that his aim was to recover them for the English.[131] This hit on a major cultural truth. The achievement of William Stukeley had been, it was suggested earlier, to turn the Druids into ancestors whom all the British could hold in common, whether they admired them (as Stukeley did) or not. This had presented the Welsh with a problem and an opportunity. The problem was that a general British adoption of the Druids meant that, in this respect as in so many others in which the new British identity was invoked, the major shareholders in the project would be the English. The unique Welsh claim to be the true and direct heirs of the ancient British would be further eroded, in concert with the general evaporation of traditional Welsh culture under the impact of a European modernity of which the English were the local exemplars and powerhouses. The opportunity was to re-establish a particular connection between the Druids and the Welsh which would reinforce the twin projects of reviving and consolidating a distinctive Welsh identity, and of persuading the other British nations to admire it. Iolo Morganwg, however dishonest his means, had done much to accomplish both aims. It is not clear how apparent this was to him, and how great a success he had felt his life on balance to be, as his world slowly shrank around him with his declining health. During his last three years, he, for so long the indefatigable walker, could no longer move beyond the end of his garden in Flemingston. His last literary project was a second volume of hymns in Welsh for his fellow Unitarians, but like so many others this was left incomplete when he died, surrounded by his piles of writing, at the end of 1826.[132]

By contaminating the resources of Welsh historical tradition with bogus texts, Iolo Morganwg had deliberately and repeatedly broken what was, even in his time, regarded as one of the fundamental practical rules and moral precepts of scholarship. The question of what he himself gained from this admits of no simple answer. It seems that he hoped to accomplish four different ambitions. The first was to achieve adulation and wealth for himself. In this he had more or less completely failed. He had certainly gained an impressive reputation as an authority on Welsh literature, but his personality and his political beliefs had combined to prevent that from translating into major material benefits. His second ambition had been to advance the cause of political and religious liberty, and so help to create a better human world. There had certainly been some small advances in British liberties during his lifetime, and many more and greater would follow; but it is difficult to specify any effective contributions that he himself had made to that process. His third hope had been to push his native Glamorgan into the leadership of Welsh cultural life. Here he had made a considerable impact: in the words of Ceri Lewis, the foremost living expert in the county's literary tradition, he made a hitherto unimportant part of Wales appear to be its most interesting and significant province.[133] His fourth wish had been to increase the importance of Wales within the British superstate, and to give its people an institution, and ideas, that would stimulate their culture and mightily reinforce and focus the existing attempts to recover and utilize its bardic heritage. In that, also, he had been successful, and (as shall be seen) would have a yet greater impact after his death. The impact of his own bardic skills had not brought him material riches; but it had, after a fashion, both conferred immortality on him and altered the human world.

6

⤳⤫⤶

INTERLUDE: A PAIR
OF WILLIAMS

A t this point, the broad narrative of the changing place of Druids in the British consciousness needs to be interrupted. There are various themes and issues connected to it in the Georgian period which have still not been properly considered, and can be dealt with now by a study of two Englishmen. Each has been specially associated with Druids, in different ways, and this association is best understood in the context of a particular aspect of culture. A more skittish title for this chapter would be 'From Williams to Williams', because both the men concerned were called William, and both have much in common with Edward Williams, alias Iolo Morganwg. They make natural successors to a consideration of Iolo. All three of them worked creatively with prevailing ideas about Druids, and in the process produced images of their own which were to make a great impression on posterity. They were contemporaries, and the other two, in one case certainly and in the other probably, knew of Iolo and his work. All three were excited and inspired by the French Revolution, and contributed to the ferment of radical ideas that occurred in Britain in the 1790s. One of the other two men was William Blake, equally celebrated as a poet, artist, religious mystic and prophet of national reform and renewal, whose work has always been recognized as drawing heavily on Druidical images. His broad face, with its high-domed forehead, staring, visionary eyes, and tightly pulled, resolute mouth, is one of the iconic images of Georgian art and letters. He will be set in the context of historical writings about Druids in late eighteenth-century Britain. The other was William Wordsworth, one of the leading British poets of all time and the one who wrote most often about Druids. Visually as well as in his verse, with his slim form and tapering, sensitive face with deep-set eyes, he remains one of the archetypal Romantics. He will be set against a background of hostile treatments of the ancient Druids in Georgian poetry. By this means, the place of Druids in the imagination of each, it is hoped, be properly represented, and their role in the wider culture of the time can be properly rounded out.

* * *

By the second half of the eighteenth century, the Druids featured prominently in every history of Britain, local, regional or national, that dealt with the ancient past.

They were likely to be linked to every megalithic monument, and most dramatic natural rock formations. A full treatment of references to them in the historical writings of the period, therefore, would turn into a roll-call of works dealing with ancient Britain and its remains. What will be attempted here is something more selective: to deal only with those texts that made judgements on the nature of ancient Druidry and attempted to alter or augment opinions of it.

Some of these judgements were unequivocally admiring, and a consideration of them will begin with the few which wholly or almost wholly endorsed Stukeley's view of Druids. It has been suggested that, despite his tremendous success in drawing attention to them, he convinced only a small number of people of his own interpretation of their rites and beliefs. None the less, there were at least a couple, and the one who wrote most extensively was a Wiltshire vicar called William Cooke, who published a book in 1754.[1] He repeated and endorsed Stukeley's points at length, leaving out the archaeological fieldwork but adding plenty of scriptural and classical quotation. Like his hero, he published on Druids as proof that modern sceptics and freethinkers were wrong: Christianity was the natural religion of humanity and the perfection of the one religion revealed to the first humans. Like Stukeley, also, he emphasized that the true form of Christianity was the Church of England, which had been presaged by Hebrew patriarchs and Druids alike, and to which Roman Catholicism had represented merely an interruption. In 1795 the curate of Avebury, Charles Lucas, provided an account of the megalithic complex there for the gentleman who owned it at that date. This was based on Stukeley, but added ideas from Bryant, using them to mount an argument that the temple had been built by the Druids according to the dimensions of Noah's Ark.[2] The copy in the Bodleian Library includes a sad note that these sterling intellectual efforts did not achieve their intended effect: Lucas remained on the bottom rung of the clerical ladder, dying as a country curate.

Others, more eminent as authors, took their own line. One of the earliest and most distinguished of the Georgian historians who dealt with the Druids respectfully, and at length, was the famous scholar Thomas Carte. It has been noted that in the seventeenth century proponents of a high ceremonial Church and a powerful and sanctified monarchy tended to favour Druids. An influential ancient priesthood, dignified, learned, and hedged by ritual, had an obvious appeal to such a mindset. In this, as in other respects, Carte, supporter of the exiled Stuarts and of divine right kingship, was a throwback. He dealt with Druids in the same much-read history of ancient and medieval England that repeated the legend of Edward I's persecution of the Welsh bards, and so directly inspired Gray's famous poem. He published this history in 1747, and it is a sign of how much Stukeley had put the Druids into the minds of the British by that time that Carte devoted to them the sample chapter that he sent out in the previous year to solicit subscriptions to cover the expense of publication. It stressed their political influence, even to the extent of supervising magistrates, and their exemplary way of life and moral character. He also, however, proclaimed that they had been recruited from the nobility, and so were the ancient equivalent of the House of Lords. Essentially, they were princes who had undergone training in learning and ethics at seminaries such as the one on Anglesey, and ran the state and commanded its armies as well as officiating in religion. They were, in fact, 'an order of men of the first quality, endowed with all that greatness of mind, which a noble birth, uncorrupted by vice and luxury, naturally inspires'.

Carte duly got his subscriptions, and then proceeded to take the Druids down a peg or two in the actual book. Still winging far beyond the actual historical sources on the thermal currents of his heated imagination, he accused them of using their skill in science 'to cover the ridiculousness of the charms they palmed upon people, as well as to supply the want of their efficacy in diseases'. None the less, they built 'stupendous monuments', and were initially practitioners of the true religion revealed to the first humans, offering only flowers, grain and cakes to the one deity. Later they degenerated into polytheists and idol-worshippers, and took up blood sacrifice, but indulged in these less than other pagans and, except in emergencies, only sacrificed human beings who were guilty of serious crimes. He added that they had probably picked up the habit of offering human beings at all from the unpleasant, oriental, Phoenicians. By disparaging the latter, he was signalling his distance from Stukeley, and he did so more dramatically by asserting that the Druids had built no temples until taught to do so by the Romans. Stonehenge, Avebury and similar monuments were therefore all later than the Roman conquest. In this opinion, once again, Carte was a survival from an earlier age. He held to his earlier view that Druids had been excellent judges and taught good ethics, and his affection for universities showed in his assertion that their practice of dwelling in colleges improved their manners and learning. He proudly cited everything of note that had recently been published on them – Stukeley, Toland and Rowlands – while presenting a portrait that was uniquely his own. It made them into attractive ancestors while still enabling the present-day English to feel superior to them in religion, science and morals.[3]

In the second half of the century, another leading English intellectual arrived at much the same result: Edmund Burke, a front-rank politician who also made major contributions to the philosophy of art, history and politics. His account of the development of England began by pointing out that the role of the Druids had not been exceptional, because among all primitive peoples justice was administered by the priesthood. Despite this, Burke thought that they had been unusually fine priests for their time: 'it must be owned that in general their ideas of divine matters were more exalted than those of the Greeks and Romans; and that they did not fall into an idolatry so coarse and vulgar'. He praised them also for including both sexes, equally, in their order, and having genuine learning. He believed that their religion was based on natural forces that represented the fundamental powers of the cosmos or stood symbolically for genuine theological truths: thus, the oak embodied the stability and long duration of the power of the one deity. He accused the Romans of suppressing them because they were rival sources of authority, and not because there was anything wrong with their beliefs or actions.[4]

Even as these English giants spoke well of Druidry, some Scots continued to maintain the traditionally benevolent attitude taken by their countrymen. The reputation of Scottish culture in Europe as a whole was given a tremendous boost by James Macpherson's 'Ossian' poems, which seemed to provide a new body of ancient literature, technically accomplished and deeply atmospheric, to inspire artists and writers in the present. Druids sometimes gained benefit from the general increase in admiration for old Gaelic culture which the poems produced. They were, of course, controversial from the moment of their appearance, some critics immediately suspecting (correctly) that they had been wholly or partly fabricated by Macpherson himself. This, however, had the effect of making his defenders the more intent on magnifying the virtues of the ancient society which had apparently created them. One of the foremost of these writers was Hugh Blair, who emphasized the learning traditionally credited to the Druids as proof of the sophistication of the prehistoric Scots.[5] One of the oddest was John Smith, who despite his impeccably Lowland name was minister of a parish in the authentically Highland hinterland of Argyll. In 1780 he tried to cap Macpherson's achievement by publishing more bogus bardic poetry and passing it off as the work of the ancient Gaels. As a preface, he added an account of the Druids which was based mainly on the work of Toland, removing the latter's prejudices and substituting those of Smith himself.

He began by attempting to drag back to Scotland, in the matter of Druidry, the attention which was starting to wander towards Wales. Pointing out that the Scottish Highlands had never been conquered by the Romans, he argued that the folklore of the region provided a particularly valuable source of information on Druids, being the product of a society which had included them and which had never been contaminated by foreign invasion. By mixing together Ammianus Marcellinus's ancient text with actual Highland culture, he asserted that the Druids had occupied the summit of a hierarchy which descended from them through bards, to *sennachai* or historians, and finally to *eubages*, the apprentices. In his scheme, their 'moderation' and 'mildness' meant that they kept the respect of warlike chieftains who would not have tolerated a cruel or oppressive priesthood; Smith was bidding for the sympathy of readers who disliked the pretensions of established clergy. They had a simple religion derived from the true original revelation, which venerated a single god, and believed in a devil opposed to him, and in heaven and hell. As the latter were still a part of Highland folk tales, the Greeks and Romans must simply have been wrong in crediting Druids with a belief in transmigration of souls. They were not a celibate clergy, of the sort instituted by the Catholic Church, and references in the ancient texts to Druidesses must have been to their wives. They did not sacrifice humans, something charged against them by hostile Greek and Roman writers who had mistaken for it the execution of condemned criminals. Indeed, they did not even sacrifice animals, offering flour, milk, herbs and eggs to their deity as modern Highlanders did. Smith confided to a Britain on the brink of industrial revolution the news that the Druids had been great scientists and technocrats. Pliny's reference to their wearing of serpents' eggs had been a misunderstanding of a symbol that they had carried of their knowledge that the earth was round. They had invented the telescope, mastered mechanical engineering, and probably invented gunpowder, to judge from Gaelic tales of Druids conjuring fire and summoning storms. By fighting off the pagan Romans, the Highlanders had prepared Scotland to turn more readily to Christianity: 'Druidism may have been the purest of all pagan superstitions, and perhaps the wisest of all institutions that were merely human. But our religion is divine.'[6]

These, then, were the most favourable portraits of Druids painted by British historians in the mid- to late eighteenth century. None of them went so far as to suggest that ancient Druidry might actually have been superior to modern culture, presenting it instead as an early preparation for the blessings of modernity. In addition to them, there were several authors whose treatment of Druids was either more ambivalent or less consistent; and the greatest of these was Macpherson himself, the creator of the Ossian poetry. At first sight, he should have been an obvious person to eulogize Druids, given his nationality, his Highland background, and his project of getting contemporary Europeans to respect traditional Gaelic culture. Instead he banished them from the poems. His official reason for their absence was that they had been destroyed in a civil war that had engulfed northern Britain a generation or two before the time at which the poetry had been composed. He did not, however, trouble to conceal his own satisfaction at this development, terming them 'cunning and ambitious priests' whose 'pretended intercourse with heaven' gave them too much power in civil as well as religious affairs.[7] His recent biographer Fiona Stafford has suggested that this animosity was due to Macpherson's opposition to the Presbyterian Scottish clergy of his own day, whom he saw as wielding a repressive influence over his compatriots. He therefore attacked the Druids as their ancient counterparts, preferring to identify instead with the native bards, the nearest corresponding figures to the modern literary world to which he belonged.[8]

However, his criticism of them was always qualified: in the comments on the poems quoted above, he still declared that, for priests, they had wielded their authority well: 'they never broke out into violence or oppression' (as early modern Scottish clergy had done).[9] When he came to write his own history of Britain and Ireland, he was still more generous. As Smith was to do, he used Highland customs and beliefs to fill gaps in knowledge of the Druids left by the ancient sources. According to him, their fundamental tenet was faith in a single supreme being, whose spirit was expressed in the elemental powers of nature: they were pantheists, not polytheists. Unlike the Brahmins, Macpherson continued, they credited humans with distinct individual souls. They had no concept of hell, but believed that heroic souls went on to an unusually blissful afterlife, and everybody else passed to one which, although less superlative, was still better than the mortal world.[10] As Iolo Morganwg was to be, Macpherson was at heart a reformer, who wanted to check the pretensions of contemporary churchmen and offer a vision of a kinder religion than hellfire-toting brands of Christianity.

Another prominent author whose attitudes developed with time was the northern antiquary William Hutchinson, a Durham lawyer. He dealt with them first in a guidebook to the Lake counties which appeared in 1774. Here he was already prepared to defend Druids against the charge of human sacrifice, declaring that foreigners had mistaken for that the execution of people guilty of atrocious crimes. He praised them for the justice and dignity of their conduct. However, when describing the prehistoric stone circle of Long Meg and Her Daughters, set against the green Pennine fells, he was stricken by fear of the power that unscrupulous clergy might wield in a primitive society. He 'reflected on the trembling enthusiastic multitudes who here perhaps had assembled to hear the priestly dictates touching government and moral conduct; to learn the Druids' arrogant philosophy and superstitions, and cherish an implicit faith in the immortality of man's intellectual spirit, though in transmigration to reptiles and beasts of prey. Perhaps here princes submissively have stood to hear the haughty Druid exclaiming:

> Thou art a king, a sovereign over frail men;
> I am a Druid, servant of the Gods;
> Such service is above such sovereignty.'

Going on to the equally impressive circle at Castlerigg, within sight of the majestic peaks of the Cumbrian mountains, he was equally nervous, associating their mega-liths with sacrifice.[11] Within two years, however, he had changed his mind. In the second edition of his guide, the forbidding fantasy at Long Meg had gone, to be replaced by a eulogy on the Druids for the justice and dignity of their conduct. Once more he declared that foreigners had mistaken for human sacrifice the execution of criminals. He suggested that the methods used were more merciful than those in the London of his own time: 'what Druid but would have been struck dumb with aston-ishment and horror at our Tyburn executions?'[12]

A decade later, in his great history of County Durham, Hutchinson still saw Druids as having dominated civil jurisdiction and government as well as religion, with secular chiefs elected only as temporary war leaders, and thought them well fitted to do so. He had them worshipping a god of nature in high places, without idols, and cele-brating the passage of seasons as their festivals. He reassured his readers (and, presumably, himself) that 'they seem to have practised little priestcraft, and held not the ignorance of their adherents in the bonds of superstition'. In his imagination, their stone circles had been courts of law, each stone representing a division of the local tribe, with a Druid delegate standing before it. Each session was opened with rites before a nearby altar, which had a fire kindled upon it as emblem of the divine pres-ence and was fed with sweet-smelling woods. Each Druid, in this happy picture, wore an amulet as the emblem of their deity's attributes: 'wisdom, eternity and universal love'. Hutchinson's villains were, of course, the Romans, who introduced an idolatrous pagan religion and slaughtered the Druids in order to do so.[13] Ten years beyond that, when he published the first volume of his matching history of Cumberland, he was even keener on Druidry, declaring how 'wonderfully enlightened' they and their society seemed to have been. Faced with the excesses of the French Revolution, his earlier nervousness of churchmen had evaporated and he told his readers that, although 'priestcraft' was dreadful, its opposite extreme, 'cynicism and licentiousness', was worse. A learned and pious clergy, such as the Druids had been, were recom-mended by him to keep the 'multitude' in awe.[14]

Another author whose attitudes shifted was the Hampshire vicar William Gilpin, who produced immensely influential guides to the English landscape and its monu-ments, which educated travellers into seeing the beauty and majesty in them and informed artists of the best prospects from which they might be painted. They are major texts of the developing Romantic Movement. In 1772, when making his own visit to the stone circle at Castlerigg, he decided that it provided 'strong proofs of the savage nature of the religion of those heathen priests: Within these magical circles we may conceive any incantations to have been performed ... where our ancestors, in their nocturnal orgies, invoked the spirits which rode upon the winds – the awful forms of their deceased forefathers'.[15] By the time he reached Stonehenge, necromancy had turned into piety: 'the Druid, though savage his nature, had the sublimest ideas of the object of his worship'.[16]

Others simply did not know quite what to think. An example is another clergyman, John Whitaker, who set himself the task of writing the history of his home town of Manchester, as it was growing into the first and greatest of the new cities produced by industrialization. He began by praising the Romans for having introduced Christianity to Britain and so rescuing it from a 'deep night of ignorance' represented by a Druidical religion corrupted into idol worship, even as Roman Catholicism was later to deform Christianity. He went on to qualify this condemnation by saying that Druidry had once been pure, and indeed retained to the end, almost alone among heathen forms of worship, the three sound doctrines of 'a Providence, the soul's immortality and the world's destruction'. Looking wistfully at his local Lancashire countryside, which was starting to disappear as villages united into a conurbation, he allowed his senses to be moved by what he imagined to have been the setting of the ancient religion. He visualized mighty megalithic monuments set amid a 'magnificent amphitheatre of woods', and mused that 'all must have very strongly laid hold upon that religious thoughtfulness of soul which has ever been so natural to man'. Then, getting a grip on himself, he changed tack again and reminded readers that the same religion had also contained 'the grossest impurities and the most abominable mixtures', including human sacrifice.[17]

From this middle ground, two different spectra lead out. One consists of historians who had no real interest in Druids as such, but used them as material for wider theories about the nature of religion. The most notable of these consisted of the new school of British orientalists, one product of the conquests by British arms in India during the latter part of the century. Some of the effects of this have already been noted, in Iolo Morganwg's appropriation of Hindu ideas to create his own version of Druid theology. The pattern was set in 1790 by Reuben Burrow, who said that Indian religions had spread westward across the entire ancient world, and that Stonehenge was a Buddhist temple. He concluded: 'that the Druids of Britain were Brahmins, is beyond the least shadow of a doubt'.[18] Burrow was followed by Thomas Maurice, who published six volumes on the history of India in the 1790s. As part of this work, he argued that Druidical beliefs had been derived entirely from those of the Brahmins, who likewise met in sacred groves, venerated snakes (here he was following Stukeley), and held initiatory rites in caves. He derived the word Druid itself from the Eastern term 'dervish'.[19] The same sort of argument was then repeated by Francis Wilford, with the addition that Sanskrit texts referred to sacred islands in the west, which could be identified as the British Isles and therefore taken as evidence that the ancient Indians had direct contact with the ancient British.[20]

Another kind of avant-garde intellectual argument was presented by one William Williams, a resident of Pembroke, who tried to turn the ancient Phoenicians from the transport system for the Hebrew religion from Palestine to Britain to a major civilizing force in their own right. He pointed to what he took for similarities between the Welsh and Phoenician languages and that of the Berbers, the modern natives of north-west Africa, where the Phoenicians had planted the most famous of their actual colonies. He then argued that the Druids were only the westernmost outposts of this remarkable people.[21] The most significant, and the least influential, of the 'off-beat' interpretations of Druidry was made by a quarrelsome Scottish antiquarian, John Pinkerton. In 1789 he wrote a history of his nation in which he directly attacked the now established connection between Druids and megalithic monuments, terming it 'another idle dream of antiquists'. By 'another', he meant that he regarded almost everything said about Druids as rubbish: 'this century has been overwhelmed with nonsense concerning Druidism'. In making these claims, he pointed to a very real problem that Georgian scholars had chosen to ignore or forget: that Scandinavia, a region which had never known Druids, was rich in megalithic monuments very similar to those of the British Isles.[22] Pinkerton had in fact hit the major weakness in the orthodoxy that he was attacking, and his general assessment of contemporary scholarship regarding Druids was horribly accurate. He himself, however, could do no better. Like all intellectuals of his time, he was bound to the Greek and Roman classics, medieval literature and the Bible for a framework in which to locate the early European past. He could therefore only insist that megaliths had been Scandinavian courts of justice, brought to Britain by the Vikings: an argument which had been sunk by Aubrey a century before, when he pointed out that such monuments did not correspond to Scandinavian areas of influence in the British Isles. This, and his needlessly provocative manner, rendered his arguments ineffectual.

A second spectrum of opinion which led out of the 'middle ground' of historians' attitudes consisted of those which treated Druids with outright hostility. The authors who fall into this category had reasons for taking their stance that were even more individual than those for praising Druidry. One was Edward Ledwich, a Church of Ireland vicar who published an article in 1785 in the main periodical for scholars interested in British and Irish antiquities, that published by the Society of Antiquaries. He began by declaring testily that 'on no subject has fancy rooted with more licentious indulgence than on that of the Druids and their institutions'. He went on to argue, intelligently enough, that it was now impossible to recover what the Druids themselves had thought and taught, and that all that could be done was to cite what the Greek and Roman writers said about them. Having got this far with perfect reason, he proceeded to credit only those classical authors who had recorded unpleasant things, even believing Pliny's apparent charge of cannibalism. This he defended on the grounds that savages everywhere were alike, and if Native Americans and Polynesians could engage in atrocious practices in modern times, then so could the ancient British. Grudgingly, he conceded that the megaliths were imposing, and then insisted that people as foul as the Druids could never have erected them, and that they must therefore be the work of an earlier and better period of humanity.[23] Like Pinkerton, Ledwich had come close to hitting on a major truth, but by using entirely the wrong reasoning. It may be that his position as one of the rulers of a conquered people, the native Irish, had left him with less sympathy for indigenous peoples than most of the British of his time.

Other motivations propelled a lawyer named Edward King, who published an account of ancient Britain at the end of the century. He was another man possessed of an unusually pugnacious personality, which caused him to challenge commonly accepted views, and to quarrel with fellow members of the Society of Antiquaries over procedural issues. He was also an increasingly fervent Protestant mystic, who hated Roman Catholics and looked forward to the destruction of the world by his deity. Druids stood little chance of good treatment at the hands of a writer like this, and did not get any. He conceded that they were good scientists, for their times, but only in the service of a dreadful religion, of the kind which (to him) all pagans must have practised. When describing a dolmen on Anglesey, he felt that it conveyed 'that marvellous idea of stupendous danger, and horror, which was ever in the minds of those wretched Gentiles, whose corrupt superstition destined human victims to appease their false deities'. He rejoiced that 'when we consider the vast improvements of the arts, and of the conveniences of life, which have attended our emerging from the dreadful chains and fetters of those corrupt times; that we may become sincerely and heartily thankful, to the only true and Almighty God'. Like Pinkerton and Ledwich, his animosity towards prevalent ideas made him arrive at some genuine truths, although his general framework was no more correct than those he faulted. In his case, he cast doubt on whether formations like rocking stones, or basins formed in granite boulders, or natural boulders with holes in them, had been Druidical monuments as current opinion held.[24]

Most significant were the attacks launched by a trio of Scottish writers. Scots had been early both to recognize Druids as admired ancestors and to link them to megaliths, but there had long been an opposed tradition among them, associated with evangelical Protestants such as Buchanan. After the revolution of 1688 it was the radical, Presbyterian tradition that had been dominant in the Church of Scotland, and one of its leaders in the late eighteenth century was the Edinburgh minister Robert Henry. In his history of Britain, he proved himself an apt follower of Buchanan. He owned that Druids might once have practised the true religion of Noah, but insisted that in their hands it had become 'a very corrupt system'. In his fantasy, its practitioners had lived in colleges, with their leader, the Archdruid, dwelling in great splendour in Anglesey. Like Catholic monasteries and Anglican cathedral chapters (both anathema to Henry's kind of churchman), they had been supported by rich endowments of land. In addition they had demanded fees for every religious service and exacted annual tithes, making them the wealthiest members of their society. Henry adopted Borlase's imagined system of three orders of female Druid, but added that some of these lived like Catholics in nunneries. He conceded that, as descendants of Noah, they had probably believed in true doctrines, of the one god and the immortality of the soul. None the less, he insisted, they had taught superstition to the common people, to keep them in thrall, and had eventually come to believe in it themselves, turning into pagan polytheists addicted to large-scale animal sacrifice with the addition of human victims. Henry made one curious, and influential, contribution to the main national body of Druid lore, by declaring that they had celebrated their New Year on 10 March, and that this was the time when they cut the mistletoe, as described by Pliny. It is certainly true that some ancient peoples, most notably the Romans, dated their official year, when people took up government posts, from the spring equinox, even if the new year was still popularly celebrated at the opening of January. How Henry got the Druids to hold theirs at the equinox too (where his date would fall, adjusted in line with the calendar change of 1752), he never explained. He praised the Romans for having waged war on such a dreadful religion, and called the coming of Christianity a 'more agreeable subject'.[25]

A very similar line was taken by a less prominent minister in the same Church, John Macpherson, who served a parish on the Isle of Skye. Whereas John Smith could be appointed to a living among Highlanders, and be enthused by their traditional culture, Macpherson was born into that culture, and loathed it. A convert to the strongly evangelical Protestantism more associated with the Lowlands, he campaigned against the folk beliefs and customs of the Gaelic world as remnants of paganism, and despised those who preserved them as 'the injudicious vulgar'. In keeping with this stance, he condemned Druidry as 'idolatrous superstition', fit for barbarians.[26]

Our third Scot was a writer of much greater fame and very different hue; in religious terms, indeed, almost at a polar opposite. He was David Hume, one of the leading British figures in the pan-European movement known as the Enlightenment, which urged the supremacy of reason over religious revelation in human knowledge. As part of this programme, its adherents set out both to demand the practical demonstration of all truths and to obtain an understanding of the cosmos, by pooling the best possible information on the nature of the physical universe and its inhabitants. None of this worked to the benefit of the Druids. For one thing, thinkers like Hume were naturally opposed to powerful and traditional clergy, the embodiment of that religious obscurantism to which the Enlightenment was opposed. For another, as part of the movement's commitment to human progress, its proponents reversed the biblical portrait of ancient history as one of degeneration from the true faith revealed by the deity to the ancestors of humanity. Hume and his fellows both believed in such a deity and thought this belief to be reasonable, given that the world seemed to them to have been fashioned by an intelligence according to a design. Hume portrayed primitive humans, however, as irrational and uncomprehending, ruled by passion and desire and obsessed with immediate needs and targets; rather as philosophers such as himself viewed the common people of their own time. In his scheme, they had therefore started as pagan polytheists and grown slowly to the recognition of the one true deity, as civilization and cumulative wisdom increased. Hume himself was not entirely convinced that progress was actually possible for the mass of humanity, suspecting that it might be confined to sages of his own kind, and saw in most people of his time the same disposition to ignorance and fear that he imagined had dominated earlier ages.

He thus had two objections to Druids – for being priests and for being ancient – and attacked them with unrelenting hostility. He opened the first volume of his history of England with the declaration that 'no species of superstition was ever more terrible than that of the Druids'. He imagined them as cowing their followers with the threat of excommunication and of being reborn after death in animal bodies. They kept their knowledge secret from the multitude, sacrificed human beings, and hoarded the spoils of war. They were idolaters of the worst kind, and the fact that the normally tolerant Romans had abolished them only served to show how peculiarly horrible their religion had been.[27]

Some of the same attitudes seem to have rubbed off on our last example, the English antiquarian and engraver Joseph Strutt, who pioneered research into such areas as the story of costume. His work was characterized both by sympathy for the common people (from whom he was himself drawn) and a dislike of clerics, especially of the powerful and ceremonious kind exemplified by Catholics. In his history of England he laid into Druids as masters of 'pretended miracles and mysterious doctrines', with which they had overawed the multitude. In this he held them to have been like all ancient priests, but he went on to insist that they were even worse than the others: 'all the ancient records of the known world cannot furnish a more striking view of the prevalence of superstition in the people, or the arbitrary government of the priest, than we shall find among the deluded British'.[28] Strutt's judgements were the more strident in that his research was even more superficial than that of most commentators of the age: he was just repeating, wholesale, what he found in Henry's book with some additions from Toland. None the less, he would hardly have been so attracted to, and persuaded by, these authors had he not shared some of their prejudices.

What must be clear from this survey was that historians of the Druids who published in late Georgian Britain wrote very much according to individual inclination; there were no prescribed confessional or partisan lines to be taken. Despite this, there were some predispositions, and although these were never absolute they corresponded very much to those that had been manifest ever since Druids became interesting to the British during the sixteenth century. Writers who tended naturally to favour religious ritual and a powerful and privileged clergy were inclined to admire them and present them in the best possible light. Those who preferred a religion based more on Scripture and on evangelical preaching, or personal religious revelation, were much more likely to be hostile, as was anybody who resented and opposed the pretensions of established churchmen. This pattern puts Iolo Morganwg into a still clearer perspective, as the leader of a Welsh movement to buck the trend by reclaiming the Druids for radical politics and religion. Among the English and Scots, however, the general pattern continued to hold up well, from the earliest days of the Reformation to the end of the eighteenth century. This is the context in which we may place William Blake.

* * *

Blake was a radical Protestant who worshipped in groups of voluntarily gathered enthusiasts operating outside the national Church and who shared many of the reformist hopes of the 1790s. He created and illustrated a mythical Christian history of his own, centred on Britain (and especially on the London area) and functioning as a parallel to that provided in the Old Testament. Druids featured prominently in this. In all these features he has strong similarities to Iolo; but, given the pattern that has been suggested above, it might be expected that he would be antipathetic to Druids rather than favourable. This is exactly what we find.

Blake's engagement with Druids seems to have begun in 1794, with his poem *Europe: A Prophecy*. It was immediately hostile, depicting a fallen angel seeking his 'ancient temple serpent-formed' (as Stukeley had represented Druidical Avebury), and finding its 'oak-surrounded pillars, formed of massy stones . . . placed in the order of the stars'. This place, the verses proclaim, was designed for the service of 'God a tyrant crowned', and encloses 'the Stone of Night'.[29] He returned to them in *Vala*, completed by 1803. The keynote of their religion was established here as the butchery of human beings, in an ancient London area where 'groans ran along Tyburn's brook and along the river of Oxford/ Among the Druid temples'.[30] In *Milton*, completed by 1810, the references multiplied, while remaining occasional. Blake had picked up on the notion of Druidry as the British manifestation of the original worldwide religion. What was sensationally original about his reworking of this, however, was his conviction, reached after 1800, that the religion concerned had in some sense begun in Britain. He seems to suggest in his poetry that his own island, and indeed his own native district of London and its environs, had been the setting for the early events of the Book of Genesis. Britain had therefore been both the birthplace of the human race, and of the true and original faith that it practised, and the scene of the fall of that faith into corruption, after which it was given to the rest of the world. It is not altogether clear how literally he intended this to be understood, and whether he was finding parallel correspondences for biblical events on British soil rather than simply transplanting those events to Britain.[31] None the less, the place of the Druids in this transposition of sacred history is relatively certain. They were both the priests of the first, true religion, and then the operators and personifications of the satanic form into which it turned. From Lambeth, in Blake's vision, 'stony Druid temples' spread first across the island and then over the rest of the earth, from Ireland to Peru and Japan. This vision gave strength and meaning to his haunting refrain, 'All things begin and end in Albion's ancient Druid rocky shore'. Yet it was not as the former servants of the good faith that Blake thought of Druids, but as the later servants of the devil, comparable to the exploitative industrialists of his own time:

> And the mills of Satan were separated into a moony space
> Among the rocks of Albion's temples, and Satan's Druid sons
> Offer the human victims throughout all the earth.[32]

In 1809 he supplemented his poetic references with a catalogue note, which accompanied a now lost painting, the largest and most ambitious that he ever created, on *The Ancient Britons*.[33] This was produced for none other than Iolo Morganwg's former friend and supporter William Owen.[34] Owen had supplied Blake with some of Iolo's triads, which represented a much more benevolent view of Druidry, and it is interesting to see how much Blake felt able to compromise with this in his note. He had in common with it the idea – which was after all embedded in the Bible – of a single good faith, revealed by the true god to the ancestors of all humanity, and looking forward to Christianity: 'Antiquity preaches the Gospel of Jesus'. This he argued against authors of the Enlightenment tradition, who had called into question the literal truth of the

biblical narratives at various points, terming their kind, bitterly, 'the reasoning historian, turner and twister of causes and consequences', and riposting 'away with your
reasoning and your rubbish!' As part of this picture, he also accepted the long-argued
idea that the original Druids had been upholders of the pristine ancient religion:
'Abraham was a Druid, and Noah'. Here, however, Blake made a further remarkable
departure from existing ideas. Because to him Britain was the original Holy Land, and
the Druids the original ministers of religion, the degeneration of their religion must
have taken place not after the time of Abraham, as previous authors had believed, but
before it. To him the spread of their corrupt and bloody faith throughout the world had
threatened to annihilate the human race. It was to prevent such a disaster that
Abraham had been given his special revelation as a measure taken by the deity to
restore true religion: 'Abraham was called to succeed to the Drudical age, which began
to call allegoric and mental signification into corporeal command, whereby human
sacrifice would have depopulated the earth'.[35]

In his next epic poem, *Jerusalem*, probably completed in 1820, he dealt with Druids
repeatedly for the first and last time. Once again he established their main activity as
ritual murder. At ancient Paddington

... the Druid's golden knife
Rioted in human gore
In offerings of human life ...

They remained the tools of the Fiend:

Satan his name; in flames of fire
He stretched his Druid pillars far.

Such comments recur throughout the poem, as Druids and their stone circles are
associated with howling, wailing, chaos, weeping, torture and bloodshed, and equated
with the cruel religions of Canaanites, Syrians and Philistines which the Hebrew
prophets and kings had opposed. Their 'rocky circles' offer 'permanent remembrance
of sin', and the brightest moment in Blake's legendary history comes when Jesus
'the whole Druid law removes away' from Britain. To put this point into visual
form, he embodied it, in the year 1815, in an illustration to John Milton's poem,
'On the Morning of Christ's Nativity', which spoke of the fall of the pagan deities
at the birth of Jesus. Its centrepiece was the tumbling of the spirit of Apollo, hailed
by poets and artists in Blake's time as their classical patron, from a statue of him
sculpted and erected in the Greek and Roman manner. Lest anybody miss the
relevance to Britain, he positioned an image of Stonehenge, with a smoking fire of
sacrifice in front of it, so that the vanquished god appeared to be falling from that
as well.[36]

He went further in *Jerusalem*, to equate with Druids the deists and Enlightenment
philosophers whose call for a religion based on reason, and for respect for the faiths
of other peoples, struck both at his own emphasis on direct religious revelation and at

his intense personal relationship with Christ. To such ideas he responded that such 'Greek philosophy (which is a remnant of Druidism) teaches that man is righteous in his vegetated spectre – an opinion of fatal and accursed consequence to man, as the ancients saw plainly by revelation to the entire abrogation of experimental theory; and many believed what they saw, and prophesied of Jesus'.[37] Blake took a last swipe at Druids in 'The Ghost of Abel', which was written in or soon after 1821. Once again they were the Devil's ministers, Satan promising the youthful human race that 'I will have human blood . . . By the rock and oak of the Druid, creeping mistletoe and thorn, / Cain's city built with human blood'.[38]

Even in *Jerusalem*, references to things Druidic take up a small fraction of space and are incidental to the main point of the work; to Blake they were peripheral characters, present at all because his age regarded them as the dominant figures of ancient Britain. They have, accordingly, played little part in the huge literature of criticism devoted to his work, most of it being content to state their place in his personal theology and history, as has been done above.[39] A. L. Owen has provided the most evocative summary of their role: 'without moving from the background, they are, like figures in a striking tapestry, intrusive'. Owen went on to demonstrate that several details of Blake's picture of Druidry were taken from Stukeley, while in general it opposed Stukeley's own characterization of Druidry.[40] This is hardly surprising, as Stukeley had made it the forerunner of the established Church which Blake rejected; and there is a further and more ironic relationship between Blake and his predecessors. Whereas John Toland had demonized Druids as over-mighty priests, Blake – just as radical in his attitude to political and religious norms – demonized them as deists like Toland himself.

Some attempts have been made to find a direct connection between the work of Blake and Iolo Morganwg. Peter Fisher has suggested that 'the four Zoas' in *Vala* reflect Iolo's four circles of existence, but this is no more than possible.[41] Jon Mee has demonstrated that one of Blake's employers, the publisher Joseph Johnson, was a friend of Iolo, but has done no better than anybody else to prove that the two men actually met. He has argued forcefully for the similarities in some of their ideas: a common opposition to the slave trade and to war against France, a hatred of priest-craft and a yearning for a more primitive and democratic Christianity.[42] It is easy to suggest two more: both created a luxuriant mythical history for Britain – though Blake made no attempt to root his in historical fact – and both were fervent patriots, both at the national level (Wales and Britain) and the local (Glamorgan and London). None of this vitiates the fact that their view of the Druids developed in precisely opposite directions, as Blake remained much more faithful to the Bible and to radical Protestant tradition.

It is equally hard to prove a relationship between Blake and modern Druids. Here there is one striking and incontrovertible fact: that they were neighbours. Between 1785 and 1790 Blake lived at 28 Poland Street, with Lodge No. 1 of the Ancient Order of Druids, led by Hurle, meeting in the King's Arms Tavern only two doors away.[43] Is it possible that Blake, with his interest in ancient Britain, could have been in such close proximity to the lodge for half a decade without becoming involved? Perhaps it is, for a number of reasons. First, the whole point of the lodge system was to hold meetings behind closed doors, with signs and passwords to fend off non-members and an agreement to keep all proceedings secret. The object was to ensure that no one else in the pub, let alone two houses away, would be aware of what was going on. Second, no biographer of Blake, who lived a relatively well-recorded (and extremely well-investigated) life, has found any reference to his membership, at the time or retrospectively. Third, the Ancient Order itself never claimed, at the time when its earliest history was still in memory and being written down, that the visionary artist and poet had been part of it. To be sure, that history survives only in snatches copied almost a century later, but if those included Charles James Fox then they ought to have mentioned Blake. Fourth, the view of Druids taken by the order was a wholly benevolent and admiring one, very different indeed from that of Blake, which in turn sprang from the root of his religious beliefs and instincts. Fifth, Blake was not (unlike, say, Stukeley or Toland) particularly clubbable, preferring on the whole to avoid societies and fraternities. Sixth, he never showed any exceptional enthusiasm for music, which was the main point of the order's meetings. Seventh, if the identification of Hurle made by Wilhelm North was correct, he was a pillar of the capital's Anglican parish establishment, and so part of a society and religion very different from Blake's determined nonconformity. All told, it is impossible to prove that Blake did not join the lodge, but the odds are probably against it. It may well be, after all, that he simply did not know that it was there, or did not care about it if he did.[44]

Other difficulties attend his later association with a different Druid order, the Universal Bond. In Ross Nichols's *Book of Druidry*, written in the early 1970s but published posthumously in 1990, Blake is claimed as its fifth chief, in the succession that started with John Toland and continued with William Stukeley. This is part of the foundation legend of the order, which has been examined before in this book and will be put into its own historical context later, as will Ross Nichols's considerable services to modern Druidry. As evidence for the claim, Nichols cited the similarity between some of Blake's ideas and those professed in his own order by the mid-twentieth century, and the fact that one of the poet's London homes was close to the tavern in which Toland had founded the Universal Bond.[45] It may readily be seen how slender the reasoning is in each case. Nichols also, however, proclaimed a more conclusive proof that Blake at least identified himself with Druidry: that at his trial at Chichester in 1804, for uttering alleged words against the government and in support of Napoleon, he refused to take the oath when called upon to testify, because he was a Druid.[46] This is precisely the kind of specific evidence, rooted in demonstrable source material, which a historian needs: but, on inspection, it is not there. In the surviving records of the trial, edited by G. E. Bentley Junior, Blake was never called to speak. Instead he watched as a barrister conducted his defence, breaking down the testimonies of the two people bringing the charge and constructing a picture of his own client as a loyal and orthodox member of society; which is why Blake was acquitted. His only words spoken in the courtroom were at one point to cry out ' 'tis false, 'tis false'.[47] Nichols also claimed that Blake 'mentioned that he was a Druid in the preface to one of his books',[48] but failed to specify which, and without such a reference it is hard to see what he meant. Clearly Ross Nichols admired Blake and was anxious to claim him as an ancestor: he did so repeatedly in his book, and wrote a letter to a magazine in 1971 upbraiding a contributor who had (reasonably enough) cast doubt on Blake's affection for Druids given what he had written in his poems.[49] It must be concluded, however, that to do so was to reverse the apparent truth of history, by propagating an impression that Blake identified himself, and his religion, with the Druids.

That truth seems to be that William Blake, in harmony with all the rest of his ideas and achievements, recast Druidry in a context which was radically new because it depended on a new and personal vision of Britain's place in the divine plan for humanity. In doing so, however, he provided a heterodox, but still recognizable, development of existing Protestant tradition, associated especially with its more evangelical and fervently reformist wing, which was in turn based on a fundamental reliance on the truth of Scripture.

*   *   *

Blake was not so unusual for his time in a different sense, as a poet who portrayed Druids as bloodthirsty barbarians. As we saw earlier, they were celebrated in Georgian poetry both as British patriots and as freedom-fighters, and as priests of nature and embodiments of the wisdom and goodness consequent on a close relationship with the natural world. Druidry remained, however, a rival, hostile, tradition which, like that among historians, was the preserve of a minority at this period but still flourishing. Indeed, because of the much greater prominence of Druids in the national consciousness, and the much greater number of literary references to them as a whole, the number of poems attacking them was greater than ever before.

Initially, at least, the authors, like those of historical works hostile to Druids, were aware that they were swimming against the current tide of opinion. The first to weigh in was Thomas Chatterton, who made an expedition from Bristol to view the stone circles at Stanton Drew in 1769. He was not in the best of moods, having just been ditched by his girlfriend, but this probably enhanced rather than provoked his decision to associate the monument with doom and gloom. He was young, audacious, ambitious and unscrupulous: like Iolo and Macpherson, he forged apparently early literary texts as part of his attempts to win attention and applause. His opposition to the prevalent admiring attitudes to Druidry probably reflected the same desire to make an impact by flouting orthodox taste. He reached the rings of megaliths in which both Stukeley and Wood had seen geometry reflecting the power and beauty of the universe, and pronounced:

> Joyless I hail the solemn gloom
> Joyless I view the pillars vast and rude
> Where, erst the foot of superstition trod
> In smoking blood imbued
> And rising from the tomb
> Mistaken homage to an unknown God . . .
> All hail ye solemn horrors of this scene

The blasted oak, the dusky green,
Ye dreary altars by whose side,
The Druid priest in crimson dyed,
The solemn dirges sung,
And drove the golden knife,
Into the palpitating seat of life,
When rent with horrid shouts, the distant valleys ring,
The bleeding body bends
The glowing purple stream descends
Whilst the troubled spirit near
Hovers in the steamy air
Again the sacred dirge they sing
Again the distant hill and coppic'd valley ring.[50]

Poor Chatterton! Like Iolo, he subsequently trod the way of hope and expectation to London, where both failed him. Unlike Iolo, he did not retire to the provinces when they did so, but died in the capital, as one of Britain's more famous suicides.

Two years later a clergyman called James Foot weighed in by publishing a long poem called *Pensoroso*, about the wanderings and musings of a holy man. It had actually been written back in 1760, and Foot's intention was to instruct his readers in piety and good citizenship. Its section on the Druids was designed as a direct counterblast to the sympathetic portrait of them in Mason's bestselling poem *Caractacus*. Foot conceded that he thought they had known 'some useful truths', and his hero could find something moving in the sight of one of the stone circles attributed to them, 'sublimely roof'd' by the sky. None the less, Foot felt obliged to remind his contemporaries of what he felt that too many of them had forgotten: that Druids had been tainted by dreadful rites of sacrifice. So the memory of these made the stone ring, for him, a place of 'drear remains', its ceremonies 'the bloody shambles of misguided zeal', the Druids themselves 'vile priests' with 'the butch'ring tools of heaven', and their deities 'fictitious beings of the crazy brain'. After this, Foot disclosed the true purpose of these reflections: to warn people first against the horrors of ancient paganism in general, which the Druids could be taken to typify, and then against those of Roman Catholicism, which he believed to represent a contamination of Christianity by paganism.[51]

This attack was followed a year later, in 1772, by that of another poet, Michael Wodhull, in verses mourning the disappearance of the English woodlands. This was a subject which, at the time, ought to have enlisted the Druids as allies, given their association with groves. Instead, Wodhull unleashed on them a completely uninhibited onslaught. He was a country gentleman with strong radical opinions, extending to support for complete religious toleration and, subsequently, to sympathy for the French revolutionaries. His hatred of Druidry was almost certainly due to his association of it with powerful and intolerant clergy. Once again, the poem concerned had been written years earlier, in 1763, and once again it is fairly clearly intended as a reply to Mason. Among hostile literature on the Druids, it is probably unique in accusing them, along with most of the usual vices, of halitosis:

Though in your holy grotts retired
The subtle priests with venomed breath
The thirst of homicide inspired
And urged the lingering rage of death:
To their polluted altars led
Where erst the captive youth had bled
Victim of hellish cruelty,
Devoted Mona's frantic shade
In vain implored your guardian aid
O'erthrown by Roman victory.[52]

Poets did not always take consistent attitudes to the subject. Thomas Warton has already been cited as one of those who created the early Romantic Movement, and, as such associated Druids with a reverence for the natural world which he adored. None the less, when writing a sonnet on Stonehenge, he could suddenly lash out at them as priests 'sprinkled with human gore'.[53] A parallel to Warton's combination of interests was provided by John Langhorne, the rector of Blagdon, a rural parish nestling underneath Somerset's Mendip Hills. He wrote a series of poems, at some time before his death in 1779, which turned the beauties of nature into vehicles for moral reflections. In one of these, he imagined coming across the ghost of a Druid in one of the caves with which the Mendips are filled. Immediately, he knew him as 'bloody', with a 'haggard eye-ball's hollow glare', and 'sable' hair with 'gleams of wild ferocity' darting through it. Readers who might be tempted to linger over the problem of how ferocity can gleam through hair would rapidly be distracted by the manner in which the Druid concerned 'smiled grimly' as he went about his favourite pastime, sacrificing babies.[54]

There seem to have been two different processes at work in such poetry by this date. The first was the familiar one, by which Druids could be treated as emblems of bad religion: priestcraft, paganism or Catholicism, according to the taste of the author. The second was a development within Romanticism itself. If one of its features, its celebration of the natural world, could work in favour of Druids, another, which appeared during the late eighteenth century, did not. This was the new taste for a literature that set out to entertain by emphasizing the horrifying, morbid, spooky and lurid aspects of both nature and humanity. It acquired the label of 'Gothic'. To writers in this new tradition, the disparaging ancient portraits of Druids, as priests of a gloomy and gory religion practised in shadowy groves, could be a literary gift. Their potential was further enhanced by their new association with megaliths, the very size, weight and crudity of which could provide awe-inspiring and barbaric settings for dreadful ceremonies. Until now, even those authors who had highlighted the bloodthirsty nature of Druidic religion had credited its practitioners with some dignity, and, where they drew attention to the identity of their human victims, tended to visualize them as young men. As the late Georgian period progressed, Druids began a transformation into beings literally or figuratively possessed by demons, taking an active pleasure in murder and torture and behaving as if demented. As part of this development, the innocence and vulnerability of their sacrificial victims began to be stressed as never before, to open a still greater human distance between them and their killers, and to equate the latter more readily with predatory beasts or fiends. Wodhull's 'hellishly cruel' priests with their 'venomed breath', and Langhorne's glaring child-murderer were among the first embodiments of this new breed.

By the end of the 1770s it was well established. The Oxford don Robert Holmes, holder of a number of offices in the Church of England, published an epic poem in 1778 in which he managed to equate the Roman conquest of Anglesey with the Christian conversion of Britain, as parts of the same civilizing process. The Druids whom he caricatured in it were enemies alike of heaven, humanity and sanity:

No more, th'impenetrable groves among,
With sacred spoils and idol-trophies hung,
From altars foul dark wreaths of smoke
Imbosom the religious oak
When roused by Mona's bloody-mantled priest,
Impatient homicide, his Druid-crew
With eyes of madness watch the midnight spell,
And drown with deaf'ning yell
The scream of captives stretch'd in furnace blue.
The voice of heav'n, in thunders loud,
Resounded from the rocking cloud –
Back to thy doom, thou spirit fell,
Dire Atheism, eldest-born of Hell.[55]

The fact that Holmes could equate paganism and atheism shows how deep his hostility to Druids ran, and it was a reminder that membership of the established Church was no automatic bar to such emotions. There was, however, a yet deeper significance in them. A hundred years before, Oxford University had been the centre of a movement to accord Druids both greater importance in the history of Britain and greater credit as bearers of the true religion of Noah or Abraham. Now, when the British as a whole had taken up the first idea, and many had also accepted the second, fellows of the same university seemed once again to be bucking the trend, but from the other direction. It was as if they did not wish to be associated with an accepted idea, even though they themselves had done much to create the circumstances for its acceptance. Warton (in that later poetic reference) and Holmes were both indications of this pattern, and so was a fellow of Oriel College, George Richards, who followed their work in 1791. He was reacting not only against a benevolent view of the Druids, but the fashionable idealization of indigenous peoples, above all those of the South Pacific, as noble children of nature. His purpose was to condemn both ancient and tribal cultures as savage and in need of improvement by more civilized invaders. When he contemplated pre-Roman Britain, he saw only

. . . superstition, sprung in elder time,
Wild as the soil, and gloomy as the clime.

Midst rocks and wastes the grove tremendous rose:
O'er the rude altars hung in dread repose
A twilight pale; like the dim sickly noon,
When the mid-sun retires behind the moon.
From sounding caverns rush'd the darksome flood;
Each antique trunk was stain'd with human blood.
'Twas sung, that birds in terror fled the shade;
The lightnings harmless round the branches play'd
And, in the hour of fate the central oak
Shook with the spirit of the god, and spoke.

There inevitably follow various 'direful rites', in the course of which

Rocks, by infernal spells and magic prayer,
Shook from their base, and trembled high in air.
The blasted stars their fading light withdrew;
The labouring moon shed down a baleful dew;
Spirits of hell aerial dances led;
And rifted graves gave up the pale cold dead.
Imperial man, creation's lord and pride,
To crown the sacrificial horrors, died.[56]

The ancient model behind these verses is Lucan's description of the grove near Marseilles, but it goes far beyond that; even Lucan's imagination did not stretch to levitating rocks. Oxford University in the late Georgian period is often considered a sleepy place, and yet here its members were not only anticipating what would become a general revulsion against the notion of the noble savage, but writing full-blown Gothic verse very early in that tradition.

Very few poets addressed the subject of Druids more than once, and those who did, like Warton, tended to do so in passing. One exception was the Cornishman Richard Polwhele, whom we have already encountered, praying for inspiration on the ridge of Carn Brea. He at least clearly believed that he had been heard, for he continued to produce further verses through the following three decades. In the course of this output, he repeatedly turned to the Druids for what, in a more gifted writer, would be called inspiration and increasingly denounced them as pagans. In 1777, while still a schoolboy, he was already condemning them for 'bigotry', and urging readers to adore 'mercy's tenderest God' as a result of his poetry. This is as part of a cautionary tale set beside the River Tamar on the Cornish border, in which a lone Druid, hiding in the woods after the rest of his kind have been extirpated, sacrifices his own son by mistake. The setting is, of course, an 'awful scene', with 'streaming blood of victims' staining the ground around the Druid's altar under an oak.

Polwhele's attitudes hardened further as he became a clergyman in the national Church, serving in a succession of parishes in Devon and Cornwall. Like a significant number of authors who were hard on Druids, he displayed a notable tendency to quarrels and controversy in his own life. In 1781 he wrote an ode to the Isle of Man, which, perversely by this date, he still insisted on regarding as the ancient Mona captured by Suetonius. Here he tackled head-on both the Romantic association of the Druids with a benevolent natural world, and the Gothic tendency to achieve a slightly guilty pleasure in contemplating the alleged atrocities of their religion:

> Yet when the lurid nightshade blooms
> To some lone ruin's deepening glooms
> The pensive poet steals:
> Oft as he marks the Druid groves
> And crumbling piles, his bosom heaves
> With thoughts of ancient days, and pleasing horror feels!

At this point the budding Romantic tourist is saved by a cherub, fluttering down from heaven to rebuke and reform him, saying

> 'Suppress, fond youth, the unhallow'd strain,'
> He cried, 'nor rashly thus profane
> These groves with pagan sighs:
> Rejoice, that crushed to earth, the abodes
> Of Druids, and their fabled gods,
> With superstition's frown affront no more the skies.'

Being thus cleansed of both sin and scansion, Polwhele went on to pour out further works, in which the triumph of Christianity over Druidic barbarism remained a favourite theme, until his death in 1838. One more example from them may stand as typical, being another poem on Mona, written in 1806:

> Broad the hostile flames arise
> From the reverential wood;
> Red its central gloom with blood!
> Many a white-rob'd Druid hoar
> Totters in the stream of gore;
> Meets the faunchion's [dagger's] furious blow;
> Sinking, execrates the foe;
> Or, across the cromlech's stone,
> Pours his dark mysterious moan;
> Or grasps his shrine, and hails the stroke,
> Stabb'd beneath the holy oak;
> Yelling, while the maniac maid
> Hurries down the dimwood glade;
> And uproots her bristling hair,
> Paler amid the ghastly glare!
> But lo! The scenes of other days are fled!

Yet mysterious horror fills
The long-scooped dales, where Druids bled,
And deepens the dark hills![57]

Thus demented and homicidal Druids, armed with knives and exclamation marks, were stock and fashionable figures in British verse by the time William Wordsworth began to write in the 1780s.

* * *

Wordsworth had three motivations for bringing Druids into his poetry: an interest in British history and its physical remains; a deep feeling of relationship with the natural world, to which Druidry had by now often been linked; and an upbringing in Cumberland, on the edge of that dramatic landscape of mountains, lakes and stone circles with which it had now been associated by authors such as Hutchinson and Gilpin. By the end of the eighteenth century, indeed, the Lake District had become one of the four great regions of the nation – the others being Cornwall, Wales and Wiltshire – into which Druids had become especially integrated as figures of the poetic and scholarly imagination. It is hardly surprising, therefore, that Wordsworth should include them in one of his earliest surviving works, written mostly in 1786 and 1787, during his last year at school. It consists of a series of reveries set in one of the steep valleys of the district, the Vale of Esthwaite. His imaginary encounter with Druids there shows how much the Gothic vogue in poetry had turned them, by that date, into aspects of (to Wordsworth, a literal) schoolboy nightmare:

At noon I hied to gloomy glades,
Religious woods and midnight shades,
Where brooding superstition frowned
A cold and awful horror round,
While with black arm and bending head
She wove a stole of sable thread.
And hark! the ringing harp I hear
And lo! her Druid sons appear.
Why roll on me your glaring eyes?
Why fix on me for sacrifice?[58]

In 1793 Wordsworth travelled through another now classic Druidic region, Wiltshire, tramping across Salisbury Plain depressed by the outbreak of the war with revolutionary France, to which he, like other English radicals, was opposed. During the next year he wrote the first draft of a poem that summed up his feelings. When describing Stonehenge, he dreamed of a time when

. . . oft at dead of night, when dreadful fire
Reveals that powerful circle's reddening stones,
'Mid priests and spectres grim and idols dire,
Far heard the great flame utters human moans,
Then all is hushed.

Some lines later he returned to the monument, in the same mood:

> And oft a night-fire mounting to the clouds
> Reveals the desert and with dismal red
> Clothes the black bodies of encircling crowds.
> It is the sacrificial altar fed
> With living men. How deep it groans – the dead
> Thrilled in their yawning tombs their healms uprear . . .

This far, he was repeating the image of the Gothic Druid, as priest of horror, though with more linguistic skill and poetic sensibility than his predecessors, and freed from the tyranny of the rhyming couplet. He then, however, seemed to present a more dignified and benevolent portrait:

> Long bearded forms with wands uplifted show
> To vast assemblies, while each breath of night
> Is hushed, the living fires that bright and slow
> Rounding th'aetherial field in order go.
> Then as they trace with awe their various files
> All figured on the mystic plain below,
> Still prelude of sweet sounds the moon beguiles
> And charmed for many a league the heavy desert smiles.

This magical moment of tranquillity, amid the 'desert' spaces of the plain, soon passed, and a few hundred lines later Wordsworth was back to his dreams of slaughter. In the manner of an Englishman with his political views, he held up Druids as Britain's ancient examples of the religious oppression and social injustice that still scarred its modern society,

> Though from huge wickers paled with circling fire
> No longer horrid shrieks and dying cries
> To ears of Daemon-Gods in peals aspire,
> To Daemon-Gods a human sacrifice.[59]

At some time in the late 1790s, characteristically, Wordsworth rewrote the poem, with a section on Stonehenge that emphasized, once more, its grimmer associations:

> Thou hoary Pile! Thou child of darkness deep
> And unknown days, that lov'st to stand and hear
> The desert sounding to the whirlwind's sweep,
> Inmate of lonesome nature's endless year;
> Ever since thou saw'st the giant wicker rear
> Its dismal chambers hung with living men.[60]

In or around 1805 he returned to the same subject, as part of his long autobiographical poem *The Prelude*, and once again showed the same ambivalence about the Druids of Stonehenge:

> It is the sacrificial altar, fed
> With living men, how deep the groans, the voice
> Of those in the gigantic wicker thralls
> Throughout the region, far and near, pervades
> The monumental hillocks; and the pomp
> Is for both worlds, the living and the dead.
> At other moments, for through that wide waste
> Three summer days I roam'd, when 'twas my chance
> To have before me on the dreary Plain,
> Lines, circles, mounts, a mystery of shapes
> Such as in many quarters yet survive,
> With intricate profusion figuring o'er
> The untilled ground, the work, as some divine,
> Of infant science, imitative forms
> By which the Druids, covertly expressed
> Their knowledge of the heavens, and imaged forth
> The constellations, I was gently charmed,
> Albeit with an antiquarian's dream,
> I saw the bearded teachers, with white wands
> Uplifted, pointing to the starry sky
> Alternately, and Plain below, while breath
> Of music seemed to guide them, and the waste
> Was cheer'd with stillness and a pleasant sound.[61]

Here he is, explicitly, having it both ways. He starts with an imagery of gloom and gore, but then confesses that in other moods he is 'charmed' by an alternative tradition, of the Druids as scientist priests working in harmony with the music of the spheres. He admits that this might well be just 'an antiquarian's dream' (and the antiquarian concerned would be Stukeley, Wood or Cooke), while taking the darker view as apparently more objective. None the less, he gives full expression to it. In the same work he also showed a tenderness for Druidry in a more subtle fashion: in his description of his undergraduate studies at Cambridge he not only compared himself to 'a youthful Druid', but adopted Iolo Morganwg's system of colours to denote the robes of the different divisions of the ancient Druidic order.[62]

Half a decade later, Wordsworth was back to the subject, as part of the ninth poem in his sequence *The Excursion*:

> Once, while the name Jehovah was a sound,
> Within the circuit of this sea-girt isle,

Unheard, the savage nations bowed the head
To gods delighting in remorseless deeds;
Gods which themselves had fashioned, to promote
Ill purposes, and flatter foul desires.
Therein the bosom of yon mountain cove,
To those inventions of corrupted man
Mysterious rites were solemnized; and there,
Amid impending rocks and gloomy woods,
Of those terrific idols, some received
Such dismal service, that the loudest voice
Of the swollen cataracts (which now are heard
Soft murmuring) was too weak to overcome,
Though aided by wild winds, the groans and shrieks
Of human victims, offered up to appease
Or to propitiate. And if living eyes
Had visionary faculties to see
The thing that hath been as the thing that is,
Aghast we might behold this crystal mere
Bedimmed with smoke, in wreaths voluminous,
Flung from the body of devouring fires,
To Taranis erected on the heights
By priestly hands, for sacrifice, performed
Exultingly, in view of open day
And full assemblage of a barbarous host . . .
A few rude monuments of mountain-stone
Survive; all else is swept away.

Taranis was one of the savage gods of Gaul mentioned by Lucan, that great model for eighteenth-century Gothic authors, as having been the recipient of human sacrifices. Wordsworth went on to praise Christianity for having provided almost a restoration of Paradise in the place of these horrors, with 'innocent and blest' worshippers, 'the peaceful sound of Sabbath bells' and 'a marvellous advance of good from evil'.[63] While still above the average, his verse was, as has often been noticed, falling off from the remarkable verbal pyrotechnics of the 1790s even as his youthful enthusiasm for radical causes ebbed away. This simplistic view of the Druids as dreadful heathens routed by a wholly good Christian religion seems to look forward to the pious old Tory bore that Wordsworth became, notoriously, in old age.

Such a view would appear to be confirmed by some lines on another Cumbrian landscape, 'The Pass of Kirkstone', which he wrote six years later. Here he took another swipe at past Druid atrocities, contrasted with the peace and beauty of the natural world itself. The boulders of the pass make

Altars for Druid service fit;
(But where no fire was ever lit,

Unless the glow-worm to the skies
Thence offer nightly sacrifice.[64]

With Wordsworth, however, there was no such straightforward progression and solidification of attitude. A year after writing that last poem, he produced another, inspired by a visit to the big stone circle called Long Meg and Her Daughters which had already moved William Hutchinson to two successive, and differing, fantasies. He was deeply impressed by the size and number of its stones, commenting that only Stonehenge 'can pretend to rival it in singularity and dignity of appearance'. His pleasure in the sight buoyed him up to take Stukeley's or Wood's view of such monuments. To Wordsworth the circle was a survival 'from the dread bosom of the unknown past', 'in hieroglyphic round / Forthshadowing, some have deemed, the infinite / The inviolable God, that tames the proud!'[65] Cruelty and bloodshed were for a time forgotten, and once again he was seeing philosopher-priests.

In the same year in which he saw Long Meg, 1821, Wordsworth decided to mark his new, fervent love of the established Church with a series of poems dedicated, in his own words, to 'the introduction, progress and operation of the Church in England'.[66] Given his previous record, it seems as if this would have provided an irresistible opportunity for him to lambast Druidry once more, and celebrate the triumph of early Christianity. Indeed, in the sonnet entitled 'The Trepidation of the Druids', the latter fear the coming of the new faith, which will bring 'ruin to each baleful rite' and new hope to 'the weak, the suffering'. In another, he castigates them as 'jealous ministers', who cannot see the 'primal truth'. Yet in a third, dedicated to the struggle of the post-Roman Britons against invading heathen barbarians, the surviving Druids have become allies of Christianity: 'from Cambrian wood and moss,/Druids descend, auxiliars of the Cross'.[67] What Wordsworth was doing here was drawing on two opposed traditions of the place of Druidry in British religion, which had been around since the sixteenth century. In one, they were the worst opponents of early Christianity; in the other, its greatest allies and most natural converts. He made no attempt to reconcile them or rationalize a relationship between them, being content to represent both in different poems, with an equal lack of inhibition and without any attempt to resolve the apparent contradictions thus implied.

He never in fact did so, in the few references to Druids that appeared in his work during the three decades of life that remained to him. In 1829 he wrote 'Humanity', a poem inspired by the sight of one of the rocking stones that had by then been regarded as Druidic monuments for a hundred years. He could have made this an opportunity for invective against the abuse of justice with which Toland had associated them, and which was by Wordsworth's time a long-familiar literary trope. Instead, he treated the story that criminals had been judged on their ability to rock the stone as objective and morally neutral. His concern was, rather, with the manner in which the place seemed to have returned wholly to the natural world, with the presumed human activities there long gone; and with how, 'for the Initiate', natural places could teach a wisdom that no human ever could.[68] This was one of the fundamental presuppositions of Romanticism as a cultural movement, and rather than set the Druids for or against it, Wordsworth had simply consigned them to the general category of the human race. Finally, in 1842, he published a revised version of his youthful poems about Salisbury Plain. It retained a short reference to Stonehenge as a site of Druidic sacrifice, but lacked the extended flights of fancy and poesy that he had brought to it before.[69] Neither here, nor anywhere else, did Wordsworth bother himself with the question of how Druids fitted into the scheme of history and religion mapped out in the Book of Genesis; he had no great interest in the Bible, preferring the natural world as his set of sacred texts.

Wordsworth referred to Druids in passing in other verses, at various times, but without making significant comment on them; the selections quoted above contain all his actual expressions of opinion. One of his biographers, Richard Gravil, has noted the impressive list of works on the subject that he read, or at least listed as meaning to read, including Caesar, Pliny, Tacitus, Dio Chrysostom, Lucan, Ammianus, Michael Drayton and Henry Rowlands.[70] This apparent intensity of interest, and of study, makes all the more remarkable the fact that Wordworth never achieved a personal view of Druidry. Blake clearly did, taking a particular established tradition concerning it in English culture and then both recasting it within a personal mythology that was entirely his own, and retaining all of its essential features. Our other William did not: instead he mirrored in his poetry the spectrum of pre-existing attitudes to Druids that had emerged in British culture by his time. In this manner, the poet who mentioned them most often in his work may be revealed, paradoxically, as the one who never came to a particular view of them. Druids, essentially, remained incidental to the work of both, despite their common association with each, and were included simply because they so completely dominated images of prehistoric Britain by this date. That Blake came to a more consistent and personal view of them was partly due to the fact that he, unlike Wordsworth, was an instinctual maker of myth, but also due to the much firmer basis of his own religion in the traditions of Scripture.

≥≤

7

THE APOGEE OF THE ENGLISH DRUIDS

I f the mid- to late eighteenth century was the period in which the Druids took over the British imagination in all matters that pertained to the ancient history of the island, the years 1800 to 1870 were the time when they were most dominant in that of the English. Now fully established as the leading and representative figures of the earliest British past, they featured as major players in any interpretation of that past, in English works of history, literature, art and theology. In general, the manner in which they were portrayed was a continuation of earlier attitudes, but with some important changes of emphasis. Certain aspects of Druidry which had been most celebrated during the Georgian epoch were now more muted, while others were much more prominent.

One of their eighteenth-century roles had been as patriots, uniting the different peoples of the modern British superstate in a common past and identity, and being used explicitly both as models of resistance to invaders and as prophets of British greatness. This continued far into the nineteenth century. That century opened with the complete incorporation of Ireland into the United Kingdom, a step that was hailed in part of a gigantic epic poem in honour of Alfred the Great, by Henry James Pye, into which the author felt obliged to insert a Druid. This was simply because Alfred's own society, of Christian Anglo-Saxons, contained no equivalent figure suited to taking on the now traditional Druidical role, of prophesying the might of a future United Kingdom:

> Now learn events, yet unrevealed that lie
> In the dark bosom of futurity –
> As my delighted eyes, in yon firm line,
> With friendly folds see Albion's banners join
> I view them, in prophetic vision shown,
> United subjects of a mighty throne;
> See Cambria's, Caledonia's, Anglia's name
> Blended, and last in Britain's proud fame.
> And ye, fair Erin's sons, though Ocean's tide

From Britain's shores your kindred shores divide,
That tide shall bear your mingled flags unfurl'd,
A mutual barrier from an envying world.[1]

The iconic literary portrait for writers concerned with patriotic Druids remained
Tacitus's description of the Roman attack on Anglesey; and during the 1820s, three
prominent English authors produced works inspired by this. One was the most widely
read female English poet of the century, Felicia Dorothea Hemans, who supplied a
'Druid Chorus on the Landing of the Romans' to exemplify stoical courage and devotion to the parent land.[2] Another was Thomas Love Peacock, who adroitly shifted the
climactic action to the site of the future city of London, and described how a Druid
fleeing from the slaughter on Anglesey manages to reach it before encountering
another Roman and dying at his hands. The location of his death gives particular
force to the prediction of the fall of Rome and the glory of Britain that he utters while
expiring. Peacock's Druid is crossed with the Gothic image of Druidry that had
appeared towards the end of the preceding century: he has 'robes of sable hue', sunken
cheeks, white beard and (of course) 'burning eye-balls'.[3] The third poet was the young
Alfred Tennyson, who kept his doomed Druid on Anglesey, and modelled him
directly on an Old Testament prophet speaking in the name of an angry god. He
enlarged on the pride and luxury of the ancient Romans, which in the eyes of his
Druid, as in those of a hellfire preacher of Tennyson's own time, inevitably doomed
them to destruction.[4]

In the year in which Tennyson wrote this work, 1827, the University of Cambridge
offered a prize for the best poem on the Druids submitted by an undergraduate. The
runner-up was a student at Corpus Christi College, Thomas Hankinson, and the
judges thought his effort good enough to deserve publication. It depicted a sole
survivor of the massacre on Anglesey, mourning his dead comrades in the following
terms:

We fought for thee, my country: 'twas the strife
Of desperate rage – the struggle of despair –
The last wild stroke for liberty and life
We braved the invader in his fierce career,
Thy Druid daughters with their flowing hair,
Poured in mad onset on the foe, and high
Raised the shrill shriek, and tossed the torch in air:
Thy grey rocks, echoing back their thrilling cry,
Sent the dread war-note forth – 'To death or victory':
The time will come – the veil is half withdrawn –
The future's veil of gloom – I see – I see
The horizon purpling with thy glory's dawn,
My native land! – thy sons shall yet be free –
And brave – but not in vain – thy name shall be
The rallying-shout of nations – heard afar

In distant lands, and thundered o'er the sea:
Thy blood-red standard, victory's beacon star
Shall stream with meteor flash along the clouds of war.[5]

By 1830 it must have begun to seem to any ambitious poet that the subject of the Druids on Anglesey had been done to death, but that of patriotic Druids in general was to receive a further massive boost, from an external source. This was the arrival, in 1833, of Vincenzo Bellini's opera, *Norma*. One of the masterpieces of Italian music, it had a libretto by Felice Romani, portraying Druidry as the backbone of the native resistance to the Roman occupation of Gaul. The context of its message was thoroughly Italian, reflecting Italy's contemporary plight as a nation divided into separate political entities, most of which were ruled either by foreign powers or by despotic dynasties of foreign origin. Whether it was Romani's intention or not – and the odds seem in favour of it having been so – its effect was further to inflame Italian resentment of this situation. The storyline centred on the idea that Druidic priestesses (like Roman Catholic nuns or pagan Roman Vestal Virgins, but not, as far as is known, actual Druids) were vowed to virginity. The heroine thus tragically violates two mighty prohibitions by taking a Roman governor as her lover. The plot culminates in one of the most sensational climaxes in opera, when she confesses her guilt to her people and she and her lover are burned to death together. The British embraced it with almost as much fervour as the Italians, though more slowly: after that first performance it returned to London in 1837, was translated into English in 1841, and then really took off in popularity, being staged at Covent Garden annually between 1847 and 1861.[6]

Moreover, the fact that an image or an event had become a cliché could be as much a reason for lesser authors to treat it as for the greater or more ambitious to avoid it. As such, the massacre on Anglesey remained a subject for provincial writers even as it slipped away from the centre of English culture. In 1838, a lady residing at the gracious Midland spa town of Leamington published a poem intended to raise funds for a local hospital. In keeping with her philanthropic mission, she gave her sympathy to the victims of the Romans, representing their destruction as a disaster not merely for the British but for civilization. In her vision, the Druids on the island had taught true religion, sound morality and good science, as well as poetry and law; like ideal Victorian schoolmasters. Only the arrival of Christianity, in her opinion, commenced the process of repairing the damage caused by the loss of them.[7] In the following decade another minor author, Richard Davenport, published a poem in which the dying Archdruid of Mona goes 'rejoicing to [his] eternal home', foreseeing a Britain to which rivals kneel 'with envious gaze'.[8] In 1851 a third, Esther Le Hardy, saluted the achievements of Britain in the era of the Great Exhibition, with the words of another expiring Druid, who

Bless'd her with beauty, wealth and power;
Bless'd her with virtue's richest dower;
Bless'd her with one, who turns to bless
In deep affection's faithfulness;

Bless'd those fair beings to earth has bound her,
Springing in ecstasy around her;
Bless'd those she loved, and bless'd the day
When Britain own'd Victoria's sway.[9]

If the Georgian tradition of Druids as patriots and prophets of British glory
continued to flourish into the early nineteenth century, so did that which celebrated
them as priests of nature. Even earlier than the former concept, however, it tumbled
from being a theme of first-rank authors to one left to the relatively undistinguished.
Into this category falls Edward Quillinan, who published a 'Hymn to Nature' in 1820,
hailing her as

Goddess of the green retreats,
Thee my boundless worship greets!
Every hill and every dell
Has for me a Druid cell,
Every leafy fane of thine
Holds for me a holy shrine.[10]

The prize offered by Cambridge University for a poem on the Druids seven years
later, for which Thomas Hankinson was the runner-up, was won by a Trinity College
student, Christopher Wordsworth. His entry saluted them as leaders of a good and
pure religion, which treated the whole natural world as the temple of its deity:

All hail, ye saintly band, whose souls aspire
With vows that burn, and feed the holier fire.
What though your hearths no spicy sweets exhale,
Nor scented incense loads the languid gale;
Nor marble halls are yours, nor sculptured stone,
To lure the great Creator from his throne.
But oh! 'tis yours the bright ascent to try
And soar serenely wafted to the sky:
To ope the gate, to tread the bright abode,
The gorgeous chambers of the living God.[11]

Wordsworth did not go on to make a career as a poet, unlike his great namesake
(to whom he was no relation). He entered a church of 'sculptured stone', ending his
days as Bishop of Lincoln; and lost interest in both Druids and nature. Back on
William Wordsworth's home territory of the Lake District, another minor poet was
dreaming of both at about the same time. This was William Roscoe, who published
'Lines Written in the Woods of Rydal Hall, Westmorland' in 1834. In a significant
shift of emphasis, he did not hail an undifferentiated spirit of the natural world, but
the pagan god of the district whom he presumed the Druids to have worshipped
there:

O thou that rul'st this wild of wood,
Lord of the forest and the flood,
Whose sullen voice is heard to roam
By fits amid the leafy gloom,
Where erst the rolling orb of night
Gleamed on the Druid's hallowed rite,
Spirit, we hold thy oak-crowned shrine,
And altars as of yore divine.[12]

A much more famous writer of the period – though more for novels than poetry –
was Edward Bulwer-Lytton, the first Baron Lytton, who dealt with Druids in his epic
poem on King Arthur, published in 1849. One verse makes a fleeting reference to the
ancient priests, neatly uniting the images of them as lovers of the natural world,
experts in its scientific aspects, and devotees of its divine creator. The moment comes
when a medieval knight, wandering in a forest, happens upon a stone circle and
remembers

What time in starry robes and awl, arrayed,
Grey Druids spoke the oracles of man –
Solving high riddles to Chaldaean mage,
Or the young wonder of the Samian sage.

The 'Samian sage' is Pythagoras. Bulwer-Lytton's Druids also 'lured the Brahman' to
study with them, and 'hail'd the only God':

Yea, the grandsires of our primeval race
Saw angel-tracks the earlier earth upon,
And as a ruling sun, the morning face
Of Truth more near the flushed horizon shone.[13]

Bulwer-Lytton quoted, as his evidence for their early transcendent goodness, the
triads that had actually been forged by Iolo Morganwg.

Esther Le Hardy's epic poem about Druids themselves, published in 1851, has
already been introduced above, because of its prediction of Victorian British greatness. Most of it, however, is devoted to lauding a Druidic view of the natural world
as the exquisite creation of a good deity: 'the leafy page of God'. It is propounded to
a young pupil in terms that match the Christian hymn 'All Things Bright and
Beautiful' (actually written just three years before):

Sweet child! That thy young heart may know,
By seeing how the flowers grow
Without man's help, or even care,
That God is good, and everywhere.

The story ends tragically, and in another significant cultural shift, with the central characters, a gentle old Druid and brave old Druidess, being brutally murdered by invading Christian warriors.[14]

Six years later, it was the turn of a London curate with an enthusiasm for science, Blencowe Dunn, to salute Victorian Britain's pre-eminent gathering of scientists, the Royal Society, with a eulogy to the Druids as their ancestors. He portrayed Druidry as having been effective as a means of objective knowledge because its practitioners had treated the cosmos as sacred, and so studied it with both care and reverence. He urged their modern successors to go about their work in the same spirit:

Do'st *thou* seek that truth-based knowledge
Man demands to make him sage?
Here then learn to study, stranger,
The vast universe thy college,
And thy book *her* varied page.

Dunn went on to suggest that the sun, which he believed the Druids had worshipped, might be revered again in his time as a symbol for scientific knowledge:

Full orb'd God's truth rises, routing
Ignorance, darkness, Goth and Hun,
Nations telegraph to nations,
Sects conflicting, all are shouting
'Men! It is the Sun! The Sun!'[15]

The theme of Druids as nature-priests (and nature-priestesses) had therefore become an occasional one in the literature of the age, and confined to minor poets; but it was continuing to develop. The writers who had treated it at its zenith of popularity, in the eighteenth century, had celebrated a world of lost freedom and innocence, to preach the lesson that profound truths could be learned from a close communion with nature. By the early Victoran period, those who still expressed it were starting imaginatively to identify with this presumed Druidic religion themselves.

* * *

Meanwhile, a third strand of the eighteenth-century love affair with Druids also developed throughout the early nineteenth, and with more vigour than the other two: the formation of societies and clubs that took the name of Druid. The rapid growth of the Ancient Order of Druids (AOD) and its sundering into two rival, and equally successful, groups, has already been discussed. Alongside these bodies, smaller Druid orders were founded. In 1824 an Independent Order of Ancient Druids, named to distinguish itself from the AOD, was established, and, though it subsequently failed, it was revived in 1843.[16] In 1829 a Loyal Order of Druids, presumably naming itself to dispel any lingering public distrust of secret societies, came into existence. None of its documents seem to survive before a book of its ceremonies issued in 1848 from Bolton in Lancashire, which was presumably one of its strongholds.[17] What is so significant about the rites concerned is that they embodied the ideas of Iolo Morganwg, making the order the first English group to have adopted them. These they blended with the Masonic initiation rituals used by most closed societies since the previous century.

Each lodge of the order was led by a Grand Arch, assisted by a Secretary, Stewards, Auditors (for the accounts), Tylers (to police the lodge), Bards (presumably to sing or speak poetry) and Supporters, to guard the door of the room in which they all met. Each had insignia to match his office, the Grand Arch being of course most splendidly clad, in a white robe symbolizing purity, held by a belt somehow representing truth, and with a solar symbol over it indicating leadership. An altar was maintained or erected in the centre of the room, in Masonic style, and each meeting was termed a *gorsedd*, in Iolo's fashion, and declared his motto of 'The Truth Against the World'. Gatherings opened with the order's song, to the tune of 'God Save the Queen', which praised wisdom, peace, love and charity, in the name of a benevolent creator. A candidate for initiation was told beforehand that the main aims of the order were charity and goodwill, that religion and politics could not be discussed (as in the Freemasons and most closed groups of the age), and that sober and orderly behaviour was expected of members. He was asked to state that he and his wife were both in good health and so likely to contribute to the lodge's funds for a long time before needing to draw on them. He was then led to the door of the lodge. The Druids inside welcomed him with a song, and the Grand Arch then explained that the oak tree was the symbol of fellowship. The candidate was asked to promise respect for all religious opinions. To establish the limits of these, the members then sang two more songs, one affirming belief in a 'Great Supreme', revealed in the natural world, and the other declaring faith in the biblical Jehovah. The candidate then expressed a desire to receive financial support in time of sickness, and a good funeral, and promised to promote charity and behave in an orderly fashion. After that, the others sang to the 'Divine Spirit' to help their new brother keep to what he had undertaken. He was told that the ancient Druids had been famed for their virtue, knowledge and probity but that in some respects their ways were not suited to a modern society. In particular, he learned, the modern Druids differed in having an ethic of equality and unity, expressed chiefly through the election of all officers.

The Loyal Order was thus essentially a friendly society, with an added component of music, very like the United Ancient Order that had seceded from the AOD in 1833. It also, however, had a non-denominational religious tinge, which was compatible with Christianity but not identical with it. Alongside an affirmation of belief in Jehovah was an expression of faith in an undifferentiated 'Divine Spirit' and another in a pantheistic deity, subsumed in the natural world. This highly unorthodox but inclusive religiosity was most fully expressed in the burial service included among the official rites.

Members attending were expected to wear black or blue clothes, white stockings and gloves, and the special aprons, sashes and collars of the order, copied from the regalia of Freemasonry. The Druidical note was struck by the black staves they carried, with crooks on the end (allegedly for gathering mistletoe). The one presiding was expected to have a black gown with a sash. The clergyman provided for the event would read the regular burial service of the denomination of the dead man, at the graveside, and then he and all other non-members present would be asked to retire. The person making this request did so in a set form, apologizing for the secrecy of what followed and assuring the public that it was intended to reinforce mutual brotherhood, and that the order did not represent a rival religion. Nor did it; for the words that were then read out were complementary to recognized religions of the time. They emphasized the brief and insecure nature of life, the socially levelling nature of death, and the provision of an eternal reward for virtue. The service book was then closed, and all present placed sprigs of evergreen upon it which were then tipped into the grave as a sign of hope for new life. For all the compatibility of what was said and done with set forms of religious service, it reveals how much the fraternal Druidry of the time could represent an alternative form of spirituality, which could exist within Christianity but was not part of it.

By 1853 the Loyal Order of Druids had developed enough to generate a schism, as its lodges around Leigh in the Lancashire cotton district split off to form a separate society. In 1858, Liverpool produced its own Independent Order of Modern Druids.[18] On 1 November of the same year the Ancient Order of Druids underwent its second division, when its Cheshire lodges seceded to form a friendly society, calling itself simply the Order of Druids.[19] All these new bodies testify both to the energy of mid-Victorian fraternal Druidry, and to the particular independence and self-reliance of the booming industrial communities of north-west England. In addition to these large affiliated orders, tiny groups that took the name of Druids were now founded to serve the needs of communities in both urban and rural areas. An example of the latter is the Druid Friendly Society, which established itself at the George Inn, Amesbury, in 1853. It agreed to meet each month for eating and drinking at 6.30 in the evening, for two and a half hours in winter and three in summer. Each member would pay 6d. per week to ensure medical care when needed, and a good funeral. New members could only be enrolled between the ages of eighteen and thirty-five, to ensure the minimum call on the funds, and a surgeon was engaged to treat all those living within four miles of Amesbury itself. A management committee of no fewer than fifteen persons was established, including a president, secretary and treasurer. The only thing that seems to have been Druidic about these people was their name, almost certainly suggested by the fact that Stonehenge lay inside their catchment area.[20]

Hitherto, modern societies of Druids had been exclusively male, but in 1853 a Noble Order of Female Druids was founded, at Leigh in Lancashire, apparently to accompany the male order that had appeared in the town two years before.[21] If an account of them can be trusted, it developed initiation ceremonies that were both spectacular and highly original: after (unspecified) 'usual trials of fortitude', the candidate was required to leap from a 'symbolic mountain' towards a 'double row of sharp steel spikes'. When she landed, however, a soft green surface had replaced the spikes. Assistants were at hand 'should she be prosaic enough to faint'. Lights suddenly shone to reveal 'a fairy scene of green fields, shady trees, and babbling fountains. The Grande Maîtresse and other officers were seated on gorgeous thrones, while the sisters were all clad in white and adorned with badges and scarfs of various colours.'[22]

The records of Victorian English Druid orders generally lack the sort of information most precious to social and economic historians, such as lists of members that
provide exact evidence of their social composition, or full financial accounts which
indicate how much lodges prospered or struggled. They are slightly better equipped for
the cultural historian, providing some indication of the ideology embodied in them.
The most detailed description of a public ceremony held by a Druid order to survive
from this period is an account of an outing on 23 July 1856 by the Mona Lodge of the
Ancient Order of Druids. This was actually based in Bristol, and it took advantage of
the existence on its doorstep of the great stone circles at Stanton Drew, already celebrated by Aubrey, Stukeley, Wood and Chatterton. Its members, their wives and their
friends made up a total of 150 people, who drove to Stanton in a procession of
carriages, arriving at 1 p.m. Permission had been obtained from the lord of the manor
to hold a rite in the circles. Admission to this was supposed to be reserved to the order
and those invited, but when many curious local people turned up, those in charge
wisely and generously decided to include them. The interest shown by villagers was
hardly surprising, because the members of the AOD made a spectacular sight, in their
robes and insignia, carrying wands, cups and flagons. Other objects displayed in their
parade to the stones were a bible on a velvet cushion and a representation of Noah and
his Ark. In this manner they wound through the fields to the stones and formed up in
the best preserved of the three circles, that on a spit of high land at the north-east end
of the complex, overlooking the little River Chew. There they sang a chorus, after
which their Chief Bard, a Welshman called George Jones, gave an address on the
nature of Druidry. They then chanted an ode, passed round a cup of mead and
adjourned for a meal at the house of a member who lived in the village and sportingly
fed 140 of them. Afterwards, he supplied a dance band in his orchard, which played
until nine o'clock, when the carriages were made ready for the return journey.

Jones subsequently published his speech, and a thoroughly idiosyncratic representation of Druidry it turned out to be. It was founded on the familiar idea that Druids
had practised the pure patriarchal religion of the Old Testament, which had become
corrupted with time. It was in discussing the forms that the degenerate religion had
taken that Jones showed his originality, and imagination. He declared that it had been
centred on a worship of snakes and oak trees, to prove which he quoted one of the
medieval poems attributed to Taliesin, in the original Welsh, which must have
impressed if not informed his English audience. He went on to explain that it also
involved a procession in honour of the sun every morning, and of a corn goddess
called Godo every evening. In these, he insisted, Druids had danced wildly and lacer-
ated themselves; he was apparently confusing them with the Roman priests of the
goddess Cybele. He denied indignantly that they had ever sacrificed human beings,
which he held to be a Roman lie, and insisted on their good moral character, quoting
from both Davies's book on them and Iolo's triads to demonstrate this. None the less,
he conceded that their religious beliefs had been false: 'they drank of that fountain of
sacred knowledge which had originally poured forth a pure and unpolluted stream
from its spring in the eastern world, but had become turbid and polluted as it rolled
through the dark groves of Druidical superstition'.[23]

In 1861 the newly seceded Order of Druids decided to establish a common set of beliefs by issuing a book of lectures to be delivered to members initiated into each of its three degrees, which it characterized as the 'Primitive', the 'Bardic' and the 'Noble Grand Arch'. Those attaining the first, and so entering the order, were told confidently that the last of these had been founded when Noah first stepped from the Ark and offered sacrifices to Jehovah in gratitude, under an oak tree. The ancient Druids whom he had established had been 'men of truly noble and benevolent hearts, always seeking where to administer their acts of charity and love, pouring the healing balm into the hearts of the poor and oppressed, and seeking at all times the moral, social and religious elevation of their fellow-man'. They had possessed a knowledge of mechanics superior to that of the modern British: an assertion likely to impress artisans in the industrial heartland of the new order. The newly made initiate was informed that Druids no longer functioned as clergy, but could still do the work of love by affording mutual financial support when in need. The new Bard was treated to a selection of Iolo's mythology, about his hero, Hu Gadarn, the founder of Welsh culture, and told that his duty was to replicate in miniature the work of Hu, preserving morality, peace and good in the lodge as in the world at large. The degree of Noble Grand Arch was confined to those who had been elected to lead lodges, past or present. On receiving it an initiate was reminded that his job was to provide leadership, advice and admonition, and assured that the ancient teachings of the Druids had been those of Noah handed down through his descendants in Europe.[24]

The Order of Druids seems to have been unusual in having a 'party line' in Druidic tradition. Most, as the Ancient Order had done since its earliest relevant records, seem to have left it up to members to make their own relationships with the past. Whether prescribed by an order or devised by individuals, visions of ancient Druidry held by modern Druidic fraternities and sororities, like the rites they enacted, seem to have been constantly developing. This is of a piece with the nature of the Druid orders of the mid-Victorian period, as highly successful, energetic and multiplying organizations.

* * *

When all acknowledgements have been made of these continuations of Georgian views of Druids, the period between 1800 and 1870 in England may be more readily associated with two others, which were much more commonly and prominently found in national culture. One, already reflected in the discussion of Druid orders, was the claimed descent of Druidry from the patriarchal religion of the Old Testament. The early nineteenth century was the last period in Western history in which biblical fundamentalism was the dominant means of interpreting the human past; and that fundamentalism was the more strident in that it was being increasingly undermined, especially in Britain. Decade by decade, the revelations of the brand new sciences of geology and palaeontology proved that the earth was far older than had been thought, with a much longer and more complex natural history. It became obvious that either the Book of Genesis represented only part of the story of the world, or that it had to be read at times as a metaphor rather than a literal record, or that its earliest sections, at the least, were mythology and not history. These choices provoked devout English Christians, brought up to regard the whole Bible as the word of their deity, to an outpouring of print intended to minimize the damage to its reputation. Having now been established as the main characters of the earliest history yet known of Britain itself, the Druids played a major part in this enterprise. No Christian denomination ever prescribed an orthodox interpretation of the role that they had played in religious history. Instead the work of proposing one was left to individuals, who produced between them a stream of reinforcing, overlapping or competing views.

The biblical portrait of ancient religion as a family of faiths that had degenerated from the original true one, revealed by the deity himself, was central to the period's concept of history. It was, indeed, inscribed on the front of the nation's greatest shrine to the human past, the British Museum, in the 1840s. The person responsible was Richard Westmancott, who created a façade of monumental sculpture within the pediment to illustrate 'The Progress of Civilization'. In the words of the museum's director, Sir Henry Ellis, 'Commencing at the eastern end . . . man is represented as emerging from a rude savage state, through the influence of religion . . . Patriarchal simplicity then becomes invaded and the worship of the true God defiled. Paganism prevails and becomes diffused by means of the arts.'[25] To those anxious to position the Druids in this process, considerable help was afforded by one particular activity of the heroes of the Old Testament: they had erected crude stone monuments, as the Druids were believed to have done. Indeed, the megaliths best known to the early nineteenth-century English were not on Salisbury Plain, or in the Lake District, but in the Bible. Jacob had erected two pillars of stone to commemorate places in which Jehovah had promised great things for him and for his descendants. Later he had set up another, and built a cairn, as boundary markers and places of sacrifice, and then put up a fourth monolith as a gravestone for his wife. On Mount Sinai, Moses was given a divine instruction to build altars of unhewn boulders. He promptly did so, and added a stone pillar for each of the tribes of Israel. On leading the Israelites into the Promised Land, Joshua erected twelve great stones to commemorate the event, again in response to a direct divine command. After completing the conquest of it, he set up another, under a tree (translated in the Authorized Version of the Bible as an oak), marking a sanctuary of his god. Other cairns and monoliths appear later in the Old Testament, as memorials to great people and events.[26]

A classic example of the English attempts made to fit Druids into a biblical model was the anonymous work entitled *Identity of the Religions called Druidical and Hebrew*, which was published by a member of the new University of London in 1829. In the author's reading of the ancient texts, both the Druids and the patriarchs of the Old Testament had venerated a single good deity, worshipped in groves of trees, especially oaks; had raised monoliths of stone, especially in circles; had reverenced the serpent and the bull; had believed in the survival of the soul after death; and had a similar hierarchy of priests. Elements of the same religion could be found in the traditions of the ancient Egyptians, Phoenicians, Persians, Arabs, Babylonians, Indians, Romans and Greeks, proving the biblical account of a single original faith revealed by the deity himself. Unlike Stukeley and others, this writer did not claim any special privileges for the Druids, or therefore the ancient British, as upholders of an especially pure form of that faith. Instead he equated them with the other peoples in his list, and the biblical Canaanites, as practitioners of a degenerate form of it, and credited the Jewish priesthood alone with having renewed it in a form closer to the deity's wishes.[27]

If this sort of stuff was fairly standard, there were authors who developed it into more exotic and idiosyncratic theories. One such was a London curate called John Bathurst Deane. In the early 1830s he published a set of works which argued that almost all the ancient religions of the world had been based on the worship of snakes. In the case of the Druids, this rested ultimately on Stukeley's contention that the megalithic avenues and rings at Avebury had been built by them to represent a serpent passing through a circle. Even by Deane's time, it had been realized that Stukeley had slightly distorted the physical evidence at the site to arrive at this contention.[28] This did not prevent Deane from accepting the idea and reinforcing it with observations from Stanton Drew and from stone circles, rows and avenues on Dartmoor and in the Lake District. He concluded from these that the snake had been the foremost sacred emblem of Druidry, and decided that the very name 'Avebury' had derived from the Hebrew 'Aubur', signifying 'serpent of the sun'. To this fieldwork he added the interpretations of Welsh texts made by Edward Davies, with particular reference to the Welsh affection for dragons, which could be described as super-snakes. The point of all this ingenuity, and that which he similarly expended on other ancient religions, was to prove the literal reality of the biblical story of the Garden of Eden. Behind this universal importance of the image of the snake, he insisted, lay a common memory of the one that had brought about the fall of humanity and the appearance of sin in the world, exactly as Genesis recounted.[29]

Parallel to Deane, another clergyman was developing his own, highly personal, take on Druidic religion. This was William Lisle Bowles, who served the parish of Bremhill on the edge of the Wiltshire chalklands to the west of Avebury. In his reading, the one god venerated in that religion had been that known to the Greeks as Hermes, the Egyptians as Thoth, and the Romans as Mercury. Stukeley's detection of a serpent in the plan of Avebury lay behind this as well, because twin serpents had wound around the wand that had been the symbol of both Hermes and Mercury in ancient times. To Bowles, the whole Avebury complex had been laid out to make a giant calendar, knowledge of which was believed to have been vouchsafed by the god.[30] Two decades later, another Wiltshire clergyman had come up with a different theory. This was Edward Duke, who surveyed the main megalithic monuments of the county afresh and decided that none of them were calendars, and that they were not dedicated to a single deity. Instead, they were planetaria, fashioned in honour of the heavenly bodies as a first sign of the decay of the original true religion. According to a scheme long accepted by many historians and theologians, one of the earliest steps towards the error of venerating more than one god had been to worship the planets and stars. Duke lovingly mapped out for his readers the way in which the forms of different planets could be discovered in the layout of the stones. Although he thought the Druids second-rate priests, he could not praise them highly enough as scientists: 'indubitably the wisest of the wise, the most learned of their times'.[31]

Last in this selection of clerics comes a vicar of Avebury itself, John Lockhart Ross, publishing at the end of the 1850s. Like the others, he drew ultimately on Stukeley, and, like Deane, he set the Druids in a global perspective and used them to reaffirm belief in the patriarchal faith of Genesis, and so in the truth of the book. In his view, Druids had initially preserved that faith better than any other ancient priests, and were the finest practitioners of a single religion that had been observed throughout the whole of Europe and the Near East. The villains of his story were the Phoenicians. Far from transporting the teachings of Abraham to Britain, as Stukeley and writers before him had suggested, in Ross's imagining they had brought in cruel and abominable oriental practices, including human sacrifice and the destruction of infant children. Under their influence, the Druids had been corrupted into sinful pagan polytheists. None the less, Ross expended most of his energy on celebrating the main tenets of uncorrupted Druidry, as he imagined it: the belief in a single creator god, served by angels; in the immortality of the human soul; that a person's virtues would be rewarded, and vices punished, after death; that blasphemy should be suppressed, with the death penalty; that people should not injure their neighbours and should observe high moral standards; that it was wrong to eat meat, eggs and dairy products; and that the moon should be revered, because of its apparent influence on human moods and sensibilities. Ross's Druids were, in short, pious and puritanical vegans. He concluded that these qualities had made it easy for them to accept Christianity when it arrived, purifying their beliefs and practices of the contaminating Phoenician influences.[32]

It needs to be emphasized that works of this sort were not primarily considered to belong to the world of theology or of clerical apologetics, let alone to be the fringe productions of (literally) parochial scholars, opinionated amateurs or cranks. They were, rather, at the centre of contemporary discussions of the ancient British past. Furthermore, they are merely among the most prominent of an outpouring of similar publications, covering much the same broad range of positions. Many were by Anglican churchmen, though there were still plenty by genteel lay antiquarians. Some built on the earlier theories of Bryant and Faber, with a greater quantity of comparative mythology to set beside the presumed beliefs of the Druids, in order to argue for a literal acceptance of the story of the biblical deluge.[33] Others were mainly concerned with restating the apparent links between Druidical and ancient Hebrew religious practices.[34] Some lambasted the Phoenicians, as Ross did, as wily orientals who had corrupted Druidical religion, reflecting the new regularity of contact with Islamic, Buddhist and Hindu cultures and the fear this engendered in some writers that Britain would be contaminated by them.[35] Others held to the older view, of the Phoenicians as the transmitters of the true religion of the Old Testament to Britain.[36] Some were most intent on emphasizing the learning and benevolence of ancient British Druidry.[37] Yet others, excited by the growing British dominance of India, and familiarity with it, continued the tradition of drawing close parallels between the presumed teachings of the Druids and those of the Hindu Brahmins, as vestiges of the patriarchal faith.[38] Others, in turn, used Iolo Morganwg's material to pad out their portraits of a wholesome ancient Druidic religion, derived ultimately from divine revelation; most charming was the Devonshire antiquary who suggested that the structures now classed as Iron Age hill forts had been observation platforms from which Iolo's green-robed Ovates could study the stars.[39] Artists occasionally gave visual expression to this literary genre. In 1832 the painter Jacob Thompson, and in 1845 the anonymous illustrator of Charles Knight's book, *Old England*, produced classic figures of Druids as venerable priests and sages. In 1842 and 1843, Edmund Pariss and John Herbert focused on the notion that their fundamentally decent British religion, descended from that of Noah, had made them easy converts to Christianity. Pariss filled a canvas with a scene of the Christian saint, Joseph of Arimathea, having an agreeable time winning them for his faith, and Herbert represented a similarly peaceful scene of missionary work.[40]

Occasionally, a poet would likewise portray Druids primarily as pious and decent clergy. The neatest such contribution was made by an Oxford undergraduate called Gerard Smith, as an entry for a competition held by his university in 1823 for works on the topic 'Stonehenge'. He made it a perfect back-projection of an idealized Tory Anglicanism:

> Can I not fancy all these stones upright;
> The surpliced priests, with mistletoe bedight,
> With open mouths to catch the morning air,
> And crowds on crowds with open mouths too, stare . . .
> Still swells the chorus, sweet as fragrant balm
> As country clerks chant forth the hundreth Psalm:
> Or when some fiddler plays 'God Save The King',
> And twangs with ruthless stick each tuneful string,
> Men, women, children, catch th' harmonious fire,
> And in one burst of discord the loud notes expire![41]

As this would indicate, during the first seven decades of the nineteenth century the association between Druids and megaliths remained secure in the minds of most English authors; and most commonly treated in the case of the most famous such monument, Stonehenge itself. Scholarly writers who dealt with the subject may be placed on a spectrum stretching between those who accepted the connection as proven fact,[42] and those who judged that the builders of the monument remained unknown.[43] Between lay the majority, who conceded this last view but also thought the most likely hypothesis was that which attributed it to the Druids.[44] Some of this group still paid tribute to Stukeley as the person who had been most responsible for this consensus. To illustrate both the strength and the limitations of the grip that Druids had upon the imagination of the period, however, it is most revealing not to concentrate on the most celebrated sites, but to go to the other extreme: to consider an attempt to establish a major Druidical holy place where no monument ever existed. Such an enterprise was launched at Nottingham in 1850, where an anonymous resident published a pamphlet claiming the existence of a major ancient monument within the precincts of the town.[45] Although equipped with no surviving structures dating before the Middle Ages, Nottingham is notable for its rock formations, sometimes hollowed into caves, overlooking the River Trent. In one place, which by that time had become a cemetery, some of these were combined with what appeared to be earthworks, and the nameless author allowed his imagination to play upon the site to a wonderful degree.

He had read all of the most prominent authorities on the Druids, and believed that this site represented the remains of a sacred complex of the sort described by 'Celtic' Davies, symbolizing the Ark of Noah and dedicated to Ceridwen, as goddess of corn, and her consort Hu, the sun god. In its centre he visualized the earthworks as the remains of a temple surrounded by a grove of oaks. The focus of this shrine was a tree cut into a T-shaped cross of the kind imagined by Stukeley, one arm dedicated to Esus, god of war, one to Belenus, god of light, and the trunk to Taranis, god of storms. Before this, he suggested, human victims were offered to Esus. A hollow in the rocks nearby became the private cell of the Archdruid, in which that official would meditate and instruct youth in the prime Druidic doctrines: the immortality of the soul, the eternal punishment of the wicked, and the coming of an ultimate day of judgment. These Nottingham Druids were therefore remarkably similar to Victorian hellfire Christians in their beliefs. The author of the tract, however, also equated them with the traditional cunning folk or village magicians who were just starting to die out in the period. The author went on to declare, with the same perfect confidence, that the Archdruid also taught his pupils the use of amulets, charms and philtres, remarking darkly that the superstitions thus implanted were not thoroughly eradicated even at the present day.

A small cave nearby was, the argument continued, reserved for initiation cere-monies, in which the candidates were confined in darkness and without food for three days and nights. At the close of this period, they were symbolically restored to life through a passage in the rocks. They were then immersed in a basin in the same outcrop, which had been filled with water mixed with salt, laurel, barley and flower petals. As well as Druidical baptism, such basins were (the reader now learned) used for the bathing of sick people. If they died, which – the text asserted – almost always occurred, then they were assured of a happy transmigration into a new life. Also in the complex were other caves, dedicated to individual deities, and probably a stone idol of Ceridwen, to which people had to bow, and a rocking stone to be used for legal judgments in the way suggested by Toland. The account closed with a description of the daily ceremonies carried out at the temple, to Hu at noon and to Ceridwen at midnight. Druidesses would decorate the space with oak branches, like Victorian ladies putting flowers in a church for a festival. The rites consisted of a declaration of ancient lore, followed by the singing of hymns around a sacred fire, and then the interpretation of the omens suggested by the flight of any birds nearby. Worshippers were routinely rewarded by being allowed to follow the service with 'luxury and debauch', enlivened by 'fearful shouts' set up by Druids concealed in the caves, to counterfeit the presence of mighty spirits. The account ended with a shudder of relief that 'divine goodness' had delivered the British from such errors.

The author emphasized that the site in the cemetery was only one of three in the outskirts of Nottingham which could similarly be interpreted as Druid temples, and that they furnished proof that it had been an important town even in prehistory. In making this patriotic declaration, however, he or she was testily aware that it actually ran counter to a significant body of local tradition. The caves in the cemetery had been associated hitherto not with Druids but with the established favourite hero of the shire, Robin Hood. Furthermore, there was no objective evidence for the date or purpose of the earthworks which formed the only demonstrably human part of the complex, and the locals insisted that they had been made in the recent past. The booklet therefore appealed over their heads, to the more educated inhabitants and to visitors, warning them not to believe 'idle tales' and insisting that 'verbal testimony is not always to be relied on'. It was all in vain: despite the creative power with which the writer caused that patch of the city to flower with ancient rituals, no scholar of national stature came to believe in the temple at Nottingham, and the locals stuck to Robin Hood.

To the north of Nottingham, a couple of decades earlier, a writer was at work who seems, in the context of his age, considerably more eccentric but who was to have a considerable impact on later generations. This was a wealthy country gentleman called Godfrey Higgins whose seat was Skellow Grange, a mansion near Doncaster in southern Yorkshire. The only surviving portrait of him shows an elderly fellow in natty, formal clothes, with an air of unworldly benevolence, like a philanthropic bishop. This belies the fire of reforming zeal that smouldered in him throughout the latter part of his life, and which propelled him into a series of reforming causes. His targets for improvement included the treatment of impoverished lunatics and the system of elections to Parliament. He campaigned for the abolition of restrictions on corn imports (which kept the price of bread high to benefit landowners); against the use of child labour in factories; and against limitations on the public careers of Jews and the prohibition of sports and dances on Sundays. He also called for better relations with the Islamic world. His social position, as a justice of the peace and a member of various learned societies, gave weight to his participation in these campaigns, although he was handicapped in later years by constant bad health. Many individuals of the time who were possessed of such zeal for human improvement combined it with a strong evangelical religious faith, but Higgins – as his views on Islam and Sunday might hint – was at the opposite extreme. He was a rare example among the gentry of a person who was both radical in politics and opposed to all organized religion.[46]

In 1829 he published *The Celtic Druids*, which opened with the ringing declaration that, throughout all places and times, priests had been more harmful than beneficial to humanity. Its content consisted principally of selections from the arguments of Bryant and Davies, purged of their commitment to orthodox Christianity. Like so many writers of the time, he affirmed his literal belief in a single, good, original religion and worldwide language, and in the reality of the biblical Flood. He was also traditional in personifying the Druids as practitioners of this primeval religion, who were gradually corrupted into a paganism of the sort that beset most ancient peoples, yet in their case was more worthy than the norm. On this common ground, however, he erected his own idiosyncratic beliefs. He thought that the Celtic peoples, who had produced the Druids, were a learned and enlightened group of people who had escaped the Flood by climbing the Caucasus mountains, and then spread westwards across Europe and the Mediterranean basin. His Druids had begun as wise philosophers, the natural enemies of clergy (and as such kindred spirits to himself), whose corruption had resulted from the temptations of power, turning them into a priesthood in their own right. None the less, they continued to honour the true supreme being, and to teach the necessity of performing good deeds, showing courage in battle, and loving one's nation. In his view, the appearance of Christianity actually produced a further deterioration in British religion, as the 'insidious arts' of its priests undermined patriotism, courage and the more virile virtues. Higgins conceded that the contemporary Church of England represented the best-organized faith that the world had ever known, and the most friendly to liberty, but warned that it was not immune to the corruptions inherent in a professional clergy. United with his anticlericalism was a less overt, but still powerful, misogynism, as he characterized women as the constant and natural allies of clerics in instilling fear and superstition into religion to sap the strength of free men. His book ended with the message with which it had begun, declaring that 'priests have been the curse of the world'.[47]

Interspersed with all this polemic were the sort of detailed pieces of information that would only be published by an amateur scholar who was either lacking in informed criticism by others or chose to disregard it. Thus, he concluded that the Culdees, the austere Christian monks of the early Irish and Scottish Churches, were the same people as the Chaldeans or ancient Babylonians. The name of the island containing the greatest of all their monasteries, Iona, was related to that of the Roman god Janus, the Egyptian god On, and the Hebrew Yahweh. Since Celtic peoples had once colonized northern Italy, the Roman poet Virgil, who (much later) came from that region, must have been a Druid.[48] In general, the book consisted of a large compendium of quotations from previous authors of ancient history and religion, set within Higgins's framework of prejudices and spiced with his own insights, such as those quoted above.

His subsequent reputation was, however, based more on his last, indeed posthumous, book, which was composed immediately after *The Celtic Druids* and appeared three years after his death, in 1836. This was a massive history of world religion, which set out at much greater length the nature of the primitive and good faith of which Druidry had represented a partial survival; though Higgins now thought that Buddhism was the best remaining representation. In his view it had been based on sun worship, and on a series of emanations from an original one deity, that had divided, successively, into lesser divine beings and eventually produced humans. This was the same ancient Neoplatonist view of the cosmos which had enchanted the young William Stukeley and influenced James Thomson a century before. On to this model, Higgins loaded a tale of degeneration based on a series of polarized good and evil forces, starting with the division of the one original deity into creative and destructive divinities. These polarizations included, inevitably, clergy (bad) and secular philosophers (good) and the feminine (bad) and masculine (good). Less predictable was his hostility towards Hindus (as more priest-ridden) to balance his affection for Buddhists, and his belief that black human races were morally superior to whites, and had in fact been the original humanity. He rejected Christ, as a form of pagan sun god, but admired Jesus, as a great moral teacher.

What really gave Higgins's book staying power was its central message: that the truth he revealed in it had once been known to all humanity, but had been suppressed by priesthoods for their own advantage; he accused the Roman Catholic Church, in particular, of knowing of it but concealing the evidence. None the less, he informed his readers, it had been cherished and propagated in secret by an enlightened elite. This had continued to initiate worthy people into the genuine history of humanity, so that the old lore, and the actual doctrine of the historic Jesus and of the great ancient thinkers, were saved, even if confined to a hidden few as an esoteric tradition. Higgins's view of history was certainly conditioned here by his conversion to Freemasonry towards the end of his life and he rapidly became a prominent Mason. Freemasonry's foundation myth was the claim that it had transmitted secrets passed down by initiation through a closed society ever since antiquity. To this message, Higgins joined an apocalyptic and messianic one: that the world passed through cycles of time, even as humans passed through cycles of reincarnation, and at recurrent, widely spaced, intervals a number of great souls were reborn upon the earth to act as preachers of the true faith. One such time was (of course) his own, the opening of the Age of Aquarius, in which humanity had an opportunity, by recognizing and embracing the primordial truths of the cosmos once more, to achieve reunion with the one great deity.[49]

By the standards of authors such as Deane, Ross and Bowles, or even of William Blake, this was crazy stuff, the work of a lone conspiracy theorist with an adversarial view of the world rooted in biblical teachings, and a huge sense of self-importance. None the less, there was a powerful appeal to many in the modern age in its promise of personal and cosmic liberation, for and by those who became initiates of an esoteric tradition preserving ancient wisdom for a special few. It offered a de-Christianized Second Coming, produced by the elect but redeeming instead of damning the ignorant multitude, and a secularized vision of priesthood in which those versed in the true tradition could lead humanity to salvation. Higgins was to leave his footprints through the work of many subsequent authors and societies, up to and including the present time. The oddest of all the 'theological' writers on Druids during their golden age in the English imagination, his influence was, for that very reason, to be the most enduring.

*   *   *

There was another aspect of Druidry which was also well established as a cultural theme by 1800 and which became even more important during the succeeding seven decades: that of Druids as priests of a religion of gloom, gore and horror. All the forces that had given it life were still in operation, and now reinforced by others. One was a growing acquaintance with the native peoples of Asia, Africa and Polynesia, which produced ever more and better information on their customs and beliefs. In the late eighteenth century there had been a strong tendency to idealize them, and especially the people of the Pacific islands, as relics of a lost primeval paradise, in which humanity lived in harmony with itself and with nature. Closer and more regular contact with them revealed many aspects of their cultures which Europeans found repulsive, and the reaction against the earlier admiration of them had a knock-on effect on attitudes to 'primitive' societies in general, including that of ancient Britain. However, there had been plenty of hard information available on indigenous peoples earlier which had included the less attractive features of their behaviour. The disposition to ignore it then and emphasize it now reflected a shift in European attitudes;[50] and that is where other factors, also affecting Druids, came into play.

One was the decisive technological superiority which industrialization was starting to give Europeans over the rest of humanity. Until the nineteenth century, the states of Asia and the Middle East, and some in Africa, could at the least hold their own against Europeans in military confrontation. It was during the nineteenth century that Europeans decisively acquired the ability to outshoot all others, and began as a consequence to carve up much of the rest of the globe, with accelerating speed, into colonial empires. The British took the lead in this, and provided moral justification with the claim that they would civilize and improve the physical and spiritual condition of the peoples whom they conquered. In British Christianity as a whole, imperialism combined with a response to the challenges presented by the apparent spiritual needs of the new industrial cities to produce a sense of 'mission', at home and abroad, which grew ever stronger as the nineteenth century went on. All these developments boded ill for attitudes to societies that lacked the hallmarks of Western civilization, whether in the present or the past; and the Druids were firmly associated with such a society.

For the British of the time, two areas of the world in particular became models of the interaction of civilization and savagery, or moral enlightenment and moral darkness. One was Polynesia, which had a generation before provided the classic examples of noble savages for the European imagination. The populations of four of the island groups which had been most frequently visited by Europeans – those centred on Tahiti, Hawaii, Fiji and the Marquesas – all engaged in human sacrifice at the time of their discovery. During the early nineteenth century the practice was stamped out in three of them, and its persistence in the fourth, Fiji, accompanied by savage wars between local chiefs, kept attention focused upon it. The other area was India, which had become the most glamorous, prestigious and densely populated of the British overseas possessions. There, between 1820 and 1850, their administrators engaged in a series of well-publicized campaigns against Hindu customs that they had come to regard as pernicious. Three, in particular, made a deep impression on the British public. One was *sati*, or suttee, the burning of a widow alive upon the funeral pyre of her husband. The second was human sacrifice, represented in particular by the cult of *thagi* or Thugee, in which travellers were ritually murdered as offerings to the goddess Kali, by devotees of her cult based at the temple of Bindhachal. The third was the practice of offering oneself as a sacrifice by committing ritual suicide before the image of the god Krishna in the city of Puri. The traditional method was to throw oneself under the wheels of the carriage bearing the huge statue of the god, known as the Juggernaut, as it was dragged in procession through the streets. The efforts to suppress the last two customs have made a permanent impact on the English language, in the words 'thug' and 'juggernaut'.

None of these developments were entirely uncontroversial. Just as, at the height of the eighteenth-century cult of the noble savage, there were writers who argued that savages were inherently disgusting, so now voices were still raised in favour of traditional peoples. Likewise, the suppression of long-established aspects of Hindu culture represented a conscious reversal of previous British policy, which had been to tolerate indigenous habits as no concern of administrators preoccupied solely with loyalty, order and profit. Those who supported the change felt the need to justify it, because of the risks it posed to continued acceptance of British rule by its Indian subjects.

Frequently, therefore, portrayals of Druids as upholders of superstition and barbarism represented contributions, explicit or not, to debates over the contemporary treatment of traditional cultures elsewhere in the world.

Often the linkages were explicit. In 1825 the author of a general history of the ancient world, Thomas Fosbrooke, listed appalling practices which travellers had noted among tribal peoples in various parts of the modern world. He used these to argue that they were inherent to primitive cultures, and that therefore all of them had been carried on by the Druids.[51] More frequently, writers selected comparisons with particular native societies. Back in 1799, as part of his attack on Druids, Edward King had used Captain Cook's report that human sacrifice was taking place on Tahiti as an argument for believing what the Romans had said about its presence in ancient Britain and Gaul. He then went on to write bloodshed on to the plan of Stonehenge, by naming the megalith that now lies prone in the processional avenue approaching the monument, 'the Slaughter Stone'. It had actually stood upright, and the channels now in its surface have been worn by weather, but King decided that it had functioned as an altar, with the grooves in it made by Druids to allow the blood of victims sacrificed across the stone to run off it. The name was taken up by most people dealing with Stonehenge thereafter, and still has popular currency, acting as a potent subliminal device for giving an impression of the stones as a setting for dark deeds, and of the Druids as perpetrators of them.[52] The comparison between modern Polynesians and ancient Druids could also cut the other way: when the novelist Mary Russell Mitford wove Cook's description of the sacrifices at Tahiti into a tale of adventure that she set in the South Pacific, she termed them, with horror, 'the Druid rite'.[53]

Cross-references with India were more common. If the pediment of the British Museum represented the period's most prominent display of the biblical view of early human history, the equivalent for the Indo-Druidic relationship appeared in the Palace of Westminster, alias the Houses of Parliament. In 1841 a series of wall-paintings was commissioned as decorations for the central corridor, as part of the programme of rebuilding after the fire of 1834 had destroyed most of the palace. They were given the form of a series of three 'before and after' panels, to illustrate the moral progress of the British. The middle one matched an ancient British Druid performing a sacrifice with modern administrators in British India preventing a rite of suttee.[54] Two decades later, a Cornish poet, John Harris, went further, by assuming that the Druids themselves had burned to death the widows of fallen warriors.[55] As for the suicides at Puri, the poet Stephen Prentice could contemplate Stonehenge, in 1843, and imagine:

>   when thou
> Hadst superstition redly written on thy brow,
> And wickered victims in their blazing cage
> Upheld with shrieks the glory of a creed,
> Whose crimson prop, in a benighted age,
> Was ignorance, that bade the wretches bleed
> And holocausting torture was the mead
> Of their fanaticism, murder-fraught.

That faith is gone, but has the world indeed
From blushing time a holier colour caught?
Go ask the ensanguined car of modern Juggernaught! [*sic*][56]

Eleven years later another minor poet, the Cumbrian clergyman George Newby, accused the Druids of

sad superstition and more cruel by far
Than crushed the wretch 'neath Juggernaut's cruel car.[57]

Like Prentice, the Devonshire poet Frederick Paas also invoked the Juggernaut, this time comparing it to the wicker giant in which Druids had allegedly burned victims alive. His readers were invited to identify with the Romans, as bringers of both civilization and Christianity, and his hero was a dashing Roman who rescued a British maiden from sacrifice: an action, again, evoking associations of contemporary British officers saving women from suttee. Paas's vision of Druidry was of an outwardly dignified priesthood contaminated by association with barbarism and superstition, as the Indian Brahmins were perceived to be. He portrayed the Druids themselves as

Attired in robes white as the snow,
Their silvery beards hang long below
Their waists round which encircling
Secured's a band, with crystals sparkling . . .

The assistants who served them in the poem were, by contrast, far more like Native Americans than the true Indians, with wolf-hide tunics, head-dresses of eagle feathers and necklaces of teeth: in other words, textbook savages.[58]

Scholars as well as poets invoked contemporary India in their picture of Druidry. One of these was John Kenrick, writing in a literary journal, who made a direct comparison between Roman rule over Britain and British rule over the subcontinent, praising both for combining a general religious toleration with a humanitarian crusade against cruel customs and institutions; among which he included suttee, the Juggernaut and Druidry.[59] As Britain's own tropical empire grew, comparisons between it and that of Rome, already easily made because of the prominent place of Roman literature in the educational curriculum, became ever more natural. As well as fellow imperialists, the ancient Romans had kept a professional army with strong regimental traditions and been notable administrators and engineers; they were people in whom the nineteenth-century British could easily recognize spiritual, and perhaps literal, ancestors. The temptation to identify with them against the less civilized peoples whom they conquered was very strong.[60] The atrocious practices that the Romans alleged against the Druids could now be used to justify that identification, even as they had originally been used to justify Roman aggression. One historian drew an explicit comparison between the British rebel Boudica and the leaders of the Indian Mutiny against British rule, and dismissed any sympathy for the native

British as 'maudlin sentiment'.[61] Six years after the Mutiny, in 1863, a novelist called Julia Corner published *Caldas*, about a Druid who turns against his own people, horrified by their custom of human sacrifice. He defects to the Romans, who fully reward his expectations by giving him a warm welcome and bringing the blessings of civilization to his people. Like the British confronting the cults associated with temples of Kali and Krishna, they suppress the cruel rites that had been carried on at Stonehenge, but respect the monument itself.[62]

The Midland author of a *Complete History of the Druids*, published in 1810, directly confronted the problem that some ancient sources portrayed his subjects as learned and wise, and others as bloodthirsty. He solved it by pointing to cultures in his own time which combined an aptitude for the arts and sciences with 'barbarous customs'; and here he was clearly thinking of those of Asia, of which India was the exemplar. Having thus damned Druidry by association, he could unleash his imagination on it, denouncing it as a 'cruel religion' of 'craft and superstition' and speaking of his 'awful horror, in viewing those places, where, in the gloom of the thickest woods, the Druids performed their tremendous rites, where they erected their sanguinary temples, and bathed their altars with the blood of human victims'. He both adopted and subverted Iolo Morganwg's three divisions of ancient Druidry, by claiming that the true Druids had arrived in Britain after the Bards and Ovates did. In this reworking, the Bards could be admired as poets and the Ovates as philosophers, but the Druids, as power-hungry priests, had taken over both groups and incorporated them into their degenerate faith.[63]

The twin forces of imperialism and colonialism infected views of ancient Britain in more subtle ways. The authors of a pictorial history of England accounted for the degeneration of Druidical religion by claiming that its practitioners had 'gone native'. Arriving from the Middle East as preachers of a virtuous faith, they had allowed themselves to be corrupted by the superstitions and idolatries of the local people instead of eradicating these as they should have done. The result was the horrid species of heathendom that the Romans found when they arrived, and which they exterminated in most of Britain as a service to humanity. Lest any reader still be tempted to pity them, the authors insisted that, had they been allowed to survive, the Druids would have bitterly persecuted Christianity.[64] More common in writings of the time, however, was the concept that native British religion had originally been pure and true, and was corrupted by oriental influences. This idea, illustrated above, was yet another consequence of the new British relationship with Asia.

Bound up with the imperialist theme in treatments of Druids was that of another of the greatest in nineteenth-century European culture, and especially among the British: that of progress. The rapid and unprecedented advances in technological, geological and geographical discovery gave to many a new sense of the potential of humanity to improve its lot and transform the world for the better. This view of history as a progression towards greater knowledge, power, comfort and compassion, exemplified by the British themselves, naturally privileged later periods of time over earlier. As the Druids stood at the beginning of the process, they could be deemed inherently to represent the barbarism from which Britain had ascended: the mural in the Palace of Westminster was making exactly this point in an imperialist context. Some works of the age emphasized it above all. In 1852 the most celebrated English novelist of the time, Charles Dickens, wrote a history of England designed for children. Dickens's contempt for the past was vehement, and it is no surprise that he portrayed early Britain as a land of skin-clad savages, with a 'strange and terrible religion' of superstition, fear and bloodshed. He closed this portrait with an invitation to his young readers to heave a sigh of relief that they were born into modernity: 'It is pleasant to think that there are no Druids, now, who go on in that way, and pretend to carry Enchanters' Wands and Serpents' Eggs – and of course there is nothing of the kind, anywhere.' By that last assurance, Dickens meant that there were no such things on earth as effective magical objects; he was well aware (in his terms) that savages still existed, elsewhere, who pretended to possess them.[65] Likewise, the author of a full-blown history of progress in Britain, Robert Philp, portrayed the annihilation of the Druids as a major step in that progress, as they had kept people bound by false dogmas and deceived by pretended miracles. He invited modern travellers to contemplate the newly built Britannia Bridge across the Menai Strait between Anglesey and the Welsh mainland, one of the notable achievements of Victorian engineering. The Roman soldiers crossing to Anglesey to slaughter its Druids were, he insisted, making as great a contribution to the improvement of Britain as the builders of the bridge.[66]

In the works of both Dickens and Philp lay not only a particular view of history but one of religion: both were hostile to what previous generations had termed 'priestcraft', and identified the Druids with it. Ever since the 1540s, Druids had functioned, in part, as whipping boys for whatever people considered to be bad religious behaviour: paganism, Roman Catholicism, and any established Church with powerful clergy, represented favourite examples. This tradition continued unabated through the early and mid-nineteenth century, and indeed cultural forces worked to reinforce it. The period was characterized by a sense of mission in propagating active and committed Christianity, at home and abroad. One of the most distinguished pioneering historians of Victorian culture, George Kitson Clark, declared that 'probably in no other century ... did the claims of religion occupy so large a part in the nation's life, or did men speaking in the name of religion continue to exercise so much power.'[67] They articulated, moreover, a sense of religion imbued with a particularly high moral tone, which combined with the cult of progress to underline the need to improve the condition of humanity and constantly defined itself against what its proponents held to be bad conduct. The period was also a time of growing religious toleration and diversity, in which the national Church was steadily losing its dominance of the political and educational system, and Protestant nonconformity, Catholicism and even non-Christian faiths such as Judaism were admitted with ever greater freedom to participation in all areas of British life. All these developments produced both unusual fervour and acute anxiety among many devout English Christians, which rebounded at times upon Druids. The result was that the hostile ancient portraits of the latter were now repeated, reworked and amplified more than ever before.

An extreme example of this effect is supplied by the evangelical poet Frederick William Faber, who contemplated the growing religious diversity and freedom of his time and expressed the fear that his compatriots would forsake Christianity altogether.

His ultimate dread was that they would return 'to Druid rite once more'.[68] A classic illustration of the sectarian use of Druidry is provided by the Cumbrian clergyman George Newby, quoted earlier as comparing it with Hindu superstition. Newby drew much of his concept of what Druids did from Iolo's description in the edition of the poems of Llywarch Hen. On to this, however, he grafted a view of them as a 'tyrant priesthood' obsessed with the shedding of human blood. The climax of the *gorsedd* described in his poem came when its heroine, the lovely princess Bertha, is crowned with oak leaves, stripped to the waist, bound with osiers and then stabbed through her 'beauteous bosom' by an Archdruid robed in white and crowned with a gold tiara. Newby emphasized that the spirit of these dreadful acts still survived in Christianity as Catholicism. He went on to warn readers that the current Oxford Movement in his own Church of England, which aimed at a greater element of ceremony and of physical beautification of churches, was only a stalking-horse for the Church of Rome.[69] A colleague of his in the national Church, called Francis Thackeray, who published a history of ancient Britain, accused the Druids of a 'hideously distorted' version of the true, patriarchal religion, which included 'detestable cruelty', 'abominations' of magic and astrology, and 'trifling and ridiculous' ceremonies. As his prime witness against them, this author produced the fictions of the Roman poet Lucan, who he felt had provided sufficient evidence of their 'murderous orgies'. He concluded, sonorously, that it was impossible to avoid comparing all this with Roman Catholicism, even suggesting that Druids had likewise lived in monasteries and nunneries.[70]

In an age in which the parliamentary franchise was slowly being extended downwards in society, and industrial workers were forming into unions to protect their trades, a major theme of many authors was the need to educate the masses in their new responsibilities. A correspondingly common target of such writings was the role previously played by established priesthoods in keeping the bulk of the population in a state of reverent ignorance and obedience in order to consolidate their own power. Christian clergy were often cast as the villains of this piece, and Catholics above all, but some of the stereotype rubbed off on the Druids. Dickens and Philp made full play with it, as did Iolo Morganwg's former friend Robert Southey. He credited Druids with belief in Iolo's system of reincarnation through spheres of existence, but dismissed it as 'the conceits of imagination'. To him, they had been purveyors of 'deceit and vanity', and of 'abomination'. To Toland's fantasy of rocking stones used as mechanisms for false judgments, Pliny's naked women paraded at festivals, and Strabo's human sacrifices in a blazing wicker giant, he added the assertion that Druids had demanded and received a third of the best sheep and cattle produced by British farms each year. To keep the people cowed, and subservient to their greed and lust, Southey insisted, they practised pretended magical tricks.[71]

In 1815 Samuel Rush Meyrick and Charles Hamilton Smith published a lavishly illustrated history of ancient Britain, which gave to the remainder of the century its most commonly reproduced images of Druids and their world. These were assembled with meticulous care, from all the evidence that archaeology could now join to literature. For the most famous portrait of all, that of an 'Archdruid', they took the basic image, of a bearded old man in a robe, from Aylett Sammes, and through him from

Conrad Celtis. They gave him, however, new ornaments and instruments – a golden breastplate, tiara, belt, bracelet and rings, a set of wooden message-sticks, and a golden dish, made up from a mixture of descriptions in medieval Irish literature, the writings of Iolo Morganwg, and Bronze Age objects excavated from graves and bog deposits. They set him in a shrine, constructed around an altar and a veiled prehistoric dolmen, and equipped him with a pet snake, based on the ideas of William Stukeley and Edward Davies. All this eclectic and patient reconstruction, however, was put in the book to the service of a view of Druids as a corrupt and degenerate clergy. Once again, Toland's judicial rocking stone made an appearance, as evidence of their deceitful practices to keep 'infatuated votaries' in awe. The expression of the magnificently equipped Archdruid, preparing to pronounce a judgment, is at once remote, implacable and sanctimonious.[72] The Meyrick–Smith portrait of him replaced Aylett Sammes's image to become the stock visual representation of a Druid in modern British culture. Echoes of it have already been encountered in the literature discussed above (such as in the garb of George Newby's murdering high priest), and it is the most commonly reproduced picture on the covers of books about Druids in recent years.

Even Roman Catholics themselves, so often damned by Protestants alongside the Druids, sometimes turned upon the latter, as if to demonstrate to the world that their own religion was much more wholesome. The greatest English historian the Roman Church produced in the period, John Lingard, portrayed Druids as witch doctors living 'amid the silence and gloom of the forest' and wholly ignorant of any real science or useful technology. All that they could offer by way of genuine knowledge consisted of herb lore and incantations. He accepted Iolo's fantasy that they had preached reincarnation, but called such a doctrine an 'absurd fiction', beside the Christian system of salvation and damnation. By their postures and pretences, he declared, they exercised 'the most absolute dominion' over the masses.[73]

There was yet another shift in English religious culture that reacted against Druids. The first half of the nineteenth century was the decisive period for the adoption of a completely novel humanitarian ethic by the political and social elites. Opinion, and the law, turned against such traditionally accepted phenomena as the trading in and ownership of slaves; the baiting of animals with dogs as entertainment; the exhibition of lunatics for the amusement of visitors; the keeping of imprisoned criminals or debtors in conditions of squalor and brutality; and the public execution of convicted felons. As part of this development, a new emphasis was placed on the kindlier and more altruistic aspects of Christianity, and on Jesus as a merciful and compassionate saviour. This involved, in turn, laying a much greater stress on the New Testament of the Bible, which contained the Christian message, than on the Old Testament, with its warrior deity who encouraged conquest and genocide, its acceptance of slavery and animal sacrifice, and its brutal and restrictive law code which prescribed public execution as the penalty for many offences. To strenuous Christians, to whom both Testaments were still supposed to represent divine teaching, one way of diverting attention from some of the tensions and contradictions within the biblical message was to define their faith more actively against external opponents. The prime target here was paganism, both in ancient times and among Asian, African and American peoples, which was commonly represented as a bloody, cruel, amoral and repressive set of religions. The fact that the Old Testament itself at times portrayed rival ancient cults in those terms made the tactic easier.

By playing up the charges of human sacrifice made against Druids by ancient writers, English authors could now place even stronger emphasis upon their identity as the natural enemies of Christianity, and upon Christianity as a religion that liberated people from superstition, fear and bloodshed. This contrast provided a subtext to several of the works quoted above, and acted as the main theme of others. The author of an ecclesiastical history of Britain, published in 1838, himself the minister of a Congregationalist chapel in south London, condemned the Druids as idolaters and butchers of helpless human victims. He added ominously and mysteriously that their moral doctrines included some too shocking to mention, and concluded his account with the outburst: 'Druidism . . . will be the means of leading every pious reader to adore that gracious Providence, by which our ancestors were called out of darkness into the marvellous light of the gospel of Christ. A thousand profitable reflections will naturally arise in the devout mind, while a contrast is made between the horrors of Druid-paganism and the benevolent, purifying, and saving doctrines of our divine Christianity.'[74]

The author of an essay on Stonehenge, in a London magazine, chose to illustrate this theme with an imagined portrait of a ceremony at the monument. Like the minister, he damned the Druids more by what he would not disclose about them, but implied, than by that which he actually portrayed:

> Let us await the rising of the moon from behind the sacred grove at Amesbury; so shall we see the entrance of the officiating priests, the Druids and Druidesses, and witness the solemn and hoary chief advance to the altar with slow and reverent footsteps, his face downcast, his beard long and smoothly trimmed; his clothes reaching to his knees are fastened with a girdle, to which is attached the bronze celt [i.e. an axehead]. In his hand he carries a forked stick, which fits onto the celt, and has enabled him to cut the mystic mistletoe which he holds in the grasp of his other hand. But ere the rites are accomplished and ere the victim is sacrificed, let us awaken from our dream and hail with thankfulness the advent and installation of Christianity over the fair land.[75]

Another Congregational minister, this time Robert Weaver of Mansfield, Nottinghamshire, pulled off the same trick of damning more by implication than disclosure, in the process turning the old association of the Druids with nature into a means of berating them:

> Oh! The inspiring effect of lofty hills and mountains, where all is grand and sublime; of deep and shady groves; of exalted and widely extended plains; everything above and around is calculated to inspire with awe, and in many cases with sacred dread. And, in such places, to see the Druidical priests and the Arch-Druid officiating in the sight of an assembled multitude; who can wonder that they are

carried away as they are led. Nor is even this all – the feasts upon the sacrifices –
the sports and amusements that followed, and the indulgence that idolatry in
general gave to the irregular appetites and passions – all would tend to rivet their
chains, to imprison their soul, and overspread their minds with darkness. In conclusion, well may we congratulate ourselves and glorify God for our happy state as
delivered from idolatry and as possessing the Christian revelation.[76]

There was, however, a final factor at play in the growing English tendency to prior-
itize and amplify the ancient descriptions of Druidic rites as gory and cruel. This has
already been touched upon in relation to the appearance of the taste for Gothic horror
in literature, towards the end of the eighteenth century, and its impact on descriptions
of Druids. To poets, historians and theologians alike (though especially the first),
atrocity lent colour, and so readability, to their work. This was especially true in a
period with a pronounced appetite for melodrama, which was associated with a
complex of anxieties and appetites centred on violence and sex. With the ending of
the Napoleonic Wars, an unprecedented period of European peace ensued, lasting
until the 1850s. Throughout it, the United Kingdom was kept constantly ready for
war, and engaged in brief and distant conflicts – usually successful – on the borders of
its imperial territories. The great bulk of the population was insulated from the experience of mass violence, even at second hand or a short but safe distance, in a way most
unusual in its history. This may help to explain the interest in atrocious brutality
shown in some of the literature of the age, including much of that referring to Druids.
It overlapped with an at times pronounced concern, which spanned the century, with
the power of human sexuality, and in particular that of women. There was a clear
tendency to neutralize it in literature, either by portraying women as innocent and
passive objects of male desire or by punishing them for sexual transgression. A classic
piece of double satisfaction could sometimes be achieved in the process, by which the
reader could be titillated by descriptions of the very acts which were, ostensibly, being
condemned. The portrayal of (imagined) atrocity, however deplored in the name of
Christianity and humanity, could be a very effective vehicle for sadistic entertainment.
In the Druidic context, the fate of Bellini's Norma, and of Newby's Bertha, have
already provided illustrations of some of these tendencies.

In a previous publication I have already quoted from some of the most colourful
examples of what the nineteenth-century English imagination could do, when
unleashed on the subject: Thomas Kitson Cromwell's 'fiend-like' Archdruid presiding
in a 'gloomy twilight' of megaliths and oaks; Joanna Bailey's 'crowds of terrible spectres' that attend Druid rites; Frederick Paas's altar clotted with gore, hair and brains;
N. T. Carrington's screaming women and children inside the burning wicker man;
T. F. Wilkinson's babies dismembered within shrines; T. G. Lomax's insistence that
Druids taught anatomy by dissecting living men; William Hurd's declaration that
they deflowered their own daughters; Sandford Earle's poetic chamber of horrors
laced with orgiastic sex; Thomas Miller's assertion that only the cruellest pupils were
allowed to graduate into Druidry, and that Druids gave beautiful young women the
choice between death and surrender to their desires; and William Winwood Reade's

incredible fantasy of a herb-gathering rite involving a naked maiden.[77] I shall not reprint them here, partly to prevent unnecessary repetition, and partly to avoid the charge of succumbing to the same fault that may be alleged against these authors themselves: of turning atrocity and salacity into entertainment under the cloak of higher motivations. Nor, since these examples are so spectacular in themselves, do I need to stack up any more, from the more humdrum if equally gory descriptions of imagined Druid ceremonies provided by other writers of the time.[78]

The point that needs to be made from all this is that the balance of sympathy among the English regarding Druids tipped significantly between the late Georgian and early Victorian periods, from one in which admiring images predominated, to one in which the most common attitude was hostility. Even as they occupied their most prominent position in the national imagination and dominated images of the earliest British history, they functioned mostly as figures of fear and horror.

* * *

In view of this, it may be necessary to restate that an important minority tradition remained, in which they functioned as patriotic heroes or as gentle priests of nature: at the middle of the century the saintly protagonists of Esther Le Hardy could appear in the same year (1851) as Joanna Bailey's conjurors of demons, and a year before Thomas Miller's sadistic murderers and rapists. So this survey closes with three examples of imaginative writing from the period, all published in London, which fell at neither extreme. In each case they sought to present a picture of Druids that was more mixed, complex and reflective. Almost needless to say, there is no reason for a historian to consider them any more accurate, just or realistic than the others, or to suppose that we would ever have a way of knowing if this were so. They merely supply examples of authors who were prepared to provide a more sophisticated portrait of imagined Druidry than the others.

It is significant that all three works were novels, a form that allows of extended treatment of a subject and fine shades of description and attitude. The first appeared in 1811, being the anonymous *Travels of a British Druid; or, The Journal of Elynd*. It divided Druidry into three forms, effectively the English, French and Highland Scottish, all on good terms with each other. The English Druids were fundamentally wise and devout, but a little too fond of power. They themselves believed in a good creator god and rejected the worship of idols, but to please the masses they allowed the practice of human sacrifice, which the common people expected and demanded. None the less, they refused to witness these acts themselves. Those in Gaul (alias France) were very similar, except that (as one might expect, from an author writing at the height of the Napoleonic Wars) they had become more corrupted, and officiated at the sacrifice of humans. In their customs, beauty and dignity had become mixed with ostentation and barbarism. Here is a description of a moonlit parade to a New Year festival, by the Gallic Druids visited by the story's hero:

Three of the Bards opened the procession, playing upon their golden harps. Over their white robes they wore a brown mantle, which was fastened on the shoulder; and round their waist was a girdle of the same. Near to the Bards walked groups of young men, singing the sacred songs. Behind these followed the animals to be sacrificed, and with them, two unfortunate men, whose hands were tied, and their bodies covered with branches of green oak. Then followed the sacrificers, armed with swords and lances; with the osier cage in which the wretched victims were to be burned. This was borne on the shoulders of men, each of whom carried a lighted torch. Then appeared the women priestesses; their hair dishevelled, with wildness in their locks – dancing along. At a distance from these followed the deputies of the several Gallic nations . . . They wore, as marks of distinction, different sorts of collars, bracelets and rings; some of which were of gold.

Last came the Druids, preceded by the youths whom they were currently instructing. Their Archdruid wore a crown and carried a branch of vervain. Immediately before him 'the herald walked, who wore a cap, in which were placed two wings of the swan; and in his hand was a stick entwined with serpents; both of these being hieroglyphics of the sacred order'. There is no description of the ensuing ceremonies, with the attendant acts of sacrifice, because the British Druids, of course, withdraw rather than be implicated in them.

By contrast, Highland Druidry is represented as being of an older, purer and superior kind to the English. Its leaders rule with moderation and mildness under an elected chief, and practise the true religion of Noah and the Hebrew patriarchs, worshipping the one god without altars or temples, save for stone pillars of the sort mentioned in the Old Testament. They preach the existence of heaven, hell and a devil, and offer cakes as sacrifices rather than animals, let alone humans. They teach all natural and experimental sciences, including geography, astronomy, medicine and mechanics. They wear long robes, short hair and long beards, carry wands, hang an egg encased in gold around their neck, and walk in pentagonal wooden shoes. Many of these details are taken from the earlier work of the Scotsman John Smith, whom the author of the novel made his chief authority for Gaelic Druidry, absorbing his rosy view of it in the process. On the whole, the book reads like the work of a liberal Englishman or Lowland Scot from the (self-consciously) educated classes, with a sentimental admiration of the Highlands.[79]

The second novel was effectively also anonymous, as the writer took a pen-name, 'Malachi Mouldy'. Entitled *Stonehenge: or, The Romans in Britain*, it appeared in 1842, and presented Druids who were a mixture of those portrayed by Borlase, Pliny and Iolo. They meet, white-robed, at the great monument at solstices and equinoxes, led by an Archdruid with flowing silver hair and beard, wearing an oakleaf garland and a gold tiara, a gold breastplate, a white mantle held by a gold ring, and wooden pentagonal sandals (which derived ultimately from Toland's imaginative reconstructions). He carries a golden sceptre and rides a milk-white mule, and lives in a cave in Groveley Wood, in a valley south-west of Stonehenge. His other working tools and insignia, deployed on different occasions, consist of a silver-tipped wooden wand, a necklet and breast-chain of gold wire mingled with pearls, a crystal ball, 'necromantic scissors and shears', bundles of rods or twigs carved with symbols and arranged in a frame, for divination, and rolls of astrological figures, to predict the future by the stars.

He is attended by Ovates, in light green robes, who sacrifice white cattle with knives, and Bards in sky-blue, to provide harp music. Disciples look on at ceremonies, from outside the circle, wearing a variegated costume of red, blue and green.

The Druids over whom he presides are, like those of the previous author, divided into different sects by the issue of human sacrifice. Those in France believe that it is legitimate to kill prisoners of war as offerings to the spirits of the dead. Those based in Anglesey are the worst, holding (as Tacitus had asserted of them) that the future could be divined from inspecting the bodies of sacrificial victims. Those at Stonehenge, led by our stately Archdruid, are the best, disliking the sacrifice of people as a recent innovation in Druidry. In this they are correct, for the good moral teachings that they have inherited from the distant past (exemplified by Iolo's triads) are part of the original divine revelation to humanity, rescued from the biblical Deluge by Noah and his family. Dolmens are used, as Davies had suggested, as artificial caves for the initiation of new Druids. The axis of the book's plot lies in the relationship between the Druids and the Romans, ending in the military victory of the latter. In the short term, this seems a disaster, because the conquerors, especially as personified by their debauched emperor Nero, are beyond doubt less decent than the Druids of Salisbury Plain. On the other hand, the latter's defeat is to the long-term benefit of their people, because Roman rule opens the way for Christianity, an even finer religion, to reach Britain.[80]

The last novel appeared in 1851, also from a nameless author, and bore the title *The Ancient Britains: A Tale of Primeval Life*. 'Primeval' was indeed how the Britons of pre-Roman times were seen in it, as it drew on those classical texts that represented them as savages clad in the skins of beasts. None the less, they were also given to 'peaceful meditations' and 'mystic rites'. Their Druids are shown as proud, stoical and impassive figures, with upper lips stiff enough to impress any Victorian gentleman. For lack of true religion, they cannot comfort the fear of death among their flocks, but they do strive to preserve peace and good conduct among them. Their temples consist of stone circles with an altar or dolmen in the centre of each, with an oval of small stones beside it, which contains a sacred fire tended by a Druidess. Like 'Malachi Mouldy', the author of this work made great play with Toland's fantasy of the rocking stone as the means by which Druids controlled justice, but their punishments are here confined to fines and flogging. They venerate one god, under Edward Davies's name of Hu, carry out their rites in a dignified silence, and generally oppose war, as harmful to humanity. Their main failing is, once again, their love of power, which is greater in their society than that of kings. The book's ultimate verdict on them concentrates on this: 'They communicated as much light to the Briton, and kept him in as much darkness, as suited their own purposes. They suffered his mind to be degraded and enslaved by superstition.' Hence, of course, the conclusion is a ringing endorsement of Christianity, but with a warning that the temptations of both superstition and power are still at work in contemporary society, and that the 'angel of Christian truth' has even now not fully prevailed in Britain.[81]

It would be interesting, though difficult, to carry out further research into the manner in which any of these writings affected the readers who consumed them. It is likely that there exist diaries or letters that provide some indication, but none were uncovered in the work for the current book, and to seek them would really be a task for a specialist in the society and literature of the time, interested specifically in reader reception. As it is, the matter can be tackled here only in the limited and oblique sense of how other authors used the work of their predecessors, and of the range of attitudes to ancient Druidry manifested by members of Druid orders, who presumably were likely to be better disposed towards it than most people. What can be reconstructed from the material studied here, with some confidence, is the spectrum of views taken by authors themselves; which is why this chapter has inevitably turned, more than most, into a series of book reviews. Three results seem to stand out from its investigations. The first is the one that has been repeatedly emphasized: that the period between 1800 and 1870 was the one in which Druids most completely dominated the English perception of ancient Britain. The second is that this dominance meant that they received a broad range of literary treatments, and that the authors of the age took a rich variety of attitudes to them. The third is that, for all this variety, the most common manner in which Druids were regarded in the period was a hostile one; and this drew upon some of the most important cultural currents of the age.

1 A statue of Julius Caesar, the most influential ancient author on Druids, projecting an image of capability and trustworthiness.

2 Tiberius, one of the emperors later credited with suppressing the Gallic Druids. The statue emphasises his official role as bringer of peace and culture.

3 The best-preserved portion of the enigmatic Coligny Calendar.

4 A gold torc, the emblematic neck decoration of high-status Iron Age British people, often found interred as offerings in pits.

5 John Aubrey, the progenitor of the view that megalithic monuments were Druidic, at about the age at which he discovered the Avebury circles for scholarship.

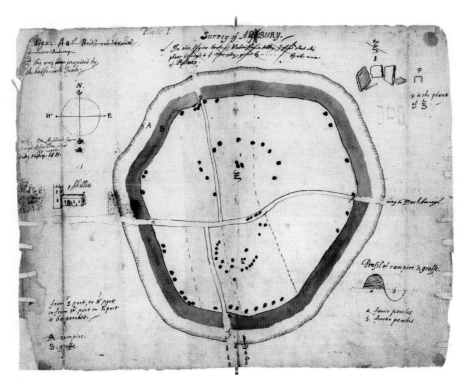

6 Aubrey's drawing of the Avebury circles, for his unpublished "Monumenta Britannica".

7 A self-portrait of William Stukeley, who made a connection between Druids and megaliths into orthodoxy, as the Druid Chyndonax.

8 Stukeley's reconstruction of Stonehenge, with pious Druids in attendance.

9 Stukeley's reconstruction of the Avebury complex at its zenith, with Druids processing in front with bunches of mistletoe and a free-range (and doomed) goat.

10 A lithograph by N. Whittock of an imagined Druidic ceremony at Stonehenge, drawing heavily on Stukeley's ideas both for the physical setting and the reverence of the proceedings. It could, however, also be read as a satire on Roman Catholicism; and note the bound prisoner.

11 A more boisterous fantasy of a Druid festival at Stonehenge, by Samuel Meyrick and Charles Smith, still very dependent on Stukeley for its images.

12 One of the most influential of all pictures of an Archdruid, published by Meyrick and Smith in 1815 and based on a mixture of Stukeley, Iolo and prehistoric artefacts.

13 Pliny's image of the Druid as gatherer of mistletoe, twinned with Stukeley's one of a priest of Stonehenge, engraved to illustrate William Mason's famous poem.

14 Druids, mired in superstition, caught mistletoe-handed by the arrival of the superior religion of Christ, in a Victorian engraving after a painting by Francis Hayman.

15 The classic medieval vision of the Biblical Flood, treated as an actual event in history, in a twelfth-century fresco.

16 Aylett Sammes's classic illustration of the 'wicker man' as a mechanism for human sacrifice, based on Caesar and Strabo. Ever since its publication in 1676, it has often been a source of inspiration for histories, novels and films.

17 Engraving from the Druids' Magazine, 1832, showing the Treasurer of the ruling Grand Lodge of the Ancient Order of Druids. He personifies the confidence, opulence and pomp of the lodge, and the whole order, on the eve of its great schism.

18 Another illustration from the same magazine, showing the officials parading into the Grand Lodge for an evening of ceremony and music.

19 Members of the Salisbury Lodge of the Ancient Order of Druids parading through the city to show support for the Great Reform Bill. The picture displays well the high public profile of the order by this date and its identification with bourgeois liberalism.

20 Robert Cruickshanks's famous caricature of Iolo Morganwg, in the chair in which he worked and (unable to lie down because of asthma) slept. One of his forged manuscripts, with his 'mystic sign' of Druidry at the top, is in his hand.

21 Thomas Gray's Bard, the epitome of Georgian Celtic romanticism, about to leap to his death in the River Conway rather than to surrender to the English.

22 William Blake's vision of an ancient British bard, inspiring his people to peace and love; consciously or not, an illustration of Iolo Morganwg's conception of how bards should have been, and might yet be.

23 W. O. Gellar's engraving of a Druid ceremony at Stonehenge, from 1832, sums up the Romantic preoccupation with drama in humanity and nature and the increasing predominance of a concept of Druidry as a religion of dementia and horror.

24 William Wordsworth, the archetypal Romantic poet of nature, and the poet who most often mentioned Druids, engaged in a suitable reverie among sublime natural surroundings.

25 The frontispiece of William Kingston's Eldol the Druid, from 1874, advertising the novel's view of Druidry as a furtive and nasty cult.

26 A Victorian illustration of the Hindu rite of sati, the burning of widows on their husbands' funeral pyres, which the British were trying to suppress in India.

27 A Hindu painting of Kali, the goddess to whom the practitioners of thagi sacrificed their human victims until British rule stamped out the cult.

28 The Rocking Stone on Pontypridd Common, with Myfyr Morganwg's Victorian Druid temple around it.

29 William Price, the most famous of all Victorian Welsh Druids, in his formal public dress, holding the torch with which he lit his baby son's funeral pyre and the crescent moon which was his symbol of Druidry. His ceremonial garb was actually a white robe.

30 The Druids (genuinely) arrive at Stonehenge, the processional corridor formed by members of the Ancient Order of Druids with hooded robes, false beards and staves, to open their huge ceremony there in 1905.

31 The head of the stone serpent threaded through the Rocking Stone on Pontypridd Common: a Victorian realisation of Stukeley's dreams of how Avebury should have been.

32 Stonehenge meets the Masons. The title page of the official magazine of the Ancient Order of Druids, 1909, combines Pliny's concept of the ancient Druids as oak priests and Stukeley's one of them as builders of megaliths, with an altar from modern Freemasonry.

MARCH, 1909

THE DRUID

OFFICIAL ORGAN
of the
A·O·D
Circulating throughout
The UNITED KINGDOM
the COLONIES
and AMERICA.

Edited by
William McAuliffe

33 Robert MacGregor-Reid holds up the ceremonial sword (its sheathing being the symbol of peace) at a ceremony on Primrose Hill, London, in 1957. Both the sword and the 'mystic sign' on the banner are part of Iolo Morganwg's legacy.

34 The Universal Bond at Stonehenge, Midsummer 1956, with Robert MacGregor-Reid presiding with staff and book. The crowding of the public around them is an ominous portent of the troubles of the early 1960s.

35 The Gorsedd of Bards of the Isle of Britain at a twentieth-century Welsh National Eisteddfod, Iolo Morganwg's greatest legacy to the world.

36 Thomas Maughan, successor to MacGregor-Reid as chief of the Universal Bond, presides over an equinox ceremony on Tower Hill in 1966.

37 Breton Bards in full glory at their own national Goursez, based on the Welsh Gorsedd and so one of Iolo's institutional grandchildren.

8

IOLO'S CHILDREN

It has been shown how the Welsh came late to an incorporation of Druidry into their national self-image, and how they then, at the end of the eighteenth century, made up for lost time by forming a strong collective relationship with it. It has also been emphasized that the most influential work to this end was carried out by the wayward genius of Edward Williams, alias Iolo Morganwg. During the nineteenth century, the relationship between Druidry and Welshness was consolidated, to make the Welsh the people of Druidry *par excellence*. Iolo's influence continued to contribute to this process, until by the end of the century he had supplied some of the main concepts and expressions of modern Welsh nationhood.

The process took various forms, one of them a literary love affair between Welsh scholarly authors and Druidry which endured throughout the period. Its main themes were all shared with Iolo, and in some cases explicitly inspired by him. The first was a belief that the ancient Druids had been wise and high-minded people who had believed in the one true god and expounded a theology of salvation by him. The second was a detestation of the Romans, as brutal invaders who propagated lies about the British in general and Druids in particular, whom they misrepresented as bloodthirsty barbarians. The third was a claim that Christianity had blended with Druidry to produce an early British Church which taught an unusually benevolent and liberal kind of Christianity, accurately reflecting the wishes of Jesus himself. The fourth was a hatred of Roman Catholicism, portrayed as the force that had taken over and largely suppressed this native Church in order to further its own corrupt power in a replay of what the pagan Romans had done to Britain. The fifth was a belief that medieval Welsh literature had preserved Druidic teachings concealed in the imagery of the bards who had composed it, who were themselves the direct heirs of Druidry. These teachings were usually held to be expressed in the triads associated with them, but actually composed by Iolo. The composite result of these ideas was a powerful new national legend, which made Welsh writings about Druids during the century much more admiring, overall, than English equivalents.[1]

A few selections from them should illustrate the point. In 1833 Angharad Llwyd published a history of Anglesey in which she provided the most impassioned of all accounts of Suetonius's attack on the island, told from the point of view of the defenders. To her, both the Druids and the black-clad women had been completely unarmed, and represented a religion of, for its time, admirable learning and piety. By contrast, the Romans were 'the most savage and unprincipled nation' that has ever 'polluted the earth', and their victims on the island 'fell a lamentable sacrifice to the most extreme outrages and fiercest cruelties ever practised, even by that nation'.[2]

Three years later there appeared a classic statement of the new Welsh foundation legend by David James, then a curate who held the living of Almondbury on the side of the Yorkshire mill town of Huddersfield. He was, however, thoroughly Welsh, and went home regularly to compete in regional *eisteddfodau*, with the bardic name of Dewi o Ddyfed. He went to great pains to prove that the Druids had practised the religion revealed by the true god to the Hebrew patriarchs, in every respect. He neatly turned the tables on English authors who identified with the Romans as fellow imperialists, by reminding readers that, according to the biblical account of the peopling of the earth, the earliest Britons would themselves have been colonists settling in virgin lands and planting the true faith: 'It is a most unpardonable mistake into which both historians and divines have fallen, to represent the aborigines of almost every country and consequently of Britain, as a group of untutored savages or half barbarians. They were all civilized, enlightened, and for the most part religious colonies, that spread from Asia to people the globe.'

James's portrait of the Druids themselves was one of wonderful scientists and mechanics, as well as fine clergy; he took another swipe at contemporary political issues by declaring that, unlike the modern established Church, the Druid system did not allow its members to hold more than one benefice at a time. His imagery is as vivid as any picture; largely because much of it *was* based on pictures, taken from Meyrick and Smith's history book, purged of the opinions of those authors and with extra material added from Iolo (above all) and other writers. Thus, every member of the Druid order wore a hooded robe in the colour of his grade, with a string of beads around his neck. All had short hair and long beards. A Druid had a crown of oak leaves, a Bard carried a harp, and an Ovate bore a staff with a golden top. To give judgment in a legal case, a Druid donned a white stole over his robe, and a girdle in which was set a crystal encased in gold. He hung a gold crescent upon his breast and added a gold tiara to his leafy crown. Before him he set a frame holding wooden staves on which legal maxims were cut.[3]

In 1851 the rector of the village of Llanllynfi, on the north Welsh coastline almost opposite Anglesey, wrote a treatise on the improvement of agriculture in which he raised the Druids' reputation as inventors to new heights. In his opinion, their respect for peace, morality and science had been such that they must, logically, have been great promoters of both commerce and farming. He thought that they had probably invented windmills, water mills and fulling mills, and machinery for the manufacturing of textiles.[4] Eight years later, a contributor to the *Cambrian Journal* credited them with a deep knowledge of electricity, hypnotism, chemistry and medicine.[5] As has been seen in the case of some English writings, in the right hands the Druids could benefit as much from the Victorian cult of science and technology as they had from the Georgian cult of nature. By 1887, it was time for them to be enlisted in a political cause, of home rule for Wales and the disestablishment of the national Church there. The author of a pamphlet calling for these reforms praised both Iolo and Stukeley for revealing the virtues of ancient British Druidry, and so the inherent abilities of the Welsh, and used the Bible to corroborate their views. In addition, he declared that King Arthur's Round Table had actually been a Druidical stone circle.[6]

The bestseller in this whole list was Richard Williams Morgan's *St Paul in Britain*, published in 1861 and going through nine editions during the next 120 years; it still exerts some influence, overt or not, on forms of modern esoteric Christianity and modern Druidry. It was the work of a Welsh churchman dedicated to proving that British Christianity was an indigenous and admirable form of religion, founded by the apostles Paul and Simon the Zealot, supported by Joseph of Arimathea, and owing absolutely nothing to the Church of Rome. In his starstruck eyes, Britain had been the holy land of remote antiquity, equivalent to Rome in modern Europe or Tibet in modern Asia, from which its Druids had gone forth to establish centres of piety and learning as far away as Greece and Egypt. It had been the fount of Greek philosophy and science, and Orpheus and Pythagoras had both been Druids. Morgan published a list of thirty-one Druidic universities, which he declared had been scattered across Britain in ancient times and had occupied the sites of most subsequently notable English cities (to which he gave actual or invented Welsh names). He claimed that these were the examples that could be recovered out of a total of forty that had once existed. In his view, Druids had led the British in an uncompromising opposition to Roman paganism, joyously received the Christian faith, and been persecuted by the Romans alongside Christians as a result. He closed by manufacturing a family tree showing the descent of Queen Victoria from the leaders of the ancient British Church.

The overwhelming Welsh appreciation of Druids, and the dominant and increasing English antipathy to them, were clearly connected. As has been emphasized, Druids had become major figures in British culture as the result of the construction of a British superstate in the years around 1700, requiring a common history. They peaked in general popularity during the second half of the eighteenth century, as that superstate proved to be a tremendous political, military and economic success. During the nineteenth century that success only increased, and Ireland was added to the United Kingdom, but all the principal peoples included within it were starting to react against the common identity to which they were expected to subscribe. By the end of the Georgian period, both the Scots and the Welsh were manifesting fears of England's dominance of the partnership, in population, resources, and the seats of political and administrative power. Although the dividends of membership of the kingdom were clearly large enough to make their continuation in it worth while, there seemed to be a real danger that they would lose their distinctive sense of identity as peoples and be turned into second-rate extensions of a national culture dominated and shaped by the English.

As a result, the first half of the nineteenth century saw a process of action and reaction, whereby all three main historic nations of Britain reinforced their own sense of cultural individuality while co-operating with ever greater dynamism and success in the common pursuit of power and wealth. The Scots developed a greater sense of their own history and nationhood, exemplified by the novels of Sir Walter Scott. They also adopted visual and musical symbols – the kilt, clan tartans and bagpipes – which could immediately signal their separate and unique identity to all who saw or heard them.[7] The Welsh, as we will see, conducted the same exercise, with equal success; and their appropriation of the Druids, as figures with whom they had a particularly close historic relationship, was a part of it. The English reaction to the Scottish and Welsh efforts to define and preserve their separate character was a complex one. On the one hand, some writers remained fully committed to a general sense of Britishness; a construct, after all, from which the English had profited most of all, as the leading partner in the consolidated kingdom. This remained a theme throughout the nineteenth century and it helped to perpetuate a sense of Druids as heroic ancestors.

Other authors, however, chose two different courses, which were both inimical to such a sense. One was to preserve a sense of Britain as the unit of loyalty, but to identify it as a modern version of the Roman Empire, with the British functioning as spiritual (and, as former subjects of the Romans, perhaps as literal) descendants of the Romans as conquerors, administrators, builders and engineers. The other, equally dismissive of Druids, was to respond to the Welsh and Scottish efforts at self-definition by stressing a distinctively English tradition, culture and character within the broader British framework. This drew directly on those roots which gave England its political origin and separate history: in the Anglo-Saxons. These Germanic settlers were credited with three different complexes of qualities especially admired by the English of the age. One comprised hardihood, courage, enterprise and acquisitiveness; the pioneer virtues much to the fore in an age in which the British were settling large areas of Canada, Australia and New Zealand. The second consisted of a practical approach to living, which concentrated on technological invention, efficient management and commercial acumen at the expense of the imaginative arts; all attributes obviously associated with the greatest period of British economic expansion. The third was made up of democracy and self-reliance, characteristics that historians of the time commonly attributed to the free German tribes who had emigrated to Britain to dispossess natives too long habituated to obedience to, and reliance on, Roman might. In these supposed ancestral traditions, English historians claimed to find the origins of their parliamentary tradition.[8] None of them were interested in finding Druids in archaic Germany, and to those who emphasized the Anglo-Saxon foundations of England (and therefore of British greatness), Druidry became either menacingly alien, or irrelevant. This attitude is exemplified by Thomas Hughes, one of those who inclined instinctively towards this separate and Germanic sense of Englishness, when discussing the White Horse carved on the chalk slope above Uffington in his native part of Berkshire. In his time it was most commonly supposed to have been made on the orders of the most notable Anglo-Saxon in modern memory, Alfred the Great. Hughes commented: 'One wouldn't care about it if it wasn't made by the Saxons and their great king. The Druids don't seem akin to us somehow.'[9]

The Anglo-Saxon sense of Englishness was in part an adversarial stance, defining itself against other peoples in the United Kingdom, and at their expense. The Scots – at least in the dominant, Lowland, areas of their country – could be incorporated within

it, by extension, as they possessed a Germanic language and their generally acknowledged commercial and military acumen nicely fitted the stereotype being assembled for
it. It could, by contrast, be readily deployed against the Welsh, especially as they reinforced their own sense of themselves as a separate people, based partly on a claimed
inheritance from Druidry. Its main target, however, and the true Other against which
nineteenth-century Anglo-Saxonism was defined, consisted of the Irish. From the
moment that Ireland was incorporated into the United Kingdom in 1801, some – often
many – of its people opposed the terms of union, campaigning or conspiring to achieve
at least a loosening of them and at most renewed independence. These actions grew
more violent, and the political and social atmosphere of Ireland more embittered, during
the middle years of the century. The realization that large numbers of the Irish were
rejecting a partnership with the British state drove many of the English who led that
state to explain such a development with resort to hostile ethnic and national stereotypes. The sturdy, efficient, reliable and well-organized 'Germanic' temperament was
increasingly contrasted with an emotional, untrustworthy and anarchic 'Celtic' one,
which at worst lacked any of the common human virtues, and at best lacked most of
those that fitted a people to govern themselves. The association of Druids with a native
'Celtic' culture in both Wales and Ireland made those English who identified with an
Anglo-Saxon sense of national origins even less likely to look on them with affection.[10]

For the Welsh, the effect of all these developments tended to progressive reinforce-
ment of the relationship with Druids. The more that English writers ceased to regard
Druidry as a valued part of their national heritage, the more incentive was provided
for Wales to claim and honour it for itself. The stronger the perceived link between
Welshness and Druidry became, the more likely it was that the English would cease
to identify themselves with Druids. It could be a perfectly circular process.

*   *   *

It has been noted how much Iolo's work runs through the Welsh attitude to Druidry
during this period; as, indeed, it featured in English writings of the same time. Once
his own difficult personality had been removed from connection with them, his representations of a bogus ancient Druidic and bardic tradition could make a still greater
impression. It was his full intention that this should be so, and he laboured in later
life to ensure them immortality even as his own body decayed. As described before,
he planted his institution, of the *gorsedd* of Bards, into both local and regional gatherings in south Wales, and tried to prepare his own unpublished writings for the press.
In both endeavours he placed great emphasis on his possession of an heir to his work,
in the form of his son, Taliesin.

No full biography exists for Taliesin Williams, but his life is the subject of a valuable preliminary study by Brynley Roberts.[11] He was born in 1787, and at first assisted
his father in the family business of stonemasonry. In 1816, he established himself in
a more comfortable and respectable career as a schoolmaster, founding and running
his own establishment at Merthyr Tydfil. It was soon the principal school in the
district. By basing himself there, Taliesin was shrewdly looking forward to the
modern destiny of Wales,[12] rather than backwards to a bardic past, for he had linked
his fortune to that of one of the principal centres of the Industrial Revolution.

Merthyr in the period was a boom town, based on the manufacture of iron. By 1790 it had four major ironworks within its boundaries or its vicinity, all using the most advanced technological processes and one of them being the largest in the world. In one generation, between 1760 and 1800, it turned from a poor upland parish of scattered farms into the largest single concentration of Welsh people on earth. By 1830 it was the focus of seven parishes, containing between them about 40,000 people and forty-four furnaces. It was the greatest of a chain of ironmaking centres founded in the same period, the 'Top Towns' that were strung along the broad trough of linked valleys that runs from north-east to south-west under the peaks of the Brecon Beacons. They owed their presence to English industrialists who had spotted the potential of the district's rich deposits of the three materials needed for the new-style furnaces: iron ore, coal and limestone. The greedy appetite of the works powered the establishment of major extractive industries in all three products, and turned the coalfield that lay beneath the steep and narrow valleys streaming down to the south-east into one of the most important, and intensively mined, on the planet. In 1788 the region had produced 12,500 tons of pig iron (the standard iron bars needed for most construction work) per year. By 1830, output was 277,000 tons, representing almost half of total British production.

This explosion of economic activity had proportionate cultural consequences. As English ironmasters had first developed the region, and output was sold through an English-dominated trading network, the English language was used for all official transactions. English and Irish immigrants also made up a large minority of the labour force at and around the furnaces. The majority of it, however, was drawn from rural Wales, and Welsh was the language most commonly spoken in house, pub, chapel and street. It was a mirror-image of the situation that had thrust the London Welsh to the forefront of the national cultural revival in the previous century. The place taken in that earlier movement by Welsh business people who worked in London was now taken largely by business people of English origin who were based in Wales. The role of outsiders, immigrants and borderlanders, noted earlier with reference to Welsh (and indeed most) cultural nationalism, was to be vividly illustrated once again. A key role was played by the families who owned and ran the most important ironworks, and who took up something of the work of patronage undertaken by medieval lords and princes. Three in particular were to exert a great influence. At Merthyr itself were the Crawshays, owners of the Cyfarthfa works which dominated the town and were initially the most important in the whole region. Nearby at Dowlais were the Guests, who overtook Cyfarthfa to make their ironworks the largest and most productive in the world. Eastwards at Tredegar were the Halls. Two of these were to make an impact on national politics, in the persons of John Guest and Benjamin Hall. Both supported the reforming Whig Party, and won themselves titles, Guest as a baronet and Hall as a baron, taking the name Lord Llanover. Hall was to earn a different kind of enduring fame by gaining direct responsibility for the rebuilding of the Palace of Westminster and having the bell of the new clock tower named after him. It has come to chime out time for the British nation, as Big Ben.

While these men looked after the politics, their wives took care of the cultural nationalism.[13] Hall married more new money, by his union with Augusta Waddington, daughter of a London family which had made its fortune in the American trade, and then seated itself in Monmouthshire. Guest wed old blood, represented by Charlotte, eldest daughter of the Earl of Lindsey. Both women embarked on a love affair with Wales and became leaders of the next wave of measures to preserve and revive a distinctive cultural identity for it. The earlier initiatives, led from London, had concentrated on recovering and restoring a national heritage in the shape of traditional literature and music, and an institution, the *eisteddfod*, to encourage new productions. Augusta took the lead in building on these and adding external symbols of nationhood, of the sort pioneered so successfully by the Scots. Her main vehicle for this work consisted of the new Welsh institution of the regional cultural association, first devised by Bishop Burgess and his team of young clergy with the aid of Iolo. Burgess's Cambrian Society of Dyfed had rapidly been followed by the appearance of equivalent bodies in north Wales, and in 1821 one was founded to cover south-east Wales. That it should be the last to appear was no accident, for that region had long been the most Anglicized and least nationalist part of the country. Monmouthshire, where the society was based (as were the Halls themselves), was technically in England. To blot out this fact, the society took to itself, instead, the medieval Welsh name for the region, Gwent. As part of this deliberate archaism, it held its regional *eisteddfodau* at medieval towns, such as Brecon, Abergavenny and Cardiff, rather than in the new industrial centres, like Merthyr, which generated much of the wealth that helped to fund such events. At the Brecon *eisteddfod* of 1823 the society made Iolo an honorary member, and invited him to act as a judge.

In the period between 1825 and 1850, Augusta Hall presented her adopted nation with a set of symbols around which a distinctive identity might be consolidated for it in the modern world. She gave it a national folk hero, in the form of the Cardiganshire outlaw and trickster Twm Sion Catti. He was already a figure of local legend, but she sponsored his conversion into a figure known to the British in general by her patronage of Thomas Jeffrey Llewelyn Pritchard, a writer who produced a bestselling novel about him. She gave Wales a national costume, designing a female dress of tall black hat, red cloak, gown and petticoat and sponsoring its adoption at *eisteddfodau*. She gave it a national instrument, by establishing the triple-strung harp (originally Italian) as the dominant instrument at such events. Finally, she gave it a national mythology, by helping to found a Welsh Manuscripts Society to carry on the work of editing and publishing medieval texts to form a common literary heritage. The greatest product of this society was a series of tales recorded in a manuscript at Jesus College, Oxford, which had been intended for publication by Owain Myfyr but was crowded out of the *Myvyrian Archaiology* by Iolo's forgeries. It was now edited by Lady Charlotte Guest and under the name of *The Mabinogion* became the best-known and most admired feature of traditional Welsh literature in the world at large.

This, then, was the impact that Welsh industrialization had upon 'high' culture; it was to have major implications for the development of modern Druidry. As important, however, was the impact on the culture of ordinary people in the ironworking and coalmining region. Life for workers there was very unusual, in comparison with that which they had known in their original homes in rural or urban areas. On the one hand, earnings were higher – those of ironworkers were three to six times those of farm labourers in west Wales, and even higher than those of farmers. There was also a much greater sense of personal freedom than in the more closed, static and traditional communities that were the norm elsewhere. On the other hand, existence was much less secure. Ironworking was a notoriously volatile industry, prone to boom and bust, and those employed in it could plunge from plenty to destitution in a matter of months. It was also physically dangerous, as the hot metal seared eyes and threatened death or disablement with any spillage or explosion. The mining industries on which it depended were equally risky, destroying lungs, providing rockfalls and pit collapses and releasing poisonous or combustible gases. The rapidly swelling and overcrowded industrial settlements mostly lacked systematic sanitation and were swept by epidemics; there was a striking absence of old people in them. By the 1810s, relations between workers and employers there were already among the worst in nineteenth-century Britain.

All this led to a profound radicalization of proletarian culture. By 1839 there were well over two hundred dissenting chapels in the region. In places like Tredegar, site of the Hall ironworks, a new one was erected almost every year. By 1831 up to a half of the select vestry of Merthyr itself – the body that represented effective town government – was made up of Unitarians or their allies, often viewed as the most radical sect of all, and the one to which Iolo Morganwg had belonged. A conservative traveller across the area in the earlier part of the century reported that 'almost all the exclusively Welsh sects among the lower orders of the people have . . . degenerated into habits of the most pitiable lunacy . . . The various subdivisions of methodists, jumpers and I know not what, who meet in fields and houses, prove how low fanaticism may degrade human reason.'[14] In 1831 Merthyr became the centre of the most successful armed uprising by workers during the nineteenth century, which won control of the area around the town for a few days and subsequently produced Wales's first working-class martyr, Dic Penderyn, who was hanged for his part in it. Eight years later, the ironworkers and colliers on the Monmouthshire side of the border launched the last full-scale popular rebellion on British soil, which will be discussed later. The coalfield produced a secret society, the Scotch Cattle, which terrorized strike-breakers and intimidated employers' agents all through the first half of the century. Merthyr was the home of Wales's first working-class press, and in the 1820s over twenty *eisteddfodau* were held in its pubs, by local societies of poets and musicians. By 1840 there were about four hundred different clubs in the industrial region as a whole, including branches of English societies such as the Oddfellows, though the English orders of Druids had not yet made an impact. This, then, was the remarkable town, and district, in which Taliesin Williams chose to settle.

His portrait shows a determined face with a tightly closed mouth and firm chin, and indeed he was a much more effective man than his father in most worldly matters, while lacking all Iolo's creative genius. Initially, his politics were as fierce; in later years he recalled that when he first arrived at Merthyr he found that most of the friends he made there had been passionate supporters of the French revolutionaries.[15] On St David's Day 1821 a local Cymreigyddion group was founded in the town to foster Welsh culture, meeting at the Patriot Inn and strongly radical in its beliefs. Two years later it established a bardic chair of Merthyr, to be competed for at an *eisteddfod*; the first was held at the autumn equinox and given Iolo's 'Druidic' name of Alban Elfed, which surely reflected Taliesin's influence. He was the secretary of the panel that administered the competition, which was held from one to three times annually for the rest of the decade; in May 1825 he presided, and a year later he won the title of Chief Bard.[16] During the business of organizing the *eisteddfodau*, he came to be partnered with clergy of the established Church, who were pursuing the contemporary project of strengthening it by aligning it with the cultural revival. This may have mellowed Taliesin, for thereafter he showed none of his father's hostility to the ecclesiastical establishment. He duly befriended the Halls and Guests and became their ally, supporting them in their reformist politics and in opposing the workers' rising of 1831.[17]

These powerful friends were to be invaluable to him in propagating his father's legacy: an intention signalled by the bardic name that he took for himself: Taliesin ab Iolo (Taliesin, son of Iolo). Almost as soon as he inherited Iolo's huge mass of manuscripts he set to work to edit and publish selections from them, as his father had intended to do. In 1829 the first appeared, *Cyfrenach y Beirdd*, a treatise purporting to date from the sixteenth century and intended to disseminate Iolo's views on the proper rules of bardic composition, and the superiority of the versification that he alleged had been used by the bards of Glamorgan. At the same time Taliesin helped to preserve his father's institution, and ceremonial structure, of the *gorsedd*. Here he was assisted by the tradition of bardic gatherings and ceremonies that Iolo had planted at Newbridge in the Taff valley, downstream from Merthyr, a decade and a half before. Newbridge was now sharing in the general development of the region, becoming a major ironworking and mining centre in its own right. As it grew into a town, one of the fastest expanding in Wales, it became another powerhouse of the native cultural revival, and signalled this by taking the Welsh name of Pontypridd.[18] As a continuing seedbed for Iolo's ideas, it possessed the advantage of two notable personalities, one animate and the other inanimate. The former was the local innkeeper, Iolo's initiate who had taken the bardic name of Gwilym Morganwg. The latter was the rocking stone, Yr Maen Chwŷf, on the eastern hillside, the region's only credible Druidic monument (though credible only by the false attribution inherited from Toland). Taliesin had himself been initiated there, and in 1827 he returned for a full-scale *gorsedd* ceremony, at which he himself presided and Gwilym read poems, one of them in memory of Iolo.[19]

In 1833 Taliesin became one of the founding members of the Cymreigyddion y Fenni, a society designed to promote Welsh cultural nationalism, modelled on those already established at Pontypridd and elsewhere and based at Abergavenny. What gave it special significance was that two of the main driving forces behind it, and mainstays of its funding, were Benjamin and Augusta Hall, and so Taliesin was drawn further into an alliance with them.[20] The following year, the *eisteddfod* movement scored its greatest success to date, when the Gwent and Dyfed regional societies joined forces to stage a huge competition at Cardiff. It was the first to be patronized by British royalty, as the guests of honour were the Duchess of Kent and her young daughter, the future Queen Victoria. Augusta Hall won the essay prize with a polemic on the importance of preserving both the Welsh language and the Welsh national costume. The latter, of course, did not actually exist at this time, and her manifesto was a key stage in Augusta's campaign to create one.[21] Taliesin was also there, ideological guns blazing. He declared the *eisteddfod* open, and proceeded to win the bardic chair for poetry with a piece on 'The Druids of the Isle of Britain'. This expounded his father's pseudo-history, turned the Romans into savage conquerors and liars, and held up the Druids as exemplars of peace, learning and piety. The speech by Taliesin's Archdruid on Anglesey, reproving the advancing soldiers of Suetonius, remains a classic image of benevolent Druidry:

> There is but one who rules the eternal skies,
> One God, One Parent, He supremely wise!
> Those deeds of bloodshed are to us unknown,
> By us abhorred, nor are our hearts of stone;
> By us no captives in the flames are slain,
> We seek no pleasure in another's pain.

Taliesin also emphasized his father's argument that the Christian bards of medieval Wales had merely been the old Druids in new guise, and made the declaration:

> May Britain's Isle the glorious and fair,
> Truth her unfailing guide, her dearest care,
> Dispense afar the Gospels' cheering rays,
> To advance her people, and adorn their ways:
> May peace e'er prosper, unassailed by strife,
> Secure in conscious purity of life.[22]

At the autumn equinox following the Royal Eisteddfod, a party of those who had attended reunited at Pontypridd. They assembled at Gwilym Morganwg's pub, the New Inn, and climbed the eastern slope of the valley, led by a harpist and a sword-bearer. At the rocking stone, Taliesin presided over a *gorsedd*, unsheathing the sword with the aid of the other initiated Bards, and then climbing the stone holding it by the point, as a sign of peace. He declared the event open, recited some of his father's triads, and initiated a series of Ovates, of whom the first was Augusta Hall. Gwilym then declaimed a poem of his own on the British Druids, from the summit of the stone.[23]

In 1838 there followed another landmark in the progress of the Cymreigyddion y Fenni, an *eisteddfod* at Abergavenny itself. This town was, and is, one of the traditional gateways to Wales, clustering around the ruins of its medieval castle at the pass that the River Usk, flowing into Monmouthshire, makes in the Black Mountains. The event opened with a grand procession led by many banners and an open carriage containing a dozen harpists, followed by members of the society itself, initiated Bards who were its guests, and – as a novelty – members of the Ancient Order of Druids, led by two Archdruids in full ceremonial dress. In this fashion, English fraternal Druidry linked up formally with the Welsh revival. The local gentry brought up the rear, on horseback or in carriages. A *gorsedd* ceremony was held in a yard behind the George Hotel, its stone circle being hastily constructed from small stones found nearby. Observers were impressed by the fact that, despite wind and rain, the Bards holding the rite remained bareheaded and shoeless throughout the proceedings, as Iolo had prescribed. Their leader this time was a guest from north Wales, William Ellis Jones, who had founded the Cambrian Society of Merioneth. He presided in a gown trimmed with purple, and a blue sash from which hung a gold star, striking a new note of sartorial ostentation at such events. One of the Bards initiated was the vicomte de Villemarqué, a visitor from Brittany who was to become the most important single leader of the modern revival of Breton cultural nationalism. Two years later, Taliesin himself presided at an equivalent ceremony held at the next *eisteddfod* at Abergavenny, and one of the Bards initiated there was the local vicar of the Halls, who was also a prominent member of the Ancient Order of Druids. Thus further links were made with the fraternal movement.[24]

It was now time to publish another instalment of Iolo's papers, and Taliesin dutifully produced it in 1840, in a book entitled *Coelbren y Beirdd*. This propounded Iolo's fantasy of a set of special alphabets based on Druidic tradition and used by the medieval bards, in conjunction with a wooden frame on which sticks engraved with the letters could be mounted. In this way, Iolo suggested, they could convey secret messages to each other when their English conquerors forbade them to use pen and ink (another of Iolo's pieces of imagined history). These were equivalents to the genuine Irish ogham alphabet, which was itself presumed at the time, and long after, to be an invention of the Druids.[25] A couple of Taliesin's more scholarly friends in the *eisteddfod* movement warned him not to publish this material until he had better proof of its authenticity. As far as Taliesin was concerned, the proof lay in his father's own collection of manuscripts; he either did not see, or chose not to believe, that it was necessary to question what sources might lie beyond those.[26] He set to work on a third collection of Iolo's material, this time a range of texts that referred directly to ancient Druidic and bardic teachings. Probably because of increasing age and ill health, he had still not submitted this to the press when he himself died in 1847. It was left to the loyal Augusta Hall to ensure that it appeared, the following year, through the Welsh Manuscripts Society that she had sponsored.[27] It was offered to the reader, without hesitation or qualification, as an edition of ancient manuscripts. In 1853 Augusta completed her good offices by purchasing the whole of Iolo's collection of texts and notes from Taliesin's heirs and depositing it at her home of Llanover Court, above the Usk downstream from Abergavenny. There she made it available to scholars, to whom it was represented as an invaluable collection of transcripts from medieval Welsh manuscripts.

Brynley Roberts has made a persuasive case that Taliesin succeeded in winning a still greater measure of acceptance for his father's portrait of the ancient Druidic and bardic tradition, and in giving an apparent stamp of authenticity to it.[28] He did this by arguing directly on its behalf, by promoting its central institution of the *gorsedd*, and by producing apparently scholarly editions of the material on which it was based. His own transparent honesty and sincerity, and ability to win and keep friends – all qualities in which Iolo himself had been lacking – did much to reinforce these achievements. He would not have been so successful, however, had he not made such powerful and supportive allies among the new industrial ruling class of his adopted district. In this respect, Augusta Hall, her husband and her friends had indeed taken on the role of the medieval Welsh princes, in acting as cultural patrons. It was not quite the result for which Iolo had hoped, at least for much of his life: that his system would become part of a new, and revolutionary, social and religious order. None the less, it represented a more traditional form of transmission and acceptance, and Iolo himself, who had, after all, dedicated his poems to the Prince of Wales, and allied with the Bishop of St David's, would probably have been happy with it.

* * *

Taliesin simultaneously honoured the other aspect of his father's intellectual inheritance, by encouraging young radicals among the common people of Wales to identify with Druidry. Two of these, in particular, came to stand out. One was Evan Davies, for whom, again, there is no full-scale biography but who has been the subject of an important essay by Huw Walters.[29] He was born on a farm in the Vale of Glamorgan in 1801, and impressed people while still a boy with his unusual intelligence and intellectual curiosity. He never went to school, but taught himself to read and write, and acquired a lasting enthusiasm for mathematics, astronomy and Welsh poetry. He spent many nights on the slope of the mountains that bounded the northern fringe of the Vale, studying the stars.[30] By the mid-1820s, he was competing as a poet in local and regional *eisteddfodau*, and this is how he must have come to Taliesin's attention; Davies won the first prize in poetry at a competition at Merthyr in 1826, which Taliesin helped to organize.[31] At the spring equinox of 1834, the older man initiated the younger as a Bard, in a *gorsedd* held at the rocking stone above Pontypridd. He was back at the stone at the autumn equinox, to assist Taliesin at the ceremony in which Augusta Hall and others were initiated.[32]

Unsurprisingly, he became an ardent proponent of Iolo's teachings, and in 1839, at an *eisteddfod* at Cowbridge in the Vale, he lectured on some of their main aspects.[33] He also found a vocation as a preacher, serving a series of chapels belonging to the Welsh Independent sect in the north of the Vale, and between 1838 and 1843 he founded and ran a Welsh cultural society to serve the area. At some point in the mid-1840s he followed the now well-beaten trail from the agricultural south to the industrial north of Glamorgan, and settled at Pontypridd. There he made clocks and watches, work which fitted that love of mechanics that caused him so to appreciate the revolutions of the heavens. In addition, he continued to preach, at an Independent chapel in the town.[34] His move brought him into closer proximity with the other man who would come to personify radical Druidry in nineteenth-century Wales. This was William Price, who was born in 1800 at Risca, where the River Ebbw flows out of the mountains on to the coastal plain of Monmouthshire.[35] Whereas Evan Davies has never risen above the level of a local worthy, and a character in studies of modern Druidry, Price has a permanent place in the national memory. He was both one of the most colourful characters in Welsh history, and one of the most remarkable in Victorian Britain. He has been the subject of several biographies, in both book and essay form. None, however, constitutes a full-length, properly referenced, published study. The most extensive, painstaking and scholarly is an unpublished doctoral thesis, now almost half a century old.[36] The published works are almost all admirable in certain respects, and progressively better in overall quality, partly because each has built on the others.[37] None, however, is lengthy, and most are not properly referenced; and the casual reader's notion of Price is also bedevilled by the existence of a lively booklet on his life which purports to be a serious biography but departs so far from the known facts, without locating any of its sources, as to seem more like a historical novel.[38] He certainly poses a problem of evidence, in that, despite a spectacularly flamboyant personality, much of his life is not well recorded. He has left few letters and no diaries or memoirs, and most of the information preserved on him was recorded by journalists, none of them writing at length or with great perception. In many ways his own outrageous personality gets in the way of historians, as it came between him and most of his contemporaries, so that none of those who have pronounced on him to date have been able to give him full sympathy. Some have concluded that he was clinically insane, while others prefer the softer term of 'eccentric'.[39] As I have argued elsewhere,[40] neither term seems wholly appropriate. He was far shrewder and more effective than most madmen, and too politically engaged, and terrifying to conservatives, to chime with the harmless and amusing oddity normally associated with eccentricity. It is a further problem in the present context that while those who have written on him hitherto have been interested in him as an oddity, or a radical, none have been concerned with him as a Druid.

Price's background was shaped by family tragedy. He was the third son, and the only one to achieve any fame, of a Monmouthshire clergyman. After a promising start, his father ruined first his social standing, by marrying a servant girl, and then his career, by going insane. He became disordered in his dress, kept snakes in his pockets as charms, carried a saw for the purpose of removing bark from trees, stood up to his neck in ponds, and sometimes went about naked. He became completely incapable of providing for his family, which was reduced to living on the charity of others, while young William's mother held it courageously together.[41] The boy grew up in a Welsh-speaking household, but learned English at school. He was a keen scholar, and, by a mixture of hard work and aid from family friends, managed to reach medical school in London and achieve a brilliant success there. Having qualified as a doctor, he returned to his native district to practise, and then followed the lure of the booming industrial communities, to settle in the Taff valley just below Pontypridd. In 1823 he became surgeon to the main chain-making plant at Pontypridd itself, being the first medical officer ever to be elected by a workforce.[42]

By the early 1830s he had become a supporter and ally of the Guests, in both politics and cultural nationalism. At the Royal Eisteddfod of 1834, directly after proceedings were formally opened by the city's aristocratic patron, the Marquess of Bute,

Price delivered an oration on Welsh history and literature. Lady Charlotte Guest thought it 'one of the most beautiful and eloquent speeches that was ever heard'. On the strength of it, he was invited to be a judge of the bardic competitions at the *eisteddfod*, in which Taliesin won his prize.[43] There is no evidence that Taliesin himself was ever directly associated with Price, but the older man's propagation of a love of Druidry must have had an impact on the younger. As well as being on good terms with the Guests, Price formed a still closer relationship with the Crawshay dynasty of ironworkers, and in particular with Francis Crawshay, a younger son who had been given the Treforest tinplate works below Pontypridd. Francis was quite a character himself, allegedly fathering twenty-four illegitimate children and naming streets after them in the ranges of housing built for his workers. He also built several chapels in the neighbourhood, and, for good measure, put up a Druidic stone circle in the grounds of his mansion at Treforest.[44]

By 1837, Price had become a leading member of the Society of the Rocking Stone at Pontypridd, which Gwilym Morganwg had founded, for in that year he paid for ten prizes of a pound each, offered by the society for essays in Welsh on moral subjects.[45] He organized classes in the Welsh language every Sunday,[46] and in 1838 he issued a circular calling for subscriptions to construct a Druidical Museum near the rocking stone, run by the same society: 'Let Y Maen Chwŷf be the banner of our heritage around which millions yet unborn shall assemble to learn the music and the language of our people.' Receipts from the museum would be used for a free school for the poor, kept by the curator. Francis Crawshay supported the scheme, but it failed to attract sufficient sponsors and Price vented his feelings by placing a declaration in the local newspaper, excoriating the gentry of the district for ignoring 'your immortal progenitors, *to whom you owe your very existence as a civilized people*'.[47]

This outburst was a danger sign. What drove Price's enthusiasm for Welsh culture was not merely an inherent pride in it, but anger. To advance the cause of Wales was also to oppose the dominant people of the island, the English, and Price was fashioned to see the world in adversarial terms. Certainly the difficulties of his family in childhood must have counted for something, because he was left with a smouldering rage and resentment, and a need for both achievement and combat. His view of the world embodied an indefatigable urge to challenge and flout social conventions. Such traits made it almost inevitable that he would become attracted by radical politics, especially of the more exciting, glamorous and activist kind. These were provided lavishly at the end of the 1830s, when the cause of Chartism suddenly took hold of the ironworkers and colliers of south-east Wales. This was a movement to establish a true democracy in Britain by granting full participation in parliamentary elections to working men, irrespective of their economic status. It is possible that Price's disappointment and humiliation over the matter of the museum led him to embrace it with a greater fervency, and, even as he published that angry letter, he was emerging as one of the leaders of the Chartists of his district.[48]

What distinguished the movement in the industrial region of south Wales and the ports that served it was a greater readiness to take up weapons to obtain the desired reforms, if they could not be achieved by peaceful lobbying. Price threw himself into both aspects of the campaign, making fiery speeches in support of it to meetings at the rocking stone, while also collecting arms to equip his own division of a rebel army: government informers reported that he had amassed seven pieces of field artillery by the autumn of 1839. Yet when the Chartists elsewhere in the coalfield and the iron district did rise, at the start of November, Price did not join them. Judging that the rebellion was badly planned and doomed to failure, he shrewdly kept both himself and his followers at home. None of them, therefore, were directly involved in the famous march that ensued, which has been justly called the last popular rebellion in British history, and which was broken by an engagement with regular soldiers at Newport in which twenty to thirty Chartists were killed or mortally wounded. None the less, Price was also clever enough to realize that he would be arrested during the wave of repressive measures that followed. He escaped to France, disguised as a woman, and remained there for a few months until the political temperature cooled and he could return home without danger.

While he was in Paris, he experienced a turning-point in his religious life. In the great collection of ancient art housed in the Louvre he came across a stone bearing an inscription in ancient Greek. In reality, it is concerned – at least partly – with the zodiac. The self-taught Price identified the carved figure upon it as one of Iolo's ancient bards, addressing the moon. He deciphered the text as a prophecy sung by a Welsh prince called ap Alun, who had once ruled the entire civilized world in about 800 BCE. It spoke of the coming of a man who would understand the true secrets of the old Welsh language and liberate the Welsh people. The fact that nobody else had heard of this person, or made (anything like) the same interpretation of the inscription, was an encouragement to Price. It turned him from a lonely and ignominious fugitive from a political disaster into somebody granted a unique revelation of vital importance to his people: for surely he was the cultural saviour whose coming had been foretold for almost three thousand years.[49]

He had left Wales a political revolutionary; he returned there a religious one. Immediately he set up as a Druid and began attracting followers. In July 1840 the Marquess of Bute, who had co-operated with him in the Royal Eisteddfod less than six years before, and was now the government's highest-ranking representative in the region, reported Price's return to the Home Office: 'His great object appears to be to spread his infidel opinions with his republicanism.'[50] Another official report stated that 'his "scholars" walk openly with a stick in their hand, about four feet in length, shaped like a bayonet, three-sided, with figures and letters on them; but not an iota of their instructions or discipline is yet known.'[51] Posterity is, alas, no wiser, save that Price's principles now included a rejection of the institution of marriage. At about this time he began to live with Ann Morgan, from Pentyrch, downstream on the Taff, and in 1842 she bore him a daughter.[52] The girl was baptized by Price himself, acting as a Druid priest, in a public ceremony at the rocking stone.[53] She was called Gwenhiolan Iarlles Morganwg, 'Gwenhiolan, Countess of Glamorgan', thereby incorporating a title into her actual name. As so often, it is not certain how much stunts like this represented serious gestures or acts of playful and provocative misrule; but it seems fairly certain that Price's longing for glory for his family reflected his desire to wipe out the shame he felt in his real familial past. After the birth of his child he took a great interest in his descent, drawing up elaborate genealogies tracing it through many generations.[54] There is no evidence that he was ever actually initiated at a *gorsedd*; it may be that he did not deign to accept a status from others which he felt to be his by hereditary right.

Throughout this period he continued to engage in Chartist politics, but it is possible both that he had lost some prestige by his failure to support the rising and that the subsequent turn of Chartism to peaceful and patient lobbying did not suit his combative personality. Certainly, he found himself bereft of local support in the mid-1840s: in 1844 he sponsored an *eisteddfod* at Pontypridd, intended to act as a show-case for his own material, for which absolutely nobody else entered. As a result, the only event held at it was his own initiation of his baby daughter, as a Bard.[55] Increasingly, he found a new outlet for his aggressive energies in litigation. It was during an appearance in a lawcourt at Bristol in 1848 that he was first noticed as having adopted the formal dress which he was to wear on secular public occasions for the remainder of his life. The *Merthyr Guardian* described him as wearing

> a beard flowing to his waist, and his hair, which has evidently not been cut for many years, descends to as great a length, but is tied up with sundry long tails, à la chinoise [in the Chinese style]. His dress consists of a jacket and trousers of emerald green, fancifully notched and scalloped, lined and pointed with bright scarlet, and adorned with numerous small gilt buttons bearing devices. His cap is of sable, of singularly quaint form, and has attached to it three pendant tails of the same fur, one falling over each shoulder of the wearer, and the third coming down to the centre of his back.

He described this to the reporter as 'the dress of the ancient Court of Glamorgan',[56] but he was never consistent on the matter. He told another journalist, forty years later, that it was the costume of ancient Bards and Druids,[57] and it was later remembered that he had informed a judge that it was the military dress of the Welsh at the Battle of Bosworth Field in 1485, and that he was descended from the man who had carried the standard of Henry VII on that day.[58] It seems to have been his own unique creation, and certainly lent additional stature to a man who stood just five and a half feet tall.[59]

During the following decade, Price continued to make attempts to assert himself as an expert on Druidry, both in argument and in ritual, with at best qualified success. In 1855 there was a procession of a Welsh nationalist friendly society, the Ivorites, through the streets of Merthyr Tydfil to a chapel where an *eisteddfod* was to be held. Somehow, the members had agreed that Price should lead it. He did so in his now habitual costume, accompanied by a half-naked Aberdare man, calling himself Myrddin (Merlin), who wore dark paint and an animal skin over his shoulders in the manner often thought typical of ancient Britons. The pair led a goat, presumably as a national emblem. The local newspaper was not amused.[60] A year later, Price wrote to the two most prestigious newspapers of the United Kingdom, the *Times* and the *Illustrated*

London News, proclaiming his rediscovery of the authentic language of ancient Britain, 'unknown to the Bards and Baronets of the present day'; the last part was probably a crack at his former ally, Sir John Guest. To prove his case he quoted from some of Iolo's forgeries and from long-obsolete works of seventeenth- and eighteenth-century continental scholarship. Both papers refused to publish his letter, and so he had it printed himself, making no discernible impact on the world of scholarship.[61]

Price's activities ought to have made those of his new neighbour at Pontypridd, the hitherto modest and respectable Bard Evan Davies, seem very conventional by comparison. Davies, however, was starting to create his own reputation for flamboyance. Two events seem to have been significant in pushing him into more extrovert and provocative ways. One was the death of his mentor Taliesin, in 1847, which gave him both opportunity and incentive to develop his own ideas. The other was to be passed over for the post of resident preacher at the chapel which he attended and at which he had preached at times. This was alleged to have left him feeling slighted, and more inclined to explore alternative forms of spirituality.[62] The first sign of these came near the end of the 1840s, when he and other members of the Society of the Rocking Stone decided to build a full-scale ceremonial site around the stone itself. They used the plan that William Stukeley had proposed (erroneously) for the Avebury complex in its prehistoric heyday: of a snake passing through a circle. The rocking stone itself was enclosed in a double ring of megaliths, fourteen in the inner circle and twenty-eight in the outer. Two avenues of smaller stones were then set up, leading to the circles from either side. One came together at the end to form the serpent's tail, the other culminated in an oval to represent its head, with two rocks for its eyes, one of which had symbols from Iolo's bardic alphabet on it. Iolo's 'mystic sign' of Druidry was set out in stones below the eyes. It was the most imposing ritual complex yet to be erected in Wales for the performance of *gorseddau* according to Iolo's specifications; and Davies was clearly the moving spirit in its construction.

Perform them, he and his friends promptly did. The first recorded ceremony in the new monument took place at midsummer 1849, for the proclamation of an *eisteddfod* at Pontypridd in the following year. Davies made it, and then thanked everybody who had assisted him in building the circles and avenues. He gave a potted history of Druidry and bardism, based on Iolo's assertions. He then declared the *gorsedd* of the rocking stone to be the oldest in the whole of Britain, with supreme authority over all the others. As part of this supremacy, it was now ready to initiate Bards, Ovates and Druids from worthy candidates drawn from the whole of Wales. In a way which would surely have warmed Iolo's heart, he predicted a new golden age for the bards of Glamorgan and Gwent.[63] The *eisteddfod* thus proclaimed was held at the summer solstice of 1850, in the new ritual site – or, in the words of its promoters, 'within the charmed circle of the court of Ceridwen, and the revealers of the coiled serpent'. The reference to Ceridwen indicates that Edward Davies had now joined Stukeley and Iolo among the influences on Evan Davies's thinking. At ten o'clock a large crowd of people from all over Monmouthshire and Glamorgan gathered in front of the New Inn at Pontypridd and formed a procession. At its head was a white banner decorated with gold, and then a carriage containing a harpist, followed by 'the broad banner of the Gorsedd of the Bards of the Isle of Britain', the supreme body which was now claimed to be based at the rocking stone. The banner was azure, and bore in gold Iolo's 'mystic sign' and his motto 'The Truth Against the World'. Following were the existing Bards, among them Davies, bearing a sheathed sword by its point as a sign of peace. Davies opened the proceedings with a prayer composed by Iolo, although – characteristically – the latter had left it in manuscript with the claim that it was the work of Talhaiarn, the earliest known Welsh bard, from whom no actual compositions have survived. He had written three slightly different versions, all of them edited by his son Taliesin and published in his posthumous volume in 1848. The one most commonly known now in English runs

Grant, O God, thy protection
And in protection, strength
And in strength, understanding
And in understanding, knowledge
And in knowledge, the knowledge of justice
And in the knowledge of justice, the love of it
And in the love of it, the love of all existences
And in the love of all existences
The love of God, and all goodness.

This is vintage Iolo Morganwg, expressing the very best of his idealistic vision, in all its generosity; it made an appropriate opening to such an occasion, and Davies seems to have used it to open *gorseddau* henceforth. He followed it with a song in praise of the Bards of Britain. Initiations followed, and two of those whom he admitted as Ovates were the composers of the words and the tune of what was to become the Welsh National Anthem, 'Hen Wlad fy Nhadau'. At the close, Davies announced that the next *gorsedd* would be held there at the autumn equinox. The company then adjourned to the New Inn for lunch, and reconvened at the market hall of Pontypridd at six o'clock, for the bardic competitions.[64]

From this point onward Davies seems to have held regular ceremonies at the rocking stone, and his tendency to grandeur, already manifest in his claims for his own *gorsedd*, became more pronounced. In 1851 he became the first known person ever definitely to expel a Bard permanently from the official company of those initiated at a *gorsedd*. The victim had committed the sin of accepting a cash prize in an *eisteddfod* held at Dowlais, site of the Guest family ironworks. Evan Davies declared him 'excommunicated through the tail of the serpent [of the rocking stone complex], and driven to the brook, and from the brook to the river Taff, and from the river Taff to the sea, and from the sea to the state of evil, and from the state of evil to Annwn, and from Annwn to the water closet of Lucifer'.[65] At midsummer 1852 he mounted the rocking stone again, for his followers to invest him with the title of Archdruid of the Isle of Britain. His symbol of rank was what some commentators called a crystal, allegedly found inside a prehistoric burial chamber and termed a 'Druid's egg', of the sort made famous by Pliny; though some thought it the shell of an ostrich's egg.[66] He claimed that in taking the name of Archdruid he was functioning as the heir of Taliesin Williams, who had in turn inherited the dignity from his father Iolo, who had in turn claimed to be the last of the properly initiated Bards of Glamorgan, who had alone preserved the ancient Welsh bardic tradition. With it, he assumed a more glorious bardic name, Myfyr Morganwg, which can be translated as 'the scholar of Glamorgan'; and it is by this that he is usually known to history.[67]

It was perfectly credible to put himself into an apostolic succession of bardic leadership that passed through Iolo and Taliesin, but nobody before Myfyr had claimed the title of Archdruid of Britain; both Williamses had been content merely to take the role of presiding and officiating Bard at particular *gorseddau*, as Myfyr had done hitherto. The name of Archdruid had indeed been assumed in a Welsh context before, at regional *eisteddfodau* held in Anglesey since 1832. It was used by David James, 'Dewi o Ddyfed', author of the celebrated pseudo-history of ancient British Druidry. The historian of the *eisteddfod* movement, Dillwyn Miles, has suggested that he was influenced by the title given to lodge leaders of the English fraternal Druid orders. As a clergyman working in England, James was in a good position to know these, as would Myfyr himself, if he met the English Archdruids who participated in the Abergavenny *eisteddfod*. In addition, the setting of the events at which James used the name, in Anglesey, would have concentrated the minds of those present on ancient Druidry. There is no evidence, however, that James employed it as anything other than an alternative to that of presiding Bard, to be relinquished as soon as the rite was over. Myfyr was acting without precedent by claiming the title permanently for himself, as a further symbol of the complete supremacy of his own *gorsedd*.[68]

In 1853 he staged a performance that had nothing to do with Druids or Bards, but seemed intended to wind up his old co-religionists of the chapels. He had handbills distributed through Pontypridd announcing that, on the nearest Sunday to midsummer, a prophecy spoken by the biblical prophet Isaiah would be fulfilled on the rocking stone. Hundreds of people appeared to see this, some with the notion that Isaiah himself was expected to manifest. Myfyr Morganwg appeared in a carriage containing two long white poles, which were carried by companions on to the stone. From its summit, Myfyr recited an 'ancient prayer' (presumably the one by Iolo quoted above), and then a hymn was sung to the music of a harp. He then preached a sermon on Isaiah, as a great bard, and on the true god as a fount of peace. Then his assistants uncovered the tops of the poles, to reveal, suspended from them, 'several irons', which he assured the onlookers were swords beaten into ploughshares and spears into pruning hooks, as the prophet had predicted would come to pass. Most people present were amused, and cheered, but some held the whole presentation to have been a cheap stunt, and after this resentment and criticism of Myfyr began to grow in Pontypridd.[69] It was now a moot point whether he or William Price would prove to be the most outrageous figure in Victorian Welsh Druidry.

* * *

It was shown earlier that Iolo's portrait of Welsh history provoked disbelief and opposition among some of the more informed of his compatriots, from the moment that it appeared. One critic in particular, John Jones, had suggested techniques of source analysis that could commence the work of dating key texts and putting them into their cultural context. In the decades following Iolo's death, doubts continued to be voiced concerning the authenticity of his material, although they were more muted and tended to be expressed verbally rather than in print;[70] the leaders of Welsh cultural nationalism found Iolo's view of the past too convenient to be neglected. In the mid-nineteenth century, however, a new movement began for the more rigorous and sceptical treatment of Welsh history and literature, and (like so much else) it was centred on Merthyr Tydfil. It was started by a brilliant young scholar called Thomas Stephens, who had settled in the town to work as a chemist, pursuing his literary interests as a hobby. In 1848 he pulled off his first success, at an *eisteddfod* at Abergavenny sponsored by, among others, the Halls, and with the Prince of Wales as guest of honour.[71] There he won the essay prize with a critical overview of medieval Welsh texts, which he published the next year under the title *The Literature of the Kymry* (i.e. the Welsh).

With good reason, this book is commonly regarded as marking the beginning of the systematic and objective study of its subject. It argued that the poetry credited to the earliest bards was in fact the product of various periods. Some of it seemed indeed to belong to the time in which the poets concerned were said to have lived. Much, however, was a great deal later, and this included the body of mystical verse attributed to Taliesin and Myrddin which had been used as a source of Druidical teaching. Had it indeed been composed in the fifth and sixth centuries, as had been assumed, then there was indeed a strong likelihood that it had incorporated such teaching. From internal evidence, however, Stephens thought that none of it could be earlier than the tenth century, and some could even be as late as the thirteenth. He also noted that instead of preaching peace, as Iolo had insisted that the medieval bards had done, the work of the historical Welsh poets usually glorified war.

He tried to soften the implications of these discoveries by declaring that 'it is certain that the influence of Druidic ideas is observable' in the medieval poetry. He went on to say, however, that this was 'not the real Druidism of history', but a much altered and refined descendant of it. He concluded that 'there was probably as much difference between the moody and tyrannical Druid of reality, and the gentlemanly Druid of the age of chivalry', as there was between the latter and the democratic Druidry preached by Iolo. Both of the last two varieties of Druid, in Stephens's opinion, were effectively fictions, visions of ancient Druidry dreamed up in much later, and altered, times: 'they were psychological – not historical – truths'. In his reading, the medieval bards had created a vision of how ancient Druids should have been, in order to secure for themselves the respect, as a separate and learned caste, that they considered had been given to the Druids. Furthermore, this vision was the preserve of a sophisticated elite, with no reflection in society at large: their 'new Druidism was a thing of limited significance, and so obscure as to require explanations'. It had the effect of further dividing professional bards from ordinary people.

Stephens went on to consider the view of Druidry propagated by Edward Davies, and became the first critic to point out that he had not only misdated his key sources, but mistranslated some of them. He threw another sop to those who wanted to treat the texts as a reflection of Druidic belief by declaring that 'there is no reason to doubt' that some memory of the ancient doctrine of transmigration of souls was preserved into the thirteenth century. He then, however, countered the effect of this, yet again, by concluding that such a memory was so faint as to be reduced to scraps of folklore rather than surviving as a doctrine. He concluded with an analysis of one of the most famous texts in question, 'Preiddeu Annwn', pointing out that the language in which it was written did not develop before the twelfth century, and that it was 'not a theology but a romance'. All in all, he managed to undermine the credibility of medieval Welsh literature as a source for Druidry, wholesale, without launching a full-scale attack on the memory of Iolo. He suggested that Iolo had touched up some of his representation of the bards with wishful thinking, but placed the responsibility for most of the distortions on the medieval authors themselves. At the same time, he attributed honourable and understandable motives to them for their development of a false, recreated, vision of what Druids had been.[72]

In 1852–3, Stephens stepped up the attack, with a series of articles in a Welsh-language journal that called into question Iolo's claims for the *nod cyfrin*, the 'mystic mark' consisting of three lines diverging from a single point. Iolo had, as described, come to make this the most important visual symbol of his invented Druidic and bardic tradition, representing its creation myth. Stephens could find absolutely no basis for this in genuine historical sources, and said so. Furthermore, for the first time he revealed his irritation with some of his contemporaries who were developing Iolo's ideas further, referring slightingly to 'the rocking stone barefoots' at Pontypridd. This, naturally enough, infuriated the leader of those 'barefoots', Myfyr Morganwg, who was at this very moment using Iolo's mythology as one of the foundations for the system of which he now claimed to be supreme chief. Myfyr, however, simply did not possess the scholarship to reply effectively.[73] Much worse, for people of his cast, was to follow in 1858, when a scholar whose principal interests lay in Egyptology, David Nash, published a book entitled *Taliesin*.

This went over the same ground that had been covered ten years before by Stephens, but with still more detailed linguistic and literary analysis, and striking straight at all the most sensitive implications of the subject which his predecessor had skirted. Nash started by ridiculing a selection of recent books that had taken for granted both the central importance of Druids to ancient British history and the assumption that modernity now possessed a good knowledge of their teachings. He also made an all-out attack on Edward Davies, whose books he summed up as 'monuments of misapplied learning'. He then went on to restate, with further argument, Stephens's discovery that the main medieval texts that appeared to refer to Druids and their doctrines all dated from the twelfth century or later. In a striking anticipation of conclusions that successors were to reach again in the 1990s, he pointed out that even some of the poems that might have been authentically sixth-century (and had nothing to do with Druidry) seemed to contain later additions. He dwelt mercilessly, and hilariously, on what he claimed to be Davies's mistranslations. In one of several examples, Davies had taken the archaic Welsh word 'archaeddon' to signify 'the ark of Aeddon'; it actually just meant 'archdeacon'. A line that Davies had read as a mystical reference to rebirth – 'without the stall of the cow of transmigration, without a luxury in the world' – became a homely country proverb: 'without the cow-stall there would be no dung-heap'. He was equally unsparing of both Iolo and his son Taliesin, describing the bardic alphabets that the former had devised and the latter had published as 'monstrous impostures'. Iolo's assertion of a founding hero for Welsh culture called Hu Gadarn was unpicked and exposed as fallacy.

Like Stephens, Nash argued that the prose and verse works on which previous authors had relied most heavily for evidence of Druidry were not only very late but designed as entertainments, not expositions of religious belief. He pointed out that 'Preiddeu Annwn' refers to incidents from other medieval romances, and seemed to be a collection of references to heroic tales, not to a mythology. The story of the birth of Taliesin, *Hanes Taliesin*, was the single most important source for those seeking evidence of the Druidic doctrine of transmigration. Nash pointed out that not only was there no evidence that it dated from an early period, but that it referred to magical shape-shifting, of a sort found in popular stories all over the world, rather than progressive rebirth of a soul. He concluded that 'there is no more necessity for seeking a hidden meaning in the tale of Taliesin than in that of Cinderella'. Nash concluded by discarding even the shreds of consolation that Stephens had left those who still wanted to believe in a connection between ancient Druids and medieval bards: he pointed out that there was not a single undoubted reference to Druids in Wales between the first and the twelfth centuries, and suggested that the references to Druids that even Stephens had accepted in medieval literature were in fact to philosophers or sages instead.[74]

Stephens and Nash together had delivered a devastating attack on the basis for the new nationalist myth of Welsh history, and they had done so in English, to ensure the widest possible audience. None the less, there were inbuilt limitations to the impact it could achieve. Very few people were sufficiently expert in medieval Welsh to be able to judge the points at issue. This being so, most readers would have to fall back on their own prejudices, and the two books were too novel, iconoclastic, inconvenient and (in Nash's case) shockingly rude to command immediate assent from many. By the end of the following decade, influential figures had appeared in each of the British realms to minimize the damage they might do. England produced Matthew Arnold, the scholar and poet who, amongst much else, laboured to persuade his compatriots to value the Celtic literatures, as figures like Gray had done before. In 1867 he published a series of lectures that he had given a few years before, in his capacity as Professor of Poetry at Oxford. He immediately attacked Nash as 'too absolute, too stationary, too much without a future' in his scepticism. He then went on to praise Stephens for a more generous spirit, and to recommend the *Myvyrian Archaiology* (Iolo's forgeries and all) as the key book of Welsh medieval texts. He dealt with Nash's argument of a long gap in references to Druids by suggesting that the Welsh might have referred to them in literary works which had disappeared. Whereas Nash had shown that there was no good reason to think that the story of Taliesin referred to the Druidic doctrine of transmigration, Arnold proposed that there was no proof that it did not. He declared that the characters in the tales edited by Lady Charlotte Guest, as *The Mabinogion*, seemed to be more archaic than those from most medieval literature, and so appeared to be evidence of an older stratum of tradition. This opinion was, of course, based on a complete personal ignorance of what Welsh society of the eleventh and twelfth centuries was actually like. Arnold had no expertise in medieval Welsh, and indeed in the same book he proclaimed his belief 'in the need to extinguish Welsh as an everyday language' in the present. None the less, his airy opinions may have done much to reassure people that they could ignore many of the arguments made by Stephens and Nash.[75]

He was followed in the next year by a Scottish scholar of equivalent stature, William Skene. Skene complimented Stephens and Nash on inaugurating a new school of criticism which submitted medieval Welsh poetry to proper analysis. He joined the attack on Davies, commenting that 'it would probably be difficult to find a stranger specimen of perverted ingenuity and misplaced learning' than his work. He added that almost all of Iolo's documents 'must be viewed with some suspicion, and that very careful discrimination is required in the use of them'. He did not, however, inform readers of how they were to discriminate, and held out some latitude in the term 'almost'. Furthermore, he judged that neither Stephens nor Nash had proved conclusively that some of the mystical poems credited to Taliesin, and portions of those attributed to Myrddin, did not date from the sixth century.[76] This weakened the whole basis of their case.

Elsewhere in Britain, therefore, the challenge presented by the new critics was rapidly diminished in force. Within Wales, opposition to it was co-ordinated from within the entity which had by turns been Iolo's own foe and ally: the established Church.

* * *

The prime mover in this opposition was a clergyman called John Williams, from Ruthin in the north-eastern mountains. He had been ordained in 1835 and given a curacy at Llanfor near the head of Llyn Tegid, one of the largest lakes in central Wales. This was a prime site for regional *eisteddfodau*, and Williams immediately identified with the cultural nationalism that they embodied; the following year, when he was still just twenty-five, he published a book that enhanced the developing contemporary myth of the Welsh past. It enlarged on the familiar argument that the ancient British Church had been completely independent of that of Rome, and far superior in quality; and that Roman Catholicism had subjugated it in the course of the Middle Ages and attempted to eradicate knowledge of it. Williams suggested that the surviving native tradition of a finer kind of Christianity had fed into the Reformation and been revived in the Protestant Church that he himself served.[77] This love for an imagined native Christianity gave him a similar love for the Druids who, according to the evolving nationalist myth, had contributed so much to it. In 1842 he won the essay prize at an *eisteddfod* at Swansea, with an argument against the belief that they had offered human sacrifices. Significantly, it was based substantially on information provided by Iolo Morganwg, and repeated Morganwg's argument that the so-called sacrifices were just executions of people who had committed serious crimes. He had begun to use the bardic name 'ab Ithel', 'descendant of Ithel', after a medieval archdeacon of that name whom he claimed as an ancestor.[78] The following year all this work won him a transfer to a better curacy, at Nercwys in the north-east where the last slope of the Clwydian mountains comes gently down to meet the coastal plain of Flintshire.[79]

There he became even more active as a scholar. He was one of the two main moving spirits in the foundation of a Cambrian Archaeological Society to foster knowledge of Welsh history and prehistory, and a journal to publish its findings, *Archaeologia Cambrensis*. He also published a second, and larger, history of the early British Church, making extensive use of Iolo's assertions to restate his earlier arguments, and to declare that under the Druids, the Britons had been 'really an enlightened people, far advanced in civilization and intellectual development'.[80] In 1849 he managed to gain appointment to a living of his own, the parish of Llanymawddwy, south of Llyn Tegid in the very heart of the Cambrian mountains. In career terms it was a promotion; in practical respects, a disaster. His new job was one of the toughest that his Church could inflict on a minister, giving him responsibility for an impoverished community set in some of the harshest terrain in Britain. The financial proceeds were naturally meagre, and the work exhausting for a conscientious pastor, as poor ab Ithel certainly was. Repeatedly he visited the sick and troubled, walking on winter nights when the weather was too bad for riding. He was sometimes swept off his feet by streams in flood, and began to experience fainting fits; once he passed out in the middle of a sermon. A mere three years after taking up residence he suffered a complete breakdown in health, and was thereafter never really fit again.[81]

He was now caught in the same trap as 'Celtic' Davies had been half a century before. If he wanted to escape to an easier post, he needed to impress patrons even more than he had done hitherto; and this was most readily achieved by the scholarship that was in any case one of his main interests. To make greater efforts in that world, however, was to place a still greater strain on a body that was already starting to break. In view of this, it is both admirable and tragic that he pushed himself even harder than before. He edited key texts of medieval Welsh literature for the Welsh Manuscripts Society. In 1852 he fell out with his colleagues in the Cambrian Archaeological Association; he claimed that they had become tools of the Welsh based in London, while it seems that they were unhappy about his growing attachment to Druidry. Within a year he had founded a new society to rival it, the Cambrian Institute, with its own periodical, the *Cambrian Journal*, of which he was editor. Augusta Hall gave him free use of the collection of manuscripts amassed by Iolo, which she had purchased, and he continued to base his view of Druidry on them. Between 1849 and 1856 he published a series of articles quoting their information on the Druids' use of megalithic monuments, theology, and contributions to the making of Christianity.[82]

By this time he had made contact with Myfyr Morganwg, whom he immediately respected as a scholar, as few others did, and they became allies in the effort to defend and extend Iolo's heritage. In 1855 ab Ithel's health broke down so badly that he was given two years of leave from his parish duties, and he used these to the full for his wider enthusiasms. In August of that year he held a *gorsedd* of Bards on the common land of the nearest thing to a town near his parish, Dinas Mawddwy. He used his own money to hire a marquee, provide prizes for displays of bardic arts, and buy blue, green and white ribbons to tie on to new Bards, Ovates and Druids. Indeed, he proceeded to initiate several of these, in flagrant disregard of the fact that he was not actually yet an initiate himself.[83] At the summer solstice of 1856 he attended a ceremony held by Myfyr at the rocking stone above Pontypridd, swallowing whole the mythology that his host had by now built around it, based on the traditions bequeathed by Iolo and Edward Davies. Like the latter, Myfyr saw the stone circle and the boulders at its centre as the 'cradle of Ceridwen' and the 'ark of Noah'. Officiating on the summit of the rocking stone, he now represented himself as the embodiment of the divine solar power and the personification of Menw, Iolo's first man. He told his audience that the Welsh had received the original divine revelation more fully than the ancient Hebrews, and that all Christians should study the Welsh bardic tradition in order to understand their own religion. He then initiated five new Bards, including (at last) ab Ithel himself, before the proceedings were rained off. Ab Ithel went home to publish a rapturous account of the ceremony in his *Cambrian Journal*, concluding that the bardic literature of Wales revealed 'the pure and simple elements from which all disguised fables and the religious systems of the whole world sprang'.[84]

By the following year, he and Myfyr were co-operating to plan something never before attempted by the Welsh cultural revival: an *eisteddfod* with competitors and judges from all over the nation. It was held in the following year, at Llangollen, which was one of the most accessible places in the country as it was set in the central portion of Wales but virtually on the English border. This was a device, on ab Ithel's part, to reinvigorate the regional *eisteddfodau* of mid-Wales, his own area, which had recently come close to collapse. The fact that it took place at all was a great achievement, and set a precedent which was rapidly followed, with the establishment of a national council in 1860 to arrange a single annual National Eisteddfod for Wales, to be held alternately in the north and south of the country. The official song adopted for it was 'Hen Wlad fy Nhadau', from Pontypridd, which had been given prominence at Llangollen and as a result was launched on its course to become the National Anthem. All this was, very clearly, the consequence of the lead given by ab Ithel, but he himself was firmly excluded from any influential position on the council. This was because of his behaviour and that of his allies at Llangollen.

First, there was the matter of profit. Ab Ithel had suggested that a bardic tiara in gold be awarded, with an extra gift of £30, for the best work on 'the Bardo-druidic system of the Isle of Britain'. This tremendous prize was duly given to ab Ithel himself, for more material copied from Iolo's papers. Several other awards were made to members of his family, and the substantial surplus of cash generated by the whole event was pocketed by him and the two other promoters, fellow curates who happened to be his friends. Then there was a question of ethics. A prize was offered for the best essay on Madoc, a twelfth-century Welsh prince who had allegedly settled in America. This story had experienced a new surge of popularity among the Welsh after the recognition of American independence in 1783, as it apparently gave them a particular and early connection with the new nation. Iolo had duly jumped on this bandwagon, and forged some documents that appeared to corroborate the tale.[85]

When the entries came in, there could be no doubt that the very best was that offered by Thomas Stephens of Merthyr, the great revisionist scholar of medieval Welsh literature. The problem was that, true to character, he had expertly and conclusively debunked the story, proving that it was actually an early modern legend. When the moment came to award the prize, the judges declared Stephens's entry disqualified, on the grounds that it had undermined national tradition.[86]

Finally, there was an issue of style. From Iolo's time, coloured ribbons had been tied on initiates in *gorseddau* according to the grade awarded to them, and occasionally an individual, like the presiding Bard at Abergavenny in 1838, would strike a more flamboyant note in costume. In general, however, participants wore normal dress. In his programme notes for the Llangollen *eisteddfod*, ab Ithel regretted that there were no formal robes for bardic ceremonies, especially as the Victorian friendly societies were now accustomed to sport flags, sashes and other regalia on public occasions. At Llangollen, the three grades of the *gorsedd* paraded to the stone circle behind banners in the colours associated with them by Iolo, and wore matching robes. Four young female Ovates wore dresses 'of an ancient Welsh style, and, on their heads, chaplets of mistletoe, oak leaves, ears of corn and leeks'. A Welsh lawyer living in Surrey turned up in clothes of rainbow hue.[87] Ab Ithel appointed himself to preside, in Druidical white, and opened the proceedings with a speech on the history of bards, taken from Iolo. Myfyr was also robed in white, as Archdruid, with his 'Druid's egg' hung around his neck. They continued to wear these costumes on the official platform of the *eisteddfod*, before a crowd of four to five thousand people. There, however, the show was stolen by William Price, also up from Pontypridd even though he was not – as far as anyone knew – an initiated member of a *gorsedd* and may not even have been invited. He sported 'a short velvet jacket or hunting suit, with an enormous foxskin cap, sword, and flowing beard'. With him was his teenage daughter, under her full given name of 'Gwenhiolan Countess of Glamorgan', wearing 'a long scarlet robe with the paternal head dress of a foxskin'. She sat 'silent, cold and unimpassioned among her voluble and wondering sisters'. Their presence, to some observers at least, gave the proceedings an air of mockery, rather than solemnity, and furnished a large additional helping of ammunition to those who deplored ab Ithel's taste for ritual trappings.[88]

Ab Ithel now set to work to publish more of what he believed to be the authentic teachings of the ancient Druids and their successor the British Church, as preserved in Iolo's manuscripts. Between 1858 and 1860 he printed a long essay on the subject by Iolo himself, as a series of instalments in his *Cambrian Journal*.[89] He then issued a mass of information on the beliefs and organization of the Druids and Bards, as contained in Iolo's manuscripts, in a thick volume put out by the Welsh Manuscripts Society in 1862.[90] The contents were all, like the final volume of his father's papers edited by Taliesin Williams, provided in English, to reach the widest possible audience. He gave them the name *Barddas*, meaning 'bardcraft', or, more elegantly, 'bardistry'. In his introduction, he made a determined argument for the authenticity of the material, against all the doubts that had by now been cast upon it. He pointed out that the language used seemed to be genuinely archaic, that Iolo professed himself unable to understand the sense of some passages, and that some texts occurred in more than one version, with internal inconsistencies. He emphasized, in addition, that Iolo referred at times to specific manuscripts as his originals, even if these could not now be traced. Ab Ithel also declared that Iolo's own character had been that of a person incapable of forgery.

In this he had been greatly aided by a book published over ten years before, by a now elderly man called Elijah Waring, who had known Iolo in the latter's own old age. It consisted of a set of recollections of him, which portrayed him as a lovable and high-principled man, eccentric, prickly, opinionated and a little naïve, but immensely learned and possessed of tremendous integrity. It did indeed provide a good portrait of half of Iolo's character, completely missing the brilliant and unscrupulous deceiver and the fomenter and preserver of quarrels. Instead, with colour and skill, it represented a person incapable of any conscious duplicity.[91] Coupled with the efforts of Taliesin and ab Ithel to defend Iolo's memory and perpetuate his heritage of learning, Waring's memoir effectively shifted the spotlight of enquiry off the man. It seemed now easy to believe that older manuscripts lay behind Iolo's information, however ancient, and however accurate, that information actually was. Between Taliesin's *Iolo Manuscripts* and ab Ithel's *Barddas*, English readers now had at their disposal most of what Iolo Morganwg had wished the world to believe about the Druids.

Alongside his efforts on behalf of Iolo's tradition, ab Ithel continued to edit genuine medieval texts for the Welsh Manuscripts Society and to publish devotional works. In 1857 he had returned to his gruelling duties in his parish. None of these efforts earned him promotion within his Church or appointment to a university post, although he had hoped for either of these. In part this was probably because his personality – self-promoting, flamboyant and dogmatic – and his affection for odd ideas, and even odder friends, troubled his superiors as it did other leaders of the *eisteddfod* movement. It must also have counted, however, that he was a zealot in a Welsh nationalist cause which the leaders of his Church regarded at best with ambivalence. The mid-nineteenth century saw a sharpening of debate over the place of Welsh culture, and especially of the Welsh language, in the British superstate. It was reflected in the comments of Matthew Arnold, above. Their critics maintained that both language and culture acted as barriers to Welsh people in achieving full participation in the United Kingdom and its empire, and profit from it. Their defenders – who were by definition in a minority among the British – insisted that they gave a valuable sense of collective worth and identity to the Welsh, which made them more effective participants in wider enterprises and also protected them from more systematic exploitation by and subservience to the English majority in the kingdom. The established Church was governed from England, and between the 1720s and the 1870s the bishops chosen for Wales did not include a single one who was both born there and spoke Welsh. Many, like Iolo's temporary ally Burgess, were ambitious Englishmen using their appointment as a stepping-stone to more prestigious English sees. None of *yr hen bersoniaid llengar*, the 'old literary parsons' who had identified themselves with the national cultural revival, won accelerated preferment as a result of their efforts. It is no wonder that in the course of the century the Anglican Church in Wales earned itself the nickname among nationalists of *yr hen fradwres*, 'the old traitress', or that by 1851 three-quarters of the people of Wales worshipped in dissenting chapels, rather than parish churches.

Ab Ithel's efforts at least got him out of the mountains. A redrawing of boundaries moved his parish into the diocese of Bangor. As luck would have it, its Bishop was a newly appointed man, sympathetic to him, who offered him a more comfortable parish. It was Llanenddwyn, tucked safely on to the coast of Merionethshire in a milder climate with gentler gradients, and with a handsome pair of prehistoric dolmens conveniently accessible by the main road. Ab Ithel moved there in 1861, and in that same year a regional *eisteddfod* held in the ruins of Conway Castle honoured him for his services to Wales, with the presentation of an inscribed drinking-horn, made after a medieval pattern. It was all too late, for he was now a dying man, and lasted only a year after his move to the coast. He passed away with a second volume of *Barddas* still incomplete; what there was of it, consisting of more of Iolo's notes on early bardic privileges and organization, was purchased and published by a London firm over ten years later.[92] That completed the posthumous propagation of Iolo Morganwg's work.

On the whole, this work had been rescued quite effectively during the mid-Victorian period, and those who wished to use it could reasonably feel that it had at least the benefit of the doubt. Likewise, the medieval poems credited to Taliesin and Myrddin could still be used as evidence for ancient Druidry, with ways found round the objections lodged by Stephens and Nash. Where the revisionists had truly scored was in reducing the reputation of 'Celtic' Davies. Having emerged in the first decade of the century as one of the foremost experts on Druidry, he was now being relegated to the margins of respectable scholarship; once again, Iolo was winning victories after his death that he had been denied while yet living.

*   *   *

Ab Ithel's most impressive legacy, although one with which he came to have such an ironically cool relationship, was the National Eisteddfod. Its history has now been well researched by Dillwyn Miles, on whom the following account essentially relies.[93] The first such event, organized by a committee of three hundred members founded in 1860, was held at Aberdare in 1861. Its tone was established from the beginning as non-political and also non-sectarian, so that any of the nation's denominations could be represented among promoters, competitors or audience. Seven years later, the committee collapsed in a welter of financial problems, and the *eisteddfod* movement broke into regional meetings again. Most of these included Iolo's *gorsedd* ceremony, and from 1860 those in north Wales had began to use the title of 'Archdruid' and the insignia of a sash, for the person presiding. By the 1870s this was generally a Denbigh clockmaker and Wesleyan Methodist lay preacher called David Griffith, who used the bardic name of Clwydfardd, after the river valley in which Denbigh lies. He had tremendous energy, often walking thirty miles to attend a religious meeting and celebrating his eighty-first year by climbing to the top of Mount Snowdon. In 1876 he officiated at an *eisteddfod* at Wrexham, and claimed the title of Archdruid of the Bards of the Gorsedd of the Isle of Britain, mirroring and rivalling that already held for over three decades by his fellow poet and clockmaker, Myfyr.

Although by now long customary, the *gorsedd* still aroused ambivalent feelings in commentators, and some participants. In 1860 a prominent participant in Welsh cultural events, Thomas Gee, was initiated as a Druid at one held in front of the ruins of Denbigh Castle. An observer noted that he 'was dragged by two Bards, I presume, within the *gorsedd*, as a drunken man is dragged by two members of the police force ... Mr Gee staggered, protested, and would not be a Druid; but Clwydfardd shouted "Get him in; let him be a Druid." Mr Gee was got in, and made a Druid.' Matthew Arnold, visiting from England, saw the ceremony at the 1864 National Eisteddford, in the gracious northern coastal resort of Llandudno: 'The *gorsedd* was held in the open air, at the windy corner of a street, and the morning was not favourable to open-air solemnities ... The presiding genius of the mystic circle, in our hideous nineteenth-century costume, relieved only by a green scarf, the wind drowning his voice and the dust powdering his whiskers, looked thoroughly wretched; so did the aspirants for Bardic honours; and I believe, after about an hour of it, we all of us, as we stood shivering round the sacred stones, began half to wish for the Druid's sacrificial knife to end our sufferings'.

By the end of the 1860s, leaders of Welsh culture were much more concerned with the collapse of the National Eisteddfod than with opinions regarding anything that happened at one. Once again it was the Welsh living in England who came to the rescue, just as they had started the modern *eisteddfod* movement a century before. The main traditional society of the London Welsh, the Cymmrodorion, was refounded in 1873, and in 1880 it hosted a meeting of prominent Welshmen at Freemason's Tavern, near Covent Garden, to discuss a revival of the National Eisteddfod. An association was established to carry out the work, and held its first event in the following year, at Merthyr Tydfil. The controlling association met at the Castle Hotel, and accepted as its president Clwydfardd, with his title of Archdruid. This, of course, swept aside the claims of Myfyr Morganwg, and on the latter's own home territory, but Clwydfardd was in better health, had more experience of different *eisteddfodau*, and was a much more congenial and conventional character, having nothing in fact out of the ordinary about him apart from his wish to be an Archdruid. He celebrated with an improvised *gorsedd* at the end of Merthyr's market-place, using bricks to make the ceremonial circle for lack of any rocks. The ritual sword was borrowed from a passing soldier. Things were not much more impressive in 1883, when the National Eisteddfod was held at Cardiff. Clwydfardd had to conduct the *gorsedd* in a field next to the engine shed of the Taff Vale Railway Company. The proceedings had to be shouted, over the racket of the shunting locomotives on one side and a showground on the other; but those involved bravely persevered.

Clearly, things needed to improve, and they had by the time that the National Eisteddford met outside Wales, in Liverpool, in 1884. The Archdruid and his train decided to imitate the regalia paraded by Freemasons, and so all sported pale blue sashes and aprons embroidered with Iolo's 'mystic sign'. The Bards and Ovates wore robes in their grade colours. They were rewarded for these efforts with a grand setting, and grand guests, at the National Eisteddfod held at Caernarvon in 1886. At a *gorsedd* inside the spectacular medieval castle, Clwydfardd initiated the Lord Mayor of London as an Ovate, with the name of Gywddon, taken from Iolo's legendary history. Two years later, at Wrexham, a captain retired from the Royal Denbigh Rifles presented the members with his sword, to function as a regular one in the rite whereby peace was proclaimed at the opening of a meeting. At that event a permanent committee was also established to run the *gorsedd* at each National Eisteddfod, led by the Archdruid.

During the 1890s the ceremonies became still more imposing and ornate. The stone circles set up for them were starting to be made of real megaliths, as tall as a human, and left in place after the *eisteddfodau* were over, so that they could be reused if the event returned to that town or city. As such they became permanent monuments to modern Welsh nationalism, and to Iolo's dreams, and probably the first megalithic structures ever erected by Druids. In 1890 it was decided, at last, that standard robes in the grade colours, as advocated by ab Ithel over thirty years before, should be adopted by all members. They featured at the *gorsedd* which opened another National Eisteddfod at Caernarvon, held in the square in front of the castle in 1894, the making of them having been funded by a trio of aristocrats led by the Marquess of Bute. In a special ceremony on that occasion, Clwydfardd tied green ribbons round the arms of the Prince and Princess of Wales and their daughters Victoria and Maud, initiating them as honorary Ovates. The future Edward VII was given the simple and appropriate bardic name of 'Iorwerth Dywysog', 'Edward the Prince'.

Clwydfardd died in the following autumn, and was succeeded as Archdruid by Rowland Williams, the minister of an Independent chapel, who had been born in Anglesey. He bore the initiatory name of Hwfa Môn. Williams had a tremendous voice – reputed to make 'the hills echo' – and an absolute personal belief that the ceremonies revealed by Iolo had been handed down from ancient times. Plans pressed ahead all through the winter to increase their pomp still further by decking out their members in a regular ceremonial dress. To design the latter, the organizing committee commissioned Hubert Herkomer, Slade Professor of Fine Art at Oxford and one of Britain's leading painters, himself a member of a German family which had arrived in England via America.[94] He produced a standard series of robes, in the bardic blue, Ovate green and Druidic white. To these was added, in 1899, a specially crafted sword to replace the one presented by the Denbigh soldier. It had a crystal in its hilt, representing mystery, and Iolo's 'mystic sign' engraved into it, to represent the creator deity. The handle was copper gilt, with a steel hand-guard and a copper dragon, the emblem of Wales. The scabbard was of wood, carved with various mottoes in Welsh, including Iolo's own, 'The Truth Against the World', and the last line of his prayer, which now opened every *gorsedd*: 'God and all goodness'. Finally, Herkomer furnished the Archdruid with a crown of office, made of metal wrought with oak leaves and acorns, a breastplate (modelled on that in the famous drawing in Meyrick and Smith's old book), and a sceptre with a crystal head.

The standard robes and the Archdruid's costume were revealed to the world at a ceremony held to proclaim the next year's National Eisteddfod, in a park at Newport in 1896. The more modest tastes of the mid-Victorian era had been affronted by the sight of ab Ithel and his friends in their finery, but even the trappings designed by Herkomer were now not enough for the gaudier and more extrovert style of the imperialist Britain of Victoria's Diamond Jubilee. At the *gorsedd* that opened the actual National Eisteddfod of 1896, the man holding the office of its herald, Thomas

Thomas, presented the company with an official banner. It had a sky-blue background embroidered with gold with oak leaves and mistletoe for Druidry and leeks for Wales. On the upper part was a dragon rampant in the centre of a radiant sun, three rays of which formed the 'mystic sign', with the *gorsedd* mottoes woven between them. In the lower half was a circle of crystals representing the ceremonial stone ring, with the word 'Heddwch', 'Peace', woven within. The herald had also designed a horn, the 'Hirlas', for the ceremonial presentation of drink to the leading members. It was ready in 1899, paid for by a leading Welsh nobleman, Lord Tredegar from Monmouthshire, and commissioned from Sir William Gascombe John of the Royal Academy. He made it from the horn of an African buffalo, with a silver cover showing a Druid playing a harp, surrounded by five dragons curled round semiprecious stones. On its side was a massive silver dragon holding a crystal in its claws. The now customary ceremony that opened each National Eisteddfod was turning from an event into an institution, a true central 'Gorsedd of the Bards of the Isle of Britain'.

The Cardiff National Eisteddfod of 1899 had a *gorsedd* circle designed by Thomas Thomas, in two rings with the outer one a hundred feet across. Its stones still stand, outside the National Museum of Wales. Within that imposing setting, the institution now acquired a new, international role among the developing Celtic nationalist movements. A Gorsedd Llydaw, a national *gorsedd* for Brittany, had been founded the previous year, and a delegation now arrived from it to pay its respects to the older and more magnificent Welsh body that had inspired it. At the same meeting the first Cornish member was initiated. The national Gorsedd which opened the Eisteddfod of 1902, at Bangor on the north coast, was the most impressive to date. It held no fewer than three successive ceremonies, in a stone circle guarded by twelve Bards, each standing by a megalith, and two Keepers stationed by each entrance. Hwfa Môn presided, standing on the central stone, surrounded by colleagues representing the five traditional divisions of Wales. The meeting approved new rules for the admission of members, establishing annual examinations in Welsh music and poetry in which candidates could qualify for initiation. Three thousand onlookers watched a local brass band lead the robed members in procession to the ritual circle. A university professor uttered Iolo's prayer, and a new piece of equipment, an official trumpet, sounded a fanfare. In another recent innovation, a robed lady presented a sheaf of wild flowers and fruits to the Archdruid as symbols of the natural bounty of Wales. Another presented the Hirlas to him, filled with the ritual drink. At Bangor, also, the Gorsedd was given supreme control of the whole Eisteddfod movement. Henceforth its consent was required for the holding of any *eisteddfod*, national or local, and it could choose the subjects for competition in the local events. Its development was complete: it had become what Iolo had designed it to be, the central institution of Welsh culture.

* * *

It remains to return to Pontypridd and see what had happened to the most colourful of all Victorian Welsh Druids, operating largely outside the umbrella of the *eisteddfod* movement. During the central decades of the century, Myfyr Morganwg had been developing his concept of Druidry from a framework within which the bardic arts could be celebrated and cultural nationalism pursued – which is how Iolo had designed it – into something like an alternative religion. In one sense this was a short step to take. It has already been noted that observers branded the industrial valleys of south Wales a breeding ground for new sects, which the more conservative regarded with horror and alarm. By the early Victorian period, the area had become famous for *crach-pregethwyr*, 'quack-preachers', more generously characterized as religious entrepreneurs, operating in a free market and founding congregations among any who would follow them. Even at the present day, Pontypridd preserves twenty-one different houses of worship. Furthermore, William Price had already, at the opening of the 1840s, forsaken Christianity for a form of Druidry practised in public at the rocking stone and with acolytes being trained in it; though the latter do not seem to have lasted long. In addition, this was an age in which religious and historical orthodoxy included belief in an original worldwide religion, revealed by the true god, of which Druidry was an aspect. By claiming to revive this, Myfyr could make a case that he was no heretic or infidel, merely getting back to basics by recovering the good religion of the parents of the human race. None the less, to most people in his place and time what he did looked very heterodox indeed, especially as he propagated and sustained it over a number of decades, in both books and public ceremonies.

There were three main books published between 1860 and 1875.[95] They were in Welsh, and furthermore in a more than usually convoluted style, so that anybody who does not read the language well can only view Myfyr's ideas through the impressions of others. His personal theology was based on Stukeley, the Bible, and a series of books concerning Eastern religions. The most important of the last was the tenth volume of the learned journal *Asiatic Researches*, founded to foster British knowledge of Eastern culture. In this he found the article by Francis Wilford, mentioned before, which suggested that the British Isles had been the sacred islands mentioned in some Hindu traditions. The conclusion was that ancient Druidry and Indian cultures had been very closely related. Myfyr followed this up by acquiring a translation of the great Hindu text, the Rig-Veda, and works on ancient Mesopotamian and Egyptian religion.[96] He decided that Christianity was based on the Indian legend of the ninth incarnation of the god Vishnu, and that 'the Indian system of religion is Druidism in conclusion'.[97] This was a linkage that had been made by a few British orientalists since the 1790s, but Myfyr took it much further. He mapped the Hindu divisions of godhood on to ancient Druidry, telling an admiring ab Ithel that the sun had been its symbol of divinity, and that the rites of the summer solstice represented the deity as creator, those of the winter solstice portrayed him as destroyer, and those of the equinoxes honoured him as preserver. Projecting Christianity on to Druidry, in turn, he declared that at midwinter the sun was believed to descend into the primeval chaos of Annwn, to be reborn after three days.[98] In a series of pairings, he related deities from Welsh and Irish mythology to Hindu deities, biblical patriarchs and characters from the works of Iolo and Edward Davies.[99]

Myfyr infused this syncretic religion into the ceremonies which accompanied the *gorseddau* which he continued to hold in the temple he had constructed around the rocking stone, at the solstices and equinoxes. These flourished through the 1870s and into the 1880s, and Myfyr must have made an imposing figure at their centre, in his white robe with his pendant 'egg', and a flowing beard like a Hebrew prophet, black as jet in his youth and white as snow in old age. Details of them, however, only survive during their last few years. At the rites of midsummer 1878, with a mistletoe sprig in his buttonhole, he offered a prayer to an imagined Welsh goddess called Celi, as the creatrix 'of the sun, moon, stars and universe'. At least one person present confused this being with the Hindu goddess Kali; and, indeed, this may have been precisely Myfyr's intention. During these meetings he regularly initiated newcomers and guests of both sexes into his circle, including some American visitors.[100] Indeed, he obtained a doctorate in civil law from the United States, though admittedly from an organization that sold such qualifications under a specious academic front.[101] The summer solstice ceremony of 1878 attracted a large crowd, both of participants and of observers, and at the following spring equinox another throng turned out, despite bitterly cold weather. Myfyr had been billed to speak about 'the tripod of Apollo', but in the event he was too ill to attend. His son stood in for him as 'Under Archdruid' and made a ringing speech inviting the Welsh to return to the shrine of their ancestors. More American visitors were initiated as Bards and given written diplomas to prove it, signed by three of Myfyr's friends.[102] His son was called to officiate again at that winter solstice, before another large gathering which 'presented a weird appearance in the floating white mist'.[103] Myfyr's enforced absences, and an apparent loss of interest by his son, began to have a corrosive effect on the rites. Only four people turned out for the spring equinox of 1881, and Myfyr himself was ill again. None the less, 'the usual religious rites and prayers' were conducted, facing 'the life point in the east', led by a friend of Myfyr's carrying 'the wand of the Gwyddon' (Iolo's original British priests and magicians) as a sign of office. The circle around the rocking stone was declared to be the temple of Hu the Mighty, Iolo's invented hero whom Edward Davies had identified as the sun god of the Druids.[104] At the summer solstice of that year, the old man bounced back into action, very dapper in a light grey suit and white hat. He initiated as Bards a parish clergyman, with a living at Gorseinon on the edge of the Gower Peninsula, and a New Yorker. He kept his sense of crowd management to the last: 'While this business was in progress a heavy shower of rain fell, and the Archdruid, improving the occasion, referred to it as a blessing upon them.'[105] This was, however, the final occasion at which he is recorded as being present and indeed the last rites which his group is known to have performed at the stone took place at midwinter 1882.[106] In addition to conducting these ceremonies, Myfyr built a small observatory on top of one of the mountains above Pontypridd, so that he could study the stars in the manner of a classical Druid. He also remained a competent poet and harpist, his music being much in demand for local events.[107]

For all the qualifications made earlier, there is no doubt that what Myfyr was doing was very remarkable for his time. His apparent praise of Kali was being uttered well within living memory (including his own) of the British campaign to stamp out the most savage aspects of her cult in India. He was invoking pagan deities by name, in a society which, however religiously fragmented, was still Christian in its outlook and contained large numbers of fervent adherents of forms of that faith. He was doing so, moreover, in full public view for anybody who wished to watch and listen. His activities are a clear example of how much anybody who wished to practise a pagan religion could get away with in late nineteenth-century Britain. He certainly attracted open hostility from chapel preachers; one reason why his books are now so scarce is that his enemies encouraged their flocks to buy them up and burn them. At the Llangollen Eisteddfod he had been rigorously questioned about his beliefs by a group of ministers, several of whom opposed them as contrary to Christianity; the debate ended when he refused to proceed further with it.[108] His local enemies attacked him in newspapers and books,[109] and ordinary people in general were said to find him 'too profound in his philosophical speculations' to be readily understood. He repaid opposition in measure, with a dogmatic certainty leavened with ferocious sarcasm.[110] On the other hand, he clearly drew on much friendship and goodwill in his locality. Some educated people respected him, and one likened him to 'an aged neglected Kimmerian [Welsh] Homer moving about Pontypridd'.[111] Among those who attended his rites were several major poets,[112] and (as noted) his *gorsedd* at the rocking stone may be deemed in some measure the birthplace of the Welsh National Anthem. The hostility to him in some chapels was due in part to his success in attracting members of their congregations.[113] In some ways he lived too long; for the last five years of his life he was too infirm to work, let alone to act as an Archdruid, and was maintained by a subscription among his followers, which raised £140, and a pension awarded by two local aristocrats, one being the Marquess of Bute.[114] He also retained intermittent cordial relations with the National Eisteddfod, although launching attacks on the conduct of it at other times. In 1867 he was invited to mount the central stone at the *gorsedd* ceremony held as part of the National Eisteddfod at Carmarthen, and in 1883 he was graciously introduced on the platform of the one at Cardiff as 'the Archdruid of Wales'.[115] His funeral in 1888 was perfectly orthodox, as he was buried in the public cemetery at Pontypridd, with the local vicar reading the service of the established Church. It attracted a large crowd of local people and Welsh literary figures.[116]

Myfyr must have died more happily in the knowledge that he had a clear successor. This was a local journalist called Owen Morgan, a farmer's son from the south bank of the Rhondda. He took the bardic name, and pen-name, of 'Morien', claimed by some nineteenth-century Welsh historians to be the native name of the late Roman heretic Pelagius. Pelagius was a Briton by birth (though he wrote in Rome), who had preached that humans could obtain salvation through their own efforts. He was often hailed by the same historians as a leading proponent of the kinder and more authentic version of Christianity that they credited to the native British Church, and through this, in many cases, to the Druids. Morien was in his youth an elegant, handsome, round-faced man with a neat, dark beard; in old age he shaved this off to present the image of a bald and bespectacled sage, with corrugated cheeks and sagging jowls. He was a prominent member of the bardic *gorsedd* at the rocking stone by 1877,[117] and almost certainly wrote the admiring reports of the ceremonies there during the following four years, which appeared in the newspaper for which he worked. It was he who wrote to the Marquess of Bute, asking him to come to Myfyr's financial aid in his old age.[118] He immediately claimed the title of 'Archdruid of the Isle of Britain' in succession to him, informing not only the local paper but national journals such as the *Pall Mall Gazette*.[119] There is no doubt that this is what Myfyr himself would have wanted, as he formally bequeathed the younger man his Druidic 'egg', and his writings and papers, 'knowing as I do that he is the best qualified to deal with them properly and to make the Druidic philosophy of our Cambrian ancestors known to the world'.[120]

What is not clear is how much Morien actually did to fulfil this office. There seems to be no record of any actual ceremony that he conducted at the rocking stone, though it is possible that these were now so much taken for granted that they went unreported. At the very next National Eisteddfod, held at Wrexham in north-east Wales in the summer of 1888, Morien was recognized as 'Archdruid of the Gorsedd of the Maen Chwŷf', and invested with the rank of a Druid of the National Gorsedd and appointed to its committee. Clwydfardd was, however, left with the grander title of Archdruid of Britain, and it was ruled that, although all the existing Bards, Ovates and Druids initiated by Myfyr's circle at the rocking stone would be regarded as full members of the National Gorsedd, no new initiates of it would be. Morien clearly accepted all this. When the National Eisteddfod came to Pontypridd, in 1893, its Gorsedd met at the rocking stone, and Morien formally gave Clwydfardd the right of precedence there. Touchingly, the Archdruid from north Wales was by then himself so old that he had difficulty in climbing on to the stone to conduct the proceedings.[121] How much Morien would have wanted to carry on Myfyr's religion may be doubted, for, once his mentor was safely dead, he belittled it and its followers in print. As well as emphasizing the unpleasant rancour with which Myfyr held his beliefs, he spoke of his 'strange services' and condemned his followers as 'men of no religion', devoid of 'true reverence for God and humble faith'.[122] If he felt this about the spiritual aspect of the rites that had been celebrated at the rocking stone, and no new bardic degrees could now legitimately be awarded there, it is easy to see why he may not have bothered to continue them. What is undoubted is that he constantly encouraged the bardic arts at Pontypridd, being prominent in a lively circle of poets and musicians which met at an auctioneer's office in the town.[123]

On the other hand, he wrote extensively on ancient Druidry, making a very personal and idiosyncratic reconstruction of it; in this sense he kept faith fully with Myfyr's dying wishes, and also with his own bardic name, which was, after all, that of a heterodox theologian. He was another example of an author who, like Aubrey and Iolo, was incapable of writing a book in the normal sense of the word. True to his profession as a journalist, he tended instead to turn out what were effectively articles – short, disconnected reflections on different aspects of a subject – and then collect and bind them together under a common title. At no point did he make a clear and systematic exposition of his ideas, so that a reader must piece them together from fragmentary and often overlapping or repetitive statements. This way of working lends an oracular atmosphere to his writings – as if they were the work of a sage too profound and unworldly to need to explain things simply for the unenlightened – which may have been deliberate. He was also capable of blurring the boundary between fact and fiction as ruthlessly as Iolo, and with far less subtlety: when writing a history of Pontypridd and its neighbourhood, he completely invented a major battle in which the natives defeated the Romans, in order to make up for a dearth of early events.[124] His date and place of birth may never be known with certainty, as he concealed both in order to have the power to make himself whichever age he chose.[125]

Morien's own background was in Calvinistic Methodism, and he formally remained a member of that denomination.[126] It is not certain, therefore, how much his writings about Druidic belief represented a theological position that he himself professed; though they certainly read like one, and a very, very unorthodox one at that. There is no full-length study of his life or work; like Myfyr, he has been made the subject of a lively exploratory essay, though one more restricted in scope.[127] His ideas were published in five books and pamphlets, spanning the period from 1890 to 1911.[128] All are in English, ensuring them a much greater readership, and longevity, than Myfyr's, and indeed the most substantial was republished in the late twentieth century by a London society as a contribution to the recovery of 'lost knowledge'.[129] Some of Morien's theories were relatively self-contained, such as that concerning the Gorsedd of Bards of the Isle of Britain, Iolo's invention which was becoming the senate of the National Eisteddfod, and in which Morien himself had been given a place. He declared both that King Arthur's legendary round table had in fact been the *gorsedd*, and that the latter was the origin of the English Order of the Garter, which had appropriated its traditions as part of a campaign to wipe out Welsh independence.[130]

Much of Morien's reasoning was of this kind, although not usually so easy to follow. He delighted in finding apparent linkages between previously separate phenomena, based on external similarities of form, enabling him to match up words in different languages and images in different pieces of art. One of the more straightforward runs as follows, starting with the name Iona, borne by the Scottish island on which had flourished the most famous of all the early Christian monasteries of the Gaelic world:

> Iona or Jonah signifies Dove, and the Great Fish, which swallowed Iona or Dove, is one of the three Oriental Symbols of the instrument of the Queen of Heaven, namely: a Rocking Stone, a Boat, a Dolphin, a name signifying Delphos, a Greek name signifying the womb, the womb in this instance being that of the Queen of Heaven, mother of the Sun's baby boy . . . The Bards calling the boat Llun (Image) and the Latins, deriving their name of the Moon, namely Luna, from the Druidic Llun, and the Solar Boy being described as in the Llun, gave rise to the old legend of the Man in the Moon.[131]

Another example concerns the name 'Iao', known in magical tradition since it was used in Greek texts from late antique Egypt as that of a deity or powerful spirit; the usual interpretation of it is that it signified the Hebrew 'Yahweh', alias Jehovah. Morien's starting-point was Iolo's 'mystic sign', which he proceeded to elucidate by a comparison of points of the Welsh language with modern Hindu custom, modern British administrative symbolism, medieval heraldry and the Bible:

> It is called Tri Sul – a Welsh name – throughout India, and is inscribed with chalk on the forehead, the middle line being red: 'And they shall see his face, and his

NAME shall be on their foreheads.' Rev. 22.4. In the Diadem of Wales it is the plumes of three feathers, and the word's Ich Dien are Eich Dyn, or your Virile Power. As the Government mark of Great Britain is called the Broad Arrow. It is, including the sun's circle, represented by the head and face of the Prince of Wales, IAO, hieroglyphically rendered. Cynun is a title of the sun on each June 25th, and we say Cain is the sun bearing this title. When Cain was born, Eve (Venus) his mother, is represented by a saying, 'I have had a man who is the IAO', meaning the sun with the Winged Wand or Name in his head.

Morien proudly added to this statement, 'In the foregoing pages we have solved the IAO mystery, which has puzzled the profoundest scholars of many countries, from the earliest ages of authentic history.'[132] He was dimly and uneasily aware that some modern scholars doubted the authenticity of some of the material on which he most heavily relied. Any systematic engagement with the arguments of such as Stephens and Nash was beyond him, so instead he tried to discredit them with side-swipes, using arguments from apparent parallels of the sort quoted above. In one of these, he accused Nash of having 'stupidly' translated the name Adda, in medieval Welsh poems, as that of the biblical Adam. In fact, he declared grandly, and with no need of further exposition, it was the Persian 'Ad Hama', meaning 'Lord Sun'.[133]

The influence of Iolo is readily apparent in the passages quoted above, but sharp-eyed readers will already have spotted another, crucially important for Morien's system of interpretation: that of Edward Davies. In particular, he had drawn heavily on an aspect of Davies's vision of Druidry which was in harmony with one of the prevailing scholarly constructs of his age, and which had an especially heavy impact on the field of comparative religion. It may be remembered that, unlike Iolo, Davies had laboured to employ the most advanced and fashionable intellectual models of this time. One of them – Bryant's theory of the omnipresence of traditions of the biblical flood – has been mentioned. Another was that which found the key to all ancient and primitive religion in an interplay of complementary female and male forces, which between them gave rise to all life. Unlike most other theories concerning the nature of ancient religious belief, this was based on material artefacts rather than literature. It was galvanized, in particular, by the rediscovery of the buried Roman cities of Pompeii and Herculaneum, and the revelation of the number of phallic symbols apparent in the art and portable objects of the citizens. These were then related, in turn, to the accounts of Hindu religious culture starting to arrive as a result of the British conquests in India, with its equally heavy emphasis on the sacred nature of male and female sexual symbols. Four scholars drew attention to this pattern during the last two decades of the eighteenth century. Two were French, at least in origin: Pierre François Hugues, the self-styled Baron d'Hancarville, and Charles François Dupuis. Two were British: Sir William Jones, the Welshman who has already been encountered as a modern Druid and pioneer of oriental scholarship, and the Englishman Richard Payne Knight. All painted a picture of ancient worship as concerned primarily with generation and creation, embodied in a great complementary pair of female and male deities. It is also significant that all of them regarded such a religion with sympathy. This varied in degree. Jones merely urged his readers to consider the sexual symbolism of Indian religion with an open mind, as a bold recognition of cosmic truths. D'Hancarville, however, recommended a revival of the ancient reverence for sex as a means of liberating modern society from unnecessary inhibitions. Knight went still further, to use the ancient evidence in an open polemic against both orthodox morality and Christianty, holding the latter itself to be a misunderstanding of an ancient phallic cult. Dupuis took the idea furthest, to produce the classic religious text of the most extreme French revolutionaries, arguing that all revealed religions were 'the daughters of curiosity, ignorance, self-interest and imposture'. This was because a single, all-powerful moral deity was a late invention of a humanity which had earlier reverenced a nature based on the interplay of male and female, active and passive, generative forces. He also denounced Christianity as a misunderstanding, of an allegory of the progress of the (male) sun through the yearly cycle.[134]

These ideas, of an ancient paganism based on a complementary duality of goddess and god centred upon sexual union, have fed through European thought ever since. They have played a major part in constructing modern paganism. Edward Davies, of course, was set on defending Christianity, not discrediting it, but he was too keen on staying abreast of current thinking to avoid embodying this fashionable dialectic in his portrait of ancient Druidry. This accounts for the cosmic polarity he sees in that religion between a fertilizing sun god, Hu, and a receptive and life-creating goddess of the earth and moon, Ceridwen. Morien developed Davies's idea on a grand scale, bringing in ideas from Myfyr and further themes from the old Welsh story *Hanes Taliesin*. He also altered Ceridwen's name yet again, to 'Cariadwen', which translates still more convincingly as 'beloved and beautiful one', thus taking it even further from the form, and sense, in which it features in the medieval poems. To Morien, this departure was a restoration of a more authentic rendering and more sublime truth. His cosmology consisted of a cascade of divine emanation or essence, or, more prosaically (and, sometimes, in his writings, literally), semen.

It began with the heavenly god Cêli, alias Celu, alias Coelus, whose sperm descended into the womb of the earth goddess Cariadwen, alias Cêd, alias Isis, which Morien held had been represented symbolically as a ship, an egg or a cauldron (giving him vast potential for detecting its presence in ancient and medieval art and literature). This coupling produced the sun god, Hu, alias Arthur, alias Pan, alias St George. Hu in turn sent forth his sperm, in the form of divine words, which became personified as Christ, alias Apollo, alias Taliesin, the representative of the sun's life-giving warmth on earth. Cariadwen had, however, independently produced a son of her own, Avagddu, alias Pluto, alias Satan, alias Set, who personified darkness and destruction and so was automatically opposed to Hu. She also gave birth to a beautiful daughter, Crairwy, alias Diana, spirit of the moon and of the virgin earth. To Morien the most important festival of the Druids had been at midwinter, when they acted out the annual destruction of the sun's old body by the force of darkness, and his rebirth in a new one from the womb of Cariadwen. The spring equinox commemorated the fertilization of Crairwy by Taliesin (alias Christ), whose power to give life had been conferred by his consumption of three drops of semen (or seminal words) emanating from his father, the sun. Morien dealt with the question of the fate of the soul by adopting, wholesale, Iolo's progressive rebirth through circles of existence. He kept a place for the biblical Jesus, as a separate character from the divine Christ, being a British Druid sired directly by the sun god, who had fertilized the human woman Mary. In Morien's view of history, Jesus had succeeded in turning the ancient world from worshipping the ageing sun of autumn to venerating the new one of spring, and, on his death, was identified with that young sun himself.[135] He could find evidence for this ancient system almost anywhere: the modern coat of arms of the Corporation of Portsmouth, a star above a crescent, became in his eyes 'the sun rising from the sacred ark of Druidism'.[136]

The most delightful aspect of Morien's writings, and the one which caused his normally laboured prose suddenly to take on colour and energy, was their re-enchantment of the landscape around Pontypridd. The district was in fact unusually devoid of signs of ancient occupation, having only a few burial cairns and meagre earthworks. The good stuff was either lower down in the Vale of Glamorgan or higher up in the Brecon Beacons. Yet Morien made the valleys of the Taff and Rhondda blossom with primordial rites, by projecting his idea of Druidry, and his own experience of the land, on to them. He imagined a winter solstice ceremony in which people costumed as Cariadwen and Taliesin commenced a ritual chase, of the latter by the former, at the rocking stone. They ran down the hillside to the River Taff, symbolizing the Styx, river of the underworld. They were ferried across this as Druids stood on both banks, costumed as hobgoblins and satyrs, carrying flaming torches and chanting dirges to represent the cries of ghosts. The chase continued uphill to a mountain lake, a journey which symbolized that through the circles of rebirth. The priest taking the part of Taliesin then took refuge in a cave, from which he re-emerged 'with a loud melodious shout – cry of the birth . . . in white and his brow dazzling with a golden crown with radiating gold beams'.[137] On the day of the winter solstice, Morien made his Druids gather on one of the main local mountains, Dinas, to watch the sunset, holding that it represented the fall of the sun god, mortally wounded by the spirit of darkness. As it did so, 'the vast multitude crowded to the western edge of the mountain, and there poured forth groans and tears in pious sympathy with the supposed sufferer'. At dawn three days later, 'myriads' of them gathered again on the surrounding mountain tops and 'shouted their joy and sang in vast bowing choirs' to see the sun reborn.[138] It would be lovely had Morien ever recreated any of these ceremonies, if not with myriads, at least with a few companions, but there is no apparent evidence that he did.

An especially amusing and endearing aspect of his talent for imaginative projection was his disbelief that the ancient Britons, any more than the modern Welsh, could have existed without fragmenting into quarrelling sects. The villains of this piece of his pseudo-history were the Phoenicians, whom he portrayed as having sailed in from the east with all sorts of wrong ideas and corrupted the original, pure, British Druidry. They taught that the dead returned to a shadowy underworld instead of being reborn through the circles of life, that Taliesin was the child of earth not of sun, that the rebirth of the sun was in March, not December, that burnt sacrifices were necessary to religion, and other perversions of true doctrine.[139] Two cairns above the Taff valley south of Pontypridd were identified by Morien as sacred platforms erected by rival groups of Druids, to practise their respective rites in sight of, and despite, each other (like chapels in his own time).[140]

While Morien sometimes cited sources, mostly passages of Iolo's writings, much of his account of ancient Druidry was simply asserted as fact, and at times implied to be a tradition handed down by word of mouth in his region. He triumphantly concluded his first book with the claim 'Thus we have revealed the marvellous lore of the ancient Druids, preserved, most of it orally, by the bards of Glamorgan, the direct descendants and representatives of the priests and philosophers of heroic Siluria [south-east Wales] . . . So we have been the instrument to dispel the clouds, and to reveal beyond the gloom of time, the entire Druidic system of religion.'[141] He died at the end of 1921. His obituary in the local paper for which he himself had worked was affectionate but condescending. It declared that his 'volubility and emphasis of expression . . . always impressed and sometimes bewildered', that he had no academic training and was not 'a profound scholar', and that his 'genius for company' was balanced by his 'somewhat tumultuous manner'.[142] Furthermore, unlike Iolo Morganwg, Taliesin Williams and Myfyr Morganwg, he made no apparent effort to find an heir. With him, the Druidic tradition of Pontypridd came to an end.

* * *

Before it did so, however, the succession of remarkable characters who had gathered at the rocking stone had secured their greatest triumph, and made their principal contribution to British history. They had done so in the person of the most marginal, and hitherto least effective, of them: William Price. His triumphant appearance at the Llangollen *eisteddfod* of 1858 had been swiftly followed by the nadir of his entire career, precipitated by a new scheme of his to build a museum and school at Pontypridd. Land for the purpose had been leased to him in 1853 by the ironmaster, and patron of Welsh culture, Sir Benjamin Hall. Eight years later, Price had both run out of money for the work and fallen out with the Halls. In 1861, Augusta, who had treated other champions of Welsh nationalism with such generosity, summarily evicted him from the land, leaving him with full responsibility for the debts owed to the builders. Price was ruined, and had to flee to Paris, for the second time in his life and in still more ignominious circumstances.[143]

He had always responded furiously to failure, and this one, his worst, seems to have caused something like a nervous breakdown. He wrote hysterical letters, full of capitals, underlining and ridiculous claims. In one, to the Lord Mayor of London, he called himself 'I Arglwyt Deheudir Cymry', which in his own 'reconstructed' antique Welsh language seems to read 'Lord of the Southern Welsh'. He called his father 'Lord Rhys of Caerphilly' and termed the mayor his father's steward, demanding back from him his father's staff, cross and New Testament, and warning him that the British government would cease to exist before the end of the year.[144] Another letter was sent to a printer, ordering him to produce a declaration that Price alone understood the nature of ancient literature, which was all based on Welsh: 'All the Greek Books are the Works of the Primitive Bards, in our own Language!!!!!!! . . . Homer was born in the hamlet of Y Van near Caerphili. He built Caerphili Castle . . . the oldest Books of the Chinese confess the fact!!'[145] These are the only things that he wrote which could truly be termed demented, and marked the saddest part of his story.

Yet, once again, he bounced back. In 1866 he returned to Wales to pick up the pieces, an old man with no home, no reputation, and no family life, for his partner Ann Morgan died at this time and his daughter had moved out. He eventually settled at Llantrisant, a small town to the south-west of Pontypridd and of a very different kind. It was not in a valley but on the saddle between the two peaks of the last of the Black Mountains, rising isolated from the edge of the Vale of Glamorgan. It was not a modern industrial community but a medieval one, with fragments of a Norman castle and small twisting streets. Here he remade his life. He built up a new medical practice, and all those who have written on his life have acknowledged or conceded that he was an excellent doctor. He performed difficult and advanced surgery, gave great satisfaction to customers, and became known for his generosity to those who were both poor and sick. Tales abounded of the courage and wit with which he dealt with the greedy and pretentious. He remained a political and social radical, supporting the demands and the strikes of local industrial workers, campaigning for the rights of unmarried mothers, and advocating vegetarianism. And he found a new companion of the heart, in the form of a farmer's daughter called Gwenllian Llewelyn, aged twenty-one, who moved in with him soon after he passed his eight-ieth year, and remained with him for the rest of his life.[146]

He also continued to practise Druidry. His own sources for it seem to have been even fewer than those employed by Myfyr: in his will, the books that he owned consisted of Stukeley's volume on Stonehenge, the *Myvyrian Archaiology*, a French antiquarian work of the early eighteenth century, and Dupuis's revolutionary polemic on the origins of religion.[147] These were, none the less, all powerful and influ-ential texts, and to them he added scraps of information from elsewhere and his own, inimitable, personal vision. In 1871 he published an account of the doctrines of the ancient Druids, which is even more difficult to read than those by Myfyr or Morien. It was written in his own 'authentic' ancient Welsh, and its mode of expres-sion, even in expert translation, is especially convoluted. Its title means *The Will of My Father*: once again, Price's troubled childhood was striking home. The father in this case seems to be a deity, the fount of the whole cosmos, who was born from an egg laid by a serpent. The notion of the universe as hatched from a cosmic egg appears in the ancient Greek Orphic hymns, which Price combined with the pagan Norse tradi-tion of a giant serpent that twines about the earth. This father deity, the text continued, directs the motions of the sun, which is the living god of the apparent world. Some sense of Price's style can be gained from a passage on the nature of ultimate divinity:

> For he, from his own brain, literally sends the sun through the moon onto the seas and onto the earth from his right hand in a cold egg as the Eternal Prince, over the sons of H H Th ... the Welsh of the Royal state, the Welsh of Monmouth and Glamorgan in the year 1871 according to belief. His will was revealed from his cold egg.

Even more than Morien's religious writings, those of Price read more like a prophet speaking in trance than a theologian making an argument; which was probably the intended effect. Much more lucid were the political and nationalist sections of this testament, in which Price called on the Welsh to reject the European, and Christian, culture that repressed them, and return to their native roots.[148]

The book sank without trace – nobody even seems to have thought it worth burning – and ten years passed before Price was again noticed as doing anything Druidic. It seems to have been his romance with Gwenllian which precipitated him into more such activity. They were married in a Druid ceremony at the Pontypridd rocking stone on 4 March 1881.[149] Two weeks later came the equinox, and Price led a procession through the streets of the town's suburb of Treforest. He wore a white robe over his usual red-lined trousers, with his equally habitual fox-fur cap on his head, and a large flag of crimson silk streaming from a rod on his shoulder. The person who recorded this scene, writing in the local paper, went on to describe how 'the whole town were at their doors, and many followed the strange visitor, among them three respectable women representing the Three Graces. Having reached the Rocking Stone, the doctor mounted it exactly at noon; and, addressing the sun, he proceeded to speak in the strange Welsh (it was supposed) of the pre-Adamite epoch. The audience was in convulsions of laughter; but not a smile was on the performer's face.'[150] The details of Price's garb and actions all ring true, but there was more than a drop of poison mixed into the account; it was almost certainly by Morien, smarting from the poor turnout for the rite of his own group of Druids (that of Myfyr) the previous day, which he had also just explained away in the paper. He plainly regarded Price as an interloper and competitor. It may be noted that the article fudges the question of how many in the crowd that Price drew were actually his collaborators, and how many curious spectators. The 'Three Graces' certainly sound as if they were part of the act. Nor can the reference to the derision displayed by the spectators be entirely trusted. Price was back at the rocking stone for the winter solstice of 1882, and once more it was almost certainly Morien who sniped at him in the newspaper. He sneered at Price as 'the "hissing egg" celebrity' (presumably a reference to his doctrine of the cosmic egg). The article went on: 'As usual the modern Thoth appeared in the circle in full canonicals, and carrying a red banner, on which was the mystic symbol of the "bru" of the goddess Anian. He spluttered . . . a song he called "The Will of His Father".' The author went on to contrast this rite with that, on the following Sunday, of the 'regular' Druids of Myfyr's group, whom he credited, by contrast, with orthodoxy and sobriety.[151] Again, this was almost certainly Morien, engaged in a range war.

The doctor's life continued in triumphant fashion into 1883, when Gwenllian presented him with a son, whom he named 'Iesu Grist', 'Jesus Christ', partly following his habitual taste for provocation, and partly as a sign of the high hopes he had for the boy. These ended swiftly, as the child died of convulsions at the age of five months, in early January 1884. This personal tragedy accidentally ensured Price his own immortality, at least in historical memory.[152] One of his beliefs was that the burial of corpses was 'barbarous', and burning them the only wholesome and decent method of disposal. This reflected both the obsessive hygiene which was part of his success as a doctor and his commitment to an imagined ancient Druidry. Many people had, in fact, reached a similar conclusion regarding the benefits of cremation by this date, and a pressure group had been formed in 1874 to make it legal in the United Kingdom. Hitherto, however, all its efforts had failed. Price chose to ignore this fact and to burn his son's body himself. Utterly in character, he began to do so early on the evening of Sunday 13 January, at precisely the time when people would be crowding out of the chapels. He did so upon the summit of one of the two peaks which rise on either side of Llantrisant, so that in the darkness of the winter night the flames would show for miles. He may simply have been deranged by grief, as he had been in 1861, and neither noticing nor caring about the possible consequences of his actions. On the other hand, he may have been assuaging his emotional pain, in part, by challenging local society to a fight.

If so, he certainly got one. A crowd surged up the hill, and found Price in his white ceremonial robe, arms outstretched, in front of the fire. He was chanting one of the medieval poems attributed to Taliesin, in the version of it published in the *Myvyrian Archaiology*. What caught the attention of the crowd, however, was the sight of a dead child in a container among the flames. Price's life and liberty were saved by what – unless he had calculated the odds with almost superhuman cunning – were two tremendous pieces of luck. First, the police arrived before he could be beaten up or lynched, and took him into custody. Second, the body of poor little Iesu was rescued before it was burnt too far for an autopsy to be successfully conducted, so that a coroner could pronounce him dead from natural causes. None the less, Price was rapidly tried for the act of attempting to cremate a corpse. The combination of bereavement and the pressure of his predicament should have reduced a genuine madman to raving incoherence. Instead, he met the challenge with cool intelligence. Just as he was admirable in a medical emergency, so he had always been an excellent performer in a courtroom; and this was his finest hour. He did not talk about Druidry, but defended his action on legal and hygienic grounds. What really saved him was another great piece of luck: that he had a sympathetic judge, who was prepared entirely to endorse his main argument, that, if cremation was not explicitly permitted in British law, then there was no law either that explicitly forbade it. He was acquitted, and in being so established the *de facto* legality of what he had done. Within three months the first public crematorium in the kingdom was under construction (in Essex), and the mode became first an important, and then the normal, means for the disposal of the British dead. On returning from the courtroom in Cardiff to Llantrisant, Price was welcomed home by a cheering crowd. He triumphantly completed the cremation of his son on 14 March, watched by large numbers of people on the slopes below the peak.

Price now had genuine, and well-deserved, fame: even Morien, who had been preparing to crow over his downfall, admitted himself impressed.[153] Like a monarch, he struck a medal to commemorate his victory, selling three hundred copies of it at threepence each. It was oval in shape and bore upon it a goat and a snake. Price explained that the shape represented the cosmic egg, and the snake the world serpent who had laid it, while the goat was an emblem of Wales but also stood for Price himself, who had been made a scapegoat for the cause of cremation.[154] Invitations now came in to address public meetings on his beliefs, which, perhaps unfortunately, he accepted. One was at Blaenau, up in the valleys, in March. He was billed to speak on the ancient Britons, but chose instead to discuss cremation and his recent trial. What was more startling was that he then removed his outer clothing to reveal an outfit resembling a set of long combinations, made of red cloth embroidered with green letters from his bardic alphabet. In one hand he raised a pole, with horns representing the crescent moon, and a red streamer hanging from it. He then sang a Welsh song about the meaning of his costume, and the performance ended.[155] He repeated it at an exhibition hall in Cardiff in the following month. Here he spoke about his view of the cosmos, but the journalist who recorded the occasion clearly did not understand him: 'the lecturer connected his early ancestry with the contents of the Goose's Egg, and declared, amid wondering amusement on the part of the hearers, that 3,700 years ago his birth was registered'. There are echoes here of the Orphic egg, and of a belief in a predestined fate, but for lack of a more sympathetic or perceptive witness, or a better delivery on Price's part, it is impossible to elucidate them. What was vividly and plainly remembered, once more, was his act of undressing on stage.[156] After that, the invitations seem to have dried up.

Price's own life, however, continued triumphantly. Soon after his acquittal in court, Gwenllian became pregnant by him again, and later in the year she gave birth to another boy, also called Iesu Grist. This time the child survived, and was followed two years later by an equally healthy daughter, named Penelopen.[157] In the summer of 1888, a local journalist came out to his home to interview him, and the series of articles that resulted represent the best portrait that survives of Price, at any point of his life.[158] He received his visitor dressed in the latest version of his formal costume, of white tunic, green trousers with scarlet stripes, scarlet waistcoat with brass buttons, and (of course) the huge fox-fur cap. His streaming hair and beard were now snow white, but his back was still straight, and he had a ferocious, piercing look which dissolved into a kindly smile. His home was sparsely furnished, with three or four growling dogs stretched out before the fire. Gwenllian made a tall and imposing presence. Price announced that he was the true successor to Myfyr Morganwg, who had died a few months before, as Archdruid of Britain. He called Myfyr 'a very clever old man, and well read', but added cryptically that 'he did not understand'. Of Morien, his rival in the Archdruidical succession and Myfyr's designated heir, he was naturally more contemptuous: he knew 'nothing of Druidism', as he could not decipher the ancient bardic hieroglyphs as Price knew how to do. Price did not, in any case, need any succession from Myfyr to confirm his rank as Druid, because he claimed that through his father, one of a long line of Druids. To underline this, he explained that his father had been baptized in a special house in Monmouthshire, 'the only place where the Druids baptized their sons', by a clergyman who happened to own a particular local estate. Those who possessed that land, proclaimed Price, had always been Druids with a special power to baptize. He himself claimed to have been the only Druid in his generation of the family, though his sister had been one 'at heart'. Once again, he was making up for the tragedy, hardship and humiliation consequent upon his real paternity.

Price also announced that in ancient times it had been the Druids who chose the king of their country, giving him the title *Mab Duw*, 'son of God'. He proudly showed off his little son Iesu, who sported a miniature version of his own fox-fur cap, predicting that the boy would reign over the earth. He recalled the tablet he had seen at the Louvre in his first exile in France, which had been the foundation of his own interpretation of Druidry. Now he said that it had predicted the second coming of Christ, with the implication that his son would be the fulfilment of this. He still went occasionally to the rocking stone at Pontypridd to hold rites consisting usually of chanting 'a song of the Primitive Bard to the moon', which he now saw as the chief object of veneration by the ancient Druids. He was swift to emphasize, however, that this was not an act of worship, for he recognized no power in the cosmos greater than humanity itself. He also believed that the only true immortality lay in one's children, and that he would live on through the person of his son; again, his tremendous sense of family inheritance and pride, bequeathed to him by his troubled childhood, came through.

In 1892 he erected a pole over sixty feet high, bearing his now standard Druidic symbol of a crescent moon, on the mountain top where he had burned the body of his first son. It was also intended to mark the spot on which he wished to be cremated himself, when his time came, and did not need to stand long. He died in the following January, just short of his ninety-third birthday, and his last act was to sip a glass of champagne. His cremation was watched by about 20,000 people, and attended by his son, in a full little replica of his own costume, and Gwenllian, Gwenhiolan and Penelopen, who wore different versions of traditional Welsh dress.[159] This spectacular event confirmed his reputation as a mixture of local oddity and local hero. Ballads to celebrate him circulated for a few years after his death,[160] an exhibition on his life was held at Cardiff in 1896, and a pamphlet biography on him was published to accompany it, based mostly on the newspaper articles of 1888.[161] These salutations exhausted Morien's reserves of generosity, and he wrote two petulant newspaper articles, protesting that Price had been no true Archdruid and that this honour belonged to Morien himself, in an apostolic succession extending back six hundred years.[162]

*   *   *

Despite all his great hopes, Price was no more successful than Morien in leaving an heir to his Druidry. Gwenllian's attachment to his ideas did not long survive him, and she had both her children baptized into a Christian denomination; Iesu Grist, understandably, became Nicholas. She subsequently made a regular marriage to a road inspector employed by the county council. None of Price's offspring achieved anything of real distinction, though Penelopen came closest by being decorated for her services to nursing; certainly none showed any wish to be Druids.[163] By 1940 the author of the first approximation to a proper biography of him, Islwyn Nicholas, could say he was 'now forgotten in Wales'.[164] At the present day that is certainly true of Taliesin Williams, Myfyr Morganwg and Morien, outside a small circle of scholars. None has an entry in the current *Dictionary of National Biography*. Myfyr gets a mention in the town museum of Pontypridd, though more with reference to his activities as a poet than as an Archdruid. There is not at this moment any equivalent display there for Morien, nor a commemoration of Taliesin at Merthyr. John

Williams ab Ithel is remembered only in histories of the Welsh National Eisteddfod, and even in these he has not entirely escaped a reputation for over-enthusiasm and self-promotion. If any of them deserve to be remembered, it is as examples of what was possible for the nineteenth-century Welsh imagination.

William Price's fate has been very different, as Islwyn Nicholas's pamphlet began a celebration of him which has swelled steadily ever since. The society of the late twentieth century, which placed an increasing value on determined and courageous individualism, found proportionately more and more to admire in his flamboyant nonconformity. Short works upon him, almost all in a popular format, have continued to multiply. He has his place in the *Dictionary of National Biography*, and has become the main historical hero of Llantrisant. Visitors to the town in the year 2006 could find a plaque to commemorate him, supplied in 1947 by the Cremation Society; a statue of him in the town centre, unveiled in 1982; a memorial garden named after him, opened in 1992; and an exhibition dedicated to him, complete with waxwork, in the heritage centre. He has become one of the great Welshmen of all time, with a more modest, but secure, place in the story of Britain.

Meanwhile the rocking stone still sits quietly in a public park above Pontypridd, having featured in the tale of Victorian Welsh Druidry almost as a personality in its own right. By 1950 most of the stone avenues around it had been destroyed by unknown persons, but a local outcry prevented further damage and resulted in the restoration of Myfyr's monument.[165] At the present day it has become once again the focus for occasional ceremonies by modern Druids and other kinds of pagan. In Julian Cope's beautifully illustrated and passionately written tribute to the landscape and ancient monuments of Britain, published in 1998, it takes its place as a ritual centre (with the implication that it has been one from ancient times).[166] Yet, in a sense, it has fallen asleep. The stone itself seems to have lost the ability to rock, and so the very feature which drew so many remarkable people to it, for so long, has apparently disappeared.

⮎⮌

9

THE DOWNFALL OF
THE DRUIDS

B y 1860, Druids had dominated perceptions of the ancient British past for over a
hundred years, and a wide range of imaginative uses had been found for them in
that capacity. Whether they were turned into sages or savages, heroes or villains, they
were central to the earliest parts of the island's story. This situation was now to change
very suddenly, but before examining why this was so it may be helpful to prepare the
way by identifying authors who, even in the heyday of interest in the ancient Druids,
sought to marginalize or discount them.

Such authors approached this common end from various directions. A few could,
depending on one's viewpoint, be characterized either as colourful proponents of
markedly original ideas or as cranks. The most remarkable was a Wiltshire man
called Henry Browne, who decided that both Stonehenge and Avebury had been built
before Noah's Flood. He developed Stukeley's idea, that the two stone avenues
winding to and from the Avebury circles represented a snake, to suggest that the
monument had been built by Adam himself, as an awful reminder of the harm done
by the serpent in Eden. Browne pointed out that, according to the Book of Genesis,
Adam had lived for 930 years and so would have had ample time in which to accu-
mulate enough descendants to carry out the work. By contrast with the religion of the
biblical patriarchs, which represented to him the highest thoughts of which humanity
was capable, he accused the Druids of 'the most slavish superstition'.[1] His fundamentalist attitude to Scripture aside, Browne did good work: he drew accurate plans of
Stonehenge, and he and his son acted as unofficial caretakers there for decades,
protecting the stones from damage by sightseers.[2] Furthermore, his fundamentalism
was itself popular with many at this time; his tract, published in 1823, went through
eight editions within the next half century.[3]

A different constituency for the depreciation of Druids lay in the spiritual heirs to
the very poets who had eulogized them a generation or two before: the main exemplars of the movement known as Romanticism. This had now reached its climax, with
the production of some of the best-known verse, by some of the most famous poets,
in the whole canon of English literature; but, with one exception, these poets were not
keen on Druidry. The exception was, of course, Wordsworth, whose boyhood in the

Druid-haunted landscape of the Cumbrian mountains had rooted them in the relationship with nature and history that was central to much of his work. Even he,
however, was at best ambivalent about them. Of the other great names in the group,
Coleridge and Shelley ignored them, and Byron dismissed them:

The Druids' groves are gone – so much the better:
Stonehenge is not – but what the devil is it?[4]

Keats affected to find their presumed monuments depressing. In 'Hyperion' he
described the ancient gods as being:

like a dismal cirque
Of Druid stones, upon a forlorn moor,
When the chill rain begins at shut of eve,
In dull November, and their chancel vault,
The heaven itself, is blinded throughout night.

It seems as if the very prominence of the Druids in contemporary culture caused these
self-consciously avant-garde writers to disdain them as bores.

More attention was paid to them by the most famous romantic visual artists of the
Victorian period, the Pre-Raphaelites, but there was still very little of it, and what was
given turned out to be bitterly hostile. Holman Hunt displayed his fierce Christianity,
and ignorance of history, in a painting with one of the longest titles and most ludicrous subjects in Victorian art: *A Converted British Family Sheltering a Christian Priest
from the Persecution of the Druids*. Only one other artist in the group, Edward Burne-
Jones, dealt with them, and in a short story rather than a picture. Published in his
youth, it provided a riposte to writers who doubted that the Druids engaged in human
sacrifice, by having such a sceptic, on holiday, encounter a Druid's ghost. The latter
confesses that such bloody work was one aspect of the tyranny that his kind had
wielded, after succumbing to the temptations of power.[5]

Another set of opponents to the contemporary excitement over Druids consisted of
a handful of English authors who still doubted the connection between them and
megalithic monuments. In the circumstances of the time, these had to be self-
consciously heterodox, and usually took pride in setting themselves against the
prevailing trend of opinion. As a group, they were marginal to the contemporary
world of historians and antiquaries, but had some individual distinction; they
included the prominent Shakespearean scholar, J. O. Halliwell.[6] The common core of
their argument lay in the complete lack of any association between Druids and megaliths in the ancient literature, and they tended, in addition, to be provoked by the
wilder historical speculations or fantasies that the prevailing preoccupation with
Druids had produced. Halliwell put the case most resoundingly: 'There is certainly no
evidence, and, as far as I can see, no probability, that a single Druidical monument or
relic of any description is now to be found in Great Britain. Even with regard to
Stonehenge itself, the theory of it being a temple of the Druids is unsupported by the

least evidence.'[7] It is typical of this group, however, that, although he scored an archaeological bull's-eye with that statement, his own interpretation of the monuments was completely mistaken; he declared that stone circles had merely been boulders that had supported the sides of vanished burial mounds. It is significant that all of these authors published in the 1850s and early 1860s, indicating that by that date some ambitious English writers were growing weary of the general preoccupation with the Druids as key figures in perceptions of ancient Britain.

A different line of attack was mounted by another self-consciously heterodox tradition of writing, which revived the early modern argument that the megalithic monuments of Britain dated from the post-Roman period. The key author here was an Oxford don, the Dean of Merton College, called Algernon Herbert; ironically, he was descended from the Earls of Pembroke, one of whom had been a notable patron of William Stukeley. At Oxford, he carried into new realms the antipathy towards Druids manifested by that university since the late eighteenth century, which contrasted markedly both with their general popularity at that time and with its own earlier advocacy of them as the pupils of Abraham. In a series of books published between 1836 and 1849, Herbert put them into a completely novel context.[8] His starting-point was the medieval Welsh literature, which he thought, as so many had by now suggested, contained traces of ancient Druidic belief. His dislike of Druids, however, led him to reverse the usual sympathies of writers who held this position; instead of concluding that this gave the bardic verse concerned even more importance, he held that the Druidic association had contaminated it with bad doctrine. To him, it represented 'an open paganism without the dissembling cloak of Christianity', and 'devilry and hocus-pocus'.[9]

He developed this opinion into a theory that the Druidry of prehistoric times had managed to survive the Roman period under cover, and had flourished anew once the restraining and civilizing rule of Rome was removed. Indeed, in his view the revived Druid religion was even worse than before, incorporating as it did elements from Mediterranean mystery religions brought in by the Romans, such as that of Mithras, and sub-Christian heresies like Gnosticism. One of the gods of this new paganism, transfigured from Mithras himself, he declared to be Arthur, later turned into the human hero; likewise, Merlin was in fact the Gnostic Antichrist in disguised form. Thus heated, Herbert made his own readings of enigmatic lines in the bardic poetry to prove that the post-Roman Druidic 'doctrine was imparted to the aspirant amid horrifying and intimidating orgies, and under the sanction of a self-imprecated curse binding him to silence'.[10] In advancing these arguments, he had four main targets. One was religious toleration: 'God is intolerant and a jealous God, because all worship but that of him is at variance with his unapproachable supremacy.'[11] The second was Iolo Morganwg, whose political liberalism and religious radicalism were alike anathema to Herbert and whom the latter branded a forger and an ignoramus. Like others among Iolo's detractors, while doing this he unwittingly employed some of Iolo's forgeries to build his own case. The third consisted of children's history books which gave a benevolent view of Druidry, and which he considered dangerous nonsense. The fourth of his targets was the Irish, as he denounced their patron saint Patrick as no Christian but a Mithraic priest. As part of his polemic, he declared megalithic monuments to have been crude and barbaric attempts to match the elegant buildings of the cultured Romans, erected in the dark age of the post-Roman Druid revival. His invective here was trained on Stukeley, whom he termed a purveyor of 'lies and forgeries'.[12] Herbert's theories generally earned unfavourable reviews, gaining some slight support only among writers who shared his religious prejudices.[13] They also inspired or encouraged a few lesser figures to devote books or articles to arguing that British megaliths were from the Roman or 'Arthurian' periods. By the 1860s this was an established, if minor, theme in British historical writing.[14]

The most powerful and significant strand in early nineteenth-century Druido-scepticism, however, was represented by Scots. This is the more remarkable in that Scotland had, after all, been the British nation in which both enthusiasm for Druids and association of them with megaliths had appeared earliest. As these twin phenomena got built into the cultural life of the new British superstate Scots had continued to express them, now in unity with the other British peoples. This tradition persisted into the early part of the new century. In particular, the prominent perform-ance of Highland soldiers in the Napoleonic Wars provoked celebrations of a native military tradition going back to the opening of history, in which patriotic images of Druids played a full role. The author of a history of Scotland published in 1807 lauded their ability to teach people moral virtue and a love of native country and of liberty. Like many a Scot before him, he argued that the inhabitants of the Highlands had been the only people in Britain to resist Roman conquest successfully. This he now built upon, to suggest that this resistance had a religious component, as the Druids strove to defend their purer religion against contamination by Mediterranean paganism.[15] Eight years later a poet made a direct link between the warriors who fought Rome and those who opposed Napoleon:

> The land of hills and heroes, long,
> When Roman deeds but live in song,
> Will boast its ancient liberty.
> And other tyrants, worse than haughty Rome,
> When they, like her, in Freedom's name will come,
> Shall feel as thou has made her feel,
> The Highland arm, and Highland steel,
> In undiminished energy.[16]

In 1831, a Fellow of the Society of Antiquaries of Scotland wrote a history of the Highlands, which likewise highlighted the propensity of their ancient Druids to teach justice and the immortality of the soul, and to incite young men to be brave and virtuous.[17]

By then, however, times were changing. The Scots were fully embarked on the process of acquiring and establishing new symbols of national identity which marked them off from the other British peoples, and which was to inspire the Welsh to a similar effort. The new Welsh identity, as has been emphasized, was marked by a very strong incorporation of the figure of the Druid. It was also suggested that the growing

English hostility to Druids as ancestral figures may well have been, in part, a reaction to Welsh enthusiasm for them. It seems likewise to have been no coincidence that, just as the Welsh were identifying so strongly with Druids, the Scots began to jettison them altogether. This reaction was strongly represented by the figure who summed up and propagated the new Scottish nationalism more than any other: Sir Walter Scott. In 1819 he published one of his great chain of historical novels, *The Pirate*, which was set in the Northern Isles of Scotland. Its dramatic climax occurred amid the huge prehistoric stone circles of Orkney, and here there should have been ample opportunity for Scott to capitalize on the now standard associations between these monuments and Druidry, and between the latter and Scottish patriotism. Instead, he remarked tepidly that some attributed them to the Druids and others to the Goths or Vikings, but that nobody could be sure (and, he implied, it did not matter).

When he came to contribute pieces on Scottish history to the *Edinburgh Encyclopaedia*, a dozen years later, he had sharpened this lack of warmth towards Druids into an all-out attack on the importance fashionably attributed to them. He began by declaring that 'respecting them, and their religion, antiquarians have indulged in many opinions, and advanced many circumstances as facts, which are totally unsupported by any authority or evidence'. In his opinion, 'so far from deserving the high and enthusiastic praises bestowed on them for their learning, they were ignorant and extremely barbarous in their manners, and gloomy and cruel in their superstitions'. He enlarged on this by pointing out that there was no evidence that they had any connection with the biblical patriarchs, or Greek philosophers, and plenty, in the ancient sources, that they had been savage pagan polytheists. Nor, he added, was there any proof that they had built or used megalithic monuments or made any worthwhile contribution to Scottish history.[18]

Another feature of the early nineteenth century which sounded warning of a new Scottish determination to marginalize or banish Druids was a revival of the hypothesis that the megalithic monuments of northern Scotland – at the least – had been built by the Vikings. This drew strength from the strong political, cultural and commercial connections which Scotland had always maintained with Scandinavia, and which were, because of its geographical position, greater than those of other parts of the British Isles. Such contacts focused attention on a puzzling loose end that had been left dangling by the Georgian integration of Druids and megaliths. It was clear that Denmark and Sweden contained many megalithic monuments that were, in form, and therefore in date, apparently very similar to those elsewhere in Western Europe. No ancient author, however, had claimed that Druids ever existed in that region. The similarity of the Scandinavian and British monuments had been the major prop of the theory argued by some writers in the sixteenth and seventeenth centuries that English stone circles had been built by Danish invaders. By the mid-eighteenth century this had been rejected by almost all scholars, but it was now being revived by a series of Scottish authors anxious to diminish the association of their national past with Druidry.[19]

None of these writers on Scotland, including Scott himself, were capable of basing their arguments upon detailed references to archaeological evidence, but they were followed, in the middle of the century, by two compatriots who were. One was

Sir Daniel Wilson, the person who actually coined the term 'prehistoric',[20] and the other John Stuart. In the course of the 1850s and 1860s they produced between them a string of books which made a common case: that Druids should be left out of the record of the Scottish past. Stuart's advocacy of this was based on the striking stone circles of Aberdeenshire, with a massive recumbent boulder in the southern arc of each, which may well have first inspired the Scots to identify such monuments as ancient temples. Excavation was now revealing that some of these had human remains interred inside the ring of stones, which enabled Stuart to argue (wrongly, as it turned out) that they had in fact been burial sites and not religious monuments at all. Both he and Wilson also asserted (this time correctly) that the stone chambers commonly known in recent times as dolmens were likewise used for burial, and therefore were not Druid altars as modern tradition had commonly held. Wilson emphasized how little was known of the Druids, and declared that 'after the devotion of so many learned and ponderous volumes to the attempted elucidation of Druidism, the subject has lost little of its original obscurity'. He went on to highlight the complete lack of any certain connection between them and megaliths. Instead he proposed that stone circles and chambered tombs be assigned to a period of the remote past in which the peoples later to develop into the Celts and Scandinavians all built them; though he used an analogy from later Viking culture to suggest their probable use for political assemblies like the Norse 'things'. Wilson became the first scholar to suggest (in 1851) that Druids should be redefined as a shadowy priesthood who belonged to the very last stages of prehistory, shortly before the Romans turned up. Stuart agreed that they had nothing to do with prehistoric stone monuments, and used the medieval Irish sources to declare that they had simply been pretended magicians, serving barbarous tribes.[21]

The old and the new views of Scottish prehistory came face to face in 1863, following the publication of a thoroughly old-fashioned book by a clergyman, John Pratt. He summed up most of what had been said of Druids by scholars in the later eighteenth century and added a few insights from 'Celtic' Davies, under the impression that by doing so he was bringing the accepted record thoroughly up to date.[22] His book was promptly flattened by a long essay in the *Edinburgh Review*, which began by showing how few and how unreliable the ancient sources for Druidry were. It then repeated the now recurrent charge that there was nothing to associate Druids and megalithic monuments, and drew on the Welsh revisionist scholarship, associated with Stephens and Nash, to separate them in turn from the medieval bardic literature. The piece drew the crushing conclusion that 'the place they really fill in history is indefinite and obscure; and that the attempt to give a more precise form to these traditions by ingenious conjectures has been for the most part unsuccessful'.[23]

The views of people like Pratt outlived the decade, even among relatively well-educated Scots with a keen interest in antiquities. In 1872 a short-lived society was founded at Oban, the principal mainland port that served the southern Hebrides, to foster knowledge of the history and prehistory of the region. At its first meeting, two papers were read on the Druids, which took as established fact their role as builders of stone circles and leaders of the rites for which the circles had been designed. This is hardly surprising, for the author's notions of ancient Scotland were based firmly on eighteenth-century texts, and above all on the Ossianic poems of Macpherson.[24] None the less, there is no reason to doubt the opinion of Peter Rowley-Conwy, the principal historian of the Victorian adoption of the concept of prehistory, that by the end of the 1850s most leading Scottish antiquarians had accepted the arguments of Wilson's book.[25] The latter conformed to what those intellectuals now wanted to hear.

* * *

It has been suggested that the readiness with which the Scots had begun to dismiss the Druids had much to do with the importance now attached to them by the Welsh and English. In the cases of Wilson and Stuart, however, a different aspect of Scotland's traditional connection with Scandinavia was also of importance to their position. Research into the Scandinavian past had always been driven by traumas in the present. In the sixteenth century, Sweden had declared its independence from Denmark, and thereafter the two states had been locked in a fierce rivalry. This was very good for scholarship, for it drove inhabitants of both to create nationalist histories, and, as Denmark gradually got the worst of the conflict, such efforts became proportionately greater there. In particular, its scholars made a national survey of ancient monuments, which acted as a direct inspiration to John Aubrey to attempt something similar for Britain. Then, as the struggle subsided and the region in general turned into a backwater in European politics, so in turn its scholars dropped into the background of intellectual culture. What altered this situation was the humiliation the Danes received following the Napoleonic Wars, when they ended up on the losing side and handed over (to Sweden) another of their great traditional possessions, Norway. Being thus shamed and weakened, and with their southern borders menaced by the growing power of Prussia, the Danes embarked on a frenetic new attempt to fan the flames of patriotism, by reinforcing a sense of their own distinctive past. Unlike many other European peoples, they had no Greek or Roman texts to provide even the slightest glimpse into their own origins, and the Book of Genesis seemed to have even less to say to them than to most northerners. What they had, instead, was the material record left by the most remote antiquity of their country. The collective symbol of this, and of the historic nationhood that they were now vaunting, consisted of the national museum opened in Copenhagen in 1819.

It was organized according to a principle which had been suggested at times by various European scholars ever since the early eighteenth century: that the archaeological record showed a progressive development of ancient technology from stone tools and weapons to successors made first of bronze and then of iron. During the previous fifty years it had been Danes, in particular, who had discussed this idea, and it was now built into the new museum by its first curator, Christian Jurgensen Thomsen. Over the succeeding two decades he gradually applied it to monuments as well as to objects, making it the organizing principle of Danish prehistory as a whole. In this work he was increasingly aided by his assistant, and eventual successor, Jens Jacob Asmussen Worsaae, who has been called the first professional archaeologist. Worsaae also commenced the work of separating out real from bogus ancient monuments. In particular, he argued that rocking stones were natural creations, and not associated with early humans at all. In 1848–9 the main books of both men were translated into English, and so British scholars at last had at their disposal an alternative means of making sense of the remote past than that provided in the Bible.[26]

For it to become really effective, the Book of Genesis itself had finally to be removed from the world of history to that of myth and symbolism; and that development came suddenly at the end of the 1850s. For five decades, evidence had been accumulating, in Britain, France and Belgium, that the various strata of rocks that made up the earth had been deposited slowly, over vast periods of time, allowing for no rapid sequence of cosmic creation and no globe-altering catastrophes such as Noah's Flood. In the same countries, and in the same decades, excavations were also suggesting that stone tools were found in association with the bones of extinct animals; so that humanity itself had a place in this long and slow development of the present world. What prevented acceptance of these new ideas was partly the difficulty of achieving final proof from what were often complex and disturbed archaeological deposits, and partly the lack of systematic co-operation between the scholars who studied them, in their respective nations. The barrier was broken between September 1858 and November 1859. First the report was published of the discovery of an undisturbed cave at Brixham, on the south Devon coast, in which fossil animal bones and early human tools were, beyond doubt, found mixed together. Then, in the following May and June, a trio of British scholars informed various learned societies of the results of a visit they had made to France, to discover whether sites there showed the same pattern. They could now confirm their absolute certainty that this was the case. Further data were added at meetings in the remainder of the year, from other English excavations, and in November Charles Darwin published *The Origin of Species*. This unveiled to the world a theory that accounted for the development of life forms through a process of natural adaptation and selection, which fitted the new data revealed by geology and archaeology and made the Book of Genesis redundant as an account of how the world came into being. The British scholarly establishment was now largely convinced by the new ideas, and during the following few years a succession of books carried them to a wider public. In 1863 an Irish anatomist called William King announced that other species of human than our own had existed in the past, and gave the first of these to be identified the name of Neanderthal Man.[27]

Darwin's theory of evolution filled the gap in natural history that had been left by the evaporation of literal belief in the Book of Genesis. The gap in ancient history was plugged by the Danish three-age system, and the first full integration of that into the British past was made by Wilson in 1851. There were two aspects of the system that made it especially attractive to Victorian minds. One was that, like evolution, it fitted so neatly into their pre-existing celebration of intellectual and technological progress. It suggested that their most remote ancestors were already embarked on the process of ever-increasing knowledge of and control over their environment; a process which had just made a huge further leap with full industrialization. This reinforced sense of the story of humanity as one of cumulative self-improvement could be assimilated to evangelical Christianity, with only a few changes of emphasis. The technological and military prowess of the contemporary British had already been hailed as a sign of special favour to them on the part of the Christian deity, and as an admirable vehicle for the propagation of his worship. In the decades after 1860, British theologians developed the theory of 'progressive revelation', by which humanity was preordained by the creator deity to discover more and more truth about the nature of the universe by successive stages. In 1868 one of the age's most prominent British churchmen, John Henry Newman, declared that 'Dr Darwin's theory *need* not then be atheistical, be it true or not; it may simply be suggesting a larger idea of Divine prescience and skill'. Darwin himself agreed, telling his readers that 'I see no good reason why the views given in this volume should shock the religious feelings of anyone.'[28] After all, the concept of cumulative progress as a divine mechanism had already been recommended to the British by no less a figure than Victoria herself. In 1851, the year of the Great Exhibition, she told her subjects that 'The progress of the human race resulting from the labour of all men ought to be the final object of the exertion of each individual. In promoting this end we are carrying out the will of the Great and Blessed God.'[29] Its marriage with the theory of evolution was exemplified by the person who was, more than anybody else, to establish for modern British archaeology the proper techniques for excavating a site. He was a retired military man who had inherited a fortune and taken the name of Augustus Pitt-Rivers. In 1887 he told a meeting of the Archaeological Association that 'if man was created originally in the image of God, it is obvious that the very best of us have greatly degenerated. But if on the other hand we recognise that we have sprung from inferior beings . . . we are encouraged to hope that with the help of Providence . . . we may continue to improve.'[30]

The other aspect of the three-age system that held an appeal for the British of the time was the association that could be made between it and the growing contemporary preoccupation with racial differences. This was one inevitable product of the dramatic expansion of colonial empires, which set up Europeans as rulers of huge populations of other peoples. Theories that characterized the former as inherently endowed with superior qualities of management, enterprise and technical aptitude went a long way towards providing a moral justification for the acquisition and exploitation of colonial possessions. To some extent, the Book of Genesis had provided a brake on these, as it proclaimed the common ancestry of all humanity as a special creation of the one true deity. Racial differences, and arguments for the superiority of certain races, had therefore to be based on the lesser distinction of a subsequent divergence from that common origin, in the course of which some had degenerated more than others.[31] The new theory of evolution removed that restraint, opening up European thought to the possibility that the different races of humanity might in fact be entirely distinct, with no mutual ties of descent or creation. A racist model was built into the three-age system at the beginning, for Thomsen and Worsaae had both asserted that each new age of technology had been introduced to Denmark by peoples coming from the east, who had conquered and subdued the existing inhabitants.[32] Those accustomed to viewing the remote past in a biblical framework did not need to make many leaps of the imagination to assimilate this idea: the Book of Genesis was merely being replaced by the Book of Joshua as the primary text for prehistory.

The 1860s and 1870s therefore witnessed both the acceptance of the three-age system for prehistory by the British intellectual establishment, and a struggle over how exactly it was to be interpreted and assimilated to contemporary preoccupations. First off the mark had been Sir Daniel Wilson, who had integrated the Danish ideas with British material almost as soon as the former were published in English. His great book on the prehistory of Scotland was issued in 1851, with a second and revised edition in 1863, and incorporated the suggestions of the Scandinavian scholars concerning race as well as those concerning periods of human development. These suggestions had been influenced by another international intellectual fashion, the science, or pseudo-science, of craniology, according to which the different races of humanity were distinguished by the shapes of their skulls. In particular, the Danes, and scholars among their neighbours, the Swedes, had highlighted a difference between long-headed and round-headed peoples. In part, they were doing so in order to resist German claims to Danish territory, which depended partly on the notion that the territory concerned was originally settled by a Germanic race.[33] Wilson tried to assimilate all this new information to what seemed to be the evidence for the ancient Scottish past. As a deeply religious man, he wished to retain the concept of one original human race, created according to Genesis; but thereafter it was the divergence of humanity, which was again compatible with the biblical tradition, on which he placed most emphasis.

He assigned all the megalithic remains – tombs, circles and rows – to the earliest age of humanity, when stone tools were used. He then raised the question of whether the people of this period were of a different race to those who succeeded them, and who had a technology based on bronze. He admitted that the existing information about skeletal remains was too sparse to provide a basis for firm conclusions, but he went on to make some provisional suggestions and – like the Danes – clearly wanted a strong racial element in his view of the remote past. He proposed that the Stone Age people of Britain had been long-headed, and their Bronze Age successors short-headed. This enabled him to identify thoroughly with the latter, as equivalents of the British settlers of North America, Australia and New Zealand in his own time. He had the courage of his convictions, emigrating himself in 1853 to become one of the founders of Canadian academic scholarship. In his reading of the evidence, the stone-using inhabitants of the island had been superstitious savages, making little attempt to exploit its resources and practising a shamanistic religion based on a view of the natural world as teeming with spirits, equivalent to that of modern Siberian and American natives. The bronze users had therefore brought with them not just a new type of tool but a new mentality, amounting to an industrial revolution and a complete reworking of the land: 'The forests rang with the axe and the wedge; the low grounds were gradually cleared of their primeval forests; and the fruits of patient industry were substituted in part at least for the spoils of the chase.' Wilson identified the Bronze Age people as Celts, and credited them with having had an organized priesthood, as befitted their higher state of development. He thought the Druids might have been a part of this, and went further to speculate that aspects of the older and more primitive beliefs might have been absorbed by the newcomers as part of

Druidry. This, in his eyes, would explain why the medieval Irish stories portrayed Druids as magicians rather than priests, and so easier to equate with tribal shamans and medicine men. Wilson did not, however, want his readers to identify the Scots too closely with Celts, and so with the modern Irish. He suggested that a further invasion of yet more civilized, Germanic, tribes had taken place towards the end of prehistory, and that they had brought with them the use of iron. He also suggested that these newcomers had settled Britain south of the Scottish Highlands, and exerted an influence on the culture of the Celtic tribes remaining in northern Britain. In this fashion he projected back into prehistory a sense of common identity between the English and the Lowland Scots, with the Scottish Highlanders brought safely into their orbit and the Irish left out in the cultural cold.[34]

The situation that had thus been achieved by 1860 was a repetition of that which had obtained in the early modern period: Scottish scholars, influenced by continental ideas, had arrived at a concept of prehistory which was subsequently to be adopted by the other British peoples. In this case, it was to take two decades instead of two centuries for the process to be completed, but, once again, well-connected English authors were needed for the transfer of ideas to succeed. In this case, the closest equivalent to the part played previously by Stukeley was undertaken by a young man, heir to a banking fortune and the title of baronet, with a broad, domed forehead, deep-set, piercing eyes, and a full beard of the sort fashionable at the time. This was John Lubbock, who had acquired a personal interest in prehistory, and ample time and funds with which to indulge it while waiting to inherit the family firm.[35] He read and travelled extensively, to absorb the very latest opinions about ancient Europe from French, German, Swiss and Scandinavian savants. He learned Danish in order to understand fully the new literature pouring out in that language. By the mid-1860s he was ready to work up what he had learned into a form suitable for his compatriots. Lubbock grew up on the ideas of Charles Darwin, who was a family friend and acted as something of a father-figure to him. He had immense energy and a proportionate appetite for knowledge; he wore boots with elastic sides, claiming that it was possible to learn a language in the time which most people took to lace up their footwear. He was also a person with strong, liberal political opinions, and an intense interest in preserving the surviving remains of the national past for posterity and in advancing the welfare of ordinary people in his own time. Among his achievements, he played a leading part in securing the legal protection of ancient monuments and the establishment of bank holidays, and weekly days on which shops closed early to give the public more leisure. He became president of the Working Men's College in London, to promote the education of common people. After he inherited the family bank in 1865 he gave increasing time to the management of that, and to his political career; but his enduring love of prehistory was signalled by the title he chose on being awarded a peerage in 1900: Baron Avebury.[36]

Lubbock's campaign to introduce the new ideas to his nation took two forms. First, he promoted a visit to England by one of the Scandinavian professors who had recently made the running in the interpretation of the European past: the Swede, Sven Nilsson. In June 1865 Nilsson read a paper on Stonehenge to the Ethnological Society in

London, of which Lubbock was president, and which was published in the society's transactions. It began by dismissing the Druids as the builders of the monument, arguing that no ancient author had identified them as worshipping the sun – on the movements of which Stonehenge was clearly orientated – or building megalithic structures. He proposed that they had arrived much later in prehistory, with new immigrants from the European mainland. Being now stuck for people who might actually have built Stonehenge, he brought back the Phoenicians, arguing for this the undoubted evidence of sun worship in ancient Syria, which they might have brought to Britain.[37] This lecture attracted a great deal of attention.[38] What Lubbock liked most about Nilsson's ideas, however, was their downplaying of the role of new races and of invasions in the technological progress of prehistoric Europeans. Nilsson gave Europeans more credit for the ability to invent new processes themselves to improve their own material and intellectual condition. This accorded precisely with Lubbock's ambitions for modern humanity, and he gladly produced an English translation of Nilsson's main book on Scandinavian prehistory, in 1867, and wrote an admiring preface for it.[39] Within a year, it had gone through three editions.

In 1865, he published his own views, in one of the most influential works of Victorian scholarship, the archaeological equivalent of Darwin's *Origin of Species*: a book called *Pre-Historic Times*. It applied the partitioning of prehistory into technological ages to Europe in general, with special reference to Britain, but it made one enduring addition. This was to divide the Stone Age into old and new parts, the former, or Palaeolithic, corresponding to the Ice Ages and a lifestyle of nomadic hunter-gatherers, and the latter, or Neolithic, to the succeeding period of farming, pottery and the making of polished stone tools. He thought that some burial mounds could date from the Neolithic, but that most, and the megalithic monuments, including Stonehenge and Avebury, were erected in the Bronze Age. He thought, furthermore, that they were the work of the native British, politely agreeing with Nilsson that the Phoenicians had reached Britain, but then pointing out that these were an Iron Age people and so could not have arrived until after the monuments had been built.

What was most striking about the book, however, was its theory of progression. It ignored the Bible completely, and dismissed the Druids as irrelevant. Instead it emphasized the savagery of the ancient British, and indeed of hunter-gatherers and simple farmers in general. The fact that unburnt and cremated human bones, and those of animals, were sometimes found together in prehistoric burial mounds was worked up by Lubbock into a portrait of large-scale human sacrifice. In his opinion, dogs, horses, slaves and perhaps wives had all been killed to accompany the dead person in whose honour the mound was being raised. He went on from this to make a tour of peoples who had a Stone Age or Bronze Age technology in the world of his own time. Drawing selected features from accounts of them sent back by European explorers and missionaries, he concluded that they all had repulsive habits and beliefs, with no sign that they had degraded from a higher state of civilization. In his opinion, all humanity had developed out of beasts and long retained bestial ways after developing human bodies and minds. Modern cultures that preserved ancient lifestyles were survivals of what had once been the universal condition of humankind, and as retarded in their moral development as they were in technology: 'There is indeed no atrocious crime, no vice recorded by any traveller, which might not be paralleled in Europe, but that which is with us the exception, is with them the rule.'[40] In this, however, Lubbock found hope for the future, as much for modern 'savages' as for the inhabitants of 'developed' societies such as his own, as 'it shows that both our minds and our bodies may improve. Happiness is certainly increased by civilisation, with security, nourishment, health, humanity. Science will improve our condition and religion our morality, but education and affluence will remove the worst impulses to sin.' He informed his fellow Victorians that they were themselves 'but on the threshold of civilisation', and could go forward together (pulling the rest of the world after them) into a future in which ignorance, cruelty and crime might all be eliminated.[41]

Lubbock's stress on the essential unity of humanity, and its common potential for self-improvement, ran counter to the growing tendency to divide peoples on the basis of race and to suggest that different strains of human being had different abilities. In the context of British archaeology, however, this tendency was now given a new impetus by a Yorkshire doctor, John Thurnam, who divided his enthusiasms between the excavation of ancient monuments and a quest for better understanding of the ailments of his patients. Over time, it was mental illness that came to preoccupy him most. In 1851 he was appointed superintendent of the newly built Wiltshire county lunatic asylum, a posting which placed him in an area exceptionally rich in ancient burial mounds. His two preoccupations came together in the unearthing and study of prehistoric human skeletons, and especially the skulls. In 1849, when he was still in Yorkshire, he published an essay which showed how swiftly he had read the English translations of the new works of Danish prehistory, and in particular those sections which suggested that skulls could be used to identify racial characteristics. He proposed that such investigations be extended to England, and embraced the Scandinavian theory that earlier kinds of human had short oval skulls, and that later and more culturally advanced settlers were marked by longer heads. He admitted that he had seen very few ancient British crania, but joyfully commented that these did indeed seem to correspond to the more 'primitive' kind, being short and oval, with narrow, receding foreheads. He then added a dimension of class prejudice to that of race, by commenting that such physical signs of savagery or retardation survived into later times among 'persons from the lower and less cultivated ranks' of English society.[42]

Thurnam continued to amass data from further excavations, and in 1865, alongside Lubbock's *magnum opus*, he published a huge book of his own, a two-volume study of ancient British skulls carried out in partnership with a fellow surgeon, Joseph Barnard Davis. It was prefaced by a survey of British prehistory, which was, for its time, quite old-fashioned. It gave a prominent place to Druids, interpreting them in biblical terms as the savage heathen priests of a religion which had once been the good one of the Old Testament patriarchs and had been corrupted by contact with Phoenician, Greek and Roman paganism. It devoted some imaginative colour to reconstructing their rites, from hints in Roman texts, especially with regard to the part played by women, whose 'songs and dances were protracted through the night. They decked themselves with the leaves and branches of ivy, or . . . shared in the same rites naked'. The meat of the book lay in its analysis of the skeletal remains. Thurnam and Davis concluded that there was no evidence for a succession of different races in British prehistory. They proudly reported that no trace had been found of Neanderthals or other 'inferior' hominids, and that all the early British seemed to be of the same, modern, species. Although long-headed people were at first more common than short-headed, both types could be found in every age of technology. They added, callously, that since the native Irish, the most primeval race which had survived into the contemporary British Isles, lacked long skulls these could not in themselves be taken as a sign of backwardness. They also warned that elongated heads might have been not a natural feature but the result of deliberate flattening, of the sort carried out by some Native American cultures. On the whole, they concluded cheeringly, the ancient British seemed to have been of uniform race and to have had better mental and moral powers than the lowest sorts of humanity in the present world (such as the Australian Aborigines). None the less, the stock had certainly improved, both by natural selection and because of the arrival of superior peoples in historic times, such as the Romans and English. Both authors were able to declare confidently that the shapes of the skulls of the latter revealed yet greater intelligence and self-control.[43] In general, therefore, they harmonized with Lubbock's view of the national past.

Within a few years, however, Thurnam had jettisoned Davis and changed his ideas yet again. In the late 1860s he read a series of papers on the classification of ancient burial mounds to the Society of Antiquaries. The society published them in two instalments in 1869 and 1871 and they were to be far more influential than anything Thurnam had written before.[44] He opened with a scathing attack on the reputation of Stukeley, demoting him from one of the most respected of Georgian antiquaries to one of the least reliable: 'in no other works of his time is there such a mixture of minute original observation with crude and ill-founded conjecture and hypothesis, and there are none probably which require to be used with so much caution'.[45] He proposed to abolish the association made by Stukeley between prehistoric tumuli and Druids. Using fieldwork from some of the same monuments, on which Stukeley himself had based his conclusions, he proposed a totally different classification. To the Neolithic he assigned the long mounds, often covering stone chambers, which his predecessor had termed long barrows. To the succeeding Bronze Age he dated the smaller round tumuli, usually with a primary grave under the centre and often containing cremations, to which the name round barrows had been given.

In these conclusions Thurnam was undoubtedly correct, and his twin essays marked indeed a significant, and permanent, advance in the understanding of British prehistory. He proceeded, however, to draw more, which departed further from the evidence, and threw away the caution with which he had analysed the same material in his earlier book. He declared that the long barrows had been the work of a more primitive race with longer and narrower skulls. Furthermore, they had been both smaller and more savage than their successors. The dismembered skeletons that he found in some long barrows – which are now thought to be the result of burial practices designed to remove the flesh before deposition – he interpreted as the remains of human sacrifices and cannibal feasts to mark the funerals of chieftains. In this he would certainly have been influenced by the reports coming back to Britain from observers of certain native societies such as those in Fiji and West Africa, which were alleged to have these practices. As evidence, however, he used derogatory passages in Roman authors about barbarian practices, stretched to cover the ancient British. The bronze-using people who raised the round barrows were now represented as a different race, taller and with rounder heads. They were, however, not much better behaved: he concluded that the presence of children's bodies next to some burials was evidence for infanticide, and that female cremations in some mounds were the results of rites of suttee. He then posited the arrival of a third people who ushered in the Iron Age and whom he identified with the Belgae, a tribal confederation mentioned by Julius Caesar. He used the presence of Roman coins on some long barrows – now interpreted as offerings left by Romano-British visitors – as proof that the aboriginal people who built them had lingered in certain areas into historic times. All three races had therefore been present in the island during the Roman period, occupying different points in the hierarchy under the imperial rulers, with the Neolithic aborigines at the bottom and on the margins. It was a situation, of course, which reflected that existing in India and other parts of the Victorian British Empire.

By the 1880s this view had become the scholarly orthodoxy. The decade opened with the publication of another landmark text of the developing discipline of archaeology: *Early Man in Britain* by William (soon Sir William) Boyd Dawkins, best known as an excavator of Palaeolithic cave sites. This began with a declaration which showed how completely and how easily motifs from the Book of Genesis had been fused with the new view of prehistory based on technologies, races and invasions. It asserted that ancient Britain had been characterized chiefly by two phenomena: a series of advances in material culture, and a westward progress of successive waves of people 'over Europe from their ancient Eastern home, from the birthplace of the nations . . . the mystic Garden of Eden'. Dawkins then distinguished two such waves in particular, the earlier being the 'Iberic', and the later being the 'Celtic' and 'forming the vanguard of the great army of the Aryan invaders'.[46] Whence, then, had these new terms come, here applied so confidently to prehistoric races? The answer is, from classical literature and from linguistics. In fact, there was just one ancient text at stake, by our old friend Tacitus: a passage in which he described the inhabitants of Britain in his time as being of different tribes with distinctive physical traits. Thus, the Caledonians in the far north tended to have red hair, and the Silures, in what is now south Wales, to be swarthy-faced and have curly hair. Tacitus admitted that it was uncertain whether these characteristics had developed within the island or were a consequence of the peoples concerned being descended from separate groups of immigrants. He himself, however, guessed that the latter was true. In that case, he thought the Caledonians might have arrived from Germany, the Silures from Iberia (now Spain and Portugal), and the tribes of south-eastern Britain from Gaul, as the people of those other regions had equivalent characteristics.[47]

Late Victorian scholars seized on his surmise, and tended to treat it as stated fact. The comparison of the curly-haired and swarthy-complexioned Silures with Iberians could be made to fit neatly into a new genetic and linguistic model: that the Basques of modern Iberia were the best candidates to be proposed as the most ancient people still surviving in Western Europe. They were, for those looking for a fit with (selective) British evidence, satisfyingly dark in complexion and (allegedly) small in stature, and so could be joined with Tacitus's Silures and Thurnam's Neolithic long-barrow builders. The term 'Aryan', by contrast, came from India, where it had been used to characterize invaders from the north who had subdued and partly replaced the existing inhabitants of the peninsula before the opening of history. Since the end of the eighteenth century, it had been noted that there was a clear relationship between the language they had used and the dominant linguistic group in historic Europe. From this, the label 'Indo-European' had been coined for this family of languages and, in the more race-conscious late nineteenth century, the word 'Aryan' was increasingly being applied to the warrior peoples who were supposed to have carried those related languages west into Europe and south into India, from a hazy original homeland somewhere in the Asian steppes. The century was one of developing nation states, of which race and language were regarded as the two primary foundations and distinguishing characteristics; so it was easy to regard them as synonymous. Furthermore, for British scholars, the fact that the earliest surviving inhabitants of India, the Dravidians, tended to be smaller and darker than the Aryans who invaded and took over their land seemed to provide a clear parallel for what might have happened in Britain.

Dawkins's model for British prehistory was one of invasion red in tooth and claw. First came the Palaeolithic hunters and cave-dwellers, who were driven out by the Neolithic settlers, a small remnant of them maintaining their traditional way of life on the northern fringe of the world as the Eskimos. He now put together Thurnam's data with the Basque comparison to suggest that the new settlers were small, dark-haired people divided into small, warring tribal communities with savage practices, comparable to modern Native Americans and Africans. These he saw as dispossessed in turn by the bronze users, Thurnam's bigger, rounder-headed race whom Dawkins identified as the Celts, and to whom he awarded fair hair and blue eyes as additional characteristics. Their small dark predecessors were, he suggested, driven into mountainous corners to become the Basques, Tacitus's South Welsh, and (for good measure) the native inhabitants of south-west Ireland, who were noted for their dark hair. None the less, he magnanimously conceded, most European peoples showed a mixture of fair and dark features, and of sizes, suggesting a considerable mixing of the two races. He credited the Celts with having introduced a new religion, centred on the worship of fire, with cremation burials, round barrows and stone circles, including Avebury and Stonehenge. Finally, in his scheme, more Aryan peoples poured into Europe, represented in Western Europe by the Germanic race, even bigger and fairer than anybody before them. Some of this race reached Scotland (in homage to Tacitus) to become the Caledonians; thereby, incidentally, rescuing the Scottish Highlanders from any possibility that they might be identified, because of their common language and folklore, with the Irish. In none of this account of the ancient past were the Druids mentioned at all.[48]

For the rest of the century Dawkins's model was the standard one; indeed, it was not wholly abandoned until the 1970s.[49] It equated technological advancement, military strength and moral superiority in a manner deeply satisfying to the British of the age. One further important refinement was made to it in 1882 by the great expert in Celtic languages, Sir John Rhys. As it stood, the scheme pushed the Welsh and Irish together as 'Celts', since they spoke related languages and so were presumed to be of kindred races. Given the increasingly bitter struggle of many of the Irish to separate themselves from the United Kingdom, and the resentment of them by the British in general as a result, this was inconvenient. The problem was overcome by separating them in prehistory. According to Rhys's revised scheme, the 'Iberian' Neolithic inhabitants of Britain had been pushed into the far north by the Bronze Age newcomers, to become the shadowy people known to the Romans as Picts. At that time it was believed – again on grounds that have now been shown to be shaky – that the Picts had possessed a different language and culture, which could qualify them for membership of the earlier race. Their conquerors had been the first wave of Celtic people, the Goidels, who had spoken a language ancestral to Gaelic and whose descendants were the Irish. Later a new, and culturally more advanced, Celtic immigration had occurred, by the people known to Caesar as the Belgae, who linguists now decided had spoken the ancient language which they had come to label Brythonic, the ancestor of modern Welsh, Cornish and Breton. These had taken over most of the island, were dominating it when the Romans arrived, and subsequently produced the Welsh nation.[50] A safe space was thereby created between the two different Celtic cultures of the modern British Isles. This construction, like the basic sequence of ethnic groups and invasions on to which it was grafted, was to be repeated as fact in works on British prehistory – and so reproduced in historical novels – for almost a hundred years.

The obvious question to be asked is why the Druids were not assimilated to it. Given their previous importance in the British historical imagination, it seems at first sight strange that they were disregarded or marginalized by the proponents of the new prehistory. They could easily have been incorporated into the new model in different ways. After all, Wilson, who had introduced it, had thought it possible that Druidic tradition had incorporated elements inherited from the earliest inhabitants of the British Isles. Lubbock could have made them an example of the way in which his home-grown savages developed, by generating an established priesthood with set dogmas of the sort that many writers, since ancient times, had thought the Druids to have been. They were prime candidates for the leaders of the new, fire-worshipping religion introduced by the Celts at the start of the Bronze Age; which would have reunited them with stone circles. One respectable scholar of the late Victorian period consistently made a case for keeping them in the prehistoric frame in just such a way. This was A. L. Lewis, who immediately (in 1871) suggested that the Druids had been the priests of the Celtic 'nations' who had, according to the newly emerging orthodoxy, introduced bronze technology and erected most of Europe's megalithic monuments.[51] Two decades later, he was still trying to make the same argument; and doing so, it should be owned, with perfect logic given the state of information in his time. He agreed that megalithic monuments could well be very early in their date, but that both the artefacts found inside them, and the legends associated with them in historic times, suggested that they had continued to be used through most of prehistory.

Moreover, there was no decisive evidence that chambered tombs and stone circles had been built by different races. Some stone circles clearly showed alignment with the sun, which matched what ancient writers had said of the Druids' interest in the heavens. Hence, the Druids could still fairly be associated with them, even if they were not necessarily the founders of the tradition of building such monuments. Lewis noted, however, that anybody who attempted to make that association was now 'resented with a ferocity which seemed to embody almost as much racial antipathy as antiquarian zeal'.[52] He himself, however, was not made the object of any such ferocity, for his temperate, carefully posed and prominently published arguments were – it seems – totally ignored. He was so far out of the mood of the time that his colleagues simply chose not to notice what he was saying.

A snapshot of the same effect at a local level can be found by returning to the circles at Stanton Drew, Somerset, in 1877, on the occasion of a visit to them by the Bristol Cymmrodorion Society, which represented the Welsh settled in that city. It was welcomed by the local vicar, who did his utmost to reconcile the old and new teachings of prehistory. He began by reminding his guests of the Old Testament parallels for the erection of megalithic monuments, and of the fact that ancient texts had credited the Druids with the study of heavenly bodies. He pointed to the manner in which certain prehistoric circles and rows could be plausibly said to have alignments with the movement of sun, moon or stars. He suggested that the Druidic religion, and the building of such monuments, could therefore have been introduced to Britain by the Celts, migrating from their ancestral lands in Asia and bringing with them the religion of the Hebrew patriarchs. All this counted for nothing with the vice-president of the visiting society, a medical doctor, who replied brashly that the stones were 'certainly' not Druidic, as too little was known about the origin, nature and beliefs of the Druids to credit them with anything.[53]

As none of the scholars who constructed the new view of British prehistory articulated directly their reasons for wishing to usher the Druids out of sight, these can only be surmised from the context in which they were working; but it is relatively easy to do that. Druids had been too completely absorbed into the old, biblically based, model of the ancient past, which the new authors were setting out to displace. In this sense, the previous century of scholarship had actually been too successful in integrating them into a history that took its essential structure from the Book of Genesis. Knowing that this history was thoroughly implanted in the British imagination at all social levels, proponents of the new model felt the need to dissociate it from the old wherever possible, to give it the maximum possible impact. Noah's Flood and the Druids had to go out together, as part of the process of reformation, evangelism and conversion; they were, effectively, icons that needed to be demolished. It gave an additional force to this process that the new ideas were being propounded, on the whole, by new people. Scholars like Wilson, Lubbock and Dawkins were making their name with the revelation of the reconfigured view of the past. They were also representing a further secularization of British scholarship. As has been emphasized, before 1860 clergymen were central to writings upon the ancient past, as an extension of their vocation as proponents and interpreters of the divine word as revealed in Scripture.

That role disappeared rapidly with the displacement of the Bible as the basic work of world history. This did not mean that clerics immediately ceased to be prominent in research into British history and prehistory; on the contrary, they long retained a position in it. They were, however, increasingly consigned to the local level, or to the margins of the national one. In the longer term, they began to vanish even there; the proportion of clergy in the Somerset Archaeological and Natural History Society (which seems typical) was 20.3 per cent in 1876 and 3.8 per cent in 1930.[54] The running in scholarship was now made by people from the other professions: bankers, medics, soldiers and – increasingly – laymen appointed to full-time positions of research scholarship in universities and museums. The Druids, as priests, were being ousted as part of a whole, millennia-old, tradition that had fused religion with the writing of ancient history, both in its emphasis and in its personnel.

This point is highlighted by the appearance of yet another book in that pivotal year 1865, which witnessed the publication of *Pre-Historic Times* and *Crania Britannica*. It was of a very different hue, being *Our British Ancestors: Who and What Were They?*, by Samuel Lysons. Lysons was a Gloucestershire rector, and a prominent and active antiquarian, excavating and recording prehistoric burial mounds to a standard as good as most achieved at his time. His book was a full-scale attack on the new prehistory, opening with the ringing declaration that the Bible was the highest guarantee of all truth. He then went on to ridicule Iolo Morganwg's account of Druidic theology, and Darwin's theory of evolution, as equally ill founded in good evidence. He attacked the three-age division of prehistory, on the grounds that use of stone tools (allegedly) persisted among some European tribes even into historic times and that metal and stone artefacts were sometimes found together in prehistoric graves. He then restated the view of Druids as practitioners of a slightly degenerate version of the true religion of the Old Testament patriarchs, spread by the descendants of Noah's son Japhet. As such, they retained enough revealed truth to prepare Britain for the coming of Christianity. Lysons then proceeded to make a case study of one of the Neolithic long barrows that he had excavated, the elaborate stone-chambered one in his own Cotswold parish of Rodmarton, known to the locals as Windmill Tump. He showed, step by step, how its layout accorded with the religion that featured both in biblical texts and in ancient accounts of Druidry.[55]

He proved, in fact, to be an isolated reactionary, whose protests were ignored by the pace-making scholars whose works appeared alongside and after his. None the less, the manner in which he emphasized the Druids, as major components of the vanishing orthodoxy that he was striving to rescue, indicates why his ideological opponents were equally ready to banish them.

* * *

It remains to be seen how much the changing orthodoxy was absorbed into British culture in general during the final third of the nineteenth century. Two statements by different commentators may serve to frame the problem involved. One was by James Rust, a minister of the Church of Scotland writing in 1871, who began by admitting that the Druidic interpretation of megalithic monuments was already discarded by 'nearly all the great archaeologists of the present day'. The admission was a sorrowful one, in that Rust, as a clergyman of the old school, thought that the interpretation should be salvaged. He pointed out that stone circles could still be best interpreted as ritual monuments, and that the medieval Irish legend of Maigh Slecht seemed explicitly to link Druid worship with a ring of idols. He suggested in addition that the absence of any association between Druids and circles in the ancient sources might be explained by the fact that most of the latter dealt with Gaul, not Britain, and that only the Druids in the latter may have habitually erected megaliths.[56] None the less he acknowledged that, even by that date, his views would be treated as redundant. The second commentator was also a clergyman, but English, of very different views, and writing at the end of the century. This was H. N. Hutchinson, who produced a popular textbook on British prehistory down to the end of the Bronze Age, which embodied the now standard scholarly orthodoxy as laid out by Dawkins. He added that 'it is a thousand pities that, in the face of so much striking evidence, both from tradition and from archaeology, as well as written history, schoolmasters and others should persist in putting the Druid as the first actor on the stage of human events in Great Britain'.[57] This is the other face of the scholarly rejection of the Druids: that, even by the late 1890s, its proponents believed that it had made little impact, even on educated members of the general public. It remains to be seen how much this is reflected in the surviving sources.

It is worth bearing in mind that, where stone circles and rows were concerned, everybody in the period was operating in a vacuum of evidence. Thurnam's discovery, that long barrows were Neolithic and round barrows (generally) Bronze Age, could be sustained from excavated material. The freestanding megaliths, however, had thus far yielded few comparable objects that could be used to place them in any part of the three-age scheme. The necessary work was not, in fact, accomplished until the next century, when the British Association set up a committee to determine the matter by pooling all the available evidence and obtaining more. By 1915 enough artefacts had been amassed, especially from Harold St George Gray's excavations at Avebury, to draw the conclusion that most stone circles were built in the late Neolithic or early Bronze Age.[58] What had happened during the previous fifty years was that most scholars of prehistory had agreed to evict the Druids from them without knowing to whom they could be assigned. This is plain not merely from the writings of major figures, but from the work of their less distinguished colleagues. The typical essay or book on stone circles published in the late nineteenth century describes the form of the monuments concerned without mentioning Druids or attempting to position them in any particular period.[59]

Writings on megaliths in general, however, emanated from people with a special interest and expertise in them, who could be expected to be most fully abreast of current scholarly opinion. It is more instructive to look at changing attitudes to a celebrated local monument, in which a slightly wider cross-section of society is represented. Such a case study is provided neatly by the circles and avenues at Stanton Drew. Something of the conflict of views is conveyed by the account of the visit of the Bristol Cymmrodorion Society, given above. An examination of late Victorian publications on them reveals the same shift in progress. In 1867 a contributor to the journal of the local archaeological club could still assign them to the Druids, embracing in particular Deane's theory of serpent-worship, which was based in turn on Stukeley's books. A handbook on the stones issued in 1888 suggested that they were monuments of 'superstition or religion' erected by Neolithic people who could best be compared to the most primitive of modern Indian tribes. A guidebook in 1896 had the Dawkins picture by heart, assigning them to a people migrating from the east before the main 'Aryan' invasion occurred.[60] In that same year a more extended work, by an expert in West Country megaliths, warned readers not to join the recent assault on the memory of those who had ascribed them to the Druids. He gallantly declared that those earlier authors, 'if they erred from defect of knowledge, or from giving too loose a rein to fancy had, after all, good grounds for some of their conclusions'. After this piece of generosity, however, he went on to suggest that there were, as yet, no grounds for conclusions at all: the structures at Stanton could not be dated or linked to any particular culture, and there was no intrinsic sign of their purpose, so 'all is conjecture'.[61] It may be concluded from this that the changing scholarly views had made a deep impact, at least on educated society in Bristol and Somerset, by the end of the century.

Stonehenge is another matter. For one thing, it looks so different from any other megalithic monument, having stones that were smoothed and worked into shape and fitted together with a woodworker's techniques. This long suggested that it belonged to a different time from that of the unworked stones that went into other circles and chambered tombs. It also mattered a lot that Stonehenge was so famous, attracting attention from people who knew little about prehistory in general and were not much acquainted with other ancient monuments. This meant that writings upon it were both much more varied in their views and represented a much broader range of social, cultural and intellectual groups. Certainly its date and purpose remained much debated even among leading proponents of the new, Druid-free, view of the ancient past. Lubbock, for example, thought that it was built in the Bronze Age, while Thurnam attributed it to the Belgae, touted as the leading people of Iron Age Britain.[62] All that united prehistorians who embraced the new ideas was that it was pre-Roman, but that left open the question of where it was to be positioned, in what were now regarded as three very different periods from the Neolithic onward.[63] The impatience and frustration provoked by these arguments in some informed readers was expressed by a rising star of British archaeology: Arthur Evans, subsequently to become a knight, and the discoverer of the Minoan civilization of Crete. In 1889 he bluntly asserted that all existing theories concerning Stonehenge were 'mere beating of the air'. He ventured to admit that 'after all, perhaps we may yet find ourselves once more in Druid company, but we must at least arrive there by the methods imposed by modern science'.[64] The matter only appeared to be resolved in 1901, when the owner of the stones allowed one of them, which was leaning at a dangerous angle, to be straightened. This work afforded an opportunity for archaeologists to dig underneath it, supplying evidence that the main part of the structure was either Neolithic or from the very early Bronze Age.[65]

Some Victorian authors, clearly, never left Druid 'company' where Stonehenge was concerned. One of them, by a marvellous irony, was Charles Darwin himself, who must not have read the new prehistorians he had helped to inspire, and referred to the monument as Druidical in 1881.[66] Lubbock's feelings could not have been improved by a pamphlet written by a female admirer of his, and dedicated to him, which then proceeded to say that Britain's stone circles had been erected by Hebrews migrating from the Holy Land, in worship of 'the one true God'.[67] Until the end of the century, authors of books on Stonehenge continued confidently to repeat the old Druidic orthodoxy, often adding the biblical patriarchs and the Phoenicians, as had been done for two hundred years.[68] In 1886 the *Times* newspaper carried an article which acknowledged that the purpose and date of the monument were both 'hotly disputed among the learned', but said that it was 'all but certain' that Druids had built Stonehenge, the main problem being whether modern people should admire or deplore it.[69] In the same year, *Punch* magazine, more satirically as was its wont, had a cockney tourist collide with an archaeologist among the stones, who

> . . . pattered a proper blarney
> About Druids, and sickles, and mizzletoe, slortering stones and such stuff,
> Till I asked 'im if tuppence 'ud stash 'im; an' sent 'im away in a 'uff.[70]

Downmarket of these in the world of journalism, the *Daily News* cheerfully called Stonehenge 'the Druid's temple', without any sense of hesitation or complication, in the very last year of the century.[71] Some further indication of popular belief may be found in the guidebooks to the monument which began to be produced locally as visitors to it increased with improved transport systems and technologies in the last quarter of the century. There was as yet no 'official' guide, as entry was still free, unrestricted and unsupervised – the unofficial guardians, the Brownes, were now gone – so these booklets were sold in nearby towns. What is apparently the first to survive, from 1882, showed an awareness of theories of Nilsson and Lubbock, but still stated that Stonehenge was 'generally credited' to the Druids, who had been a bad lot. Two others followed in 1894. One, by a Wiltshire vicar, held that the scholarly beliefs about it were now so varied that nothing of any certainty could be concluded. The other pronounced confidently that the monument had been the work of the Druids, who had practised a religion with many admirable qualities.[72]

The new views, likewise, had not got through to Lady Antrobus, wife of the actual owner of Stonehenge and the land around it at this period. In 1900 she published her own guide, in which, struggling to show her appreciation of differing scholarly opinions, she held that it had been either a 'Great Druidical Temple or (as some hold) Phoenician Observatory'. She herself preferred the former theory, and proceeded to imagine the monument 'in happy, thoughtless Pagan days. Druid priests and priestesses forming grand processions; crossing the rushing Avon and winding up from the valley to Stonehenge, clothed in pure white and holding gleaming sickles in their hands, chanting hymns on their way to perform the sacred rite of cutting the mistletoe. Perhaps they sang and chanted through the short summer night, waiting for the sun to rise . . . probably this was the signal for sacrifice, the death of the victim, and the appeasing of wrathful gods.'[73] In the material published on Britain's greatest prehistoric monument, therefore, there is ample justification for the complaint made by Hutchinson, that by the end of the century many people who claimed to be informed were still making Druids central to their view of British prehistory.

One success scored by the new prehistorians consisted of seeing off challenges from other avant-garde ideas; and of these the greatest was that fostered by Algernon Herbert, that megalithic monuments were post-Roman. The main proponent of this in the late nineteenth century was a Scottish architectural historian called James Fergusson, who assembled a great deal of interesting comparative data about similar monuments erected in other parts of the world. His basic arguments, however, were the same as those always employed by proponents of this hypothesis: that no Greek or Roman author ever associated Druids with stone temples or noticed any impressive native monuments in Britain.[74] Proponents of the new system of prehistory, based on the ages of technology, saw in his work a combination of serious error and an erudition and skill in argument that gave it great potential appeal. They accordingly mounted against it a ferocious onslaught of criticism,[75] sustained for decades. Lubbock himself attacked it twice, exposing the complete lack of any real supporting evidence for it, while its most vehement opponent was a respected archaeologist from the Channel Islands, Frederick Collings Lukis, who called for every copy of Fergusson's main book on the subject to be 'committed to the flames'. The campaign seems to have worked, for, although the post-Roman theory was sometimes cited by local authors as one of a number of contending views of British megaliths,[76] it never made any deep impression on the public. Nor was any fresh momentum given to it by the support of a young surveyor who published a detailed study of the structure, mathematics and astronomical alignments of Stonehenge in 1880, and concluded that they indicated either a pre- or a post-Roman date.[77] His views, by contrast with those of Fergusson, were more or less ignored, and he went off to become one of the founders of the modern discipline of Egyptology, as Sir Flinders Petrie. He retained till the end of his life the opinion that the monument was the burial site of the post-Roman British kings, because of his wish to believe literally the long-discredited pseudo-history of the medieval author Geoffrey of Monmouth. This was, however, regarded indulgently by others as one of the many eccentricities of the great man.[78]

It is also notable that the expulsion of Druids from the centre of orthodox British prehistory caused a contraction of the sphere of monuments that could be attributed to any prehistoric human activity. Between the early eighteenth and the mid-nineteenth century, as discussed earlier, it had been common to treat a range of natural geological phenomena – curiously shaped rock outcrops, basins in boulders and on crags, and (especially) rocking stones – as having been fashioned by the Druids as shrines and idols. This interpretation had begun to be disputed during the first half of the nineteenth century, but in the 1850s it was still possible to find authors championing such striking formations as Druidical constructions.[79] After the Danish scholars had dismissed them, however, they finally disappeared from the archaeological record of the British, and the arguments and assumptions concerning the activities of the Druids were withdrawn to structures that seemed beyond doubt to be the work of ancient human hands.

What is especially revealing about this whole pattern of reaction is the contrast it makes with the Georgian period. Within a few decades of the scholarly acceptance of Stukeley's argument, that the Druids had built Britain's megalithic monuments and should be regarded as the leading figures of national prehistory, this idea had been taken up enthusiastically in all parts of the nation and at all levels of society. This was because they could be hung on all sorts of existing mental pegs. They were, after all, already familiar figures to many of the educated British, although hazily so. They were rooted in classical literature, and the work of assimilating them to the Bible had already begun. They could readily, if spuriously, be visualized, because of the stock image provided by Aylett Sammes. The ancient references to them could be converted to a range of useful functions: they could be seen as exemplars of patriotism, home-grown wisdom, piety and technical skill, love and understanding of nature, appreciation of the performing arts – or of barbarism, cruelty, priestcraft and heathenism.

By contrast, the nameless, faceless peoples who roamed through the new British prehistory had no familiar correspondences in the popular mind, no matter how people like Dawkins tried to link them to images from Genesis. They could not be associated with biblical characters – in fact, they had come on stage as part of a clearing away of Scripture as a literal source for British history – and they were beyond the orbit of ancient literature. They had left no visual portraits of themselves, just as they had left no writings. They could be viewed, in fact, only through the representations of prehistorians who themselves disagreed over their precise identities, movements and dates. It is no wonder that the general public hung on to Druids, even while the new scholarly establishment was urging it to abandon them and ridiculing those who failed to oblige.

* * *

If Druids proved to be more tenacious than the proponents of the new prehistory had expected or wished, then the Book of Genesis had a still more effective hold on the Western imagination, reasserting its influence in a range of subtle ways. One was to give a new power to the ancient myth of Atlantis. Now that Noah's Flood was disappearing from works on world history and geology, the biblical deluge reappeared as the one that drowned the lost civilization of which Plato had spoken. In this guise, the land of the Atlanteans had been the home not just of yet another ancient culture, but of the most developed and influential of early times, thereby allowing its end to fill the emotional space of the biblical Flood much more effectively. Furthermore, it seemed to be better based in historical records, as it was apparently reported as fact by one of the most respected of ancient Greek philosophers. In addition, it had a particular appeal for British and (especially) American minds, because it positioned this putative advanced and doomed civilization comfortably close to their own shores, relieving them of the need to look to the Near East for the key developments in the human story.[80] Propelled by American enthusiasm, its impact on British prehistory first became visible in the 1890s, when two writers produced pamphlets arguing that Stonehenge had been built by refugees from Atlantis.[81]

More subtle, but none the less discernible, was the lingering influence of Genesis on archaeologists. Its echoes in the work of Dawkins have been noted. The basic plan that

Genesis provided for the earliest history was that of the populating of Europe by peoples spreading from a common point of origin somewhere in the east. These, according to the model, brought with them a common religion, which produced the first ceremonial monuments and subsequently fragmented, and degenerated, into the different pagan traditions recorded across Europe and the Middle East at the opening of history. By the early twentieth century this model had reappeared among continental prehistorians in two rival forms. One, associated particularly with the Swede Oscar Montelius, held that all that was good in European thought and technology had come out of the Near East. The other, promoted especially by the German Gustav Kossina, turned the shadowy Indo-Europeans or Aryans, a hypothetical race created by scholars from the evidence of linguistics, into the new children of Japhet, spreading civilization in their wanderings from an original, single homeland. The pre-Indo-European peoples of Europe became in this model the equivalent of the sinners drowned in the biblical Flood, except this deluge had become one of humanity, as the superior Indo-Europeans eradicated or absorbed the natives whose lands they occupied.[82] The extreme British reconfiguration of the Genesis model was provided between 1911 and 1936 by the 'diffusionist' school led by the anatomist Grafton Elliot Smith and the anthropologist William Perry. This argued that world civilization had been created by Egyptian missionaries and entrepreneurs, who had spread a common religious system, common cultural attitudes and common technological development around the world from their homeland. This school differed from the others, however, in that it did not regard the ideas and techniques that were spread as necessarily beneficial to humanity; it had kept the structure of the Genesis myth while inverting the morality.[83]

Such attitudes also rebounded on mainstream British archaeologists in the first two-thirds of the twentieth century. Perhaps the greatest of all was Gordon Childe, the principal synthesizer of European material among them, and the most active and influential generator of interpretative concepts and methods of explanation. Between 1925 and 1957 he repeatedly reconsidered the means by which the successive periods of European prehistory had been formed. Faced with the two continental models, he veered between them. In the 1930s and 1940s, appalled by the racist use that the Nazis had made of the concept of clever, robust, conquering Indo-Europeans, he threw all his weight behind the Montelius theory: that in prehistory light had only shone from the Near East. In his reading, missionaries from that region had taught the peoples of early Europe everything about successive improvements in technology, and also brought it the religion associated with the building of megaliths. In the 1920s, before the Nazis came to power, and the 1950s, when they had been defeated, he modified this to emphasize that Europeans had made creative use of the Eastern ideas they had received. In this alternative view, likewise, he portrayed the fount of civilization in the Near East as having been cut off, eventually, because of the degeneration of its religion into priestcraft and superstition.[84] All these notions had been found before, in eighteenth- and nineteenth-century models of the arrival of the patriarchal Hebrew religion in Europe.

They were taken further in the mid-twentieth century by other leading figures in British archaeology. Glyn Daniel and O. G. S. Crawford propagated the idea that the megalithic tombs of Neolithic Western Europe, the earliest stone monuments in the region, were erected as temples of a religion brought by missionaries, colonists or prospectors from the eastern Mediterranean.[85] The source of this megalithic religion had shifted from Syria and Palestine to Crete and the other Aegean islands, the carriers of it had become Bronze Age seafarers rather than the Phoenicians, and its deity had become a single, benevolent, Great Goddess, rather than a single, benevolent, Great God. None the less, the basic model was that proposed by Stukeley and many scores of authors in the century after his time. Only the Druids had been removed from it.

It is hardly surprising that this should be so. After all, Druids had been central figures of the British historical imagination for only about a hundred years before the scholarly establishment turned against them. By contrast, the Bible had been the foundation of the concept of the ancient past, held by most literate Europeans, for one and a half millennia. That modern experts in prehistory should slip so easily into modes of thought that echoed it is a sign of how embedded they remained in traditional culture. It is also, however, a sign of how badly lacking they were in alternative points of reference, in the new world of Stone, Bronze and Iron Ages in which they now found themselves.

10

⋙⋘

DRUIDIC AFTERGLOW

This chapter is devoted to the fortunes of themes and institutions which had evolved in British culture during the heyday of Druids as figures in the national imagination, in the period following the eviction of the Druids from their central status. In the late nineteenth and twentieth centuries, some novelists, poets, religious writers, societies and national institutions continued to work with images of them in the forms developed during their period of maximum national significance. They often did so to considerable effect, and with a proportionate impact on contemporary society. What had changed was that a general concept had become a group or individual one: but one which, none the less, is very revealing of the cultural and social trends of the time.

* * *

The most important group that had formed its identity around the obsolete view of Druidry was the Gorsedd of the Bards of the Isle of Britain, which managed the Welsh National Eisteddfod. It had grown steadily in splendour and importance even as the British preoccupation with Druids, on which it had been based, was eroding away. That erosion was, moreover, only one problem with which the Gorsedd had to reckon, because, in addition, its own rites and historical claims were founded directly on the forgeries of Iolo Morganwg. It therefore faced both a general and a specific difficulty in weathering the transition to the twentieth century. For much of the nineteenth, as has been described, the challenge to the trustworthiness of Iolo's version of history had been more or less contained. In the 1890s, however, just as the Gorsedd was acquiring standard robes and regalia, a rising Welsh scholar called John Morris Jones launched a fresh attack on its authenticity as an ancient or medieval institution, in a series of journal articles.[1] It did not help matters that Jones subsequently became one of the leading experts in the Welsh language and literature, and received a knighthood, and that he was hostile to the Gorsedd as an institution.[2] His view of Iolo was vindicated in the 1920s by the research of a younger literary scholar of equal prowess, Griffith John Williams. Williams was the first person to combine the two characteristics that were needed to verify or disprove Iolo's claims: an interest in Iolo himself and a deep knowledge of the bardic literature of medieval and early modern Glamorgan on which Iolo had drawn. Williams's work spanned the period between the 1910s and the 1950s.[3] None the less, his first major publication, in 1926, was enough to destroy the nineteenth-century myth of Iolo as an honest if eccentric individual. He was revealed instead as a skilled and deliberate deceiver. Once again, Williams had a personal investment in attacking the credentials of the Gorsedd, deeming it a constricting and conservative influence on modern Welsh literature.[4] Jones was understandably triumphant at his news, commenting that 'the impostor has been caught' and describing Iolo as 'a hateful man'. He went on to express his fear that 'it will be another age or so before our literature and history are clean of the traces of his contaminated hands'.[5]

However, the impact of these developments on the Gorsedd was postponed, and to some extent cushioned. For one thing, Williams's revelations were not made until the new century was over a quarter run. Furthermore, in a sense Jones seemed to give with one hand what he took away with the other. While attacking Iolo, he also turned his scholarship and scorn on the revisionist historians of Welsh literature from the mid-nineteenth century, and especially the most extreme of them, D. W. Nash. He agreed with him that Edward Davies's translations from the medieval texts had been ridiculous, but thought that those by Nash had also been faulty; indeed, he doubted whether the meaning of much of the verse credited to Taliesin could ever be known. Having said that, he proceeded to argue both that there had been a genuine sixth-century bard called Taliesin, and that the 'mystical' poetry recorded under his name rested on genuine ancient myth. Indeed he went further, to specify that in that case it could well embody genuine Druidical teaching after all, especially regarding the fate of the soul.[6] Jones therefore seemed to have restored the credentials of medieval Welsh literature as the only surviving material that gave access to Druidic teaching. He did so for more than forty years; not until 1960 did an equivalent giant in another generation of Welsh scholars, Sir Ifor Williams, finally prove that only a dozen of the 'Taliesin' poems could date to an early period, and none of these contained the 'mystical' material.[7]

Help also came directly to the Gorsedd for a time, from an altogether different scholarly source. This was represented by the leading astronomer of Edwardian Britain, Sir Norman Lockyer, who studied the plan for an ideal *gorsedd* circle drawn by Iolo in one of his manuscripts, and decided that the alignments of the stones matched the night sky as it would have been in the late Neolithic period. He was able to inform the Royal Institute of South Wales, meeting at Swansea in 1907, that 'in my opinion your Gorsedd in Wales is a thing forty centuries old ... It makes the Gorsedd I take it just about the oldest thing that we have on the planet connected with any human activity past or present.' He then went on to say that alignments based on the layout of the Gorsedd circle matched some that could be found in the plans of 'genuinely' prehistoric stone circles in Cornwall, of Stonehenge, and of the ancient Egyptian temple at Luxor. He mocked archaeologists for their ignorance of astronomy, which blinded them to these truths.[8] In fact what he was demonstrating was that an expert in one discipline should not interfere recklessly in the affairs of another; as Iolo's forgeries were subsequently proved, Lockyer's alignments had to be coincidental. Members of the Gorsedd, however, were understandably elated and grateful, and initiated him into their company with the bardic title of Gwyddon Prydain, 'the Magician of Britain'.[9]

Reactions of Welsh cultural nationalists to questions of the antiquity of the Gorsedd therefore developed slowly over time. Rowland Williams, 'Hwfa Môn', Archdruid from 1894 to 1905, took a fundamentalist attitude, asserting Iolo's claims against all comers.[10] In the years following his death, two pamphlets were published that took the same line.[11] Just over a decade later, however, things had become a great deal more hesitant and temperate. In 1921 the reigning Archbishop of Wales, as president of the Cambrian Archaeological Association, addressed that society on Druids. He still held them up as worthy ancestors of modern Christian clergy who had possessed a vocational programme of study and training unique in the ancient world and had taught the immortality of the soul. He used Tacitus's description of the Druids and women on Anglesey to argue that both male and female members of their order had special robes, again like established Christian clergy. He considered it possible that they had indeed coloured medieval Welsh Christianity, and pointed to the poems credited to Taliesin, once again, as evidence for this. Finally, he suggested that the National Eisteddfod might be an echo of an ancient Druidic festival, 'in shadow if not in substance', and that the Gorsedd resembled what could be surmised of ancient 'Celtic' assemblies, something which 'favours belief in the antiquity of its origin'.[12] This was all comforting, hypothetical and never mentioned Iolo.

Two years later, the current Recorder, or secretary, of the Gorsedd went still further in caution and equivocation. He disavowed all claims that it closely resembled the bardic gatherings of the Middle Ages, and admitted that its name was itself modern. None the less, he felt that it had preserved something of the spirit of the ancient bardic order, and that bardic contests were themselves pre-Christian in origin. He then issued an invitation to all the staff of Welsh colleges, and all graduates of the University of Wales, who could prove their knowledge of Welsh history and literature, to seek membership.[13] This was about as flexible and reasonable as it was possible to be at that time. Against this, however, may be set a string of publications by Welsh authors, from the 1900s to the 1930s, which reasserted the nineteenth-century myth of Druidry virtually in its entirety. With varying emphasis, they represented the Druids as having been great scientists and practitioners of a wise and noble religion, of which the Welsh could be proud, and of which the Gorsedd was in some fashion a descendant. All, likewise, drew heavily on Iolo's mythology to prove their points.[14] These private and individual polemics gave the impression that nothing had changed since the 1850s. They skirted rather than engaged with the criticisms of the ideas that they were repeating. They would have been deeply reassuring to anybody worried by those criticisms but not much acquainted with them, and seemed plausible, in their confidence, to anyone approaching the subject for the first time.

The Gorsedd itself did not need them in order to survive. The argument made by its Recorder in 1923 was one that virtually proofed it against challenges to its historical authenticity: that in some way it represented the spirit of medieval Welsh and ancient British bardic assemblies and contests, rather than arguing for any direct continuity with them. Furthermore, it had by now stacked up a continuity, and a tradition, of its own, far exceeding any living memory, and could fairly claim to justify itself by the job that it did in administering, and adding glamour to, the National Eisteddfod. In 1937 it merged with the National Eisteddfod Society which had organized that event since its revival, to form a ruling council to oversee all aspects of the Eisteddfod. Its quantity of ceremony increased still further. In 1931 the English journalist H. V. Morton attended a ceremony, and reported unkindly that he had spotted a microphone hidden in a bunch of green leaves on the central stone, and that the wind whipped aside the robes of participants to reveal 'trousers of serge and tweed and pin-stripe'. Perhaps in response, members wore more flamboyant dress beneath the robes thereafter, with flashes of gold lamé, and white shoes, and sported crowns of laurel. In 1959 the author of a letter to the *Western Mail*, the paper for which Morien had worked, likened the Archdruid to 'a cross between a Pharaoh and a Roman senator'. In 1947 the Herald Bard acquired a staff of office decorated with oak leaves and mistletoe, and in 1954 the Gorsedd added two silver trumpets, which had been used at the coronation of Elizabeth II in the previous year. The queen was herself a member, having been initiated as an Ovate in 1946, with the name of Elisabeth o (*sic*) Windsor. Her husband, the Duke of Edinburgh, received the same rank in 1960, using his lesser title of Earl of Merioneth to give him the name of Philip Meirionnydd. In spiritual terms, the Gorsedd remained where it had been placed in the mid-nineteenth century, as an expression of anybody who believed in 'God'. In practice, its Druid component functioned as an expression of modern Welsh Christianity. Most of its Archdruids in the early and mid-twentieth century were clergy, including Methodists, Congregationalists, a Baptist and a Church of Wales minister.[15] It was entirely in accordance with this tradition that the Welshman Rowan Williams was initiated as an honorary Druid in 2002, with the name Rowan ap Neirin, after being made Archbishop of Canterbury.[16]

In 1928 it produced a satellite institution in Britain, being the Cornish Gorseth of Bards, or Gorseth Kernow, formed as an expression of and a stimulant to the cultural nationalism of Cornwall even as the Gorsedd and National Eisteddfod are to that of Wales. At the National Eisteddfod of 1928, eight Cornishmen were initiated as Bards, in order to form a nucleus for the new organization, and at the autumn equinox of that year the Archdruid led a delegation from Wales to Cornwall to establish it. The Gorseth has met annually in all peacetime years since, functioning as a mixture of *gorsedd* and *eisteddfod*. It has never had any Druids or Ovates, consisting wholly of Bards. The reason for this is not discussed in any of the extant literature, and may simply reflect a desire for streamlining suitable for a smaller nation. If there was any conscious wish to distance the institution from Druidry, this has been muted in practice by the fact that many of its meetings have been held in the prehistoric stone circles in which Cornwall abounds; the inaugural one took place at the Nine Maidens near Boscawen-Un.[17] To some extent the distinction still makes the Gorseth less directly relevant than the Gorsedd to a history of representations and re-creations of Druids. None the less, its rites and symbols are modelled directly on those of the Welsh body, and therefore on the work of Iolo; in that sense, Gorseth Kernow is another of his children.

In the last part of the twentieth century, the Gorsedd continued to flourish, coming further to terms with its historical past while consolidating and developing its role as the ceremonial face of the National Eisteddfod. The former work was carried out largely in a pair of books published in 1978 and 1992 by the Herald Bard, Dillwyn Miles.[18] These traced, in meticulous detail, the actual history of both the Eisteddfod and the Gorsedd, making plain both the roots of the former in medieval Welsh tradition and the origin of the latter in Iolo's vision for his homeland. They provide a wonderful resource for historians and an honourable and honest account of the growth of the twin institutions, richly justifying both in terms of their actual achievement over two centuries. The enduring popularity of the Gorsedd ceremony was attested by the large crowds that it has continued to draw on each occasion on which it is performed: the performers number hundreds and the spectators thousands. In the course of the twentieth century it was repeatedly revised in details. For readers who have never seen it, the following is the form which it took in the 1970s, and which still seems to be current.[19]

The circle is still formed of twelve stones, with the flat one, the Maen Llog, in the centre as a platform for the Archdruid. Facing it at the eastern side of the ring is the Maen y Cyfamad, the Stone of the Covenant, at which the Herald Bard stands, and behind this are the Meini'r Porth, the portal stones, guarded by purple-robed officers. The portal stone on the right of the entrance points to the midsummer sunrise, and that on the left to the midwinter one. The shadows thrown by these three eastern megaliths make up Iolo's 'mystic sign' representing the name of the creator deity. The ceremony opens with a fanfare of trumpets from the Maen Llog, followed by Iolo's prayer. The Archdruid, wearing a mother-of-pearl robe with the bronze and gold regalia of his office, then ascends the Maen Llog and lays his hand on the partially drawn Grand Sword, calling 'A Oes Heddwch?', 'Is There Peace?' This he does three times, sheathing the sword each time the reply 'Heddwch!', 'Peace!', is echoed by the surrounding Gorsedd members and crowd.[20] The Archdruid then receives from a lady the Hirlas Horn filled with drink to symbolize the welcome to the Eisteddfod from the locality in which it is held. He is also handed Y Flodeuged, a sheaf of wild flowers presented by a younger woman representing the youth of Wales, attended by a group of small girls who then perform a floral dance within the circle. Both women wear long cloaks of vermilion trimmed with gold over white silk gowns, and flowing head-dresses of gold lamé. The dancers wear short green tunics with chaplets and garlands of wild flowers. Around stand the Bards in blue, Ovates in green, Druids in white, Eisteddfod officials in purple, and trumpeters and banner-bearers in crimson. If Iolo could come back from the dead for a short while to witness this, he would probably have jibbed at the pomp, and wondered what the children were doing. Overall, however, it is almost certain that he would have been thrilled to see that his creation had endured so well and was still being enacted with such enthusiasm before so many people.

The Gorsedd rites have served, more than any other factor, to retain and reinforce a sense of special connection between the modern Welsh people and Druidry. This is the more striking in that, historically, the Welsh were the last British people to begin to take an interest in Druids, an interest that can largely be attributed to the wayward genius of Iolo Morganwg.

* * *

After the Gorsedd, the most significant sort of institution which had been inspired by the Georgian love affair with Druids was the club or society, and this continued to flourish all through the late nineteenth and early twentieth centuries. The oldest of all, the Ancient Order of Druids, repaired the losses sustained in the secession of the Order of Druids in 1858, founding new lodges across Britain and (in the 1860s) a string across Australia. The Order of Druids grew alongside its parent, expanding into south-eastern England and Scotland even though its heartland remained in the northern and central English industrial areas. By 1871, it had 55,151 members in 955 lodges, and by 1927 the total membership had risen to 160,000.[21] This was despite losing its lodges around Sheffield, which formed an order of Equalized Independent Druids in 1892.[22] The previous breakaway group from the Ancient Order, the United Ancient Order, also grew in numbers, and repeated the experience of its parent by suffering secessions in turn. Before the end of the nineteenth century, some of its northern lodges departed to found new Druidical friendly societies based in Sheffield and Manchester. It had become the first order bearing the name of Druid to make serious inroads into the population of the south Welsh coalfield and ironworking area; but most of its lodges there rebelled, to created a third successor society.[23] Alongside this family of organizations, completely new Druidical bodies of men or women continued to be founded until the end of the Victorian era: the 1870s alone produced another Loyal Order of Druids, a Loyal Order of Modern Druids and a United Order of Modern Druids.[24]

In a sense, such organizations had already survived one challenge to the premise on which they were based, because they had spread with undiminished momentum during the period in which English public opinion in general became hostile to Druids. With the coming of the new prehistory, in which Druids were declared to be marginal and uninteresting, the Druidic societies preserved their position by the adoption of a number of strategies. One was to reorganize. In 1888 the Ancient Order finally dealt with the continuing accusations made against it of excessive central control and elitism, by removing all vestiges of government by the original lodge in London. It transferred overall leadership to a national board of management composed of former leaders of lodges, which met at a London hotel.[25] The former Grand Lodge closed down altogether for twenty years, which dramatically confirmed the devolution of power. In its place provincial lodges became the dynamic parts of the order, and one of the most successful was the Albion, based at Oxford. It secured as its patron a prominent aristocrat, the Duke of Marlborough. This gave it an especially notable publicity coup on 10 August 1908, when it held a ceremony under a group of oaks in the park of the Duke's seat at Blenheim, in which it initiated his relative, the future Prime Minister Winston Churchill, who had already made his mark as a soldier, author and politician.[26] The United Ancient Order modernized in a different fashion, by turning itself into more of a family organization. In 1876 it founded a parallel order, composed entirely of women, and in 1910 it established branches of its own body for women and for the children of members. The female branch operated exactly like the male order, save for additional admonitions, in the speeches made to new members, on the importance of motherhood in producing new Druids. The children were equipped with simple ceremonies and with lectures on the ancient Druids as exemplars of noble conduct.[27] The newer orders were both rigorously democratic and added extra benefits to those given by the old: in 1898 the Sheffield Equalized Independent Druids' Friendly Society was governed by a council composed of a delegate from every lodge, and paid money to help members travel to find work, as well as for sickness, disablement and burial.[28]

An extension of reorganization, on a much wider scale, was for orders to co-operate with each other. This process was initiated from abroad, and was one result of the expansion of both the Ancient and the United Ancient Order into America during the nineteenth century. The American divisions of both orders inherited none of the residual bitterness lingering from the great schism of 1833, and had good relations with each other. In 1858 the Grand Secretary of the American United Ancient Order proposed to the parent bodies of both organizations in Britain that they reunite in a federal structure (similar, in fact, to that of the United States themselves). The Ancient Order and United Ancient Order attempted to oblige twice during the late nineteenth century, but could not agree on a means. Again, foreign intervention was needed to achieve this. Among the American members of the orders had been a number of Germans, who had subsequently returned to Germany and founded Druid societies of their own there, in imitation of those that they had found in the New World. From Germany, these spread out to Denmark, Sweden and Switzerland. As the twentieth century opened, and tension grew between the European Great Powers, some of the German Druids decided to foster international links between modern Druids, as a practical gesture in support of the brotherhood of humanity that their orders preached. They were led by Herr Fricke, the recognized spokesman of all the German Druid groups, who approached his American counterparts with a proposal for a common association. The Americans set up a meeting of British and German representatives of the United Ancient Order at Hull in 1906, and joined them for a further one at Munich in 1908. In 1913 all three groups met again in London, and this time they were joined by delegates from the Ancient Order and from the Manchester society that had seceded from the United Ancient Order. With them were Australian and New Zealand Druids, and the combined assembly founded an International Grand Lodge of Druidism.[29]

In the following year, of course, world war broke the connections that had just been formed; but they were remade after it ended. The Grand Lodge ruled that members of the orders represented in it were permitted to visit each other's lodges and attend major events organized by them. Once more the Germans proved to be especially enthusiastic about such contact. The president of the Grand Lodge in the early 1930s was a Hamburg schoolmaster called Hugo Wiese, Noble Grand Arch of the German Order of Druids, who was prominent at British events.[30] He and his supporters published the first guide to the world's Druid orders in 1931.[31] Unhappily, they were now not only the most conspicuous Druids in the world, but the most vulnerable. In 1933 they issued a formal declaration of support for the newly installed Nazi government when it took power, as a bulwark against Communism.[32] This gesture, which reads as passionately sincere, was both mistaken and futile. Hitler's regime subsequently set to work to stamp out German Druidry, in common with other closed societies which might, possibly, become centres of independent thinking. Poor Wiese was arrested, and died of the treatment that he received in custody. None the less, the greater co-operation among Druids that he and his compatriots had pioneered survived in the English-speaking world.[33]

Another survival strategy was to glamorize ceremonies further. By the end of the nineteenth century, the older orders were investing still more heavily in costumes and props. In the Ancient Order, robes had become general for members, as had bushy white false beards for ceremonies. There was a flurry of alarm in 1911 when it was suspected that borrowed beards might harbour tuberculosis germs, but this was soon allayed.[34] By the 1920s, the most important officers of the order sported crimson hoods on their white robes.[35] Costume in the United Ancient Order of Druids seems to have developed in parallel, so that by 1906 members were expected to attend rites wearing special robes and collars and carrying staves, while the presiding officer was prescribed a long sky-blue hooded robe, with a string of glass beads and a long beard.[36] The initiation ceremony used by the order from the 1890s to the 1920s began with the candidate being brought to the door of the lodge and declared to have been proposed, seconded and accepted for membership. He was then admitted and led to the chair in which the Archdruid of the lodge sat. The brethren performed a song commencing 'Hark! Hark! Stranger's footsteps our lodge are approaching . . .' The Archdruid then informed him that philanthropy was 'the basis and bond of Druidism', and that the secret signs and symbols by which members could be recognized were designed to prevent abuse of it. The candidate had to declare that he would protect those secrets and conform to the order's rules, and never degrade or injure it. Another chorus ensued, commencing 'See the flames arise . . .' The Archdruid then told him that the ancient Druids had been the most enlightened people of their time, and held to a purer worship than any other. The new Druid was now taught the permanent sign, countersign, handshake and token of the order, its rules, and its password which was changed every three months. He also received a diploma of acceptance, and his new brothers sang a final number, starting 'Brother, you're welcome here . . .'[37] Such rites would presumably have had a strong impact on new members, making them feel that they were now part of an order of considerable importance and antiquity.

Another strategy was to put fraternal Druidry still more prominently in the public eye, and the most dramatic example of this was the colonization, by some Druids, of Stonehenge. At the start of the twentieth century, the monument had been enclosed at last by a fence, with admission through a gate staffed by a custodian, on payment of a fee. This was the work of the current owner of the land on which it stood, Sir Edmund Antrobus, and was initially controversial as some people argued that what was effectively a site of national importance, traditionally open to all, should not be turned into a source of private profit. Antrobus's main defence, of course, was the straightforward one of legal possession, but his action in enclosing the stones had been propelled by developments in public access to the area. Improvements in roads, and in the technology of transport, were making the stones much easier to reach, and so the number of visitors was rapidly growing. This in turn raised issues about the safety of the structure, especially after one of its megaliths blew over in a gale as the century began. The permanent restriction of access was therefore represented both as a means of preserving Stonehenge against further collapse, and of raising funds to do so. It also, however, made possible, for the first time, the formal booking of it, through the owner, as a space for private events.

The first Druid group to do this was the Ancient Order, which took it over for a day in August 1905 for a mass initiation ceremony. In all, 259 new members were initiated, one of them being Antrobus himself and others being the mayors of Ipswich and West Ham. Antrobus would certainly have been impressed by the sheer size of the turnout, seven hundred of the order appearing, and (perhaps) even more by the illustrious nature of some of the members. The Dukes of Marlborough and Leeds were both present, as was the Earl of Warwick. Members who did not possess their own false beards were equipped by a famous costume hire firm. A marquee was pitched as a venue for a formal luncheon before the ceremony, with a brass band providing music. Carts brought in 'tremendous piles' of food. 'Hundreds and hundreds' of spectators arrived for the event, and, although they were confined behind the fence during the rites, they were admitted to the monument without the usual payment once these were concluded. Those initiated were brought in blindfolded to the stones, and then returned to sight when they had taken the oath of loyalty to the order (*en masse*) and spoken the password, 'Light'. They saw (in the words of a London journalist who had sneaked among them) the presiding Archdruid, in robes and beard 'the very image of Father Christmas', standing before an altar on which a blue fire – produced by methylated spirits and saltpetre – burned fitfully. He held a battleaxe uplifted in his right hand, while round him stood other Archdruids with golden sickles. The Bards around sang one of their set choruses:

See, see the flames arise!
Brothers now your songs prepare!
And ere their vigour droops and dies
Our mysteries let him share!
  Let him share!
And let him know your songs divine,
And let him know the mistletoe
  And Togodubiline!
  And Togodubiline!

It had been intended to give a sprig of evergreen to each initiate, but there was not enough to go round. There followed another song with the chorus 'All round the oak', and the tale of Togodubiline was told. A further ceremony concluded the rites, the Archdruid standing on a beer crate to conduct it, and everybody could retire to the marquee once more to disrobe (and remove beards), and enjoy tea, 'including four kinds of the best cake'.[38]

The event was covered in local and national newspapers, but not usually with respect, especially in the latter. One London paper called the Druids there 'as many figures of fun as have probably ever been seen together in any gathering of humanity'.[39] The journalist who sneaked into the ceremony noted mixed reactions to the Druids among the general public. The citizens of Salisbury, where many of them stayed on the night before the gathering, apparently looked on them with 'intense suspicion', and imagined them as 'unholy'. The huge crowd of onlookers at Stonehenge cheered and laughed throughout the proceedings. No such reactions were recorded to the parades by Druid orders through towns and cities in the early nineteenth century, or to their visits to Stanton Drew. It is possible that the heavier investment in distinctive costumes, by the end of the century, made the Druids seem more alien to the populace; or it may be that in the earlier cases they were active within a local community to which they belonged, or were contributing to it financially and as a spectacle. In 1905 the Ancient Order seemed more to be invading a district and taking it over, and this also drew the attention of a national press which was more inclined to be ribald. It is just possible, however, that more of a gulf had opened between the Druids and society in general.

Four years later, the Royal Gloucester Lodge of the same order returned quietly to Stonehenge, for two initiations. There was now a hiatus in visits, caused by the war, and then in 1925 the Ancient Order returned, three hundred strong, having chartered a special train to bring half of them from London. In 1931 it was time for the United Ancient Order to appear, with a grand event to celebrate the centenary of the rebellion which had led to its foundation. It arrived with members from Germany, Norway and New Zealand and guests from other Druid orders, at home and abroad: Hugo Wiese was especially prominent among the latter, and spoke in honour of England (rather than Britain) as the birthplace of ancient Druidry. The focus of the rites was the installation of another president and vice-president, for the whole order.[40] After this, until the end of the 1930s, individual lodges or provincial lodges of both the Ancient Order and the United Ancient Order held ceremonies at the monument at some point every year. These gatherings were suspended during the Second World War, but resumed as soon as it ended.[41]

The meetings at Stonehenge after the First World War were no longer arranged with Antrobus but with the national body, the Office of Works, into whose custody the monument had passed. They were agreed and staged with equal ease. In many ways these fraternal bodies were a custodian's dream. They applied for permission to hold their ceremonies well in advance, expressed public gratitude to the Office for it, avoided times of maximum visitor pressure on the site, and paid entrance fees, which – for a large meeting – could amount to a substantial sum. Their proceedings were dignified occasions, which onlookers from the general public might enjoy (from outside the fence). They contained nothing likely to offend even conservative observers. Well-known Christian hymns were sung, such as 'O God, Our Help in Ages Past' and 'All People That On Earth Do Dwell', and prayers were offered. Speeches were made that extolled charity, fraternity and patriotism. The biggest were covered by newspapers, and treatment of them grew more rather than less supportive with time. In 1925 a local newspaper, the *Salisbury Journal*, printed the whole of the Ancient Order's version of the National Anthem:

Hail! Mystic Light Divine,
May'st Thou ne'er cease to shine
Over this land.
Wisdom in thee we find
Beauty and strength combined
Druids are ever joined
In heart and hand.
Come then, ye sons of light,
In joyous strain unite,
God save the King!
Long may Our Monarch reign,
King of the azure main:
Druids respond the strain,
God save the King![42]

As has been noted,[43] it was a great, and potentially uncomfortable, irony that modern Druids had arrived at Stonehenge just as archaeologists were evicting the ancient Druids from it. None the less, the actual impact of the new prehistory on the modern orders was reduced and refracted in various ways. Those orders which had developed private mythologies that were completely out of touch with real fact continued to repeat them. Presumably some members did so with tongue firmly in cheek, while others did so ingenuously. The Ancient Order (as illustrated at Stonehenge) preserved its completely imaginary founder, Togodubiline, telling initiates now that he was the son of a British bard, Tacitus Magallas, who had been killed on Anglesey when the Romans took the island, and a Druidess called Sensitoria Roxiana. In a neat Druidic parallel to the story of Moses, he was found as a baby by fleeing Druids, having been abandoned beneath an oak tree, and brought up by them. He went on to become a famous philosopher and scientist, and among his more convivial discoveries was the secret of brewing beer(!)[44]

Some members of the modern orders felt the need to keep abreast of new scholarly thought as well, and by 1907 some of the Ancient Order, in particular, knew that the ancient Druids were no longer credited with raising megaliths. They got round this problem in a number of ways. One was to suggest, cleverly and credibly, that Druids might have used monuments that had been raised long before, and that they could have retained ideas and practices from the original megalithic religion.[45] At the huge gathering at Stonehenge in 1925, the Imperial Grand Archdruid of the Ancient Order informed members that it was not known for certain when the stones had been erected or whether ancient Druids had ever worshipped there, but that it was likely that they had.[46] Another tactic – especially important in the ceremonies – was to draw on those classical sources that emphasized the wisdom and benevolence of Druidry. In interpreting these, they continued to call on three centuries of tradition – not itself objectively disproved – which had portrayed it as a religion that taught reverence for a single good deity, the immortality of the soul, a reward or punishment after death for behaviour during life, and the importance of justice, benevolence and learning as exemplars of human behaviour.[47] Yet another compensatory tactic was to bring in ideas from the writings of Iolo Morganwg, to take the place of those from Genesis and eighteenth-century notions of ancient Britain. Both the Ancient and the United Ancient Order had done this by the 1920s.[48] It was, of course, another spectacular mistiming, as this was the very point at which Iolo was conclusively exposed as a forger. None the less, Iolo's key writings were all in English, while those that exposed him were all in Welsh, so the impact of the latter on the rest of Britain was both delayed and muted. By 1932, it is true, one of the most erudite of the Ancient Order had got wind of them. This was Wilhelm North, an impressive historian of the Ancient Order itself, who published two articles on the ancient Druids in a London newspaper. He declared that the theories of authors like Stukeley had been 'a pure fairy tale', that Iolo's triads had been revealed as bogus, that medieval Welsh literature was too late and too Christian to be relevant, and that the ancient texts were unreliable and hard to understand. His basic message was that orders like his own had by then justified their existence in their own right.[49]

All this said, another reaction of members of the Victorian Druid societies to changing scholarship was simply to ignore or reject it, and this was more common than the subtle and informed responses summarized above. It was also more official. In 1909 one of the United Ancient Order published a pamphlet for the instruction of his colleagues and of other Druid groups. He declared resoundingly that there was still no reason to doubt that Druids had built Stonehenge and all other megalithic monuments, and had done so according to tenets learned from the Old Testament patriarchs. He added, for good measure, that his order was the oldest friendly society existing in Britain, and had been at its zenith at the time when the Romans arrived.[50] Between the 1900s and the 1920s, the order's official instructions for its highest officers, issued by the national board of directors, repeated the traditional belief that Druids had been monotheists, practising a wise and benevolent religion. The instructions then claimed that they had met in a *gorsedd* of the modern Welsh kind, and believed in moral tenets expressed in the triads composed by Iolo. Furthermore, they called the ancient British hero Caractacus, who had resisted the Romans, a leader of the order, and made a medallion portraying him the token by which members could be recognized.[51] During the 1930s, the initiation ceremony of the Order of Druids declared that its founder had been Noah, and repeated the sixteenth-century myth that Druidry had been brought to Europe by his son Japhet. In 1936 one member published a history of the order which contained the same assertions.[52]

From the 1900s to the 1930s, articles in the official journal of the Ancient Order, which recognized that archaeologists no longer associated Druids with megaliths, were interspersed with others dogmatically restating the connection.[53] In the period between the world wars, the basic initiation ceremony used by the order informed all initiates that it was older than the Persian magi, the priesthood of Babylon and the Brahmins of India.[54] At some point near the end of the 1920s, one of the order's lodges decided to publish an information pack on the history of Druidry, which had been compiled by one of its members in the early years of the decade for the further instruction of the newly initiated. It propounded as fact a lush pseudo-history, mixing together Noah, Japhet and the universal patriarchal religion, Iolo's mythology, a Druido-Christian native British Church, Stonehenge and megaliths, Pythagoras, Borlase's Druidesses, and much more, with a seasoning of what seems to be pure original fantasy. As part of this, it claimed the descent of the Ancient Order in unbroken succession from a secret society founded to preserve Druidry from persecution by the medieval Catholic Church. These teachings were subsequently adopted by the whole order as educational texts; most worrying, for a historian, is that they were still being issued to newcomers in the 1990s.[55]

The later twentieth century proved to be a difficult period for fraternal and sororal Druidry of the sort that had fared so well all through the nineteenth. In the 1950s it disappeared altogether from Stonehenge, in circumstances which will be discussed later. With this, it largely vanished from the public gaze altogether, and so from that of the historian. The welfare state removed most of the need for traditional friendly societies, and the conviviality of lodge nights must have waned as competing forms of entertainment multiplied, that could involve entire families. The changing British economy spelled doom for the manufacturing industries, and the communities that depended on them, on which the orders had heavily drawn. In a sense, their integration with Victorian Britain had been too complete, and when the framework of that Britain finally collapsed in the mid-twentieth century, they were caught up in its ruin. None the less, the role of the independent insurance society reappeared near the end of the century, with the decline in value of national pensions and health services. Furthermore, in a world of increasingly rapid change, social institutions with a proven antiquity, if only above a hundred years, could provide reassuring symbols of stability and survival. It seemed possible by the 1990s that the old-style modern Druid orders might have a new lease of popularity.

The actual results have been mixed. The United Ancient Order, ironically, was destroyed by what might otherwise have been an asset: its identity as a friendly society. In the last decade of the twentieth century, new government regulations were adopted for such bodies, to which the order could not adapt. It dissolved a few years before the century ended. The splinter of the Order of Druids in Sheffield, however, succeeded in making the transition and survives as the Independent Druids' Friendly Society. Meanwhile, the oldest of all, that founded by Henry Hurle and his friends in 1781, continues to function with every sign of success, opening lodges to visits from the general public and co-operating in national meetings with other kinds of modern Druid. It may, indeed, become an Ancient Order, in the true sense of the words.

* * *

Meanwhile, traditional literary images of Druids endured different fortunes in the decades on either side of 1900. New portraits of Druids as patriotic heroes virtually disappeared as the Welsh appropriated them, the Scots disowned them and a sense of peculiarly Anglo-Saxon identity eroded the English sense of connection to ancient Britain. The stress must be on the word 'new', as older works that celebrated them as patriots, and in particular the poem by William Cowper, continued to circulate. None the less, the contrast between the heavy use of Druids as heroic ancestors in England and Scotland between 1750 and 1850, and the almost complete lack of it during the late Victorian period, remains striking. In 1861, Bellini's opera *Norma* finally vanished from the regular repertoire of the Royal Opera House,[56] and eight years later its heroic nationalism was sent up in a comic parody. This was *The Pretty Druidess*, an early work of William Schwenck Gilbert, who was to go on to become one of the definitive figures of late nineteenth-century England, as half of the partnership of Gilbert and Sullivan. In his reworking, the contribution of Norma and her fellow priestesses to the overthrow of Rome consists of making clothes to be sold at a fête to raise funds for the resistance movement, and of attempting to convert the invaders to their own faith. They are, in short, perfect reflections of pious and philanthropic Victorian ladies. Nobody dies at the climax, because it turns out that every single Druidess has taken a Roman boyfriend as Norma has done, making the traditional prohibition on doing so unworkable. The Druids are a mockery of greedy and pompous Anglican clergy, most of them concerned with the details of their ritual garb, with passing on to their curates as many duties as possible, and with a love of good dinners. Their chief opens a ceremony with the solemn invocation:

Now lo the mystic sucking-pig draw near,
Uncork the sacerdotal ginger beer!
Incomprehensible rice pudding try!
Attack the sacrificial rump-steak pie![57]

Another resolutely unheroic, and self-indulgent, Druid chief – probably inspired by Gilbert's – is found in a pantomime produced in 1891 and set on the Isles of Scilly. The sage concerned informs some invading Vikings (the action gloriously telescopes history) that he achieves visions by consuming enough plum pudding. He is also anxious to tout for custom:

Magic or spells, I hope that here you'll buy them;
And on the cheapest terms I will supply them.
To send by train or parcel post I'm happy,
So please address, Arch Druid, Tresco Abbey.[58]

Things seemed to change during the further upsurge of patriotic fervour and anxiety during the Boer War, with the appearance of two resounding employments of Druidry in the loyal cause. Both, however, turn out to be the products of the continuing Welsh enthusiasm for it. One was *Britain's Greatness Foretold*, by Marie Trevelyan, a novel about Boudica's rebellion which openly equated its heroine with Queen Victoria. It built upon Cowper's long-famous ode, which it treated as an authentic historical document rather than a Georgian fantasy. The author opened the book with a vehement affirmation of faith: 'In wonder I studied the ancient Druidic creed, so pre-eminently patriotic that it was systematically misrepresented and marked out for extirpation by the Roman government. I observed that the spirit it infused into the Britons under their able and intrepid commanders, contributed to render the slow progress of Roman arms in Britain a solitary exception to the rapidity of their conquests in other parts of the world.' Trevelyan portrayed their creed as so compatible with Christianity that the first British Christians also rallied to Boudica's banner, against the common pagan enemy represented by Rome. Appropriately for a female novelist (and in the wake of *Norma*), Druidesses were prominent characters in the story, making their bases in caves or towers and turning up at Boudica's court to lead graceful maidens in singing choruses. On the whole, its concept of Druidry was taken from Iolo Morganwg, seasoned with the work of Morien; again, the Welsh influence was vital, and, indeed, Marie Trevelyan was an author particularly associated with Wales. Trevelyan's Druids still, shamelessly, use megalithic monuments as their temples, and, on the defeat of Boudica, all turn Christian to continue the resistance to Rome in a spiritual form.[59]

Four years later, a 'Welsh opera' appeared, entitled *Eos and Gwevril* and featuring Druids who combined full-blooded patriotism with belief in a happy life after death. Classical authors had remarked that such a belief gave the peoples of Gaul courage in risking death in battle, and the librettist of the opera, one Thomas Vincent, rather cleverly combined this with the Eastern doctrine of reincarnation. Iolo himself had, after all, done this a century before, and the concept had become much more generally familiar by Vincent's time with the spread of Buddhist and Hindu ideas to Britain from its Indian possessions. Touchingly, some of the spirits of those who had given their lives for their country were represented as having been reborn as trees growing from it; so, of course, gaining a much longer life – of a sort – in exchange for that which they had sacrificed.[60]

The opera went on to have its Druids prophesy the fall of Rome and the eventual greatness of Britain, in the manner of so many since Cowper's did; but they were the very last to do so. A decade later, the carnage of the First World War had begun, and it was to make such nationalist bombast unfashionable in mainstream British culture. When the Second World War came, and enemy legions massed again in earnest against the shore of Britain, various heroes were recalled from the British past to help rally resistance. There were, however, no Druids among them; they had finally passed out of the general British consciousness as symbols of patriotism.

The fate of Druids as exemplars of an informed and caring relationship with the natural world was rather different. During the first two-thirds of the nineteenth century this theme, like that of patriotic Druidry, had retained a regular, if minor, presence in English letters. In the following sixty years it sustained this role. In some respects the relatively slight use of Druids as priests of nature was more marked in those later decades, because the English idealization of, and passion for, the rural world became ever more intense as a reaction to increasing urbanization and industrialization. The main ancient figures to whom late Victorian and Edwardian writers turned as symbols, however, were drawn from classical mythology and consisted above all of the god Pan and the nymphs and other attendant spirits of trees and waters. These were characters from a familiar and beloved literature, with none of the ambivalence, confusion and controversy that had always adhered to the Druids. It was a commonplace in Victorian verse to associate oak trees with Druidry, but the Druids themselves were always offstage in these similes and metaphors: they were simply a way of saying that the trees concerned were extremely old, and represented living connections to previous ages and so an organic link between a rapidly changing present and a rapidly disappearing past. This general context of neglect makes even more significant the few specific references to Druids as nature-worshippers that did appear.

In 1880 a scientist, John Eliot Howard, addressed the Philosophical Society of Great Britain on the manner in which – in his reading – Druidry had taught the presence of a divinity within the entire natural world: the doctrine to which John Toland had given its modern name of pantheism. Howard still believed that they had been the builders of stone circles, which he considered to have been temples of nature, made of unworked stones, open to the sky and innocent of any idols or other images that would have attempted to reduce the powers of the cosmos to a visible and solid form. Howard much applauded this, affirming that 'Pantheism in its refined form seems to me to be the highest effort of the natural mind in religion.' Once again, his impression of what Druids believed was drawn ultimately from Iolo, and he himself was left uncertain how much he should admire them. At one point he emphasized that their creed was inferior to Christianity in its view of the afterlife: 'Pantheism may seem attractive in the hour of prosperity, but it has no remedial feature for the hour of adversity, no consolation against the darkness of the grave.' At another, he gave full credit to them for an appreciation of the beauties of nature which he passionately shared and found lacking in formal Christian worship: 'I must confess that for myself I so far share their prejudices that I should prefer the breezy air of the Wiltshire downs to the atmosphere of Westminster Abbey'. In the end he came down on the side of Christianity, holding that pantheism had more potential to be corrupted into idolatry, as people too easily redirected their worship to natural phenomena themselves from the divinity that (in Howard's opinion) inspired and produced them.[61]

As before, the view of Druidry as nature-religion was expressed far more often in poetry. Some authors of this shared the ambivalence of Howard. One of the few Scots of the time who still retained an affection for Druids, Evan McColl, acknowledged that Christianity was the truer religion, but still gave the old priests credit for some truth, in their love of natural beauty. On an island traditionally associated with them in Loch Awe, that long and lonely stretch of water amid the mountains of Argyll, he reflected that

By nature sole instructed, here of yore
The Druid taught his votaries to see
In day's bright orb the great creative power
To which he oft, adoring, bent the knee
Beneath the branches of some old oak tree
Towering above yon circle of grey stones:
Grateful to God that better light have we,
Let us tread reverent o'er the Druid's bones,

And own, whate'er his faults, he reasoned well
In choosing in this paradise to dwell.[62]

Other poets of nature were much less temperate in their admiration for Druidry. In 1869 one of the many minor writers who sprinkled the period with verses, Robert Leighton, paid several tributes to Druids, as people who had loved the woods of Britain as much as he. This gave him an affection both for the megaliths with which, at that date, they were still commonly associated, and for the religion which they practised, as part of a timeless recognition of divinity in the world of nature. He visited Orkney, and the tall remaining stones of the circle at Stenness in the centre of the island, and affirmed his sense of unity with its builders:

O Druid! We are one; I feel thy thoughts
Now climbing up to God. The *form* of thought
Goes with the age – the thought is for all time
As stones, grass, sun the same.[63]

In the 1880s others of his kind echoed these feelings. Henry Sutton also found something genuinely holy about a massive natural boulder, which he unhesitatingly believed must have been sacred to Druids, and felt that they had a religion in common:

Well might the Druid old bow down with awe,
And deem thee, when thy uncouth form he saw,
An altar cut by Nature's hand in stone,
That her God might be worshipped thereupon
More largely and in more majestic ways
Than on those lesser ones which mortals raise . . .
And though thou who wast, ages gone,
An awful altar, now art but a stone,
Yet let my song to God our Maker be
As solemn fire to rise once more with thee.[64]

The following year, Harwicke Rawnsley published a collection of sonnets, some of which commemorated a visit to Cumbria, and places that had been familiar to Wordsworth. In one of these, along the coastline, he found a prehistoric standing stone which, like his fellows poets, he immediately attributed to Druids. Like them, he thought it a monument to a still enduring natural religion:

If Seascale's copse and oaks of Drigg have waned
And pearls no longer at thy feet are laid,
From Esk to Duddon by the votary brought;
Still to thy stone of help is reverence chained,
With sense of lonely watching, and the thought
Of silent faith – here vows anew are made.[65]

If the usage was not accidental, there was quite a clever, and significant, sleight of language here, because Victorian writers more commonly held that it was sacrificial victims, not reverence, that should be considered to be 'chained' to Druid stones, and that they were monuments of slaughter, and not of 'help'. In 1897 John Tabb published a passionate little tribute to a Druid as a person who enjoyed a unique understanding of, and sense of identity with, the natural cycle of things:

> He alone
> The sunshine and the shadow and the dew
> Had shared alike with leaf, and flower and stem.
> Their life had been his lesson; and from them
> A dream of immortality he drew
> As in their fate foreshadowing his own.[66]

What this chain of texts expressed between them, with mounting intensity, was something that had featured in some earlier British poetry but appeared here with a new directness: a personal sense of reverence for the presumed works and beliefs of the Druids and an impulse to identify with them and embrace them. This sense was now stripped of any of the earlier linkage of Druidry with Hebrew religion or Neoplatonist philosophy which had helped to give it respectability in earlier works. These imagined Druidic beliefs were valued on their own terms, as something natural and organic. Such a valuation accompanies, and outweighs, the more obvious import of their verses: that the authors were either unaware of, or indifferent to, the developments in scholarship that had officially stripped the stones of which they wrote of Druidical associations. They represent a bridge between the early Romantic portrayal of Druids as nature-priests and the late twentieth-century appearance of Druidry as an actual religion of nature.

The First World War destroyed much of the British taste for sentimental nature poetry, but an admiration for Druids as pagan priests connected with the natural world persisted, in a more raw and full-blooded form. One illustration of this came in Rutland Boughton's opera *The Immortal Hour*, first staged at Glastonbury in 1920. The story was based on one composed, taking themes from medieval Irish mythology, by the Scottish author William Sharp. Sharp had written both in his own name and, with far more success, under the assumed one of a Hebridean woman, Fiona Macleod. In the latter guise, he was perhaps the most influential writer to mirror Scottish culture at the end of the nineteenth century, as Sir Walter Scott had been in its early decades. As such, he showed all the dislike of Druids that most of his compatriots had manifested since Scott's time. Writing as himself, he reviled them as heathens and savages, at one point portraying them as crucifying Christian missionaries.[67] Writing as Fiona, he pointedly ignored them, even when, as in the case of the early Irish setting of *The Immortal Hour*, the context seemed to cry out for them. This makes it all the more significant that Boughton put them quite lavishly into the opera he made of Sharp's play. In particular, they appeared in procession and singing a liturgy. No longer did they call upon the Old Testament god of authors anxious to show that they had practised the religion of the Hebrew patriarchs, or even on the pantheist, non-denominational deity of other Victorian authors. Instead they addressed their prayers to the pagan deities of ancient Ireland, led by 'sky-set Lu who leads the host of stars', and to the elemental powers of nature. One sung blessing has a ring of genuine invocatory power. It is actually the work of William Sharp, writing as Fiona Macleod,[68] but whereas he intended it to be a freestanding verse, Boughton put it into the mouths of his assembled Druids, and so made it part of their liturgy:

> By the voice in the corries where the Pole-Star danceth,
> By the voice on the summits the dead feet know,
> By the soft, wet cry where the Heat-Star troubleth,
> By the plaining and moaning of the sigh of rainbows.
> By the four white winds of the world
> Whose father the golden sun is,
> Whose mother the wheeling moon is,
> The North and the South and the East and the West,
> By the four good winds of the world
> That man knoweth, that One dreadeth, that Lu blesseth,
> Be all well on mountain, moor and lea,
> On loch face and lochlan and river,
> On shore and shallow and sea.[69]

It cannot be coincidental that Boughton himself was a notable social and political radical who flouted the norms of his time in various different ways, including by rejecting Christianity. His followers attracted a similar reputation: at the time when his *Immortal Hour* was first staged, it was rumoured in Glastonbury that the young actresses and actors who performed in it (themselves mostly Londoners) had the habit of running up the Tor, the hill that dominates the town, 'to greet the dawn in a state of pagan undress'.[70]

A juvenile parallel to the opera was provided in 1939 by a Welsh author, Alvin Langdon Coburn, in the shape of a play designed for children and called *Fairy Gold*. Its hero is a wise Archdruid, served by the spirits of the four elements, who is pitted against an evil witch. He is, very clearly, a priest of nature, declaring that 'All the world is my concern. The world and its loveliness is my deep concern. The beauty of the dawn and the stars at eventide. The silver shimmer of the waves, the rustle of the wind in autumn leaves, the smell of the new rich earth turned by the plough, fire's warmth in winter's cold: all these are my delight. Yet beyond these there is a deeper, richer joy, as when the soul sweeps upward on its flight to its true home.' His ultimate allegiance is to 'God', whom he hails with the prayer composed by Iolo and used to open the Welsh Gorsedd. His human allies are the white-robed priestesses of Ceridwen, a goddess represented in 'Celtic' Davies's terms as the great deity of the natural world, who manifests herself in the play at a prehistoric dolmen. She speaks of the 'love of God', and wishes the gifts of justice, love and inspiration to girls initiated into her mysteries. The play promises the coming of a golden age in which humans can reclaim the ancient Druidic wisdom. It ends, of course, with victory over the witch, but she is not destroyed; instead she undergoes a change of heart and herself becomes a priestess of Ceridwen.[71] In place of Boughton's full-bodied polytheist paganism, what is suggested here is a theology which had surfaced at times in Christian tradition ever since antiquity, whereby the one true god had appointed a female subordinate to look after the affairs of the world, and especially of the natural world. It is still notable that, despite the reassuring references to a good and ultimately powerful 'God', Ceridwen effectively displaces Christ.

The same decade brought forth a novel from a passionate Scottish nationalist, Neil Gunn. It was set in an early medieval Scotland in which the old religion of Druidry still lingered alongside Christianity, and was indeed reviving in the face of the new menace from the Vikings. Gunn followed the traditional line that it had been a dark faith, of blood sacrifice, and yet he still came out thinking it superior to that of Christ. This was because it was more fully native to, and integrated with, the land, and bound up with the lives of the human inhabitants: 'it ran with their blood as it had run with the blood of their ancestors'. Furthermore, it sanctioned natural human pleasures, and sexual pleasure in particular, in a way that Christianity did not. The implication of the book was that Druidry had been a more generous religion, which answered more to human needs, and that this perhaps made a bit of bloodshed worth while.[72]

The image of Druids as nature-priests therefore underwent some development between the middle of the nineteenth century and that of the twentieth. The holy places attributed to them – human-made as well as purely natural – were reinvested with a lingering sense of real sanctity, and their religion was recognized both as genuinely pagan and as having enduring allure. There was a new sense abroad, at scattered times and places, that the religion of the Druids had been admirable in itself, needing to be assimilated neither to the Hebrew patriarchs or Greek philosophers nor to a heightened sense of the presence of the familiar creator deity in natural things. It prepared the way for the appearance of a fully formed modern pagan Druidry at the end of the twentieth century.

* * *

Over the same period, the tradition that had related Druids to Old Testament religion and Greek philosophy remained very much alive. This is not surprising in view of what was suggested earlier about the very slow absorption by the general public of the new ideas concerning prehistory. During the last third of the nineteenth century, fresh books were published by amateur scholars which repeated the traditional views wholesale, and apparently in genuine ignorance of changing intellectual fashion.[73] A striking example of this effect persisting into the new century is provided by one of the most celebrated ritual magicians of the Victorian period, William Wynn Westcott. He was both the leader (Supreme Magus) of the Societas Rosicruciana in Anglia, the Rosicrucian Society in England, which had been established for the recovery and study of arcane wisdom, and one of the two leaders of the Hermetic Order of the Golden Dawn, designed for the study and practice of ceremonial magic. In 1908 his lecture on the meaning of the Avebury circles was published, and turned out to be based on a careful study of texts that were all at least fifty years out of date, including Stukeley (whom he termed 'definitive'), to whom were added 'Celtic' Davies, Deane and Duke.[74] Bound up with these old ideas for most of these writers, of course, was the confident attribution of megalithic monuments to Druids, which was given a longer afterlife by the fact that the increasingly popular maps published by the Ordnance Survey continued to mark stone circles as 'Druidical' until the 1920s. In 1914 an estate agent wrote a guidebook to Stonehenge which still credited it to the Druids, without any sense of controversy.[75] More startling is the description of what was clearly a Neolithic or Bronze Age timber circle, discovered outside Glasgow in 1939. A local man wrote a pamphlet appealing to have the site preserved, as it was threatened by the construction of a new highway, and characterized it as that of a 'Druid temple'. This would be less remarkable had he not been a Fellow of the Society of Antiquaries of Scotland, the nation's main association for archaeologists.[76]

Alongside those who repeated the old view in innocence were others who chose to uphold it stubbornly in the face of the new scholarly orthodoxy. In 1903 an otherwise obscure individual called Arthur Ireland wrote a booklet on Stonehenge in which he summed up the different views concerning its builders and then declared (without seeing need for further elucidation) that the 'strongest proofs' still supported the 'Druidical circle theory'.[77] Two years later a lawyer called Sebastian Evans wrote his own book on the great Wiltshire monuments, in which he declared that the mathematical precision that he claimed to find in them made a Stone or Bronze Age date for them impossible. He therefore credited them once more to the Druids, as acknowledged masters of science.[78] Those who wanted to cling to the old model received powerful support from Sir Norman Lockyer, the eminent astronomer, who proceeded to interfere in the matter of Stonehenge as he did in that of the Welsh Gorsedd. In both cases, he used his undoubted understanding of the heavens to defend traditional beliefs, and drew completely erroneous conclusions. In 1901 he argued that the skill of the Druids in astronomy (which he simply assumed) needed a long period to develop, and so they had probably existed in Britain from the time of the stone circles, after all.[79] In 1906 he published a book that identified the megalithic monuments of Britain, from their alignments on the heavens, as part of a single great sun-worshipping religion which had originated in Egypt and Babylonia and been brought to Western Europe by the Phoenicians. It had been served, throughout its range, by astronomer-priests, who evolved in Western Europe into the Druids. This was really just a secular version of the theory that the Phoenicians had brought the true religion of the Old Testament to Britain, and the two were tied together more closely when Lockyer drew attention to the megaliths mentioned in the Bible as the Hebrew manifestations of the same religion.[80] His dating was, of course, way out – the Phoenicians were two millennia younger than the megaliths – and the material finds of archaeology support none of his contentions; but to those inexpert in the subject, his great fame as a scientist lent weight to his ideas.

In addition to these works, there were others produced by people who either explicitly or apparently knew of the developments in scholarly prehistory, but chose simply to ignore these as part of a general rejection of orthodoxy. Three were particularly

popular. In 1925 E. O. Gordon produced a fantastic vision of the prehistory of
London, based on a mixture of Iolo's writings and the medieval pseudo-history of
Geoffrey of Monmouth. It peopled the streets, squares and hills of the metropolis
with Druids, finding evidence of their colleges, temples, assemblies and seats of justice
in every district.[81] The second was by a former naval officer, Lawrence Roberts, who
had taken ordination on retirement. His aim was to show that the British had been
favoured above other European nations in being prepared to receive the Gospel by
the wise and good religion of their Druids. It was based on a large number of obsolete nineteenth-century works, above all *Barddas*, though his reference to 'Robert
Stukeley' as a great authority indicates that he had not read some of them very carefully.[82] The third was by a vicar of Glastonbury, Lionel Lewis, who also drew heavily
on Iolo to argue that some of the most prominent historic features of his town, as he
still supposed the megalithic monuments of Britain to be, were the work of Druids.
These prepared the way for the establishment of a great Celtic Church, based at
Glastonbury, by St Joseph of Arimathea in the first century, which became the base
for the conversion of Western Europe.[83] No doubt the success of these works derived
from their combination of patriotism and apparent historical certainty. Like that of
Gordon, echoes of them are still found now in works of esoteric spirituality. Indeed,
occasional books continue to appear from Christian writers which restate the old
belief in a single, good, universal faith, of which Druidry was the British component
and Jesus the greatest representative, and which may be detected by hidden messages
encoded in written texts and monuments.[84]

*   *   *

A still more resilient aspect of the early nineteenth-century preoccupation with
Druids was the hostile portrait of them as priests of a barbarous and bloodthirsty religion. This was less vulnerable than the others to swings of cultural fashion. For one
thing, it seemed to be more firmly based in ancient texts. For another, it retained two
considerable uses to authors in any period: as a means of extolling one's own religious
beliefs (and thereby often of smearing those of others) and as a means of titillating
readers with images of sex and horror. This depiction remained a subject for poetry.
Some authors treated it concisely, such as the devout Scotsman, John Stuart Blackie,
praising his hero St Columba in 1890:

> For the Druids worshipped demons,
> Gods of earth and air and sky,
> Peopling land and peopling water
> With the glamour of a lie.[85]

In 1914 another overtly Christian poet, G. K. Chesterton, handled the same subject
with equal brevity and hostility, but more lightness of touch:

> The Druids waved their golden knives
> And danced around the oak
> When they had sacrificed a man;

But though the learned search and scan
No single modern person can
Entirely see the joke.[86]

Other poets were anything but concise. In 1885 one in Manchester published an
epic on the Roman conquest of his region which made a curious medley of images of
Druids as heroic patriots and barbaric heathens. They are certainly shown as brave
and devoted to preserving the freedom of their land, preferring at the end to jump
into the sea rather than submit to foreign rule. It is equally emphasized, however, that
the Romans ultimately represented the superior cause, because they were the vehicles
by which Christianity was introduced to Britain. To push the point home, the Druids
are shown as joyously sacrificing Christians as blasphemers against their own religion,
and the Archdruid is struck down by lightning – wielded, it is clearly implied, by the
true deity – as he is raising a knife to dispatch another. The poem closes with a single
bard surviving from the Druid entourage, who accepts the faith of Christ and turns
his skills to the singing of hymns.[87]

In the period between 1870 and 1914 novels were replacing poems as vehicles for
storytelling, and this was true in the treatment of Druids as of any other subject. Once
again, it was the image of them as monsters which proved most alluring to authors,
and which served various different motives. Three novels in particular point up the
changing uses of it. The first is *Eldol, the Druid*, written by William Kingston and
published in 1874. It excoriates Druids as servants of a cruel and bloodthirsty supreme
god who demands human victims and treats both inferior divinities and mortals as his
slaves. They burn people alive in wicker giants representing their idols – a scene
described in detail in the story – and terrify the rest of the population into obedience
to their every wish by teaching that those who do not oblige them will be reborn after
death in the bodies of snakes or toads. They also practise mysterious 'immoralities, too
terrible to be named . . . in the name of religion'. The Romans too are condemned as
pagans and idolaters, and the two religions are, indeed, held to be derived from the
same false and contaminating Eastern faith, that denounced by the Old Testament
prophets. None the less, both have their uses in the providential history ordained by
the true god. Druidry still has elements that are superior to Roman paganism, and so
good Druids are readily drawn to Christianity when Roman rule allows the latter to
spread to Britain. They set up a particularly pure version of the faith of Christ, which
remains in the British spirit during the long centuries of renewed idolatry imposed by
the Roman Catholic Church, and flowers again as the Protestant Reformation.[88]

The second was *The Count of the Saxon Shore*, the work of Alfred Church, a
clergyman who became the Professor of Latin in the new University of London. It
appeared in 1887. Its Romans are (at their best) dignified, civilized and, since the
story is set at the end of their rule, Christian. The Irish are 'severely bigoted' pagans,
while the Anglo-Saxons are also heathen, but inherently a much more decent lot, and
only possessed of the wrong religion because of their ignorance of the true one. No
such excuse can be accorded to the Druids, who linger in secret among an untrustworthy native population, hungering for a return to their old days of power and ritual

slaughter. Their favourite victims are young women of noble birth, and the climax of the tale is the rescue of one of these, from being killed at Stonehenge in the moonlight, by a loyal Saxon slave.[89] Similar concerns feature in Sidney Sedgwick's *A Daughter of the Druids*, from 1904. Once more the setting is late Roman rule, with the devilish priests still surviving in hiding. For a secretive and persecuted sect, Sedgwick's Druids invest heavily in costume and equipment, wearing white robes with 'curious' embroidered or painted designs, and wreaths of oak leaves in their hair. They carry 'ugly' curved daggers in girdles around their waists (to make sacrifices) and worship in timber round-houses. Their vital piece of ritual technology is a square bronze altar, seven feet long on each side, wrought with figures of deities. It has rings to which to bind victims, and a channel down the centre to allow blood to run away, and is always encrusted with gore from the victims and ash from sacrificial fires. This is, however, only for routine religious observances. Major festivals require the slow roasting alive of a mass of victims of both sexes, in a wicker figure of a woman hung over a fire at the full moon. The deities to whom these offerings are made are remarkably eclectic, being drawn from cultures across ancient Europe and the Near East: 'Wodin', Thor and Astarte, 'goddess of night'. Again a maiden is at the centre of the action, but this time as the daughter of the Archdruid, and a priestess in her own right. Despite her unpromising relatives and job description, she is really a nice girl, most interested in the gathering of healing herbs. It is she who saves the hero from sacrifice, having fallen in love with him, thereby paving the way for events that end in the slaughter of all the Druids by the Roman rulers, and the imposition of law, order and decency.[90]

These three works typify the shift in novelistic portraits of evil Druids during the period. All were concerned to celebrate the triumph of Christianity over paganism. Kingston's, however, belonged to an older world, primarily concerned with celebrating British Protestantism and lambasting its opponents, Roman Catholicism and the heathenism of tribal peoples. The concerns of the other two are those of a later age, of an imperial British state menaced by nationalism among the subject peoples of its colonies and socialism among the growing industrial proletariat at home. The Romans are viewed with a new sympathy, made easier by the fact that the stories are set towards the end, or just after the end, of their rule in Britain. The concern is with the preservation of stability and civilization, against both invaders and ungrateful and treacherous subjects, and Druids exemplify the survival of repulsive beliefs, and murderous intentions among an outwardly compliant conquered population.

Three other works of the period fit into this latter model. One is Hugh Kay's *Saint Kentigern*, which was concerned with the struggle to restore stability and propagate Christianity after the collapse of Roman rule. The Druids in it are reduced to a few fanatical groups, but are still hungry for 'horrid virgin sacrifices': once again, young women are prominent, either as symbols of purity, vulnerability and innocence that forces of evil seek to destroy or as points of weakness in pagan society by which goodness may enter.[91] Another is Florence Gay's *The Druidess*, set in the same period. Once again, Druidry lingers as a menace beneath the surface of an outwardly Christian society. Its rites are wild and exciting, but savage, including sacrifices of bulls and humans, worshippers who go into frenzies and gash their bodies with flints, and warriors who strip naked and dance with weapons in their hands. Christianity, by contrast, is shown as inherently a religion of sweetness and kindness. The Druidess of the title is an anti-heroine, who converts to the better faith, but reverts to her old one and pays for this with her life. The comment of the narrator on this development is that 'this woman was a Druidess, and daughter of Druids, and they are reared in vice and cruelty . . . love and honour are closed books to them'.[92] There may be a general colonial message here about natives, but it could have had particular force because in this case the treacherous native happens to be Irish. The third work is Agnes Strickland's *The Druid's Retreat*, which again celebrates the blessings of established Roman rule, equating the Druids with wild beasts who prey on the young and weak. It proclaims that by the fourth century of Roman Britain 'children, who only three centuries before, would have shrunk in terror from the forests where the oaks waved their giant branches, now played fearlessly beneath their shade'. The point of the book, of course, is that the lack of fear is misplaced, for Druids still lurk in hidden places and keep up their acts of ritual murder.[93] In this as in their treatment of other subjects, historical novels vividly point up the anxieties of the English middle class in late Victorian and Edwardian England.

Musical Druids could be just as unpleasant. The worst were probably in an opera called *The Druid*, published by J. M. Capes in 1879 and devoted to the tragic career of one who comes to doubt the necessity of human sacrifice and is blinded by his fellows as a punishment. He then suffers a double misfortune when the pagan Roman conquerors kill his daughters, who have converted to Christianity; but the prospective triumph of this faith is held out as the consolation for all the suffering.[94] Lighter musical fare aimed other kinds of blow. In 1899 two authors produced a play enlivened with songs, called *The Druid's Elect*. Its purpose was satirical, and it used its portrait of ancient Druidry to attack a new target: Spiritualists, who were lampooned as frauds playing on popular credulity in the way that churchmen had been held to do by anticlerical writers (again, often using Druids) since the sixteenth century:

We carry on the priestcraft for this poor benighted race
With a slow impressive manner and a sanctimonious face
From a sacrificial offering to the paying of accounts
They always find the ready while we settle the amounts . . .
With raps and solemn music and a tin of phosph'rous paint,
We can raise the tortured spirit of some dear departed saint;
With a hidden cinematoscope and twenty megaphones
We can make the dreaded oracle give forth its measured tones.[95]

Just as before, professed works of serious history could be equally imaginative. Indeed, as Druids were pushed towards the margins of interest by scholarly historians and prehistorians, those authors who continued to deal with them as figures of purported non-fiction were as unrestrained as any mid-Victorian author; and a very significant range of contemporary animosities were revealed in the process. A clutch of works from the years around 1900 may serve to point this up. In 1897, the leading historian of Worcestershire, John Willis-Bund, published a history of Welsh Christianity in which he treated of Druids. One principal concern of his was to praise the Welsh at the expense of the Irish. The former, in his view, were descended from the 'Brythonic' Celts, who had an 'easy-going polytheism', associated with an attractive sense of the sacred in the natural world. The 'Goidelic' Celts, from whom the Irish were descended, had absorbed Druidry from the older and more primitive peoples of the British Isles, whom they had conquered before the Brythons turned up. It was a 'stern, cruel form of belief', with prominent use of human sacrifice. Willis-Bund's Druids had exerted an 'immense' influence over 'an ignorant and excitable people'. This rested on their supposed magical powers, so that Christian saints became their natural opponents and vanquishers; here Willis-Bund was drawing heavily on the images of them in medieval Irish literature of the sort that was at last becoming readily available in English translation.[96]

In 1904 there appeared a textbook on 'Celtic Britain', from a far greater scholar but an equally unreliable historian, the leading philologist Sir John Rhys. Rhys pressed home the belief that the British ('Brythonic') Celts must have been too decent to have embraced Druidry. Instead, he suggested that at the dawn of history the British Isles had contained three different races. There were the Brythonic Celts, practising an acceptable, 'Aryan' polytheism like that of ancient Greece and Rome, the non-Celtic aborigines 'under the sway of Druidism', whose dark, old religion it was, and the more inferior and susceptible Goidelic Celts, 'devotees of a religion which combined Aryan polytheism with Druidism'. To Rhys, therefore, Druidry became a magical system associated with inferior peoples, equated with the shamanism of modern Lapps and Siberians. He turned the resistance to the Romans on Anglesey, as portrayed by Tacitus, into a clash between civilization and a 'non-Aryan' savage religion lingering in a corner of Wales. This scheme also enabled him to suggest that the black-dyed naked women of whom Pliny had spoken need not have anything to do with the 'true' British. Having credited the Irish with a much greater susceptibility to the bad old ways, he made a condescending nod towards the French. In his view, their Celtic ancestors had also been guilty of imbibing savage religious habits from the inferior native population; but they had turned it into something much more civilized, even if not as estimable as the ways of the clean-living Brits. Rhys's book was published by the Society for the Propagation of Christian Knowledge; it was, incidentally, reissued in 1996.[97] In 1907 an amateur historian, Rice Holmes, produced a book on Caesar's invasions of Britain. By then, in his opinion, it had become perceived as a 'common view' that Druidry had been the religion of the Neolithic, non-Aryan (and so technologically and morally inferior) population of Western Europe. It was, accordingly, both cruel and backward-looking. With an imperialist's glance at modern Hindus (and, perhaps, at Catholics as well), Holmes declared that, as a priestly caste, Druids had been 'naturally opposed to all innovation'. They were the enemies of the true faith of the modern British: that of progress.[98]

It may be noted that this 'common view' ran directly contrary to that now expressed by leading prehistorians. It incorporated the whole of the new scheme of successive races and technologies, introduced by invasions, but reversed the role of the Druids:

instead of turning up in the baggage of the late-coming Aryan Celts, they had been there since the Neolithic era, contaminating every subsequent wave of arrivals *except* the Aryans. Whence had this idea come? The answer is, from another of the emerging scholarly disciplines of the period: the study of folklore. As this had developed, in Germany and Britain during the late nineteenth century, it was heavily dependent on the theory of survivals. This theory had been derived in turn from the most successful of all the new branches of learning, the science of geology, which had dethroned the Bible as the chief record of the remote human past. Victorian and Edwardian folk-lorists believed that, just as strata were laid down in the rocks through successive geological ages, the customs and beliefs of common people, and especially of stable, rural communities, were likewise accumulations of ages of developing tradition. As such, they were thought to contain traces of ancient religion and cosmology preserved in modern society like fossils in stone, which could be recovered by scholars. In this manner, a study of contemporary or recent folklore could provide insights into beliefs that had existed before the advent of writing provided sources for historians to study and that could not be understood from the material remains that were the province of archaeologists.[99] The new folklorists were thus making a very high claim for their discipline, and staking out a territory for it in which they alone could function as the experts: another stage in the process of appropriation, exploitation and exclusion of knowledge that had been under way since geology had proved literary sources to be wholly inadequate for the understanding of the past. As the folklorists depended for their importance on the theory that religious beliefs survived social change better than most, it was necessary to turn the Druids into a prime example of this, and to put them near the beginning, and not at the end, of the successive ages of prehistory.

It was Sir John Rhys himself who instituted this process, as a scholar who allied folklore with linguistics, and he did so in a book published in 1882. It was there that he first put forward the idea that Druidry had been the religion of the aboriginal natives of Britain, with which the Gaelic Celts made compromises but the stouter Brythonic Celts did not.[100] In 1890 it was taken up enthusiastically by one of the leaders of the new folklore studies, George Lawrence (later Sir Lawrence) Gomme. Gomme pointed out that certain modern Indian hill tribes contained individuals who combined the roles of priest and judge as the Graeco-Roman texts had portrayed Druids as doing. Since these surviving 'primitive' people were believed to have been in India before the Aryans or Indo-Europeans arrived there, this seemed to indicate that the possession of such figures was indeed pre-Aryan. Gomme concluded that Druids 'supply us, in fact, with the British evidence for what is so apparent in India, that the non-Aryan races have forced upon their Aryan overlords a position as priests to the still feared gods of nature'.[101] This talk of forcing and fearing indicates something seen in the work of Rhys himself, and of Willis-Bund: that, as a primitive religion left over from a savage race, Druidry did not recommend itself to those who took the folklorists' view. Indeed, two years later Gomme tainted it further, with another bold suggestion. He drew attention to the trials for witchcraft which were a feature of early modern Europe, and the accusations of horrific rites, involving cannibalism, child sacrifice and sexual orgies, that had been made in them. Authors had been suggesting since the 1820s that the people against whom these accusations had been levelled might have been practitioners of a surviving pagan religion. Gomme now put forward the idea that the religion concerned had been Druidry, and every bit as dreadful as the hostile ancient authors had depicted it. As the religion had evolved during the Middle Ages, the male Druid had been replaced as leader by a female adept, the witch priestess, but its foul practices and beliefs had been preserved until suppressed by the early modern authorities.[102] This was the doctrine of survivals, with a vengeance.

In making this suggestion Gomme was, once again, drawing on existing ideas. The theory that he was putting forward had appeared in a book published almost forty years before, by a Scottish antiquary called Jonathan Forbes Leslie. Scots had particular reason to take an interest in the witch trials, which had been much more numerous in their nation, and resulted in a much higher death toll than in the rest of the British Isles. Furthermore, they had been more closely associated with a devil-worshipping religion. Leslie saw Druids as the embodiment of primitive and savage religion, their most prominent characteristics being 'mystery and cruelty, two commonly associated elements of ancient sacerdotal power and man's debasement'. To the various methods of human sacrifice already attributed by ancient authors to the Gallic tribes, Leslie confidently added crucifixion, and made all of them common to the peoples who had Druids. It was a short step from this to declaring that later Scottish witchcraft and superstition was but a continuation of Druidic religion; which meant, in turn, that all the dreadful deeds alleged against early modern Scottish witches could be laid against Druids as well. He held up Tacitus's famous portrait of the black-robed women on the shore of Anglesey, and concluded that it provided a perfect image of witches at work, of the sort that had lingered into early modern times.[103]

Experts in Gaelic culture made another contribution to a disapproving linkage between ancient Druidry and later magical beliefs. The new discipline of folklore was deeply ambivalent towards its own source material, some practitioners clearly regarding the lore and customs that they collected as generally delightful and fascinating, while others saw them as hallmarks of ignorance and error. In the 1880s the author of a book on a region of the Scottish Highlands deplored what he viewed as the continuing addiction of its inhabitants to divination and magic. He associated this with the portrait of Druids as magicians given in the medieval Irish sources, and rued the fact that their influence seemed to linger among the people whom they had once deluded: 'the Druidical ideas as held by the Gael, if the witchcraft alluded to is worthy of the name of ideas, tincture all their superstitions'.[104] In 1891 the compiler of a major collection of the folklore of the Isle of Man took this further, declaring the Druids to have been 'mere magicians and medicine men'. He continued that, although they themselves had been (fortunately) suppressed by Christianity, 'their beliefs survived as those of magicians, enchanters, sorceresses, witches, or those regarding those figures'.[105] Gomme was therefore drawing on an established body of material when linking Druidry to witchcraft. Both could be held up as enemies of the civilized and the modern; another example of secularization and updating of traditional Christian attitudes.

Even when detached from witches, the Druids remained a means by which those who recorded and disliked aspects of modern folklore could castigate these as false beliefs. In 1891 a Scottish clergyman published an article forthrightly entitled 'Highland Superstitions'. He blamed these folk traditions on the lingering influence of long-vanished Druids, and went into a remarkable flight of fancy in which he imagined the rites in which Druids had indulged. These included the slow roasting of women alive in wicker idols, while 'young, innocent, beautiful maidens were dragged to the altar and sacrificed to the powers above'. Most inventively, he informed his readers that the Druids had told their people that shooting-stars were the spirits of particularly illustrious dead Druids; his evidence for this was that some Highlanders of the present day believed that such stars were souls bound for eternity.[106] Twenty years later, a much more famous Scottish cleric tackled the subject. This was J. A. MacCulloch, respected both as a folklorist and as a scholar of Celtic literatures. He opposed the ideas of Rhys and Gomme that Druidry was necessarily a pre-Aryan survival confined ultimately to the wrong kind of Celt, pointing out that there was plenty of apparent evidence that all the Celtic peoples appreciated bloodshed and magic of the sort credited to Druids. The fact that Rhys had been a patriotic Welshman while MacCulloch was himself a Gael may not have been entirely dissociated from this difference of opinion. MacCulloch's own attitude to Druids was itself no more kindly. He rejected the idea that their wisdom could have amounted to anything more than superstition, declaring that their astronomy was probably just astrology and that if they had believed in the survival of souls they were unlikely to have attached any ethical aspect to the progress. He concluded that there was no clear evidence that they had held any advanced or admirable doctrines, and dismissed them as specialists in delusion, represented by magic and myth.[107]

This selection of sources should indicate that the figure of the demonic Druid continued to flourish in the British literary imagination – enlisted in contemporary causes – until the eve of the First World War. After that it went into steep decline, for a number of possible reasons. One was a fall in the religious temperature of society, which made Druidry a less attractive means to proclaim the virtues of Protestant Christianity and to attack its perceived enemies. Another was the horrific and sustained bloodshed of the war itself, which diminished the appetite for imagined atrocity. Within the narrower world of scholarship, folklore rapidly lost ground as a discipline as its doctrine of survivals was discredited, while archaeology gained in strength; so a view of prehistory that relegated Druids to the margins was upheld. In general, it might be said, a preoccupation with Druids had been one of the hallmarks of nineteenth-century Britain. Like other characteristics of that age, it was well sustained under the Edwardians but shrank notably in the very changed world produced by the Great War.

There seem, in fact, to be very few manifestations of the hostile image of Druids from the 1920s and 1930s. From the former decade comes a book by an amateur historian, Hadrian Allcroft, who suggested that Druidry had in fact been a political organization, designed to gain and concentrate power by infiltrating and taking over one society after another. As such, it was displaying 'German' characteristics, which had crept into Gaul shortly before Caesar arrived there; so Allcroft was apparently projecting the rising Nazi party back into ancient times.[108] Seemingly, nobody else took up this idea. From the 1930s come two other items. One was a perfect throwback to Victorian evangelism, a novel called *In the Grip of the Druids* by a spinster, Beth Coombe Harris. Designed to educate children in the need to embrace a fervent Christianity, it portrays the adventures of a native family in Roman Britain eluding the attempts of Druids to acquire them for sacrifice. The efforts made to capture them are the more determined in that they have brought back Christianity from Rome, which the Druids are determined to keep out of Britain lest it stir up the people against their tyranny. In a glance at the realities of continental European politics at the time of publication, those awaiting sacrifice are confined in concentration camps. They are rescued from being burned alive by the arrival of heroic Roman soldiers, who kill all the Druids and set fire to their sacred groves. A retired naval officer contributed a foreword, adding a warning to its juvenile readers against the evils of Roman Catholicism. The impact of this book should not be underestimated; it apparently became a favourite prize in Sunday schools.[109] The other work was a play, published by T. B. Morris in 1938 and called *Druid's Ring*. The ring concerned is a prehistoric stone circle, standing above a modern farmhouse. The point of the plot is that the dark deeds committed there by Druidical hands in the past have somehow contaminated it, and its malign influence seeps down into the home beneath it, to warp the minds and lives of the inhabitants.[110] Such works, though few, served to keep alive hostile images of Druids through the early twentieth century.

Images like this were to flower again, in some cases spectacularly, after the Second World War, but the context for the development was a different and distinctively late twentieth-century one. For the present, it is sufficient to note that condemnatory attitudes to Druids, which had been such a feature of the previous three centuries and reached an apogee in the nineteenth, became much less prominent between the world wars.

*   *   *

There was one final aspect of the British preoccupation with Druids during the late Georgian and early Victorian periods which was to have significant consequences in the early twentieth century; and it was one that developed even as that preoccupation was waning. It arose from three of the strongest impulses in Victorian culture: a desire for increased knowledge of, and control over, the world; a yearning for continued faith in an original divine plan for the universe and a special divine revelation to humanity; and a continued joy in clubs and societies with a controlled membership. These features came together, from the 1860s, in the foundation of organizations dedicated to the recovery of ancient wisdom, and especially of a kind, already represented by the traditions of Freemasonry, that was alleged to have been handed down in closed circles of initiates. Two of these have already been mentioned: the Societas Rosicruciana and the Hermetic Order of the Golden Dawn. The Theosophical Society was another. Druidry was easily assimilated to the world-picture of these groups, as the British version of the ancient knowledge that they were attempting to recover; but the lack of any definite body of doctrines associated with it made it less

useful to them in practice than old philosophies and religions that had possessed a
literary tradition. Only one Victorian esoteric society is said to have been founded in
their name: the Ancient and Archaeological Order of Druids, allegedly founded in
1874 by Robert Wentworth Little and restricted to Freemasons.[111]

By the early twentieth century, the offspring of these Victorian societies had
diffused and multiplied sufficiently to establish occultism as a British subculture.
Authors within it or influenced by it now began to attempt to reconstruct or imagine
ancient Druidic rites, as counterparts to those being enacted in the closed, initiatory
groups of modern magicians. In doing so, they self-consciously bade to make Druidry
a significant force in the mental world of British occultists. The first to undertake this
work was Dudley Wright, an otherwise little-known person who published a book on
Druids in 1924 which became an item in most major public libraries and presumably
acquired a proportionately large private readership. He restated the old view of
Druidry as the primordial religion of the Old World, held in common with the
Persians, Babylonians, Hebrews, Brahmins and Egyptians. He also repeated another
well-established tradition, that it had easily been blended with Christianity to
produce a benevolent and admirable Celtic form of that religion. For the religious and
moral content of it, he relied mainly upon Iolo's writings, with some input from those
of Davies. He was aware that Druids were no longer regarded as the builders of stone
circles, but, as circles featured prominently in Iolo's depiction of Druidry, he declared
that 'it may be taken for granted' that they used them. He also repeated Toland's old
idea that rocking stones had been employed by them as instruments of judgment.

For his accounts of the hidden rites of his subjects, he depended, of necessity, upon
fantasy, but he possessed that in full measure. At one point he described the initiation
ceremony of a novice, set in a cave. Three officers led it: 'Cadeiriath', the chief,
standing in the east, 'Goronwy', representative of the moon goddess Ceridwen, in the
west, and Fleidwr Flam, representative of the sun god Hu, in the south. Here was
Edward Davies's imagined Druidical religion, cast into a ritual form influenced by
Freemasonry; as a sure sign of the influence of the latter, the north, viewed in Masonic
tradition as the place of darkness, was left empty. The candidate took an oath of
secrecy, as in all modern esoteric traditions, and was clad in a crown of ivy and a
robe coloured in sections of blue, green and white. These were Iolo's colours for his
three divisions of the Bardic and Druidic order, put into one garment and held to
symbolize truth, hope and light respectively; and over this a pure white tunic was
donned. The candidate was examined to ensure that he truly was male, as – in a
manner that echoed Freemasonry and most of its Georgian and Victorian imitations
– women were excluded from the mysteries. His hair was shaved back into a crescent
above his forehead from ear to ear, a detail that Wright would have known from his
reading as the tonsure of early medieval Welsh and Irish Christian monks. In addition, he was expected to grow a beard and keep his hair short. The ordeal of the initiatory process consisted of being shut into a coffin for three days, to signify death and
rebirth. On being released, the candidate had to be led blindfolded into a company of
Druids who chanted a hymn to the sun, and was then taken nine times around the
space while they shouted, clashed vessels and screamed to frighten him. He then took

a second and yet more binding oath, and was immersed in water and hauled out of it into a blaze of light. Finally, he was presented to the Archdruid, who received him seated on a throne, and retired into a forest to commence his studies. Wright informed his readers that, if successful, the initiate would rise through five more grades during the twenty-year training that Caesar had said was needed for a full Druidical training. He would then be allowed to wear the multicoloured robes that Toland had said were the mark of Druids, and the ornaments shown in the famous conjectural portrait of an Archdruid by Meyrick and Smith.[112]

In 1925 it was the turn of one of the contributors to Britain's foremost journal to deal with esoteric teachings: the *Occult Review*. He wrote on the ancient Druids, and made Iolo's system, in his case specifically *Barddas,* the source of all that he had to say. He concluded his summary with the spiky remark that the Druids appeared to have exerted far more genuine influence upon the people of Britain than any established Church had done since.[113] In 1928 the work of reclaiming esoteric Druidry was taken up by an author who achieved as great a circulation as Wright and who is much better known as a public figure: the Scottish journalist and nationalist Lewis Spence. He boasted that his book on the subject was the first to approach it in a 'scientific manner' and in 'the light of modern research'. Indeed, he did his utmost to reconcile the portrait of prehistory produced by the new archaeology with the writings of Iolo and interpretations of medieval Welsh poetry. As, however, he relied mostly on the last two sources, the result was ultimately as imaginative as that of Wright. It did not help matters that, apparently as an act of faith, he declared that he believed Iolo's *Barddas* to 'have been handed down from an immense antiquity'. Likewise, he rejected the scholarly consensus that the account of ancient British history found in Geoffrey of Monmouth was a twelfth-century fabrication. Rather than argue a case, he simply proclaimed that 'from the first I almost instinctively adopted the theory of its derivation from ancient Cambrian and Breton sources', and turned it into another body of evidence for the nature of Druidry. He also praised Davies and Morien, and accepted their reconstruction of Druidic doctrine, shorn arbitrarily of all the linkages that both of them had made to the Bible.

Spence reasserted the existence of a single original religion that had covered the whole of Neolithic Europe and the Near East, and which had spread from a single point. It was, however, not that of the Bible and had not come from Palestine. He characterized it, in the new archaeological terms, as a cult of the dead, which had developed in north-west Africa and been carried to Britain by the small, dark Iberian people who were currently regarded as its New Stone Age inhabitants. In Britain, however, it had developed into a uniquely elaborate and sophisticated form, turning the island into 'the Tibet of the ancient world'; here Spence made his own patriotic reply to the admiration for Buddhism which had developed in Britain from the 1880s. He had also adopted the Rhys and Gomme view that Druidry was essentially the religion of the Neolithic, passed down to all later waves of immigrants. In his formulation, however, it grew into an admirable one, as the life-loving and life-affirming Celts turned a veneration of the spirits of the dead into a means of countering and overcoming the human fear of death. By contrast, he characterized the

Romans as merciless conquerors and plunderers, but also as failures in their mission to stamp out Druidry. In his vision, it had survived to re-emerge in strength after the end of Roman rule and to evolve into the purest form of British Christianity, opposed to all that Protestants later disliked most in Roman Catholicism. As such, it attracted further suppression from a now Christian Rome, but lingered in sufficient strength to leave Druidic mythology 'virtually unimpaired' in medieval Welsh literature; thereby licensing Spence to use the latter freely as a source for Druidic teachings and to give the greatest possible credence to what Iolo had seemed to take from it. He also accepted an early modern legend that Welsh sages had founded a college at Oxford before the university was established there, identifying these in turn with Druids.

Spence based his reconstruction of a Druidic initiation rite on one enigmatic medieval Welsh poem, which he interpreted as a veiled account of such a ceremony: 'a definite attempt on the part of the initiates of some mystical society, to explore the underworld plane'. In his reading, the candidate acted out a journey into an immortal Otherworld of the sort found in medieval Welsh and Irish literature, which Spence equated with both Iolo's Annwn, the place of the refashioning and rebirth of souls, and the astral plane on which modern occultists claimed to travel in spirit form. The initiate was first enclosed in a cell within a tumulus, which echoed Davies's interpretation of prehistoric chambered tombs as initiation spaces and enabled Spence to identify the fairyland of British folk tradition – often located in hollow hills – with the spiritual Otherworld of the Druid adepts. The ordeal also acted out what Spence, building on Morien, took to be a central part of Druidic theology, a myth of how its principal god, Hu or Arthur, representing the sun, had descended into the underworld to obtain power over death. The initiate was then cast adrift in a vessel on the sea, an idea also put forward by Morien and ultimately based on the early modern story of the birth of Taliesin. Those who passed the first test and survived the second could become Druids. By 'reconstructing' rituals such as this, Spence claimed to have provided the British with the true 'Secret Tradition' of their land, one capable of matching any of the currently respected teachings of India and China. He accordingly called on them to study it instead, and to 'restore and rebuild the ruined edifice of British mysticism, as rendered conformable to Christian belief by the bards'. This, he proclaimed, would be 'eminently to our psychic advantage'.[114]

Spence himself was to change these views. Twenty years later he published a book devoted to Druids, in which he based his observations on the classical and Irish sources, and explicitly rejected most of what he had said before. Out went Iolo, the Welsh poetry, a connection with stone circles and any claims for a sophisticated and admirable Druidic theology or for any significant connection between one and medieval Irish or Welsh Christianity. In came a primitive cult of oak trees, mixed up with a thunder god, sacred kingship and human sacrifice.[115] What is more interesting here, and much more difficult to document, is the question whether anybody in early twentieth-century Britain was trying to act out an esoteric Druidry, based on initiation into closed societies, of the sort that he and Wright had imagined. There seems to be a complete dearth of historic evidence for this. Even the Ancient and Archaeological Order of Druids, cited above, is less well attested than at first seems.

Little, its founder, is well known in the history of British occultism as the first Supreme Magus of the Societas Rosicruciana. Knowledge of it, however, seems to depend on a few lines in a single book, published in 1975. Some solid evidence was apparently provided for the order's existence there, with the comment that items of its regalia were preserved in the Museum of Freemasonry in London.[116] The museum, however, now seems to have no record of any such objects, and the author concerned almost certainly did not see them herself. Being a woman, she would have found it almost impossible to gain access to those collections.[117] She was clearly given this information by members of a twentieth-century Druid order, which will be discussed later in this book, and at a time when that order was engaging in a wholesale invention of history.[118] Nothing seems to be known, moreover, about the membership or duration of the Ancient and Archaeological Order, or what it actually did.

An extreme illustration of this problem was provided in 2004, with the publication, from a local press in Leicestershire, of *The Druidic Order of the Pendragon*.[119] The contents of this book were presented as a set of papers left by a body of Druids that had survived in such secrecy that it is recorded nowhere else. They were published by Nick Farrell, who explained that he had inherited them from a Leicestershire man, a former civil servant who had an ardent personal enthusiasm for paganism and ritual magic. Farrell had met him in 1978, and he had died at an advanced age in 2001. He had left the papers to Farrell specifically for publication, in the hope that this would bring about the revival of the order concerned, to which he had belonged in the 1930s and 1940s. He claimed that he had been initiated into it in 1931, at which time it numbered about twenty and met either on a Derbyshire farm or at the home of the leader in Loughborough. The leader concerned, known as the 'Merlin', ruled it absolutely, and it was badly disrupted when the current 'Merlin' was killed in 1943, and his archive destroyed, by bombing. No new order was founded, and no more people initiated into the group, although the existing membership continued to perform rites for six more years, and to meet until 1965, when five remained. Farrell's contact lived long enough to be the last survivor. As Farrell presents them, the papers concerned are in the hand of his own informant, who claims to have copied and modernized those that he received in the 1930s. He also, however, claims that some of the documents in the collection he received can be dated back to the 1850s, while not explaining how or why. Farrell has not himself, as far as I know, allowed anybody else to examine any of them, and he conceals the identity of his informant. As far as a historian is concerned, therefore, the trail of evidence at present begins and ends with Nick Farrell himself.

The mythical history of the order, as given in the papers, states that it was descended directly from Druids who had preserved their pagan beliefs in secret all through the Middle Ages, moving between various places in southern Britain, including some with great legendary associations such as Tintagel and Sherwood Forest. The papers state that the existence of the order could be securely verified back to the year 1765, but do not explain how. They also state that in 1780 its traditions were written down for the first time, and subsequently revised in 1843, 1880 and 1932, before being finally updated by the man who bequeathed the papers to Farrell.

In this final form, they certainly, as Farrell emphasizes, embody a unique system. It claimed that its members were a surviving third of the ancient Druid order, which had been divided into Priests, Bards and Pendragons. The latter depended for their power and identity on 'the serpent force and the energies of the land', had twin serpents tattooed on their arms, and provided the true spiritual energy for rituals. Fortunately, therefore, it was they who had survived the Middle Ages and become divided in turn into three ascending grades: Measog, Ovates and Druids. The first were expected to understand the physical world, the second the underworld and the third the celestial world. The whole order was controlled by a council made up of three representatives from each grade, an Archdruid and his expected successor. Each grade had particular teachings attached to it, addressing such subjects as divination, animal spirits, a secret alphabet, magical weapons, astrology and set rituals. The order celebrated eight seasonal festivals in each annual cycle. The creation myth commenced with a supreme deity called Oinacos ('the One United'), who produced three other beings, Ather, the Father, power of light, Mather, the Mother, power of night, and Amrhan, the Song. The seed of Ather became the sun and the egg of Mather became the moon. Amrhan asked Oinacos to sacrifice him so that he might enter all creation and give it life, and humans subsequently created specific goddesses and gods from the spiritual force of Amrhan.

Distinctive the system may be, but there is nothing in it that seems recognizably older than the 1980s. Some of the elements are characteristic of that decade: the title of 'Merlin' as given to a succession of Druid leaders, and the tattooing of serpents on the arms of initiates of his religion are motifs found in Marion Zimmer Bradley's novel, *The Mists of Avalon*, published in 1982. The emphasis on serpent power as representing the natural energies of the earth developed from the publication of John Michell's *The View over Atlantis* in 1969, and the eight festivals are those of the modern pagan ritual year, as established in the late 1950s. The preoccupations of the grade teachings are very much those of the pagan and magical spirituality of the last two decades of the twentieth century; while the three progressive grades, each with its own identity and teachings, are similar to those of the Order of Bards, Ovates and Druids as re-established in 1988. All these features may perhaps be accounted for in terms of further updating by Nick Farrell's informant himself, but when the sections of the teachings that seem to reflect recent concerns and motifs are stripped away, there seems to be nothing left that can be matched to those of the nineteenth or early twentieth centuries. As a system for use by contemporary pagans and magicians it is admirable; but a historian cannot, without better evidence, associate it with any earlier period.

*   *   *

All these aspects of Druidry, then, can be represented as surviving after 1860 as significant relics of the importance Druids had enjoyed in the British imagination during the previous century. The twentieth century was also, however, to produce distinctively new cultural forms in Britain that reflected or involved Druids; and these represent the subject matter of the rest of this book.

11

❧ ❧

THE UNIVERSAL BOND

On Midsummer's Eve, 23 June 1912, five men arrived at Stonehenge, dressed in white robes embroidered with designs, and tall white turbans, in the manner of orientals. This is, indeed, what they presented themselves as being. Their leader, a tall and strongly built individual with a bushy black moustache, introduced himself as Ayu Subhadra, 'the messenger from Tibet', and his company included 'Mr Karkhushru J. Tarachand, a Persian gentleman'. They proclaimed that they represented 'the Universal Bond of the Sons of Men', and had come to the monument on an annual pilgrimage. At sunrise they processed around the altar stone, repeating set phrases of liturgy. They then sang some hymns and completed their service with a confession of faith. This whole procedure was repeated by them at eleven o'clock, after which they disappeared. Although so few in number, and brief in appearance, they made a considerable impact, having a full description of their rites published in the local newspaper, and a briefer one, with staged photographs, in a national one.[1] As national journalists did not normally hang around Stonehenge at midsummer during this period, it may be suspected that the Universal Bond had specially invited the papers to report the occasion. Perceptive observers of the confession of faith would have noted that it was a remarkable mixture of Christianity, Islam, Judaism, Buddhism and Zoroastrianism. In this curious manner, the first distinctively twentieth-century Druid order made its début performance before the public.

Three obvious questions spring to mind for a historian: what were people doing at Stonehenge at all, during midsummer, at this period; what was the Universal Bond; and what were its members doing there in particular? The first is easily answered, having lately been the subject of research by, successively, Chris Chippindale, Adam Stout, and Andy Worthington.[2] Together, they have put together the following picture. The habit of gathering at the stones to watch the midsummer sunrise was in origin a distinctively late Victorian phenomenon. It had not yet appeared in 1860, when the Earl of Caernarvon decided to wait there for the sunrise and found himself alone. By 1868, however, groups of people were present, and they turned into hundreds in the course of the 1870s. By the end of the century Devizes pubs were staying open all night to serve people bound for the monument. If the sky was clear and the solstice fell at a weekend, up to three thousand people were present. Some came from formal institutions, like the Devizes cycling club and Marlborough College. Some were figures of local authority, such as the headmaster of Dauntsey Agricultural School, and these would sometimes give a speech, after which the National Anthem would be sung. The bulk of the crowd, however, tended to be comprised of local working-class people, and was often unruly, climbing on the stones and breaking bottles against them. A few policemen were put on duty, but were not sufficient to control such behaviour. By 1885 the local newspaper was already calling for 'interference to preserve the peace, and apparently interference of an energetic character'.[3] That was supplied when Sir Edmund Antrobus fenced off the stones and imposed an admission charge in 1901. His right to do so was challenged in court, and the judge, on ruling in his favour, was especially swayed by the need to protect Stonehenge from proletarian revellers. In the words of one commentator, he was 'evidently under the impression that the vulgar population had, by their destructive propensities, disqualified themselves as visitors to a place of antiquarian interest'.[4] Numbers attending the sunrise initially dropped as a result, though they crept back up to two thousand in 1908, with the coincidence, once again, of good weather and a weekend date. Still, by now the gatherings had acquired a routine character, and ceased to attract much notice from the press; that is, until the Universal Bond turned up.

One problem arising from this story, which needs to be tackled here, is why the custom arose. The answer needs to be surmised from externals: when an observer in 1875 asked those attending why they were there, he 'failed to elicit any intelligible reason . . . except that . . . tradition told them that at Stonehenge something unusual was to be seen at sunrise on the morning of the summer solstice'.[5] What can be proposed is a twofold process. One part of it was provided by growing education and literacy among ordinary people during the period, to which the swelling number of guidebooks to Stonehenge catered. This enabled the alignment between the stones and the summer solstice sunrise, first noted by Stukeley and long familiar to scholars, to reach a wider audience. The other factor consisted of technological advances which allowed them, once informed, to reach the stones in time to be able to start work later the same morning. The crucial one here was the invention of the bicycle, by which many, and sometimes most, of those attending actually arrived. During the 1900s this was supplemented and reinforced by the appearance of motor vehicles. A second point is that, although those attending were indeed generally locals, from the beginning there were some people from the capital: of thirty-five present in 1872, four were Londoners.[6] A third is that the custom took off around 1870; in 1868 just four individuals were present to watch the sunrise, all from the Bath Natural History and Antiquarian Field Club and so scholars of the old sort rather than members of the general public.[7] By 1872, not only were the thirty-five present who have already been mentioned, but they were apparently ordinary people, and one observer noted that in good weather it was now customary for them to gather.[8]

The questions of what the Universal Bond was, and what its members were doing at Stonehenge, can also be answered, though with more complexity and difficulty. Something the newspaper reporters did not grasp, or at least did not emphasize, was that the group of apparent orientals were not, at least in the main, from the East at all. The 'messenger from Tibet', Ayu Subhadra, was actually a Scotsman called George Watson Reid who had already passed through a long history of religious and political experience before he appeared in the role of a Buddhist avatar.

*   *   *

Much of that history has now been pieced together, by Alan Seaburg, Bruce Aubry and Adam Stout.[9] The first two were mainly concerned with aspects of Reid's career which lie outside those of the present book, and so complement it. Dr Stout's interests, by contrast, have exactly matched my own, and his work has provided the indispensable launch-pad for my research into the subject. Reid first appears in 1888, working in the Glasgow docks. Bruce Aubry and Adam Stout have both made gallant attempts to discover any solid facts about his earlier life, and come up with none. Reid himself told several stories about it, but wherever they can be checked against surviving evidence they seem to be false. As a result we shall never know where or when he was born, or how he grew up: the only certainties are that he was a Scot who initially made his living, in some fashion, from the sea.[10]

By 1889, at any rate, he is firmly in the historical limelight, as a fiery orator campaigning with absolute dedication and tremendous energy for the trade union movement. In that year he helped to organize a seamen's strike on the Clyde, and then moved on to Hull to set up a new union there in rivalry with the existing one. This, of course, brought him into conflicts, which were compounded by his difficult personality. He was fined for physical assault and censured for intemperate language, and eventually expelled from his own union. He promptly moved to New York and picked up his career as an agitator, getting the dock workers there to join an international union. In doing so, however, he claimed to have authority from the British trade unions. When it was discovered that he had none, this, combined with the same behaviour that had brought him down at home, resulted in his dismissal from the American labour movement in 1891. Unabashed, he went straight into national politics, acquiring American citizenship so that he could stand for Congress. In 1892 he did so, for the short-lived Populist Party, which effectively declared war on the rich. He polled 1 per cent of the vote, and this further failure ended his American career, for by 1893 he was apparently back in Britain.[11]

Adam Stout has noted that Reid's sojourn in New York probably catalysed his spiritual interests, for in later life he paid tribute to one of its residents called Thomas Lake Harris. Harris was a Spiritualist, an adherent of the movement that had arisen in America in the mid-nineteenth century and focused on communication with discarnate entities, including the dead. He was also an advocate of simple and natural living, and of Universalism, a Christian creed which had started in eighteenth-century Britain but was by now mainly confined to New England, with a few small outposts in British cities. It depended on the concept of a rational and benevolent natural world, ordered by a good god. It held forth the prospect of the triumph of good over evil, the salvation of all souls, and the reconciliation of all religions.[12] Certainly, having failed as a labour leader and a politician, Reid now turned his radical enthusiasms to the moral renewal of humanity. In 1893 he published, from a 'Proletarian Publishing

Company' in London, his first pamphlet, *The Natural Basis of Civilisation*. It inveighed against militarism and profiteering, called established political parties corrupt, and accused governments of being 'responsible for every evil which curses and blights the happiness of the country, destroys the happiest of homes, and brutalises and degrades the people'. He called for their replacement by communes, voluntarily organized by ordinary people. Underpinning this view of politics and society was one of the natural world as essentially good, and all the evils of life as the product of human degeneracy and, in particular, of individual selfishness and greed. He gave credit to most of the world's great traditional religions as forces for virtue, offering the hope of salvation to humans. On the other hand, he also emphasized that socialism and anarchism were superior modern counterparts to them: 'The Anarchist and Socialist would make a heaven and destroy a hell. The Christian would destroy a heaven and support a hell.' In addition, he advocated a return to natural living, declaring nine-tenths of the machinery of his day injurious and calling for the use of water and air power and the reclamation of waste land.[13]

He now disappears completely for thirteen years. In later life he claimed at unspecified points of his past to have made remarkable travels, especially in India and Tibet, and to have fought in foreign wars. There is plenty of room in this lost period for such exploits to have taken place, but the context of his interest in the East developed later in his career, and there is no reason to believe that his martial experiences were any more real than the naval service he had claimed earlier. When he resurfaces in the records, in September 1906, it is in very different circumstances. He is a middle-class man of comfortable independent means, married and living in the affluent Sussex town of Burgess Hill. How he came by his money is not known: a simple explanation might be that his wife and his fortune arrived together.[14] There is also, however, one mighty clue to something else of significance that had occurred during the missing period. He had taken an additional name, 'MacGregor', pinned just behind his surname.

The spelling of this new, Highland, name, is especially important, for it matches the one adopted (likewise from choice) by one of the greatest ritual magicians of modern British history, Samuel Liddell MacGregor Mathers. With Westcott, mentioned earlier, he was one of the two leading figures in the Hermetic Order of the Golden Dawn, and he was the composer of its rites. There is no need to speculate about a relationship between Reid and Mathers, because one is well recorded. In an unpublished manuscript, Reid paid tribute to Mathers, by name, as 'our teacher and friend of many dream studies'.[15] The work concerned was inscribed as that of 'Frater A. I. of the Golden Dawn Temple Isis-Urania', the main body of the order, and the one which Mathers had led and, after the schisms that broke the order into rival groups from 1900 onward, continued to claim to lead. 'Frater' was the usual title for a male member, and the initials A.I. stood for the magical name that was taken upon initiation. Nor is there any doubt that Reid himself was the Frater concerned, for he identified himself as such in a poem that he wrote to a fellow initiate of the Golden Dawn, and an even more famous magician than Mathers: Aleister Crowley. He inscribed it, in or around the year 1913, in a book of Crowley's own poetry. Recognizing that Crowley had by then become a figure of considerable controversy, he offered him support against the world, as somebody who had wisdom, looked to heaven, and brought gladness to humanity.[16] It probably matters that Crowley had emerged, for a time, as Mathers's main supporter in the Golden Dawn after the schism of 1900. We can add to all this evidence a memoir by Reid's son, Robert, which states that his father had been a pupil of Mathers.[17] It seems, therefore, that at some point between 1900 and 1906 Reid studied under Mathers and was initiated by him into the Golden Dawn. This experience impressed Reid so much that he incorporated part of his teacher's name into his own, in perpetuity.

With Reid, of course, nothing is so simple. There is something odd about the reference to 'dream studies' in his tribute to his mentor. It is possible that their relationship occurred only in the spirit realm, or (more bluntly) in Reid's own mind, and that his initiation was a fiction, claimed to boost his standing among occultists. None the less, there is no doubt about Mathers's influence on him, and his change of name may be attributed to it. That influence took a particular form, displayed in Reid's own writings: of introducing him to the study of the Hebrew Cabbala, as filtered through Mathers's famous book on the subject. Reid made specific admiring reference to the latter. His own recorded use of it took the form of three unpublished treatises, which together represent a personal attempt to reconstruct the original religion revealed to humanity, like so many made in the previous few centuries.[18] Gone was the dismissal of religion as a spent or antagonistic force, which he had shown in 1893: instead the 'sceptic' is called as great an enemy of universal brotherhood as the 'dogmatist', and materialism denounced as inimical to a true understanding of the nature of being. Reid's new system had an important place for Christianity, holding that Christ had indeed been an emanation of the First Cause of all creation, and present 'from the very foundation of the world'. Those parts of the Christian message that denounce greed, selfishness and cruelty were now harnessed to Reid's former creed of moral renewal through socialism. The political and social reform of the human race was now linked to a restoration of the unity 'of God and Man'.

Druids also make their probable first appearance in his writings here. He related prehistoric stone circles, which he assumed both to be Druidical and to have a standard number of megaliths in each, to the Cabbala. He treated Druidry, however, as merely one corner of a universal and true ancient faith of which Buddhism, Taoism and Shinto were also aspects. The Cabbala was recommended as the key to all of them, by which the old understanding of nature and divinity could be recovered. None of these manuscripts can be dated, though the longest is an early draft of a work published in 1910. In none of Reid's writings after 1908 does he show the same preoccupation with the Cabbala and Mathers, so it seems fairly certain that they derive from an earlier period, soon after his change of name, when the influence of the great magician was still strong.

On his reappearance in 1906, Reid had a second new enthusiasm, to which he devoted part of his new-found fortune: natural medicine. He began mobilizing people in this cause, as he had done before for trade unionism, founding a British Nature Cure Association with a monthly journal, the *Nature Cure*, pitched at 'all Food Reformers, Vegetarians, Temperance Enthusiasts, Anti-Vivisectionists, Anti-Vaccinists and believers in Simple Life ideals'.[19] These indeed remained the main preoccupations of the magazine, and so presumably of the association, for some years. From the start, however, Reid's universalist theology also crept into its pages. In the first issue, he declared that 'God is too big and too good to belong to any church'.[20] In 1907 the *Nature Cure Journal* proclaimed the intention to establish a 'Simplicitarian Church', dedicated to 'good health conditions' and a common religion of 'the fatherhood of God and the brotherhood of man'.[21] At this point he was still casting around for gurus to guide him. The first to appear in 1907 was an Indian mystic, visiting London, to whom Reid devoted six admiring pages in the *Nature Cure Journal*. The next group was embodied in the Kosmon Church, based in the London suburb of Balham, followers of an American dentist called John Ballou Newman, to whom holy teachings had been revealed in visions back in 1882. Reid recommended this organization in turn, and serialized Newman's writings in his magazine. It is easy to see why they appealed to him, for they preached selflessness, brotherhood, love of a benevolent natural world, and religious unity.[22] In 1908, a new influence entered his life: Allan Bennett, the first Englishman to be ordained as a Buddhist monk, who returned to England that summer to preach his new faith. Significantly, Bennett was another initiate of the Golden Dawn, and protégé of Mathers. Reid extolled him in turn in the pages of the *Nature Cure*, and chaired the farewell meeting held by Bennett before his return to the East.[23] Bennett's Buddhism became for Reid the finest expression he had yet heard of his own ideal of universal love and reconciliation. His centre of spiritual gravity moved in accordance: Christianity and the Cabbala were now of secondary importance to the traditions of Persia, India and Tibet. He had come to regard the Himalayas as the place to which ancient peoples such as the Egyptians and Pythagoreans had gone for instruction.[24]

By now Reid was anxious to become a religious teacher in his own right, and had begun to serialize, in the *Nature Cure Journal*, his own sacred text, *The Holy Book of Umvali*; the last word stood for 'Universal Majesty, Verity and Love Infinite', one of his enduring expressions for divinity. It purported to be a translation of existing sacred texts, by 'the Brother Teachers', and aimed to promote 'Health, Happiness, Humility, Holiness' and to do so by mixing Vedic, Egyptian, Buddhist, Shinto, Confucian, Christian and Islamic tenets in a harmonious whole. It took light as its symbol of goodness, peace and wholesomeness, and called on readers to hear the cries of those made poor and hungry by greed.[25] Extracts from it were published regularly in the journal between 1908 and 1909, till, by the latter year, health and natural living were causes that Reid was anxious to shed in order to concentrate on religion.[26] His journal ceased publication in March 1909, and his association died with it. The following year, he published a full-length book, *The Path That Is Light*, to function as the sacred text of a new universal religion. With it he took a new pen-name, and a new persona, as 'the Tathagata [monk] Ayu Subadra' (later reformulated as 'Subhadra').

The volume was presented as a mixture of Vedic, Parsee, Buddhist and Islamic wisdom, compatible with the essentials of the Christian message. Most of its contents were alleged to be translated from a text used by a group called the Wandering Brothers of the Universal Bond, who roamed the region between Persia, China and Mongolia. Two figures in particular were held up as teachers and models. One was 'the Master Kapilya', a bearded sage who had died in Baghdad in 1846 and was hailed as the author of *The Holy Book of Umvali*. He was quoted as preaching the need to annihilate self and reach Nirvana. 'Kapilya' went on to explain that some great souls who had qualified themselves for bliss chose to remain on earth for love of it, as the Mahatmas. Their followers on earth were an elect group led by a Holy Brotherhood. The other guru eulogized by the book was its putative author, Ayu Subhadra himself, 'the Chosen Servant of the Holy Brotherhood of the Elect', said to be a Tibetan monk who lived by begging from door to door in the Himalayas. He preached a creed by now very familiar from Reid's previous writings, of the goodness of nature and of the single true god, and of the need for humanity to embrace altruism, pacifism and temperance, and respect the sacredness of all life. The book seemed to leave no doubt that he was a real person, and included a picture of him, as a young Buddhist monk with austere, sensitive, clean-shaven features; looking nothing like Reid. There is equally little doubt that Reid was writing in his name, which he indeed kept as a *nom de plume* for many years, in a variety of contexts, as well as presenting himself under it at Stonehenge in 1912. It is possible that both he and Kapilya were 'spirit guides' to Reid, disembodied beings who were very real to him in vision and who spoke through him even as Newman had 'channelled' his revelations. Behind both stood the much greater figure of Helena Blavatsky, the founder of Theosophy in the 1870s, who claimed likewise to receive messages from Mahatmas in the Himalayas. None the less, the book gave a consistent impression of both Kapilya and Ayu Subhadra as real and solid beings, one dead and one living, and both completely separate from the identity of Reid himself.[27] In that sense, it was a huge fraud.

It was not just a statement of theology and philosophy, and a call for moral renewal, but the service book for a new religion, of 'The Universalist Churches and Temples'. It included declarations and hymns to 'the Lord' against hatred, oppression and exploitation, in which Jesus was downgraded to the role of an admirable human. There was a new version of the Christian Lord's Prayer, denouncing hunger and poverty, and a creed, which declared belief in the sacredness of all life, the unity of all religious ideals, and reverence for all that was noblest in humanity. Services were to be led by Reid (or 'the Tathagata') himself, speaking invocations, preaching, and sprinkling worshippers with water to purify them; there was a special emphasis on healing the sick.[28] The obvious question here is whether any real organization existed to enact them. It seems that one did. By 1909 the British Nature Cure Association had branches in London and the gracious provincial towns of Bournemouth and Leamington Spa. Reid credited the latter, established by a Mrs Emily Cox-Davies, with special attributes, calling it, in Buddhist terms, 'the first temple of the Sangha' (the faithful adherents of the true beliefs).[29] In large part this distinction might just have been a practical one, meaning that it had its own meeting hall, whereas the other branches had to make do with municipal property hired for the night, and each other's homes.[30] None the less, it turned into a religious group, surviving the collapse of the association of which it had formed part to mutate into the first known of Reid's universalist churches. Presumably the London one made a similar transition, without formal premises, until about 1913 when Reid bought a house in Clapham to function as its temple.[31]

When he and his companions met the press at Stonehenge in 1912, therefore, it was clearly in a bid to publicize their new religion and attract further members. The fact that there were only five of them may act as an indication that hitherto their recruitment had been at a proportionately modest level. This was, almost certainly, not Reid's own first visit to Stonehenge. His son Robert, many years later, told a journalist that he himself had first seen the stones in 1909, with his father; and this was the year of the record turnout for the midsummer sunrise, which may have been the event that drew them.[32] Reid also had friends who were more interested in the monument. One of these can be identified,[33] an Irishman called John Barry O'Callaghan, who had died in 1909. He was a journalist and businessman by profession and a campaigner for Irish independence, who was also a social reformer of Reid's kind. His greatest personal enthusiasm, however, was not for religious subjects but for politics: he was president of the Rational Reform League, which sought a new equality in the structures of government and taxation. His memorial service was attended by socialist leaders such as Keir Hardy and John Burns, and his funeral was without any religious ceremony.[34] By 1913, however, as Reid's own interests had changed, he was starting to reinvent O'Callaghan as a priestly figure, with a special connection to Stonehenge.

There were a number of reasons why Reid and his friends should have chosen the monument for their first publicity stunt. It had great fame as a sacred place and obvious potential as a stage, and it seemed possible to arrange a ceremony there without difficulty. It had an obvious connection with the sun, the greatest source and symbol of that light which was currently the prime symbol of divinity and virtue in Reid's new faith. It appeared to be an outstanding physical memorial to that universal ancient religion that he claimed to be reviving. He and his people did not, however, arrive there as Druids, and neither of the newspaper reports identified them as such. Instead they came as universalists, with the formal title of the Universal Bond, and the main emphasis of their faith was placed upon the East, in costume, liturgy and titles.

* * *

By 1913, Reid had found a new guru-figure, and the centre of his religious gravity was accordingly shifting again. The person concerned was Charles Rosher, significantly another former member of the Golden Dawn. Whereas Allan Bennett had planed off from occultism into Buddhism, Rosher had headed into mystical Islam. In 1911 he had championed the cause of the Moroccans, against French imperialism, and by 1912 had taken up that of the Senussi Order. This was an Islamic sect that had been established at Mecca in 1837, as an attempt to renew the spiritual springs of Islam with an austere and unworldly piety. It opposed the use of military force, established lodges for communal living, and worked ultimately for a complete regeneration of religious and moral life throughout the Islamic world. As such, it became especially opposed to European imperialism, especially in North Africa and the Sahara, as a rule over Muslims by infidels. The British and French, gradually annexing most of this vast region in the late nineteenth century, came to return the hostility. For a long time the Senussi owed their survival to the fact that their main base was in Libya, the one part of Africa that remained under the rule of a Muslim power, the Turkish Empire. In 1910, however, the Italians began to conquer it, and to suppress the Senussi as part of the process.[35] As represented by Rosher, therefore, they provided Reid with an ideal cause at that moment: a pacifist, mystical, communal group who were very credible victims of imperialism and capitalism, and who filled out the Islamic corner of his universalist faith very neatly.

Back in 1907, when Reid was preparing to launch a 'Simplicitarian Church', he had promised a journal called the *New Life*, to act as its mouthpiece. Now, six years later, when he had actually got a church of his own, he published that periodical. Only one issue is known to exist from this period, but it runs to hundreds of pages.[36] It shows how much of an impact Islam had made on Reid's consciousness in the three years since he issued *The Path That Is Light*. Buddhism is still prominent in its pages, but mystical Islam is now declared to be 'the living succession of the Ancient Druid Faith'. There are plenty of articles on different aspects of it, and salutations to the Muslim world as representing the ideals of tolerance and brotherhood better than the West. Reid even expressed his intention of moving his base from Britain to an Islamic territory, as better fitted to receive his message. In particular, he intended to visit the Senussi at their last stronghold in the Sahara, declaring himself their chief representative in Europe, with the name of 'Abu Magrigor'. He stated that a party of his British comrades had already gone to join them; and that fifteen of them (three of them named) had died and been buried at their desert base. If this was true – and there seems no way of establishing whether it is – it was a moving and tragic gesture of international and inter-faith solidarity. In keeping with his ideological shift, Reid now substituted the name 'Allah' for that of 'God' at various points of his religious liturgy. His organization itself had not yet acquired a fixed name, being referred to variously as 'the Universal Bond', 'the Sacred Bond of the Sons of Men', 'the Universalist Church' and 'The Holy Brotherhood of the Elect'.[37] Druids were present in a few of the journal's ideological statements, but functioned, as before, as long-dead British representatives of a universal faith that now survived only much further east.

What is also very plain in these pages is the developing conflict over Stonehenge. Reid had declared in 1912 that he intended to make his rites there an annual event, and he meant this. The owner, Sir Edmund Antrobus, had other ideas. He had plainly no objection to ceremonies as such amongst the stones, having participated in the huge one staged by the Ancient Order of Druids in 1905 and allowed members of that order back since. The Universal Bond, however, was quite a different matter. It offended him as a landowner, having failed to ask his permission to hold its ceremony, let alone to involve journalists, in 1912. It also offended his conservative political instincts, as a group of people flaunting exotic dress and articulating views that challenged social norms. In preparation for the summer solstice of 1913, therefore, he had a notice fixed to the turnstile that gave access to the monument, forbidding any political or religious meetings inside it. Reid's response was to pay his entrance fee obediently at dawn, and then march around the interior single-handed, chanting the words of his liturgy. For good measure, he returned to the gate at noon to utter a solemn invective against the keeper and policemen guarding it, calling on 'Almighty God and his angels' to send 'pestilence and affliction' upon them.[38] At this point the law of private property and the English class system proved as beneficial to him in some respects as they had been adversarial in others. The land to the south of Stonehenge was owned by another member of the ruling elite, Lord Glenconner, whose wife, Pamela, had acquired a most opportune, and enduring, affection for Reid and his followers. As a result, they were allowed to camp on it, a mile away from the stones, affording them a secure base and refuge in the neighbourhood and a site on which to enact alternative rites that midsummer. The site concerned was a double Bronze Age burial mound, which became known as the 'Double Circle'.[39]

It had been intended that Reid would commence his tour of North Africa and the Middle East immediately afterwards, but it does not seem that it was ever made. Instead his life took a different course. His new interest in the Muslim world ebbed away, and Charles Rosher disappeared from his circle. What remained was the Universal Bond, based in London and Leamington, and the seasonal battle over Stonehenge. In 1914 that battle was renewed with vigour, this time under the eyes of several newspaper reporters and about three thousand of the general public: perhaps the largest crowd yet assembled to watch the solstice sunrise. Once more Reid paid his way into the monument before dawn, this time accompanied by nine other men and two women. As before, he proceeded to chant prayers, but on this occasion a policeman called on him to obey the prohibition of religious services. When he ignored them, he was thrown out, and began to harangue the people outside. Only about a hundred of the huge throng that had turned up for the sunrise had been able or willing to pay to go among the stones. Reid now took their side, denouncing the fencing of the enclosure as a denial of public right. Hundreds then attempted to break through the fence, but the police were present in force, and prevented them. Reid promised to return the next year with ten thousand followers and enforce free entry for all. He and his group came back twice later in the day to hold ceremonies, repeating the liturgy of 1912 outside the perimeter fence.

In his invective against the turnstile attendants Reid included a new historical claim: that delegates of his order had come to Stonehenge to worship ever since 1643.[40] This was clearly impossible, for not only is there no trace of any religious activity there by the Universal Bond before the previous year, but before 1910 Reid had not yet formed a religion to practise anywhere. So where did the date come from? It was apparently from a piece of furniture. On setting up his new temple at Clapham, Reid had acquired for it an antique wooden table, which now represented the focus for rituals and which had the date concerned carved upon it. This seems to have been turned, very swiftly, from a coincidental acquisition into a tangible link with an imaginary past for Reid's new spiritual tradition.[41] The latter was still not represented as Druidry, or taken as such by journalists; instead newspapers identified its practitioners as 'sun-worshippers', and they themselves claimed kinship with the ancient religion of Persia.[42]

The following year Reid was indeed back, though with his usual handful of companions rather than the promised thousands. Once again he was ejected from the enclosure for trying to stage a ceremony, and once more he tried to incite the crowd outside to oppose the enclosure of the stones. This time he won no sympathy from it, and departed. It was the first occasion on which Reid began primarily to take on the role of a Druid, apparently in response to his order's increasing association with Stonehenge. In character, he informed the crowd that he was the chief of all the Druids of England, or (in another version of his speech) of Europe, and a journalist termed his order the 'latter-day Druids', as well as the 'Universal Bond of the Sons of Men'.[43]

At this point the whole situation altered: Antrobus died, and Stonehenge was put up for sale by his heir. It was bought by a local lawyer, Cecil Chubb, who had married money and was setting himself up as a landed gentleman. Another Wiltshire man later described him as a 'red-faced bounder', and 'a classic example of the '20s profiteer' with his cigar and spats.[44] He must, however, also have been a genial fellow, in comparison with the haughty and prickly Sir Edmund, because he solved the problem of the Universal Bond by giving them exactly what they wanted. At midsummer 1916 he allowed them to enter the stones and hold no fewer than four ceremonies; all the publicity had aided them, and their numbers had now swelled to about thirty. There was a large police presence in case of trouble, but none occurred. Instead the crowd, numbering about a thousand, heard Reid preach on how Druidry was the 'one root of religious life', which sought 'to call man back to Nature, so he can look through Nature, to Nature's God', and so to 'the Brotherhood of Man'. He emphasized that to join or recognize it did not require them to leave their existing faiths.[45]

Perhaps because of wartime conditions, there is no record of his presence in 1917, but in 1918 he was back with gusto, to hold another five services between sunset on 20 June and the evening of the 23rd. He no longer showed any interest in those shut out beyond the fence, and had effectively taken control of the members of the public inside it: when some climbed on the megaliths, he called on them to respect the monument as a temple, and come down; which they did. His sermons were heard in attentive silence, and reported in detail in a local newspaper. In this last year of world war, he told his audience that Druidry was a remnant of the oldest of religions, and also the faith that now most genuinely worked for peace on earth.[46]

These experiences completed the transformation of Reid's self-image and that of his order. In 1915 he published his last pamphlet as Ayu Subhadra;[47] hereafter, he spoke before the world as an Archdruid. In 1918 the Universal Bond acquired a new official name, blazoned across headed notepaper: 'An Druidh Uileach Braithreachas', Gaelic (the Scotsman Reid's preferred 'Druidic' language) for 'the Universal Druid Brotherhood'.[48] The older one was still used informally and as an alternative, but its spiritual substance had changed. Its holy places were no longer Tibet or Mecca, but sites now associated – at least in legend – with either Druids themselves or the 'Celtic' Christianity supposed by some to be derived from them: Stonehenge (now given the Gaelic name of Cathair Ghall), Iona and Glastonbury.[49] After so long and colourful a spiritual wandering, Reid and his people had found a stable identity at last, as Druids.

* * *

In October 1918 the position of the Universal Bond at Stonehenge seemed to be secured permanently, as Cecil Chubb presented the monument to the nation, receiving as reward the title of baronet to cement his new position in society.[50] To have the stones taken out of the capricious hands of private individuals, and lodged in those of a state which Reid, as a socialist, viewed as the custodians of the general public, seemed to guard against any future difficulties.

Instead, the Universal Bond discovered that their greatest security had actually lain in private property owned by sympathizers. Those civil servants now directly responsible for Stonehenge, the staff of the Office of Works, had neither animosity nor goodwill towards the Bond. Instead, they viewed its members as rather eccentric members of the general public. Their first memorandum on the issue was issued by the Inspector of Ancient Monuments in June 1919. He termed Reid's Druids merely 'curious persons', who did no harm and caused no outrage and should be allowed to hold services at the stones on the same terms as before. The problem that developed was over what, exactly, those terms had been; and between 1919 and 1924 relations between the Office and the Universal Bond were marked by constant, and bitter, acrimony.[51] The first issue was that each time the Office granted permission to the Druids to hold a set number of ceremonies, they asked for more. Thus, in 1919 it was agreed that they should be able to hold four 'services' (as Reid now termed his rites) at the summer solstice and on the following day. Once this was arranged, Reid proceeded to demand further ceremonies on two additional days. In 1920 he wanted six days of rituals, and the next year raised his bid to eight. The second difficulty concerned the payment that the Universal Bond should make for admission. The Office, viewing them as ordinary members of the public, initially expected them to pay the usual fee. Reid and his companions, on the contrary, regarded themselves as very special members of the public, with a unique spiritual role to carry out at the stones on behalf of the nation. As such, they expected, at the least, to pay a greatly reduced rate. Only in 1922 was a compromise reached that was even temporarily acceptable to both sides, and it was one that represented a considerable concession on the part of the Office: that each Druid would pay in advance the standard fee for a single visit, which would then allow entry for four successive rites inside the monument.

Another problem was that of policing. The Druid ceremonies attracted crowds, not all of whom, significantly, were friendly to the Druids themselves, and so there was a real risk of disorder. Police cover, however, cost money, and there was a further wrangle between the Office of Works and the Wiltshire constabulary over who would bear the cost. In the end, the local police very reluctantly agreed to provide the extra constables without any payment. In addition to all these flashpoints, Reid and his companions expected the custodian and police to maintain not merely their physical safety but their dignity. They regarded themselves effectively as a priesthood serving the nation, and any mockery or insults to them as sacrilege, to be punished by the authorities. At the midsummer sunrise of 1922, before most of Reid's Druids had arrived at Stonehenge, a group of young officers from a nearby army base staged a burlesque of one of their rituals, wearing white sheets and false beards. The custodian regarded this as harmless fun, but the Bond's leadership, on hearing of it, regarded it as an intolerable insult, and severed relations with the Office for two years. As a result of all these disagreements, the Druids of the Universal Bond only actually celebrated inside Stonehenge at midsummer in two of the first five years in which the monument was in public ownership. They still arrived in the area at that season, but celebrated instead in their stronghold and sanctuary around the 'Double Circle' on Lady Glenconner's land.

There is no doubt that, in their dealings with the civil servants, they made things much more difficult for everybody by the manner in which they presented their case. They needed to bargain and cajole. What they did instead was to bluster, demand and lie. In the course of these years they informed the Office of Works that it was they who had maintained and protected the monument during the long years before it was enclosed, paying their own guardians to care for it. They declared that until 1913 Antrobus had allowed them to hold all the solstice ceremonies that they were now requiring, and without interference. For good measure, they warned the civil servants that Reid's curse on Antrobus had been followed by the latter's death. They also elaborated their own mythical history, claiming that the records of their order went back to 1643 (the date on the table in its Clapham temple) and its traditions to 'pre-Roman days'. They demanded that the custodian of Stonehenge be replaced with one of their own members, and the official guidebook to the monument with one written by themselves.

In making these claims and demands, the order was also squaring up to a new group of rivals at the stones: archaeologists. On acquiring Stonehenge, the Office of Works had undertaken two major responsibilities for it: to make the surviving structure safe, and to sponsor excavations that might provide greater knowledge of its date and purpose. It approached the main national body of British archaeology, the Society of Antiquaries of London, for a good person to undertake the job, and was sent William Hawley, a retired military man and experienced excavator. Hawley commenced work in 1920, stabilizing the megaliths and digging among and around them. Reid told his followers at the Double Circle, and members of the public who came to view the rites there, that this was desecration of a holy place, which would reveal no information of value. He may well have been perfectly sincere in these beliefs, but the whole tone of his order's communications with the Office suggests that he also deeply resented the presence of any authority on the history and purpose of the monument other than himself.

In the same period the Bond's rites and organization developed to fill the role which it was now seeking for itself. It retained its earlier eclecticism, hailing 'God' as 'Ahura Mazda, Brahma, Zeus and Jove', but added new Christian elements, including praise for the Ten Commandments and elaborate imagery based on the Cross. There were plenty of hymns, some written by Reid himself but others from the standard English repertoire, including 'Lead Kindly Light'. What remained constant was Reid's basic message of the need of humanity to reunite with each other and with the divine. In his speeches, to crowds at Stonehenge and the Double Circle, Reid now sounded like a mixture of a socialist politician and a preacher from a dissenting congregation, of a sort who would be familiar to many Wiltshire people. He accused the Church of England of failing to relieve the poor and claimed that Christ had come to save the working class from oppression. He informed his audience that the kingdom of God was within every human being, and that Druids would make England 'God's land' again. It helped their public image that he and his followers now shed their Eastern robes and adopted the garb of the long-familiar Ancient Order of Druids, putting on white robes with crimson hoods. Like the Ancient Order, also, they organized themselves into 'lodges', one based at Clapham and the other at Leamington, reflecting their traditional centres of membership.[52]

The year 1924 appeared to bring 'God's land' much closer to people like Reid, because the first Labour government was elected in the United Kingdom, a cause that he and his order had supported wholeheartedly. Reid himself, in fact, had become the leader of the local branch of the Labour Party in Clapham, and worked hard for it. A new First Commissioner of Works was duly appointed, and seemed to be one with whom Reid could do business, being a good-natured, chunkily built Yorkshireman who had started work in a textile mill at the age of eight, and been radicalized by the wage reductions imposed by employers. His name was Frederick Jowett.[53] The two of them met in July, and Reid was granted a whole new set of requests, including eleven days' worth of ceremonies inside Stonehenge at midsummer, and more rites at the equinoxes. Each Druid would be charged only one entrance fee per festival. The concession that would prove to be most controversial, and would pitch the Universal Bond into the national limelight, was that the order would be allowed to inter a small portion (about a seventh) of the cremated ashes of each of its deceased members within the monument. This had apparently happened in Cecil Chubb's time, though the evidence for this rests wholly on claims made by the Bond to the Office of Works; and it has been seen how much reliance can be placed on these. There is testimony that some ashes had been scattered by the Bond at the stones at that period, but not that they had been put into the ground.[54] At any rate, Jowett agreed to this as well, with some sensible provisos: that the ashes were put only into the topsoil, and kept outside the circles of stones themselves. It was a workable and amiable arrangement, which Jowett could make binding on his subordinates. Both he and Reid, however, had reckoned without the archaeologists.

Thus far, certainly, they had been represented by the regular, mild-mannered and unobtrusive presence of Colonel Hawley, going about his continuing excavations. In Wiltshire as a whole, however, archaeology was the concern of one of the most powerful and dynamic of the county societies founded under Victoria for the investigation of the English past. The custodian of Stonehenge tipped off a member about the agreement to allow the interment of ashes. He chose his man well: a retired vicar called George Engleheart. Engleheart was a person of enthusiasms, of which gardening and archaeology were the chief, and of conservative religious views: he had converted to Roman Catholicism on retirement. He also loved controversy, not least with fellow antiquarians: his obituary in a Wiltshire paper included the admission that 'his views on the subject were not always accepted by the majority of archaeology students'.[55] He was opposed on principle, furthermore, to the ideas that Stonehenge had been either a temple or connected with the movements of the sun. He had decided that it was a tomb.[56] The news of the concessions to the Druids could not have reached anyone more likely to oppose them with the utmost fury. At the next meeting of the Wiltshire Archaeological Society, Engleheart called the agreement with Jowett 'an almost unbelievable outrage on a national monument' by 'one sect'.

He was seconded by Frank Stevens, keeper of the Salisbury and South Wiltshire Museum and author of the official guide to Stonehenge. Stevens insisted that the prestige of British archaeology was now at stake, and he invited his fellows to consider the impact on continental scholars if they allowed the monument 'to become the scratching ground or burial place of a rather obscure sect of which they knew nothing'. The motion to launch a protest was carried unanimously in one of the most crowded meetings that the society had ever known.[57]

The proprietary tone of the statements is unmistakable. The ongoing archaeological work at the monument had given both the national and the local communities of archaeologists a new sense of responsibility for, and emotional investment in, the site. The Universal Bond now seemed, according to one's position, either to be challenging this, or to provide a splendid opportunity for the newly emerging discipline of prehistoric archaeology to test its strength. The Wiltshire Archaeological Society first worked through Parliament, putting up its local MP to question Jowett in early August. When the First Commissioner stood firm, the society orchestrated a national campaign among all concerned with British prehistory, to force him to change his mind. It took the form of a bombardment of political figures and newspapers with angry letters, and the authors spanned the range of experts and interest groups, including local antiquaries, Oxford dons, surviving giants from the Victorian era like Sir William Boyd Dawkins, and pioneers of the new-style professional archaeology which incorporated aerial photography and systematic field surveys, such as O. G. S. Crawford. They wrote both as individuals and as institutions, the latter including the Society of Antiquaries and the Royal Archaeological Institute. They stressed, to differing extents, three arguments: the tremendous potential damage that would be done to the archaeology of Stonehenge by disturbance of the ground; the lack of any connection between the historical Druids and the monument; and the character of the Universal Bond as an outfit made up of cranks and impostors. Much of the first of these depended on misunderstanding and misinformation. What had actually been agreed was that only a seventh of the contents of an urn of cremated ash should be deposited, in areas already dug over by Hawley. Some of the protesters seemed to think that entire cremations or even whole bodies would be dug into the site, at any point. None the less, the outrage expressed was all the greater for such errors, and the impression on the public accordingly the worse. The archaeologists also at times took care to distinguish the Universal Bond from more important and respectable modern Druid societies such as the Ancient Order of Druids, with the implication that the latter could use the monument for ritual for the benefit of all; the Ancient Order took the hint, and formally distanced itself from the Universal Bond. The matter became a national preoccupation in the 'silly season' of comparative absence of serious national news during the August holiday period.

The employees of the Office of Works carefully compiled cuttings from most of the newspapers that published letters, articles or editorials on it, and these rapidly and consistently expressed hostility to the Druids and to Jowett for pandering to them.[58] There was a minority opinion, which mocked archaeologists as self-important spoilsports, cut off from ordinary people, but this was no more favourable to Reid and his followers. They certainly suffered from a basic social prejudice against them as non-conformists or eccentrics, but they did not help their own cause. They might have won much more sympathy, and bolstered Jowett, by presenting themselves as well-intentioned and humble folk, attacked by pompous and overbearing intellectuals who were anxious to gain control of ancient sites and bully everybody into accepting their authority. Instead they chose Reid's habitual tactics, in adversity, of bombast and bluster. They claimed to be the oldest religious body in the modern world, and to have 68,000 members worldwide, with particular strength in Brittany and the United States. They denied that archaeologists had any greater privileges at, or expertise in, Stonehenge than themselves, and indeed insisted that they were superior, because they were united in their views and confident in their assertions, whereas the scholars were divided and admitted their ignorance of a precise date and purpose for the monument. It was added that all holders of the higher ranks in the Universal Bond had to pass an examination in astronomy, of which archaeologists were wholly ignorant.

The Universal Bond also carried out an enormous further embellishment of its own mythical history. Reid informed the Society of Antiquaries that it had grown out of a 'Haemus Lodge', which had existed long before the seventeenth century, when the famous philosopher and scientist Francis Bacon had been a member. It may be recalled that the order had only acquired lodges a year or two before; the name 'Haemus' was probably gained from reading or hearing of the published letters of William Stukeley, whose London home was given that nickname. Reid now declared that Stukeley himself had become chief of the order in 1720 and that the line of chiefs had then descended in unbroken succession to himself. Among its early members, he claimed various radicals of the English Civil War period, including the 'Leveller' leader John Lilburne and the 'Digger' leader Gerrard Winstanley, as well as John Aubrey and John Toland. Among the later members, he named 'Celtic' Davies, Charles Dickens, the royal Duke of Kent (Queen Victoria's father) and the Duke of Sussex, Godfrey Higgins, Charles James Fox, Iolo Morganwg, William Price, William Morris, Dante Gabriel Rossetti and a string of modern religious and social radicals. What Reid was clearly doing here was making a list of historical figures whom he personally admired, and co-opting them, posthumously, as members of his organization. He claimed that he and his Druids had known about all the discoveries made at Stonehenge by Hawley long before the archaeologists did. He taunted the archaeologists with doing nothing but damage to the monument and the other prehistoric sites around it. The privileges granted by Jowett had been given because the Commissioner had swallowed a completely bogus claim made by the order: that they had held services at the stones annually from before living memory. The Bond went on to state that Antrobus had supported them against archaeologists when the latter had objected to them in 1900.[59] Making claims like this was a dangerous game to play. A Wiltshire newspaper which had accepted the point that the deposition of ashes was not likely to do any damage was alienated by the assertions of a long history of Druid celebrations at Stonehenge on the summer solstice; local people knew perfectly well that they were a recent development.[60] Likewise, to include individuals like Charles Dickens and the Duke of Kent, who had well-recorded lives, as Druids, was to invite the ridicule and contempt of an informed audience such as the Society of Antiquaries.[61]

Above all, by making outrageous historical claims and presenting themselves as the true experts on, and custodians of, Stonehenge, Reid and his companions came over as even more self-important and unreasonable than the prehistorians, and with far less justification. Only one newspaper printed a letter stating their case, out of seventy that Reid claimed to have been sent by him and his people,[62] though journalists at times summarized their views. The *Times* and *Daily Chronicle* did send reporters to see the temple at Clapham, which they described as having as its focus the handsome carved oak table, wrought with signs of the zodiac and the date '1643', bearing a large Celtic cross with a suspended red lamp always burning before it. Neither newspaper, however, took up the Druids' cause.[63] Jowett felt that the case against the Bond was unreasonable, as what had actually been agreed could not possibly damage anything or anybody. The intention of the Druids was to deposit a small quantity of the ashes of one member in the top of one of the so-called Aubrey Holes that circled the stones. These were Neolithic burial pits, which may originally have been dug to hold timber posts, and the holes selected for the rite had already been excavated by Hawley. The pressure of both learned and journalistic opinion on the government was, however, becoming overwhelming. On 5 September Jowett gave way, and withdrew permission to inter any ashes at the monument. Reid and his henchmen sent infuriated letters to him and the Prime Minister, vowing never to submit to the decision and withdrawing the support of their order for the Labour Party. It no doubt helped this change of allegiance that, by the following year, Reid had been forced to resign as leader of his local branch of the party because of 'anti-democratic and irregular' behaviour.[64] At Stonehenge his order was left with only a fraction of the concessions that it had been granted by the new government: the right to hold four services at midsummer, each member paying an entry fee of half the usual price for every one. The one and only appearance of the order in the national consciousness had proved to be a disaster.

In 1956, when carrying out excavations at Stonehenge, Richard Atkinson found fragments of what he took to be a Victorian glass bottle, containing the ashes of a human being whom he thought to be (on unknown evidence) a 'Chief Druid'. It was outside the main circle, near the outlying megalith called the North Station Stone, and placed just under the turf to avoid disturbing any layers further down; and perhaps, also, for ease. There was a note with these, saying that the bottle had been interred 'by ceremony of BEMA'.[65] This is almost certainly a relic of the Universal Bond, the only group that expressed a desire to bury cremated ashes at the site during the period.[66] Whether it was deposited in the time of Chubb's ownership, as the Bond claimed, or whether it was sneaked in under cover of darkness, in defiance of the ban of 1924, will never be known. Atkinson gallantly reburied the remains where they had been found. They presumably rest there still, as a tangible link with an affair from which, at the present remove of years, nobody seems to emerge with much credit.

* * *

No single matter had united the world of British archaeology until that time so actively and comprehensively as this one, which may appear to us now as a non-issue:

the wish of a tiny Druid order to inter a few ashes in the topsoil of areas already exca-vated. It was a classic case of making a mountain out of a molehill; but then Reid's megalomania had made the Universal Bond into a molehill that pretended it was a mountain. He had attacked the archaeologists' presence at Stonehenge from the beginning, and set out quite deliberately to turn his order (which meant, effectively, himself) into the foremost public authority on the significance of the world's most famous prehistoric monument. The complete futility of this ambition did not diminish the determination and ferocity with which he had pursued it. In that sense, the national community of archaeologists had apparently done him the honour of taking his challenge seriously. The truth, of course, was otherwise: for the most part, the archaeologists were taking advantage of the Universal Bond to tighten their grip on the national view of the past. It has been mentioned that, ever since the 1860s, the orthodoxy among prehistorians had been that the ancient Druids had nothing to do with Stonehenge or other megalithic monuments, and that those prehistorians had expressed great bitterness at the failure of much of the general public to hear them on the matter. The publicity campaign mounted over the issue of the burial of ashes provided a splendid opportunity for them to put their message across in a broad range of newspapers. There were other benefits to be gained from the mass effort. The president of the Society of Antiquaries, the Earl of Crawford, told his colleagues that to have allowed the Universal Bond their wish would have been to open the door to any who claimed kinship with the ancient Druids to use the monument for similar rites. The exclusion of all such groups left archaeologists (specifically those appointed by his own society) as the only people allowed to disturb any ground around the stones. Their work, and therefore 'the really scientific investigation of the site', could therefore proceed without interruption or competition.[67] Similarly, the action taken by the Wiltshire Archaeological Society was just one of a number that it carried out in the 1920s in an attempt to ensure that nothing happened at the county's ancient monuments that did not have at least its approval and usually its leadership. These will be discussed later.

It is interesting, in this context, to note how scholarly views of Stonehenge and of the Druids developed during this period. When the government took over custody of the monument in 1919 it commissioned Frank Stevens, the museum curator at Salisbury, to produce an official guidebook to it, and he did so immediately. It remained the only guide sold at the site throughout the 1920s and 1930s, and, though slightly revised over time, did not alter in its essentials.[68] Stevens addressed three issues in particular. First, he assigned the building of the monument to the Neolithic, which he held – and as subsequent research has confirmed – to be the great age for erection of megalithic monuments in the British Isles. Second, he emphasized how little could still be understood of it, though it seemed at present most likely that it was a temple, and linked to worship of the sun; again, this suggestion stands up at the present day. Third, he sought to dispose of Druids, either as the builders of Stonehenge or as figures worthy of respect for any other reason. Citing a single Irish source in support of his surmise, he declared them 'likely to be mere "wise men" or "witch doctors", with perhaps a spice of the conjuror ... Theirs it would be to

summon the rain clouds and to terrify the people with their charms.' He then said
that both archaeologists and astronomers agreed that Stonehenge was constructed
long before their time, and perhaps by a different race. He recognized that Sir
Norman Lockyer was a respected astronomer who continued to associate them with
the monument, but represented him as isolated and eccentric in doing so.

The official government guidebook was therefore, in part, a document which
undermined any justification for the presence of Reid and his modern Druids at the
monument. The controversy over the burial of ashes had the additional effect of
sharpening the attitude of unofficial guidebooks towards them. Two of these were
published in 1924. One, issued at the Wiltshire county capital of Trowbridge,
assigned Stonehenge to the Neolithic and ignored Druids completely. The other was
in a series of guides to different English monuments produced by a Cheltenham
publisher, and took the offensive, blaming 'the imaginative' Stukeley for 'the notorious
Druid theory, which was responsible for much squandering of precious sentimentality
in the nineteenth century'. The anonymous author acknowledged that it was 'quite
probable' that Druids had used the monument for their ceremonies, even though
they did not build it, but then went on to point out the total lack of actual evidence
for this.[69]

One problem that the controversy brought home to archaeologists was the lack of
any full-scale book dealing directly with Druids which contained the new model of
prehistory. One of the most distinguished of British scholars, Sir Thomas Kendrick
of the British Museum, was provoked to provide one, and the result, entitled simply *The
Druids*, appeared in 1927. Designed for the broadest possible readership, it presented
itself as 'a complete and well-documented summary of the whole of the pertinent material' and 'a sober outline of fact'. This was directly contrasted with the 'prodigious
amount of rubbish' which 'has been written about Druidism, particularly that worst and
insidious variety that masquerades as deep and recondite learning'. Kendrick denied
that there was any connection between Druids and most megalithic monuments, or any
chance that Druidic tradition could have been preserved through the centuries that
separated the disappearance of the ancient Druids from the appearance of their modern
counterparts. Indeed he emphasized, with some justice, that modern Britain had no
separate, rival, popular set of beliefs concerning Druids, opposed to those of scholars:
those voiced by people like Reid were just those of previous archaeologists, 'or their
ancestors', which were now out of date. He argued that the evidence now suggested
most strongly that Druidry was the religion of the Celtic invaders of Western Europe,
and developed by them there as a fusion of their own traditions with those of the
peoples whom they conquered. He portrayed it as 'the elementary superstitions of
simple folk', bereft of real scientific knowledge, profound theology or philosophy,
or impressive places of worship. Both ancient and modern Druids were thus thoroughly
put in what Kendrick took to be their place.[70]

These attitudes rubbed off on publications concerned with the other great Wiltshire
monument that had become associated with Druids: the circles and avenue at Avebury.
In 1923 a naval surgeon gave the world his own theories concerning their purpose.
Even twenty years before, these would have been full of Druidical references; now

there were none. Instead, he interpreted Avebury as a shrine to the reproductive powers of nature, represented by the heathen gods Moloch and Baal denounced by the Old Testament prophets. In his reading, it had been abandoned, with the religion it had served, upon the arrival of the Celts.[71] Once again, an attempt was being made to bring the Bible back into British prehistory, but this time without the Druids. In 1930 a semi-official counterpart arrived: a guide to the monument written by Maud Cunnington, one of the leaders of the Wiltshire Archaeological Society. It derided Stukeley's interpretations, never mentioned Druids, and assigned the circles firmly to the Neolithic or Bronze Age.[72] At the end of the decade, an avowedly official guide-book was published, produced by the wife of the current owner and excavator of Avebury, Alexander Keiller. Although the Cunningtons and Keillers were rivals in a struggle to dominate the public perception of Wiltshire archaeology, the two booklets were essentially similar in their approach. The second was just ruder, both to the prehistoric builders, who were characterized as 'primitive' and superstitious, and to Stukeley and his successors: 'You may have heard all kinds of stories about sun worship, serpent worship, and so on, but there is absolutely no foundation for any of these tales, which have been put about by people with more imagination than knowledge.'[73]

There was, however, a way by which Druids could be allowed back into Stonehenge, although in a much reduced role, and it had been signalled by the guide-book from Cheltenham: that they used the monument for their ceremonies, even if they had not built it and if it was already one or two millennia old by their time. Kendrick himself took this quite far, suggesting that it had actually been rebuilt by the Druids in its present form, which is why it looked so different from other stone circles, and, with its lintels, seemed to show knowledge of Greek and Roman archi-tecture. He concluded that the monument might therefore 'very fairly be called a temple of Druidism'. He went on, moreover, to suggest that some Neolithic cham-bered tombs, at least in France, might have been repaired or even built by Druids, and that the newly discovered monument nicknamed 'Woodhenge' had been their work. This consisted of a timber round-house, or (more likely) concentric rings of wooden posts, excavated by Maud Cunnington a mile from Stonehenge itself. Kendrick felt that it might have been an artificial imitation, made by the Druids, of a sacred grove.[74]

Similar ideas were subsequently championed by the Cunningtons themselves and their friends, and contained in a book published by R. H. Cunnington in 1935. He disagreed with Kendrick over Woodhenge, holding that to be much older, and the present structure of Stonehenge to be an Iron Age imitation of it. On the late date of the major Stonehenge circles, however, they were agreed, and Cunnington went further. He suggested that the monument might indeed have been the temple of the Hyperboreans mentioned in ancient Greek texts, and that its 'inception may after all have been due to that romantic Order, the Druids'.[75] Such ideas were anathema to George Engleheart, the arch-enemy of Reid's Druids, who deplored the fact that by 1933 they were held by several of his most prominent colleagues in the Wiltshire Archaeological Society, including both Cunningtons and a group he nicknamed 'the Devizes school', after the town that contained the society's headquarters and museum.[76] In a way, the scholars concerned were projecting back into prehistory the role of modern Druids themselves, as a set of latecomers who had made Stonehenge into their own temple.

* * *

Meanwhile, the Universal Bond was left to make what it could of the small remnant of concessions from Jowett, and these led to another disaster. In 1925, for the first time in the decade, Reid's Druids chose to stage a ceremony in Stonehenge at the solstice sunrise itself, when the maximum number of people would be present. Indeed, the crowd that gathered, mostly outside the fence, was the largest in living memory. Under the terms of the agreement, the Bond's members could enter the stones at half-price, on production of a letter from Jowett directing this. For some reason, Reid's own son, Robert, was unable or unwilling to show the letter to the custodian, and an argument broke out. Either because of impatience with the delay in allowing entry to the stones, or because Reid and his son incited them to do so (statements differ over the matter), about a hundred of the crowd outside the gate then forced their way in without payment. Reid was able to deliver an invocation as the sun rose, followed by a speech, though a companion who sang a hymn was jeered by the spectators. Reid and his fellows returned for a full-scale service at noon and for another oration delivered by Reid in the evening. The atmosphere between the Druids and the Office of Works had, however, been further embittered. Showing remarkable patience, the Office was prepared to try to make the same arrangements work for the following year, but the Bond was not. Its leadership sent a letter denouncing the civil servants for failing to punish both the custodian and the police, and threatening to start another riot. Instead, and wisely, it withdrew from Stonehenge altogether for two years.[77]

In that time, it camped and worshipped at midsummer on the land of Lady Glenconner (now Grey); one of the many ironies of Reid's career was that he preached socialism with such fervour while remaining dependent on old-fashioned aristocratic patronage for a base near Stonehenge. The standard format for the gatherings was a rite in the morning followed by a set-piece address by Reid in the evening. The nature of the former was even more clearly allied to Christianity, with the singing of well-known hymns and readings from the Bible. Although denunciations of the Office of Works and the government had now joined his usual material, Reid's orations covered the same basic ground as before. He condemned modern society as characterized by greed, selfishness and exploitation, and predicted the coming of 'the time of God', when poverty and war would be abolished. In his view, the traditional churches had betrayed both Christ and humanity, while his Druids kept faith with both. Hundreds of local people came to hear these speeches, and it is easy to see why: their call for apocalyptic social regeneration, in a union of socialism and Christianity, would have struck a receptive chord among many working people in the era of the General Strike and growing economic instability.[78]

During this period, Reid continued to rework his own personal mythology, and to publish his beliefs. Another issue of the *New Life* was brought out in 1927, which claimed that the order had held services at Stonehenge since the Tudor period. It also took a swing at the Ancient Order of Druids for distancing itself from the Universal Bond so firmly during the burial controversy.[79] The Bond now claimed that the founder of the Ancient Order, whom it misnamed 'Anthony Hurle', had been expelled from its own ranks in 1791, for wishing to introduce 'alcohol and ribald mirth' in place of spirituality. It now identified its faith firmly as the Celtic Christianity that nineteenth-century legend, building on sixteenth-century roots, had derived from Druidry. As part of this latest shift, it expressed a new hostility to Roman Catholicism as a worse and rival faith, and took credit for having caused the Protestant Reformation. None the less, it expressed respect for the teachings of Buddha and all faiths that sought to unify humanity, and still proclaimed its ideal to be 'Universal Brotherhood'.[80]

In 1928 the Bond came back to Stonehenge for midsummer, and proceeded to do so for the next four years, without any difficulty. The basic reason for this remarkable change was the replacement of its arch-enemy, the custodian, with a new man who looked on them with much more favour. It helped also that negotiations with the Office of Works were taken over by Reid's son, Robert, who, despite his appearance at the centre of the trouble in 1925, was a person of much more easy and diplomatic temperament. Permission to hold services was smoothly and politely requested, and given. After the experiences of 1925, the order avoided the solstice itself, preferring to hold services at dawn, noon and sunset on one of the neighbouring dates. In 1931 the entrance fee was reduced still further for Reid's Druids, to a half-price single payment that covered the entire day.[81]

The number of the Universal Bond who attended the Stonehenge rites now reached its maximum under Reid's leadership, being just over fifty in each year. Adam Stout has argued plausibly that they represented the majority of the order's active membership at that time; as one piece of evidence, visitors who called at its main temple at Clapham, at midsummer 1930, found it locked up because everyone was away at Stonehenge.[82] Most were from London, which was clearly now the main centre of the organization. Compared with the hundreds who turned out for the ceremonies of the Ancient Order and United Ancient Order, let alone the hundreds of thousands in their world membership, this certainly left the Universal Bond as a minor group of modern Druids. None the less, over fifty people could make an impressive enough showing among the stones. Unlike the older English orders, the Universal Bond had always admitted women on theoretically equal terms, and they took part in the ceremonies, although they were never as prominent in Reid's organization as the men. The rites themselves followed a fairly standard pattern.[83] The robes sported by the order now signalled a hierarchy of office. Reid and three other senior members of this body were the only celebrants allowed to wear wholly white robes, the symbol of purity and unity. They were capped by pleated white headdresses. Other leading members, with the title of Past Arch, taken from the Ancient Order, wore red hoods (red being the symbolic colour of wisdom), purple robes (mixing the hues of wisdom and understanding), white surplices and golden girdles. All others worked in normal dress.

The ceremonies began before daybreak, with the 'Rite of the Golden Dawn', a name which, of course, suited both the hour and Reid's roots in ritual magic. A confession of faith was proclaimed at the Hele Stone, which stands at the entrance of the earthwork surrounding the monument, and then all the celebrants clasped hands around the recumbent Slaughter Stone between the entrance and the main circles. They moved round it sunwise three times, chanting. Once in the centre of the stones, they sang the 'Song of Dawn' as the sun rose. A charcoal fire was kindled in a gilded brazier beside the Altar Stone. Five notes were then struck on a gong, to symbolize the five trilithons of Stonehenge and the five senses of humanity. Reid's massive figure presided over the rites – he now weighed over two hundred pounds without having run to fat[84] and sported a long walrus moustache. He led the others in taking 'communion' in bread and wine, another sign of the increasing assimilation of his Druidry to Christianity. The wine was drunk from a silver cup, or 'grail', which each Druid, led by Reid, raised when standing beside the Altar Stone. They all returned later that morning, at eleven o'clock, and rekindled the brazier, burning oak leaves on it as an offering to the souls of dead members of the order. Their names were spoken and a 'sacristan' lit a long taper in memory of each. Reid stood behind the Altar Stone, with his robed Druids in front of him and those without robes, and the public, gathered behind him. Hymns were sung to the music of a harmonium, with lengthy responses. At the end, Reid turned to the south, lifted his face and hand to the sun and invited both living and dead to stand before 'the throne of Love's Illimitable Light'. Both the dawn and the late morning rites attracted between one and five hundred spectators, including American tourists, press reporters and (occasionally) a film crew; sometimes more than now attended the solstice sunrise itself. As before, once Reid himself was allowed into the stones on preferential terms, he showed no interest in the public beyond the fence. Conversely, now that the Office of Works was apparently treating the Universal Bond with respect, journalists and spectators had begun to do so again.

The impression that these events were largely a pedestal for Reid himself was strengthened during the rest of the day, which was given up to speeches by him. In the afternoon he lectured at Stonehenge on the history of Druidry, to his members and anybody else who would listen. In the evening he delivered a set-piece oration at the Double Circle to the south, where he and his people still camped. Up to three thousand people gathered to hear him, and the Amesbury brass band provided music for the hymns that were sung afterwards in a brief service conducted in the midst of the crowd by the robed Druids. Passages from the Bible accompanied these, and they ended with Iolo's prayer, taken from the Welsh Gorsedd; Reid had now started to read Iolo's writings and incorporate them into his practice of Druidry.[85] Reid's evening speeches hammered away at the theme of the apocalyptic Second Coming of Christ to reform society completely and do away with poverty and oppression. He summed up the doctrine of Druidry as the need to give food and employment to all, and the need of each human to know his or her own self, and to recognize and experience God within himself or herself. To drive home the identity of Druids with Christians, he declared that the reason why the Romans had persecuted the former was the fervour with which they had taken up the latter's message, which so well suited their existing beliefs. At one point he insisted that the number of stones at Stonehenge was equal to that of the fish caught by Christ's apostles when he ordered them to cast their nets. Once more it may be argued that, to many of those listening, what he was saying must have seemed a natural outgrowth of the dissenter tradition of British Protestantism, and one well suited to the mood of the times, as the nation settled into the Great Depression.

The Universal Bond thus seemed to have achieved a stable and respectable routine; but with Reid things could never remain the same for long. For all his professed abhorrence of physical violence, he could not live without adversaries to be reviled and threatened. These could be abstract figures (those who ground the faces of the poor), but he also needed specific targets. He was still fulminating against the Ancient Order of Druids and the archaeologists, and it was only a matter of time before he quarrelled with the Office of Works again. The cause this time was provided by his order's magazine itself. A single copy of it was published at midsummer each year, for sale to the public at Stonehenge and the Double Circle. In 1930 and 1931 some of those who bought it were, unsurprisingly, offended by the views it expressed. The friendly custodian suggested that the order proof itself against their complaints by seeking formal permission from the Office to sell its literature; and this was a fatal error. The Office had a policy of prohibiting the sale of any on the site except the official guidebook. It enforced this with genuine impartiality – the works of the Wiltshire Archaeological Society were banned as well as those of the Druids – but that is not the way Reid saw the matter. The official guidebook was, after all, that by Frank Stevens, which both denigrated the ancient Druids and denied that they had any connection with Stonehenge; to Reid, it was the bluntest and most succinct expression of all that he detested in modern archaeology. To deny him the right to sell his order's magazine was to deprive him of any written right of reply and give a monopoly to a view of the monument which he believed to be completely false.[86] At midsummer that year, the Universal Bond held its usual three services, but Reid made clear to spectators and journalists that they would be the last at Stonehenge because of this latest outrage inflicted on his order.[87]

Reid added that he would continue to stage his midsummer rites at the Double Circle, as during previous feuds with the Office of Works; but times had changed. His protectress, Lady Grey, had died in 1928. Her son, the new Lord Glenconner, was willing to tolerate the continued presence of the Druids on his land, and would probably have given them sanctuary on it indefinitely. Reid, however, now pushed his luck by informing the public, on withdrawing from Stonehenge, that his order proposed to erect an exact replica of the monument at the Double Circle, for use in its ceremonies. This was probably never a feasible project, but the Wiltshire Archaeological Society and the *Wiltshire Gazette* took it seriously and protested at the disturbance that such building work would create in an area of major archaeological interest. Glenconner, whom Reid had clearly not consulted about the matter, refused permission for it, and the rift between them deprived the Universal Bond of its vital base near Stonehenge. Reid never returned to the area. The monument was left entirely to the Ancient Order and United Ancient Order, who hired it for rites with increasing regularity through the 1930s.

It may be that Reid was growing weary of being a Druid, as his restless spirit was leading him into yet new enterprises. In 1928 he had bought a hundred acres of land in Sussex, on which he built a holiday camp and health farm for fellow radicals – 'men and women in the vanguard movement of politics and religion'.[88] Furthermore, his religious centre of gravity was shifting yet again. Just as Stonehenge had led him into identifying himself as a Druid, so the loss of the opportunity to worship there now caused him to shed that identity. After 1932 he never seems to have referred to himself as a Druid. The Clapham temple became known as 'the South London Universalist Church', and its liturgy was reshaped yet again. It still stated belief in the union of the human race and in the humanity of Christ, but became even more Christian, terming Jesus 'the author and perfector of our faith'. Gone were all references to Buddhist or Muslim terminology, and indeed any interest in other religions. The list of 'prophets and pioneers' honoured in it was now confined to a succession of leaders of the formal Christian denomination of Universalism.[89] The official name of the Universal Bond of the Sons of Men had now become 'the Universalist Church, British Circle'.[90]

As part of his process of sloughing off Druidry, and in keeping with his bellicose character, Reid quarrelled with and disinherited his own son. This breach was largely due to his promotion of another leading supporter, Arthur Peacock, as his spiritual heir in place of Robert.[91] Peacock has left an autobiography, and it is easy to see from it why he and Reid were attracted to each other.[92] The younger man was a keen socialist, drawn to the older one by his energy and vivid rhetoric and also by his profession of a radical spirituality. He found Reid's creed attractive because of its emphasis on love and universal salvation, and he swallowed his historical claims completely. This absolute loyalty and admiration gave the older man the disciple that his autocratic temperament craved. In addition, Peacock's fundamentally Christian instincts chimed well with Reid's own drift in the 1930s back towards a religion based more firmly on that tradition, of which his son (as shall be seen) certainly did not approve. It may well be, indeed, that Peacock's inclinations acted as an encouragement to Reid in that drift; in which case he was following in the steps of Mathers, Bennett, Rosher and those before who had acted as powerful influences on Reid's thought.

It may also be true that Reid was at last growing old, and his energy and interest in his order were starting to wane. Whatever the precise impact of all these changes, the Universal Bond was already starting to show signs of decay by the mid-1930s: an American who had visited it in 1935 recalled that it 'seemed to be struggling'.[93] Things got much worse with the coming of war. The camp in Sussex was requisitioned by the army, cutting off Reid's main source of income and dispersing members of his order still further; when another American visited the Clapham church in the autumn of 1943, he found Peacock acting as minister to one old man. In August 1944 a flying bomb destroyed the building with all its contents.[94] Once the war ended, Reid and Peacock set to work to pick up the pieces, consecrating a new church on the estate in Sussex, but the old man's time had finally run out. He died in August 1946; the certificate that recorded this gave his occupation as 'Minister of Religion'.[95]

The biographer of George Watson MacGregor Reid, Adam Stout, has called him 'the most fantastic fabulator' and 'one of the most inspirationally different characters I've ever come across'.[96] I have written of him that he was 'a bully, a braggart and a charlatan', but also 'a visionary of heroic and generous ideals, capable of inspiring great devotion in others'.[97] Clearly he was a giant character, physically and spiritually, and clearly, also, his successive changes of religious tone and emphasis were in pursuit of an absolutely consistent vision, of the ending of poverty and oppression on earth. As such, inevitably, he has dominated this chapter, but its central concern has been with the story of his order. There is little or no 'internal' evidence of its nature and workings. Its archive was completely destroyed by the bomb that removed its headquarters.[98] What personal papers remained to Reid were bequeathed to his wife and Peacock, neither of whom had much interest in Druidry.

What this chapter has sought to show is how much can be learned about a modern religious group from 'external' sources alone; from its publications, letters written by its members to outsiders, and observations made on it by journalists and other commentators who encountered it. As such, it is a study in the invention of tradition, and a micro-history of how a modern religion can develop and progressively create and recreate a past. It is also a study of how, back in the 1910s and 1920s, a self-conscious spiritual counterculture could relate to and react with dominant structures and norms. It is an illustration of how a small number of people could, once linked to a famous prehistoric monument, make a considerable impression on national consciousness. It also describes and analyses an important phase in the growth of engagement with the national heritage by both the state and archaeology; in this respect the Universal Bond acted as a flashlight shone upon both bodies of people to reveal features of their ambitions and attitudes that would otherwise have been concealed. Finally, even more than other parts of this book, it is a refutation of the statement made by Stuart Piggott in 1968: that the nature of modern Druid orders makes the writing of a true history of them 'virtually impossible'.[99]

12

DRUIDS AND
ARCHAEOLOGISTS

The Universal Bond was to survive the death of its founder, and it was to continue to draw public attention, in a greater and more consistent measure than before. Again it would be an agent and a subject of national controversy, always associated with the world's most celebrated prehistoric monument. Again it was to achieve an adversarial relationship with the established world of scholarship, in a manner which is revealing of the nature of both parties and of the wider social and cultural context in which they operated. It was not, however, to be the same relationship, with the same results, for by the mid-twentieth century all three entities – the Druids, the archaeologists and the parent society and culture – had altered in nature.

* * *

Reid's order split into two main groups upon his death. One was the continuation of his Universalist Church in London, now led by the old man's designated heir, Arthur Peacock. In 1951 Peacock finally gave up the struggle to renew it and became a minister of the Unitarian Church in Wandsworth instead. He therefore achieves the distinctive but melancholy significance of having been the last Universalist parson in the United Kingdom.[1] The second group was formed out of those members of Reid's order who wished to continue within a specifically Druidic tradition. It was the Ancient Order of Druid Hermetists (AODH), led by another Londoner, called G. W. Smith. Smith, like Peacock, had met Reid through the Labour Party, and then been drawn into his spiritual interests. He subsequently paid tribute to Reid for having taught him everything about both Druidry and socialism.[2] Smith's order was in existence from the late 1930s, long before Reid's death, and the need for it is an indication of how much the old chief had himself abandoned a Druid identity by that time. Its name was a neat indication of its ambitions, for it blended a reference to the oldest modern Druidical society, the Ancient Order of Druids, with another, to occult tradition, for the Hermetic texts were one of the main bodies of ancient mystical teaching to survive in the European world.

According to a story that was circulating in the 1950s, it had been founded in London in 1926 as an offshoot of the Dublin branch of the Hermetic Society, a Victorian body founded to recover and synthesize wisdom from Western esoteric traditions.[3] This may be the case, but by the time it emerged into the historical record it was showing no sign of interest in the Hermetic Society or any of its personalities. Its public début was at midsummer 1938, with the first appearance of its magazine, the *Pendragon*. The name of this was itself a bow towards the Arthurian legend, and the declared purpose of the new order was to demystify occultism 'in such a practical manner as will render its application to everyday life and action'. Although it never mentioned Reid, it was clearly in harmony with his ideals, aiming to educate its initiates to work for a new era of peace and happiness and calling the objective of modern Druidry 'the Universal Spiritual Brotherhood of Humanity'. Its ethics were based in the triads composed by Iolo Morganwg, which it believed to be the work of the ancient Druids.[4]

From 1938 it began to celebrate the summer solstice at Stonehenge, at first very unobtrusively. On 21 June in that year and the next just five members appeared, in ordinary dress, and for very brief rites, unnoticed by the press.[5] Its profile rose when it became the only Druid group to hold ceremonies anywhere near the monument during the Second World War, and it now showed both a gift for seizing attention and a delicate tact. It held its recorded wartime ceremony in 1943 away from the date of the solstice itself to avoid attracting crowds. It also held it at the Double Circle, rather than at Stonehenge itself, having remade with the landowner, the heir of Lady Glenconner, that invaluable friendship that Reid had thrown away a decade before. A private ceremony was held at dawn on 20 June and repeated before a group of about thirty members of the public two days later. It emphasized the need to strive, after the ending of the war, to bring about a new age of beauty, wisdom and universal love to replace that of cruelty and terror which had now reached its apotheosis in the world conflict. In doing so, the AODH neatly scored three targets: it opposed the spirit of war itself, according to Reid's old ideals; it held out the hope of a better world when peace returned; and it provided another stirring example of the determination of the British to preserve their traditional customs and habits through the heart of the conflict.[6]

In the year after the war ended, 1946, the AODH celebrated the return of peace with fervour, holding sunrise rites at the Double Circle on 21 and 23 June. At noon on the 23rd it performed for half an hour at Stonehenge, with twelve members all now robed solemnly in white. It introduced Iolo's ceremony, from the Welsh Gorsedd, of the ritual sheathing of a sword, to mark the ending of the world war. More of Iolo's influence was visible in the conclusion of the ceremony in the invocation of the 'One Divine Spirit' under the Welsh name of 'awen', which both medieval and modern Welsh bards had taken to mean inspiration, usually with the implication that it had a divine source. As part of the democratic hue of Smith's order, all present then in turn put on a crown of oak leaves. The custodian of the monument was impressed by the good behaviour of those taking part.[7]

When Reid died a few months later, the Ancient Order of Druid Hermetists was in a perfect position to assume the original name of his order, as 'the Druid Universal Bond',[8] while Peacock preferred to use its later one, the British Circle of the Universalist Church. Smith's order thus became, to all intents and purposes, the most obvious successor group to Reid's original one as it had been in the 1920s.

Immediately, it began to enlarge its presence at Stonehenge, giving four services between dawn and evening of 22 June 1947. The participants now numbered sixteen, drawing a crowd of spectators of over forty and a recording crew from national radio.[9] The next year, 1948, competition arrived, with the return of the fraternal orders to Stonehenge after their wartime absence; and this time the focus was on the summer solstice itself. First two hundred of the Ancient Order of Druids, from a Sussex lodge, performed on 19 June. Then a Royal Arch Chapter of the same order of Druids, also from Sussex, got an hour of rites on the afternoon of 20 June, for a group numbering about a hundred, including wives and children. Not to be outdone, some of the United Ancient Order appeared on the evening of the 21st. The Universal Bond was in danger of being completely overshadowed.

Clearly this mattered to it, because it quickly took action to grab and keep the midsummer limelight, by booking itself in at the hour of dawn and sunrise on 21 June, when the maximum number of the public and journalists would be present. It also fielded a larger number of members – thirty – and with more pomp. The Office of Works gamely agreed to keep Stonehenge open all night for the first time, and Smith and his people held a vigil there through the dark hours, singing songs and hymns. They informed journalists that they represented the reunion of the full former order of George Watson MacGregor Reid, after years in which it had been scattered, and marked the occasion with a return to the graded ceremonial garb of his days. Once more some members wore red hoods and some purple robes, while Smith was robed in the white of purity and universal brotherhood. He now administered communion, as Reid had done. He and his companions also introduced more ritual elements from the world of ceremonial magic, and especially from those used by the Hermetic Order of the Golden Dawn. The four cardinal points of the compass were honoured and given elemental correspondences. A leading Druid clad in a red hood stood on the eastern side of the rites to represent the element of air, a yellow-hooded one stood to the south to represent fire, a black-hooded one was to the west, for earth, and a grey-hooded one to the north, for water.[10] The result was a complete success, as the national press recorded the dawn rites of the Universal Bond in detail, and not those of the other orders, the custodian was impressed by the dignity of the proceedings, and a crowd of two hundred watched with respectful interest. Smith thanked it at the end for its orderly behaviour. He and his companions returned for a further ceremony later in the day, before the United Ancient Order turned up. The liturgy neatly blended Christian and pagan themes, speaking at one moment of a single supreme divine being, and at another of the material world as being in the custody of a sun god and an earth goddess. Reincarnation was stated to be the fate of the human soul, and Iolo Morganwg was quoted on the primitive equality of the human race.[11] Henceforth, Smith's Universal Bond held the central position at the annual gathering to watch the midsummer sunrise, and it became the modern Druid order of which the public was most aware.

In pushing for attention in this manner it was almost certainly reacting to more than a threat from the older Druid orders. It was facing a challenge from a brand new one, dangerously close to itself. It may be remembered that Reid had a son of his own,

Robert, who had supported him actively in his Druidic rites in the 1920s, and been disinherited in the 1930s. Robert continued to take his Druidry seriously, joining Smith's AODH and remaining with it through most of the 1940s.[12] He also, however, regarded himself as the rightful heir of the old chief, and his exclusion from his material and spiritual inheritance clearly rankled. This pride in his family, and natural ambition, was signalled by the manner in which he began to hyphenate his surname with the one that his father had assumed, to give it the more gentrified form of 'MacGregor-Reid'. His feelings seem to have come to a head after the old man died, and coincided with those of former followers of the latter who were either personally fond of Robert or unhappy with Smith's leadership, or both. It mattered to Robert's sense of his position, and of the legitimacy of his cause, that several of them came from the former lodge of the Universal Bond in Leamington Spa, which George Watson Reid had himself recognized as the first one ever formally established to enact his religion. It could therefore claim to be the senior division of the order, and some of its people resented the way in which the London membership had eclipsed it.[13] At the winter solstice of 1946, the disaffected former followers of Reid gathered at the home of the oldest of them, in Bristol, together with some newly found allies. The Leamington group formally claimed the status of Mother Lodge of the order, conferring on itself some kind of leadership, and proclaimed Robert MacGregor-Reid to be the new chief of the Universal Bond. To reinforce its credentials, it announced a new creation myth: that it had been founded by John Toland himself at a meeting in London in 1717. According to the new mythology, a conference of Druids had chosen Toland as chief of a new federated Druid order over which the lodge now based at Leamington was to preside. From that moment until 1946, the succession of chiefs of the order had been continuous, and Robert was now the latest to be elected. The body thus formally invented at that meeting in 1946 now took both the names that Reid had given to his order: 'An Druidh Uileach Braithreachas' and 'The British Circle of the Universal Bond'. With calculated affront to its rivals, it also added another, grander and simpler: 'The Druid Order'. It had proved itself to possess boldness, and a capacity for historical fantasy, every bit as remarkable as those of Reid himself.[14]

The rebellion was slow to gather momentum, and in the next year Robert was fully occupied in establishing his position. In July 1948 his order consolidated its identity further by issuing its first handbook of ceremonies.[15] By 1949, it was ready to take its place at Stonehenge. In May that year it declared its existence to the Office of Works, claiming to be the true order of the Universal Bond, and to have affiliations with groups in North and South America, Scotland, Ireland and continental Europe. It asked for permission to hold three ceremonies in the monument, at dawn, noon and evening; but as some gesture of accommodation with its rivals, it requested a date in early July, tactfully avoiding the midsummer period. The Office agreed, though it coldly directed that the rites concerned had to be brief and informal, and that a reduced entrance fee could be paid only if the participants numbered over thirty.[16] In November that year, Robert and his supporters agreed to transfer their headquarters from Leamington to London, where a new Mother Lodge would be established, with a Grand Council to govern the whole order.[17]

Smith's group struck back by raising its own profile at Stonehenge still further. It asked for and got additional services there at the autumn equinox of 1949 and New Year's Day 1950, and requested them on no fewer than four more dates in the remainder of 1950. It also warned the Office of Works not to grant any requests from Robert's group, whom it now denounced as impostors. At the same time, the venerable Ancient Order of Druids was making its own rites at the monument more spectacular. For the midsummer of 1950 its district lodge for South-East London designed one to involve almost four hundred of its members, with music provided by a portable organ and two solo singers. It included a piece of drama in which one of the company, representing an ancient Druid, offered himself to be judged for offences against the rules of the order, and passed between twin fires of purification before being restored to favour. Six hymns were to be sung, in addition to the order's version of the National Anthem (as sung at the stones in the 1920s), followed by an address by the presiding Druid on the universal nature of sun-worship throughout the history of humanity. The props required for the rites consisted of three urns to hold fires, six wooden swords, twelve torches to represent the signs of the zodiac, and a total of thirty-one candles, set in patterns to represent the sun and moon and a star. The civil servants responsible for Stonehenge struggled with all these requests as well as they could. They tried to limit Smith's group to only two more days of ceremony that year, and ignored its invectives against that of Robert MacGregor-Reid, who was once more allowed three services on a date in early July. They let the Ancient Order stage its extravaganza, on condition that the public was allowed into the enclosure to watch, and that the Druids kept away from the stones. Then they realized that it wanted the same date as Smith's people, and had to arrange for them to celebrate at different hours.[18]

After that, things got worse for the hapless officials. Smith proved himself every bit as stubborn as his mentor Reid had been when encountering opposition to his wishes. Ignoring the ruling of the Office, he pushed for celebrations in the stones at both equinoxes and the midsummer of 1951, and the civil servants gave way on condition that he asked for only two dates per year in the future. MacGregor-Reid's order asked for its usual day in July, and warned that it would bring a larger group than before, including a number of American guests. The Office agreed, if it would enact two services instead of three. The International Grand Lodge of Druidism booked in for 29 June, and sent hundreds of delegates to the rite, representing orders in eight nations, including the Ancient Order, United Ancient Order and Order of Druids in the United Kingdom. In 1952, MacGregor-Reid's Druids requested three services again on their annual visit in July, whereupon Smith protested that he should be given more, as compensation for this indulgence of rebels. The next year MacGregor-Reid raised the stakes again, by applying to the Office to hold three services on the summer solstice itself, including the dawn one, that pole ritual position which Smith had so adroitly occupied. Once again, the officials struggled to be reasonable, granting the dawn ceremony to Smith once more, but giving the noon and sunset bookings to his rival. This judgment of Solomon endured for two years, and resulted in the Office being bombarded with invective from Smith and protests from his competitors. It ended, unexpectedly, with the physical collapse of Smith himself in June 1954. He was suddenly taken mortally ill, and there was nobody in his group capable of succeeding him. The group's dawn ceremony at the solstice that year was cancelled, and it fell apart after his death. Robert MacGregor-Reid was suddenly left as the leader of the only surviving successor group of the original Universal Bond, and at the summer solstice of 1955 he smoothly took over the conduct of dawn and noon ceremonies at Stonehenge. He had, after all, reclaimed the entire spiritual inheritance of his father.[19]

* * *

Three major questions need to be posed and answered about Robert MacGregor-Reid and his order in its heyday of the 1950s: what sort of person was he; what beliefs did he and his fellow Druids hold and what rites did they enact; and how did their relationship with the general public and the civil service develop after they assumed such a prominent position at Stonehenge?

In body and mind, MacGregor-Reid was very much his father's son: a man of commanding physical presence and powerful personality who enjoyed leading from the top. He also sported a prominent dark moustache, though it was of the toothbrush rather than the walrus style. Rather unfortunately, his physical bulk tended to spread sideways rather than being balanced, as in his father's case, by muscle and height. The artist Ithell Colquhoun, who regarded him with affection and respect, still commented on the 'bulky white-draped figure' he made at Stonehenge, and how he would 'wallow' his way to the stones to jeers of 'Moby Dick!' from bystanders.[20] Colquhoun also recorded his enthusiasm for ritual magic, summed up in his exclamation to her, 'Doesn't it occur to you that the Druid Order is the survivor of the Golden Dawn?' As part of his attempt to establish connections between the two bodies, MacGregor-Reid told her and others about the former existence of various Druidical groups in the world of ritual magic of which no record survives: the Ancient and Archaeological Order of Druids, mentioned before, a mysterious 'Nuada Temple' in London in the 1910s, and a Druid lodge led by the occultist John Brodie-Innes, called 'An Tigh Geatha Darrach', 'The Gate House of the Gods'.[21] How far any of these existed outside the realms of fantasy, it is now impossible to say.[22] MacGregor-Reid professed a respect for Aleister Crowley, whom he claimed to have met on a number of occasions.[23] What is certain is that the desire to link modern Druidry to Victorian ceremonial magic was a common concern of those who had gathered round Smith in the AODH. An issue of Smith's magazine, published in 1953, included a pseudo-history in which a Mount Haemus Grove had been founded at Oxford in 1245 and continued until the late nineteenth century, when it had been taken over by occultists. According to this article, the same people had led the Theosophical Society, the Golden Dawn, and the Universal Bond, which had itself grown out of the Mount Haemus Grove. Ithell Colquhoun, who recorded this information and who knew more about late Victorian occultism than most people, remarked that the people listed as these leaders actually represented individuals whom the Druids now wished to claim as ancestors, in a piece of wish-fulfilment.[24]

In other ways MacGregor-Reid could be distinguished from his father. He could be every bit as self-assertive, audacious and ruthless, as Smith found to his cost, but was better at negotiation and diplomacy, as he had already shown on behalf of his father in the 1920s. It helped a lot that he had to work for his living. Whatever capacity the older Reid had ever possessed for holding down a regular job was rendered beside the point when he came into private money. By disinheriting his son, he forced him to continue, till the end of his life, to earn his keep, and it must have helped (when dealing with the Office of Works) that Robert eventually became a civil servant himself.[25] For all the traumatic relationship that the two men had achieved by the last decade of the elder one's life, Robert remained, officially at least, proud of George Watson Reid and his legacy. After all, he claimed to be his true heir, by both blood and election, and to have restored the order that his father had founded.

Robert's talent for diplomacy produced another striking feature of his order that set it apart from the older Universal Bond: his love of building bridges between it and other groups and prominent individuals. In part, this was driven by his need to outclass Smith, but it was retained long after his victory over him. The meeting that appointed him as chief, in 1946, included a retired colonial administrator called Gerald Gardner, who remained a prominent member of MacGregor-Reid's order during the early 1950s.[26] Gardner went on to become the main publicist, and perhaps the main creator, of the modern religion of pagan witchcraft, called Wicca. By 1950, contact had been made between MacGregor-Reid and sympathetic individuals in Scotland, Ireland and Wales, who were willing to be associated with the order and give the impression that it had a membership that spanned the British Isles. The one who agreed to lend his name to it in Scotland was none other than Lewis Spence, the most famed of all authors on the occult secrets of ancient Druidry.[27] In 1951 the order entertained as its guests at Stonehenge the famous occultist and former friend of Crowley, Gerald Yorke, and two clergymen of the Church of England.[28] By 1956 it had picked up another of Crowley's followers, his biographer Charles Cammell, who was invited to preside over a ceremony at Stonehenge.[29]

What turned out to be the most spectacular result of MacGregor-Reid's policy of outreach involved the Goursez of Brittany, the body that represented Breton cultural nationalism in the manner of the Gorsedd of Bards in Wales, and had been directly inspired by the latter. In the 1950s, leading members of the Breton body began to develop links with Druid orders in both France and Britain, including the Universal Bond, whom they joined for a rite at Stonehenge. MacGregor-Reid and friends, in turn, visited the Goursez. By contrast, the Welsh Gorsedd had firmly turned its back on such links after an occasion, in the late 1940s, when the reigning Archdruid and Herald Bard accepted an invitation to appear, in their robes, at a Wessex festival held in a house in Dorset. No record has apparently survived of the English Druids they encountered there, but the visiting Welshmen found them 'weird and heretical'. The Gorsedd's board of management decided to forbid any further such contacts lest they bring it into disrepute. When the Ancient Order of Druid Hermetists, who may have been the offending people in Dorset, extended an invitation to visit, it was flatly turned down.

The clash between the policies of the two national bodies came to a head in 1963, when a man was re-elected as Archdruid of the Welsh Gorsedd who was a former Methodist minister and secretary of the British and Foreign Bible Society. He immediately issued a demand to the Goursez that it maintain relations only with the Gorsedd itself and the Cornish Gorseth, and with no other bodies. He added another, that membership of all three groups be restricted to professed Christians. This was, unsurprisingly, rejected by the Goursez as an unreasonable interference in its affairs, and the Gorsedd promptly severed links with its Breton offspring. The schism lasted until 1971, when the Cornish Gorseth brokered a peace treaty between the Welsh and the Bretons. It took the form of a surrender to most of the points required by the Welsh Archdruid. The local autonomy of the three national bodies was reaffirmed, but the Gorsedd was granted supreme authority over the rules and practices of all three. Moreover, all agreed to accept 'the absolute necessity of guarding our respective gatherings against intrusion by alien and non-Celtic elements and personnel'. With this declaration, the rift between the Welsh, Cornish and Breton institutions inspired by Iolo Morganwg, and the English Druid orders, became absolute.[30] In part it was a reflection of modern Celtic chauvinism, but it also ensured that a body that could count the Queen and the Duke of Edinburgh, and (latterly) the Archbishop of Canterbury, among its initiates could not be accused of keeping disreputable company.

So what were the 'heretical' beliefs held by the Universal Bond by the 1950s? They rested in part on a steadily developing historical myth, communicated to the public in a series of handbills and pamphlets. It commenced with the claim that the order had been founded by John Toland in 1717, with Stukeley as his successor in the leadership. By 1950 this had been reinforced by the declaration, originally made by the elder Reid, that all the Druid societies that had been founded in the eighteenth and nineteenth centuries had been offshoots of the Universal Bond. It added a claim that the Victorian esoteric orders, such as the Societas Rosicruciana, had likewise been derived from the Bond.[31] This legendary history enabled it by the mid-1950s to add two new names for itself to its already extensive list: 'The Most Ancient Order of Druids' and 'The Ancient Druid Order'. In 1951 the list of chiefs descending in unbroken line from Toland and Stukeley was further elaborated, with the addition of the names of those who had allegedly led the order in the mid- and late nineteenth century. They were three Victorians who had propagated the idea of a universal religion and of the reunion of humanity – William Carpenter, Edward Vaughan Keneally and Gerald Massey; the list culminated in O'Callaghan, whom Reid had built up posthumously into a mentor, and in Reid himself. In the case of the first three, the new Universal Bond was clearly doing what Reid had done in claiming former members, and co-opting figures whom its leaders admired. It was also, however, paying homage to Reid's constant ideals.[32] The finishing touches to the pseudo-history were added in the late 1950s or early 1960s.[33] The list of chiefs stretching between Toland and MacGregor-Reid was completed by filling the gap between Stukeley and Carpenter with men who were known to have written about Druids or been associated with the eighteenth-century revival of interest in them. All, to fit the ideological hue of the Universal Bond, were social, political or religious radicals, and usually all three. The obvious omission was Iolo Morganwg, perhaps because he had become so firmly associated with the Welsh Gorsedd, or perhaps because word had reached the Bond that he was now discredited as a forger. In his place were substituted one of his followers, David Samwell, and William Blake.

The order was now given a complete mythical prehistory as well as a history. This was prefaced by Iolo's pseudo-history of ancient Britain, inserted into the modern mythical history of Atlantis, from which all the mystery schools of the ancient world were said to derive.[34] Spence's story of a Druidic presence at medieval Oxford was repeated, and added to the AODH's account that the Mount Haemus Grove had been founded there in 1245, to revive Druidry in England. It was claimed that this same Grove had been behind the Scientific Revolution of the seventeenth century, inspiring the foundation of the Royal Society and Greenwich Observatory, and that John Aubrey had led it. Aubrey was now credited with advising Toland to undertake his great work of unifying all the five branches of surviving British Druids in 1717, with royal approval, to found the Universal Bond. Subsequent members or associates of the order had included the Victorian novelists Bulwer-Lytton and Charles Kingsley. All this provided the grounds on which a society that had actually formed between 1910 and 1918 could claim precedence over all the older and larger modern Druid orders, and assert itself if necessary against historians and prehistorians. It was also, however, a reflection of special circumstances. Just as the older Universal Bond, under Reid, had tended to create and augment a historical mythology when challenged by archaeologists or civil servants, so the more elaborate and rather different reconstructed order had been the creation of adversity. Robert MacGregor-Reid's disinheritance, seizure of power by a coup, and long feud with the group from which he had seceded, all made him and his supporters particularly conscious of the need for a legitimizing lineage.

At the same time, the position the order was taking towards prehistoric monuments pushed it ever further away from what had long been scholarly orthodoxy. Indeed, it was adding interpretations of landscape features that had never been orthodox. In its 1951 'souvenir brochure', issued for the summer solstice, the editor listed a number of monuments as obviously or probably the work of the ancient Druids. It was not surprising, though controversial, to see Stonehenge and Avebury there, but the list also included the Georgian folly at Swinton in Yorkshire, apparently under the impression that it was ancient. It also added the 'Glastonbury Zodiac', a putative temple of the stars which had been identified in Somerset by an artist called Katherine Maltwood in the 1920s, formed out of a series of landscape features that dated from very different periods. Belief in it has always remained the preserve of a relatively small number of mystics.[35] The ancient Druids were, unsurprisingly, characterized in both the public and private literature of the order as marvellous scientists, especially of astronomy, and guiltless of human sacrifice: this was represented as a Roman libel against them. They were portrayed as the timelessly ancient priests of the British, whom the Celts adopted when they reached Britain. Much of their customs and teachings, as portrayed by MacGregor-Reid's Universal Bond, were taken straight from the writings of Iolo Morganwg: the three divisions of the order into Bards, Ovates and Druids, with robes of blue, green and white respectively, the circles of existence through which souls were reborn, the emphasis on complete pacifism, the Gorsedd Prayer, and so forth.[36] The order may have rejected Iolo as an ancestor, but it still relied heavily on his teachings, perhaps because its members no longer realized that they were his.

The order's private set of rites, as composed by MacGregor-Reid in 1948, left those working them in no doubt that by joining his order they were entering an elite. They contained the frank directive to be aware that 'the people of the world are all more or less well-meaning, and that they are more or less stupid'. The main initiation ceremony in the rites was modelled on one of the Hermetic Order of the Golden Dawn. It proclaimed that the aim of the initiate was to return to 'the Light of Our Father' and 'the peace of God', and 'to learn of the doctrines of Nature and to discover the wondrous principles by which All is governed'. This quest, for the hidden wisdom that illuminated the workings and purpose of the universe, had been that of the late Victorian esoteric orders, from the Theosophical Society and the Societas Rosicruciana onward. Christians would be reassured by the employment of the Cross as the prime symbol of 'love's unity' in the rites. They would find a further familiar point of reference in the declaration that Druids aimed at 'the diffusion of the Great Primal Revelation'. It would also have been a comfort, both to those in established faiths and those who preferred a philosophical to a religious tinge to their spiritual ambitions, to be told that Druidry was a science and not a cult, which demanded independent thought and sought the secrets of nature. MacGregor-Reid was obviously trying to please as many people as possible. Like the Golden Dawn and its successor orders, but unlike the older Universal Bond, MacGregor-Reid's order had not only initiations but magical names, which each member took on initiation and by which he or she was generally known to fellow initiates.[37]

A series of instructions survive, composed by MacGregor-Reid for delivery to new members, which elucidate various points in the identity and self-image of the Universal Bond, both in his time and before. They begin with the uncompromising statement that the Bond was 'a most ancient order of seers, sages and instructors, who cling to the wisdom and mercy message of the most ancient faith'. Its object was 'spiritual elevation and the amelioration of the burdened and enslaved'. It had existed since prehistory, and 'always upheld the banner of freedom against tyranny in whatever shape this appeared, clerical, political or social'. Then, however, MacGregor-Reid disclosed the way in which this impressive history was compiled: by declaring that every 'wise and spiritually enlightened person belongs to it by right of her or his nature', even if not actually aware of its existence. The order could therefore claim the spiritual membership of absolutely anybody whom its present leadership happened to admire in the past; which is surely how the elder Reid had co-opted people like Charles Dickens and the younger compiled his list of chiefs of the order since Toland. MacGregor-Reid admitted that very few of these wise and enlightened people were actually aware, even now, that a society existed to promote their ideals. He closed his first address by informing newcomers that they had to place unquestioning belief in anything that their instructors in the order told them, or it would be impossible for them to receive proper guidance. It seemed that the Universal Bond's unwavering commitment to freedom did not extend to the right for its members to argue with anything that its leaders said.

The public rites of MacGregor-Reid's order are well recorded. The standard set at Stonehenge, for midsummer, began with an all-night vigil held in the car park. At midnight a procession was made to the Double Circle, for the sake of old times, where participants formed a circle and joined hands for a few minutes, then heard a short address. As dawn approached, the Druids gathered by the altar stone for an invocation and a blessing. They then filed around the exterior of the monument, in the manner of Smith's Universal Bond, to the four points of the compass where the elemental symbols – bread and salt, water, a rose (for air) and a brazier of fire – had been left. An offering of oak leaves was made to the fire. At the Heel Stone, the outlying monolith of the monument, each placed a hand on the surface of the stone and renewed a personal covenant with divine fatherhood and motherhood. They then proceeded to the centre of the stones and placed the elemental symbols on a white linen cloth spread upon the ground there. All held hands while the presiding member proclaimed, to the point where the sun was due to rise, that humanity should prepare for the 'Restoration', and earth for the 'coming of the Great Peace'. A series of songs, prayers, hymns and invocations followed, as day broke and the sun rose.

At noon, everybody returned for a similar procession, with the addition of the drawing and sheathing of a sword at one of the megaliths, and the proclamation of peace to the four quarters, as symbolized by this action. In the centre, the presiding member (usually MacGregor-Reid himself) placed a crown of oak on his own head, and then all others present crowned themselves with it in turn. Once again, the transference of ritual acts from the AODH is obvious, as is the borrowing of that concerning the sword from the Welsh Gorsedd.[38] In the late 1950s, the order instituted a further ceremonial innovation which was to have a lasting impact on modern Druidry. Iolo Morganwg had written of a 'mystic word', with which his creator deity had produced the cosmos (imitating the Gospel according to St John). The Universal Bond now decided that the word concerned had been 'awen', one which in medieval Welsh literature signifies creative inspiration. Iolo had also (naturally enough as a poet and forger) been fond of this word, and MacGregor-Reid's Druids began to speak or chant it in chorus at Stonehenge, to represent the power of creation.[39] By now, also, the order regularly recited Iolo's prayer, as used by the Welsh Gorsedd, in an English translation, at both dawn and noon rites.[40]

In 1956, the year after its triumph in taking pole position at Stonehenge, the order instituted two more annual seasonal ceremonies. The administrative base of the whole organization, and the home of most of its members, including the chief himself, was in London. From that year onward therefore, it began to stage ceremonies at the equinoxes on Tower Hill, opposite the Tower of London. This was the most celebrated medieval monument in Britain, just as Stonehenge was the most famous to be left from prehistory. It was a setting that was both prominent in historical terms and eye-catching in the present, and it had, moreover, associations with medieval Welsh legend, which might still be presumed to be 'Druidical'. The head of Bran the Blessed, one of the greatest heroes of that legend, was said to have been interred on Tower Hill for a time. At the spring equinox of 1956, the main officers of the order and their followers, twelve strong, assembled on the pavement opposite the Tower and formed a circle. The hour was noon, symbolically appropriate for a sun-honouring tradition but also, being on a weekday, ensuring the attention of lunchtime crowds.

What followed was a mixture of the elder Reid's Druidry with the Welsh Gorsedd. From the former came the opening invocations, spoken by MacGregor-Reid himself.

Most of the actual rites were taken directly from the Gorsedd. They opened with the presentation of the sheathed sword to the four quarters, as a symbol of peace, followed by Iolo's prayer. At the core of rites was the presentation of a horn carrying drink, imitating the Welsh 'Hirlas', by a robed woman to the presiding Druid. At that first rite in 1956 the horn contained cider and was carried by a pretty twenty-year-old secretary from Kensington, 'her auburn hair bound with a circlet of twisted gold'. Instead of flowers, as in Wales, the chief was then presented (by the same woman) with some seeds, which he scattered on the ground, calling them seeds of love, plenty and goodness for humanity. Another detail missing from the Gorsedd was that the lady who made the presentations was termed the representative of the goddess Ceridwen, 'the Earth Mother'; though this was just to borrow from a different Welshman, 'Celtic' Davies. At the autumn equinox, the same ceremony was repeated, save that the chief Druid was given fruits and not seeds.[41]

It was one annual rite at Stonehenge, however, which was to fix public attention on the Universal Bond once more and propel it into renewed national controversy. This was the dawn ceremony at the summer solstice. Having seized this from its rivals, MacGregor-Reid's order swiftly rediscovered the problems inherent in it. Any Druid group who held a service then was bound to attract the mass media, giving it a high public profile, and a proportionate prestige and ability to recruit. On the other hand, this was also the one occasion on which the public turned up in large numbers, and the chances of a collision between them and the Druids were greatly increased. Druids who performed rites at Stonehenge on any other date were likely to be free from trouble and to have a smooth relationship with the Ministry of Works, as the former government Office had now become. This was a pattern to which the Ancient Order and the United Ancient Order had always adhered. On the other hand, they were also likely to go unnoticed by all but a small number of people, and to a group as ambitious for fame and growth as Robert MacGregor-Reid and his supporters, this was intolerable. They discovered the full potential of the problem in the very next year after they secured the right to appear at the stones for the solstice sunrise: 1956. The trouble arose because of the presence of several military bases near Stonehenge, on Salisbury Plain, which contained, inevitably, a large number of ebullient, aggressive and (in peacetime) rather bored young men. These had already given the Universal Bond difficulties in the 1920s, and now they did again. By sunset on 20 June a crowd of two thousand had already gathered around the stones. It included hundreds of drunken soldiers, some of whom were setting off thunderflashes – low-level explosives – purloined from their camp. When the Druids, now fifty strong, started their procession to the Double Circle soon after midnight, the servicemen closed around them, shouting insults and hurling some of these devices. They caused no injuries but a great deal of alarm. Matters were brought under control before dawn by the arrival of military police, who arrested one or two ringleaders and then kept watch to prevent further trouble. The incident was reported in national and local newspapers, with general sympathy for the Druids and admiration for the dignity with which they had withstood the attack and the courage with which they had subsequently enacted their ceremonies at dawn, noon and sunset. The Universal Bond itself asked the Ministry of Works to exclude all members of the general public henceforth from the monument while its dawn ceremony was in progress. The Ministry, however, did not feel able to do this.[42]

The following year, the military police appeared at dusk before the solstice, and guarded the Druids all through the night. The soldiery showed their resentment by substituting ridicule for violence, as they had done a generation before. A group of sergeants from the Royal Artillery donned white blankets and carried forked sticks to stage a parody of a Druid rite, while young officers shouted abuse at the members of the Universal Bond. More insults were hurled by members of the civilian public, youths who were now being attracted to the stones by the prospect of excitement and trouble. Two musical bands, playing the latest teenage craze of skiffle, competed with each other from opposite sides of the monument. When the Druids sounded a horn to greet the sunrise, a jeer went up from the crowd. Once more, there was considerable attention from the mass media, and once again it was sympathetic to the Druids, who were turning into symbols of English order and tradition under attack from the forces of indiscipline and irreverence which conservative commentators were increasingly starting to deplore in the nation's adolescents. By now the Ministry of Works was becoming seriously worried. It discussed the complete closure of Stonehenge at the solstice, but concluded that this move would be unpopular and could backfire, if the rowdy elements of the public decided to force an entry. Instead it resolved to floodlight the stones all through the night of 20–21 June, in order to deter troublemakers. This, initially, proved effective.[43]

The effect was, unhappily, short-lived. In 1959 the skiffle groups were back in greater numbers, and full volume, and university students reinforced the military in providing a supply of young men looking for mischief. The Druids were met, in the words of one journalist, by 'a great blast of jeering and barracking from the assembled youth'. The crowd numbered about 1,600, some of it visibly very drunk, and some climbing on to the tops of the stones. Once again, the newspapers contrasted this behaviour with the solemnity and courage of the Druids.[44] The midsummer of 1960 was worse. More youths climbed on the stones, and the jeering, cat-calling and laughter at the Druids was louder and more sustained. It was now only too clear that many of those attending were there purely to bait the Universal Bond. One newspaper commented of the crowd that 'there never was a more ribald congregation. They shouted Hyde Park witticisms, they rocked with laughter, they made undefinable [sic] derisive noises.'[45]

Matters had now reached a crisis, and the Ministry of Works was faced with some very tough decisions. One theoretical solution – that the Universal Bond voluntarily cease holding a ceremony at Stonehenge at the midsummer sunrise – was not on the negotiating table. However difficult and unpleasant the position of MacGregor-Reid and his friends had become, they were not people to back down from a confrontation. Furthermore, they enjoyed the now tremendous publicity that the occasion gave them, as the most visible group of Druids in the nation. Stonehenge had become their exclusive preserve, because after 1956 the older orders, even though they had invariably held their rites at quieter and less contentious times, had kept away from the site.

The Ministry therefore had to choose, starkly, between banning the Universal Bond at the summer solstice, banning the public, or excluding both. In reaching a decision, the civil servants found themselves operating in an altered scholarly context, and facing a third interest group. This was one that did not appear at the stones at midsummer, but had come to identify itself with them at least as much as any other. It was the one that had proved spectacularly potent the last time the activities of the Druids at the monument had become controversial, in 1924: the nation's archaeologists. Here we need to step back a while from the present story to examine changes that had occurred in the culture of the latter since they last clashed with Druids.

*   *   *

Anybody who reads through a standard history of archaeology written in the late twentieth century tends to find the same basic story in it. This is a chronicle of increasing knowledge and sophistication gained through an apostolic succession of scholarship that starts with the antiquarians of the sixteenth century. This approach is equally true of personal statements such as Glyn Daniel's Thames and Hudson volume of 1981 and team efforts such as *The Cambridge Illustrated History of Archaeology* in 1996.[46] Like any kind of history, this one defines itself in large part by what it leaves out. In most cases the omissions are implicit, in others very explicit. To Glyn Daniel, for example, by then holder of the established chair in the subject at Cambridge University, genuine scholarship was always to be contrasted with what he bluntly termed 'alternative archaeology, lunatic archaeology and bullshit archaeology'. He coupled this string of terms with the assertion that 'the good can apparently only grow with a parallel growth of the bad'.[47] In propagating this dualist view of the universe, he admitted that the good could occasionally be redeemed from the bad: for example, the great Egyptologist Sir Flinders Petrie initially subscribed to visionary interpretations of the Great Pyramid, but, in Daniel's words, he was 'fortunately . . . not for long carried away by these pyramidiocies'.[48] In this particular case, Daniel missed an important point: that Petrie would never have gone out to Egypt in the first place had he not been inspired by an evangelical Christianity that drove him to believe that the Great Pyramid revealed his god's design for the universe. He did abandon these beliefs later, but without them the man commonly hailed as the father of British Egyptology would never have got going. Furthermore, Petrie's career was saved by another Christian zealot during a subsequent phase, when a quarrel with the Egypt Exploration Fund cut off his source of money. This was a Manchester businessman, who supported him for a vital period in the hope that his excavations would prove the literal truth of the Bible.[49]

Such cross-currents do not invalidate the traditional history of the development of archaeology, and that history certainly remains one way in which that process can legitimately be perceived. They do, however, suggest the possibility of a different way of writing the history of archaeology in Britain since the nineteenth century. Some of that other picture has been indicated at places in the present book. It is a story of complexity, rivalry and social division, in which the categories of orthodox and alternative were (and are) constantly contested and redrawn. In particular, instead of emphasizing only a steady accretion of knowledge, through discovery, debate and the validation of 'good'

facts and ideas – though such an accretion has indeed occurred – it would draw attention to some other developments in the period between 1860 and 1960.

One of these was a change in the social status of leading archaeologists.[50] In Britain
the discipline had been in large part an extension of the traditional domination of
rural life by landowners and professional men, especially clergy and lawyers.
Excavation, and the interpretation of the remains found, was at once a new and
exciting kind of field sport and a confirmation of the possession of land and the interpretation of knowledge by the established social elite. This elite dominated the county
and national societies founded to promote archaeological and historical investigations, and the leading institution to conserve the physical trophies of nationhood: the
British Museum. It produced the people who led the adoption of all the intellectual
innovations which transformed humanity's view of its own remote past: above all, the
division of prehistory into Stone, Bronze and Iron Ages; the use of precise and careful
excavation techniques, with sections put through sites and plans made at each stage;
and the acceptance of the huge age of the world and the evolution of species, with the
Book of Genesis relegated at best to a symbolic truth.

It has been stressed before that these innovations produced an important shift of
power in the community of British scholars, from clergy to laity; but it was a shift
which occurred very much within the same social class. The Disney Chair in
Archaeology at Cambridge, which Daniel was eventually to occupy, was first held, in
succession, by two men who were expert in classical texts rather than field archaeology. Sir John Lubbock, the greatest individual evangelist of the new approach to
prehistory, was a baronet who grew up in a great country house and gave up archaeology for a political career that took him into the House of Lords. Augustus Pitt-
Rivers, the man who, more than anybody else, established the modern methods of
excavation, was a retired general. He inherited and increased a huge landed estate in
Dorset, and owned the monuments on which he first tested his techniques. Thomas
Bateman, the famous scholar of Derbyshire burial mounds was, like Lubbock and
Pitt-Rivers, the heir to a large fortune. The Victorian Society of Antiquaries was
reluctant to admit anyone without a genteel background and a private income. One
scholar, Charles Roach Smith, had his membership prospects jeopardized when the
news got round that he was a businessman. In the words of Philippa Levine, the
historian of Victorian archaeologists, most of them were drawn 'from a class where
education was an unquestioned privilege and leisure an ample commodity'.[51]

Into this world erupted the new wealth generated by the Industrial Revolution.
Indeed, specific archaeological discoveries that made a huge impact on the world imagi-
nation can be linked to individual commodities: indigo dug up Troy and Mycenae,
papermaking helped to uncover the Minoan civilization of Crete, and marmalade
excavated Avebury.[52] The person responsible for the last project was Alexander Keiller.
With his sports cars and skiing holidays, and his inherited fortune from a factory in
Dundee, he was the epitome of the vulgar, self-assertive new industrial plutocrat.[53]
More important to archaeology in the long run was the appearance in it of young men
from the lower middle classes, the sons of schoolteachers, colonial judges, clerks and
journalists. These had been attracted to the subject by reading about it as boys, and

became the founders of truly professional archaeology in Britain: they include such names as O. G. S. Crawford, Stuart Piggott, Christopher Hawkes, Sir Cyril Fox, Sir Mortimer Wheeler, Leslie Grinsell and Glyn Daniel himself.

At times their alliance with the new wealth was blatant: Keiller sponsored the work of Crawford, Piggott and Grinsell. At times, also, the clash between the old and new breeds of archaeologist was equally plain. When Crawford was excavating the Carneddau Hengwm megalithic tombs in Wales in 1919, he was visited by the powerful regional antiquarian society, which had been founded by John William ab Ithel a generation before: the Cambrian Archaeological Association. He heard afterwards that they had been deeply offended when he greeted them wearing a sweater and shorts instead of more formal attire. The members were mollified only when the president, the Victorian savant Sir William Boyd Dawkins, told them that Crawford must have become mentally unhinged by his experiences during the war.[54] When Reginald Smith of the British Museum came to inspect Stuart Piggott's excavations at the Trundle, a Neolithic enclosure in Suffolk, in 1928, he took care to wear a pin-striped suit, bowler hat and pince-nez spectacles. He sneered at Piggott's techniques as 'very marmalade'; a clear swipe at Keiller.[55] Leslie Grinsell's investigation of the Lambourn Neolithic long barrow in 1935 resulted in an embarrassment when the lord of the manor invited him to lunch and found that he crumbled bread into his soup.[56] More serious were the local range wars, such as that conducted by the Wiltshire Archaeological Society, and especially by the Cunningtons, designed to achieve complete control over any excavations that occurred in the county. Its members were as ruthless in waging these against interloping scholars as they were against the Druids at Stonehenge. Keiller was able to dig at the Windmill Hill Neolithic enclosure only by appointing a director for the work who was acceptable to the society (and disliked by Keiller himself). This did not remove the hostility of the members, and Keiller remarked years later that, if they had been able, the Cunningtons would have had the police expel him from the shire.[57] When an American scholar of some distinction, subsequently holder of a professorial chair at Harvard, dug up prehistoric pottery on a Wiltshire site, he was likewise confronted by the Cunningtons, who demanded that he deliver it all to the society.[58]

It is possible to make too much of the contrast between old and new archaeologists. Both were capable of joining forces against a common foe, as they did against the Universal Bond in 1924; just as the Bond itself could show unity against archaeologists but engage in a civil war of its own from 1946 to 1954. The Wiltshire Archaeological Society had its own internal feuds, manifested in the public disagreements between George Engleheart and the Cunningtons over the date and purpose of Stonehenge. Furthermore, none of the new breed of archaeologist came from the working class. Most were privately educated, and their backgrounds were firmly bourgeois. None the less, when all these qualifications are made, the gap between them and the old-fashioned antiquarians was still very real. The most self-consciously aristocratic of the new men was Mortimer Wheeler, a former army officer with a handlebar moustache, a drawling accent and a disdain for 'vulgarity'. Even he, however, was not quite what he seemed, for he had been educated at home because his family was too poor to afford school fees.

He eventually worked his way into a good state school and so got to university – but at London rather than one of the older and more prestigious pair.[59] By doing even this he surpassed Grinsell, Piggott and Fox, none of whom had any university education at all.

These men were themselves very conscious of their relatively humble social position. When Cyril Fox first met Glyn Daniel he had heard that Daniel had been an undergraduate at Cambridge and nervously expected him to have a superior manner. Fox was delighted to find that he was, instead, the son of a Welsh country schoolmaster who had got a scholarship to Cambridge from a state school. He thumped him on the shoulder and burst out 'Excellent, good yeoman stock like myself and O. G. S. Crawford and Stuart Piggott. Backbone of England, dear boy – and of Wales.'[60] 'Yeoman', in this context, was shorthand for 'middle-class'. Fox was himself the son of a bank clerk, and had started his own working life as a market gardener. It was his expertise with soil types that had got him into archaeology, through administrative work for a Royal Commission.[61] The socially grandest of the new archaeologists was probably Grahame (later Sir Grahame) Clark, a stockbroker's son who was educated at a famous private school and then at Cambridge, and spent his whole career at that university. Even he, however, felt the difference when he came up against one of the leading East Anglian archaeologists of the old genteel sort, Leslie Armstrong. He told Armstrong that some flints that the latter had called Palaeolithic were actually Mesolithic, and received the reply, 'You impudent puppy!'[62]

This confrontation sums up the paradox in the relationship between old and new. The incoming men were anxious to gain the status achieved by their predecessors, and within the same institutional, and much the same intellectual, framework. Daniel was later to describe himself as having been 'a very ordinary secondary-school boy from Wales who lapped up the magic of Cambridge, and is still deeply sensible of it'.[63] He had expected to become a schoolmaster like his father, and never ceased to revel in the grandeur and opulence of the college life of which he found himself a part instead. None the less, he and his kind had both a sense of solidarity amongst themselves and a determination to push the old guard of archaeology out of power and reputation. It was a replay of the developments of the 1860s, when the new men equipped with the Danish and Darwinian models of prehistory had turned on the familiar orthodoxies based on the Bible and classics. Daniel later recalled that both his first article and his first book were 'written in anger', being 'protests against . . . the complacency of establishment archaeology'. His bewitchment by Cambridge had not stopped him aiming his very first publication against views expressed by his immediate superior at the university, with a calculated iconoclastic savagery. He characterized these views as 'evils even more dangerous' than the destruction of archaeological evidence itself, 'namely observation so dominated by false or imprudent hypotheses that it results in a distorted version worse by far than mere blind observation or empty ideas'.[64]

It was symptomatic that the very first of the new kind of archaeologist to make an impact on the university system was Gordon Childe, an Australian who had started his career as a socialist politician. Once established in the chair of archaeology at Edinburgh University, he loved to wind up his more conventional colleagues by wearing short trousers, ostentatiously reading the *Daily Worker* newspaper, and approvingly quoting Stalin in his public speeches. One of his books, it has been suggested, 'was designed ... to scandalize the ... Society of Antiquaries of Scotland'.[65] By the time the Second World War was over, the new generation of professionals had more or less taken over the discipline, filling the dominant posts in the national museums and staffing those in the growing number of universities. Indeed, an academic career in archaeology was one that largely appeared in their generation: Glyn Daniel noted proudly that in 1927 there were seven or eight university posts in his discipline, while in 1980 there were about three hundred.[66] To celebrate this takeover, Stuart Piggott ground the faces of the old-fashioned antiquarians in the dust in a sensational article in the first national *Archaeological Newsletter* in 1948. It declared that the business of excavation and interpretation was now too complex for anybody but full-time, carefully trained, career professionals such as himself: 'the days when the Bronze Age of Blankshire could be discussed chattily by the dear vicar are gone never to return'. He told members of the county societies that the role of their members in future was to act as volunteer labour on digs led by experts of his sort.[67] This is, indeed, exactly what happened; the local power of families such as the Cunningtons had been broken, apparently for ever.

The 'official' history of the development of British archaeology, as a seamless process of increasing knowledge and expertise, therefore conceals a significant power struggle between different generations, and kinds, of 'orthodox' scholar. It also gives a misleading impression of the simplicity of the relationship between orthodox and unorthodox ideas. A significant number of the new professional archaeologists were first inspired to take an interest in ancient sites, not so much by the writings of established scholars as by the publication of Ordnance Survey maps with those sites printed on them.[68] These maps, moreover, induced a different way of looking at the landscape, encouraging the readers to relate different features to each other and to trace routes between them. This explains the proliferation of books on prehistoric tracks around 1900, and the impact of these on young readers. Stuart Piggott's introduction to archaeology came through *The Green Roads of England*, written by Hippsley Cox, a London restaurant-owner.[69] O. G. S. Crawford, as a boy, was 'profoundly influenced' by Arthur and George Hubbard's *Neolithic Dew Ponds and Cattle Ways*.[70] Both men were sponsored by Harold Peake, an amateur prehistorian of comfortable private means. Without his encouragement and support, neither would have become an archaeologist. One of Peake's ideas was that churches dedicated to particular saints represented the sites of ancient shrines, and that prehistoric roads could be traced between them. Crawford incorporated this into his very first publication on field archaeology. It was only much later, when his career was established, that he distanced himself from what he now termed 'wild theorizing' of this sort and from Peake's 'typically fantastic' notions.[71] That career had, however, been launched from a basis of such notions, which had only subsequently come to be redefined as unacceptable by professionals. Likewise, only years later did Piggott come to reject what he now called his mentor's 'wild fantasies'.[72]

Unorthodox notions, moreover, could be rooted in even the most conservative and respectable parts of the archaeological establishment. Readers may remember

Reginald Smith of the British Museum, who turned up in his pin-striped suit and bowler to sneer at Stuart Piggott's excavations in 1928. It turns out that he was a keen dowser on the quiet, believing firmly in the ability of some humans to detect the presence of underground features by psychic powers activated by the use of divining rods. Once he had safely retired, in 1939, Smith addressed the British Society of Dowsers to tell them that his rods suggested that a confluence of underground springs of water was found underneath every major prehistoric site.[73] This was a belief which was to resurface in the 1960s and 1970s as a tenet of the new 'alternative archaeology' of that later period, to which professional archaeologists were, almost unanimously, vehemently opposed.

This redrawing of the boundaries of the acceptable was an aspect of the process by which the young outsiders of the 1910s and 1920s had won their battle with the old establishment, and replaced it. Being themselves, in the main, the sons of men who worked in professions, they naturally professionalized archaeology itself. Entry to the discipline slowly became by diploma and degree, awarded through training courses that they and people like them devised. They also obtained control over the land itself, through an increasingly stringent series of Acts of Parliament restricting excavation to their own kind. As late as 1946, when a young photographer called Philip Rahtz developed an interest in archaeology, he could dig up a local Bronze Age burial mound simply by getting permission from the landowner.[74] Just over forty years later, Rahtz was Professor of Archaeology at York University and one of the nation's leading experts on early medieval sites. The course over which he presided enabled young people to gain the professional and monitored training that he himself had never received. Moreover, over the same period it had become illegal for anybody except a properly qualified professional to excavate a scheduled ancient monument. He and his kind had prised loose the millennia-old grip of the gentry and farmers on the prehistoric and historic remains of the land and imposed their own instead; and the amateur digger was pressed into their service. The Victorian antiquarians had been a social aristocracy, which for the most part ruthlessly policed entry to their company. The twentieth-century professionals were a meritocracy, but their control over entry to their ranks was even more rigorously policed.

None of this should be taken as a denunciation of the new professional archaeology. Just as the nineteenth century's genteel amateurs had carried through some of the greatest intellectual revolutions in human history, so the twentieth-century meritocrats undoubtedly brought about a tremendous improvement in the pace and accuracy with which knowledge of the past could be gained. It is only worth noting that they left future generations unable to engage with those remains as they themselves had once done. Furthermore, after they had seized power, the new archaeologists began to rewrite their own past, much as new ruling families in the early Middle Ages claimed links with former dynasties, and newly ennobled and knighted gentry families, in subsequent periods, tended to emphasize real or assumed lineages that connected them to older nobility. In this case, the genealogies devised represented the new professionals as the natural heirs of the antiquarian gentry and clergy of the old regime. This was made easier by their gradual abandonment of their earlier interest in landscape as a whole, and the route-ways across it. Instead they increasingly focused on the old regime's preoccupation with excavation and artefacts, the commodities that they themselves most closely controlled. The Druids at Stonehenge in the 1950s, therefore, were operating on the home ground of archaeologists who had turned into a professional closed shop, of a sort that had never existed before.

* * *

There was not the slightest chance that any of the new archaeologists would have any real sympathy with, or understanding of, the ideals of the Universal Bond. Adam Stout has examined the religious and cultural attitudes of the former, and shown that they ran counter to those of the Druids at many different points. In religious ideology, the new professionals divided into two groups. In one were those who felt either indifference or hostility to all forms of religion and spirituality, being themselves atheists with a greater or lesser degree of conviction and aggression, such as Childe, Crawford, Piggott, Daniel and Wheeler. In the other were personally devout and orthodox Christians, such as Clark, Fox and Christopher Hawkes. Neither was likely to respond favourably to the mysticism embodied in the Druids' teachings and rites. Furthermore, most, if not all, of the new archaeologists adhered to a view of human development as one of triumphant progress from savagery to ever increasing civilization. They differed on how inevitable they felt this improvement to have been, how much it was threatened in modern times, and whether it derived essentially from the mass of people or from elites. Still, none of them had any time for the notion of a primeval and superior wisdom available to humans in the remote past, which was embedded in much of the belief-system of the Universal Bond.[75] Nor did any of them show the slightest inclination to credit modern Druid societies and ceremonies with any value or dignity, based on their identity as parts of British culture as it had developed since the nineteenth century. The one among them best placed to do so was Cyril (later Sir Cyril) Fox, who directed the National Museum of Wales, and thus had to reckon with the existence of the Welsh Gorsedd of Bards as a long-established part of his adopted nation's public identity. He could hardly fail to do so, as before the main entrance of his museum in Cardiff proudly stood (and still stand) the megaliths of a *gorsedd* circle that had been erected in the 1890s. His public response was to ignore them, his private one to rant to Glyn Daniel that it was 'monstrous that an archaeologist should have a bogus antiquity right in front of his museum'.[76]

There was now, furthermore, a specific flashpoint between the new Universal Bond and the new kind of archaeologist: at Stonehenge, to which the archaeologists, like the Bond, had returned after a period of absence. Just as before, they had turned up much later than the Druids: whereas the Universal Bond and its progeny had been absent from the monument for just five years (1933–7), and the gap had been well filled by the older Druid orders, the archaeologists had put in no sustained appearance for over twenty. Only brief and occasional excavations were carried out at the monument between 1926, when Colonel Hawley concluded his sequence, and 1950, when the Ministry of Works invited in Stuart Piggott, partnered with a rising star of the new professional archaeology, Richard Atkinson. At regular intervals between then and 1964, they carried out a programme designed both to stabilize and restore parts of the monument, and to solve some of the remaining questions about it.[77] This was in many respects a spectacular success, in that they re-erected all the megaliths that had fallen since the end of the Middle Ages, and established the basic sequence in which Stonehenge had been constructed. The excavations were never properly published, even by the standards of the time, but resulted in a book by Atkinson which summarized the main conclusions that he had reached after the initial investigations. It appeared in 1956, and was explicitly populist, being 'written primarily for the ordinary visitor'.

Its main purpose was to set forth what Atkinson now believed to have been the phases in which the monument was constructed. These were basically correct, and have formed the departure point for studies of Stonehenge published ever since. It was also, however, a polemic aimed directly against the Universal Bond and the other Druids who enacted rites there, as it attacked most of the beliefs that they had propagated about the site. Atkinson believed, reasonably but wrongly, that the main stone circle had been erected almost a thousand years after the dates now assigned to it. He characterized it as the work of an architect who had travelled there from Bronze Age Greece and represented that more superior culture, working among natives whom Atkinson termed 'mere barbarians'. In his view they had, moreover, been warlike barbarians, led by a powerful king who commanded other bellicose chieftains and was concerned with maximizing wealth and prestige. The greatest glory of Stonehenge, to him, was that it represented 'the first incorporation of Britain, however transitory, within the orbit of the Mediterranean world, the cradle of European civilization'. There was no place here for the sophisticated, wise and peaceful native society envisaged by the modern Druids; and things got worse for them. Atkinson stated bluntly that 'there is no evidence whatever for connecting Stonehenge with the Druids, whose ceremonies and observances took place, we are told, in natural groves of trees rather than in artificial temples'. His authorities for this were, of course, selected Roman authors.

Atkinson went on to call in the collective opinion of his profession to support this dismissive view: 'It may be remarked that Druids have so firm a hold upon the popular imagination, particularly in connection with Stonehenge, and have been the subject of so much ludicrous and unfounded speculation, that archaeologists in general have come to regard them as almost unmentionable in polite society.' His references to such 'speculation' were the more disdainful in that he did not provide any further details of it. Instead, he proclaimed himself helpless in the face of popular misunderstanding and ignorance, claiming that in the minds of the masses the Druids and Stonehenge were so closely associated that 'I have no illusions that anything I may say, however forcibly, will do much to break the connection.' None the less, he did his utmost to shatter it, hammering home the point asserted by the late Victorian prehistorians – which he simply assumed to be correct – that the Druids belonged to an Iron Age culture which had not reached Britain until around 300 BCE.[78] Atkinson was too modest, though certainly sincere, in expecting that his book would make no impact on popular impressions of Stonehenge. In my own boyhood, during the late 1950s and 1960s, it was constantly cited by schoolteachers and other members of the reading public as the definitive work on the monument, and the one that conclusively disproved its connection with the Druids. The sudden and permanent cessation of the rites held by the older Druid orders at Stonehenge, in 1956, may have been precipitated by the attack on the Universal Bond there at midsummer, but may also have been induced by the appearance of Richard Atkinson's book. It seems to have brought about the decisive shift in public opinion for which scholars had striven for almost a hundred years, in breaking the lingering association between Druidry and the monument in the minds of the majority of the British.

An informed and astute reader might have noticed certain weaknesses in Atkinson's arguments. He never actually provided any evidence for the assertion that the Druids had arrived in the Iron Age, simply stating it as known fact. He glossed it, in a manner that would have impressed general readers, by saying confidently that they had been part of the La Tène culture, which had arisen in continental Europe only after 500 BCE and reached Britain two hundred years later.[79] The culture concerned, however, is identified by a particular style of metalwork, which nobody has ever related decisively to a style of religion or religious official; and indeed it would be hard to see how this could be done. Nor did Atkinson deal any more precisely with the other possible link between Druids and Stonehenge: that the former used the monument even though they had not built it. Indeed, he made rather a fudge of it. At one point he stated that it was possible that the present ruined state of the structure was due to the fact that it had been deliberately wrecked by the Romans. He then conceded that, had the Romans done this, it would have been as part of a campaign to repress the Druids, to whom the place was sacred. He added immediately that there was in fact no evidence for this, and then weakened his own assertion with the qualification that the evidence, if not entirely missing, was 'at least equivocal'.[80] What lay behind these verbal gymnastics was a simple truth: that there was absolutely no reason to believe that the ancient Druids had ever had anything to do with Stonehenge, but it was equally impossible, in the present state of the data, to prove that they had not. Atkinson was stating the former fact, while implying that it somehow disposed of the latter problem.

In fact, he had a larger problem than he acknowledged, for some of his own colleagues had suggested that there might have been some continuity of belief and personnel between the British Neolithic and the Iron Age. In 1941 Piggott himself had argued that genuine traditions of the building of Stonehenge might have survived all the way to the Middle Ages, to be incorporated in Geoffrey of Monmouth's history which had long been thought an invention. He had added that round Iron Age temples could have deliberately echoed Neolithic henge monuments, and that Stonehenge might have been reconstructed in the Iron Age. In his opinion, it was 'perhaps possible that the ancient native cults persisted in many regions little changed' and that some of the pagan temples encountered by Christian missionaries in the seventh century CE 'were products of the old Bronze Age tradition'.[81] Eight years later, Piggott repeated and amplified this view, pointing out the similarity between Bronze Age metalwork and the golden sickles that Pliny had attributed to Druids. He added that Stonehenge itself might have been repaired by them and that their religion was already ancient by the time of Caesar.[82] In the year before Atkinson's book appeared, Christopher Hawkes delivered a lecture at Oxford University, in which he argued directly that the Druids dated from before the Bronze Age and were 'the nameless priests of the old megalithic religion Celticized'. In his opinion, there had been a fundamental continuity of religious belief and personnel in Gaul and Britain from the Neolithic until the arrival of the Romans.[83]

It is important not to turn the relationship between Atkinson and the Druids into a simple one of aggressive scholarly authoritarianism asserting itself against populist forces of freedom of thought and speech. In the early 1950s the rival divisions of the Universal Bond had vied for supremacy at Stonehenge with just as much ruthlessness as that displayed by the new archaeologists in imposing control of their subject. Robert MacGregor-Reid and his followers made historical claims for their order which had at best only a symbolic truth, and forbade their initiates to question anything that their superiors taught. At least the new archaeologists expected colleagues and pupils to question and test their views, however uncomfortable they might find the process in practice. There was nothing in Atkinson's book, moreover, which explicitly condemned modern Druidry itself, or called for its exclusion from the stones. Indeed, one at least of the new breed of archaeologist showed some tolerance of it, and that was O. G. S. Crawford, in his capacity as editor of the most important journal of his profession, *Antiquity*. In 1956, when the procession of the Universal Bond was attacked by the soldiers, he called this action 'a disgraceful display of hooliganism'. He made it clear that he did not take the pretensions of the Druids seriously, but emphasized that they should be entitled to carry out their rites without molestation. He accordingly called on the army authorities to place Stonehenge out of bounds to all servicemen on the night before the solstice sunrise.[84]

This humane attitude was not to prevail, however, even in the editorials of *Antiquity*, as Crawford now retired and was replaced in control of the journal by Glyn Daniel. He brought to the pages of the periodical a new energy, and a new intolerance, turning upon the Druids the zeal and the anger that he had long deployed against predecessors in his own profession. In personal belief and instinct, as well as academic position, he was opposed to most of what they represented. His father had been a fervent Christian in the Welsh nonconformist tradition, preaching at a Congregational chapel, and the young Daniel had enjoyed his sermons, played harmonium at the chapel and taught in a Sunday school. As an adult he lost any personal faith, but continued to value Christianity as a part of tradition and good form, loyally attending the services at his college chapel. He had no time for modern spiritual movements that challenged that tradition and form and were associated with what he termed the lunatic fringes of belief.[85] Nor did his social and political attitudes chime with those of the Universal Bond. Soon after his appointment to his Cambridge fellowship he published an article asserting that humanity lacked any obvious benevolent instincts. He called on his readers to 'get away from . . . sentimental assumptions of the brotherhood of man'.[86] He was determined that *Antiquity* would henceforth be deployed not merely to propagate 'sound' archaeological views, but to condemn the bad, and to see off any rivals to his discipline.

In the case of the Druids, the perfect opportunity for this was provided by the worsening problem of the solstice sunrise gatherings at Stonehenge. In 1961 three thousand people assembled, and some of them indulged in the now customary heavy drinking, jeering at the Druids and climbing on megaliths. They left a huge litter of broken bottles behind them. Once more, press commentary was hostile to the trouble-makers but favourable to the Universal Bond.[87] It was after this midsummer's troubles that Glyn Daniel devoted his first editorial to the matter, presuming from the start that 'hooliganism' and 'neo-Druidism' were equally to blame for the problem. He noted that in the year before one of the bodies that represented the nation's archaeologists, the Ancient Monuments Board for England, had advised the Ministry of Works to make more effort to control unruly members of the public. Daniel himself now called on the civil servants to end such a 'monstrous, wicked and most undesirable state of affairs' as that prevailing at Stonehenge. He urged them to do so, however, by banning the Druid ceremony which, he insisted, represented 'antics' and 'foolish people confusing fact with fiction'. In this and a second blast of editorial passion, later that year, he called on the Universal Bond to erect its own monuments for rituals, holding that it and any other such 'unreasonable body' was free to do this.[88]

During the following winter, the people at the Ministry found that both the Ancient Monuments Board and the Chief Constable for Wiltshire now wanted the Druid ceremony to be prohibited. The key official responsible for the matter was reluctant to do so. He felt that the Druid rites were now 'time-honoured', and that those who enacted them could not fairly be held responsible for the behaviour of others. What really counted with him, however, was his perusal of the previous files of documents relating to the issue of Druidry at Stonehenge, which, like the good bureaucrat that he was, he had carefully consulted in search of precedents. There he found all the furious and threatening letters that the elder Reid and his henchmen had written in the 1920s and 1930s. He feared that, if banned, their successors would likewise 'wield a violet [sic] pen', and would force their way into the stones. He also suspected, with some justice, that the sympathy regularly shown for them by journalists since the Second World War might cause public opinion to take their side. He tested the mood of the present Universal Bond by writing to them asking if they would be willing to move their dawn ceremony away from the official date of the solstice itself. After four months, in which he sent two further letters and made a telephone call, he at last got a reply, blankly refusing. After a more threatening missive, he received an offer to hold dawn ceremonies both on the date of the solstice sunrise, the 21st, and on the following day, to divide public atten-tion, and (it was hoped) the crowds. This also, of course, doubled the Druidic presence at the stones at midsummer and so the publicity associated. The official wearily concluded that this was as much co-operation as he was going to get, and agreed, with the additional proviso that the monument would only be opened to the public an hour before dawn. This, it was hoped, would reduce the numbers present and the amount of time in which misbehaviour could take place. As a sop to public opinion, it was also decreed that no entrance charges would be levied on either morning.[89]

The strategy seemed to work at the next midsummer, of 1962, but at that of 1963 the disorderly elements in the crowd reasserted themselves in all the former ways. In 1964, therefore, the Ministry adopted the suggestion that the Universal Bond had been making since the trouble first began, and agreed to admit the Druids at dawn on 21 June but ban everybody else; the takeover mounted by Robert MacGregor-Reid's order was now complete. Two circuits of coiled barbed wire, fifty police and four guard dogs with their handlers were all installed to protect the ceremony and ensure that only the cele-brants were allowed into the circle. Daniel was livid with rage at what he called a 'craven compromise'. For the next four years, he continued to pelt both the Universal Bond and the Ministry of Works with abuse. He called the former 'bogus', 'dotty', 'ridiculous', 'silly', 'ludicrous', 'horrid' and 'nonsense', and suggested that the latter was 'riddled with secret Druids' and ought to be fined for its misconduct.[90] He was now uneasily aware that one of his former arguments, that Druids in general had nothing to do with Stonehenge, could not be sustained. He now admitted that the Iron Age kind might have been 'heirs to, if not consciously performers of, the ancient religion that swayed the megalith builders'. What he could assert instead was that they had died out completely almost two millennia before, and that the modern people who claimed their name were frauds; hence 'there are no Druids to be admitted to Stonehenge'.[91]

It was all in vain: for the time being, at least, it was the Druids who had won, over both archaeologists and the ordinary members of the public who turned up for the midsummer sunrise. The events of 1924 had been dramatically reversed. From the distance of half a century, there are certain similarities to be observed between the Universal Bond and the new professional archaeologists, alongside the obvious differ-ences and antagonisms. Both were relatively small groups of ambitious people who had emerged, in the course of the twentieth century, from outside the traditional social elites. Both were bidding for public attention and respect, because of the special relationship they claimed with their nation's ancient past, and calling for special privi-leges to be accorded them by the official agency which conserved the physical remains of that past. Both pursued those aims aggressively and self-confidently; and by the 1960s they had both done much to achieve them, within their respective spheres. What had caused the Druids to win their confrontation with archaeologists in the 1960s, when they had lost the previous one in the 1920s, was a shift of public opinion. At least as it was represented by newspapers, that opinion had been generally hostile in 1924 and generally favourable between 1956 and 1966; as the civil servants who carefully collected press cuttings in both periods were well aware. The basic priorities and instincts of journalists had not altered, but the position of the Universal Bond in relation to them certainly had. In the 1920s the Druids appeared to be forces of novelty, radicalism and heresy, so that the scholars who denounced them could appear to represent by contrast the forces of order and respectability. By the late 1950s the Druids had come to seem upholders of tradition, dignity and spirituality, and to be threatened by forces of youthful disrespect and disorder that were now frightening and angering many solid citizens.

They seemed, also, to be weathering the challenge represented by Atkinson's successful assault upon the historic association between them and Stonehenge. The favourable press notices that accompanied their appearances at the monument paid little attention to any ancient context and concentrated instead on their contributions to the present. Perhaps this attitude is best expressed, at the local level, by an article which appeared in a provincial newspaper in 1962, written by a schoolteacher. The author summed it up by declaring that 'the present-day Druids have always had a special place in the hearts of Wiltshiremen, and whatever might have been their connection with Stonehenge in prehistoric times, they have become indissolubly linked with the monument in the minds of those who live on Salisbury Plain today'. He had read Atkinson accurately, and concluded that it really no longer mattered if Druids had used the monument before the twentieth century; they were now a part of it.[92]

* * *

At this time of triumph, however, the Universal Bond was to suffer two major blows, which would mark modern Druidry profoundly for the next decade and, in many respects, for long after: a death and a book. The death was that of Robert MacGregor-Reid himself, from a heart attack in January 1964.[93] It came without expectation or warning, and so no provision had been made for a successor. Two contenders immediately emerged from the senior members of the order, both now Londoners: Thomas Maughan, a practitioner of natural medicine, and Philip Ross (usually called Ross) Nichols, who managed a private tutorial agency. An election was held, and Maughan won by a tiny majority on a second ballot. After a few months, Nichols and his faction seceded from the Universal Bond to found their own Druid organization. It was named the Order of Bards, Ovates and Druids, after the three divisions that Iolo Morganwg had given to his imagined ancient Druids.

The Universal Bond was therefore in a state of schism on the death of a chief, as it had been in 1946, although this time Nichols chose not to make the confrontation so stark. Rather than compete for space and attention at Stonehenge, he left the monument to his rival and decided to hold his midsummer ceremonies on Parliament Hill, in the north of London. He celebrated the equinoxes there as well, leaving Tower Hill to the remnant of the Universal Bond.[94] This deliberate avoidance of confrontation must have done much to reduce the bitterness of the split in the order but it was still traumatic. When Maughan led his Druids through the barbed wire cordon into Stonehenge at midsummer 1965, it was noted how reduced the company that followed him was that year.[95]

Now came the second blow: the book, written by Stuart Piggott. As suggested, Atkinson's volume on Stonehenge had apparently succeeded in breaking the popular association of the monument and Druids in prehistory. What it could not do was tackle popular perceptions of the ancient and modern Druids themselves, which were outside its scope. Indeed, there had been no scholarly work on Druids, published in a form readily accessible to the general public, since Kendrick's in 1927. The plain truth was that historians and archaeologists were not much interested in them unless modern Druids forced the subject to their attention, as they had in the 1920s. Kendrick's book had been a direct response to that last time when Druidry came to national attention. In default of a new one, the portrait of Druidic history presented to the public by the Universal Bond, through its own publications and the pens of journalists, was likely to be widely accepted. This portrait was (to recap) of a benign ancient British religion, elevated in its theology and morality and allied to a knowledge of science and technology which was advanced for its time. The charges of human sacrifice and other barbaric practices, made against Druids by some classical authors, were dismissed as Roman error or propaganda. Furthermore, it was stated, vaguely but confidently, that the ancient Druids had survived the succeeding Christian centuries in secret, and with their basic teaching intact, to resurface in the eighteenth century as the modern set of orders. The Universal Bond was the oldest of these, and had given birth to the others.

The way in which the Ministry of Works had upheld the wishes of Druids over those of archaeologists, in relation to access to Stonehenge at midsummer, gave a new impetus to the latter to discredit the Druids' claims. It was Piggott who took up the challenge. It is possible that he would have written on Druids even without the humiliation of his profession over the Stonehenge issue; but it gave both a context and an impetus to his work. He was probably Britain's leading authority on the Neolithic, and his remit included Stonehenge; which is where he had encountered the Universal Bond directly and where the clash between them lay. He had also shown a close interest in the history of his own discipline, and real prowess in researching and writing it: he was the biographer of William Stukeley, for example. Furthermore, he was a friend of Glyn Daniel, and they were as similar in personality and ideology as they were different in their appearance. Daniel was short, plump, dark and bespectacled. Piggott was tall, spare, fairer, muscular and conventionally handsome, in a bluff, square-hewn way. Both were the sons of provincial schoolmasters, who rose by their own efforts to hold famous professorial chairs in leading universities: Piggott's was at Edinburgh. Both were accordingly fiercely proud of their profession and determined to establish its absolute dominance over the investigation and writing of British prehistory. They shared a will to communicate with the public at large, as well as with colleagues, and a gift for doing so. They also had in common a natural energy, aggression and intolerance of opposition, and neither of them had any emotional or ideological points of contact with the Universal Bond.

Piggott was an atheist, with a suspicion of religion and spirituality, and projected this attitude back on to the ancient past. He thought that religious belief itself had arisen from a 'primitive misinterpretation of dreams', and shared to the full the contemporary faith in scientific rationalism as the means to human progress.[96] As he noted, the story that he was telling as an archaeologist was essentially one of improvements in technology. Material remains were, after all, what prehistoric peoples left behind to be studied. He was firmly of the opinion that they did not allow modern scholars to understand the 'ideas, beliefs, fears or aspirations' of those who had made them.[97] Although he warned readers not to condemn previous stages of human progress simply because they were less advanced,[98] he did not always heed his own advice. In 1949 he had published a general survey of British prehistory, which characterized the Palaeolithic mind as having been 'concerned with the irrationalities of mimetic magic and a superstitious belief in unseen powers'. This he related to the 'awe' and 'superstition' with which natural phenomena were regarded in 'simple cultures' at the present time, such as that of the 'Australian blackfellow'. He summed up the Neolithic villagers of Orkney as living in 'a state of indescribable filth and disorder' (actually a misunderstanding caused by the fact that those at Skara Brae had used material from an old rubbish heap to buttress their walls).[99] Reaching the Iron

Age, he warned readers that 'the strong element of barbarity in Celtic religion must not be forgotten', and supported this conclusion by referring to the Roman accounts of Druids sacrificing humans. He glossed these by maintaining that they amply justified the Roman policy of suppressing Druidry.[100]

In 1965 he published a survey of European prehistory, closing with the Iron Age. He commenced the section on the ancient Druids by saying that the literary sources for them were so poor that 'their interpretation is hazardous and can easily be nugatory'. He followed this admirable caution, immediately, by the statement that what was certain about them was that they practised human sacrifice and divination by ritual murder, and so we could also believe that they sanctioned head-hunting. His reason for crediting such accounts was his conviction that 'one of man's most deeply seated and most cherished needs is for aggression and dominance, violence and killing, directed against his fellow men'. In his view, much of human history and prehistory had 'no grander theme' than gang warfare. He then expressed his sympathy for the classical civilizations of the Mediterranean, over the tribal peoples of ancient northern Europe: 'with all their faults, the successive civilized communities of antiquity achieved an organization of man's powers, and a control of his frailties, immensely superior to anything brought about by the barbarians. To laud the barbaric virtues is to fall victim to the myth of the Noble Savage.' He insisted that inequality was natural to our species and condemned that 'eighteenth-century optimism' expressed alike in the American Declaration of Independence and the Communist Manifesto. He added that this deeply pessimistic and adversarial view of human nature was his own, but then gave it a more general currency and weight by saying that it was supported by most other 'scholars'.[101] It was certainly endorsed by Glyn Daniel, and it just as certainly ran directly counter to the ideals that had underpinned the Universal Bond from its earliest beginnings, and which were based directly on that 'eighteenth-century optimism' that Piggott so disdained.

There was not the slightest chance that Stuart Piggott would have much good to say of the ancient Druids in his book devoted to Druidry. It was most unlikely to treat the modern kind any better. There may, none the less, have been a very faint chance that he might have done so if, when studying modern Druids, he came to gain some respect for them and understanding of them even if he continued to differ from them on specific matters. He collected some of the literature issued by the Universal Bond, which is preserved in his archive, and, in the course of preparation for his book he opened a direct correspondence with Ross Nichols. Instead of creating a *rapprochement*, however, this had the reverse effect. Piggott was especially interested in the historical claims made by Nichols's order, and wanted to see the documentary evidence for them. As Nichols continued loyally to assert the claims, while failing to produce or cite anything to substantiate them, Piggott lost patience, apparently concluding (correctly) that there was no evidence to produce. He ended the exchange, and with that the last hope of a mitigation of his hostility was gone.[102]

Piggott's book was published by Thames and Hudson, a popular but respectable firm, in 1968; which meant that its commissioning editor was Glyn Daniel. It was entitled simply *The Druids*, which signalled its comprehensive nature and also its

intention of matching and replacing Kendrick's work of the same name. It demonstrated to the full Piggott's formidable prowess as an archaeologist, historian, populist
and polemicist. The book ran to over two hundred pages, with seventy-five illustrations, some never published before (the second edition was to add fifty-five more). It
dealt extensively with the material remains of the Iron Age, as known by that date, in
order to reconstruct the culture of the ancient Druids. For information on the latter
it leaned heavily on the Greek and Roman accounts, and gave credence to those
which portrayed Druids as bloodthirsty barbarian priests. Piggott conceded that they
seemed to have had some skill in astronomy and the calculation of calendars, but
argued that their scientific prowess could not match that of the Greeks. He justified
the privileging of the hostile ancient texts not only on the grounds that they were
more ample and detailed, but also because his view of human nature made them seem
much more believable than texts which admired the Druids. He did not, however, feel
that this prejudice made his conclusions more subjective. Instead, he consistently
represented it as the only sensible and realistic position to adopt, to be taken by all
right-minded people, and one that was actually held by all reputable scholars. Those
who had viewed the Druids differently, from ancient times to the present, were
portrayed by him as idealists and dreamers, out of touch with the ways of the
real world.

Although the majority of the book was concerned directly with ancient Druidry,
almost half of it was devoted to views of Druids since the beginning of modern times.
Here his attitudes were sustained, in that those who wished to believe well of the
Druids were dismissed as dreamers hankering after an imagined and unrealistic golden
age. A large part of his purpose, moreover, was to discredit modern Druidry. It was
indeed central to the book, which opened by portraying the Universal Bond holding
its rites at Stonehenge, and asking if it had any right to be there. The answer, spread
throughout the book, was of course resoundingly negative. Piggott devoted more care
and space than any previous scholarly writer to portraying the known history of
modern people who had claimed identity with Druids. In doing so he displayed at
moments a taste for vituperation as unrestrained as that of Glyn Daniel. Among other
comments, he described the various kinds of Druidry constructed since the Georgian
period as 'almost unbelievably fatuous speculations and fantasies', 'moonbeams from
the larger lunacy', 'a compelling magnet for many a psychological misfit and lonely
crank', 'a non-rational universe where every form of belief and unreason may meet',
'almost unrelieved lunatic darkness' and 'a world at once misleading and rather
pathetic' which represented 'a sad pilgrimage through error'. To the final category he
consigned not just the Universal Bond but the whole of fraternal Druidry as practised
since 1781. His main purpose was to map out the ways in which ancient Druids had
been reimagined since 1500, in a manner that broke valuable new ground; but in doing
so he made clear his scorn for them.[103] Piggott's book was a bestseller, and became the
standard work on its subject for the next twenty years. No other archaeologist or historian was sufficiently interested in the subject to tackle it in turn, and Piggott would
have been a hard act to follow. The modern Druids themselves were quite incapable of
the sort of scholarship needed to answer him effectively. He had provided the general

public with both a comprehensive history of Druids and a comprehensive denunciation of their modern forms.

*   *   *

It remains to chart the progress of both the severed portions of the old Universal Bond in the years after the schism, and the attitudes taken towards Druids in that subsequent period by the archaeologists who had attacked them. Thomas Maughan continued to lead his section of the former order to Stonehenge each midsummer, and to Tower Hill at the equinoxes, under its traditional names, including that of the Universal Bond. In 1966 the current Minister for Public Building and Works, swayed by the continuing protests of the archaeologists on the Ancient Monuments Board, decided to ban the Druids from the stones at dawn on 21 June, together with every other member of the public. He was dissuaded by his civil servants, this time seconded by the county police force, which had warmed to the Druids in the intervening years. Both argued that Maughan and his people had behaved perfectly, and had never been responsible for the bad behaviour of crowds in previous years. Furthermore, the policy of exclusion appeared to be working, as only a small number of people now turned up for the solstice sunrise – about a hundred in 1967 – which they watched peacefully from beyond the barbed wire.

This happy state of affairs was ruptured in 1969, when several hundred 'drunks and hippies' turned up to protest against the banning of most of the public from entry. The police fought a way through them to enable the Druids to get in, but many of the crowd cut the wire barrier, broke in and climbed on the stones. The response of the Ministry was to order thicker wire for the next year. The local district council, however, persuaded it to deal with the new problem by relaxing, rather than strengthening, its defences. A deal was brokered whereby the general public were admitted to the enclosure around the stones as the Druids entered it before dawn, but only the Druids themselves were allowed among the megaliths. This actually worked; although a crowd three thousand strong turned up for the solstice sunrise of 1970, its members behaved perfectly well. Maughan catered for them by addressing them between parts of the ceremony, to make sure that they understood what was happening.[104]

The new decade therefore opened well for Maughan and his order at Stonehenge; evidently it had recovered from the departure of Nichols and his supporters. In 1965 the small size of his following at the monument was all too plain, but by 1967 it was up to thirty-five, and by 1970 had swelled to fifty-three. Maughan himself made a commanding figure, robed in white with a purple ribbon of office and a shepherd's crook decked with oak leaves. In 1968 he gave an interview to a sympathetic journalist, who found him a lively, elderly man with a cream-coloured beard. His vision of Druidry was very much one of individual self-knowledge and personal growth of a sort characteristic of Western spirituality in the late 1960s and 1970s; in that sense he was in harmony with the times. He told his guest that his Druids were 'interested in the art and science of living, and in building up a man and his character'. He added, with the air of delivering a slogan, 'Man is God in the making', and expressed a belief in reincarnation. Questions relating to the order's historical connection with Stonehenge were cheerfully ducked, as Maughan explained that there was no conclusive evidence of one before the present century, but a strong oral tradition insisted that it had existed.[105]

The formal literature of the Universal Bond was more forthright. Before the 1973 midsummer rites, it issued a press release declaring that this was the 258th year since its foundation. It then reminded readers that three of its claimed former chiefs – John Toland, William Stukeley and William Blake – had all been convinced of the central importance of Stonehenge to the ancient Druids, as had Sir Norman Lockyer. It then cited a recent book by Gerald Hawkins, an amateur prehistorian who had declared, sensationally, that the monument had been a giant computer, designed, amongst other things, to predict eclipses. (Hawkins was wrong, because he had associated with each other portions of the monument that were actually from different periods.) The Universal Bond naturally hailed his book as proof that the builders of Stonehenge were indeed great scientists, as they claimed the ancient Druids to have been.[106] Between 1965 and 1968, the order published its own magazine, the *Druid*, the first issue of which opened with a historical overview produced by the two leading members, one being Maughan himself. To a historian, the most striking feature of it is its anachronism: it could have come straight out of the early nineteenth century. It mixed together the legendary story of early Britain produced by Iolo Morganwg with that summarized by William Stukeley, equating, for example, Iolo's mythical founding father, Hu Gadarn, with Stukeley's Phoenician leader Hercules. It insisted that the Druidic religion brought by this hero consisted of divine revelations given to humans long before the time of Abraham. It added that, because they possessed such a pure and genuine faith, the Druids had converted to evangelical Christianity long before the Romans arrived in Britain. The mission that it recommended to modern Druids was to restore the true and original religion and so replace the degenerate varieties that dominated the current age. Lest this sound too radical, it urged readers to bring out the best in humanity, rather than try to change it.[107]

There is much in this story that a historian cannot know; at least in the present state of the available evidence. There seem to be no accessible records of what life was like inside the order, or of what people belonged to it, why they joined, and whether their views of it altered once they had become members. At Stonehenge, it is relatively easy, at least in outline, to know what journalists, bureaucrats and Druids thought of the events at midsummer. There seem to be no accessible accounts, however, left by members of the general public who turned up there. None the less, it is possible to draw certain conclusions about the changing nature of the order, and its relationship with other groups. In some basic respects the Universal Bond of 1970 was not that of 1920 or 1930, and the shift had taken place under the leadership of Robert MacGregor-Reid. The order led by his father was dedicated, above all, to the unification of humanity, especially in religion but also in society and politics, so that war, poverty and oppression would all be eliminated from the world. There were traces of this ideal in the mission statements issued in the 1950s, but the emphasis was far more now on enabling individuals to achieve their own maximum potential. Under Maughan, this was sustained, though in this as in other respects he was doing no more than preserving what he had inherited from his predecessor. The Universal

Bond of the late twentieth century was very much that recreated by MacGregor-Reid in the years around 1950, and it did not change to any significant extent thereafter.

MacGregor-Reid also left his imprint on the other successor order to spring from his own, that of Bards, Ovates and Druids, produced by the secession of 1964. Naturally enough, this reflected more obviously the character of its founder, Ross Nichols. Like his rival Thomas Maughan, he was a relatively old man when he came to command a Druid organization, in his case aged sixty-two. He had come to Druidry late in life, joining the Universal Bond in 1954, although within two years he had already risen to be one of its most prominent members.[108] Presumably the order gave him a warm welcome, as somebody who already had more distinction than most of the existing membership: he was a graduate of Cambridge University, a respected poet and a journalist, and had been a contributor to, and the assistant editor of, the nation's most erudite magazine concerned with occultism: the *Occult Observer*. A large amount of information is now available upon his life and work, including many of his own writings, largely because of the fidelity to his memory of his eventual successor as chief of his order, Philip Carr-Gomm.[109]

Nichols's personal ideals were very much those of the earlier Universal Bond. He was a socialist and a pacifist, with a mystical love of the natural world and a special interest in the education of youth. He had an exalted sense of the position of humanity within the natural order, continuing to believe, in defiance of Darwin, that humans had been granted a special divine revelation of the sort portrayed in the Bible. His solution to this need for a special status for humanity was already provided by Theosophy: his species had evolved physically from other animals, but been recreated by higher beings, for a special purpose. His immediate hope was that humans could reconstruct and achieve that purpose by studying ancient wisdom. His ultimate one was that they might be able to communicate directly with those beings, as in the past. He believed firmly in a single deity, but held that this entity was immanent in the natural world, and could manifest in a variety of forms, male and female, including both the Christian god and the Great Mother. This freed him to continue to attend services regularly in the Anglican Church. For the same reason, he sustained the old belief that Druidry had been only one part of the universal and good primeval religion created by the original divine revelation. He could recognize aspects of that religion in a number of thinkers who were formally in different faiths but whom he could personally hail as fellow workers in the same cause, including Pythagoras, St Augustine of Hippo, William Blake, Jain holy men and Sufi mystics. He had a personal reverence for Jesus Christ as a teacher of brotherly love, altruism, self-restraint, pacifism and marital loyalty, all of which accorded with his own social and political ideals. The Christ whom he venerated, however, was not merely the biblical Messiah but a Tibetan Buddhist adept, Osiris, Horus, Adonis and a son of Zeus.[110]

Sun, light and air all featured powerfully as positive symbols and forces in his teachings, as a natural corollary of his naturist's love of fresh air and exercise in natural surroundings. Also important to his work was a passion for structure. He was never happier than when expounding the symbolism he perceived in an ancient monument, or the nature of a system of thought. His favourite technique in doing this was to appropriate and assimilate images, figures, concepts and lessons from all across the Old World, from Ireland to China, and fit them together to make a model of his own. His vision of the ancient Druids was very much as philosophers and scientists rather than as priests, and as part of his mythical history he credited modern Druids as having given a vital impetus to the Scientific Revolution of the seventeenth century, led by such figures as Newton. For his overall view of prehistory, he grafted actual archaeological discoveries on to a scheme based ultimately on the Bible (in particular, a belief in a single, true, primeval religion revealed by a divine force) and Iolo Morganwg.[111] In addition, he had a touching belief in the mythical history of the Universal Bond, which he accepted and defended loyally, in its entirety. He repeated the full list of bogus chiefs of the Universal Bond, as compiled by MacGregor-Reid and his friends shortly before he joined the order, and attempted to argue away any doubts concerning it. In the process he added further pieces of misinformation, such as that, discussed earlier, which claimed that William Blake identified himself as a Druid at his trial.[112] He admitted that Iolo Morganwg's work was controversial, but informed his audience that the latest scholarship 'has found a great deal of earlier work, possibly improved and edited, incorporated by him in his vast oeuvre, but has not really worked out which is what'. As usual he provided no source reference for this (to anybody familiar with the scholarship concerned) staggering statement. Instead, he went on to inform people – again on no visible base of evidence – that Iolo's information on the circles of existence and the 'mystic sign' were among this early and authentic material.[113]

It has been shown that a large part of the historical mythology of the Universal Bond was invented as a response to adversity. This pattern held with Ross Nichols, whose status, as a schismatic leader of a rebel group, seems to have reinforced his emotional need to emphasize the legendary history of his parent order and to position himself as a legitimate successor to it. This is, certainly, what he did. During his lifetime, his view of the Druidic past was disseminated only to his own friends and pupils in his order, and in very occasional letters to journals or newspapers.[114] It has, however, reached a much greater audience since 1990, when it was published in a posthumous edition of his writings.[115] As such, it represents probably the most comprehensive collection of misinformation on the history of Druidry ever to get into print, and long years will be needed to undo its effects. This being so, it is a shame that the historical section of Nichols's work seems to be the one most frequently quoted by Druids in conversation, to the neglect of the philosophical passages which ought better to stand the test of time. What they contain, between them, is an impressive reworking, for a late twentieth-century audience, of the eighteenth-century dream of combining the world's different traditions of wisdom to reconstruct the original revelation made by the true divinity to humanity. Just as Nichols himself, an idealist surviving from the socialism that flourished between the world wars, could identify easily with a much later youth culture, so he had put a pre-Darwinian view of the human past into a form meaningful to radicals who professed not to trust anybody who had come of age before the 1960s.

Meanwhile the archaeologists who had set themselves up as the main opponents of the modern Druids continued to flourish and to co-operate, but their relationship with the subject of Druidry followed very different courses. Stuart Piggott never returned to it in his scholarly publications, but continued to lash out at contemporary Druids far into his old age and retirement. He wrote letters to national newspapers to denounce them every time they were featured there claiming an ancient connection with Stonehenge or a modern history going back as far as 1717.[116]

The case of Glyn Daniel is rather different. After 1968 he lost interest in modern Druids, perhaps because he felt that Piggott's book had answered them completely, and certainly because he had found new targets among what he regarded as 'bad' archaeology, such as the belief that ancient monuments were built on lines bearing natural energy. Whilst his interest in modern Druids evaporated, however, his attitude to their ancient counterparts was undergoing an important shift, and in the opposite direction to that of Piggott. The latter had studiously ignored any possible relationship between them and megalithic monuments, treating these wholly as an Iron Age phenomenon. Daniel, on the other hand, now restated the connection with great force. In 1972 he gave a lecture to London University, subsequently published as a booklet, in which he looked at the way in which megalithic monuments had been venerated or reused in later periods. He announced that 'I have no doubt myself that a knowledge of some facts about megaliths and the faith of the megalith builders survived through the Roman period and the Migration period into the Christian Middle Ages.' He added, candidly, that 'it would be an amusing turnaround in our thinking if, having scoffed in a superior way at Aubrey, Stukeley and Rowlands for restoring the megaliths to the Druids, we are now restoring the Druids of history to the megaliths of prehistory. This may be too blunt a way of putting it, but I find it difficult to envisage why there should be a Christian occupation of some megalithic sites, unless a real tradition of their importance as special and sacred places was carried through the period of the Bronze Age and Early Iron Age.'[117] It was as if, having seen off the modern Druids, Daniel was now keen to appropriate for himself some of the ideas that had most deeply inspired them.[118]

He was supported two years later by Anne Ross, a close friend of Stuart Piggott, who had just made a name for herself as an expert in Iron Age and Roman-British religion. She published the view in 1974 that the Celts had actually arrived in Britain in the Neolithic, and were therefore the builders of most prehistoric stone circles; which meant that the Druids, of course, would have been the priests who served in them.[119] Such beliefs were given apparent support by the developing discipline of archaeoastronomy. During the late 1960s, a professor of engineering, Alexander Thom, had conducted many surveys of stone circles and rows, on which he based the theory that they had been sophisticated observatories, aligned on the movements of the moon and stars and built to a standard unit of measurement. This presupposed a very high degree of scientific knowledge and centralized intellectual authority at the time when they were constructed, both of which fitted some of the traditional images of Druids. It also argued strongly against the portrait of backwardness and barbarism which archaeologists such as Atkinson and Piggott had attributed to prehistoric Britain.[120] Thom's work was followed up by Euan Mackie, a former pupil of Glyn Daniel.[121] In a book published in 1977, and dedicated to Thom, he declared proven the existence of 'the hierarchical, stratified nature of late Neolithic Britain, whose upper echelons lived in special ceremonial centres, evolved a sophisticated system of observational astronomy and field geometry ... and commanded the manpower, resources and technical skill to erect some of the largest earthworks in Europe as well as a stone temple whose architectural sophistication is unmatched outside the Bronze Age urban civilizations of the Near East'.[122] The temple, of course, was Stonehenge. Mackie went on to draw the now obvious conclusion: that the priests of that society could well have been the ancestors of the Iron Age Druids, which would explain both the high reputation of Britain as a sacred place even in Caesar's time and the respect given to Druids as scientists by ancient writers.[123]

The period between 1968 and 1978 had therefore witnessed a curious dual effect. Stuart Piggott had launched a major attack on modern Druids, and especially the Universal Bond. Any special relationship between the ancient Druids and Stonehenge had been denied, the former had been depicted as bloodthirsty barbarians, and their modern counterparts had been derided as lunatics and charlatans. At the same time, Glyn Daniel, followed by other members of his profession, had restated tentatively the association between Druids and stone circles that modern Druids had long been condemned by archaeologists for making. And another discredited image of ancient Druidry, as possessed of admirable scientific ability, was being restored by professional scholars. Even as these developments occurred, the Universal Bond had succeeded in both consolidating its position at Stonehenge and surviving the schism in its membership, as both the resulting orders prospered. In a sense, there was honour on both sides.

* * *

In retrospect, the mid-1970s was a time when both aspects of that (in some respects) happy situation were to begin to alter, removing the position that all represented in it had managed to achieve. The first and most obvious change came in 1975, when Ross Nichols died suddenly of a heart attack, just as his mentor MacGregor-Reid had done. Once more, the unexpected nature of the event resulted in a Druid order being thrown into crisis, but the outcome in this case was even worse than before. Nichols had left nobody willing to keep his group functioning, and so the Order of Bards, Ovates and Druids seemed to disappear with him.[124] It appeared that the Universal Bond had survived another schism, and that one of the contending groups had seen off its rival, just as had occurred in 1954. Things were to be different this time, for the Order of Bards, Ovates and Druids was to reappear in 1988 under the leadership of Nichols's pupil Philip Carr-Gomm; but this took over a decade to occur. His rival, Thomas Maughan, survived him by no more than a year, dying in 1976, but in this case the succession was well established, eager and vigorous. The 'main' branch of the Universal Bond therefore continued as before, retaining among its other traditions the annual ceremonies at Stonehenge. It remained very much the public face of British Druidry, and the one order of which everybody in the nation, and many outside it, knew.

Its problems under its new leadership were to come from outside, and to centre, almost inevitably, on its celebrated and controversial relationship with Stonehenge. By the 1970s it had long seen off the archaeologists and contented the Ministry; instead, once again, its position would be destabilized by members of the general public, or at least of a particular subculture within that public. This was that huge movement among Western radicalized youth which was a conspicuous feature of the late 1960s, and which produced an annual rock festival in a field next to the monument. It grew up slowly between 1974 and 1980, and became the nation's most flamboyant, public and accessible showcase of the counterculture concerned: a hippie city. At its peak in 1984, perhaps a hundred thousand people attended at one point or another while the festival lasted.[125] Its focus was the summer solstice, which meant that it took place at exactly the same time as the annual ceremonies of the Universal Bond, potentially in collision with it, and presenting an apparently huge new problem for police supervision and site security. In a sense, it represented a new manifestation of the old popular tradition of gathering at the stones to watch the midsummer sunrise, but on a completely unprecedented scale and linked to a very specific new kind of social and cultural radicalism.

In the event, no dramatic problems occurred. The festival-goers were allowed to watch the Druids' dawn ceremony if they desired. More important, they were permitted, from 1979 onward, to enter the monument itself later on the same day to enact their own rites, and were in general well behaved despite their huge numbers and anti-authoritarian attitudes. By the early 1980s, the pattern of interaction took a set and repeated form. The Druids would arrive before midnight to process up to the Double Circle for their customary service of remembrance of past members. At about two o'clock they returned to the car park to rest in their coach, pulled up beside the mobile police station established for the duration of the festival. At 3.15 an advance party of them went to hold a brief vigil among the stones, and from that time a crowd of festival-goers and other members of the public began to gather outside the fence. The Druids processed in as day broke, carrying a cross, banners, a copper globe hung from three chains, a small silver cup and two sprigs of oak. Once inside, they moved about, stood still for moments, and processed again, uttering their liturgy in tones that the crowd could generally not hear. At one point they moved down to the Hele Stone for further devotions. At sunrise they were gathered in the centre of the monument, and saluted the event with the blowing of long bronze horns. These were a recent innovation, having been bought in a London street market; the archaeologist Christopher Chippindale thought they were probably Tibetan. After that the Druids processed out to their coach, to return again for a final rite at noon. When they finished, the festival-goers flooded into the stones, to hold various ceremonies of their own.[126]

This annual pattern was terminated traumatically in 1985. Two years before, custody of Stonehenge had been devolved by the government to English Heritage, a semi-independent body set up (among other purposes) to take control of all ancient and historic monuments which had by then come into the possession of the state. This body now resolved, for reasons that are not yet in the public domain, to close the monument completely at the summer solstice each year. An enormous police presence was mustered to enforce the ban, with notoriously brutal results.[127] If the manner in which this decision was reached remains obscure, its objective was always clear: to stop the festival, which was now officially pronounced to be a danger to Stonehenge and the surrounding prehistoric sites. The Universal Bond was banned as well, in order to make the extirpation of the festival possible. In other words, the authorities had taken the policy option which they had rejected in the 1960s, of excluding the Druids because of the perceived misdemeanours of the general public at midsummer. This time the Universal Bond departed quietly, and soon adopted the solution reached by other Druid orders before: of making arrangements to have special access to the stones for its cere-monies at times safely away from the summer solstice. In doing so, it bid farewell to difficulty and controversy, but also – as its leaders had formerly recognized – to public attention. It continues to flourish, but has slipped into obscurity. Having been the most dynamic, influential and important of all English Druid orders in the twentieth century, it has become one of the most isolated and reclusive.[128]

After trying out various solutions to the problem of access to Stonehenge at the summer solstice, English Heritage settled in the year 2000 on the policy of opening the monument free of charge to all comers on the night before 21 June, and main-taining this open access until a few hours after sunrise. This has worked well enough to be maintained until the time of writing. A huge, high-spirited crowd, numbering many thousands – much bigger than any of those recorded in the early or mid-twentieth century – parties in and around the stones all night. A large part of the merit of this policy, for the authorities, is that it removes any need either to allow a revival of the festival or to care about Druids. Many of the latter are present, from various recently founded groups, but they are lost among the mass of revellers. The centre of the monument is always taken over immediately by revellers, with no room provided for ceremonies. For the time being, at least, a special Druidic presence at Stonehenge at midsummer is over. In one sense that presence was a long and imposing one, spanning most of the twentieth century and making a great impact on the national imagination. In another, it was a fleeting and fitful component of modern celebrations at Stonehenge. By 2008, the general public had gathered to watch the summer sunrise there for almost 140 years, less only the gap between 1985 and 2000 imposed forcibly by the authorities. Druids had held rites there at midsummer, some-times only in tiny numbers, for fewer than half of those years. However unintention-ally, the policy adopted by English Heritage at the turn of the millennium effectively returned the situation to that which prevailed in the late Victorian period.

The new willingness of archaeologists to reconnect the ancient Druids with mega-lithic monuments disappeared more rapidly than the modern Druids from Stonehenge. In the 1980s archaeologists, astronomers and statisticians came system-atically to analyse the claims made by Alexander Thom and Euan Mackie for prehis-toric science, and rejected many of them. Most of the stellar and lunar alignments claimed by Thom were shown to be impossible to prove beyond doubt, and the scien-tific precision that he claimed to have found in their construction was challenged. What was certainly demonstrated was the undoubted interest of the people of Neolithic and Bronze Age Britain in the movements of heavenly bodies. The new generation of scholars found no evidence, however, that this was the result of a spirit of scientific enquiry which engendered an impressive amount of mathematical and astronomical knowledge, as Thom had held it to be. Instead, they concluded that it had reflected a wish to incorporate the movements of the sun and moon, and perhaps the stars, into seasonal rites designed to celebrate and propitiate the powers of the cosmos, in the manner of most traditional peoples. In this respect, the prehistoric British had been perfectly normal, and achieved nothing very remarkable.[129] Such a conclusion removed any incentive for archaeologists to credit the Druids with special knowledge, and therefore any renewed importance.

By now the people who had been the leading experts in British prehistory had, in any case, got bigger things to worry about. In the early 1970s it had become generally accepted that the system used hitherto for calculating the age of prehistoric sites, from the rate at which the radiocarbon found in them had decayed, was seriously inaccurate. Once it was corrected, the dates of periods such as the Neolithic and Bronze Age had to be revised, in the former case by over a thousand years. This knocked out the linkages made by some leading scholars – including Glyn Daniel and Richard Atkinson – between British prehistoric cultures and those of the eastern Mediterranean. In this manner, many of the conclusions of their earlier work were invalidated. This blow did not by any means terminate their careers; their past achievements were too great, and the respect in which they were held too profound. None the less, it fell at a time when their generation was starting to feel the effects of age, and they ceased to make the pace in their profession. Atkinson, Piggott and Daniel did not produce any major works on prehistory after this time, and Daniel and Piggott diverted much of their energy – in the former case almost exclusively – to writing the history of their own discipline. Daniel lost any interest in making connections between the megalith-builders and the Druids.

Their place in the forefront of British archaeology was taken by a new generation especially associated with an approach to their subject that they termed 'processual'. This depended on taking methods from the sciences of sociology and anthropology to construct models of how prehistoric societies might have operated. As such, it prioritized evidence for economic and social behaviour over that for ritual activity, and focused more on the special characteristics of specific cultures. There was no place in such an approach for a concern with Druids. The period between 1955 and 1975 now appeared to be a brief interlude, in which professional archaeology had taken an active interest in ancient and modern Druidry, if only of an adversarial kind. By 1980, that time was apparently over.

* * *

In the first chapter of this book, a brisk survey was carried out of the interpretations made of the ancient Druids by different scholars since the 1980s, emphasizing the sheer range that had been constructed on much the same evidence. It seems fitting to close this one by seeing how archaeologists in particular have treated the subject during the same period. A major landmark in Neolithic studies was the publication in 1995 of English Heritage's collation of all the data concerning Stonehenge, which laid out and analysed the available evidence to a standard never attempted before. The result confirmed that there were no structures of any sort on the site or beside it that could be dated to the Iron Age. There was little material present of any sort from that period, and relatively little sign of activity during it in the neighbourhood. A small quantity of pottery had been found, deposited at long intervals, and a young man had been buried in a ditch beside the site. These remains added up to a picture of sporadic and occasional visits to the location; there was absolutely no evidence that Stonehenge was regarded as a monument with any particular meaning, or that any sustained activity took place there during the time in which the Druids are recorded as having been active.[130] Such a conclusion harmonizes with the more general findings of Richard Bradley, currently perhaps the pre-eminent British archaeologist of the Neolithic and Bronze Age. He has made a survey of the use of English ceremonial monuments which suggests that there was virtually no continuity between the Neolithic and the Iron Age.[131]

This evidence makes a convenient fit with the manner in which professional archaeologists divide up their discipline, experts in the Palaeolithic, the Mesolithic, the Neolithic and the early Bronze Age, the late Bronze and Iron Ages, and the Roman and the early medieval periods tending to form compact blocs with relatively little communication between them. Certainly, most of them are once again interested in the evidence for ceremonial activity, as 'processual' archaeology has given way to a 'post-processual' variety in which the symbolic behaviour of people – including what is generally called religion – is a major subject of study. The symbolic systems concerned, however, tend to be reconstructed, naturally enough, within particular societies, and the question of continuities between periods is generally left open, or ignored. None the less, there seems at least to be a tacit acknowledgement that such continuities may have existed. Occasionally it is explicit, as in the work of Francis Pryor, one of the few current British archaeologists to range widely across periods (and one of the most exciting). In 2004 he declared that 'today . . . most prehistorians would accept that the religious beliefs that formed the core of Druidism had very ancient roots indeed, at least as old as Stonehenge, and probably a great deal older'. He did not name any such prehistorians, but he added as a personal testimony, with reference to the Universal Bond's ceremonies at Stonehenge in the 1960s and 1970s, 'I'm now inclined to think that the much-derided people wearing sheets actually had a better idea of what was going on in prehistory than my lecturers at Cambridge, who were unable to take a sufficiently long or broad view of the way that prehistoric beliefs arose, developed and matured through the centuries of later prehistory.'[132]

This is a heroically generous and magnanimous statement, though it does not exactly represent what the Universal Bond was saying about British prehistory. Nor is it entirely fair to Pryor's Cambridge teachers, the main one of whom was Glyn Daniel, who came to make the very point that Pryor himself was now emphasizing.[133] Despite this, it highlights an important issue. As evidence of his own for continuity of belief, Pryor began by citing the fact that one recently discovered Bronze Age timber circle, the famous 'Seahenge' in Norfolk, was made of oak, the sacred tree of the Druids. This, unfortunately, puts a great deal of reliance on a single ancient source, Pliny, for Druidic beliefs. Pryor went on to cite broader linkages of ritual behaviour across prehistory: a concern with water, with the passage of the seasons, and with the sun and the moon.[134] These are undoubted, but also common to most tradi-tional peoples. The manner in which this behaviour can be packaged, in terms of the deities venerated, the monuments associated, the ceremonies enacted, the personnel empowered, and the demands made of worshippers, can vary so considerably as to mark off entirely different religious systems. The argument is therefore important and well made, but there are limitations to it. The same comments may be applied to the work of Miranda and Stephen Aldhouse-Green, who have attempted to relate archaeological evidence taken from the whole of European prehistory to the phenomenon that historians of religion call shamanism. This is itself a very loosely defined and controversial category, invented by anthropologists and now increasingly abandoned by them as too nebulous to be useful: the Aldhouse-Greens employ it in a broad sense, to mean specialists who seem to communicate with a spirit world, while in a trance state, on behalf of their peoples. They claim to have found data from every period between the Palaeolithic and the early Middle Ages that testifies to the existence of such individuals across Northern Europe. This would make shamanism an essential (and perhaps *the* essential) component of pre-Christian religion, and the Druids feature as one aspect of it, associated with the Iron Age.[135]

This is continuity with a vengeance, but the theory is susceptible to a qualification and a challenge. The former, which does not invalidate it, is that shamanism can be repackaged into different religious forms, which otherwise have little in common. This is the same problem as with Francis Pryor's argument. The challenge is that the checklist of evidence assembled by them as possible indicators of the presence of shamanism is too long and diffuse to be wholly convincing. It includes unusual postures for bodies in burials, unusual grave goods, particular motifs in art or architecture, the presence of musical instruments, representations of human figures that show them dancing, or associated with animals, equipment for healing or divination, and several others. All of these could be interpreted as signifying things other than shamanism. The result is an exciting book, with a wealth of valuable information; and its case is very much worth stating. None the less, an argument can be made that it is inherently inconclusive.

Specialists in the Iron Age itself tend to concentrate on evidence for social, economic, technological, artistic and military activities rather than for religion, but there are two notable exceptions: J. D. Hill and Miranda Aldhouse-Green. The former has emerged as one of the most influential archaeologists of the period, and probably the leading one concerned with ritual behaviour. It was he who demonstrated, convincingly, that what had commonly been taken for deposits of rubbish on sites in southern England had been carefully structured. As such, they were not simply the remains of a daily disposal of refuse, but of 'irregular rituals which engraved a cosmology into the physical setting and daily lives of Iron Age people'. He never mentioned Druids, but his comments on the nature of the deposits have important implications for an understanding of religious practices at the time. He suggested that the bodies of animals buried whole in the deposits were probably those of sacrificial victims, and that the rarer cases of animals that had been cooked and eaten were probably of the same kind. He noted that human bodies had been treated in the same way as those of animals, and were rare enough to have represented only a minority of the population. He therefore suggested that they might have been sacrifices too.[136]

His findings were drawn upon in turn by Miranda Aldhouse-Green, who has effectively become Anne Ross's successor as the leading British expert in Iron Age and
Romano-British religious iconography. In the years from 1998 to 2001 she took a
special interest in the subject of human sacrifice during the later prehistory of
Western Europe, and decided that it had probably existed. She did so by pooling the
various claims for its existence, by pagan Greek and Roman and medieval Christian
writers, and using these to interpret human bodies from the period that had seemed
to have suffered ritualized violence or been treated in other ways that set them apart
from the norm. She acknowledged that 'almost all the archaeological evidence sugges-
tive of ritual murder is capable of alternative interpretation', but concluded that the
sheer quantity of it, from different times and places was persuasive, especially when
supported by the literary testimony.[137]

As I have stated before, these arguments are clearly both strong and well founded,
and may well represent the truth. Against them I have entered two different sorts of
reservation. One is the obvious matter of the lack of decisive proof of them, which both
proponents recognize. Furthermore, Professor Aldhouse-Green's methodology, of
mounding up disparate pieces of material data which may all be read in other ways, is
the same that she employed in her book on shamanism, and subject to the same problems. The other reservation, which I have also presented in an earlier book, is that
specialists in earlier periods of British prehistory have recently tended to interpret very
similar evidence in a different way. Neolithic and early Bronze Age sites show many
similarities to those studied by Dr Hill and cited by Professor Aldhouse-Green, but are
currently interpreted much more gently. The presence of human bones or bodies in
significant quantities in ceremonial or domestic contexts is read as remains of the
veneration of ancestors, or the representation of the human element in miniature repli-
cations of the cosmos. The mixing or close proximity of human and animal remains,
on what seems to be an equal basis of treatment, is viewed as another aspect of that
cosmic representation, or the presence of totemic beasts or personal spirit guides, or the
honouring of beloved or venerated animals. Burials that can only represent a minority
of the population are regarded as those of individuals marked out for special veneration or as spiritual representatives of the community. The unusual treatment of particular bodies is related to beliefs regarding the fate of the soul, and so on.[138]

This all makes a striking contrast with the Victorian inclination to view such
Neolithic and Bronze Age material as strong evidence for human sacrifice, being part
of a general inclination at that time to emphasize the savagery of prehistoric British
society. Such a benevolent revision of attitudes in the later twentieth century is one
consequence of a wider tendency on the part of Western scholars to look upon traditional peoples in general with greater sympathy and respect. It is also part of a movement, implicit within post-processual archaeology, to enter more into imaginative and
empathetic contact with the prehistoric peoples under study. Specific iconic finds of
the earlier, more alienated, Neolithic archaeology have now been discredited. One was
the discovery of a child's body with a broken skull near the centre of the late Neolithic
timber circles near Stonehenge, nicknamed 'Woodhenge'. It was long interpreted as
a foundation sacrifice, and the youth of the presumed victim excited additional horror

and repulsion. Recently, it has been argued that there is no actual evidence that the child's skull had been cleft by a blow; it could just as well have come apart naturally.[139] More recently still, it has been pointed out that nothing in fact dates the burial to the Neolithic; it might have been intruded into the site at a range of later periods.[140] The automatic presumption that it represented the foundation sacrifice of the monument was a product of a mindset disposed to look for such atrocities.

It may need to be stressed at this point that the mindset concerned might have been correct. There is still a possibility that the Woodhenge child was ritually killed at the construction of the monument; the point is that we shall now probably never know if this was the case, and the possibility can no longer be stated as a certainty or the burial held up as an example of Neolithic behaviour. Likewise, just as the Iron Age specialists cited could be perfectly correct in their interpretations of the archaeological data, so those in earlier periods could be too benign. There is a real chance that opinion will alter again among experts in the earlier periods, and swing back to finding sacrifice and atrocity in the same material. All that is being suggested here is that, whereas contemporary specialists in the British Neolithic and early Bronze Age have shied away from Victorian attitudes to savagery, those in the Iron Age are still, in this respect, replicating Graeco-Roman attitudes to barbarism.

Miranda Aldhouse-Green is also the author of the first all-round survey of the ancient Druids to be made by an academic scholar since Stuart Piggott. It appeared exactly thirty years after his book, in 1998, from the same publisher, Thames and Hudson, and shared his verve of expression, sure handling of the archaeological material and Europe-wide scope. Her book had more than twice as many illustrations, with much glossier reproduction. Of course, she had a lot more archaeology on which to draw. Her volume was given a slightly different, more delicate title: *Exploring the World of the Druids*. As this signalled, she recognized the lack of direct material evidence for Druids themselves, and set out instead to reconstruct all that might be known about Iron Age society and religion in general, to provide the context within which the Druids might have operated. Once again some concerns might be expressed about the methodology employed, of picking up pieces of evidence from very different geographical locations, and a range of time spans, and matching them together without a great deal of regard for individual context. In the same manner, she extracted quotations from Greek, Roman and Irish texts to augment and interpret the archaeological data, without consistently taking into account the difficulties of treating such sources as objective evidence. She recognized the problem in principle, but not always in practice. In general, her attitudes to the ancient Druids were much the same as those of Piggott, though she naturally enough showed more interest in the role of women. She found little reason to credit the Druids with great philosophical or scientific prowess, and (in keeping with her other work) plenty to accuse them of human sacrifice. Indeed, to pile up apparent material evidence of ritualized atrocity, she drew on areas such as Denmark and the Czech Republic which had never been included in the part of Europe that had Druids. They could, however, legitimately be considered part of the latter's 'world' and they gave an impression of a general commitment of North European peoples to grisly religious rites. Towards modern

Druids, she was far kinder: apart from any personal predisposition to greater generosity, she was, unlike Piggott, writing at a time when they had long been banned from Stonehenge and archaeology had no quarrel with them. A smaller proportion of her book was devoted to them, but that still provided plenty of information, some of it new, and her usual high standard of visual material. Her account of the Druidic revivals of the period between 1700 and 1980 was objective, and entirely free from abuse, and her portrait of contemporary Druids was positively warm. She gallantly gave the very last words of her book to one of them, though the effect of doing so was to underline how little those of the present resembled the (nastier and more alien) Druids of the remote past.

So, at present, archaeologists – or at least the few who are interested – have become a lot nicer to modern Druidry while remaining inclined to privilege a negative view of the ancient sort. That negative view, moreover, remains highly influential among the general public, and there seems to be no doubt that the attitudes of contemporary experts in the Iron Age are significant in sustaining or reinforcing it. The symbolic importance of Lindow Man can scarcely be overstated in this respect. Repeatedly, when discussing images of the ancient Druids with television producers, journalists, schoolteachers and other relatively informed members of the general public, I have heard this famous bog body cited as the conclusive proof that the Iron Age British practised human sacrifice. This is, as I suggested in the first chapter, a direct consequence of the way in which the British Museum has presented it, and an interpretation which, though perfectly possible, is decidedly uncertain. It also rebounds on attitudes to unorthodox religion and spirituality at the present time. In 1999 Beth Coombe Harris's 1930s novel, *In the Grip of the Druids*, was republished by an evangelical Christian company. The preface to the new edition stated that the purpose of it was explicitly to limit the influence of modern Druids, by enabling readers to perceive the essentially heinous nature of their teachings. This was to be achieved by associating them with the horrific actions of their ancient equivalents, and the preface declared roundly that, should anybody doubt Harris's portrait of those, Lindow Man represented the clear proof of it.[141]

In June 2007 the *Guardian* newspaper carried a report on the refurbishment of some of the galleries at the British Museum, an activity which left the presentation of the bog body completely unrevised. The author, Jonathan Jones, drew attention to the manner in which the label of the display connected successively the alleged triple death that the man had suffered, Druids and human sacrifice, Druids and mistletoe, and the finding of mistletoe in the man's stomach. He added that 'the last item betrays his killers – and they're still around'. He then turned his ire, by association, upon modern Druids, while declaring that the evidence of Lindow Man wholly justified the brutality of the Romans in wiping out their ancient predecessors. The article concluded with the following judgement on the exhibit: 'This treasure from our prehistory confronts us with the seduction of violence and death, the monstrosity we're inches from, the belief that a person might make a good sacrifice.' The implication was that today we are still only 'inches' from superstitious atrocity, and that contemporary Druids may be closer.[142] In such unlooked-for ways, the presentation of a museum piece does make a direct contribution to debates over religious freedom and tolerance in present-day society, and helps to form, or harden, attitudes to them.

In a sense, the major personality of this story has not been a Druid, or an archaeologist, but Stonehenge. Every time the two groups have come together there for a sustained period, there has been a collision which rebounds on scholarly literature. Each time one or the other leaves the monument, or at least leaves public view there, relations between them become more benign. Underlying the attitudes of specialists in Iron Age archaeology, however, is a deeper issue: of their situation as experts in a period on the very fringe of history. As such they have to reckon with literary sources, ancient and medieval, which may or may not have importance for their work. My own feeling is now that those sources should be completely discarded, at least for an interval, and that archaeologists should concentrate on interpreting what the material evidence for the period seems to tell us in its own right; even if a multiplicity of answers may result. In making those interpretations, however, they need to reckon with a third phenomenon, which is the hostility towards the ancient Druids manifested by most Scottish and English authors for almost two hundred years. Specialists in earlier British prehistory have indeed largely broken away from Victorian conceptions of the Neolithic and Bronze Age. Those concerned with Iron Age religion have not, because they are still influenced not merely by certain old texts but by a particular emphasis upon some of them.

CONCLUSION

T his has been a very long book, but even so most chapters have had to be slimmed
down repeatedly to keep it at a publishable length, removing much additional
material and comment. The story continues to the present day with the appearance of
new kinds of Druid order in the 1990s, reflecting changing forms of modern spirituality and countercultural politics. Since 1950, moreover, Druids have returned to
being a favourite theme of novelists, reinforced by cinema and television. Once again
there has been a clear national division, English and Scottish authors reviving in its
full blend of horror and titillation the Victorian stereotype of the demonic Druids,
while the Welsh, French and Americans are more benevolent. From the body of
information that has been treated here, it is possible to draw four fairly simple conclusions, each one representing a different perspective on the manner in which Druids
may be, and have been, treated in a British context.

The first is that an interest in Druids is one intrinsic aspect of modernity. The ancient
world – or at least that literate part of it that has left us works of history, geography and
philosophy – was barely concerned with them. That is why the total number of references to them in Greek and Roman sources can fit into about a dozen pages of fairly
large print. The Middle Ages paid them virtually no attention, outside Ireland where
they were built into Gaelic cultural memory; but then almost no outsiders read native
Irish literature until the nineteenth century. A preoccupation with Druids boomed,
across north-western Europe, just as soon as that region took on features of the broad
movement, starting in Italy, which is conventionally called the Renaissance. Indeed, that
dramatic change is a key piece of evidence that traditional items of periodization, such
as the Renaissance and the Middle Ages, still have some validity. Druids were an obvious
focus of attention for states and ethnic cultures of the kind developing between the
Rhineland and the Atlantic around the year 1500. One feature of this stage of cultural
nationalism was a quest for historic roots that identified and distinguished particular
peoples. For those occupying this region, including those inhabiting Britain, Druids were
almost the only impressive figures to be found in their most remote past; a past which
was the more undistinguished and frustrating in that the two great traditional sources for
ancient history, the Bible and the Greek and Roman classics, more or less ignored it.

Once discovered and put to work, Druids had considerable utility. The ancient sources for them may be sparse and difficult, but provide some striking images that could serve all sorts of purposes. They could be made to represent Druids as patriots, rallying native resistance against foreign enemies. They could be used to portray them as great scientists, philosophers and theologians, giving the peoples who occupied their former lands an ancestral claim to intellectual and cultural achievement. Alternatively, the same portraits could be used to chastise the present age, or civilized living, and remind both that older and simpler ways of life might nurture a superior wisdom. This employment of Druids could shade easily into two others. One was to use them as forerunners of one's own preferred kind of religion, justifying it by apparent example, parallel and precedent and causing it to appear more deeply rooted in one's native land. Another, potent from the eighteenth century onward, was to hail them as priests of the natural world, with a love and understanding of that world that could serve as an inspiration, and correction, for a modern age that had become cut off, to its great detriment, from natural living.

Conversely, negative images of Druids were just as potent. They could be held up as exemplars of everything that a person happened to fear or hate in religion, whether paganism, rival forms of Christianity, or an over-powerful priesthood. They could be used as images of savagery, barbarism, ignorance and cruelty against which to cele-brate the virtues of civilization and the triumphs of progress. As such, they could be pressed into justifications for the European mission to tame, educate and develop the rest of the planet, and their ancient suppression seen as a vital first step in the achieve-ment of that mission. From the eighteenth century onward, also, they turned into an imaginative resource for people who were challenging social and cultural norms. This could take a relatively gentle form: for example, they could be inspiring figures for societies of working men dedicated to nurturing their skill in the performing arts, especially music. There could also be a much more radical aspect, with Druids providing encouragement to people who hoped for wholesale reform of their society with the aim of producing a much greater liberty of thought, worship, behaviour and imagination. Druids proved to be very, very good to think about, for modern people attempting to remake their world with justificatory reference to an ancient past. This book could, indeed, have readily been given the title of *Thinking with Druids*.

A second perspective on the way in which the place of Druids in modern culture may be understood is by reference to the nature of the ancient sources for them. On the whole, ancient authorities on most aspects of history and geography reflect a specific tradition, which makes the accounts given relatively harmonious. Thus, peoples who are foreign to the group represented by the writers are seen as having certain stable characteristics. There is a fairly well-agreed division of historical char-acters into heroes, villains, anti-heroes and honourable enemies. Individual events are triumphs, disasters or ordeals, and specific periods are good or bad times. Such obser-vations as these certainly fail to acknowledge the complexity and subtlety with which ancient authors could write, and the shades of difference between them. None the less, on the whole, Greek and Roman authors dealt with their own past, and with the cultures and societies around them, according to certain accumulated conventions. It is therefore all the more striking that such a convention does not exist where Druids are concerned; or, if there was one, it is no longer apparent. Despite the small and brief number of ancient references to them, these references manage between them to present contrasting images. The Druids appear in some texts as barbaric, bloodthirsty and deplorable, in others as admirable, sophisticated and learned, and in yet others as a mixture of both. Furthermore, arguments can be presented against the reliability of any of these accounts. Just two were left by people who could possibly have seen Druids themselves, Caesar and Cicero. Both were unusually devious and self-interested witnesses, and Caesar has an apparent logical defect in his account.

This means that, when later ages took an interest in Druids, there existed no single, authentic and authoritative portrait of them. Instead there were a number of competing options, between which modern people could choose according to their own tastes, needs, purposes and prejudices. As a result to an extreme extent, Druids have always been a contested subject. Anybody who has sought to write about them, whether to dismiss them, disparage them, abhor them, admire them or imitate them, has had to do so despite some feature of the evidence. The fact that the traditional literary sources have been so few, so well known and (from quite an early date) so readily available, has made this appropriation and disputation all the more widespread and intense. The many-faced and controversial nature of the sources has provided easy opportunities for people to employ Druids for the wide range of purposes discussed above. At the same time they render any such employment open to challenge, provoking further debate and redeployment in a seemingly limitless process.

A third way of looking at the historical use of Druids is to point out that it has peaked in certain periods. Certainly interest in them has spanned Western Europe ever since 1500, and extended readily into at least the English-speaking lands across the oceans. Certainly, also, it has been constant in British society since the 1520s. None the less, there was quite definitely a 'Druidic century' (and a bit) in British culture, extending between 1740 and 1860. There was, beyond question, a long and important preparation for that time of greatest popularity, and a subsequent period in which aspects of that popularity retained considerable vitality and some importance. Indeed, we are still living in that latter age. Yet that span of 120 years was the one in which Druids most completely dominated the British imagination. This was, it has been suggested in this book, because of the need for a common past to the new British superstate that had been constructed by the early eighteenth century. Given the inescapable fact that the historic nations within Britain had been constructed, in medieval times, largely in opposition to each other, it was necessary to go back further, to the ancient world, to find any shared heritage: and there were the Druids, as the only impressive native figures.

Their displacement from the national imagination occurred largely because of the earlier success of efforts to integrate them into established structures of thought. The revolution in scholarship that established the three-age system as the basic model for prehistory, and the theory of evolution as the motor for the appearance and disappearance of species, swept them away as part of the older thought-world that was now being challenged and demolished. It is possible that they will be brought back, in one form or another, should future British archaeologists seek to emphasize continuity as a prime feature of the prehistoric past. For the time being, however, the division of prehistory into blocs studied by different networks of experts, the contemporary dedication to rapid change as the normal and desirable state of human affairs, and the complex and constantly altering nature of prehistoric society, as revealed by the archaeological record, all weigh against such a development.

The final way in which the relationship between the modern British and the ancient Druids can be viewed is to note how much it differed, and altered, between the respective component peoples of these islands. It was the Scots who first took them up with real enthusiasm, and first located them in the landscape by attributing to them the impressive megalithic monuments scattered across the land. The English slowly became infected by the continental and Scottish interest, and even more slowly came to accept the association of Druids with megaliths. What precipitated a general English celebration, and appropriation, of Druids was of course the construction of the new British state. English domination of this state made it much easier to employ and naturalize what had been primarily a Scottish idea, and the Druids were accordingly both Anglicized and celebrated for the remainder of the Georgian period. The Welsh were, for the first two hundred years in which Druids were being widely discussed in Britain, the people least concerned with them. The dissolution of traditional Welsh culture, and the threat of the evaporation of a distinctive Welsh identity within the new British state, changed attitudes in the course of the eighteenth century. During its second half, Welsh scholars were actively attempting to prove a special relationship between their culture and ancient Druidry, in order both to promote a sense of their pride and value as a nation and to appropriate some of the respect and interest now attached to Druids by the other British peoples. They succeeded in the first aim and failed in the second. As Druids took on an increasingly Welsh character in popular association, the Scots grew indifferent to them and promoted a view of prehistory which excluded or depreciated them. The English continued to recognize the importance of Druids to their past, but began to emphasize a negative attitude to them, which had been a vigorous minority tradition even during the Georgian love affair between the British and Druidry. As a result, an affection for Druids and a desire to emulate them became a hallmark of distinctively countercultural groups in English society. It remains that at the present day, even while they continue to be central symbolic figures within Welsh culture and have almost faded out of the Scottish national imagination.

On the whole, this process of interaction has been due to impersonal factors, or at least to those that are so much the product of collective effort and mass culture that they rise above individual opinion or action. None the less, individuals have featured prominently, indeed decisively, in it at times. Three in particular have, it has been argued, played a pivotal role in catalysing and precipitating developments: rather neatly, they were an Englishman, a Welshman and a Scotsman. None could have had the impact they achieved had not the existing social and cultural context been exceptionally favourable to their enterprises. It has been suggested that William Stukeley persuaded the English both that Druids were ancestors worth fully embracing and that they had been the builders of England's most spectacular prehistoric monuments, including Stonehenge. It was Edward Williams, alias Iolo Morganwg, who enabled the Welsh to claim the Druids for themselves and to place them at the centre of their own cultural identity. Finally, it was George Watson Reid who made the name of Druid into a vehicle and metaphor for English cultural radicalism and founded a tradition which, both by example and in a personal succession, continues to the present day. What is striking about the trio, apart from their power of personality and commitment to their causes, is that each of them has a degree of disreputability. Each was, depending on the person and the judgement of observers, either a romancer, a crank, an eccentric or a charlatan. It seems that such quirks of character may be the vital ingredient that enables a human being to push forward and succeed, with confidence and charisma, where the more scrupulous and level-headed would not venture. The history of attitudes to the Druids in Britain, like so many histories, is one in which a hall of fame and a rogues' gallery seem strikingly similar.

NOTES

As a fixed rule in all these notes, books published from 1950 onward will be shown with details of the publisher and date and place of publication; those from before 1950 will have just the place and date.

1 The Raw Material

1. Which they are in *The Celtic Heroic Age*, ed. J. T. Koch (Andover, Mass.: Celtic Studies Publications, 1997), 13–31, and translated into English. Most were also translated with a commentary in T. D. Kendrick, *The Druids* (London, 1927), 75–97, which provides the texts in their original languages at pp. 212–21. Where I have quoted directly from Latin authors in my own work, I have made my own translation, in an effort to keep even closer to the sense of the original. When quoting from the Greek I have followed Kendrick, as more literal than Koch. I have also kept to the common Western tradition of Latinizing Greek names in the body of my text.
2. Diogenes Laertius, *Vitae*, introduction, section 1.
3. Julius Caesar, *De bello gallico*, VI.13–18.
4. For a recent analysis of Caesar's stylistic tricks, see David Braund, *Ruling Roman Britain* (London: Routledge, 1996), 41–66. It is summed up in the sentence (on p. 49) that 'Any understanding of Caesar's campaigns in Gaul and in Britain requires not so much an appreciation of his military strategies as an awareness of his literary strategies.'
5. Caesar, *De bello gallico*, V.12.
6. Ibid., VI.25.
7. By Fustel de Coulanges, in *La Gaule romaine* (Paris, 1891), 3.
8. Suggested by Daphne Nash, 'Reconstructing Posidonius's Celtic Ethnography', *Britannia* 7 (1976), 124; and Kendrick, *The Druids*, 81–2.
9. Also suggested by Nash, and in J. J. Tierney, 'The Celtic Ethnography of Poseidonios', *Proceedings of the Royal Irish Academy* 60 (1959–60), 189–275; A. L. Owen, *The Famous Druids* (Oxford: Oxford University Press, 1962), 16; and Stuart Piggott, *The Druids* (London: Thames and Hudson, 1968), 109.
10. Quoted in Suetonius, *Julius Caesar*, 56.4.
11. Piggott, *The Druids*, 111; Nash, 'Reconstructing Posidonius's Celtic Ethnography', 126; Miranda Green, *The Gods of the Celts* (Gloucester: Sutton, 1986), 14; David Rankin, 'The Celts through Classical Eyes', in *The Celtic World*, ed. Miranda J. Green (London: Routledge, 1995), 29.
12. Sean B. Dunham, 'Caesar's Perception of Gallic Social Structures', in *Celtic Chiefdom, Celtic State*, ed. Bettina Arnold and D. Blair Gibson (Cambridge: Cambridge University Press, 1995), 114–15; Bernhard Maier, *The Celts* (Edinburgh: Edinburgh University Press, 2003), 65–6.
13. Cicero, *De divinatione*, I.XVI.90.

14. Dunham, 'Caesar's Perception of Gallic Social Structures', 114–15.
15. Cicero, *Pro Fonteio*, XIII.21.
16. Kenneth S. Sacks, *Diodorus Siculus and the First Century* (Princeton, NJ: Princeton University Press, 1990), 73–6.
17. Diodorus Siculus, *Bibliotheca historicae*, V.21–32.
18. The o' prefix just signalled to Greek speakers that the 'v' was pronounced like a modern 'w' in the manner of the Latin of the time. Readers wondering why I should pay such attention to a tiny grammatical point will discover in later chapters that it was to cause (so far) two hundred years of modern linguistic confusion. I am grateful to my colleague Robert Fowler for confirming the purpose of the diphthong. For the reconstruction of the Gallic 'vatis', see Dáithí Ó hÓgáin, *The Sacred Isle: Belief and Religion in Pre-Christian Ireland* (Woodbridge: Boydell, 1999), 72.
19. Strabo, *Geographica*, IV.4.4–5.
20. Ibid., IV.5.1–3.
21. Ibid., IV.4. 5–6.
22. Ibid., IV.1.1.
23. Ibid., IV.4.2.
24. Pomponius Mela, *De situ orbis*, III.2.18–19.
25. Ibid., III.6.48.
26. Kendrick, *The Druids*, 84, 87.
27. Tierney, 'The Celtic Ethnography of Poseidonios'.
28. Piggott, *The Druids*, 92–8; Nash, 'Reconstructing Posidonius's Celtic Ethnography', 125–6; Rankin, 'The Celts through Classical Eyes', 29.
29. Peter Berresford Ellis, *The Druids* (London: Constable, 1994), 50–69; Jane Webster, 'The Just War: Graeco-Roman Texts as Colonial Discourse', in *TRAC 94: Proceedings of the Fourth Annual Theoretical Roman Archaeology Conference* (Oxford: Oxbow, 1994), 6–7.
30. Piggott, *The Druids*, 116.
31. Jane Webster, 'At the End of the World', *Britannia* 30 (1999), 8.
32. The standard modern edition of the fragments of Posidonius contains no material at all which refers to Druids: *Posidonius*, ed. I. G. Kidd (Cambridge: Cambridge University Press, 3 vols, 1988); see especially the comments in ii. 308–10.
33. Inspired by Nash, 'Reconstructing Posidonius's Celtic Ethnography', 112–36.
34. Suetonius, *Claudius*, XXV.5.
35. Pliny, *Historia naturalis*, XXX.13.
36. Ibid., VII.1.11.
37. James Masters, *Poetry and Civil War in Lucan's 'Bellum Civile'* (Cambridge: Cambridge University Press, 1992), 25–9.
38. Frederick M. Ahl, *Lucan: An Introduction* (Ithaca, NY: Cornell University Press, 1976), 71.
39. Lucan, *Pharsalia*, I.449–58, III.399–452, VI.415–830.
40. Hugh Last, 'Rome and the Druids', *Journal of Roman Studies* 39 (1949), 1–5; Maier, *The Celts*, 66.
41. Last was answering Arnaldo Momigliano, A. D. Nock and R. G. Collingwood; more recent authors in the same tradition have been J. F. Drinkwater, 'For Better or Worse? Towards an Assessment of the Economic and Social Consequences of the Roman Conquest of Gaul', in *The Early Roman Empire in the West*, ed. Thomas Blagg and Martin Millett (Oxford: Oxbow, 1990), 210–19; and Drinkwater, *Roman Gaul* (London: Croom Helm, 1983), 38–9; Nash, 'Reconstructing Posidonius's Celtic Ethnography', 125; Webster, 'The Just War', 6–7.
42. Drinkwater, *Roman Gaul*, 39.
43. Tacitus, *Annales*, XIV.30.
44. Tacitus, *Agricola*, XVIII.4.
45. E. W. Black, 'The First-Century Historians of Roman Britain', *Oxford Archaeological Journal* 20 (2001), 415–28.
46. Braund, *Ruling Roman Britain*, 144. On p. 151 Braund suggests that Tacitus may have invented not only episodes but actual characters, including the heroic British chief Calgacus, who features so prominently in Tacitus's *Agricola* and has long occupied a proud place in the annals of Scottish nationalism. This attitude is now apparently general among scholars of Tacitus: Holly Haynes's study of his work is called *The History of Make-Believe* (Berkeley: University of California Press, 2003). It makes a striking contrast with the view taken by classicists a generation ago: R. M. Ogilvie, for example, introducing the revised Loeb Classics Library edition of

the *Agricola*, in 1970, called it 'a factual, accurate and balanced account' (on pp. 16–17), without doing much to defend any of those epithets and while admitting that Tacitus put speeches into characters' mouths.

47. Tacitus, *Agricola*, V.1.
48. Pliny, *Historiae naturalis*, XVI.249.
49. Ibid., XXIV.103–4.
50. Ibid., XXIX.12.
51. Piggott, *The Druids*, 125.
52. For the various botanical interpretations, see the footnotes to this part of the *Historiae naturalis* in the edition by John Bostock and H. T. Riley, published in 1861.
53. Pliny, *Historiae naturalis*, XXII.2.
54. Ibid., V.8.45, VI.35.195. VII.I.11, VII.2.23–5.
55. Ibid., VII.7, 15; XXVIII.23.79–80.
56. Mary Beagon, *Roman Nature: The Thought of Pliny the Elder* (Oxford: Oxford University Press, 1992), 23–4.
57. J. Reynolds, 'The Elder Pliny and his Times', in *Science in the Early Roman Empire*, ed. Roger French and Frank Greenaway (London: Croom Helm, 1986), 1–10.
58. Pliny, *Historiae naturalis*, VII.130.
59. See especially ibid., XXX.1–8.
60. Webster, 'At the End of the World', 10–11; Kendrick, *The Druids*, 88–90.
61. Nora K. Chadwick, *The Druids* (Cardiff: University of Wales Press, 1966), 35; Graham Webster, *The British Celts and their Gods under Rome* (London: Batsford, 1986), 26.
62. Piggott, *The Druids*, 105–6.
63. Ó hÓgáin, *The Sacred Isle*, 71.
64. Ronald Hutton, *The Druids* (London: Hambledon Continuum, 2007), 94–6.
65. J. Rives, 'Human Sacrifice among Pagans and Christians', *Journal of Roman Studies* 85 (1995), 64–85; quotations from pp. 66, 68–9.
66. Lautaro Roig Lanzillotta, 'The Early Christians and Human Sacrifice', in *The Strange World of Human Sacrifice*, ed. Jan N. Bremmer (Leuven: Peeters, 2007), 81–102; quotation from p. 81. I am very grateful to Jan Bremmer for the gift of this book.
67. Dion Chrysostom, *Orationes*, XLIX.
68. Clement of Alexandria, *Stromata*, I.15.70–1.
69. Hippolytus, *Philosophumena*, I.25.
70. Diogenes Laertius, *Vitae*, introduction, sections 1 and 5.
71. Ammianus Marcellinus, XV.9.4–8.
72. Valerius Maximus, II.6, 10.
73. The basic modern authorities are J. A. Philip, *Pythagoras and Early Pythagoreanism* (Toronto: Toronto University Press, 1966); Walter Burkert, *Lore and Science in Ancient Pythagoreanism*, trans. Edwin L. Minor (Cambridge, Mass.: Harvard University Press, 1972); *The Pythagorean Sourcebook and Library*, trans. Kenneth Sylvan Guthrie and ed. David R. Fideler (Grand Rapids, Mich.: Phanes, 1987).
74. Tierney, 'The Celtic Ethnography of Poseidonios'; Nash, 'Reconstructing Posidonius's Celtic Ethnography', 125–6; Rankin, 'The Celts through Classical Eyes', 29.
75. *Historia Augusta*, 'Alexander Severus', LIX.5; 'Numerianus', XIV; 'Aurelianus', XLIII.4–5.
76. Ausonius, *Commemoratio professorum*, IV.7–10, X.22–30.
77. Piggott, *The Druids*, 92–8.
78. Ellis, *The Druids*, passim.
79. Chadwick, *The Druids*, esp. xviii, 28, 91.
80. Anne Ross, *Pagan Celtic Britain* (London: Routledge, 1967), 52–6; and with Don Robins, *The Life and Death of a Druid Prince* (London: Rider, 1989), passim; Ross, 'Ritual and the Druids', in *The Celtic World*, ed. Green, 425; Ross, *The Druids* (Stroud: Tempus, 1999), passim.
81. Barry Cunliffe, *Iron Age Communities in Britain* (London: Routledge, 1991), 518–20; Miranda J. Green, *The Gods of the Celts* (Gloucester: Sutton, 1986), 26–8; *Exploring the World of the Druids* (London: Thames and Hudson, 1997), 31–3; and *Dying for the Gods: Human Sacrifice in Iron Age and Roman Europe* (Stroud: Tempus, 2001), passim; also see A. P. Fitzpatrick, *Who Were the Druids?* (London: Weidenfeld, 1997), 10–38.
82. Jean-Louis Brunaux, *The Celtic Gauls* (London: Seaby, 1988), 60–4.

83. Hilda Ellis Davidson, *The Lost Beliefs of Northern Europe* (London: Routledge, 1993), 97–8.
84. Webster, 'At the End of the World', 1–20.
85. This approach was suggested in Cunliffe, *Iron Age Communities*, 518–20; and Ross and Robins, *Life and Death of a Druid Prince*, passim. Books with titles like Miranda Green's *Exploring the World of the Druids* tend in practice to be mainly explorations of the evidence for Iron Age ritual.
86. Keith Parfitt, 'Deal', *Current Archaeology* 125 (July 1991), 215–20. For an example of use of this find to support accounts of the Druids, see Ross, *Druids*, 65–9.
87. Andrew Fitzpatrick, 'Druids: Towards an Archaeology', in *Communities and Connections*, ed. Chris Gosden et al. (Oxford: Oxford University Press, 2007), 302–6.
88. Philip Crummy et al., *Stanway: An Elite Burial Site at Camulodunum* (Society for the Promotion of Roman Studies: Britannia Monograph Series 24, 2007), 250, 444–5.
89. Philip Crummy et al., 'Stanway: An Elite Cemetery at Camulodunum', *British Archaeology* (March–April 2008), 28–33.
90. Jean-Louis Brunaux, 'Gallic Blood Rites', *Archaeology* 54.2 (2001), 54–8.
91. 'Headless Warriors', Channel Five television programme, 17 Oct. 2003.
92. *www.ribemontsurancre.cg80.fr/Rapport%202002/chapitre01.htm* and *www.somme-tourisme.com/ uk/decouvrir/avisiter/archeologie/archeologie_ribemont-sur-acre.asp*. Accessed 20 June 2007.
93. Jean-Louis Brunaux, 'Le Sanctuaire gaulois de Gournay-sur-Aronde', published in Bulletin 56 (2002) of the Archaeological and Historical Company of Boulogne-Conchy-Hainvillers. I am very grateful to David Lee for a copy of this paper.
94. Ibid., 1–2.
95. Drinkwater, *Roman Gaul*, 38–9.
96. Anthony King, 'The Emergence of Romano-Celtic Religion', in *The Early Roman Empire in the West*, ed. Thomas Blagge and Martin Millett (Oxford: Oxbow, 1990), 220–41; quotation from p. 234.
97. John Creighton, 'Visions of Power', *Britannia* 26 (1995), 285–301.
98. A. P. Fitzpatrick, 'Night and Day', *Proceedings of the Prehistoric Society* 62 (1996), 373–98.
99. Fitzpatrick, 'Druids: Towards an Archaeology', 287–318.
100. And that is exactly what the report concluded: *Lindow Man*, ed. I. M. Stead et al. (London: British Museum, 1986).
101. The classic text on these is P. V. Glob, *The Bog People*, trans. R. Bruce-Mitford (Ithaca, NY: Cornell University Press, 1969).
102. E.g. Green, *The Gods of the Celts*, 128; *Exploring the World of the Druids*, 53; *Dying for the Gods*, 196, 201; Cunliffe, *Iron Age Communities*, 518; *English Heritage Book of Iron Age Britain* (London: Batsford, 1995), 100; *The Ancient Celts* (Oxford: Oxford University Press, 1997), 102; Ralph Merrifield, *The Archaeology of Ritual and Magic* (London: Batsford, 1987), 24; Jane Webster, 'Sanctuaries and Sacred Places', in *The Celtic World*, ed. Green, 450; Mike Parker Pearson, *The Archaeology of Death and Burial* (Stroud: Sutton, 1999), 70–1; Timothy Taylor, *The Buried Soul: How Humans Invented Death* (London: Fourth Estate, 2002), 145–69; Ross and Robins, *Life and Death of a Druid Prince*, passim.
103. J. A. J. Gowlett et al., 'Radiocarbon Accelerator Dating of Lindow Man', *Antiquity* 63 (1989), 71–9; R. A. Housley et al., 'Radiocarbon Dating of the Lindow III Bog Body', in *Bog Bodies*, ed. R. C. Turner and R. G. Scaife (London: British Museum, 1995), 39–46; P. C. Buckland and K. F. Barber, 'Two Views on Peat Stratigraphy and the Age of the Lindow Bodies', in *Bog Bodies*, ed. Turner and Scaife, 47–51; Rick Turner, 'Dating the Lindow Moss and Other British Bog Bodies, in *Bog Bodies, Sacred Sites and Wetland Archaeology*, ed. Bryony Coles et al. (Exeter: Wetland Archaeology Research Project, 1999), 227–34.
104. R. C. Connolly, 'Lindow Man', *Anthropology Today* 1.5 (1985), 15–17. Dr Connolly's views are implicit in his contribution to the British Museum report but were completely ignored in its conclusions. He has since reiterated them in a television interview, screened in the programme 'Overkill' in the Horizon series on BBC2, 2 April 1998, without receiving any more attention from Iron Age specialists. In an interview on 2 October 2003 he repeated them to me, adding that the British Museum team had given more weight to the hypothesis of ritual killing than he believed the pathology of the body to warrant. He provided direct testimony on this matter to *The Times* on 22 March 2004, as a contribution to the debate described in n. 106.
105. Robert G. Scaife, 'Pollen in Human Palaeofaeces; and a Preliminary Investigation of the Stomach and Gut Contents of Lindow Man', in *Lindow Man*, ed. Stead et al., 126–35; Don

Brothwell, *The Bog Man and the Archaeology of People* (London: British Museum, 1986), 96; T. G. Holden, 'The Last Meals of the Lindow Bog Men', in *Bog Bodies*, ed. Turner and Scaife, 76–82; R. G. Scaife, 'Pollen Analysis of the Lindow III Food Residue', in *Bog Bodies*, ed. Turner and Scaife, 83–5.

106. I published these views as the 'Commentary' section in the *Times Literary Supplement* (30 Jan. 2004), 12–13. This drew a reply from J. D. Hill, the curator at the museum with direct responsibility for the body, who defended the traditional interpretation in the 'Commentary' section of the same journal on 5 March, p. 15. I then argued against his points in a letter to the 12 March edition, p. 15, after which the exchange ceased. In *The Times* on 22 March, p. 8, Dr Hill was quoted as saying that 'Even if the interpretation of ritual killing is wrong, he's the best-preserved prehistoric or Roman Briton there is'. This statement seemed to admit of some new element of doubt in the matter – in which case my argument seems to have been tacitly accepted – but the same article credited me with dismissing any suggestion of ritual murder and wanting the museum to remove the body from exhibition. Both statements were completely false, so it may be that Dr Hill was misquoted as well.

107. Green, *Exploring the World of the Druids*, 8, 37, 89.

108. Piggott, *The Druids*, 116; P.-M. Duval and G. Pinault, *Recueil des inscriptions gauloises, 3: Les calendriers* (Paris: Supplement à Gallia 45, 1986).

109. Garrett Olmstead, *The Gaulish Calendar* (Bonn: Habelt, 1992).

110. Ibid.: quotations from p. xi; *A Definitive Reconstructed Text of the Coligny Calendar* (Washington, DC: Institute for the Study of Man, 2001).

111. Stephen C. McCluskey, *Astronomies and Cultures in Early Medieval Europe* (Cambridge: Cambridge University Press, 1998), 54–60; quotation from pp. 58–9.

112. Brunaux, *The Celtic Gauls*, 46.

113. Significantly, the two anonymous archaeologists who acted as readers of this book for Yale University Press adopted exactly opposite stances on this point, and urged me to exactly opposed amendments of my text.

114. For what follows, see the list of references in Ronald Hutton, *The Pagan Religions of the Ancient British Isles* (Oxford: Blackwell, 1991), 147–9.

115. J. P. Mallory, 'The World of Cu Chulainn', in *Aspects of the Tain*, ed. J. P. Mallory (Belfast: Universities Press, 1992), 153.

116. For a concise summary of these conclusions, see Mallory, 'The World of Cu Chulainn', and Ruari Ó hUiginn, 'The Background and Development of Tain Bo Cuailnge', in *Aspects of the Tain*, ed. Mallory, 32–62.

117. Classic examples of all this may be found in the Irish Life of Berach, the Latin Life of Cuimine Foda, Muirchú's Life of Patrick, *Tochmarc Etain*, *Togail Bruidne Da Derga*, *Serglige Con Culaind*, *The Siege of Drom Damghaire*, *Agallamh na Senorach*, *Cóir Anmann* and *Echtrae Chonlai*. Editions of or quotations from these texts may be found in *Lives of Irish Saints*, ed. Charles Plummer (Oxford, 1922); *Vitae sanctorum Hiberniae*, ed. Charles Plummer (Oxford, 1910); *St Patrick: His Writings and Muirchú's Life*, ed. A. B. E. Hood (London: Phillimore, 1978); *Early Irish Myths and Sagas*, ed. Jeffrey Gantz (London: Penguin, 1981); Eugene O'Curry and W. K. Sullivan, *On the Manners and Customs of the Ancient Irish* (2 vols, Dublin, 1873); *The Colloquey [sic] of the Elders*, ed. Standish O'Grady (Lampeter: Llanerch, 2000); P. W. Joyce, *A Social History of Ancient Ireland* (London, 1903), ii. 225, 228; and *Ancient Irish Tales*, ed. Tom Pete Cross and Clark Harris Slover (London, 1938).

118. O'Curry and Sullivan, *Manners and Customs*, ii. 205–8.

119. See, for example, 'The Hostel of the Quicken Trees', 'The Pursuit of the Gilla Dacker', 'The Pursuit of Diarmid and Grania', 'The Chase of Slieve Cuillin' and 'The Chase of Slieve Fuad', in *Old Celtic Romances*, ed. P. W. Joyce (Dublin, 1920).

120. *The Cycles of the Kings*, ed. Myles Dillon (Oxford, 1946), 12–13.

121. *The Celtic Heroic Age*, ed. Koch, 193.

122. Ibid., 28; *The Tain*, ed. Thomas Kinsella (Oxford: Oxford University Press, 1970), 60; Kim McCone, *Pagan Past and Christian Present in Early Irish Literature* (Maynooth: An Sagart, 1990), 135; *Vitae sanctorum Hiberniae*, ed. Plummer, clx–clxiii (which provides several examples).

123. Ellis, *The Druids*, 70–90, 157–67; Ó hÓgáin, *The Sacred Isle*, 72–96; Christian-J. Guyonvarc'h, *The Making of a Druid* (Rochester: Inner Traditions, 2002); John Minahane, *The Christian*

Druids (Dublin: Sanas, 1993). For earlier expositions of the idea, see the summary in McCone, *Pagan Past and Christian Present*, 19–21.

124. For example, Guyonvarc'h, *The Making of a Druid*, presents one text, *Immacallam in dá Thuarad*, 'The Colloquy of Two Sages', as the unique survival of a work of Druidic teaching; it had formerly been regarded by scholars as a game of question and answer between an old and a young poet, wrapped up in metaphors.

125. To remain with the above example, Guyonvarc'h, while raising some fascinating possibilities, fails to demonstrate any of the following propositions: that the content of the text concerned is any older than its current, Middle Irish, form; that the metaphors in it can be decoded as he asserts; and that it has (indeed) anything to do with Druids at all. McCone, *Pagan Past and Christian Present*, represents a strong, fairly recent, argument against the whole concept that ancient Druids turned into medieval poets: see especially pp. 227–8.

126. *The Second Battle of Moytura*, ed. Whitley Stokes, *Revue celtique* 12 (1891), 91.

127. *Vitae sanctorum Hiberniae*, ed. Plummer, clviii.

128. The medieval hagiographies concerned can be found in *Lives of Irish Saints*, ed. Plummer; *Vitae sanctorum Hiberniae*, ed. Plummer; *Adomnan's Life of Columba*, ed. A. O. Anderson and M. O. Anderson (London: Nelson, 1961); and *Life of St Declan of Ardmore and Life of St Mochuda of Lismore*, ed. P. Power (Irish Texts Society 16, 1914). Patrick's Druid-busting activities will be discussed below; but they are also celebrated in law tracts: *Ancient Laws of Ireland*, ed. W. Neilson Hancock (Dublin, 1865–1901), i. 2, 15, iii, 29; *Thesaurus Palaeohibernicus*, ed. Whitley Stokes and John Strachan (Cambridge, 1901), ii. 322.

129. When Michael O'Clery wove another such episode into an existing life of Ruadan: *Lives of Irish Saints*, ed. Plummer, ii. 319–20.

130. *St Patrick: His Writings and Muirchú's Life*, ed. Hood, 86–8.

131. These comparisons are highlighted by McCone, *Pagan Past and Christian Present*, 33–4.

132. Found in *St Patrick: His Writings and Muirchú's Life*, ed. Hood, and in *The Works of St Patrick*, ed. Ludwig Bieler (London: Longman, 1953).

133. *The Works of St Patrick*, ed. Bieler, 51; cf. Fergus Kelly, *A Guide to Early Irish Law* (Dublin: Institute for Advanced Studies, 1988), 198.

134. *The Works of St Patrick*, ed. Bieler, 71; cf. *Thesaurus Palaeohibernicus*, ed. Stokes and Strachan, ii. 357.

135. D. A. Binchy, 'Bretha Crólige', *Eriu* 12 (1938), 40–1.

136. *Ancient Laws of Ireland*, ed. Hancock, v. 91.

137. McCone, *Pagan Past and Christian Present*, 150, 221.

138. *The Cycles of the Kings*, ed. Dillon, 19, 28; *St Patrick: His Writings and Muirchú's Life*, ed. Hood, 86; *Lebor Gabala nErenn*, ed. R. A. S. Macalister (Irish Texts Society 1938–56), para. 19; *The Celtic Heroic Age*, ed. Koch, 193; *Córus Béscnai*, quoted in McCone, *Pagan Past and Christian Present*, 92.

139. E.g. *The Colloquey of the Elders*, ed. O'Grady, 202; *The Celtic Heroic Age*, ed. Koch, 202–4.

140. E.g. *The Cycles of the Kings*, ed. Dillon, 12–13, 37; *St Patrick: His Writings and Muichú's Life*, ed. Hood, 89; 'The First Battle of Moytura', ed. Paul Walsh, *Eriu* 8 (1916), 19; 'The Rennes Dindsenchas', ed. Whitley Stokes, *Revue celtique* 15 (1894), 430; McCone, *Pagan Past and Christian Present*, 133, 135, 153.

141. E.g. *The Taín*, ed. Kinsella, 3, 60, 84–5; *The Celtic Heroic Age*, ed. Koch, 48; *Old Celtic Romances*, ed. Joyce, 116; McCone, *Pagan Past and Christian Present*, 174, 183, 186, 189–90.

142. E.g. *Vitae sanctorum Hiberniae*, ed. Plummer, clx.

143. Ibid.

144. Joyce, *A Social History*, 231.

145. In *Togail Bruidne Da Derga* (*Early Irish Myths*, ed. Gantz, 65), and *Serglige Con Culainn* (McCone, *Pagan Past and Christian Present*, 168).

146. *Three Irish Glossaries*, ed. Whitley Stokes (London, 1862), 25, discussed at length in Ó hÓgáin, *The Sacred Isle*, 79.

147. Ibid. An argument indeed used.

148. Ibid., 80; *Three Irish Glossaries*, ed. Stokes, xxxv–vi; Eric Hamp, 'imbloc, oimelc', *Studia Celtica*, 14 (1979), 106–13.

149. *Ancient Laws of Ireland*, ed. Hancock, i. 23.

150. *The Patrician Texts in the Book of Armagh*, ed. Ludwig Bieler (Dublin: Institute for Advanced Studies, 1979), 132.

151. The cases are cited and discussed by Ó hÓgáin, *The Sacred Isle*, 86, who is inclined to identify the Druids as medics.

152. Kelly, *A Guide to Early Irish Law*, 61.

153. McCone, *Pagan Past and Christian Present*, 85–6. Ó hÓgáin, by contrast, assumes that the role of *brithemain* and Druid were interchangeable, so that references to judges in the literature can be taken as further evidence for what Druids were like: *The Sacred Isle*, 77, 81.

154. *Early Irish Myths*, ed. Gantz, 192–3.

155. *The Taín*, ed. Kinsella, 84.

156. The most recent being, predictably, Ó hÓgáin, *The Sacred Isle*, 81.

157. McCone, *Pagan Past and Christian Present*, 231.

158. *The Celtic Heroic Age*, ed. Koch, 48.

159. Joyce, *A Social History*, 235.

160. John Matthews, *Taliesin: Shamanism and the Bardic Mysteries in Britain and Ireland* (London: Aquarian, 1991), 44–6.

161. Joyce, *A Social History*, 234; Natalie Venclová, 'The Venerable Bede, Druidic Tonsure and Archaeology', *Antiquity* 76 (2002), 458–71.

162. McCone, *Pagan Past and Christian Present*, 230–1.

163. Whitney Stokes, 'The Prose Tales in the Rennes *Dindshenchas*', *Revue celtique* 16 (1895), 35–6.

164. *The Metrical Dindshenchas*, ed. Edward Gwynn (Dublin, 1924), iv. 18–23.

165. *The Tripartite Life of Patrick*, ed. Whitley Stokes (London: Rolls Series, 1887), 90–3. The Maigh Slecht story is, significantly, missing from recent scholarly studies of pagan Irish religion, but was given great prominence in earlier, less rigorous, works, such as Charles Squire, *Mythology of the British Islands* (London, 1905), 37–9; Joyce, *A Social History*, 275–6; and Lewis Spence, *The Magic Arts in Celtic Britain* (London, 1945), 52.

166. Jacqueline Borsje, 'Human Sacrifice in Medieval Irish Literature', in *The Strange World of Human Sacrifice*, ed. Bremmer, 31–54; quotation from p. 54. I repeat my gratitude to Jan Bremmer for the gift of this volume.

167. Eugene O'Curry and W. K. Sullivan, *On the Manners and Customs of the Ancient Irish* (Dublin, 1873), ii. 222.

168. Douglas Hyde, *A Literary History of Ireland* (London, 1899), 92–3.

169. Joyce, *A Social History*, 239, 275–86.

170. Kuno Meyer, 'Human Sacrifice among the Ancient Irish', *Eriu* 2 (1905), 86.

171. J. A. MacCulloch, *The Religion of the Ancient Celts* (Edinburgh, 1911), 236–8.

172. Borsje, 'Human Sacrifice in Medieval Irish Literature', 46–51.

173. Quoted from the translation in *The Celtic Heroic Age*, ed. Koch, 185–7.

174. I.e. in works from Joyce, *A Social History*, 240, and *Vitae sanctorum Hiberniae*, ed. Plummer, to Green, *Exploring the World of the Druids*, 101.

175. Their works are much discussed in the literature cited below, but see particularly Eoin MacNeill, 'Archaisms in the Ogham Inscriptions', *Proceedings of the Royal Irish Academy* 39C (1929–31), 34 (the source of the quotation); and R. A. S. Macalister, *The Secret Languages of Ireland* (issued by the Armorica Book Company, in St Helier, Jersey, 1976). MacNeill and Macalister worked alongside each other in the early twentieth century.

176. This concept was most full-blown in non-academic works that will feature later in this book, but for a relatively recent scholarly restatement of the association between ogham and trees, confident, absolute and second-hand, see Fergal McGrath, *Education in Ancient and Medieval Ireland* (Dublin: Special Publications, 1979), 30.

177. Howard Meroney, 'Early Irish Letter-Names', *Speculum* 24 (1949), 19–43. This also cites the work of Graves, mentioned below.

178. All this is in Meroney, but for alternative, though closely overlapping, correspondences see Damian McManus, *A Guide to Ogam* (Maynooth: An Sagart, 1991), 31.

179. *Lives of Irish Saints*, ed. Plummer, i. 33; Matthews, *Taliesin*, 44–5.

180. A. T. Lucas, 'The Sacred Trees of Ireland', *Journal of the Cork Historical and Archaeological Society* 68 (1963), 16–54.

181. Fergus Kelly, 'The Old Irish Tree-List', *Celtica* 11 (1976), 107–24.

182. Anthony Harvey, 'Early Literacy in Ireland', *Cambridge Medieval Celtic Studies* 14 (1987), 1–15; McManus, *A Guide to Ogam*; Catherine Swift, *Ogam Stones and the Earliest Irish Christians* (Maynooth: An Sagart, 1997).

183. With the sources above, see James Carney, 'The Invention of the Ogam Cipher', *Eriu* 26 (1975), 53–65; Jane Stevenson, 'The Beginnings of Literacy in Ireland', *Proceedings of the Royal Irish Academy* C89 (1989), 127–65; Patrick Sims-Williams, 'Some Problems in Deciphering the Early Irish Ogam Alphabet', *Transactions of the Philological Society* 91.2 (1993), 133–80.

184. *Armes Prydein*, ed. Sir Ifor Williams and Rachel Bromwich (Dublin: Institute for Advanced Studies, 1972), 12–13.

185. Patrick Sims-Williams, 'The Early Welsh Arthurian Poems', in *The Arthur of the Welsh*, ed. Rachel Bromwich et al. (Cardiff: University of Wales Press, 1991), 51–2.

186. E.g. in Karen Louise Jolly, *Popular Religion in Late Saxon England* (Chapel Hill: University of North Carolina Press, 1996), 6, 87, 101. I am very grateful to Philip Carr-Gomm for first drawing my attention to the significance of this term.

187. Most recently in *The Celtic Heroic Age*, ed. Koch, 276–8.

188. For a recent example of the sort of dispute that can develop among experts dealing with a supposedly very early text, see *The Gododdin of Aneirin*, ed. John T. Koch (Cardiff: University of Wales Press, 1997); O. J. Padel, 'A New Study of the "Goddodin"', *Cambrian Medieval Celtic Studies* 35 (1998), 45–56; Padel and G. R. Isaac, 'Gweith Gwen Ystrat and the Northern Heroic Age of the Sixth Century', *Cambrian Medieval Celtic Studies* 36 (1998), 61–70; and Padel, 'Readings in the History and Transmission of the "Gododdin"', *Cambrian Medieval Celtic Studies* 37 (1999), 55–78. One rare case of a poem especially favoured by those questing for Druid wisdom that has been analysed by an expert in medieval Welsh literature is the one commonly known as *Preiddeu Annwn*, 'The Spoils of Annwn'. Marged Haycock, '"Preiddau Annwn" and the Figure of Taliesin', *Studia Celtica* 18/19 (1983–4), 52–78, concludes that it was the work of a sophisticated court poet in touch with the latest elements of Christian learning and could have been written at any point between the ninth and twelfth centuries. She comments on its language that 'I cannot see anything which is genuinely and convincingly archaic.' This is the more significant in that the poem has generally been regarded as older than other works in the selection quoted as evidence for ancient Druidry.

189. And here's one that I made earlier: Ronald Hutton, *The Pagan Religions of the Ancient British Isles* (Oxford: Blackwell, 1991), 170–1.

2 The Druids Take Shape

1. Noel L. Brann, 'Conrad Celtis and the "Druid" Abbot Trithemius', *Renaissance and Reformation* NS 3.1 (1979), 16–28; Frank L. Borchardt, *German Antiquity in Renaissance Myth* (Baltimore, Md.: Johns Hopkins University Press, 1971), 127. I am grateful to my former colleague A.V. Antonovics for the latter reference.

2. Brann, 'Conrad Celtis'; Borchardt, *German Antiquity in Renaissance Myth*, 20, 106–7.

3. Ibid., 145–6, 169–71; T. D. Kendrick, *The Druids* (London, 1927), 17–22.

4. All neatly summarized in R. E. Asher, *National Myths in Renaissance France* (Edinburgh: Edinburgh University Press, 1993), 44–87.

5. Jean Picard, *Le Prisca Celtopedia* (Paris, 1556), 35–72.

6. Noël Taillepied, *Histoire de l'Estat et Republique des Druides* (Paris, 1585).

7. Asher, *National Myths in Renaissance France*, 90–107; D. P. Walker, 'The "Prisca Theologia" in France', *Journal of the Warburg and Courtauld Institutes* 17 (1954), 204–59.

8. This identification had been made, precociously, by the fifteenth century: A. L. Owen, *The Famous Druids* (Oxford: Oxford University Press, 1962), 31–2.

9. Sébastian Rouillard, *Parthenie* (Paris, 1609).

10. François Rabelais, *The Heroic Deeds of Gargantua and Pantagruel*, ed. D. B. Wyndham Lewis (London: Dent, 1929), ii. 84.

11. Taillepied, *Histoire*, 83, tried to get round this by arguing that Caesar had meant Brittany and not Britain; but his ploy apparently had little influence.

12. I have used the 1531 translation of this work into Scots, by John Bellenden: Hector Boece, *The Chronicles of Scotland*, ed. R. W. Chambers and Edith Batho, ii (Scottish Text Society 3rd series 10, 1936), 72–4.

13. A fact first noticed by Owen, *The Famous Druids*, 31

14. George Buchanan, *Rerum scoticarum historia* (Edinburgh, 1582), 56.

15. John Spottiswoode, *The History of the Church of Scotland* (London, 1655), 3.
16. Geoffrey Keating, *The History of Ireland*, ed. Patrick S. Dinneen (Irish Text Society, 1908), ii. 348–51. The passage concerning Druid altars is missing from other editions of Keating, such as that made by John O'Mahony and published at New York in 1866, and as I had relied on these, I would not have spotted it had it not been quoted in John Matthews, *Secrets of the Druids* (New York: Black Dog, 2002), 17–18. As no source reference was given there, I asked John for one, and Caitlín Matthews immediately replied with it: a fine example of the way in which more 'populist' works based on Celtic literature can be of real service to the more academic kind. For the context of Keating's work, see Bernadette Cunningham, *The World of Geoffrey Keating* (Dublin: Four Courts, 2000).
17. Humphrey Llwyd, *The Historie of Cambria*, ed. David Powell (London, 1584), 7. See also Abraham Ortelius, *The Theatre of the Whole World*, trans. W.B. (London, 1606), fos xlvi–xlix.
18. Brit. L, Add. MS 14925, fos 23–5 (translation of Price's *Historiae Brytannicae defensio*).
19. This is very apparent in the works by Llwyd and Price cited above. See also Llwyd's *Cronica Walliae*, ed. Ieuan M. Williams (Cardiff: University of Wales Press, 2002).
20. Maurice Kiffin, *Deffyniad Ffydd Eglwys Loegr a Gyfieithwyd I'r Gymraeg*, ed. W. P. Williams (Bangor, 1908), xi.
21. Bod. L, Aubrey MS 13, fo. 240 (Vaughan to Aubrey).
22. Alexander Barclay, *The Shyp of Folys* (London, 1509), fo. cxxii.
23. Owen, *The Famous Druids*, 28, makes a good case for this.
24. *Polydore Vergil's English History*, ed. Sir Henry Ellis (Camden Society, 1846), 17–18, 50; quotation on p. 18.
25. John Leland, *Commentarii de scriptoribus britannicis* (Oxford, 1709), 1–4.
26. John Bale, *The Actes of Englysh Votaryes* (London, 2nd edn, 1550), fos 12–14.
27. John Bale, *Scriptorum illustrium maioris Brytanniae catalogus* (Basle, 1557), 4.
28. Johannes Caius, *De antiquitate cantabrigiensis academiae* (London, 1568), 18.
29. Matthew Parker, *De antiquitate britannicae ecclesiae* (London: 1605 edn), 4, 6.
30. All this was established by Annabel Patterson, *Reading Holinshed's 'Chronicles'* (Chicago: University of Chicago Press, 1994).
31. Raphael Holinshed et al., *The First and Second Volume of Chronicles* (1807 reprint of 2nd edn, London, 1586), i., 33–41, 63–5, 430, 494; v. 52.
32. Ortelius, *Theatre of the Whole World*, fos xlvi–xlix.
33. Stuart Piggott, 'William Camden and the "Britannia" ', *Proceedings of the British Academy* 37 (1951), 199–217.
34. William Camden, *Britannia* (London, 1586), 11.
35. Camden, *Britannia*, trans. Philemon Holland (London, 1610), 4, 12–14, 68, 149.
36. Origen, *Homiliae in Ezechielem*, ed. Marcel Borrett (Paris: Editions du Cerf, 1989), No. IV, ch. 1, lines 154–6.
37. Such as Selden (for whom see below) and Edward Stillingfleet, *Originae britannicae* (London, 1685), 5.
38. Dated by E. H. C. Oliphant, *The Plays of Beaumont and Fletcher* (New York: Phaeton, 1970), 131–5.
39. Henry Fletcher, *Bonduca*, I.i. lines 42–3 and III.i. lines 12–14. I have used the edition by Cyrus Hoy, in *The Dramatic Works in the Beaumont and Fletcher Canon*, ed. Fredson Bowers (Cambridge: Cambridge University Press, 1970), iv.
40. *The Poems of Thomas Carew*, ed. Rhodes Dunlap (Oxford University Press, 1949), 177.
41. *The King and Queen's Entertainment at Richmond* (London, 1636), 21.
42. Thomas Nashe, *The Terrors of the Night* (London, 1594), sig. B4.
43. *The Witches of Northamptonshire* (London, 1612), sig. A3. I am grateful to Madeleine Harwood for this reference.
44. Tacitus by Sir Henry Savile in 1591 and Richard Greneway in 1598, Pliny by Philemon Holland in 1601, and Caesar by Sir Clement Edmondes in 1604.
45. Ortelius, *Theatre of the Whole World*, fos xii–xiii.
46. John Speed, *The Historie of Great Britaine* (London, 1614), 167–8, 204.
47. William Slatyer, *The History of Great Britanie* (London, 1621), 17.
48. *The Works of Michael Drayton*, ed. J. William Hebel (Oxford: Blackwell, 1933), ii. 218–19; iv. 2, 180, 207–8; Michael Drayton, *Poemes* (London, 1606), sig. B.

49. *Works of Michael Drayton*, ed. Hebel, iv. 124–92.

50. John Selden, *Jani Anglorum facies altera* (London, 1610). Having failed to gain access to a copy of this original, I have used, like several authors on Selden before me, the English translation, 'The Reverse or Back Face of the English Janus', in *Tracts written by John Selden*, ed. Redman Westcot (London, 1683), 13–18, 93.

51. Nathaniel Bacon, *An Historical and Political Discourse of the Laws and Government of England* (London, 1689), 3.

52. Graham Parry, *The Trophies of Time: English Antiquarians of the Seventeenth Century* (Oxford: Oxford University Press, 1995), 95–129; Paul Christianson, *Discourse on History, Law and Governance in the Public Career of John Selden, 1610–1635* (Toronto: Toronto University Press, 1996), 11–86.

53. Sir Edward Coke, *Le Tierce Part des Reports* (London, 1602), preface. I am grateful to Benjamin Carter for this reference.

54. John Milton, 'Lycidas'; p. 70 in *The Poetical Works of John Milton* ('Imperial' edn, London, 1889); and 'Mansus'; p. 263 in *The Poems of John Milton*, ed. John Carey and Alastair Fowler (London: Longman, 1968).

55. John Milton, *The Doctrine and Discipline of Divorce* (2nd edn, London, 1644), sig. A4; and *Areopagitica*, ed. Ernest Sirluck, in *Complete Prose Works of John Milton: Volume Two* (New Haven, Conn.: Yale University Press, 1959), 551–2.

56. John Milton, *The History of Great Britain*, ed. French Fogle, in *Complete Prose Works of John Milton: Volume Five* (New Haven, Conn.: Yale University Press, 1971), 60–1, 75.

57. Francis Godwin, *A Catalogue of the Bishops of England* (London, 1615), 19–20, 26, 33.

58. Richard Broughton, *The Ecclesiastical Historie of Great Britain* (Douai, 1633), 17, 207, 240.

59. Thomas Fuller, *The Church-History of Britain* (1655), ed. James Nichols (London, 1886), i. 5–9; Peter Heylyn, *Certamen Epistolare* (London, 1659), 343; Thomas Fuller, *The Appeal of Injured Innocence* (London, 1659), 54–5.

60. Inigo Jones and John Webb, *The Most Remarkable Antiquity of Great Britain* (London, 1655), 2–7.

61. Elias Ashmole, *Theatrum chemicum Britannicum* (London, 1652), sigs A2–3.

62. Edmund Dickinson, *Delphi Phoenicizantes* (Oxford, 1655), 32–40.

63. Owen, *The Famous Druids*, 70–1, quotes Anthony Wood as an authority for this, and the story was also put about by John Locke: Bod. L, Wood MS F39, fo. 277 (Aubrey to Wood).

64. Thomas Smith, *Syntagma de druidum moribus* (Oxford, 1664).

65. This account by Aubrey has been quoted in part or published in full many times: one of the earliest complete appearances was in *Wiltshire: The Topographical Collections of John Aubrey*, ed. John Edward Jackson (Devizes, 1862), 314–15. I have consulted the original text, in Bod. L, MS Gen. Top. c. 24, fos 23–4, 39, being the famous manuscript of Aubrey's *Monumenta Britannica*. An edition of this by John Fowles and Rodney Legg was published in 1980–2, and has been subjected to fierce criticism: cf. the reviews by Aubrey Burl in the *Wiltshire Archaeological and Natural History Magazine* 77 (1983), 163–6, and Michael Hunter in the *Times Literary Supplement* (28 Nov. 1980), 1362, and the comment by Stuart Piggott, *Ancient Britons and the Antiquarian Imagination* (London: Thames and Hudson, 1989), 165. I shall say only that I found it unsuitable for the particular questions that I wished to answer, and so provide all references to the manuscript itself.

66. Bod. L, MS Gen. Top. c. 24, fos 24–5, with additional information from Peter J. Ucko et al., *Avebury Reconsidered* (London: Unwin Hyman, 1991), 15–28, 265–7.

67. See n. 96, below.

68. Bod. L, Aubrey MS 12, fo. 51v (Browne to Aubrey).

69. Bod. L, MS Gen. Top. c. 24, fo. 25.

70. Ibid., fo. 80.

71. Anthony Powell, *John Aubrey and his Friends* (London, 1948), 101–2.

72. Ibid., 127–9.

73. See the library catalogue reprinted in Powell, *John Aubrey and his Friends*, 295–303. His copy of Smith, *Syntagma*, is now in the Bodleian.

74. Bod. L, Wood MS F39, fo. 277 (Aubrey to Wood).

75. Bod. L, MS Gen. Top. c. 24, fo. 80.

76. Ucko et al., *Avebury Reconsidered*, 20, 28, 265–7.

77. As he states in Bod. L, MS Gen. Top. c. 24, fo. 80.

78. Ibid., fos 27–8, 80–93.
79. The best biographies extant are still Powell, *John Aubrey and his Friends*, and David Tylden-Wright, *John Aubrey: A Life* (London: HarperCollins, 1991). By contrast, Michael Hunter, *John Aubrey and the Realm of Learning* (London: Duckworth, 1975), is the major study of his work.
80. Bod. L, MS Gen. Top. c. 24, fos 25–6.
81. Bod. L, Wood MS F39, fo. 340 (Aubrey to Wood).
82. Bod. L, MS Gen. Top. c. 24, fo. 39.
83. Anthony Wood, *Historia et antiquitates Universitatis Oxoniensis* (Oxford, 1674), 1–2.
84. Thomas Jones, *The Heart and its Right Sovereign* (London, 1678), 542–3.
85. Sir William Temple, *Works* (London, 1731), ii. 531.
86. *The Fairfax Correspondence*, ed. G. W. Johnson (London, 1848), i. cxxiii–cxxv.
87. Aylett Sammes, *Britannia antiqua illustrata* (London, 1676), 100–5, 261–8.
88. Ibid., 101, 105.
89. For this enterprise, see Stuart Piggott, 'William Camden and the "Britannia" '; and Parry, *The Trophies of Time*, 331–57.
90. There is, notoriously, no proper biography of him, the nearest thing being the short study by Frank Emery, *Edward Lhuyd F.R.S. 1660–1709* (Cardiff: University of Wales Press, 1971). I present his name as it was printed at the time, following the custom of most historians, but some prefer alternative spellings; it is of course an early modern version of the one that is 'Llwyd' in the original Welsh and 'Lloyd' in English.
91. By Glyn Daniel, 'Edward Lhwyd: Antiquary and Archaeologist', *Welsh History Review* 3 (1967), 346–8.
92. And has been specifically examined in Ronald Hutton, *Witches, Druids and King Arthur* (London: Hambledon and London, 2003), 2–12.
93. This process is summed up in Parry, *The Trophies of Time*, 336–7.
94. The original letters from Garden are in Bod. L, Aubrey MS 12; they have been published by Michael Hunter, *The Occult Laboratory: Magic, Science and Second Sight in Late Seventeenth-Century Scotland* (Woodbridge: Boydell, 2001), 119–41.
95. Bod. L, MS Gen. Top. c. 24, fos 94–102.
96. Quoted in Hunter, *John Aubrey*, 188.
97. Toland's physical appearance at this time is described in a source quoted by Justin Champion, *Republican Learning: John Toland and the Crisis of Christian Culture* (Manchester: Manchester University Press, 2003), 215.
98. Of the various summaries of Toland's early life, perhaps the neatest is that of Robert E. Sullivan, *John Toland and the Deist Controversy* (Cambridge, Mass.: Harvard University Press, 1982), 1–5.
99. Bod. L, Tanner MS 25, fos 138, 140, 154 (Gibson to Tanner). This story is told in Stuart Piggott, *William Stukeley* (London: Thames and Hudson, 2nd edn, 1985), 83–4.
100. Robert W. T. Gunther, *Life and Letters of Edward Lhwyd* (Early Science in Oxford Series, vol. XIV, Oxford: privately printed, 1945), 278.
101. Quoted in Champion, *Republican Learning*, 93.
102. Bod. L, Wood MS F51, fo. 9 (Aubrey to Wood).
103. Quoted in Piggott, *Ancient Britons and the Antiquarian Imagination*, 141.
104. Bod. L, MS Gen. Top. c. 24, fo. 18 (Tanner to Aubrey). Bod. L, Wood MS F39, fo. 277 (Aubrey to Wood) proves that the manuscript in its present form dates after July 1694.
105. Powell, *John Aubrey and his Friends*, 239–40, 288.
106. Bod. L, Tanner MS 25, fo. 134 (Gibson to Tanner).
107. Bod. L, Ashmole MS 1817B, fos 365–8 (two letters from Woodward to Lhuyd).
108. *Camden's 'Britannia' Newly Translated Into English*, ed. Edmund Gibson (London, 1695), 107–10, 637–8, 673–5, 681–3. Recent admirers of Lhuyd have tended to emphasize his attempts to distance himself from the theory, as part of a process of eulogizing him as a forerunner of a modern archaeology which came to reject it: Daniel, 'Edward Lhwyd', 346–8; Emery, *Edward Lhuyd*, 61; Hunter, *John Aubrey*, 202. I am more inclined to stress the favourable consideration that he invited for it.
109. Spotted by Owen, *The Famous Druids*, 174.
110. Ibid., 154.
111. *Camden's 'Britannia' Newly Translated*, 673.
112. William Sacheverell, *An Account of the Isle of Man* (London, 1702), 145–75.

113. James Wallace, *An Account of the Isles of Orkney* (London, 1693), 27. The letter drawing Aubrey's attention to this reference is printed in Hunter, *The Occult Laboratory*, 157.
114. Hunter, *John Aubrey*, 224–5.
115. Sibbald's relationship with Martin is recorded by Toland in a note on his copy of the latter's book, Brit. L, C.45. c.1, vi.
116. Martin Martin, *A Description of the Western Isles of Scotland* (2nd edn, London, 1716), 102–4.
117. Ibid., 9, 105–6.
118. Owen, *The Famous Druids*, 109–13. I have not been able to trace the letter, as Owen provided a false source-reference for it; unfortunately not the only time that such misprints occur in his admirable book. The account of Highland beliefs has been printed in Hunter, *The Occult Laboratory*, 62–3.
119. Ronald Hutton, *The Stations of the Sun: A History of the Ritual Year in Britain* (Oxford: Oxford University Press, 1996), 218–25.
120. Robert Sibbald, *The History of Fife* (Edinburgh, 1710), 25.
121. As noted irritably by Alexander Gordon, *Itinerarium septenrionale* (London, 1726), 167.
122. A point well made by Parry, *The Trophies of Time*, 354.
123. Ibid., 345–55; Emery, *Edward Lhuyd*, 1–27.
124. *Camden's 'Britannia' Newly Translated*, 675.
125. Henry Rowlands, *Mona antiqua restaurata* (Dublin, 1723). Some of Lhuyd's replies to his letters are printed in Gunther, *Life and Letters of Edward Lhwyd*, 427–31, 439–42, 472–4, 480–3.
126. One of these circulated drafts survives as Bod. L, Carte MS 108, fos 59v–93v. Another, of the earlier part of the book, was doing the rounds as early as 1708: Piggott, *William Stukeley*, 179.
127. Charles Edwards, *Hebraismorum Cambro-Britannicorum* (London, 1675).
128. Geraint H. Jenkins, *The Foundations of Modern Wales 1642–1780* (Oxford: Oxford University Press, 1987), 223.
129. Rowlands, *Mona Antiqua*, 45.
130. Ibid., 34–106, 268–9; quotation, again, on p. 45.
131. Ibid., 267–70.
132. *A Collection of Several Pieces of Mr John Toland*, ed. P. Desmaiseaux (London, 1726), i. 4, 31.
133. His sources in this category are analysed by Justin Champion, 'John Toland, the Druids, and the Politics of Celtic Scholarship', *Irish Historical Studies* 32 (2001), 321–9.
134. Alan Harrison, 'John Toland (1670–1722) and Celtic Studies', in *Celtic Languages and Celtic Peoples: Proceedings of the Second North American Congress of Celtic Studies*, ed. Cyril J. Byrne, Margaret Harry and Pádraig Ó Siadhail (Halifax, NS: Halifax University Press, 1992), 565.
135. Leslie Ellen Jones, *Druid Shaman Priest* (Enfield Lock, Middlesex: Hisarlik Press, 1998), 130.
136. Brit. L, Add. MS 4465, fo. 13; *A Collection of Several Pieces of Mr John Toland*, i. 8.
137. Ibid., 8–16; quotations on p. 8.
138. Ibid., 21–31.
139. Ibid., 46.
140. Champion, *Republican Learning*, 218–26; Robert Sullivan, 'John Toland's Druids', *Bullan* 4.1 (1998), 19–42.
141. Brit. L, Add. MS 4465, fo. 16 (Toland to Chamberlayne); and Add. MS 4295, fo. 27 (the reply).
142. Brit. L, C.45. c.1. The antiquary Joseph Ames later copied all these jottings into his own copy of Martin's text, now Bod. L, Gough Scotland 185.
143. *A Collection of Several Pieces of Mr John Toland*, i. 61–113.
144. Ibid., 105–7.
145. The ancient sources for Hyperborea are Pindar, Hellanicus, Herodotus, Diodorus Siculus, Aelian, Pomponius Mela, Pliny and Pausanias. The most important and frequently quoted are Pindar, *Pythians*, X.29–43; Diodorus Siculus, *Bibliotheca historicae*, II.47; Pomponius Mela, *Chorographia*, III.36–7; and Pliny, *Historia naturalis*, IV.89–91.
146. A delightful point first spotted by Owen, *The Famous Druids*, 81.
147. Ibid., 119–83.
148. I have used the English edition brought out in London in 1751, which is far more readily available than the original.
149. Pp. 13–17, 63–4 and 95–6 of the 1751 edition.
150. Stephen H. Daniel, *John Toland: His Methods, Manners and Mind* (Kingston and Montreal: McGill-Queen's University Press, 1984), 212–25; David Berman, 'The Irish Freethinker', in

John Toland's 'Christianity Not Mysterious': Text, Associated Work and Critical Essays, ed. Philip McGuiness, Alan Harrison and Richard Kearney (Dublin: Lilliput Press, 1997), 220–8; Margaret Jacob, *Living the Enlightenment: Freemasonry and Politics in Eighteenth-Century Europe* (Oxford: Oxford University Press, 1991), 61, 91–3; Robert E. Sullivan, *John Toland and the Deist Controversy* (Cambridge, Mass.: Harvard University Press, 1982), 201–2. Champion, *Republican Learning*, 241–3.

151. Champion, *Republican Learning*, 243.
152. E.g. Jones, *Druid Shaman Priest*, 130–45; Jenkins, *Foundations of Modern Wales*, 250; Harrison, 'John Toland (1670–1722) and Celtic Studies', 574; Piggott, *The Druids*, 143.
153. Ross Nichols, *The Book of Druidry*, ed. John Matthews and Philip Carr-Gomm (London: Aquarian, 1990), 99–101.
154. Rowlands, *Mona Antiqua*, 29.
155. This is to adopt the reading of Toland made in Champion, *Republican Learning*, and Sullivan, *John Toland*.
156. Champion, *Republican Learning*, 69–70.
157. Summed up with particular concision in John Toland, *Letters to Serena* (London, 1704), 130.
158. A point well made by Patrick McGuinness, 'The Peculiar Contradictions of John Toland', *Times Literary Supplement* 27 Sept. 1996, 14–15.
159. Sullivan, *John Toland*, 184–6; Champion, *Republican Learning*, 167–89.
160. John Leland, *Collectanea*, ed. Thomas Hearne (Oxford, 1715), vi. 59.
161. Thomas Twining, *Avebury in Wiltshire* (London, 1723).
162. It is displayed at his seat of Canons Ashby; I am grateful to Mary Anne Garry for pointing this out to me.
163. Represented, successively, by Edmund Hickergill, *Priest-Craft* (London, 1706), 9; Aaron Thompson, *The British History, Translated into English from the Latin of Jeffrey of Monmouth* (London, 1718), lxxiii, xcviii; John Woodward, *Remarks upon the Antient and Present State of London* (London, 1723), 25.
164. E.g. James Arbuckle, *Snuff* (Glasgow, 1717), 24; Elizabeth Boyd, *Truth* (London, 1740), passim.
165. For an example of it, see *British Curiosities in Nature and Art* (London, 1713), 12.

3 The Druids Take Over

1. Much, but not all, of what follows has been rehearsed in Ronald Hutton, 'The Religion of William Stukeley', *Antiquaries' Journal* 85 (2005), 381–94.
2. Stuart Piggott, *William Stukeley* (London: Thames and Hudson, 1950 and 1985); references are to the second edition.
3. Aubrey Burl, *Prehistoric Avebury* (New Haven, Conn.: Yale University Press, 1979), 47–50; Penelope Lively, *The Treasures of Time* (London: Heinemann, 1979), 3, 13, 42.
4. Peter Ucko, Michael Hunter, Alan Clark and Andrew David, *Avebury Reconsidered* (London: Unwin Hyman, 1991), 39–92.
5. David Boyd Haycock, *William Stukeley: Science, Religion and Archaeology in Eighteenth-Century England* (Woodbridge: Boydell, 2002).
6. Ucko et al., *Avebury Reconsidered*, xiii.
7. To which I can now add a treatise on Druids, dating from his later years to judge by the hand-writing, in the library of the Wiltshire Archaeological and Natural History Society at Devizes.
8. *The Family Memoirs of the Rev. William Stukeley. Volume One*, ed. W. C. Lukis (Surtees Society, 1882)(henceforth SS 1), 228.
9. National Archives of Scotland, GD 18/5030/14 (Roger Gale to Sir John Clerk). I am very grateful to Sir John's descendant, Sir Robert M. Clerk Bt., for permission to quote from this collection.
10. SS 1, 77, 106.
11. Wiltshire Record Office, 383/907/2.
12. Freemasons' Hall, London (henceforth FH), MS 1130 Stu (1); quotations from p. 1.
13. Wellcome Trust Centre, London (henceforth WTC), MS 4722, p. 1.
14. Wiltshire Archaeological and Natural History Society Library, Devizes (henceforth WANHSL), Commonplace Book of William Stukeley.
15. Brit. L, Lansdowne MS 688, fos 12–13.

16. Piggott, *William Stukeley*, 41–51.
17. WANHSL, Commonplace Book, p. 19.
18. Piggott, *William Stukeley*, 53–6.
19. The nature and publication of the find are discussed in T. D. Kendrick, *The Druids* (London, 1927), 20. The antiquarian was Jean Guenebault, writing in 1623.
20. E.g. *The Family Memoirs of the Rev. William Stukeley. Volume Two*, ed. W. C. Lukis (Surtees Society 76, 1883) (henceforth SS 2), 232; and *Volume Three*, ed. W. C. Lukis (Surtees Society 80, 1887) (henceforth SS 3), 246; John Nichols, *Illustrations of the Literary History of the Eighteenth Century* (London, 1817), ii. 772.
21. The volumes are Bod. L, MS Eng. Misc. c. 323 and Cardiff Public Library (hereafter Cardiff Public L), MSS 4.253 and 4.26. The first two contain notes that they were commenced in 1723. Peter Ucko's team decided that the whole project was started in the previous year, from the date of 7 December 1722 on a self-portrait intended as the frontispiece to one volume, but the making of the picture may have preceded the inception of the work: Ucko et al., *Avebury Reconsidered*, 52.
22. Cardiff Public L, MS 4.26, p. 111; and see also p. 123.
23. Ibid., 67.
24. Ibid., 117.
25. Ibid., 3–5.
26. Ucko et al., *Avebury Reconsidered*, 75–6.
27. Bod. L, MS Eng. Misc. c. 321, fos 17–22 (quotation on fo. 20).
28. Cardiff Public L, MS 4.253, p. 108.
29. Ibid., 86.
30. Ibid., 2. For this concept among Stukeley's predecessors and contemporaries, see Frank E. Manuel, *The Eighteenth Century Confronts the Gods* (Cambridge, Mass.: Harvard University Press, 1959), 85–102.
31. Cardiff Public L, MS 4.26, p. 18.
32. Ibid., 94–5.
33. Cardiff Public L, MS 4.253, p. 147.
34. Bod. L, MS Eng. Misc. c. 323, p. 99.
35. If so, it is significant that, after his conversion, Stukeley famously made 'deists' his chief targets in controversy: SS 3, 267.
36. Manuel, *The Eighteenth Century Confronts the Gods*, 57–133. Haycock, *William Stukeley*, 136–64, provides a valuable and perceptive reconsideration of these controversies and Stukeley's relationship with them. Where we differ is in my contention that the relationship changed profoundly.
37. If Stukeley was a deist at this period, it would perhaps explain his lingering affection for Toland in later years, noted by Haycock, *William Stukeley*, 182–4.
38. FH, MS 1130 Stu (supplementary papers).
39. Ucko et al., *Avebury Reconsidered*, 81, 87, 89.
40. I am very grateful to Chris Chandler of the National Monuments Record for confirming this, and to Joshua Pollard for suggesting that I approach the Record for information.
41. The fullest description of his work at Barrow is in WTC, MS 4720. Other notices of it, reflecting its importance to him, are FH MS 1130 Stu (2); William Stukeley, *Abury: A Temple of the British Druids . . .* (London, 1743), 92–6; SS 2, 298; and SS 3, 380–5.
42. FM, MS 1130 Stu (2); Stukeley, *Abury*, 96; SS 2, 63–4.
43. How much later is hard to say. From SS 3, 38–5, it seems that the concept may not have been complete until 1739, but the other sources at notes 34 and 35 suggest a much earlier date.
44. Cardiff Public L, MS 4.26, p. 111.
45. FH, MS 1130 Stu (3).
46. Bod. L, MS Eng. Misc. c. 323, pp. 68, 132, 138, 172–3, 230–2, 249–55; Cardiff Public L, MS 4.26, 41. As all these notes are undated, it is impossible precisely to track this development in his thought. Ucko et al., *Avebury Reconsidered*, 89, believed that they had done so, by finding a note about the image of the winged circle and snake on the back of a reconstruction of part of the Avebury complex drawn on 15 May 1724. The note is, however, a later addition to the field paper: Bod. L, Gough Maps 231, fo. 31v.
47. Bod. L, MS Eng. Misc. c. 113, fo. 137.
48. SS 1, 105–6.

49. Piggott, *William Stukeley*, 76.
50. National Archives of Scotland, GD 18/5023/3/29 (Alexander Gordon to Sir John Clerk).
51. Ibid., GD 18/5030/6 (Roger Gale to Clerk).
52. Joan Evans, *A History of the Society of Antiquaries* (Oxford: Oxford University Press, 1956), 75–6.
53. National Archives of Scotland, GD 18/5030/6 (Gale to Clerk).
54. Ibid., GD 5023/3/25 (Gordon to Clerk).
55. SS 1, 106.
56. Ibid., 198–9.
57. Ibid., 208–9.
58. Bod. L, MS Eng. Misc. c. 113, fo. 137.
59. SS 1, 208–9.
60. Piggott, *William Stukeley*, 77.
61. Haycock, *William Stukeley*, 192.
62. SS 1, 216–19.
63. Haycock, *William Stukeley*, provides a fine analysis of this debate and of the involvement of some of Stukeley's own social circle on the anti-Trinitarian side.
64. SS 1, 220.
65. Ibid., 210–12.
66. Ibid., 235, 237; SS 3, 266–7: Bod. L, MS Eng. Misc. c. 323, p. 132; Stukeley, *Abury*, 57–63.
67. Bod. L, MS Eng. Misc. e. 650; and e. 554, fos 434–69.
68. William Stukeley, *Stonehenge: A Temple Restor'd to the British Druids* (London, 1740), 1–2; and see also *Abury*, 102 and Bod. L, MSS Eng. Misc. e 403 and e. 667/4.
69. Stukeley, *Stonehenge*, 1–2, and *Abury*, iii; FH, MS 1130 Stu (12); WTC, MS 4720.
70. Piggott, *William Stukeley*, 99–102.
71. FH, MS 1130 Stu (7). See also WTC, MS 4720.
72. FH, MS 1130 Stu (2, 4, 5, 9); Bod. L, MS e. 553, fos 242–303. In later life he recalled discussions of the temple of Jerusalem with Newton in the 1720s (SS 1, 62, 78), and it was certainly a considerable topic of conversation among the learned world of London in that decade: Eileen Harris, 'John Wood's System of Architecture', *Burlington Magazine* 131 (1989), 101–7. In view of all this, it is the more noteworthy that it is given no special importance in Stukeley's writings of this period, in sharp contrast to those composed later.
73. FH, MS 1130 Stu (4, 5, 11, 12, 14, 17); Society of Antiquaries, MS 806.
74. WTC, MS 4722; quotation on p. 1.
75. Cardiff Public L, MS 4.253, p. 111.
76. FH, MS 1130 Stu (10).
77. Bod. L, MS Eng. Misc. e. 379.
78. E.g. FH, MS 1130 Stu (10, 12); Bod. L, MSS Eng. Misc. d. 450 ('Windsor', 'The Druid', 'Druid Song'); e. 135, fos 14–17; and e. 138, fos 47–8; Wiltshire Record Office, 383/907/2; SS 1, 408–9; SS 2, 8, 55, 63–4; SS 3, 179, 211, 380–2.
79. Bod. L, MS Eng. Misc. e. 403; Society of Antiquaries, MS 806; Cardiff Public L, MS 2.370; SS 1, 408–9; WANHSL, uncatalogued manuscript, 'The Druids', passim.
80. SS 1, 294. Stukeley's letter to Gale, outlining his ideas, is in SS 1, 463, and the treatise itself survives as WTC, MS 4724.
81. Piggott, *William Stukeley*, 182; Haycock, *William Stukeley*, 222–4.
82. Quoted in Evans, *History of the Society of Antiquaries*, 130.
83. In Haycock, *William Stukeley*, 235–58.
84. Ibid., 124–5; cf. Christopher Chippindale, *Stonehenge Complete* (London: Thames and Hudson, 1983), 75–86.
85. A process chronicled in Esther Moir, *The Discovery of Britain* (London: Routledge, 1964).
86. Francis Grose, *The Antiquities of England and Wales* (2nd edn, London, 1785), vi. 39–44; William Gilpin, *Observations on the Western Parts of England* (London, 1798), 78–81; Richard Joseph Sullivan, *Tour through Different Parts of England, Scotland and Wales* (1798), reprinted in *The British Tourist's or Traveller's Pocket Companion* (London, 1809), iii. 32; John Hassell, *Tour of the Isle of Wight . . .* (1790), reprinted in *British Tourist's or Traveller's Pocket Companion* 369. Since writing this chapter, I have read Rosemary Sweet, *Antiquaries: The Discovery of the Past in Eighteenth-Century Britain* (London: Hambledon and London, 2004), 133–4, where the influence of Stukeley on late eighteenth-century guides to Stonehenge is also noted.

87. William Hutchinson, *An Excursion to the Lakes in Westmorland and Cumberland* (London, 1774), 98–9.
88. This is also noted in Sweet, *Antiquaries*, 135–6, where it is observed that references to Druids in the volumes peaked in the 1780s.
89. Stukeley, *Stonehenge*, preface.
90. This is, at any rate, how I interpret his remark to Borlase in SS 2, 55.
91. All this is based on Eileen Harris, 'John Wood's System of Architecture', *Burlington Magazine* 131. 1031 (Feb. 1989), 101–7, as is much of what follows, with important material added from Tim Mowl and Brian Earnshaw, *John Wood: Architect of Obsession* (Huddersfield: Amadeus, 1988), 5–89.
92. Mowl and Earnshaw, *John Wood*, 90; Harris, 'John Wood's System of Architecture', 106.
93. Sir John Soane's Museum, manuscript version of *The Origin of Building*, fos 87–9.
94. Mowl and Earnshaw, *John Wood*, 169.
95. This is in accord with his published statement that he 'began to take a plan of them, on the 12th of August 1740': John Wood, *An Essay towards a Description of Bath* (2nd edn, London, 1749), 148. It would also accord with his letter to his patron Oxford in December, enclosing his plan of the site with an apology for the long delay in sending it: Brit. L, Harleian MS 7354, fo. 1.
96. Bath Central Library, Manuscript of John Wood, *The Origin of Building*, fos 169–70.
97. Mowl and Earnshaw, *John Wood*, 11, 23–4.
98. Bath Central Library, Manuscript of *The Origin of Building*, fos 169–70; quotation from fo. 169v.
99. Brit. L, Harleian MSS 7354 and 7355 (Wood's reports to Oxford).
100. Mowl and Earnshaw, *John Wood*, 159.
101. John Wood, *The Origin of Building* (Bath, 1741).
102. It is interesting in this regard that in 1790, when the precinct of the Roman temple at Bath was discovered, it was found to have had a relief of a moon goddess on one wall. This does seem, however, to be an example of coincidence rather than clairvoyance. Wood's generation had long become accustomed to the idea that the first lapse of humans into idolatry from the true religion of the patriarchs consisted of worshipping the sun and the moon: it is found in major continental scholars such as Kircher, and in the work of Toland and Stukeley alike. Furthermore, if Britain were to be Hyperborea as Wood wished, its inhabitants had primarily to venerate the sun god Apollo as Hyperboreans did. It may be that his attention was fixed on goddess-worship at Bath by the spectacular discovery, in 1727, of a bronze head of a female deity below Stall Street. This was, however, from a statue of the city's genuine presiding divinity, Sulis Minerva, goddess of war, vengeance, healing and the hot springs, and not of a Phoenician moon goddess: Barry Cunliffe, *Roman Bath Discovered* (London: Routledge, 1971), 9–88.
103. Wood, *An Essay towards a Decription of Bath*, passim.
104. John Wood, *Choir Gaure* (Oxford, 1747).
105. This is all argued in Brit. L, Harleian MS 7354.
106. For Stukeley's attachment to it, see Piggott, *William Stukeley*, 40.
107. Which he defended in both *An Essay towards a Description of Bath*, 106–7 and *Choir Gaure*, 9–12.
108. Mowl and Earnshaw, *John Wood*, 185.
109. SS 1, 337; SS 3, 275, 277.
110. Harris, 'John Wood's System of Architecture', 107.
111. Stukeley took sixteen years to come across it, by which time his friend the Bishop had never heard of it.
112. Mowl and Earnshaw, *John Wood*, 186–92. For previous suggestions, see John Summerson, *Heavenly Mansions* (London, 1949), 87–110, and Stuart Piggott, *The Druids* (London and New York: Thames and Hudson, 1968), 149–52.
113. What follows, unless specifically stated otherwise, is based on P. A. S. Pool, *William Borlase* (Truro: Royal Institution of Cornwall, 1986), which, as well as being a good overall biography, prints or summarizes the relevant Borlase MSS preserved at Penzance.
114. SS 2, 57.
115. Pool, *William Borlase*, 89.
116. An expression coined by Hugh Trevor-Roper, who famously remarked that a fertile error can prove to be more profit to scholarship than a sterile truth.

117. Pool, *William Borlase*.
118. SS 2, 55–8.
119. Pool, *William Borlase*, 103–46.
120. Willam Borlase, *Antiquities, Historical and Monumental, of the County of Cornwall* (Oxford, 1754); quotation from p. vi.
121. Pool, *William Borlase*, 129.
122. Borlase, *Antiquities*, 53, 60–1, 121.
123. Ibid., 19–55, 333–5.
124. Pool, *William Borlase*, 148.
125. Borlase, *Antiquities*, 68–167.
126. Ibid., 107–23.
127. Leslie Ellen Jones, *Druid Shaman Priest* (Enfield: Hisarlik, 1998), 157–8.
128. Borlase, *Antiquities*, 61.
129. Ibid., 123–4.
130. Robert Hunt, *Popular Romances of the West of England* (London reprint, 1916), 49–51.
131. This is in the Duke of Devonshire's collection in Chatsworth House. It was reproduced in the illustrations to Ronald Hutton, *The Druids* (London: Hambledon Continuum, 2007).
132. William Diaper, *Dryades* (London, 1713), 15, 32.
133. Its position in the canon was firmly established by the time of Hoxie Neale Fairchild's *The Noble Savage* (New York, 1928), 57–90.
134. 'Liberty', Book IV, lines 626–33.
135. The biography of Thomson that I have used is James Sambrook, *James Thomson 1700–1748: A Life* (Oxford: Oxford University Press, 1991).
136. Brit. L, Egerton MS 1950, fos 4–5v (Pope's notes).
137. Published in London in 1747.
138. Joseph Warton, *Odes on Various Subjects*, ed. Richard Wendorf (Los Angeles: University of California Press, 1979), x.
139. Ibid., 39; from 'To a Lady Who Hates the Country'.
140. *The Poetical Works of Thomas Warton* (London, 1805), 39.
141. James Thomson, *The Castle of Indolence* (1748), Canto II, verses xxxiii–lxiii.
142. A point first spotted by Owen, *The Famous Druids*, 175–6.
143. Sambrook, *James Thomson*, 257.
144. William Collins, 'Ode to Liberty' (1747), lines 109–12.
145. The poem and its context were studied in J. M. S. Tompkins, 'In Yonder Grave a Druid Lies', *Review of English Studies* 22 (1946), 1–16.
146. P. L. Carver, *The Life of a Poet: A Biographical Sketch of William Collins* (London: Sidgwick and Jackson, 1967), 177.
147. Ibid.; Sambrook, *James Thomson*, 257.
148. Joseph Warton, *An Essay on the Writings and Genius of Pope* (London, 1756), 7.
149. Edward D. Snyder, 'Thomas Gray's Interest in Celtic', *Modern Philology* 11 (1913), 559–61.
150. Gray's correspondence, quoted in Owen, *The Famous Druids*, 148.
151. The classic recent work on this is Linda Colley, *Britons: Forging the Nation, 1707–1837* (New Haven, Conn.: Yale University Press, 1992).
152. The equivalent classic here is much older: Edward D. Snyder, *The Celtic Revival in English Literature* (Cambridge, Mass.: Harvard University Press, 1923).
153. Snyder, 'Thomas Gray's Interest in Celtic', 567.
154. Sam Smiles, *The Image of Antiquity: Ancient Britain and the Romantic Imagination* (New Haven, Conn.: Yale University Press, 1994), 48–61.
155. *Fragments of Ancient Poetry* (London, 1760); *Fingal* (London, 1762); *Temora* (London, 1763). Macpherson's impact on attitudes to Celtic-speaking cultures and ancient Britain was analysed by Snyder, *The Celtic Revival*, 86–9.
156. Quoted in the entry on Mason in the *Dictionary of National Biography*, 438.
157. Snyder, 'Thomas Gray's Interest in Celtic', 561–4; Owen, *The Famous Druids*, 147–51.
158. William Mason, *Caractacus* (London, 1759), 1–14, 71.
159. Snyder, 'Thomas Gray's Interest in Celtic', 565; William Mason, *Caractacus* (York, 1777).
160. Thomas Gisborne, *Elegy to the Memory of the Rev. William Mason* (London, 1797), 9.
161. William Gilbert, *The Hurricane* (London, 1796), 43–4.

162. In 'Elfrida', published in William Mason, *Poems* (London, 1764), 98.

163. *The Poetical Works of Thomas Warton*, 21, 110.

164. Whether Waity and Tait knew it or not (and it seems that they did not), Goldsmith had condemned Druids as a high-handed theocracy in his *History of England* (London, 1771), i. 6–7.

165. Willam Waity and John Tait, 'The Druids' Monument', quoted in Owen, *The Famous Druids*, 178.

166. *Stone Henge. A Poem Inscribed to Edward Jerningham, Esq* (London, 1792).

167. Thomas Maurice, *Netherby: A Poem* (Oxford, 1796), 5–10.

168. William Julius Mickle, *Poems, and a Tragedy* (London, 1794), xxviii.

169. 'The Genius of Carnbre', in (Richard Polwhele), *The Fate of Llewellyn* (Bath, 1777), 53–4. Polwhele did indeed continue a career as a poet (among much other writing), though not, alas, a particularly inspired one.

170. It is still there, in a churchyard laid out in 1914.

171. [John Ogilvie], *The Fane of the Druids: A Poem* (London, 1787); and *The Fane of the Druids: Part the Second* (London, 1789).

172. Fairchild, *The Noble Savage*, 57–139; quotation from p. 119.

173. John Abraham Fisher, *The Masque of the Druids* (London, 1774); quotation from p. 28.

174. Snyder, *The Celtic Revival*, 111–16.

175. Henry Brooke, *Cymbeline*, V, iv–x, in *A Collection of the Pieces Formerly Published by Henry Brooke, Esq* (London, 1778), Part IV, 394–408.

176. David R. Coffin, *The English Garden: Meditation and Memorial* (Princeton, NJ: Princeton University Press, 1994), 119–20.

177. William Cowper, 'Boadicea', in his *Poetical Works*, ed. H. S. Mitford (Oxford: Oxford University Press, 4th edn, 1967), 310–11.

178. Richard Hingley, *Roman Officers and English Gentlemen* (London: Routledge, 2000), 74–7.

179. William Sotheby, *Cambrian Hero* (London, 1800).

180. Richard Llwyd, *Beaumaris Bay: A Poem* (Chester, 1800), 20–1.

181. Dr Darwin, 'Address to the Swilcar Oak', *European Magazine* (March 1800), 226.

182. George Cumberland, *An Attempt to Describe Hafod* (London, 1796), 10–11.

183. Moir, *The Discovery of Britain*, 148.

184. David Haycock, ' "A Small Journey into the Country" ': William Stukeley and the Formal Landscapes of Stonehenge and Avebury', in *Producing the Past: Aspects of Antiquarian Culture and Practice 1700–1850* (Aldershot: Ashgate, 1999), 76–7.

185. Coffin, *The English Garden*, 117–18.

186. Ibid., 121–2, where the structure is wrongly called a stone circle; Henry Seymour Conway, 'Description of a Druidical Monument in the Island of Jersey', *Archaeologia* 8 (1787), 386–8. I visited the stones at Templecombe in 1967, by kind permission of the then owners.

187. The house is Ty Newydd. I visited the monument by kind permission of the owner in 1967.

188. Coffin, *The English Garden*, 118–19.

189. Ibid., 118, 121.

190. Glyn Daniel, *Megaliths in History* (London: Thames and Hudson, 1972), 41–2.

191. Brian Davison, *Old Wardour Castle* (London: English Heritage, 1999), 18–21.

192. Coffin, *The English Garden*, 123–6.

193. Richard Warner, *A Tour through the Northern Counties of England and the Borders of Scotland* (Bath, 1802), ii.178.

4 The Druids Take Flesh

1. Llwyd, *Beaumaris Bay*, 21.

2. Ross Nichols, *The Book of Druidry*, ed. John Matthews and Philip Carr-Gomm (London: Aquarian, 1990), 96–102; quotation from p. 97.

3. *http://www.neopagan.net/AODbooklet.html*. Accessed 25 June 2005.

4. Anthony Powell, *John Aubrey and his Friends* (London: Eyre and Spottiswoode, 1948); David Tylden-Wright, *John Aubrey: A Life* (London: HarperCollins, 1991).

5. Nichols, *Book of Druidry*, 97–8.

6. Brit. L, Add. MS 4295, fo. 18.

7. Stephen H. Daniel, *John Toland: His Methods, Manners and Mind* (Kingston and Montreal: McGill-Queen's University Press, 1984), 212–15; David Berman, 'The Irish Freethinker', in *John Toland's 'Christianity Not Mysterious': Text, Associated Work and Critical Essays* (Dublin: Lilliput Press, 1997), 228; Robert E. Sullivan, *John Toland and the Deist Controversy* (Cambridge, Mass.: Harvard University Press, 1982), 15, 28, 202.

8. Nichols, *Book of Druidry*, 100.

9. John Toland, *Pantheisticon* (English translation, London, 1751), 95–6.

10. [James Anderson], *The Constitutions of the Freemasons* (London, 1723), 197.

11. All this is chronicled in Piggott, *William Stukeley*, except the Freemasonry, of which the records are in FH, MS 1130 Stu (additional notes).

12. *The Family Memoirs of the Rev. William Stukeley. Volume One*, ed. W. C. Lukis (Surtees Society, 1882) (SS 1), 365; SS 3, 348–9.

13. Cardiff Public L, MS. 2.370, fo. iii; Bod. L, MS Eng. Misc. d. 450, 'The Druid'; and d. 454, fo. i.

14. SS 1, 82–5, 408–9; FH, MS 1130 Stu (10, 12); Bod. L, Eng. Misc. d. 450, 'Druid Song'; and e. 138, fos 47–8.

15. *The Family Memoirs of the Rev. William Stukeley. Volume Three*, ed. W. C. Lukis (Surtees Society, 80, 1887), 211; Bod. L, MS MS Eng. Misc. e. 135, fos 14–17.

16. Cardiff Public L, MS 2.370, fo. iii.

17. William Stukeley, *Palaeographia sacra* (London, 1763).

18. Bod. L, MS Eng. Misc. d. 454, fo. 1.

19. Peter Clark, *British Clubs and Societies 1580–1680* (Oxford: Oxford University Press, 2000).

20. Mrs Pritchard, 'The Druidical Society', *Transactions of the Anglesey Antiquarian Society and Field Club* (1925), 63–8; M. F. Jolliffe, 'The Druidical Society of Anglesey 1772–1844', *Transactions of the Honourable Society of Cymmrodorion* (1940), 189–99.

21. *Sir William Jones: Selected Poetical and Prose Works*, ed. Michael Franklin (Cardiff: University of Wales Press, 1995), 58.

22. Michael J. Franklin, *Sir William Jones* (Cardiff: University of Wales Press, 1995), 53–63; quotation from pp. 62–3.

23. Copies of the surviving issues of the *Druids' Magazine* are kept in the British Library and the Wellcome Institute. I wrote to the Grand Secretary of the present Ancient Order of Druids, explaining the nature of my research and requesting assistance for it, especially with regard to archival materials, and received no reply; for which there are various possible honourable reasons.

24. Hugo Wiese, G. Wolf Stoll and Karl Roeder, *Handbuch des Druidenordens* (Munich, 1931), 146–9.

25. Wilhelm North, *Who Was Henry Hurle, the Founder of the A.O.D.?* (London, 1932). A copy of this pamphlet is preserved in John Goodchild's splendid collection underneath Wakefield Central Library.

26. Ibid., n.p.

27. Ibid.; *The Druid* 4.3 (June 1909), 52, and 5.3 (July 1909), 71. Copies of this journal are held in the British Library.

28. *The Druid* 5.4 (Aug. 1909), 83.

29. This is all surmised from the detailed accounts of meetings in the 1820s and 1830s, provided in the *Druids' Magazine*.

30. *The Druid* 5.3 (July 1909), 71.

31. Ibid. and 5.4 (Aug. 1909), 84.

32. These data are taken from the *Druids' Magazine* 3 (1832), and *Ancient Order of Druids: Address, Constitutional Laws, Choruses and List of Lodges* (n.d., but clearly from 1820s). A copy of the latter survives in Birmingham Central Reference Library.

33. *The Druid* 3.7 (Sept. 1909), 100.

34. Ibid., 5.3 (Aug. 1911), 35.

35. Jacob Stanley, *An Address to the Lodges of Druids, Odd Fellows . . .* (Wednesbury, 1813); quotation from p. 1. A copy survives in the John Rylands Library, Manchester.

36. 'Runt and Pitcher', *The Cat Out of the Bag!* (London, 1824), 10–12. A copy exists in the British Library.

37. Cited at n. 30.

38. North, *Who Was Hurle . . .?* n.p.

39. The *Druids' Magazine* 3 (1832), frontispiece and p. 137. Both were published in Ronald Hutton, *The Druids* (London: Hambledon and London, 2007).
40. Now in the Salisbury and South Wiltshire Museum, and also reproduced in Hutton, *The Druids*.
41. The *Druids' Monthly Magazine* 1 (1833), 21.
42. This summary is based on issue 3 of the *Druids' Magazine* and issues 1–4 of the *Druids' Monthly Magazine*, plus *Ancient Order of Druids: Address . . .*, elucidated at points by Ted Williams, 'Ancient Order Druidism', *The Druids' Voice* 4 (Winter 1994), 7. I have the copy of the last of these journals in my own archive.
43. What follows is based on P. H. J. H. Gosden, *The Friendly Societies in England 1815–1875* (Manchester: Manchester University Press, 1961); and Simon Cordery, *British Friendly Societies 1750–1914* (London: Palgrave Macmillan, 2003), supplemented by John Frome Wilkinson, *The Friendly Society Movement* (London, 1886) and *Mutual Thrift* (London, 1891); and Martin Gorsky, 'The Growth and Distribution of English Friendly Societies in the Early Nineteenth Century', *Economic History Review* 2nd series 5 (1998), 489–511.
44. *Druids' Monthly Magazine* (Oct. 1833 supplement), 269.
45. *Druids' Magazine* 3–4 (1832–3); *Druids' Monthly Magazine* 1–2 (1833–4). Copies of the latter are held in the British Library.
46. *Constitutional Laws of the United Ancient Order of Druids* (London, 1846). A copy exists in the Worcestershire Record Office, 705: 550/4600/6 (i) (BA 4600).
47. Preserved in the same box as the *Constitutional Laws*, above.
48. What follows is based on *Ancient Order of Druids: Address, Constitutional Laws, Choruses and List of Lodges* (London, 1843). A copy exists in Birmingham Central Reference Library.
49. The earlier issues of this are cited and located above. The British Library holds those of the *Druids' Monthly Magazine* up to 1846.
50. *Druids' Monthly Magazine* 1 (1834), 212.
51. Thomas Johnson, *History of the Ancient Druids* (Bradford, 1835). A copy survives in the British Library.

5 Iolo Morganwg

I am very grateful to Mary-Ann Constantine for reading through a draft of this chapter.

1. What follows is based on Geraint H. Jenkins, *The Foundations of Modern Wales 1642–1780* (Oxford: Oxford University Press, 1987), 217–50, 424–6; Prys Morgan, *A New History of Wales: The Eighteenth-Century Renaissance* (Llandybie: Christopher Davies, 1981), 13–82, 119–28; and Dillwyn Miles, *The Royal National Eisteddfod of Wales* (Swansea: Christopher Davies, 1978), 1–38.
2. Prys Morgan, 'From a Death to a View: The Hunt for the Remote Past in the Romantic Period', in *The Invention of Tradition*, ed. Eric Hobsbawm and Terence Ranger (Cambridge: Cambridge University Press, 1983), 63; Morgan, *A New History of Wales*, 108.
3. Evan Evans, *Some Specimens of the Poetry of the Antient Welsh Bards* (London, 1764), i. 18.
4. Ibid., ii. 18.
5. Morgan, 'From a Death to a View', 63.
6. John Thomas, *A History of the Island of Anglesey* (London, 1775), 15–16.
7. Thomas Carte, *A General History of England* (London, 1747), 45–6.
8. *A Description of Stonehenge, Abiry, Etc* (Salisbury, 1783).
9. Elizabeth Ryves, *Hermit of Snowden* (Dublin, 1789), viii.
10. Quoted in Rosemary Sweet, *Antiquaries: The Discovery of the Past in Eighteenth-Century Britain* (London: Hambledon and London, 2004), 142.
11. William Warrington, *The History of Wales* (London, 1786), 11.
12. Lest there be any misunderstanding on this score, I shall state my own abilities in this respect. I have a grasp of the basic structure of the Welsh language, including the famous mutations that provide the toughest challenge for an English-speaker, and can translate short and simple passages. Although that is a good beginning by the standards of most non-Welsh Britons, I am unable to deal confidently with complex constructions or lengthy works, and so effectively

cannot read most of the sources for Druidry in Welsh. It is thus very fortunate for me that, with a few notable exceptions that I shall point out, the majority of the relevant literature was either composed in English or has been translated.

13. Griffith John Williams, *Iolo Morganwg a Chywyddau'r Ychwanegiad* (London, 1926); Williams, *Traddadiad Llenyddol Morganwg* (Cardiff, 1948), and Williams, *Iolo Morganwg: Y Gyfrol Gyntaf* (Cardiff, 1956).

14. Ceri W. Lewis, *Iolo Morganwg* (Caernarfon: Gwasg Pantycelyn, 1998).

15. Prys Morgan, *Iolo Morganwg* (Cardiff: University of Wales Press, 1975).

16. *A Rattleskull Genius: The Many Faces of Iolo Morganwg*, ed. Geraint H. Jenkins (Cardiff: University of Wales Press, 2005). Notable earlier productions from the project include Geraint Jenkins, *Fact, Fantasy and Fiction: The Historical Vision of Iolo Morganwg* (Aberystwyth: University of Wales Centre for Advanced Welsh and Celtic Studies, 1997); and 'The Urban Experiences of Iolo Morganwg', *Welsh History Review* 22.3 (2005), 463–98; and Mary-Ann Constantine, *'Combustible Matter': Iolo Morganwg and the Bristol Volcano* (Aberystwyth: University of Wales Centre for Advanced Welsh and Celtic Studies, 2003). I was entertained by Professor Jenkins and his partners at Aberystwyth in May 2005, when I delivered a paper to them, and found it an extremely exciting and valuable experience. Since then I have kept up exchanges with them, and in particular with Mary-Ann Constantine, to my continued pleasure and profit. Nowhere in England could I have found a group of people who so fully shared the interests and enthusiasms that have gone to make up the present book. This relationship was sustained when I revisited the Centre to speak just before delivering the book, and learned of the publication by it of two more collections on Iolo: *Bardic Circles: National, Regional and Personal Identity in the Bardic Vision of Iolo Morganwg*, ed. Cathryn A. Charnell-White (Aberystwyth: University of Wales Press, 2007), and *The Truth against the World: Iolo Morganwg and Romantic Forgery*, ed. Mary-Ann Constantine (Aberystwyth: University of Wales Press, 2007). In addition, the Centre has just produced *The Correspondence of Iolo Morganwg*, ed. Geraint H. Jenkins, Ffion Mair Jones and David Ceri Jones, published by the same press.

17. Cathryn A. Charnell-White, 'Women and Gender in the Private and Social Relationships of Iolo Morganwg', in *A Rattleskull Genius*, ed. Jenkins, 364–6.

18. Jenkins, *Fact, Fantasy and Fiction*, 5–7.

19. Morgan, *Iolo Morganwg*, 1–5.

20. Ceri W. Lewis, 'The Literary Tradition of Glamorgan down to the Middle of the Sixteenth Century', in *Glamorgan County History: Volume III*, ed. T. B. Pugh (Cardiff: University of Wales Press, 1971), 449–54.

21. Ceri W. Lewis, 'The Literary History of Glamorgan from 1530 to 1770', in *Glamorgan County History: Volume IV*, ed. Glanmor Williams (Cardiff: University of Wales Press, 1974), 535–641; Morgan, *Iolo Morganwg*, 1–2.

22. Charnell-White, 'Women and Gender', 364–6.

23. Elijah Waring, *Recollections and Anecdotes of Edward Williams* (London, 1850), 5.

24. Morgan, *Iolo Morganwg*, 5–7; Dillwyn Miles, *The Secret of the Bards of the Isle of Britain* (Llandybie: Gwasg Dinefwr Press, 1992), 43–4.

25. Jon Cannon and Mary-Ann Constantine, 'A Welsh Bard in Wiltshire', *Wiltshire Archaeological and Natural History Magazine* 97 (2004), 78–88.

26. Morgan, *Iolo Morganwg*, 8–9; Miles, *The Secret of the Bards*, 44; Charnell-White, 'Women and Gender', 367–70.

27. Geraint Phillips, 'Forgery and Patronage: Iolo Morganwg and Owain Myfyr', in *A Rattleskull Genius*, ed. Jenkins, 403–12.

28. Generally known now as William Owen Pughe, because he added the last name to his own on coming into an inheritance in 1806; but we are concerned here almost wholly with his career before that date.

29. Phillips, 'Forgery and Patronage', 412; Glenda Carr, 'An Uneasy Partnership: Iolo Morganwg and William Owen Pughe', in *A Rattleskull Genius*, ed. Jenkins, 443–4.

30. Carr, 'An Uneasy Partnership', 440; Phillips, 'Forgery and Patronage', 412–13.

31. Started by a letter from Owen o Feiron, in *Gentleman's Magazine* 59.2 (1789), 603–5.

32. Ibid., 976–7.

33. Miles, *The Secret of the Bards*, 45, says that he used the name from 1784, while Charnell-White, 'Women and Gender', 379, states as firmly that he adopted it on his return to London in 1791,

and Geraint Jenkins agrees, putting the date of adoption as 'around 1790': Geraint Jenkins, 'On the Trail of a Rattleskull Genius', in *A Rattleskull Genius*, ed. Jenkins, 13.

34. Morgan, *A New History of Wales*, 141–2.
35. Mary-Ann Constantine, ' "This Wildernessed Business of Publication": The Making of "Poems Lyric and Pastoral" ', in *A Rattleskull Genius*, ed. Jenkins, 139.
36. Damian Walford Davies, *Presences That Disturb: Models of Romantic Identity in the Literature and Culture of the 1790s* (Cardiff: University of Wales Press, 2002), 139–49; which is followed for most of the next two paragraphs: all the quotations provided may be found in this text.
37. Constantine, ' "This Wildernessed Business of Publication" ', 123.
38. William Owen, *The Heroic Elegies and Other Pieces of Llywarch Hen* (London, 1792), xx–lxii.
39. Ceri W. Lewis, 'Iolo Morganwg and Strict-Metre Welsh Poetry', in *A Rattleskull Genius*, ed. Jenkins, 89–90.
40. It would greatly have helped Iolo's own assimilation of these ideas that the main contemporary scholar of Indian culture, Sir William Jones – mentioned above as the leader of the modern Druids of Cardigan – had himself been a member of the metropolitan Welsh literary colony: Michael J. Franklin, 'Sir William Jones, the Celtic Revival and the Oriental Renaissance', in *English Romanticism and the Celtic World*, ed. Gerald Carruthers and Alan Rawes (Cambridge: Cambridge University Press, 2003), 20–37.
41. Owen, *The Heroic Elegies*, xxxviii.
42. This was first spotted by A. L. Owen, *The Famous Druids* (Oxford: Oxford University Press, 1962), 198.
43. Owen, *The Heroic Elegies*, lv, lvii.
44. Rachel Bromwich, *'Trioedd Ynys Prydain' in Welsh Literature and Scholarship* (Cardiff: University of Wales Press, 1969), 1–21.
45. Miles, *The Secret of the Bards*, 59.
46. Owen, *The Heroic Elegies*, l–li.
47. It is sometimes asserted that Cardiff Public Library, MS 3.104, vol. 6, no. 12, a letter from William Owen to Edward Davies, provides a detailed description of the meeting. What it actually describes, however, is Iolo's bardic system, as about to be published in *The Heroic Elegies*. Some gathering seems to have taken place, as Iolo later published a poem that he claimed to have read at it, in his *Poems, Lyric and Pastoral, in Two Volumes* (London, 1794), ii. 193–216.
48. *Gentleman's Magazine* 62.2 (1792), 956–7; *Morning Chronicle*; and *Woodfall's Diary*. Cuttings of the last two accounts survive in Iolo's papers in the National Library of Wales, and were published in William Ll. Davies, 'David Samwell (1751–1798)', *Transactions of the Honourable Society of Cymmrodorion* 1926–7, 99–102. The quotation below is from the *Gentleman's Magazine*.
49. Waring, *Recollections and Anecdotes*, 44–5; Miles, *The Secret of the Bards*, 62.
50. *The Times* (1 Jan. 1793). I am grateful to Adam Stout for this reference.
51. Miles, *The Secret of the Bards*, 66, mentions a *gorsedd* on Primrose Hill at the autumn equinox of 1793, 'said to have been attended' by the Prince of Wales and Anna Seward, but cites no source.
52. Davies, 'David Samwell', 98–9.
53. Constantine, ' "This Wildernessed Business of Publication" ', 138.
54. Williams, *Poems, Lyric and Pastoral*, ii. 194–244.
55. Lewis, 'The Literary History of Glamorgan from 1530 to 1770', 545–6.
56. Williams, *Poems, Lyric and Pastoral*, i. xix.
57. Ibid., ii. 194.
58. Ibid., i. xix.
59. Ceri W. Lewis, 'The Literary Tradition of Glamorgan', 614–15.
60. Williams, *Poems, Lyric and Pastoral*, i. xxi.
61. Caroline Franklin, 'The Welsh American Dream: Iolo Morganwg, Robert Southey and the Madoc Legend', in *English Romanticism and the Celtic World*, ed. Carruthers and Rawes, 78, 223.
62. Williams, *Poems, Lyric and Pastoral*, i. xi–xxi.
63. Ibid., xix.
64. Constantine, ' "This Wildernessed Business of Publication" '.
65. Waring, *Recollections and Anecdotes*, 1–23, 54, 116.

66. Phillips, 'Forgery and Patronage', 414–18; quotation from p. 418.
67. Ibid., 419.
68. *The Myvyrian Archaiology of Wales*, ed. Owen Jones, Edward Williams and William Owen Pughe (London, 1801–7).
69. Phillips, 'Forgery and Patronage', 418–22; Morgan, *A New History of Wales*, 83–4.
70. Bromwich, '*Trioedd Ynys Prydain' in Welsh Literature and Scholarship*, 21–5.
71. Phillips, 'Forgery and Patronage', 420–2; Carr, 'An Uneasy Partnership', 457–60.
72. National Library of Wales, MS 13145A; quotation from p. 205. These rules were published in 1803.
73. Elwyn Davies, 'Iolo Morganwg (1747–1826): Bardism and Unitarianism', *The Druids' Voice* 3 (1993), 21–6. I have a copy of this journal in my archive. Also see Waring, *Recollections and Anecdotes*, 35.
74. Branwen Jones, 'Iolo Morganwg and the Welsh Cultural Background', in *A Rattleskull Genius*, ed. Jenkins, 47.
75. Jenkins, *Fact, Fantasy and Fiction*, 5–9.
76. Brynley F. Roberts, ' "The Age of Restitution": Taliesin ab Iolo and the Reception of Iolo Morganwg', in *A Rattleskull Genius*, ed. Jenkins, 467–9.
77. National Library of Wales, MS 13144A, pp. 227–39, 242–4, 385–6, 390.
78. What follows is taken from *Barddas*, ed. John Williams ab Ithel i (Llandovery, 1862), xxxiv–lxxxi, 17–53, 163–419 and ii (Llandovery, 1865), 13–99; and *Iolo Manuscripts*, ed. Taliesin Williams (Welsh Manuscripts Society, 1848), 430–8.
79. *Barddas*, ed. ab Ithel, ii. 37.
80. Ibid., i. xvi.
81. Miles, *The Secret of the Bards*, 67; Cardiff Public Library, MS 3.104, no. 17, William Owen to Edward Davies, 22 Jan. 1798.
82. Miles, *The Secret of the Bards*, 63–70.
83. S. C. Hall, *The Book of South Wales* (London, 1861), 223.
84. Miles, *The Secret of the Bards*, 63–70; Roy Denning, 'Druidism at Pontypridd', in *Glamorgan Historian. Volume One*, ed. Stewart Williams (Cowbridge: D. Brown, 1963), 139; National Library of Wales, MS 21178E, Gwilym Morganwg to Taliesin Williams.
85. Dillwyn Miles, *The Royal National Eisteddfod of Wales* (Swansea: Christopher Davies, 1978), 46–53; Geraint Jenkins, 'The Unitarian Firebrand, the Cambrian Society and the Eisteddfod', in *A Rattleskull Genuis*, ed. Jenkins, 269–92.
86. Cardiff Public Library, MS 3.82, Burgess to Edward Davies, 25 Aug. 1819.
87. Miles, *Secret of the Bards*, 70, 81–6; Jenkins, 'The Unitarian Firebrand', 290–1.
88. This is based on [W. J. Rees] 'Memoir of the Rev. Edward Davies', *Cambrian Quarterly Magazine* 12 (1831), 408–36; and Frank R. Lewis, 'Edward Davies 1756–1831', *Transactions of the Radnorshire Society* 39 (1969), 8–16.
89. [Rees] 'Memoir'; Cardiff Public Library, MS 3.104, vol. 6, no. 28, Owen to Davies, 16 March 1802.
90. Edward Davies, *Celtic Researches* (London, 1804); quotations from p. 119.
91. The basic story of it has been laid out in Moira Dearnley, ' "Mad Ned" and the "Smatter-Dasher": Iolo Morganwg and Edward "Celtic" Davies', in *A Rattleskull Genius*, ed. Jenkins, 425–52.
92. Cardiff Public Library, MS 3.86, Davies to Owen, 26 March 1792.
93. Dearnley, ' "Mad Ned" and the "Smatter-Dasher" ', 427–8; Cardiff Public Library, MS 3.104, vol. 6, no. 12, Owen to Davies 13 Aug. 1792.
94. This has now been quoted many times. It seems to have been first printed in Morgan, *A New History of Wales*, 115–16.
95. Edward Davies, *Elisa Powell, or, Trials of Sensibility* (London, 1795), i.183.
96. Cardiff Public Library, MS 3.104, vol. 6, no. 4, Iolo to Hardinge, 29 May 1804.
97. Dearnley, ' "Mad Ned" and the "Smatter-Dasher" ', 433–5.
98. Ibid., 436.
99. Edward Davies, *The Mythology and Rites of the British Druids* (London, 1809), 5, 33, 56–7.
100. Ibid., 436–41. I have quoted directly from Iolo's letter in the *Cambrian Register* 3 (1818), 382.
101. [Rees], 'Memoir', 430.

102. Bryant's book was published in London in 1774–6. The most convenient summary of his life is in the entry by Dennis R. Dean, in the *Oxford Dictionary of National Biography*.

103. Faber's book was *A Dissertation on the Mysteries of the Cabiri* (2 vols, 1803). His life is summed up in the *Oxford Dictionary of National Biography*.

104. Dennis Dean, in the *Oxford Dictionary of National Biography*: see n. 102 above.

105. On which see Sir Ifor Williams, *Lectures on Early Welsh Poetry* (Dublin, 1944); David Dumville, 'Early Welsh Poetry: Problems of Historicity', in *Early Welsh Poetry: Studies in the Book of Aneirin*, ed. Brynley F. Roberts (Aberystwyth: University of Wales, 1988), 1–16; and G. R. Isaac, 'Gweith Gwen Ystrat and the Northern Heroic Age of the Sixth Century', *Cambrian Medieval Celtic Studies* 36 (1998), 61–70.

106. The material in the following paragraph is taken from Edward Davies, *The Mythology and Rites of the British Druids* (London, 1809), 85–410.

107. The oldest version surviving is in National Library of Wales, Peniarth MS 111, written in about 1610. Sir Ifor Williams decided that 'the prose is definitely medieval, with the orthography modernised, but still retaining older forms here and there', and with post-medieval poems inserted: *Lectures on Early Welsh Poetry*, 60. He does not, however, say how early or late the medieval forms are.

108. This derivation of Williams's is discussed and approved by Rachel Bromwich, in her edition of *Trioedd Ynys Prydein* (Cardiff: University of Wales Press, 1978), 308.

109. Quotation on p. 492 of Davies, *Mythology and Rites*.

110. [Rees], 'Memoir', 434–6.

111. William Owen, *The Cambrian Biography* (London, 1803); for example, Hu Gadarn is on pp. 178–80.

112. Edward Jones, *Musical and Poetical Relicks of the Welsh Bards* (London, 1794), 2–9; and *The Bardic Museum* (London, 1802), iii–ix.

113. Prys Morgan, 'Iolo Morganwg and Welsh Historical Traditions', in *A Rattleskull Genius*, ed. Jenkins, 252.

114. Benjamin Heath Malkin, *The Scenery, Antiquities and Biography of South Wales* (London, 1807), i. 191.

115. Peter Roberts, *The Early History of the Cymry* (London, 1803), 85, 151; William Probert, *The Ancient Laws of Cambria* (London, 1823), passim.

116. William Richards, *The Welsh Nonconformists' Memorial* (London, 1820), 1–70.

117. John Hughes, *Horae Britannicae* (London, 1816), i. 145–307, passim.

118. Theophilus Jones, *A History of the County of Brecknock* (Brecon, 1805), 199–213.

119. Phillips, 'Forgery and Patronage', 421.

120. John Jones, *The History of Wales* (London, 1824), 185–262.

121. Ibid., 236.

122. David Williams, *The History of Monmouthshire* (London, 1796), 18–27; quotations from pp. 22, 25–6.

123. 'Observations on Certain Discrepancies of Opinion among some of our Modern Archaiologists upon the Character of Druidism', *Cambrian Register* 3 (1811), 9–10. This is quoted and analysed in Dearnley, ' "Mad Ned" and the "Smatter-Dasher" ', 440.

124. Morgan, *A New History of Wales*, 122–3.

125. Robert Southey, *Madoc* (Edinburgh, 1805), xi. 108–16, 453–523.

126. Richard Colt Hoare, *The Itinerary of Archbishop Baldwin through Wales* (London, 1806), ii. 317–18; and *The Ancient History of North Wiltshire* (London, 1819), 65–83.

127. The name of the paper is lost, but the letter is preserved in the Wiltshire Archaeological and Natural History Society Library, Devizes, Cuttings Collection, vol. 1, p. 15.

128. Samuel Rush Meyrick and Charles Hamilton Smith, *The Costume of the Original Inhabitants of the British Islands* (London, 1815), 17–36.

129. Such as Samuel Greathead, 'Inquiries respecting the Origin of the Inhabitants of the British Islands', *Archaeologia* 16 (1812), 95–122; and Charles Hulbert, *The Religions of Britain* (3rd edn, Shrewsbury, 1826), 10–42.

130. J. Britton et al., *The Beauties of England and Wales* (London, 1814), xv. 371–3, 703–14.

131. Benjamin Vale, *A Lecture on Ancient Druidism* (London, 1824).

132. Waring, *Recollections and Anecdotes*, 116.

133. Ceri W. Lewis, 'Iolo Morganwg and Strict-Metre Welsh Poetry', 92.

6 Interlude: A Pair of Williams

1. William Cooke, *Inquiry into the Patriarchal and Druidical Religion* (London, 1754).
2. [Charles Lucas], *The Old Serpentine Temple of the Druids, at Avebury* (Marlborough, 1795).
3. Thomas Carte, *A General History of England* (London, 1747), 30–70; quotation from p. 35. The 'proposal' for the work is printed as a preface. In the notes to this chapter, biographical details for the authors discussed are taken from the *Oxford Dictionary of National Biography*, unless stated otherwise.
4. Edmund Burke, *An Abridgement of English History*, in his *Works* (new edn, London, 1813), x. 186–202; quotation from p. 194.
5. Hugh Blair, *A Critical Dissertation on the Poems of Ossian* (Edinburgh, 1763), 12.
6. John Smith, *Gallic Antiquities* (Edinburgh, 1780), 1–85; quotation from p. 85.
7. James Macpherson, *Fingal: An Ancient Epic Poem* (London, 1762), x; and Macpherson, *The Poems of Ossian: A New Edition* (London, 1773), ii. 215–21; quotations from p. 215.
8. Fiona J. Stafford, *The Sublime Savage: A Study of James Macpherson and the Poems of Ossian* (Edinburgh: Edinburgh University Press, 1988), 162.
9. Macpherson, *The Poems of Ossian*, ii. 215.
10. James Macpherson, *An Introduction to the History of Great Britain and Ireland* (London, 1771). I have used the third edition, of 1773, with the Druids on pp. 209–43. For an earlier, English, author who took much the same attitude, see Tobias Smollett, *Complete History of England* (London, 1757), i. 9–17.
11. William Hutchinson, *An Excursion to the Lakes in Westmoreland and Cumberland* (London, 1774), 98–9, 148–9.
12. Ibid., 112–13.
13. William Hutchinson, *The History and Antiquities of the County Palatine of Durham* (Newcastle, 1785), i, ii–iv; quotations from p. iii. I am grateful to Owen Davies for sending me copies of these passages.
14. William Hutchinson, *The History of the County of Cumberland* (Carlisle, 1794), i. 4–5.
15. William Gilpin, *Observations, Relative Chiefly to Picturesque Beauty* (3rd edn, London, 1792), ii. 28.
16. William Gilpin, *Observations on the Western Parts of England* (3rd edn, London 1808), 80.
17. John Whitaker, *The History of Manchester* (London, 1771), 393–6.
18. Reuben Burrow, 'A Proof that the Hindus had the Binomial Theorem', *Asiatic Researches* 2 (1790), 487–97.
19. Thomas Maurice, *Indian Antiquities*, i (London, 1793), part iii, 491, and vi (London, 1796), part i, sig. B.
20. Francis Wilford, 'Essay on the Sacred Islands in the West', *Asiatic Researches* 8 (1805), 11–152, and 11 (1810), 245–368.
21. Letter to the *Gentleman's Magazine* 61 (1791), 106–8.
22. John Pinkerton, *An Enquiry into the History of Scotland Preceding the Reign of Malcolm III* (London, 1789), i. 17–18. For Pinkerton's place in the intellectual society of his day, see Rosemary Sweet, *Antiquaries: The Discovery of the Past in Eighteenth-Century Britain* (London: Hambledon and London, 2004), 138–40.
23. Edward Ledwich, 'A Dissertation on the Religion of the Druids', *Archaeologia* 7 (1785), 303–22.
24. Edward King, *Munimenta Antiqua* (London, 1799), 113–345; quotations from pp. 209, 235.
25. Robert Henry, *The History of Great Britain* (London, 1771), i. 91–122; quotations from pp. 92, 122.
26. John Macpherson, *Critical Dissertations on the Origins, Antiquities, Language, Government, Manners and Religion of the Ancient Caledonians* (London, 1768), 341–6; quotations from pp. 344, 346.
27. David Hume, *The History of England. Volume One* (London, 1761), 4.
28. Joseph Strutt, *The Chronicle of England* (London, 1779), i. 189–200; quotations from pp. 189–90.
29. As Blake's poems have been published in so many editions, reference to them here will be by title, section and line: thus, the passage here is from *Europe, a Prophecy*, plate 10, lines 1–102.
30. *Vala, or The Four Zoas*, 'Night the Second', lines 37–40.

31. I am very grateful to my colleague at Bristol University, the leading Blake scholar David Punter, for making this possibility plain to me.

32. *Milton*, plate 6, lines 20–5, plate 11, lines 116–18; and see also plate 9, lines 2, 14.

33. For which see *Blake Records*, ed. G. E. Bentley Jnr (2nd edn, New Haven, Conn.: Yale University Press, 2004), 307–8.

34. Peter Ackroyd, *Blake* (London: Sinclair Stevenson, 1995), 305; Ruthven Todd, *Tracks in the Snow* (London: Grey Walls Press, 1946), 49–52; Arthur Johnston, 'William Blake and "The Ancient Britons"', *National Library of Wales Journal* 22 (1981–2), 304–20.

35. 'A Descriptive Catalogue', in *Poetry and Prose of William Blake*, ed. Geoffrey Keynes (London, 1941), 578, 609–10.

36. It is illustrated as one of the plates in Raymond Lister, *The Paintings of William Blake* (Cambridge: Pevensey Press, 1986).

37. *Jerusalem, the Emanation of the Giant Albion*, chapter 2, plate 27, lines 48–50, 55–8; plate 46, line 14; plate 50, lines 1–2; chapter 3, plate 52, lines 11–16; plate 57, lines 5–7; plate 63, lines 1–4, 8–9, 23–5; plate 66, line 84; plate 67, line 1; plate 69, lines 38–40; plate 89, lines 30–4; plate 92, lines 23–6; plate 93, line 25; plate 98, lines 47–50.

38. 'The Ghost of Abel', plate 2, lines 13–20.

39. This is equally true of such prominent Blake scholars as Denis Saurat, Northrop Frye, George Mills Harper, Peter E. Fisher, Jon Mee and Jason Whittaker; though to say as much is not to undervalue the elegance and perception with which they have written on the subject.

40. A. L. Owen, *The Famous Druids* (Oxford: Oxford University Press, 1962), 224–36; quotation from p. 227.

41. Peter E. Fisher, *The Valley of Vision: Blake as Prophet and Revolutionary*, ed. Northrop Frye (Toronto: University of Toronto Press, 1961), 36.

42. Jon Mee, ' "Images of Truth New Born": Iolo, William Blake and the Literary Radicalism of the 1790s', in *A Rattleskull Genius*, ed. Geraint H. Jenkins (Cardiff: Cardiff University Press, 2005), 173–93.

43. Ackroyd, *Blake*, 98; *Blake Records*, ed. Bentley, 743–4.

44. Todd, *Tracks in the Snow*, 52, cites an early nineteenth-century medal belonging to the United Ancient Order of Druids, which was (by the 1940s) reputed to have been designed by Blake. He thought the representation of Stonehenge on it did bear some resemblance to the stone circles drawn by Blake for *Milton* and *Jerusalem*. While this is certainly evidence, it is clearly inconclusive, and does nothing to get round the problems listed against Blake's involvement with the order.

45. Ross Nichols, *The Book of Druidry* (London: Aquarian, 1990), 103–4.

46. Ibid., 98.

47. *Blake Records*, ed. Bentley, 167–88. The fact that Nichols referred to the court that tried Blake as the assizes, when in fact it was the quarter sessions, indicates that he never saw any records of it himself and was repeating a story heard from somebody else. I have not, however, come across it in any other source.

48. Nichols, *The Book of Druidry*, 98.

49. As well as references above, see ibid., 20, 148, 233, and the magazine exchange, in the *International Times* 111 (26 Aug.–9 Sept. 1971), 16–17 and 115 (21 Oct.–7 Nov. 1971), 15. While Nichols's enthusiasm is touching, and understandable, it is hard to look with equanimity on his systematic spreading of false data, and his attempts in the process to discredit more careful researchers, such as the scholarly biographer of Blake, Kathleen Raine, and the unfortunate contributor to the magazine, as ill informed. I would not strike so hard at his pronouncements about Blake, had I not – like the claim that Toland founded the Universal Bond in 1717 – heard them repeated as fact by so many people.

50. *The Complete Works of Thomas Chatterton*, ed. Donald S. Taylor (Oxford: Oxford University Press, 1971), i. 379–80.

51. James Foot, *Pensoroso* (London, 1771); quotations from p. 164.

52. Michael Wodhull, *Poems* (London, 1772), n.p., 'Ode to the Dryads'.

53. *The Poetical Works of Goldsmith, Collins and Thomas Warton*, ed. George Gilfillan (Edinburgh, 1854), 269.

54. *The Poetical Works of John Langhorne*, ed. J. T. Langhorne (London, 1804), ii. 41.

55. Robert Holmes, *Alfred: An Ode* (Oxford, 1778), 10–11.

56. George Richards, *The Aboriginal Britons, A Poem* (Oxford, 1791), 19.

57. Richard Polwhele, *The Fate of Lewellyn* (Bath, 1777), 35–44; and *Poems* (London, 1806), i. 8, and iii. 7–8.

58. William Wordsworth, 'The Vale of Esthwaite', lines 25–34.

59. William Wordsworth, 'A Night on Salisbury Plain', lines 91–4, 181–6, 191–8, 424–7. His account of how he came to write the poem is in the 'Advertisement' to 'Guilt and Sorrow', which he published in 1842.

60. William Wordsworth, 'Adventures on Salisbury Plain', lines 154–9.

61. William Wordsworth, *The Prelude*, Book 13, lines 312–19.

62. William Wordsworth, *The Prelude*, ed. Ernest de Selincourt (Oxford: Oxford University Press, 2nd edn, 1959), 74–5.

63. William Wordsworth, *The Excursion*, Book 11 ('Discourse of the Wanderer, and an Evening Visit to the Lake').

64. William Wordsworth, 'The Pass of Kirkstone', lines 1–20.

65. William Wordsworth, 'The Monument Commonly Called Long Meg and Her Daughters, near the River Eden'.

66. *The Poetical Works of William Wordsworth*, ed. Ernest de Selincourt and Helen Darbishire (Oxford, 1949), iii. 557.

67. William Wordsworth, 'Trepidation of the Druids'; 'Druidical Excommunication'; and 'Struggle of the Britons against the Barbarians'.

68. William Wordsworth, 'Humanity', lines 1–15.

69. William Wordsworth, 'Guilt and Sorrow'.

70. Richard Gravil, *Wordsworth's Bardic Vocation 1787–1842* (Basingstoke: Palgrave Macmillan, 2003), 19–20.

7 The Apogee of the English Druids

1. Henry James Pye, *Alfred* (London, 1801), 153.

2. Felicia Dorothea Hemans, *Poetical Works* (Oxford, 1914), 165.

3. Thomas Love Peacock, 'The Genius of the Thames', for which I have used the 1927 London edition of his *Works*, vi. 123–9.

4. Alfred, Lord Tennyson, 'The Druid's Prophecies', for which I have used the 1987 Longman edition of his *Poems*, edited by Christopher Ricks, i. 116–20.

5. Thomas Edwards Hankinson, *The Druids* (Cambridge, 1827), reprinted as 'The Druid's Lament' in his collected *Poems* (London, 1844); quotation from p. 11 of the former and p. 327 of the latter.

6. The English version of Romani's libretto was published in London in 1841; its British performance history is discussed in Sam Smiles, *The Image of Antiquity: Ancient Britain and the Antiquarian Imagination* (New Haven, Conn.: Yale University Press, 1994), 108–9.

7. *The Druid and Holy King* (Leamington Spa, 1838) (anonymous, but actually by Sarah Hamilton).

8. Richard Alfred Davenport, 'The Dying Druid', reprinted, from an unnamed periodical that had appeared 'some years' before, as an appendix to Esther Le Hardy, *Agabus* (London, 1851), 153–6.

9. Ibid., 124.

10. Edward Quillinan, *Woodcuts and Verses* (London, 1820), 24.

11. Christopher Wordsworth, *The Druids* (London, 1827); quotation from pp. 9–10.

12. William Stanley Roscoe, *Poems* (London, 1834), 74.

13. Bulwer-Lytton, *King Arthur* (1849). I have used the 1875 edition, where the passage appears on p. 272, the commentary on pp. 365–6.

14. Le Hardy, *Agabus*; quotation from pp. 24–8.

15. C. Blencowe Dunn, *The Modern Druid* (London, 1857). A copy is held in the British Library.

16. It is in the list of nineteenth-century Druid orders held in the John Goodchild Collection at Wakefield Public Library, Yorkshire.

17. *Rites and Ceremonies of the Loyal Order of Druids* (Bolton, 1848). A copy is preserved in the John Goodchild Collection.

18. From the list in the John Goodchild Collection.

19. J. W. Shaw, *Historical Notes on the Order of Druids* (Manchester, 1936), 1–3. A copy of this work is in the John Goodchild Collection.

20. *Rules to be Observed by the Members of the Druid Friendly Society* (Salisbury, 1853). A copy survives in Salisbury Public Library.

21. It is in the list in John Goodchild's collection.

22. J. Frome Wilkinson, *Mutual Thrift* (London, 1891), 130.

23. George Jones, *Druidism Historically Considered* (Bristol, 1856); quotation from p. 15. A copy is held by the National Library of Scotland.

24. John Hoyle, *Lectures* (Manchester, 1861).

25. J. Mordaunt Crook, *The British Museum* (London: Allen Lane, 1972), 126–7.

26. Genesis 28:18–19; 31:44–54; 35:14–20; Exodus 20:21–5; 24:4; Joshua 4:3–23; 7:26; 24:26–7; II Samuel 18:17–18.

27. *Identity of the Religions Called Druidical and Hebrew* (London, 1829).

28. Sir Richard Colt Hoare, *The Ancient History of North Wiltshire* (London, 1819), 65–83.

29. John Bathurst Deane, *On the Worship of the Serpent* (London, 1830; 2nd edn 1833); 'Observations on Dracontia', *Archaeologia* 25 (1834), 188–229.

30. William Lisle Bowles, *Hermes Britannicus* (London, 1828).

31. Edward Duke, *The Druidical Temples of the County of Wilts* (London, 1846); quotation from p. 28.

32. John Lockhart Ross, *Traces of Primitive Truth in the Principal Nations of the World* (London, 1858), 92–102; 'Druidism in Connection with Wiltshire', *Wiltshire Archaeological and Natural History Society Magazine* 5 (1859), 149–92; 'The Picts', *Wiltshire Archaeological and Natural History Society Magazine* 6 (1860), 224–44.

33. E.g. L. Vernon Harcourt, *The Doctrine of the Deluge* (London, 1838).

34. E.g. John Kitto, *Palestine: The Bible History of the Holy Land* (London, 1841), 341–55.

35. E.g. Benjamin Vale, *A Lecture on Druidism* (London, 1824); Thomas Stackhouse, *Two Lectures on the Remains of Ancient Pagan Britain* (London, 1833); 'An Oxonian', *Thaumaturgia* (London, 1835), 75–90.

36. E.g. *The London Hermit's Tour to the York Festival* (York, 1811), 117–35; H. Barry, *Caesar and the Britons* (London, 1831), 16–39; Henry Lawes Long, *A Survey of the Early Geography of Western Europe* (London, 1859), 100–95.

37. E.g. Joseph Cottle, *The Fall of Cambria* (London, 1811), i. 70; Samuel Seyer, *Memoirs Historical and Topographical of Bristol and its Neighbourhood* (Bristol, 1821), 88–92; Mary Martha Sherwood, *The Druids of Britain* (London, n.d. but *c.* 1840); H. E. Grover, *A Voice from Stonehenge* (London: Cleaver, 1847); Martin Farquhar Tupper, 'A Discourse on British Druidism', *Sharpe's London Journal* (1849), 156–60; Julia Corner, *The Ancient Britons* (London, 1850); *The Religion of Ancient Britain Historically Considered* (London, 1846).

38. E.g. J. H. Williams, 'On the Druidical Remains of the Ancient Britons', *Transactions of the Bedfordshire Architectural Society* (1853), 406–27; 'Stonehenge', *London Magazine* 3rd series 1 (1828), 195–204; Meadows Taylor, 'Cairns, etc., in the Dekhan', *Transactions of the Royal Irish Academy* 24 (1862), 329–62.

39. E.g. William T. P. Shortt, *Collectanea Curiosa Dumnonia* (Exeter, 1842), 19–27. Other cases of use of Iolo's material will be noted in different contexts below, and in addition there is James Yeowall, *Chronicles of the Ancient British Church* (London, 1847), 6–9, and E. S. Appleyard, *Welsh Sketches: First Series* (London, 1853), 1–36.

40. Listed by the master of this field: Smiles, *The Image of Antiquity*, 104–5.

41. Gerard Edwards Smith, *Stonehenge: A Poem* (Oxford, 1823); quotation from pp. 4–5.

42. S. R. Clark, *Vestigia Anglicana* (London, 1826), i. 1–5; Sir F. Palgrave, *A History of England: Volume One* (London, 1831, with later eds 1850 and 1868); Charles Knight, *Old England* (London, 1845), i. 3–10; George Matcham, *Stonehenge* (London, 1851); Beale Poste, *Britannic Researches* (London, 1853), 282–9.

43. 'A Visit to Stonehenge', *The Leisure Hour* 94 (1853), 657–61.

44. James Eason, *Conjectures on that Mysterious Monument of Ancient Art, Stonehenge* (Salisbury, 1815; 2nd and enlarged edn, 1820); Sir Richard Colt Hoare, *The Ancient History of South Wiltshire* (London, 1812), 140–73; J. Britton, *Account of Stonehenge* (London, 1842); 'The Great Mystery on Salisbury Plain', *Sharpe's London Magazine* (1847), 216–18; Walter Thornbury, 'A Strolling Poet's Ride to Stonehenge', *The National Magazine* (May 1859),

292–6. [F. W. Zillwood], *Stonehenge* (London, 1855); W. Michael, *Stonehenge* (London, 1864); Sir Henry James, *Plans and Photographs of Stonehenge* (Southampton, 1867).

45. *A Guide to the Druid Temple in the Church Cemetery, Nottingham* (Nottingham, 1850). A copy survives in Nottingham University's Hallward Library.

46. This sketch is based on Higgins's entry in the *Oxford Dictionary of National Biography*, the preface to the Philosophical Research Society's 1977 reprint of *The Celtic Druids*; Leslie Shepard, 'The "Anacalypsis" of Godfrey Higgins', *Theosophical History* 1 (1985), 46–63; and Joscelyn Godwin, *The Theosophical Enlightenment* (Albany: State University of New York Press, 1994), 76–80.

47. Godfrey Higgins, *The Celtic Druids* (London, 1829); quotations from the preface and p. 299.

48. Ibid., pp. 32, 191–3, 198–9.

49. Godfrey Higgins, *Anacalypsis, an Attempt to Draw Aside the Veil of the Saitic Isis* (2 vols, London, 1836).

50. A point made by the first scholar to study the phenomenon comprehensively: Hoxie Neale Fairchild, *The Noble Savage* (New York: Columbia University Press, 1928).

51. Thomas Dudley Fosbrooke, *Encyclopaedia of Antiquities* (London, 1825), 768–89.

52. Edward King, *Munimenta Antiqua* (London, 1799), 208–9. His responsibility for the name 'Slaughter Stone' was noticed by Leslie Grinsell, *The Druids and Stonehenge* (Guernsey: Toucan, 1978), p. 11.

53. Mary Russell Mitford, *Christina, the Maid of the South Seas* (London, 1811), 33–4.

54. T. R. S. Boase, 'The Decoration of the New Palace of Westminster, 1841–1863', *Journal of the Warburg and Courtauld Institutes* 17 (1954), 341.

55. John Harris, *Luda: A Lay of the Druids* (London, 1868), 31–2.

56. Stephen Prentice, *Tintern and Stonehenge* (London, 1843), 33–4.

57. George Newby, *Henllywarc: or The Druid's Temple* (London, 1854), 13.

58. Frederick Paas, *The Archdruid: An Historical Poem* (Sidmouth, 1830); quotations from sigs C and E.

59. John Kenrick, 'Serpent Worship and the Age of Stonehenge', *Prospective Review* 727 (Aug. 1851), 299–307.

60. For which see Norman Vance, *The Victorians and Ancient Rome* (Oxford: Blackwell, 1997); and Richard Hingley, *Roman Officers and English Gentlemen* (London: Routledge, 2000).

61. Quoted in ibid., 82.

62. Julia Corner, *Caldas: A Story of Stonehenge* (London, 1863).

63. [T. G. Lomax], *A Complete History of the Druids* (Lichfield, 1810); quotation from p. 4.

64. George Lillie Craik and Charles MacFarlane, *The Pictorial History of England* (London, 1844), i. 59–74.

65. Charles Dickens, *A Child's History of England* (London, 1852), 1–10; quotation from pp. 4–5.

66. Robert Kemp Philp, *The History of Progress in Great Britain* (London, 1859), 45–54.

67. George Kitson Clark, *The Making of Victorian England* (London: Methuen, 1962), 20.

68. Frederick William Faber, *Poems* (London, 1857), 273.

69. Newby, *Henllywarc*.

70. Francis Thackeray, *Researches into the Ecclesiastical and Political State of Ancient Britain under the Roman Emperors* (London, 1843), i. 1–40; quotations from pp. 27, 33, 35, 36.

71. Robert Southey, *The Book of the Church* (London, 1824); quotations from pp. 4–5.

72. Samuel Rush Meyrick and Charles Hamilton Smith, *The Costume of the Original Inhabitants of the British Islands* (London, 1815); quotation from p. 18, illustration on p. 28.

73. John Lingard, *A History of England* (3rd edition, London, 1835), i. 19–26; quotations from pp. 21, 25.

74. Thomas Timpson, *British Ecclesiastical History* (London, 1838), 9–12; quotation from pp. 11–12.

75. 'The Great Mystery on Salisbury Plain', 218.

76. Robert Weaver, *Monumenta Antiqua* (London, 1840); quotation from pp. 154–5.

77. Ronald Hutton, *The Druids* (London: Hambledon Continuum, 2007), 110–18.

78. E.g. William Augustus Miles and John Fitzgerald Pennie, both quoted in Barry M. Marsden, *The Early Barrow Diggers* (Stroud: Tempus, 1999), 42–3, 95; Thomas Stokes Salmon, *Stonehenge: A Prize Poem* (Oxford, 1823), 5–6; J. H. B., 'Stonehenge', *Gentleman's Magazine* 91.1 (1827), 631–2; C. H., 'Stonehenge', *Gentleman's Magazine* 102.1 (1832), 452; John Marshall,

The Druid's Talisman (London, 1845); *The Poetical Works of William Lisle Bowles*, ed. George Gilfillan (Edinburgh, 1855), i. 105.

79. *Travels of a British Druid; or, The Journal of Elynd* (London, 1811); quotations from pp. 30–3.
80. Malachi Mouldy, *Stonehenge: or, The Romans in Britain* (3 vols, London, 1842).
81. *The Ancient Britons: A Tale of Primeval Life* (London, 1851); quotations from pp. 321–2.

8 Iolo's Children

1. Apart from the titles discussed below, see Jonathan Williams, *Druopaedia* (Leominster, 1828); J. Roberts, *Druidical Remains and Antiquities of the Ancient Britons* (Swansea, 1842); John Williams, *Gomer* (London, 1854); and *An Essay on the Megalithic Structures in Auvergne* (London, 1857); J. G. Pym ap Ednyfed, *A Half Hour with the Druids* (Caernarvon, 1859); Jane Williams, *A History of Wales* (London, 1864), 4–10; John Jones Thomas, *Britannia Antiquissima* (Melbourne, 2nd edn, 1866), 101–51. An apparently unique example of a Welsh author who accepted the general English view that the Druids had once held the true patriarchal religion but become seriously corrupted was D. Lewis, 'An Essay on the Mythology of the Ancient Britons', *Transactions of the Cymmrodorion* 2 (1828), 98–121. Significantly, he was both an early contributor and tried to use Graeco-Roman sources to balance Iolo's evidence.
2. Angharad Llwyd, *A History of the Island of Mona* (Ruthin, 1833), 32–50; quotations from pp. 38, 49. A copy exists in the library of Queen's College, Oxford.
3. David James, *The Patriarchal Religion of Britain* (London, 1836); quotation from p. 39.
4. John Jones, *On the State of Agriculture* (London, 1851).
5. G. T., 'Vulgar Errors', *Cambrian Journal* 6 (1859), 151–5.
6. 'Griffith', *The Welsh Question and Druidism* (London, 1887). A copy survives in the British Library.
7. For a convenient potted discussion of this, see Ronald Hutton, *Witches, Druids and King Arthur: Studies in Paganism, Myth and Magic* (London: Hambledon and London, 2003), 2–5.
8. On all this, see Krishan Kumar, *The Making of English National Identity* (Cambridge: Cambridge University Press, 2003); Hugh A. MacDougall, *Racial Myth in English History* (Montreal: Harvest Home, 1982); *Englishness: Politics and Culture 1880–1920*, ed. Robert Colls and Philip Dodd (London: Croom Helm, 1986); Richard Hingley, *Roman Officers and English Gentlemen* (London: Routledge, 2000); Gerald Newman, *The Rise of English Nationalism* (London: Weidenfeld and Nicolson, 1987).
9. Thomas Hughes, *The Scouring of the White Horse* (Cambridge, 1859), 44.
10. The place of Druids in the cultural dimensions of the modern Irish nationalist revival is a huge subject in itself, for which I came across scores of sources during the research for this book. It deserves a historian based in Ireland and with a profound knowledge of the Old and Middle Irish sources on which the revival was largely based.
11. Brynley F. Roberts, ' "The Age of Restitution": Taliesin ab Iolo and the Reception of Iolo Morganwg', in *A Rattleskull Genius*, ed. Geraint H. Jenkins (Cardiff: University of Wales Press, 2005), 461–79.
12. What follows is based on Gwyn A. Williams, *The Merthyr Rising* (London: Croom Helm, 1978); David J. V. Jones, *Before Rebecca: Popular Protests in Wales 1793–1835* (London: Allen Lane, 1973); and *The Last Rising: The Newport Insurrection of 1839* (Oxford: Oxford University Press, 1985); and the resources of the Cyfarthfa Castle Museum, the Merthyr Heritage Centre, the Pontypridd Museum and the Rhondda Heritage Centre.
13. What follows in the next two paragraphs is summarized in Hutton, *Witches, Druids and King Arthur*, 5–8, with a list of source references. Some material has been added here from Dillwyn Miles, *The Royal National Eisteddfod of Wales* (Swansea: Christopher Davies, 1978), 51–2, and *The Secret of the Bards of the Isle of Britain* (Llandybie: Gwasg Dinefwr Press, 1992), 92.
14. Quoted in Williams, *The Merthyr Rising*, 80.
15. Letter from Taliesin to the *Merthyr Guardian*, 3 Jan. 1835.
16. Williams, *The Merthyr Rising*, 85; David Morgans, *Music and Musicians of Merthyr and District* (Merthyr Tydfil, 1922), 207–8.
17. Williams, *The Merthyr Rising*, 75, 97.
18. It took this name in 1856, but to avoid confusion I shall use it henceforth.

19. Miles, *The Secret of the Bards*, 70.
20. Ibid., 95; Roberts, ' "The Age of Restitution" ', 471.
21. Miles, *The Secret of the Bards*, 92.
22. Henry Bruce, *The Prize Translation of the Welsh Ode on the British Druids by Mr Taliesin Williams* (London, 1835). A copy survives in Cardiff University Library.
23. Miles, *The Secret of the Bards*, 21.
24. Ibid., 95–6. Mary-Ann Constantine has an excellent paper on Villemarqué's relationship with the Welsh revival, which is currently awaiting publication.
25. *Coelbren y Beirdd*, ed. Taliesin Williams (Llanymddyfri, 1840).
26. Roberts, ' "The Age of Restitution" ', 474–5.
27. *Iolo Manuscripts: A Selection of Ancient Welsh Manuscripts*, ed. Taliesin Williams (Liverpool, 1848).
28. Roberts, ' "The Age of Restitution" ', 477.
29. Huw Walters, 'Myfyr Morganwg and the Rocking-Stone Gorsedd', in *A Rattleskull Genius*, ed. Jenkins, 481–500.
30. Morien, *History of Pontypridd and the Rhondda Valleys* (Pontypridd, 1903), 85.
31. Walters, 'Myfyr Morganwg', 484–5.
32. Miles, *The Secret of the Bards*, 71.
33. Walters, 'Myfyr Morganwg', 485.
34. Morien, *History of Pontypridd*; and obituary of Myfyr in the *Western Mail* (24 Feb. 1888).
35. National Museum of Welsh Life, MS 50/5128 (Price's chart of his family tree).
36. John Cule, 'Dr. William Price (1800–1893) of Llantrisant: A Study of an Eccentric' (Cambridge University MD thesis, 1960).
37. T. Islwyn Nicholas, *A Welsh Heretic: Dr William Price, Llantrisant* (London, 1940); Brian Davies, 'Empire and Identity: The "Case" of Dr William Price', in *A People and a Proletariat: Essays in the History of Wales 1780–1980* (London: Pluto, 1980), 72–93; Dean Powell, *Eccentric: The Life of Dr William Price* (Llantrisant: privately published, 2005). The last of these is, as suggested, the best, not least for its superb illustrations. It deserves a new edition with full source references.
38. Cyril Bracegirdle, *Dr William Price: Saint or Sinner?* (Llanrwst: Gwasg Carreg y Gwalch, 1997).
39. John Cule, as a trainee medic, not only pronounced him mad but diagnosed his illness as 'paraphrenia'. Brian Davies called him 'unquestionably not sane' (p. 92), and Dean Powell dubbed him 'eccentric' on his title-page but opened his study with the statement that 'few can dismiss claims that insanity prevailed' in Price's makeup (p. 3).
40. Ronald Hutton, *The Druids: A History* (London: Hambledon Continuum, 2007), ch. 6.
41. Cule, 'Dr. William Price', 23–31.
42. Ibid., 41–72; Powell, *Eccentric*, 29.
43. Powell, *Eccentric*, 137–8.
44. Ibid., 32–3.
45. Cule, 'Dr. William Price', 139.
46. Powell, *Eccentric*, 45.
47. Ibid., 40; Roy Denning, 'Druidism at Pontypridd', in *Glamorgan Historian. Volume One*, ed. Stewart Williams (Cowbridge: D. Brown, 1963), 140. I have added material from the advertisement, reprinted in the *Cardiff Times* (23 June 1888).
48. For a general account of what follows, see Jones, *The Last Rising*; for Price's part, Cule, 'Dr. William Price', 73–98.
49. Denning, 'Druidism at Pontypridd', 142–3; Powell, *Eccentric*, 52–8; *Cardiff Times* 16 June 1888.
50. National Archives, HO 40/57 (Bute to Normanby, 22 July 1848).
51. Quoted in Davies, 'Empire and Identity', 76.
52. Cule, 'Dr. William Price', says she was born in 1840 or 1841, but she was two years old in 1844 (for which see below).
53. Museum of Welsh Life, MS 50/5130.
54. Ibid., and MS 50/5129.
55. Davies, 'Empire and Identity', 90.
56. Quoted ibid., 78.

57. *Cardiff Times* 16 June 1888.
58. Cule, 'Dr. William Price', 16.
59. Powell, *Eccentric*, 17.
60. *Cardiff and Merthyr Guardian*, quoted ibid., 69.
61. National Library of Wales, MS 935C, fo. 57 (Price's letter).
62. *Western Mail* 24 Feb. 1888.
63. Walters, 'Myfyr Morganwg', 488–9.
64. Miles, *The Secret of the Bards*, 71–3.
65. Ibid., 72.
66. Meic Stephens, 'Sober Facts Too Much For Owen', *Pontypridd Observer* 3 Jan. 2002, 17.
67. Walters, 'Myfyr Morganwg', 489–90.
68. Miles, *The Secret of the Bards*, 90; Miles, *The Royal National Eisteddfod*, 141.
69. Morien, *History of Pontypridd*, 88–91; *Western Mail* 24 Feb. 1888.
70. See, for example, Roberts, ' "The Age of Restitution" ', 474.
71. Miles, *The Secrets of the Bards*, 96.
72. Thomas Stephens, *The Literature of the Kymry* (Llandovery, 1849); quotations from pp. 114–17, 188, 203.
73. Walters, 'Myfyr Morganwg', 493–4.
74. D. W. Nash, *Taliesin: Or, the Bards and Druids of Britain* (London, 1858); quotations from pp. 7, 35, 183, 259–60.
75. Matthew Arnold, *On the Study of Celtic Literature* (London, 1867); quotations from pp. iv–v, 12–13.
76. William F. Skene, *The Four Ancient Books of Wales* (Edinburgh, 1868); quotations from i. 8, 32.
77. John Williams, *The Church of England Independent of the Church of Rome in All Ages* (London, 1836).
78. John Williams, *An Essay, on the Question 'Whether the Druids Offered Human Sacrifices'* (Bala, 1842).
79. [James Kenward], 'Ab Ithel', *Cambrian Journal* 9 (1862), 273–332.
80. John Williams, *The Ecclesiastical Antiquities of the Cymry* (London, 1844); quotation from p. 38.
81. Ibid., 208; and *Cambrian Journal* 10 (1863), 32–62; Miles, *The Royal National Eisteddfod*, 55.
82. John Williams, 'Druidic Stones', *Archaeologia Cambrensis* NS 1 (1849), 1–9; Williams, 'Druidism', *Cambrian Journal* 2 (1855), 261–8; Williams, 'Druidism Typical of Christianity', *Cambrian Journal* 3 (1856), 343–56.
83. Miles, *The Secret of the Bards*, 97.
84. [John Williams], 'Congress of Bards, Pontypridd', *Cambrian Journal* 3 (1856), 201–4.
85. Prys Morgan, *A New History of Wales: The Eighteenth-Century Renaissance* (Llandybie: Christopher Davies, 1981), 122–3.
86. Ibid., 153–5; Miles, *The Royal National Eisteddfod*, 55–7.
87. J. G. Pym ap Ednyfed, for whom see above at n. 1.
88. Ibid., 56; Miles, *The Secret of the Bards*, 99–100, 202–3; [James Kenward], 'Ab Ithel', *Cambrian Journal* 11 (1864), 55–66, 113–40, 268–80.
89. In issues 5 (1858), 161–9, 353–63; 6 (1859), 10–29, 132–41, 241–55; and 7 (1860), 7–21.
90. *Barddas: Or a Collection of Original Documents, Illustrative of the Theology, Wisdom and Usages of the Bardo-Druidic System of the Isle of Britain*, ed. J. Williams ab Ithel (Llandovery: Welsh Manuscripts Society, 1862).
91. Elijah Waring, *Recollections and Anecdotes of Edward Williams* (London, 1850).
92. *Barddas. Volume Two*, ed. J. Williams ab Ithel (London, 1874).
93. Miles, *The Royal National Eisteddfod*, 57–83, 141–2; *The Secret of the Bards*, 102–37, 204–9.
94. William Gaunt, *Victorian Olympus* (London: Jonathan Cape, 1952), 135.
95. Myfyr Morganwg, *Hynafiaeth y Delyn Mewn Cysylltiad â Gorsedd Hu neu Drwn y Beirdd* (1860); *Gogoniant Hynafol y Cymmry* (1865); and *Hynafiaeth Aruthol y Trwn neu Orsedd Beirdd Ynys Brydain a'i Barddas Gyfrin* (1875).
96. Walters, 'Myfyr Morganwg', 495.
97. Morien, *History of Pontypridd*, 85.
98. Ab Ithel, 'Druidism', *Cambrian Journal* 2 (1855), 261–8.
99. Walters, 'Myfyr Morganwg', 496.

100. Wirt Sykes, *British Goblins: Welsh Folk-Lore, Fairy Mythology, Legends and Traditions* (London, 1880), 277–8; *Pontypridd District Herald* 29 June 1878.
101. Walters, 'Myfyr Morganwg', 497.
102. *Western Mail* 23 March 1879.
103. Ibid., 21 Dec. 1879.
104. Ibid., 20 March 1881.
105. Ibid., 20 June 1881.
106. Ibid., 27 Dec. 1882.
107. *Central Glamorgan Gazette* 28 March 1930.
108. Walters, 'Myfyr Morganwg', 491.
109. Ibid., 496.
110. Morien, *History of Pontypridd*, 88.
111. Ibid.
112. Walters, 'Myfyr Morganwg', 490.
113. Ibid., 496.
114. Ibid., 497.
115. Miles, *The Secret of the Bards*, 73.
116. *Western Mail* 29 Feb. 1888.
117. Pontypridd Museum, Certificate of Acceptance into the Gorsedd, 1877.
118. *Western Mail* 24, 25, 27, 28 and 29 Feb. 1888.
119. Ibid., 27 Feb. 1888.
120. Walters, 'Myfyr Morganwg', 498.
121. Miles, *The Secret of the Bards*, 126, 130.
122. Morien, *History of Pontypridd*, 97.
123. Denning, 'Druidism at Pontypridd', 143.
124. Something noted ibid., 144, and by Stephens, 'Sober Facts Too Much For Owen', 17.
125. Denning, 'Druidism at Pontypridd', 144.
126. Ibid.
127. John Michael Greer, *Phallic Religion in the Druid Revival* (Lewes: Order of Bards, Ovates and Druids, 2004), also at *http://druidry.org/pdfs*. I myself feel that Morien's thought was more complex and subtle than is suggested here, but this is still fine pioneering work that brings out the excitement and importance of its subject.
128. Owen Morgan (Morien), *The Light of Britannia* (Cardiff, 1890); Morgan, *Guide to the Gorsedd or Round Table and the Order of the Garter* (Cardiff, 1890); Morgan, *History of Pontypridd*; Morgan, *The Royal Winged Son of Stonehenge and Avebury* (published also under the title *Kimmerian Revelations* (Pontypridd, n.d.); Morgan, *A History of Wales* (Liverpool, 1911). All of these are held either in Cardiff University Library or Pontypridd Public Library.
129. *The Royal Winged Son*, reissued as *The Mabin of the Mabinogion* by Thorsons for the Research into Lost Knowledge Organization in 1984. This paperback reissue of a period piece is undoubtedly of help to scholarship, and the people responsible do not make any comment on whether the contents should be treated as genuine history.
130. This is the main argument of *Guide to the Gorsedd*.
131. Morien, *The Royal Winged Son*, 159.
132. Ibid., 93–5.
133. Ibid., 103.
134. The classic texts are William Jones, *On the Gods of Greece, Italy and India* (London, 1784); Pierre, Baron d'Hancarville, *Recherches sur l'origine, l'esprit et les progrès des arts de la Grèce* (Paris, 1785); Richard Payne Knight, *Discourse on the Worship of Priapus* (London, 1786); and Charles Dupuis, *L'Origine de tous les cultes* (Paris, 3 vols, 1795); quotation from i. viii. They are discussed in Peter Funnell, 'The Symbolic Language of Antiquity', in *The Arrogant Conoisseur*, ed. Michael Clarke and Nicholas Penny (Manchester: Manchester University Press, 1982), 50–64; Partha Mitter, *Much Maligned Monsters: The History of the European Reaction to Indian Art* (Oxford: Oxford University Press, 1977), 1–149; and Joscelyn Godwin, *The Theosophical Enlightenment* (Albany, NY: State University of New York Press, 1994), 1–35.
135. This cosmology is scattered, in fragments, through all of the five books cited in note 128, but the two key works are *The Light of Britannia*, where it is embryonic, and the *The Royal Winged Son*, where it is fully developed.

136. Morien, *The Royal Winged Son*, 165.
137. Ibid., 15–24. In *The Druids*, ch. 6, I got confused by Morien's double description of this rite, and substituted the River Rhondda for the Taff as the Styx. Anybody who knows Pontypridd well, as I do now, will realize that this is impossible.
138. Morien, *The Royal Winged Son*, 61, 119–20, 224. It is typical of Morien to put the three complementary sections of this rite so many pages apart.
139. Ibid., 23, 27–8, 119–20, 133–5.
140. Ibid., 133–5.
141. *The Light of Britannia*, 417.
142. *Western Mail* 17 Dec. 1921.
143. This story is well told in Powell, *Eccentric*, 72–5.
144. Printed in Cule, 'Dr. William Price', 182–4. More of these are printed on pp. 162–81.
145. Quoted in Powell, *Eccentric*, 71.
146. Nicholas, *A Welsh Heretic*, 30–34; Cule, 'Dr. William Price', 227–43; Powell, *Eccentric*, 3, 79–80.
147. The will is printed in Cule, 'Dr. William Price', 318.
148. A full translation of the book is printed in ibid., 195–219.
149. Cule, 'Dr. William Price', 244.
150. *Western Mail* 23 March 1881.
151. Ibid., 27 Dec. 1882.
152. The sources for what follows are collected, and the details reconstructed, in Cule, 'Dr. William Price', 250–305.
153. *Western Mail* 15 and 25 Jan., 3 April 1884.
154. *Cardiff Times* 16 June 1888. One of these medals is preserved in the Museum of Welsh Life, at St Fagan's near Cardiff, along with the final version of Price's formal dress.
155. *Western Mail* 13 March 1884.
156. *Cardiff Times* and *South Wales Weekly News* 12 April 1884.
157. Powell, *Eccentric*, 95.
158. *Cardiff Times* 19 and 26 May, 9, 16 and 23 June, 1888.
159. Powell, *Eccentric*, 103–18.
160. Ibid., 118 ('The Cremation of Dr Price'); Museum of Welsh Life, 'Lines on the Death and Cremation of the Grand Old Welshman Arch-Druid Doctor Price'.
161. *The Late Dr Price (of Llantrisant)* (Cardiff, 1896). A copy is held at the Cyfarthfa Castle Museum, Merthyr Tydfil.
162. Powell, *Eccentric*, 115–16.
163. Ibid., 124–7.
164. Nicholas, *A Welsh Heretic*, 7.
165. 'Druidical Symbol is Being Despoiled', *Pontypridd Observer* 4 March 1950.
166. Julian Cope, *The Modern Antiquarian* (London: Thorsons, 1998), 289.

9 *The Downfall of the Druids*

1. H. Browne, *Remarks on the Origin and Character of the Serpent and Temple at Avebury* (Devizes, 1823); quotation from p. 23.
2. Anon., *Our Holiday at Laverstock House Asylum* (London, 1860), 27–39. A copy survives in the library of the Salisbury and South Wiltshire Museum.
3. The eighth was published at Salisbury in 1867. A sample of them is preserved in the library of the Wiltshire Archaeological and Natural History Society at Devizes.
4. Lord Byron, *Don Juan* (London, 1823), canto XI, stanza xxv.
5. Edward Burne-Jones, 'The Druid and the Maiden', reprinted from the *Oxford and Cambridge Magazine* (1856), in *From the Isles of Dream*, ed. John Matthews (Edinburgh: Floris, 1993), 69–106.
6. Thomas Beesley, 'The Rollright Stones', *Transactions of the North Oxfordshire Archaeological Society* 3 (1853–5), 61–73; G. D. Barber Beaumont, *Suggestions on the Ancient Britons* (London, 1854), 5; J. O. Halliwell, *Rambles in West Cornwall* (London, 1861), 97–8, 113, 155.
7. Halliwell, *Rambles*, 155.

8. Algernon Herbert, *Britannia after the Romans* (London, 2 vols, 1836–41); Herbet, *An Essay on the NeoDruidic Heresy in Britannia* (London, 1838); Herbet, *Cyclops Christianus* (London, 1849).

9. Herbert, *Britannia after the Romans*, i. iv, xlv.

10. Herbert, *The NeoDruidic Heresy*, 38.

11. Ibid., 26–7.

12. This quotation is from Herbert, *Cyclops Christianus*, 108.

13. See the notices in the *Prospective Review* 727 (Aug. 1851), 299–307; *Quarterly Review* 91 (1852), 273–315; *Christian Remembrancer* (July 1852), 1–19; *Gentleman's Magazine* NS 32 (1849), 483–91.

14. John Rickman, 'On the Antiquity of Avebury and Stonehenge', *Archaeologia* 28 (1839), 399–419; Beale Poste, *Britannic Researches* (London, 1853), 282–9; James Fergusson, review article in *Quarterly Review* 108 (1860), 200–35; A. Stark, *Stonehenge* (Gainsborough, 1862). Some of these authors were only 'lesser' in the immediate context: Rickman was a distinguished statistician and civil servant, while Fergusson was to go on to make a prominent career as a wayward antiquary, and will be met again in this book.

15. George Chalmers, *Caledonia: Or an Account, Historical and Topographic, of North Britain* (London, 1807), 69–77.

16. *The Druid, or The Vision of Fingal* (London, 1815), 10.

17. James Logan, *The Scottish Gaël* (London, 1831), ii. 313–93.

18. Walter Scott, *The Pirate* (1831); I have used the 1860 Edinburgh edition, with the relevant passage at ii. 347–8; 'Druids', in *The Edinburgh Encyclopaedia: American Edition* 4 (1832), 767–75; quotations from p. 767. A copy exists in Cambridge University Library.

19. These writers were identified by Daniel Wilson, *The Archaeology and Prehistoric Annals of Scotland* (Edinburgh, 1851), 109, as Burry, Hibbert, Scott and Macculloch, but I have not yet been able to trace the works concerned.

20. Though both the French and the Danes had got there first. Of these, Peter Rowley-Conwy has argued convincingly that it was the Danish adoption of the expression 'forhistorisk', from the 1830s, which lay directly behind Wilson's usage of the English equivalent: *From Genesis to Prehistory* (Oxford: Oxford University Press, 2007), 44.

21. Wilson, *Archaeology and Prehistoric Annals*, and *Prehistoric Annals of Scotland* (London, 1863); quotation from the former book, p. 104; John Stuart, *Sculptured Stones of Scotland* (2 vols, Aberdeen, 1856 and 1867), i. i–xvii, and ii. xxii–xlii.

22. John Pratt, *The Druids* (Aberdeen, 1861).

23. John Hill Burton, 'Druids and Bards', *Edinburgh Review* 118 (1863), 40–70; quotation from p. 70.

24. Duncan Clerk, 'The Druids and Bards', and 'Decline and Fall of the Druids', *Transactions of the Lorn Ossianic Society* (1872–3), 10–24.

25. Rowley-Conwy, *From Genesis to Prehistory*, 137–76.

26. Glyn Daniel, *A Short History of Archaeology* (London: Thames and Hudson, 1981), 55–61; Rowley-Conwy, *From Genesis to Prehistory*, 37–81.

27. Chris Stringer, *Homo Britannicus* (London: Allen Lane, 2006), 25–40.

28. David Newsome, *The Victorian World Picture* (London: John Murray, 1997), 208–15.

29. James Morris, *Heaven's Command: An Imperial Progress* (London: Faber, 1973), 199.

30. A. H. L. F. Pitt-Rivers, 'Inaugural Address to the Annual Meeting of the Archaeological Institute', *Archaeological Journal* 44 (1887), 276.

31. A point strongly made by Colin Kidd, *British Identities before Nationalism* (Cambridge: Cambridge University Press, 1999), 290.

32. Peter J. Bowler, *The Invention of Progress: The Victorians and the Past* (Oxford: Blackwell, 1989), 77.

33. Rowley-Conwy, *From Genesis to Prehistory*, 60–5, 77–81.

34. Wilson, *Archaeology and Prehistoric Annals*, 104–353; quotation from p. 205.

35. To suggest this is not to assert that Lubbock single-handedly brought the new view of prehistory to victory; which would be a travesty of the truth. It became the orthodoxy between 1860 and 1880 because of the efforts of a small but dynamic group of archaeologists, supported by a few prominent geologists and naturalists: Rowley-Conwy, *From Genesis to Prehistory*, 235–85. What is emphasized here is the prominent part played by Lubbock in communicating it to a very wide public, as well as being the first English person to establish it within a clear overall framework.

36. *Oxford Dictionary of National Biography*, sub 'Lubbock, John'; Jonathan Rose, *The Intellectual Life of the British Working Classes* (New Haven, Conn.: Yale University Press, 2001), 128–32; *The Life-Work of Lord Avebury (Sir John Lubbock), 1834–1913*, ed. Adrian Grant (London, 1924), esp. 14–24.

37. Sven Nilsson, 'Stonehenge', *Transactions of the Ethnological Society* NS 4 (1866), 244–63.

38. E.g. John Timbs, *Nooks and Corners of English Life, Past and Present* (London, 1867), 14; *The Illustrated Guide to Old Sarum and Stonehenge* (Salisbury, 1882), 46 (there is a copy in the library of the Wiltshire Archaeological and Natural History Society).

39. Sven Nilsson, *The Primitive Inhabitants of Scandinavia* (London, 1867); for the ideological background, see Daniel, *Short History of Archaeology*, 113.

40. John Lubbock, *Pre-Historic Times* (London, 1865), 1–472; quotation from p. 465.

41. Ibid., 473–92; quotations from pp. 481, 490.

42. John Thurnam, 'Description of an Ancient Tumular Cemetery', *Archaeological Journal* 6 (1849), 123–36.

43. Joseph Barnard Davis and John Thurnam, *Crania Britannica* (London, 1865); quotation from p. 119.

44. John Thurnam, 'On Ancient British Barrows', *Archaeologia* 42 (1869), 161–244, and 43 (1871), 285–544.

45. Ibid., 1869, pp. 163–4.

46. W. Boyd Dawkins, *Early Man in Britain* (London, 1880), 4.

47. Tacitus, *Agricola*, XI.

48. Dawkins, *Early Man in Britain*, 233–497.

49. For early adoptions of it, by very different authors, see James Kenward, 'The Keltic Element in England', *Proceedings of the Birmingham Philological Society* 2 (1881), 309–42; Charles I. Elton, *Origins of English History* (London, 1882), 95–176; C. R. Conder, *Heth and Moab* (London, 1883); Pitt-Rivers, 'Inaugural Address', 261–77; A. H. Keane, *Ethnology* (Cambridge, 1895).

50. John Rhys, *Early Britain: Celtic Britain* (London, 1882); and Rhys, *Early Ethnology of the British Isles* (Edinburgh, 1891); Samuel Rawson Gardiner, *A Student's History of England* (London, 1890), 1–25; John Rhys and D. Brynmor Jones, *The Welsh People* (London, 1900), 1–36.

51. A. L. Lewis, 'Megalithic Monuments', *Journal of Anthropology* (1871), 286–96. See also his preceding pamphlet, *On Certain Druidical Monuments in Berkshire* (London, 1870), in which he makes the same points with relevance to a local case study. A copy exists in the Haddon Library, Cambridge.

52. A. L. Lewis, 'Stone Circles of Britain', *Archaeological Journal* 49 (1892), 136–54; quotation from p. 136.

53. Reported in the *Bristol Daily Post* 9 July 1877.

54. Kenneth Hudson, *A Social History of Archaeology* (London: Macmillan, 1930), 18–19.

55. Lysons's book was published at Oxford.

56. James Rust, *Druidism Exhumed* (Edinburgh, 1871); quotation from p. vi.

57. H. N. Hutchinson, *Prehistoric Man and Beast* (London, 1896); quotation from p. 206.

58. 'Report of Committee on the Age of Stone Circles', *Nature* 17 Oct. 1901, 615; Sir C. Hercules Read et al., *The Age of Stone Circles* (London, 1915).

59. There are, of course, far too many of these to list in notes: they can easily be sampled by reading through successive volumes of transactions of the numerous local antiquarian or archaeological societies of the period, or through the shelves of books, tracts and offprints in the library of the Wiltshire Archaeological and Natural History Society. A rare example of such a publication which does consider Druids (to dismiss them as irrelevant) is R. N. Worth, 'Were There Druids in Devon?', *Report and Transactions of the Devonshire Association* 12 (1880), 228–42. Another is 'Rollright Stones', *Transactions of the Bristol and Gloucestershire Archaeological Society* 16 (1892), 38–40, which describes an excursion made by this society to that famous group of megaliths. Participants were met by the Keeper of the Ashmolean Museum (and future discoverer of the Minoan civilization) Arthur Evans, who began by telling them to forget about the Druids. It is notable that Thomas Wise, 'Remarks on Celtic Monuments', *Transactions of the British Archaeological Association* 33 (1877), 158–69, went as far as India to find parallels for a possible priesthood among the 'Celts' who built stone avenues and circles, but never mentioned Druids. Just occasionally an article is found in such a source which innocently repeats the old association between them and megaliths as if nothing had changed, such as W. Beresford, 'Conjectural

Traces of the Druids in the North Staffordshire Moorlands', *The Reliquary* 15 (1875), 138–40, and H. A Botwood, 'The Druids in Shropshire', *Midland Antiquary* 2 (1883), 10–14. A copy of the former survives in the British Library, and of the latter in the National Library of Scotland.

60. H. M. Scarth, 'On the Megalithic Remains at Stanton Drew', *Proceedings of the Somersetshire Archaeological Society* 14.2 (1867), 161–72; C. Lloyd Morgan, *The Stones of Stanton Drew* (Bristol, 1888); H. T. Perfect, *Guide to Stanton Drew and its Ancient Stones* (Bristol, 1896).

61. Charles William Dymond, *The Ancient Remains at Stanton Drew* (privately published, 1896); quotations from pp. 25, 33.

62. Neatly compared in Edward T. Stevens, *Jottings on Some of the Objects of Interest in the Stonehenge Excursion* (Salisbury, 1882), 103–4.

63. For which see Thomas Wise, 'Remarks on Celtic Monuments', *Journal of the British Archaeological Association* 33 (1877), 158–69; Anon., 'Age of Bronze', *Edinburgh Review* 147 (1878), 437–74; Anon., 'Greywethers', *Cornhill Magazine* 53 (1886), 72–81; Joseph Anderson, *Scotland in Pagan Times: The Bronze and Stone Ages* (Edinburgh, 1886), 134–8, 267; Edward Clodd, 'Stonehenge', *Daily Chronicle* 26 Aug. 1899.

64. Arthur J. Evans, 'Stonehenge', *Archaeological Review* 2.5 (1889), 312–30; quotation from p. 312.

65. William Gowland, 'Excavations at Stonehenge', *The Times* 20 Dec. 1901; and 'Recent Excavations at Stonehenge', *Archaeologia* 58 (1902), 37–82.

66. Charles Darwin, *The Formation of Vegetable Mould* (London, 1881), 156.

67. Mrs Gordon, *Old Times in Britain* (n.p., n.d.).

68. L. Gidley, *Stonehenge* (Salisbury, 1873; 2nd edn 1877, 3rd edn 1893); J. H. Parker, 'Stonehenge', *Wiltshire Magazine* 17 (1878), 37–8; A. J. Church, *Early Man in Britain* (London, 1889), 8; William A. Judd, *Stonehenge* (Maddington, Wiltshire, 1893); Judd, *Notes of a Trip to Stonehenge* (Gillingham, 1896); Edmund S. Maskelyne, *On the Purpose, the Age and the Builders of Stonehenge* (Bath, 1898). All these titles, and those in n. 72 below, may be found either in the library of the Wiltshire Archaeological and Natural History Society, or in that of the Salisbury and South Wiltshire Museum. In addition, J. F. Hewitt, *The Ruling Races of Prehistoric Times* (Westminster, 1895), reflects on Stonehenge in similar fashion in i. 149, 175–6 of his work, which is in the Bodleian Library.

69. Wiltshire Archaeological and Natural History Society Library, Devizes, Cuttings Collection, i. 67.

70. Ibid.

71. 'Stonehenge for Sale', *Daily News* 4 Sept. 1899.

72. *The Illustrated Guide to Old Sarum and Stonehenge* (Salisbury, 1882); Edward H. Goddard, *Stonehenge: Handbook and Guide* (Devizes, 1894); Goddard, *Lancaster's Stonehenge Hand-Book* (Salisbury, 1894).

73. Lady Antrobus, *A Sentimental and Practical Guide to Amesbury and Stonehenge* (Amesbury, 1900); quotation from p. 18.

74. Fergusson's major work on the subject was *Rude Stone Monuments in All Countries* (London, 1872).

75. R. J. King, review in *Quarterly Review* 142 (July 1876), 142–60; Edward Duke, *The Age of Stonehenge* (Salisbury, 1887); William Long, 'Stonehenge and its Barrows', *Wiltshire Archaeological and Natural History Magazine* 16 (1876), 94–109; Anon., 'Prehistoric Archaeology', *British Quarterly Review* 56 (1872), 443–89; John Lubbock, 'Secret of the Druidical Stones', *Athenaeum* (1866), 18, 95, 136, 172; and review in *Nature* 5 (1872), 386–7; W. C. Lukis, review in *Archaeological Review* 5 (July 1888), 352–4; Charles Philip Kains-Jackson, *Our Ancient Monuments and the Land Around Them* (London, 1880).

76. Such as that of Edward Goddard, above. An isolated case of a local antiquary who took up Fergusson's theory with enthusiasm was Andreas Edward Cockayne, *Bakewell and its Vicinity* (London, 1888), 119–32. He did so, however, to reinforce the new orthodoxy that Druids could not possibly have erected megaliths.

77. William Matthew Flinders Petrie, *Inductive Metrology* (London, 1877), 153; and *Stonehenge* (London, 1880).

78. Margaret S. Drower, *Sir Flinders Petrie* (London: Gollancz, 1985), 350.

79. John Palmer, 'Rock Temples of the British Druids', *Antiquity* 38 (1964), 285–7.

80. The most important work in the development of the modern Atlantean myth was that of the American Ignatius Donnelly, in the 1880s.

81. A. P. Sinnett, *A New Theory of Stonehenge* (London, 1893); H. W. Estridge, *The Origin of Stonehenge* (Minety, Wiltshire, 1894).

82. These debates are summarized in Bruce G. Trigger, *Gordon Childe: Revolutions in Archaeology* (London: Thames and Hudson, 1980), 21–30.

83. Grafton Elliot Smith, *The Ancient Egyptians and their Influence upon the Civilization of Europe* (London, 1911); Smith, *The Influence of Ancient Egyptian Civilization in the East and America* (Manchester, 1916); Smith, *The Ancient Egyptians and the Origins of Civilization* (London, 1923); Smith, *In The Beginning: The Origin of Civilization* (London, 1928); Smith, *The Diffusion of Culture* (London, 1933); W. J. Perry, *The Children of the Sun* (London, 1923); Perry, *The Growth of Civilization* (London, 1924).

84. Childe's changing ideas are examined in Trigger, *Gordon Childe*, and Barbara McNairn, *The Method and Theory of V. Gordon Childe* (Edinburgh University Press, 1980).

85. For the development of this, and all source references, see Ronald Hutton, 'The Neolithic Great Goddess: A Study in Modern Tradition', *Antiquity* 71 (1997), 91–9.

10 Druidic Afterglow

1. They were published in *Cymru* in 1896, and are discussed in John Daniel, *The Philosophy of Ancient Britain* (London, 1927), v–xv.

2. Noted in Dillwyn Miles, *The Royal National Eisteddfod of Wales* (Swansea: Christopher Davies, 1978), 88.

3. His main books were *Iolo Morganwg a Chywyddau'r Ychwanegiad* (London, 1926), *Traddadiad Llenyddol Morganwg* (Cardiff, 1948) and *Iolo Morganwg: Y Gyfol Gyntaf* (Cardiff, 1956).

4. Miles, *The Royal National Eisteddfod*, 88.

5. Quoted and translated by Mary-Ann Constantine, 'Pious Frauds and Perjurers', in *Fakes and Forgeries*. ed. Peter Knight and Jonathan Long (Cambridge: Scholars Press, 2004), 131. I am very grateful to Dr Constantine for giving me a copy of this paper.

6. John Morris Jones, *Taliesin* (London, 1918), esp. 19–26.

7. Sir Ifor Williams, *Lectures on Early Welsh Poetry* (Dublin, 1944), and *Canu Taliesin* (Cardiff: University of Wales Press, 1960).

8. Norman Lockyer, *Antiquity of the Gorsedd* (Swansea, 1907); quotation from p. 4.

9. Ibid., preface.

10. Miles, *The Royal National Eisteddfod*, 82–3.

11. J. Griffith, *The Gorsedd of Britain* (Swansea, 1906); J. W. Hayes, *Yn Gorsedd Beirdd* (Swansea, 1910). Copies of these are kept in the Swansea Local Studies Library.

12. A. G. Edwards, 'Druidism', *Archaeologia Cambrensis* 7th series I.ii (1921), 157–69; quotations from pp. 168–9.

13. Beriah Gwynfe Evans, *The Bardic Gorsedd: Its History and Symbolism* (Pontypool, 1923). A copy is kept in Cardiff University Library.

14. D. Delta Evans, *The Ancient Bards of Britain* (Merthyr Tydfil, 1906); Sir John Daniel, *The Philosophy of Ancient Britain* (London, 1927); William Evans, *The Bards of the Isle of Britain* (Red Wharf Bay, Anglesey, 1930); D. Jeffrey Williams, *Druidic Teachings* (London, 1934); Isabel Hill Elder, *Celt, Druid and Culdee* (London, 1938). The last of these became a very common book in British public libraries, and had gone through four editions by 1962.

15. Miles, *The Royal National Eisteddfod*, 83–125, 142–7; quotations from pp. 91–2, 115.

16. The historical significance of which was commemorated by Prys Morgan, 'Archbishops and Archdruids', *The Historian* 76 (2002), 28–32. I am grateful to my colleague William Doyle for lending me a copy of this article.

17. Miles, *The Royal National Eisteddfod*, 90; Den Toll [Hugh Miners], *Gorseth Kernow* (Penzance: Gorseth Kernow, 1978); *Souvenir Programme of the Gorsedd of the Bards of Cornwall* (privately published, Lelant, 1953). A copy of the latter survives in Stuart Piggott's archive at Oxford University's Institute of Archaeology.

18. Miles, *The Royal National Eisteddfod*, and *The Secret of the Bards of the Isle of Britain* (Llandybie, Gwasg Dinefwr Press, 1992).

19. Miles, *The Royal National Eisteddfod*, 136.

20. Though observers who do not speak Welsh may have problems in working out what is going on. When my former pupil Rob Penn, turned professional writer, attended the Gorsedd ceremony in

the early 2000s, he initially heard the exchange as 'Who has a headache?', to which the reply is 'Headache'. He was, however, rescued by a headset provided for those who need one, which gave a translation: Rob Penn, *The Sky is Falling on Our Heads: A Journey to the Bottom of the Celtic Fringe* (London: Sceptre, 2004). Rob takes his place in a long succession of foreigners who have found some cause for ribaldry in the Gorsedd: remember Matthew Arnold and H. V. Morton.

21. P. H. J. H. Gosden, *The Friendly Societies in England 1815–1875* (Manchester: Manchester University Press, 1961), 48–9; J. W. Shaw, *Historical Notes on the Order of Druids* (Manchester, 1936), 50.

22. From the list of Victorian Druid orders kept in the John Goodchild Collection at Wakefield Central Library.

23. This was the Independent United Ancient Order of Druids, Monmouthshire and Welsh District. A souvenir booklet of its biennial conference, held at Cardiff in 1913, is kept in Cardiff Central Library.

24. All in the list of orders in the John Goodchild Collection.

25. *Ancient Order of Druids: Introductory Book* (London, 1889).

26. *Oxford Times* 15 Aug. 1908; *The Druid* 7.2 (1908), 110–11. The British Library keeps a copy of the latter.

27. John Goodchild Collection, United Ancient Order Archive, certificates for initiates, and books of ceremonies for the various grades and divisions, 1896–1930.

28. *Rules of the Sheffield Equalized Independent Druids' Friendly Society* (Sheffield, 1898). A copy is preserved in the British Library.

29. *The Druid* 1 March 1907, 11–12; Ted Williams, 'A Brief Treatise on the History of International Ancient Order Druidism', *The Druids' Voice* 4 (1994), 8–9.

30. *The Druids' Journal and Monthly Gorsedd* NS 7.2 (1933), 50. A copy is held in the British Library.

31. Hugo Wiese, G. Wolf Stoll and Karl Roeder, *Handbuch des Druidenordens* (Munich, 1931).

32. *The Druids' Journal and Monthly Gorsedd* NS 7.5 (1933), 117.

33. Williams, 'A Brief Treatise', 9.

34. *The Druid* 5.4 (1911), 51.

35. *Salisbury and Winchester Journal* 19 June 1925.

36. John Goodchild Collection, United Ancient Order Archive, *Lecture for the Inauguration of Past Arches* (Hull, 3rd edn, 1906).

37. John Goodchild Collection, United Ancient Order Archive, *Ceremonies to be Used in All Lodges* (Hull, 1897). For the texts and music to the songs used in the Ancient Order, several of which were shared with the United Ancient Order, see P. G. A. Hudson and Charles Benedict, *Choruses as Sung in the Grand Lodge of the Ancient Order of Druids* (London, 1903); there is a copy in the British Library.

38. The quotations are from the *Morning Leader* report, which was reprinted whole, with further details, in the *Devizes and Wiltshire Gazette* 31 Aug. 1905.

39. *The Sphere* 2 Sept. 1905.

40. *The Times* 18 June 1931.

41. The letters between the various orders and lodges, and the Office of Works, are preserved in the National Archives, WORK 14/2135–6. Newspaper reports of the largest ceremonies are found in the notes above and below this one. See also *The Druid* 3.7 (Sept. 1907), 102.

42. *Salisbury and Winchester Journal* 19 June 1925.

43. By Christopher Chippindale, *Stonehenge Complete* (London: Thames and Hudson, 1983), 172.

44. Order of Bards, Ovates and Druids Archive, *Ancient Order of Druids. Ritual of Primitive Degree*. I am very grateful to Philip Carr-Gomm for sending me a copy of this.

45. Done at once, in 1907: *The Druid* 1 (1907), 1. A copy is held in the British Library.

46. *Salisbury and Winchester Journal* 19 June 1925.

47. See the books of rituals in the John Goodchild Collection, United Ancient Order Archive.

48. United Ancient Order material as at n. 44. Order of Bards, Ovates and Druids Archive, *Lecture on Emblem* (I am grateful to Philip Carr-Gomm for the gift of a copy of this); *The Druid* 2 (1907), 1–2.

49. Wilhelm North, 'Druidism in England', *East London Observer* (24 Sept. and 5 Oct. 1932).

50. Edwin Harris, *A Short History of the Druids* (Rochester, 1909).

51. John Goodchild Collection, United Ancient Order Archive, *Lecture for the Inauguration of Past Arches*.

52. Shaw, *Historical Notes*, passim.
53. *The Druid* 2–5 (1907–11); and *The Druids' Journal and Monthly Gorsedd* NS 7.1–9.12 (1933–5), passim.
54. *The Sphere* 2 Sept. 1905.
55. Henry Cox, *The Ancient Druids* (n.p., n.d). I am very grateful to Jim Milton for presenting this to me.
56. Sam Smiles, *The Image of Antiquity* (New Haven, Conn.: Yale University Press, 1994), 109.
57. William Schwenck Gilbert, *The Pretty Druidess* (London, 1869); quotation from p. 28. A copy is held in the British Library.
58. Arthur Daubeny, *The Arch Druid of Tresco* (Cambridge, 1891); quotation from p. 19. A copy survives in the British Library.
59. Marie Trevelyan, *Britain's Greatness Foretold* (London, 1900); quotation from p. x.
60. Thomas Vincent, *The Arch-Druid's Song from Eos and Gwevril, a Welsh Opera* (London, 1904), n.p. A copy is kept in the British Library.
61. John Eliot Howard, *The Druids and their Religion* (London, 1880); quotations from pp. 31, 40–2.
62. Evan McColl, *The English Poetical Works*, ed. A. Mackenzie (Toronto, 1883), 198–9.
63. Robert Leighton, *Poems* (London, 1869), 87, 89.
64. Henry Septimus Sutton, *Poems* (London, 1886), 52.
65. Harwicke Drummond Rawnsley, *Sonnets Around the Coast* (London, 1887), 88.
66. John B. Tabb, *Lyrics* (London, 1897), 183.
67. William Sharp, *Poems and Dramas* (London, 1910), contains his 'Druid' poems, 'St Christopher of the Gael', 'A Record (A Fragment)', 'Euphrenia' and 'Two Old Yews'. The crucifixion scene is on p. 176. The edition of *The Immortal Hour* that I have used is the one published at London in 1922.
68. 'The Rune of the Four Winds', now conveniently posted on the web at *http://www.sundown. pair.com/SundownShores/HillsofDream/poems.htm*. I owe this reference to David Miley, of Maryland.
69. Rutland Boughton, *The Immortal Hour* (London, 1920), 112–14.
70. Michael Hurd, *Immortal Hour: The Life and Period of Rutland Boughton* (London: Routledge, 1962); quotation from p. 72.
71. Alvin Langdon Coburn, *Fairy Gold* (London, 1939); quotation from p. 7.
72. Neil Gunn, *Sun Circle* (Edinburgh, 1933); quotation from p. 191.
73. E.g. John Pym Yeatman, *The History of the Common Law of Great Britain and Gaul* (London, 1874), i. 52–9; J. Clark, 'Druids and Druidism', *Hawick Archaeological Society Transactions* 1878, n.p. (a copy is preserved in the National Library of Scotland); A. Scott, *The Celts and Druids* (North Shields, 1894). A copy survives in the British Library.
74. W. Wynn Westcott, *Abury and its Connection with Serpent-Worship* (privately printed, 1908); a copy is kept in the library of the Wiltshire Archaeological and Natural History Society.
75. William Burrough Hill, *Stonehenge: An Appreciation* (Southampton, 1914).
76. Ludovic McLellan Mann, *The Druid Temple near Glasgow* (London, 1939).
77. Arthur J. Ireland, *Stonehenge* (London, 1903), quotations from p. 2. A copy is preserved in the Society's library at Devizes.
78. Sebastian Evans, *From Stonehenge to Avebury and Beyond* (privately printed, 1905). A copy exists in the library at Devizes: see n. 74, above.
79. Norman Lockyer, 'An Attempt to Ascertain the Date of the Original Construction of Stonehenge from its Orientation', *Nature* 65 (Nov. 1901), 55–7. For the latest dating of the monument, see *Stonehenge in its Landscape*, ed. Rosamund M. J. Cleal, K. E. Walker and R. Montague (London: English Heritage, 1995).
80. Norman Lockyer, *Stonehenge and Other British Stone Monuments Astronomically Considered* (London, 1906). For another attempt by an eminent and inexpert author to restore the old model in the face of the new, see Sir William Preece's essay, 'Egyptians and Celts', *Celtic Review* 1 (1905), 97–103. It also argues that Egyptians and Druids had the same religion, while identifying it as that of the pre-Aryan race with whom the new prehistory had populated Neolithic Britain.
81. E. O. Gordon, *Prehistoric London* (London, 1925).
82. Lawrence Graeme Allan Roberts, *Druidism in Britain*. I have used the fourth edition, published in London in 1935.
83. Lionel Smithett Lewis, *St Joseph of Arimathea at Glastonbury*. I have used the seventh edition, published in London by James Clarke in 1955.

84. The classic example is Gordon Strachan, *Jesus the Master Builder* (Edinburgh: Floris, 1998).

85. John Stuart Blackie, *A Song of Heroes* (London, 1890), 81. See also his *Messis Vitae* (London, 1886), 175–84. Other poetic works in this vein, from the period after 1870, include Ruden Berkeley Wriostheley Noel, *The Collected Poems*, ed. John Addington Symonds (London, 1902), 320

86. G. K. Chesterton, *The Collected Poems* (London, 1933), 213.

87. Middle Wood Kirkbride, *The Arch-Druid* (Manchester, 1885). A copy is held by Cambridge University Library.

88. William H. G. Kingston, *Eldol, the Druid* (London, 1874); quotation from p. viii.

89. Alfred Church, *The Count of the Saxon Shore* (London, 1887).

90. Sidney N. Sedgwick, *A Daughter of the Druids* (London, 1904).

91. Hugh Kay, *Saint Kentigern: A Tale of the Druids and of Early Christianity in Scotland* (Glasgow, 1891); quotation from p. 5.

92. Florence Gay, *The Druidess* (London, 1908); quotation from p. 195.

93. It is bound with Agnes Strickland, *Guthred* (London, 1876); quotation from p. 54.

94. J. M. Capes, *The Druid: An English Opera in Three Acts* (London, 1879).

95. G. B. Carvill and Gervase Bailey, *The Druids' Elect* (London, 1899); quotation from p. 2.

96. J. W. Willis-Bund, *The Celtic Church of Wales* (London, 1897); quotations from pp. 103–4.

97. John Rhys, *Celtic Britain* (London, 1904); quotations from p. 70. The 1996 reprint was by Random House.

98. T. Rice Holmes, *Ancient Britain and the Invasions of Julius Caesar* (Oxford, 1907); quotations from pp. 289 and 293.

99. For a convenient, if largely derivative, summary of this development, see Ronald Hutton, *The Triumph of the Moon* (Oxford: Oxford University Press, 1999), 112–31.

100. This was the first edition of *Celtic Britain* (London, 1882), 67.

101. George Lawrence Gomme, *The Village Community* (London, 1890), 103–4.

102. George Lawrence Gomme, *Ethnology in Folklore* (London, 1892), 58–62.

103. Jonathan Forbes Leslie, *The Early Races of Scotland and their Monuments* (Edinburgh, 1866), passim; quotation from p. 68.

104. Robert Angus Smith, *Loch Etive and the Sons of Uisnach* (2nd edn, London, 1885), 280–91; quotation from p. 291.

105. A. W. Moore, *The Folk-Lore of the Isle of Man* (Douglas, 1891), 77.

106. The article was published in the *Celtic Review* in 1891; I read it in the reprinted version as a pamphlet: Alexander MacGregor, *Highland Superstitions* (Stirling, 1901), 8–12; quotation from p. 10.

107. J. A. MacCulloch, *The Religion of the Ancient Celts* (Edinburgh, 1911), 293–318.

108. A. Hadrian Allcroft, *The Circle and the Cross* (London, 1927), i. 308–15.

109. The original text was published at Stirling in 1937; my information about Sunday schools is in the 1999 reprint by Mayflower Christian Books.

110. T. B. Morris, *Druid's Ring* (London, 1938).

111. Described in Ithell Colquhoun, *Sword of Wisdom: MacGregor Mathers and the Golden Dawn* (London: Spearman, 1975), 120. But see later for the doubts hanging over this assertion.

112. Dudley Wright, *Druidism: The Ancient Faith of Britain* (London, 1924).

113. George Austin, 'The Druids', *Occult Review* 41 (1925), 297–302.

114. Lewis Spence, *The Mysteries of Britain* (London, 1928); quotations from pp. 5–6, 19, 109, 190.

115. Lewis Spence, *The History and Origins of Druidism* (London, 1949).

116. Colquhoun, *Sword of Wisdom*, 120. The accompanying statement, that this was the order into which Sir Winston Churchill was initiated, is flatly wrong: see p. 318 above.

117. I am very grateful to Andrew Tucker, Assistant Curator of the Museum of Freemasonry, for this information and the work that lies behind it.

118. This was the Universal Bond, or Ancient Druid Order, and its own references to the Ancient and Archaeological Order will be found in its publications from the 1950s, listed and analysed in Chapter 12 of the current book.

119. *The Druidic Order of the Pendragon*, ed. Colin Robertson (Loughborough: Thoth Productions, 2004). 'Colin Robertson' is the pseudonym adopted by Nick Farrell for his alleged informant, to keep the latter's true identity concealed at his own request.

11 The Universal Bond

1. *Salisbury and Winchester Journal* 29 June 1912, from which all quotations are taken, and the *Sphere* 29 June 1912.
2. Christopher Chippindale, *Stonehenge Complete* (London: Thames and Hudson, 1983), 156–64; Adam Stout, 'The World Turned Upside Down: Stonehenge Summer Solstice before the Hippies', *3rd Stone* 46 (2003), 38–41; Andy Worthington, *Stonehenge: Celebration and Subversion* (Loughborough: Alternative Albion, 2004), 14–19.
3. *Salisbury Journal*, quoted in Stout, 'The World Turned Upside Down', 40.
4. Quoted ibid., 41.
5. *Notes and Queries*, quoted in Worthington, *Stonehenge*, 16.
6. . Anon., 'Stonehenge', *All The Year Round* 10 Aug. 1872, 299; William Beck, 'Sun Worshippers', *The Antiquary* 2 (29 June 1872), 1578.
7. Anon., 'Excursions', *Proceedings of the Bath Natural History and Antiquarian Field Club* 2 (1868), 73–4.
8. Beck, 'Sun Worshippers'.
9. Alan Seaburg's paper was eventually published as 'The Last Two Universalist Parsons in the United Kingdom', *Transactions of the Unitarian Historical Society* 23.2 (April 2004), 530–62, but I read it as a manuscript copy very kindly sent to me by Philip Carr-Gomm. R. Bruce Aubry's essay is an apparently unpublished memorandum dated 1986, a copy of which I received, again, because of the generosity of Philip Carr-Gomm. Adam Stout's work has appeared as 'Choosing a Past: The Politics of Prehistory in Pre-War Britain' (University of Wales, Lampeter, Ph.D. thesis, 2004), 132–85, to be published in revised form by Blackwell in 2008; and *Universal Majesty, Verity and Love Infinite: A Life of George Watson MacGregor Reid* (Lewes, Sussex: Order of Bards, Ovates and Druids, 2005), available on the Internet at *http://druidry.org/pdfs/fifth_mt_haemus_lecture.pdf*. He sent me successive drafts of each of these pieces, and supplied me with encouragement and information throughout my research.
10. Aubry, *George Watson MacGregor Reid*, 1–3; Stout, *Universal Majesty, Verity and Love Infinite*, 2–3. The autobiographical essay is in 'Makers of the Union, Part III', *Seafaring* (13 April 1889), 4–5.
11. Aubry, *George Watson MacGregor Reid*, 4–17; Stout, *Universal Majesty, Verity and Love Infinite*, 4–5.
12. Stout, *Universal Majesty, Verity and Love Infinite*, 9–10.
13. George W. Reid, *The Natural Basis of Civilization* (London, 1895); quotations from pp. 8, 10. I am very grateful to Adam Stout for sending me a copy; as previous writers have always held the publication date to be 1893, I take the one given inside the booklet to be an error.
14. Stout, *Universal Majesty, Verity and Love Infinite*, 12. As Alan Seaburg has proved, the modern Druid belief that he invented the tonic wine Sanatogen, propagated in Ross Nichols, *The Book of Druidry* (London: Aquarian, 1990), 107, is a myth: Seaburg, 'The Last Two Universalist Parsons', 537.
15. Warburg Institute, Gerald Yorke Collection, NS 29, G. W. MacGregor Reid, 'The Message of the Paths that Lead unto the Place called Beautiful', n.p.
16. Warburg Institute, Gerald Yorke Collection, NS EE2, fo. 288.
17. Ibid., NS 18 (22), R. M. Reid, 'The Legend of Aleister Crowley'.
18. Ibid., NS. 29–31, 'The Message of the Paths'; 'Revelation'; and 'The Fourth Gospel'.
19. *The Nature Cure Annual* (1907–8), xiii. Copies of the journal are kept in the Bodleian Library.
20. *The Nature Cure* 1 (1906), 15.
21. *The Nature Cure Annual* (1907–8), xiii; *The Nature Cure Journal* (1907–8), 5, 188–9.
22. *The Nature Cure Journal* (1906–7), 235–64; (1907–8), 1–6, 19–21, 121, 235, 263–4, 290–3 440, 478–81, 636.
23. Ibid., 407, 418–20, 435–42, 530–1, 584, 651.
24. Ibid. (1909), 367–8.
25. Ibid. (1907–8), 408–12, 533–4, 610–14; (1908), 117–18; (1909), 56–7, 180–1.
26. Ibid. (1907–8), 363.
27. Ayu Subhadra, *The Path That Is Light* (London, 1910), 1–11, 84–7, 128–208.
28. Ibid., 11–24, 48, 122–4. Reid made another putative translation from Tibetan – which there is no evidence that he could actually ever read – in the name of Ayu Subhadra, which was published posthumously as *The Udanavarga* (London, 1946). It consisted of poetry, seemingly

by Reid himself, praising the true god as protector of the poor and patron of universal broth-erhood and despising the ways of the world. The introduction restated the author's credentials as somebody who had lived in a Tibetan monastery and expressed hostility to other British Buddhists for not practising the more authentic branch of the faith as he did; plainly they had not recognized his credentials.

29. *Nature Cure Journal* (1908), 83; (1909), 198, 233, 367–8.
30. Ibid. (1909), 26–30.
31. Stout, *Universal Majesty, Verity and Love Infinite*, 17–18.
32. *Manchester Guardian* 23 June 1959.
33. *The New Life* (1913), 335.
34. *The Nature Cure Journal* (1909), 96–7, 229–332.
35. For the Senussi, see Rosita Forbes, *The Secret of the Sahara* (London, 1921); I am very grateful to Philip Carr-Gomm for this reference. For Rosher's role, see Stout, *Universal Majesty, Verity and Love Infinite*, 20–22.
36. The copy is damaged and imperfect, only half of it remaining. It is in the archive of the Order of Bards, Ovates and Druids, and I am very grateful to Philip Carr-Gomm for sending me a photocopy.
37. Ibid., 228–52, 271–3, 276, 311–28.
38. Ibid., 275–6, 335–8.
39. For Pamela Tennant, Lady Glenconner, see Stout, *Universal Majesty, Verity and Love Infinite*, 33.
40. *The New Life*, 275.
41. On this see Stout, 'Choosing a Past', 144.
42. *Salisbury Journal* 27 June 1914; *Wiltshire Gazette* 25 June 1914; *Daily Mirror* 23 June 1914; *Evening News* 22 June 1914; *Salisbury Times* 26 June 1914.
43. The reports are in the *Salisbury Times* (28 June 1915) and *Salisbury and Winchester Journal* (29 June 1915); the former discusses the *London Evening News* report in detail.
44. Institute of Archaeology, Oxford University, Stuart Piggott Archive, letter from John Bowle to Glyn Daniel.
45. The *Salisbury Times* report is discussed in Stout, 'Choosing a Past', 150–1. See also the *Salisbury and Winchester Journal* 24 June 1916.
46. *Salisbury Times and South Wilts Gazette* 28 June 1918.
47. Ayu Subhadra, *When All the World's at Peace* (London, 1915).
48. Discussed by Stout, 'Choosing a Past', 151.
49. Made clear on the same notepaper, first recorded on 29 May 1919, in National Archives, WORK 14/2135.
50. See Bowle's letter to Daniel, above, and the deed of gift in Wiltshire Record Office, 2860/20.
51. What follows is based on National Archives, WORK 14/2135, documents between 12 June 1919 and 22 June 1923; *Salisbury and Winchester Journal* (26 June 1920, 23 June 1922, 22 and 29 June 1923); *Salisbury Times* (25 June 1920); *Wiltshire Gazette* (23 June 1921); Wiltshire Archaeological and Natural History Society Library, Devizes, Cunnington Cuttings Book 11.
52. WORK 14/2135, five documents dated 3 to 16 June 1921, plus the 1921 Declaration of the Universal Bond and the issue of the *New Life*.
53. His autobiography is *What Made Me a Socialist* (London, 1925).
54. See *The Times* (30 Aug. 1924), and the papers in WORK 14/2153, for 1919 to 1924. Note, however, the first letter from Thomas Ireland, dated 29 May 1919, in which he states that the ashes had hitherto been scattered on the Glenconners' land, and not at Stonehenge.
55. *Wiltshire Gazette* 19 March 1936.
56. Adam Stout, pers. comm., 19 Oct. 2004.
57. *Times* cutting, undated, in Cunnington Cuttings Book 11, in the society's library; *Wiltshire Gazette* 21 Aug. 1928.
58. They are kept at the back of WORK 14/2135. The Wiltshire Archaeological and Natural History Society made its own collection, now in Cunnington Cuttings Book 11 in its library. In addition, see the *Wiltshire Gazette* (28 Aug. and 4 Sept. 1924); *The Times* (12 Sept. 1924); *London Evening News* (29 Aug. 1924); and *Daily Chronicle* (31 July 1924).
59. All this is found in the letter to the *Salisbury Journal*, below, *The Times* cuttings in the Cunnington Cuttings Book 11, and the letters and declarations in WORK 14/2135, 14 June to 17 Sept. 1900.
60. *Wiltshire Gazette* 4 Sept. 1924.

61. See the comments in the *Antiquaries' Journal* 5 (1925), 225.
62. Printed in the *Salisbury and Winchester Journal* 29 Aug. 1924. Its author, Arthur Thomas ap Llywellyn, was another example of continuity with the old Nature Cure Association, the Sheffield branch of which he had led in 1907. He was described then as being 'of no creed or sect': *Nature Cure Annual* (1907–8), 221.
63. *Times* 28 and 30 Aug. 1924; *Daily Chronicle* 30 Aug. 1924.
64. Aubry, 'George Watson MacGregor Reid', 20.
65. Chippindale, *Stonehenge Complete*, 204.
66. 'Bema' was one of the sections of liturgy used by the Universal Bond, at least by the late 1920s or 1930s: *Salisbury and Winchester Journal* 25 June 1943, 7.
67. 'Anniversary Address', *Antiquaries' Journal* 5 (1925), 224–7; quotation from p. 224.
68. Naturally enough, Stevens's own musem, at Salisbury, has the successive editions of his *Stonehenge Today and Yesterday*, from 1919 to 1938, in its library. The quotation is from pp. 67–8 of the first edition.
69. George Landown, *Stonehenge* (Trowbridge, 1924); *Stonehenge Past and Present* (Cheltenham, 1924). Both works are held in the library of the Wiltshire Archaeological Society.
70. T. D. Kendrick, *The Druids* (London: Methuen, 1927); quotations from pp. vii–ix, 121.
71. Christopher Harvey, *The Ancient Temple at Avebury and its Gods* (London, 1923). A copy exists in the library of the Wiltshire Archaeological Society.
72. M. E. Cunnington, *Avebury* (Devizes, 1930). A copy is held by the same library.
73. This is quoted and discussed by Stout, 'Choosing a Past', 136–7.
74. Kendrick, *The Druids*, 146–93; quotation from p. 151.
75. R. H. Cunnington, *Stonehenge and its Date* (London, 1935), 125–31; quotation from p. 131.
76. George Engleheart, *Iron or Bronze?* (Devizes, 1933).
77. *Salisbury and Winchester Journal* 26 June 1925; National Archives, WORK 14/2135, nine documents dated 17 June to 13 Aug. 1925; *Wiltshire Gazette* 25 June 1925; *The Times* 22 June 1925; *Western Daily Press* 22 June 1925.
78. *Salisbury and Winchester Journal* 2 July 1928.
79. National Archives, WORK 14/2135, seven documents dated from 16 March 1925 to 23 April 1927.
80. *The New Life and Druid Journal* (Special Issue, Summer Solstice, 1927). A copy exists in the library of the Wiltshire Archaeological Society.
81. National Archives, WORK 14/2135, fourteen documents dated 4 June 1928 to 16 May 1931.
82. Stout, 'Choosing a Past', 152–3.
83. What follows is based on the *Illustrated London News* (29 June 1929); *Salisbury Times* (28 June 1930); George Long, *The Folklore Calendar* (London, 1930), 141; *Salisbury and Winchester Journal* (29 June 1928, 28 June 1929, 27 June 1930, and 26 June 1931).
84. *South Western Star* 16 Aug. 1946.
85. For this see especially *The New Life and Druid Journal* (Summer Solstice 1930), in the British Library. Copies of the magazine for 1929 and 1931 are preserved in WORK 14/2135, as is the issue for 1931.
86. WORK 14/2135, four letters dated 28 April to 13 May 1932.
87. For Reid's statements and actions at midsummer 1932, see the *Salisbury and Winchester Journal* (1 July 1932), for article and letter from Arthur Peacock, *Wiltshire Gazette* (24 and 30 June, 7 and 19 July 1932); *Salisbury Times* (22 July 1932); *Sunday Express* (19 June 1932); *Wiltshire Times and Trowbridge Advertiser* (2 July 1932).
88. Seaburg, 'The Last Two Universalist Parsons', 560–2; Arthur Peacock, *Yours Fraternally* (London, 1945), 108–9.
89. *Service Book of South London Universalist Church* (n.d., but clearly from 1930s or 1940s). I am very grateful to Philip Carr-Gomm for the gift of a copy of this work. For the Universalist background, see Seaburg, 'The Last Two Universalist Parsons', 530–40.
90. W. MacGregor-Reid, *The Garden of God* (London, 1944).
91. Harvard University, Andover-Harvard Theological Library, letter from Reid to Robert Cummins, 24 April 1942. I am very grateful to Philip Carr-Gomm for the gift of a photocopy.
92. Peacock, *Yours Fraternally*.
93. Andover-Harvard Theological Library, William J. Arms to Cummins, 20 Jan. 1942.

94. Seaburg, 'The Last Two Universalist Parsons', 530–3; Andover-Harvard Theological Library, sixteen letters to Robert Cummins, dated between late 1941 and mid-1946. I am very grateful to Philip Carr-Gomm for sending me photocopies of all this correspondence.
95. *South-Western Star* 16 Aug. 1946; *Clapham Observer* 16 Aug. 1946. I am very grateful to Philip Carr-Gomm for a copy of Reid's death certificate.
96. Stout, 'Choosing a Past', 180; Stout, *Universal Majesty, Verity and Love Infinite*, 1.
97. Ronald Hutton, *The Druids* (London: Hambledon Continuum, 2007), 181.
98. Seaburg, 'The Last Two Universalist Parsons', 539.
99. Stuart Piggott, *The Druids* (London: Thames and Hudson, 1968), 180.

12 Druids and Archaeologists

1. Alan Seaburg, 'The Last Two Universalist Parsons in the United Kingdom', *Transactions of the Unitarian Historical Society* 23.2 (2004), 550–62; Harvard University, Andover-Harvard Theological Library, Robert Cummins to John Kielty, 18 Nov. 1950.
2. *South-Western Star* 16 Aug. 1946.
3. Colquhoun, *Sword of Wisdom*, 119–20.
4. *The Pendragon*, Midsummer 1938. A single copy survives in the British Library; I am grateful to Adam Stout for sending me a photocopy he had made of it. Hooper published several books to propagate his ideas, which are held by the Bodleian and British libraries.
5. National Archives, WORK 14/2135, contains the letters granting permission.
6. *Salisbury and Winchester Journal* 25 June 1943.
7. Ibid., 28 June 1946; National Archives, WORK 14/2136, three documents dated 20 May–23 June 1946.
8. First used in Smith's letter to the Office of Works, 7 May 1947, archived in WORK 14/2136.
9. See three other documents, dated 9 May–22 June, in the same file, and the *Salisbury and Winchester Journal* 27 June 1947.
10. The Golden Dawn correspondences put earth in the north and water in the west, so the AODH was deliberately establishing its own, distinctive, system.
11. WORK 14/2136, five letters and two press reports dated 20 May–21 June 1948; *The Pendragon and Druid Guardian* Summer Solstice, 1948. A copy of this magazine, containing the liturgy, survives among Stuart Piggott's papers in the Institute of Archaeology at Oxford University.
12. Wiltshire Record Office, 2860/22, 'The Summer Solstice Celebration of the Druid Order'.
13. Ibid.
14. Ibid.; Archive of the Order of Bards, Ovates and Druids, Instrument of Appointment of Robert MacGregor-Reid. I am very grateful to Philip Carr-Gomm for a copy of the latter document.
15. A copy is in the Williamson Collection at the Museum of Witchcraft, Boscastle, Cornwall. I am very grateful to Graham King for allowing me access to this.
16. WORK 14/2136, letter from Neil to Office 31 May 1949, and reply.
17. Wiltshire Record Office, 2860/21, 'The Summer Solstice Celebration of the Druid Order'.
18. WORK 14/2136, nine documents dated 6 Sept. 1949–29 May 1950.
19. Ibid., twenty-two documents dated 29 March 1951–9 Jan. 1955.
20. Colquhoun, *Sword of Wisdom*, 117–18.
21. Ibid., 117–25, 182–3; letter from MacGregor-Reid to Gerald Yorke, communicated to me by Adam Stout, 3 April 2007.
22. I have had various exchanges with Adam Stout on this subject, and he remains deeply sceptical about the last-named group, at least.
23. Warburg Institute, Gerald Yorke Collection, NS 18 (22), R. MacGregor-Reid, 'The Legend of Aleister Crowley'.
24. Colquhoun, *Sword of Wisdom*, 125–7. Alas, it seems that she did not think enough of Druidry to preserve any of the magazines that she cites in her text: none exist in her archive at the Tate Gallery, amongst a large collection of material relating to paganism and the occult.
25. Wiltshire Record Office, 2680/20, press release 1964.
26. He signed the Instrument of Appointment at n. 14. For his later activities as a Druid, see Doreen Valiente, *The Rebirth of Witchcraft* (Custer, Wash.: Phoenix, 1989), 40, and later in this chapter.
27. Wiltshire Record Office, 2860/22, 'The Summer Solstice Celebration of the Druid Order'.
28. Derek Taylor (ed.), *Stonehenge and the Druids* (London: Universal Bond, 1951), 14–18.

29. *Daily Mail* 20 June 1956.
30. Dillwyn Miles, *The Royal National Eisteddfod of Wales* (Swansea: Christopher Davies, 1978), 120–1, 125–6; and Miles, *The Secret of the Bards of the Isle of Britain* (Llandybie: Gwasg Dinefawr Press, 1992), 222; Amy Hale, ' "In the Eye of the Sun": The Relationship between the Cornish Gorseth and Esoteric Druidry', *Cornish Studies* 8 (2000), 182–96.
31. Wiltshire Record Office, 2860/22, 'The Summer Solstice Celebration of the Druid Order'.
32. Taylor (ed.), *Stonehenge and the Druids*, 5.
33. In a pamphlet entitled *The Ancient Druid Order: The British Circle of the Universal Bond* (London: Universal Bond). It is undated, but from internal evidence published between 1956 and 1963. A copy is kept in the Wiltshire Local Studies Library at Trowbridge.
34. What follows is based on *The Ancient Druid Order*, as n. 33 above, and *The Most Ancient Order of Druids* (London: Most Ancient Order of Druids, n.d., but mid- or late 1950s), and *The Timestones of the Druids* (London: British Circle of the Universal Bond, 1960), copies of both of which survive in Stuart Piggott's archive at the Institute of Archaeology, Oxford University.
35. Taylor (ed.), *Stonehenge and the Druids*, 12–13, 20.
36. *The Ancient Druid Order*, 8–9; Archive of the Order of Bards, Ovates and Druids, *The Rites, Ceremonies and Services of the Druid Order. Part One* (London, 1948), and Ariovistus, 'Druids'. I am very grateful to Philip Carr-Gomm for copies of the latter two documents.
37. *The Rites, Ceremonies and Services of the Druid Order*, 1–5.
38. Wiltshire Record Office, 2860/22, 'The Summer Solstice Celebration of the Druid Order'.
39. The current melodic custom, of chanting it in unison on a long-drawn-out note, was apparently instituted by Philip Carr-Gomm in the early 1990s: Philip Carr-Gomm, pers. comm. 26 Nov. 2007.
40. *Stonehenge and the Summer Solstice* (London: Most Ancient Order of Druids, n.d.). A copy of this survives in Stuart Piggott's archive.
41. *The Ceremony of the Spring Equinox* (London: Supreme Grand Council, The Druid Order, 1956) (a copy of this is held in the Wiltshire Local Studies Library at Trowbridge); *The Druid Order: The Ceremony of the Autumn Equinox* (London; The British Circle of the Universal Bond, 1956) (a copy of this survives in Birmingham Reference Library). The spring ceremony of 1956 was reported at length in the *Daily Express* 21 March 1956.
42. *Salisbury Journal* 22 June 1956; *Daily Telegraph* 22 June 1956; *Southampton Echo* 21 June 1956; National Archives, WORK 14/2136, two reports and a cutting 20–21 June 1956.
43. WORK 14/2136, five reports and memoranda 21 June 1957–19 June 1958; *Salisbury Journal* 28 June 1957.
44. *Daily Telegraph* 14 July 1959; WORK 14/2136, file of press cuttings from June 1959; *The Times* 22 June 1959; *Manchester Guardian* 23 June 1959 (which supplies the quotations). The notion that Druids had been persecuted by Canute was embedded in the order's legends by the 1950s, and was based on a famous law code issued by that king that forbade various pagan practices. This was, however, directed against the recent Viking settlers in England, and not Druids: see Ronald Hutton, *The Pagan Religions of the Ancient British Isles* (Oxford: Blackwell, 1991), 298.
45. Quotations from the *News Chronicle* 22 June 1960 and *Evening Standard* 21 June 1960, with added material from the *Daily Telegraph* 22 June 1960.
46. Glyn Daniel, *A Short History of Archaeology* (London: Thames and Hudson, 1981); Paul Bahn (ed.), *The Cambridge Illustrated History of Archaeology* (Cambridge: Cambridge University Press, 1996).
47. Daniel, *Short History of Archaeology*, 196.
48. Ibid., 117.
49. Margaret S. Drower, *Flinders Petrie* (London: Gollancz, 1985), 27–33, 127.
50. What follows in the next two paragraphs is based mainly on Philippa Levine, *The Amateur and the Professional: Antiquarians, Historians and Archaeologists in Victorian England, 1838–1886* (Cambridge: Cambridge University Press, 1986); Peter J. Bowler, *The Invention of Progress: The Victorians and the Past* (Oxford: Blackwell, 1989); and Barry M. Marsden, *The Early Barrow-Diggers* (Stroud: Tempus, 1999).
51. Levine, *The Amateur and the Professional*, 54.
52. These having made the fortunes achieved or inherited by Heinrich Schliemann, Sir Arthur Evans and Alexander Keiller, respectively, and then applied by them to these famous campaigns of excavation.

53. Lynda J. Murray, *A Zest for Life: The Story of Alexander Keiller* (Wooton Bassett, Wiltshire: Morven Press, 1999).

54. O. G. S. Crawford, *Said and Done: The Autobiography of an Archaeologist* (London: Weidenfeld, 1955), 149–50.

55. Glyn Daniel and Christopher Chippindale (eds), *The Pastmasters* (London: Thames and Hudson, 1989), 23.

56. L. V. Grinsell, *An Archaeological Autobiography* (London: Sutton, 1989), 10–11.

57. Murray, *A Zest for Life*, 33–5, 75.

58. Crawford, *Said and Done*, 106.

59. Jacquetta Hawkes, *Mortimer Wheeler* (London: Weidenfeld and Nicolson, 1982), 1–53.

60. Glyn Daniel, *Some Small Harvest* (London: Thames and Hudson, 1986), 11.

61. Charles Scott-Fox, *Cyril Fox: Archaeologist Extraordinary* (Oxford: Oxbow, 2002), 1–116.

62. Brian Fagan, *Grahame Clark* (Boulder, Colo.: Westview, 2001); quotation from p. 45.

63. Daniel, *Some Small Harvest*, 57.

64. Ibid., 216; Glyn Daniel, 'The "Dolmens" of Southern Britain', *Antiquity* 11 (1937), 183–200; quotation from p. 183.

65. Bruce G. Trigger, *Gordon Childe: Revolutions in Archaeology* (London: Thames and Hudson, 1980), 17–19.

66. Daniel, *Short History of Archaeology*, 195.

67. Stuart Piggott, 'Archaeology and the Amateur', *Archaeological Newsletter* 1 (April 1948), 1–2.

68. Scott-Fox, *Cyril Fox*, 2–20; Crawford, *Said and Done*, 28; Grinsell, *An Archaeological Autobiography*, 4–5; Daniel and Chippindale (eds), *The Pastmasters*, 34–5.

69. Daniel and Chippindale (eds), *The Pastmasters*, 20.

70. Crawford, *Said and Done*, 28.

71. Ibid., 28–70; Daniel and Chippindale (eds), *The Pastmasters*, 22.

72. Ibid.

73. First noticed by Kathryn Denning, 'On Archaeology and Alterity' (Sheffield University Ph.D. thesis, 1999), 75–6.

74. Philip Rahtz, *Living Archaeology* (Stroud: Tempus, 2001), 52. I am very grateful to Philip for the gift of his autobiography, marking many years of friendship in which a great man from an older generation showed kindness to a bad boy from a later one.

75. Adam Stout, 'Choosing a Past: The Politics of Prehistory in Pre-War Britain' (University of Wales, Lampeter, Ph.D. thesis, 2004), 93–131, 134–5.

76. Glyn Daniel, *The National Museum as a Mirror of Ancient Wales* (Cardiff: National Museum of Wales, 1983), 16.

77. Christopher Chippindale, *Stonehenge Complete* (London: Thames and Hudson, 1983), 179–205.

78. R. J. C. Atkinson, *Stonehenge* (London: Hamish Hamilton, 1956); quotations from pp. xiv, 77–8, 91, 164, 179–80.

79. Ibid., 179.

80. Ibid., 179–80.

81. Stuart Piggott, 'The Sources of Geoffrey of Monmouth: II. The Stonehenge Story', *Antiquity* 15 (1941), 305–19.

82. Stuart Piggott, *British Prehistory* (Oxford, 1949), 195.

83. C. F. C. Hawkes, 'Prehistory and the Gaulish Peoples', in J. M. Wallace-Hadrill and John McManners (eds), *France: Government and Society* (London: Methuen, 1957), 7–16; quotation from p. 16.

84. *Antiquity* 30 (1956), 131.

85. Daniel, *Some Small Harvest*, 1–20, 51, 193, 201–2; Stout, 'Choosing a Past', 134.

86. Glyn Daniel, 'Anti-Christ and My Cat Toby', *Exposure* (Christmas Miscellany, 1944), 21. I owe this reference to Adam Stout.

87. *The Times* 22 June 1961; *Salisbury Journal* 23 June 1961.

88. Glyn Daniel, 'Editorial', *Antiquity* 35 (1961), 171–5, 260–2.

89. National Archives, WORK 14/2789, memoranda 2 Feb.–2 March 1962.

90. Ibid., report 23 June 1962; *The Times* 2 June 1964; Glyn Daniel, 'Editorial', *Antiquity* 38 (1964), 165–6; 40 (1966), 168–9; 42 (1968), 171.

91. Ibid., 40 (1966), 168–9.

92. *Southern Evening Echo* 15 June 1962.

93. Wiltshire Record Office, 2860/20, press release, Jan. 1964, and letter from Ross Nichols to a member, 30 Jan.; Ross Nichols, *The Book of Druidry*, ed. John Matthews and Philip Carr-Gomm (London: Aquarian, 1990).

94. This story is told from the point of view of Nichols, in his *Book of Druidry*, 112–13.

95. Wiltshire Record Office, 2860/22, unattributed newspaper cutting, 21 June 1965.

96. Stuart Piggott, *The Progress of Early Man* (London, 1935); quotation from p. 40.

97. Stuart Piggott, *The Dawn of Civilization* (London: Sunday Times, 1962), 15.

98. Ibid.

99. David Clarke and Patrick Maguire, *Skara Brae* (Edinburgh: Historic Scotland, 2000).

100. Piggott, *British Prehistory*, 47, 101, 195.

101. Stuart Piggott, *Ancient Europe* (Edinburgh: Edinburgh University Press, 1965), 15–19, 230, 256–80.

102. The correspondence is preserved in the Piggott archive at Oxford University's Institute of Archaeology.

103. Stuart Piggott, *The Druids* (London: Thames and Hudson, 2nd edn 1985), 9, 23, 165, 175, 180–1.

104. Wiltshire Record Office, 2860/20, J. M. Melhuish to J. B. Score, 10 July 1969; 2860/21, Ministry report 6 Jan. 1996; *Southern Evening Echo* 22 June 1967, 21 June 1969, 22 June 1970 and 22 June 1971; *Salisbury Journal* 23 June 1966; *Sunday Times* 25 June 1967.

105. Wiltshire Record Office, 2680/21, unattributed newspaper cutting, 21 June 1965; *Southern Evening Echo* 22 June 1967, 19 June 1968, 22 June 1970.

106. Wiltshire Record Office, 2860/22, press release 1973. For the context of Hawkins's book, see Chippindale, *Stonehenge Complete*,

107. *The Druid* 1 (1965), n.p.

108. He acted as spokesman to the *Daily Telegraph* journalist at Stonehenge in 1956, as reported in the issue on 22 June.

109. Nichols, *Book of Druidry*; and Nichols, 'Essentials of Druidry', *The Druid's Voice* 4 (1994), 10–11; Philip Carr-Gomm, *The Elements of the Druid Tradition* (Shaftesbury: Element, 1991); Philip Carr-Gomm (ed.), *In the Grove of the Druids: The Druid Teachings of Ross Nichols* (London: Watkins, 2002).

110. All this is based on writings and recollections of Nichols in the works listed above, and on his will in the national registry in London, plus his essay 'Scheme of Soul', *Occult Observer* 1 (1949), 40–3.

111. Ibid., 63–70; Nichols, *Book of Druidry*, 20–55.

112. Nichols, *Book of Druidry*, 76–118.

113. Ibid., 272–89; quotation from pp. 272–3.

114. E.g. to *The Times* 3 July 1965, and *International Times* Autumn 1971. The latter is reprinted in Carr-Gomm (ed.), *In the Grove of the Druids*, 80–2.

115. *The Book of Druidry*.

116. See the letters sections of the *Independent* 23 June 1989 and *The Times* 4 Jan. 1990.

117. Glyn Daniel, *Megaliths in History* (London: Thames and Hudson, 1972), 37–8.

118. And he remained keen; during our conversations in 1975–6, he told me that Druidry and stone circles might have been intrinsically linked, and that this would explain why Britain both had more such circles than any other part of Europe, and was credited by Caesar with being the home of Druidry.

119. In *The Listener* 3 Jan. 1974. During recent years Dr Ross has published a pair of popular books on the ancient Druids, *The Life and Death of a Druid Prince* (London: Rider, 1989) (with Don Robin), and *Druids* (Stroud: Tempus, 1999). They are characteristically well written, but take into account neither the difficulties with the sources outlined in the present book nor changes in archaeological opinion since the 1970s.

120. Thom's classic book is *Megalithic Sites in Britain* (Oxford: Oxford University Press, 1967).

121. Daniel, *Some Small Harvest*, 201–2.

122. Euan Mackie, *Science and Society in Prehistoric Britain* (London: Paul Elek, 1977), 2–3.

123. Ibid., 226–8.

124. Carr-Gomm (ed.), *In the Grove of the Druids*, 13; Nichols, *Book of Druidry*, 9.

125. The classic history of the festival is Andy Worthington, *Stonehenge: Celebration and Subversion* (Wymeswold, Leicestershire: Alternative Albion, 2004).

126. Chippindale, *Stonehenge Complete*, 262–3.

127. Again, the properly researched study of these is by Andy Worthington, *The Battle of the Beanfield* (Teignmouth, Devon: Enabler Publications, 2005).

128. By this I mean it does not co-operate with any other Druid orders (for example it refused to participate in the national council of Druids set up in the 1990s), does not publish books or hold public lectures, appears very little in the mass media, and does not welcome historians. Things might have seemed different to me, however, had I been a Londoner. When I asked if I could have access to the order's archive, I was told that this would only be possible if I joined it and then proved my genuine dedication to it by attending a sufficient number of its events. I did not think this unreasonable, and had no objection in principle to conforming to this requirement, but most of the meetings seemed to be held in the capital, and I live too far from that to make regular attendance easy. The response did, however, make a striking contrast with the open welcome given by the present Order of Bards, Ovates and Druids to all serious researchers.

129. This story is told in Ronald Hutton, *The Pagan Religions of the Ancient British Isles* (Oxford: Blackwell, 1991), 111–18; for the specific case of Stonehenge, see Chippindale, *Stonehenge Complete*, 216–235.

130. Rosamund Cleal, K. E. Walker and R. Montague, *Stonehenge in its Landscape* (London: English Heritage, 1995), 260–5, 337–42.

131. Richard Bradley, 'From Ritual to Romance: Ceremonial Centres and Hill Forts', in Graeme Guilbert (ed.), *Hill-Fort Studies* (Leicester: Leicester University Press, 1981), 20–7.

132. Francis Pryor, *Britain AD: A Quest for Arthur, England and the Anglo-Saxons* (London: HarperCollins, 2004), 45.

133. Pryor is more generous to Daniel in an earlier book, for HarperCollins, *Seahenge*, which appeared in 2002. On pp. 12–13 he pays tribute to the influence of Daniel's lectures, while adding that they had a 'lacklustre' quality at that time because of the great blow of the radio-carbon dating revolution. Daniel had much the same quality when I studied under him ten years later, undoubtedly reflecting the fact that he had never recovered from that shift in archaeological perception.

134. Ibid., 45–8.

135. Miranda and Stephen Aldhouse-Green, *The Quest for the Shaman* (London: Thames and Hudson, 2005).

136. His classic work on this subject is *Ritual and Rubbish in the Iron Age of Wessex* (British Archaeological Reports, British Series 242, 1995); quotation from p. 126.

137. Miranda Aldhouse-Green, 'Humans as Ritual Victims in the Later Prehistory of Western Europe', *Oxford Journal of Archaeology* 17 (1998), 169–90; and Aldhouse-Green, *Dying for the Gods* (Stroud: Tempus, 2001); quotation from p. 15.

138. Ronald Hutton, *The Druids* (London: Hambledon Continuum, 2007), 134–6, with references given on pp. 225–6.

139. Mike Pitts, *Hengeworld* (London: Century, 2000), 37–8.

140. Joshua Pollard, pers. comm., 30 Nov. 2006.

141. Beth Coombe Harris, *In the Grip of the Druids* (Southampton: Mayflower Books, 1999).

142. *Guardian* 21 June 2007. Archived at *http://www.guardian.co.uk/g2/story/0,,2107640,00.* html.

INDEX